A Book of Women Poets

A Book of

Women Poets

from Antiquity to Now

Edited by Aliki Barnstone & Willis Barnstone

Revised, and with an
expanded selection of American poets
edited by Aliki Barnstone

SCHOCKEN BOOKS • NEW YORK

Library of Congress Cataloging-in-Publication Data

A Book of women poets from antiquity to now / edited by Aliki
    Barnstone and Willis Barnstone.—Rev., and with an
    expanded selection of American poets.
        p. cm.
    Includes indexes.
    1. Poetry—Women authors.   I. Barnstone, Aliki.
    II. Barnstone,
    Willis, 1927– .
    PN6109.9.B6 1992
    808.81′0082—dc20   91-52701
        ISBN 0-8052-0997-2

The second, expanded edition is for
Barry Douglas Bruce
—A. B.

Someone, I tell you,
will remember us.
                    —Sappho

Contents

Preface to the Expanded Second Edition   xxi
Introduction   xxiii

SUMERIAN
Enheduanna (ca. 2300 B.C.)   1

AKKADIAN
Inib-sarri (ca. 1790–1745 B.C.)   9
Eristi-Aya (ca. 1790–1745 B.C.)   10

EGYPTIAN
Anonymous Hieroglyphic Texts (ca. 1500 B.C.)   11

HEBREW
Ancient Hebrew
Hannah's Thanksgiving (Samuel 2:1–10)   16
The Song of Deborah (Judges 5:1–31)   17
from Song of Songs (The Shulamite)   20

Modern Hebrew
Leah Goldberg (1911–1970)   24
Dahlia Ravikovitch (1936–)   27

NEO-ARAMAIC (PERSIA)
Traditional Song   29

GREEK
Ancient Greek
Sappho (7th–6th century B.C.)   30
Praxilla (ca. 450 B.C.)   43
Telesilla (5th century B.C.)   43
Anyte (ca. 290 B.C.)   43
Korinna (ca. late 3rd century B.C.)   44

Biblical Greek (Koiné)
The Magnificat (Luke 1:46–1:56)   46

Byzantine Greek
Kassia (ca. 840)   47

Modern Greek

Moirologia (Traditional Funeral Songs)	48
Eleni Vakalo (1921–)	50
Lydia Stephanou (1927–)	51
Lina Kasdaglis (1928–)	52
Nana Issaia (1934–)	53
Eva Mylonás (1936–)	54
Jenny Mastoraki (1949–)	54

LATIN

Classical Latin

Sulpicia (1st century B.C.)	57

Medieval Latin

Anonymous, from the *Cambridge Songs* (ca. 1000)	59
Anonymous, from the *Carmina Burana* (ca. 1200)	61

THE LANGUAGES OF INDIA

Sanskrit

Vidya (ca. 659)	62
Sila (between 700 and 1050)	63
Mahodahi (between 700 and 1050)	63
Vallana (between 900 and 1100)	64
Marula (ca. 1156)	64

Classical Tamil

Okkur Macatti (between 1st and 3rd centuries)	65
Kaccipettu Nannakaiyar (between 1st and 3rd centuries)	65
Andal (ca. 10th century)	66

Kannada

Mahādēvi (12th century)	67
Honnamma (late 17th century)	69

Marathi

Mukta Bai (13th century)	70
Jana Bai (14th century?)	71

Pali

Sumangala's Mother	71

Hindi
Mira Bai (1498–1573)   72

Telugu
Kshetrayya (17th century)   79

Kashmiri
Lal Ded (16th century?)   80

PERSIAN
   India
   Princess Zeb-un-Nissa (1638–1702)   82
   Empress Nur Jahan (?–1646)   82

   Iran
   Forugh Farrokhzad (1935–1967)   83

TURKISH
   Bayati   87

ARABIC
   Iraq
   Rabi'a the Mystic (712–801)   90
   Al-Khirniq (late 6th century)   91

   Arabia
   Al-Khansa (575–646)   92
   Laila Akhyaliyya (late 7th century)   98

   Morocco and Northwest Africa
   Ancient Songs of the Women of Fez   100
   haufi (traditional songs)   102

THE LANGUAGES OF AFRICA
   Bagirmi
   Traditional   103

   Nyasa
   Traditional   104

   Yoruba (Nigeria)
   Traditional   104

Hottentot (South Africa)
Traditional   105

Amharic (Ethiopia)
Traditional   106

Afrikaans (South Africa)
Ingrid Jonker (1933–1965)   107

CHINESE

The Book of Songs (7th century B.C.)   110
Cho Wen-chün (179?–117? B.C.)   112
Hsi-chün (ca. 105 B.C.)   113
Ch'in Chia's wife (1st century B.C.)   113
Lady Pan (ca. 48–6 B.C.)   114
Anonymous poems (ca. 206 B.C. to A.D. 220)   115
Yüeh-fu shih (1st century)   117
Ts'ai Yen (162?–239?)   118
Tzu Yeh Songs (3rd–6th century)   120
Chao Luan-luan (8th century?)   121
Anonymous Palace Women (ca. 8th century)   122
Hsüeh T'ao (768–831)   123
Yü Hsüan-chi (ca. 843–868)   124
Li Ch'ing-chao (1084?–ca. 1151)   133
Anonymous Courtesan   142
Chu Shu-chen (ca. 1200)   143
Wang Ch'ing-hui (13th century?)   146
Chao Li-hua (Ming Dynasty)   147
Huang O (1498–1569)   147
Wang Wei (17th century)   149
Sun Yün-feng (1764–1814)   150
Wu Tsao (19th century)   151
Ch'iu Chin (1879–1907)   153
Ping Hsin (1902–)   154
Li Chü (mid-20th century)   155

JAPANESE

Empress Iwa no Hime (?–347)   156
Princess Oku (661–701)   157
A Court Lady (?–671)   157
Woman of Suminoe (ca. 699)   158
Anonymous (ca. 733)   158

Anonymous (8th century)   158
Young Woman of Harima (ca. 715–719)   159
Lady Ōtomo of Sakanone (ca. 8th century)   159
Lady Kasa (mid- to late 8th century)   161
Ono no Komachi (834–880)   161
Lady Ise (875?–938?)   162
Anonymous (10th century?)   167
Izumi Shikibu (10th–11th century)   167
Lady Sagami (ca. 1000)   170
Akazome Emon (?–1027)   170
Murasaki Shikibu (974–1031)   171
Ise Tayū (11th century)   172
Ryōjin Hishō (1179?)   172
Lady Horikawa (12th century)   172
Princess Shikishi (?–1201)   173
Chiyo (1703–1775)   173
Yosano Akiko (1878–1942)   174
Mitsuhashi Takajo (1899–1972)   175
Nagase Kiyoko (1906–)   175
Fumi Saitō (1909–)   175
Kiyoko Tsuda (1920–)   176
Tada Chimako (1930–)   176
Shiraishi Kazuko (1931–)   177
Sachiko Yoshihara (1932–)   179
Takako U. Lento (1941–)   180
Kanai Mieko (1947–)   181

PROVENÇAL

France
Countess Beatriz de Die (ca. 1140)   183
Anonymous (12th century)   184

FRENCH

France
Anonymous Songs (12th–13th centuries)   185
Marie de France (ca. 1155–1189)   · 186
The Song of the Ill-Married (14th–15th century)   200
Christine de Pisan (1363–1430)   201
Louise Labé (1525–1566)   204
Marceline Desbordes-Valmore (1786–1859)   217
Marguerite Burnat-Provins (1872–1952)   218
Thérèse Plantier (1911–)   219

Joyce Mansour (1928–)   220
Yvonne Caroutch (1937–)   221
Anne-Marie Albiach (1937–)   224
Marie-Françoise Prager (20th century)   224

Belgium
Anne-Marie Kegels (1912–)   225

Switzerland
Monique Laederach (1938–)   227
Claude Maillard (20th century)   228
Denise Jallais (20th century)   228

Canada
Anne Hébert (1916–)   229

Lebanon
Nadia Tuéni (1935–)   240
Vénus Khoury-Gata (1937–)   242

Egypt
Andrée Chedid (1921–)   243

CATALAN

Anonymous (16th century)   245

SPANISH

Spain
Hispano-Arabic *jarchas* (1000–1300)   247
Anonymous Ballad (15th–16th centuries)   248
Morisco Ballad (15th–16th centuries)   249
Jewish Ballad (15th–16th centuries)   249
Anonymous Songs (15th–16th centuries)   250
Florencia del Pinar (late 15th century)   256
Rosalía de Castro (1837–1885)   257
Gloria Fuertes (1918–)   259
Julia Uceda (1925–)   261

Mexico
Sor Juana Inés de la Cruz (1648/51–1695)   262
Rosario Castellanos (1925–1974)   268
Isabel Fraire (1936–)   270

Puerto Rico
Julia de Burgos (1914–1953)   271
Elsa Tió (1950–)   274
Rosario Ferré (20th century)   275

El Salvador
Claribel Alegría (20th century)   276

Peru
Blanca Varela (1926–)   281
Lucia Fox (1930–)   284

Argentina
Alfonsina Storni (1892–1938)   285
Martha Paley Francescato (1934–)   289

Chile
Gabriela Mistral (1889–1957)   291

PORTUGUESE
Portugal
Sor Violante do Céu (1602?–1693)   294
Sophia de Mello Breyner Andresen (1919–)   295
The Three Marias: Maria Isabel Barreno (1939–),
    Maria Teresa Horta (1937–),
    Maria Velho da Costa (1939–)   296

Brazil
Cecília Meireles (1901–1964)   299
Henriqueta Lisboa (20th century)   300
Leila Miccolis (1947–)   301
Maria Amália Fonte Boa (20th century)   302

ITALIAN
Vittoria da Colonna (1490–1547)   305
Gaspara Stampa (1523–1554)   306
Ruth Domino (1908–)   308
Maria Luisa Spaziani (1924–)   309
Edith Bruck (1932–)   311
Rossana Ombres (20th century)   313

GERMAN

Germany

Frau Ava (ca. 1160) — 314
Annette Von Droste-Hülshoff (1797–1848) — 314
Else Lasker-Schüler (1869–1945) — 316
Nelly Sachs (1891–1970) — 319
Hilde Domin (1912–) — 324
Martina Werner (1929–) — 325
Petra von Morstein (1941–) — 329
Karin Kiwus (1942–) — 332

Austria

Ingeborg Bachmann (1926–1973) — 333

DUTCH

Hadewijch (13th century) — 341
Sister Bertken (1427?–1514) — 343
Judith Herzberg (1934–) — 344

POLISH

Wislawa Szymborska (1923–) — 346

RUMANIAN

Maria Banus (1914–) — 348
Magda Isanos (1916–1944) — 349
Veronica Porumbacu (1921–1977) — 350
Nina Cassian (1924–) — 351
Ileana Malancioiu (1940–) — 352
Constanta Buzea (1941–) — 353
Ana Blandiana (1942–) — 354
Gabriela Melinescu (1942–) — 354

HUNGARIAN

Anna Hajnal (1907–1977) — 356
Ágnes Nemes Nagy (1922–) — 358
Ágnes Gergely (1933–) — 360

NORWEGIAN

Astrid Hjertenaes Andersen (1915–) — 361

SWEDISH

Sonja Åkesson (1926–1977) — 362

DANISH

Cecil Bødker (1927–)   366
Inger Christensen (1935–)   368

ESTONIAN

Betti Alver (1906–)   370

RUSSIAN

Anna Akhmatova (1889–1966)   373
Marina Tsvetayeva (1892–1941)   386
Olga Berggolts (1910–)   400
Natalya Gorbanyevskaya (1936–)   402
Bella Akhmadulina (1937–)   406

NATIVE AMERICAN LANGUAGES

Nahuatl (Aztec)
Anonymous   420

Quechua (Peru)
Anonymous   421

Pampa
Anonymous   422

Chippewa
Anonymous   423

Apache
Anonymous   423

Papago
Anonymous   424

Hawaiian
Anonymous   425

Eskimo
Anonymous   426

PAPUAN

New Guinea
Buin Tribe   428
Elema Tribe   428
Boiken Tribe   428

WELSH

Gwerfyl Mechain (ca. 1460–1500)   429

ANGLO-SAXON

Anonymous Woman (ca. 800)   431
Anonymous Woman (ca. 900)   432

ENGLISH

England, United States, Canada, Australia
Mary Sidney Herbert, Countess of Pembroke
    (1561–1621)   434
Emilia Lanier (1569–1645)   435
Anne Bradstreet (1612?–1672)   438
Katherine Philips (1631–1664)   446
Aphra Behn (1640–1689)   447
Anne Killigrew (1660–1685)   449
Lady Mary Wortley Montagu (1684–1763)   451
Charlotte Smith (1749–1806)   452
Phillis Wheatley (ca. 1752–1784)   453
Elizabeth Barrett Browning (1806–1861)   460
Emily Brontë (1818–1848)   462
Christina Rossetti (1830–1894)   463
Emily Dickinson (1830–1886)   465
Ada (fl. 1836–1855)   487
Mary Elizabeth Coleridge (1861–1907)   490
Amy Lowell (1874–1925)   491
Mina Loy (1882–1966)   497
Elinor Wylie (1885–1928)   519
H.D. (1886–1961)   521
Edith Sitwell (1887–1964)   531
Marianne Moore (1887–1972)   533
Edna St. Vincent Millay (1892–1950)   552
Louise Bogan (1897–1970)   554
Stevie Smith (1902–1971)   556
Lorine Niedecker (1903–1970)   557
Kathleen Raine (1909–)   571
Elizabeth Bishop (1911–1979)   572
Josephine Miles (1911–1985)   595
Muriel Rukeyser (1913–1980)   598
Ruth Stone (1915–)   600
Gwendolyn Brooks (1917–)   606
May Swenson (1919–)   610

Amy Clampitt (1920–)   611
Mary Ellen Solt (1920–)   615
Shirley Kaufman (1923–)   625
Denise Levertov (1923–)   626
Jane Cooper (1924–)   631
Carolyn Kizer (1925–)   632
Maxine Kumin (1925–)   635
Dolores Kendrick (1927–)   637
Anne Sexton (1928–1974)   641
Adrienne Rich (1929–)   646
Sylvia Plath (1932–1963)   654
Audre Lorde (1934–)   666
Jean Valentine (1934–)   669
Mary Oliver (1935–)   671
Jayne Cortez (1936–)   673
Marge Piercy (1936–)   676
June Jordan (1936–)   677
Lucille Clifton (1936–)   679
Sandra M. Gilbert (1936–)   685
Diane Wakoski (1937–)   687
Kathleen Spivack (1938–)   691
Grace Schulman (1939–)   693
Margaret Atwood (1939–)   694
Anne Winters (1939–)   699
Linda Gregg (1942–)   702
Marilyn Hacker (1942–)   704
Sharon Olds (1942–)   705
Tess Gallagher (1943–)   707
Ellen Bryant Voight (1943–)   710
Sandra McPherson (1943–)   711
Louise Glück (1943–)   712
Shirley Williams (1944–)   715
Sandra Alcosser (1944–)   717
Maura Stanton (1946–)   719
Ai (1947–)   721
Emily Hiestand (1947–)   723
Heather McHugh (1948–)   724
Olga Broumas (1949–)   727
Olga Broumas and Jane Miller   730
Jane Miller (1949–)   730
Marianne Boruch (1950–)   733

Carolyn Forche (1950–)   734
Jorie Graham (1951–)   737
Brenda Hillman (1951–)   739
Joy Harjo (1951–)   743
Rita Dove (1952–)   744
Louise Erdrich (1954–)   747
Cathy Song (1955–)   751
Aliki Barnstone (1956–)   753
Ntozake Shange (20th century)   757
Roberta Hill Whitestone (20th century)   759
Linda Bierds (20th century)   761
Susan Howe (20th century)   763
Diana O'Hehir (20th century)   765
Katha Pollitt (20th century)   767
Mary Jo Salter (20th century)   768
Gwen Harwood (1920–)   771
Rosemary Dobson (1920–)   771
Leslie Scalapino   772

Acknowledgments   776
Index of Poets   795
Index of Translators   799
Index of Titles and First Lines   802

Preface to the Expanded Second Edition

The new pages in this expanded second edition represent only in small part the many and varied voices of American women poets. Although fine poets have emerged from other English-speaking countries, in this edition we have limited our choice of new writers to poets only from the United States. I have tried to make my principle of selection consistent with the first edition of the anthology, that is, to provide ample space for our forebears to speak. Thus, the additions of Phillis Wheatley, Mina Loy, and Lorine Niedecker, who surely belong in the canon along with Anne Bradstreet, Emily Dickinson, H.D., and Marianne Moore, were crucial choices to make. The task of deciding among the living poets was more arduous. Though we may correctly complain that poetry is not highly valued in late-twentieth-century American culture, contemporary poetry is prolific and vast in scope. Many anthologies reflect a point of view. In poetry, as in all the arts, this is an eclectic age, and I have tried to represent the highest qualities of this diversity. I hope you will hear a symphony of difference in these pages.

In reading for this book, I frequently felt Emily Dickinson's measure of poetry. It is not the only one, but it may be the best: "If I feel physically as if the top of my head were taken off, I know that is poetry." To make an anthology is in the Greek etymology of the word "to gather flowers." Let these poems inspire you to read other anthologies, support literary bookstores, open new unknown books of poems, and gather your own garland.

Aliki Barnstone

A Book of Women Poets from Antiquity to Now was published in 1980. My daughter and I had searched through foreign literatures for eight years to discover and establish a tradition, a world canon of women's poetry, beginning with the great Sumerian poet Enheduanna, the world's first known writer, preserved in cuneiform text, from ca. 2300 B.C., almost two millennia before Sappho. This second revised and expanded edition, eleven years later, is almost entirely the work of Aliki. I was the sounding board throughout but joined only during the last weeks of formulating the manuscript.

Unable to do all things at once, we decided to make this edition largely an appreciation of the renaissance of women's poetry in America. The next edition will make a pact again with the world. In addition to selecting, with difficulty and inevitable injustice, from the wealth of outstanding younger poets, Aliki's most significant act has been to give major emphasis to three poets, Phillis Wheatley, Mina Loy, and Lorine Niedecker, who died in obscurity but who reflect the highest achievement among American poets.

Willis Barnstone

Introduction

The earliest known writer in the world was a woman—Enheduanna, a Sumerian moon priestess from the middle of the third millennium B.C. Not only do we have forty-three magnificent poems by her, but also the ancient texts, for they survive on sculpted cuneiform tablets. We even know her appearance, for a detailed relief sculpture of her face survives on a limestone disk.

The one art in which women have always excelled is poetry. In the other arts, few works produced before the nineteenth century have been preserved. In poetry, from the earliest periods, the highly developed civilizations of China, Japan, India, the Middle East, and Europe have produced important women poets. And in the oral traditions of Africa, the American Indian, Eskimo, southeast and central Asia, there have always been women's songs.

This is not to say that it was easy for women to achieve recognition in poetry. Yet while the other arts were virtually closed to them, poetry required little more than a writing instrument, paper or papyrus, and the possibility of having one's work copied by later generations.

An extraordinary example of loss occurs in Latin. We know that educated women (*doctae puellae*) painted and wrote poetry, yet we have nothing but six poems by Sulpicia (1st century B.C.), tacked onto the canon of Tibullus. The fact that enormous quantities of Latin literature have been preserved, yet virtually nothing by women, means simply that the work of women was not considered worth preserving. In China and Japan, however, women poets were highly esteemed, their works studied and copied, with the result that we have a large corpus of poetry by women from the Far East. And in Greece, Sappho—though later reviled by the Church—was held to be, as Plato wrote, "the tenth Muse."

The problem of voice in selecting women's poetry is persistent. Was "Anonymous" a woman? Some well-known poets, like Christine de Pisan, often wrote in the male persona. Likewise, the central poems by the Spanish mystic Saint John of the Cross are androgynously in the voice of the woman lover. Often poems are ascribed to women, as in the "Magnificat," where the ascription has the authority of the scriptures. The poem is obviously a traditional Hebrew hymn, translated into Greek, by an unknown author, who might have been a man or a woman. Often, as in The Song of Songs, where individual poems of the fragmentary idyll are typical of love songs from Egypt and the ancient Middle East, we can only guess whether a poem is indeed a woman's song.

In making the selection for this anthology—obviously a painful process of eliminating worthy poets for the sake of essential inclusions—we have tried to balance several priorities. First, we wished to show the variety of good poetry from different languages and periods. In order to give the reader a notion of the scope of key poets—Enheduanna, Sappho, Yü Hsüan-chi, Li Ch'ing-chao, Al-Khansa, Mira Bai, Marie de France, Louise Labé, Sor Juana Inés de la Cruz, Anne Bradstreet, and Emily Dickinson—

a large selection of their work has been included. The selection process in the English, American, Canadian, and Australian section has been very difficult because of abundant material. We have included main figures, but have also wished to introduce new voices, particularly from the vital work of minority writers. In the last decade American writing has become more diverse. America the continent has begun to record its many voices from Spanish, French, Chinese, from Africa, from the Native American and the Arctic Eskimo. And so, as in a new Alexandria, we are coming full circle to reach our origins, the world.

Aliki Barnstone
Willis Barnstone

A Book of Women Poets

Sumerian

Enheduanna

Enheduanna (born ca. 2300 B.C.).   Enheduanna was a moon priestess, the daughter of King Sargon of Agade (2334–2279 B.C.) who reigned over the world's first empire, extending from the Mediterranean to Persia. Sargon is the first important leader to emerge from the half-light of prehistory into the full light of a written record; words attributed to him are recorded on cuneiform tablets from the early first millennium: "My priestly mother conceived me; secretly brought me to birth; set me in an ark of bulrushes; made fast my door with pitch. She consigned me to the river, which did not overwhelm me. The river brought me to Akki, the farmer, who brought me up to be his son. . . . During my gardening, the goddess Ishtar loved me, and for fifty-four years the kingship was mine." The detailed quality of this personal account also characterizes the writing of his daughter Enheduanna, who is the first writer, male or female, in history whose name and work have been preserved. Her personal history survives in highly politicized poems, which in their cosmic vision and ethical outrage recall Isaiah. In her poems to the Sumerian goddess of love Inanna, she speaks to a deity who has descended to earth as an ally, as a friend to help her in her need. In the poems' sensuality, surprising metaphors, and intimacy, they recall Sappho's poems to her ally Aphrodite. We have a stone disk which contains a detailed likeness of the high priestess, revealing her particular features and dress, flanked by three of her retainers. The poems presented here, preserved on cuneiform tablets, are from a sequence of 18 stanzas in a single poem, "The Exaltation of Enheduanna," addressed to Inanna. In addition we have forty-two hymns to temples whose authorship is not in question, as well as many other poems and fragments which may be hers.

Our thanks to William W. Hallo, Laffan Professor of Assyriology and Curator of the Babylonian Collection at Yale University, for his help and suggestions. The poems that follow have been adapted by Aliki and Willis Barnstone from William W. Hallo and J. J. A. van Dijk, *The Exaltation of Inanna* (New Haven: Yale University Press, 1968).

Inanna and the Divine Essences

Lady of all the essences, full light,
good woman clothed in radiance
whom heaven and earth love,
temple friend of An,
you wear great ornaments,
you desire the tiara of the high priestess
whose hand holds the seven essences.
O my lady, guardian of all the great essences,
you have picked them up and hung them
on your hand.
You have gathered the holy essences and worn them
tightly on your breasts.

Inanna and An

Like a dragon you have filled the land
with venom.
Like thunder when you roar over the earth,
trees and plants fall before you.
You are a flood descending from a mountain,
O primary one,
moon goddess Inanna of heaven and earth!
Your fire blows about and drops on our nation.
Lady mounted on a beast,
An gives you qualities, holy commands,
and you decide.
You are in all our great rites.
Who can understand you?

Inanna and Enlil

Storms lend you wings, destroyer of the lands.
Loved by Enlil, you fly over our nation.
You serve the decrees of An.
O my lady, on hearing your sound,
hills and flatlands bow.

When we come before you,
terrified, shuddering in your stormy clear light,
we receive justice.
We sing, mourn, and cry before you
and walk toward you along a path
from the house of enormous sighs.

Inanna and Ishkur

You strike everything down in battle.
O my lady, on your wings
you hack away the land and charge disguised
as a charging storm,
roar as a roaring storm,
thunder and keep thundering, and snort
with evil winds.
Your feet are filled with restlessness.

On your harp of sighs
I hear your dirge.

Inanna and the Anunna

O my lady, the Anunna, the great gods,
fluttering like bats in front of you,
fly away into cliffs.
They do not have the courage to walk
through your terrible gaze.
Who can tame your furious heart?
No lesser god.
Your malevolent heart is beyond temperance.
Lady, you soothe the reins of the beast,
you make us happy.
Your rage is beyond temperance,
O eldest daughter of Suen!
Who has ever denied you homage,
lady, supreme over the land?

Inanna and Ebih

In the mountain where you are unworshiped
the vegetation is cursed.
You have made its grand entrance ashes.
For you the rivers rise high with blood
and the people have nothing to drink.
The army of the mountain goes to you captive
of its own accord.
Healthy young men parade before you
of their own accord.
The dancing city is filled with storm,
driving young men to you, captive.

Inanna and the City of Uruk

You have spoken your holy command over the city
which has not declared:
"This land is yours,"
which has not declared:
"It is your father's and his father's,"
and you have blocked its path to you,
you have lifted your foot and left
their barn of fertility.
The women of the city no longer speak of love
with their husbands.
At night they do not make love.
They are no longer naked before them,
revealing intimate treasures.
Great daughter of Suen,
impetuous wild cow, supreme lady commanding An,
who dares not worship you?

Banishment from Ur

You asked me to enter the holy cloister,
the *giparu,*
and I went inside, I the high priestess
Enheduanna!

I carried the ritual basket and sang
your praise.
Now I am banished among the lepers.
Even I cannot live with you.
Shadows approach the light of day, the light
is darkened around me,
shadows approach the daylight,
covering the day with sandstorm.
My soft mouth of honey is suddenly confused.
My beautiful face is dust.

Appeal to the Moongod Nanna-Suen to Throw Out Lugalanne, the New Conqueror of the City of Uruk

O Suen, the usurper Lugalanne means nothing to me!
Tell An: "Have An release me!"
If you will only tell An
"NOW!"
and An will release me.
This woman Inanna will carry off this young cock
Lugalanne.
Mountain and flood lie at her feet.
This woman is powerful as he.
She'll make the city expel him.
Surely she will forget her rage against me.
Let me, Enheduanna, pray to her.
Like sweet drink let me cry freely for holy
Inanna!
Let me call to her!

Crimes of Lugalanne

I can't appease Ashimbabbar, the moon god An,
for Lugalanne came in
and changed the rituals of sacred An.
He stripped An of his temple at Eanna.
He's never walked in proper awe before King An.
That sanctuary is irresistibly attractive,

its beauty is infinite.
That sanctuary he destroyed!
He came to you, Inanna, as a friend to seduce you
as he tried to seduce his brother's wife.
O my holy, impetuous, wild cow and goddess of the moon,
throw this man out of the city
and capture him!

A Curse on Uruk

What am I in the place of nourishment
and sleep?
What am I now?
That city of Uruk has become an evil rebel
against your god.
An, make it surrender. Cut it in two!
Let Enlil curse it!
Let its whining child go without a pampering
mother.
O lady, the harp of mourning is on the ground.
Your ship of mourning is on a hostile shore,
dragged over the rocks.
When the people of the city hear my sacred song,
they are ready to die.

Condemning the Moongod Nanna

As for me, my Nanna ignores me.
He has taken me to destruction,
to the alleys of murder.
Ashimbabbar has not judged me wrong.
If he had, what do I care?
If he had, what do I care!
I am Enheduanna.
I was triumphant, glorious,
but he drove me from my sanctuary.
He made me escape like a swallow
from the window.

My life is in flames.
He made me walk through the brambles
on the mountain.
He stripped me of the crown correct
for a high priestess.
He gave me a dagger and a sword,
and said:
"Turn them against your own body.
They are made for you."

Antiphonal Hymn in Praise of Inanna

No one has sung "Let the world know!"
to Nanna
but only to his daughter, you, Inanna.
You are lofty like Heaven.   Let the world know!
You are wide like the earth.   Let the world know!
You devastate the rebellious land.   Let the world know!
You roar over the land.   Let the world know!
You smash their heads.   Let the world know!
You devour corpses like a dog.   Let the world know!
Your glance is terrible.   Let the world know!
You raise your terrible glance.   Let the world know!
Your glance is flashing.   Let the world know!
You are victorious.   Let the world know!
No one has sung "Let the world know!"
to Nanna
but only to his daughter, you, Inanna.
O my lady, this song has made you great
and exalted you.
O my lady, wife of An, I have told your fury!

Final Prayer

In the censer the coals are high
with flame for the rites.
The bridal chamber waits for you. Go in
and fill your heart!

I have done all I can do. I sang to you,
exalted lady.
What I sang at midnight
let the singer echo at noon!
Because your husband is captive,
your rage increases, your heart is never calm.

The Restoration of Enheduanna to Her Former Station

The first lady of the throne room
has accepted Enheduanna's song.
Inanna loves her again.
The day was good for Enheduanna, for she was dressed
in jewels.
She was dressed in womanly beauty.
Like the moon's first rays over the horizon,
how luxuriously she was dressed!
When Nanna, Inanna's father,
made his entrance
the palace blessed Inanna's mother Ningal.
From the doorsill of heaven came the word:
"Welcome!"

> *The fifteen preceding poems were adapted by*
> *Aliki and Willis Barnstone from the translations by*
> *William W. Hallo and J.J.A. van Dijk.*

Akkadian

MIDDLE EUPHRATES KINGDOM OF MARI

Inib-sarri

Inib-sarri (ca. 1790–1745 B.C.).   A daughter of the king Zimri-Lim, a constant theme of her letters is her unhappy residence in Aslakka and Nabur. She was probably married to Ibal-Addu.

A Letter to Her Father

Twice I have written you that I am unhappy,
my lord,
and you wrote back:
"Go and enter the city of Aslakka."

Now I have gone into Aslakka
and I am very unhappy.

For Ibal-Addu's wife is queen there!
That woman takes in gifts almost every day
from a multitude of cities,
including Aslakka,
but she forces me to sit in a corner
like a female idiot,
digging my fingers into my cheek!

WB

Eristi-Aya

Eristi-Aya (ca. 1790–1745 B.C.).   Also a daughter of Zimri-Lim, she was placed by her parents in a cloister. Much of her correspondence concerns the matter of her support.

A Letter to Her Mother

I am a king's daughter, you a king's wife.
I am furious!
Those tablets you and your husband used
to order me into this cloister,
let's forget them.
But remember this:
even warriors seized as booty in war
are treated humanely.
At least, treat me like them!

WB

Egyptian

Anonymous Hieroglyphic Texts

The Egyptian love poems (ca. 1500 B.C.), even in word-by-word literal translations, appear remarkably personal, intimate, and modern. Women's poetry of the Middle East has a main source in Egypt. Many of the lyrics recall the love fragments of the Shir Hashirim, the biblical Song of Songs.

> With candour I confess my love;
> I love you, yes, and wish to love you closer;
> As mistress of your house,
> Your arm placed over mine.
> Alas your eyes are loose.
> I tell my heart: "My lord
> Has moved away. During
> The night moved away
> And left me. I am like a tomb."
> And I wonder: Is there no sensation
> Left, when you come to me?
> Nothing at all?
>
>
> Alas those eyes which lead you astray,
> Forever on the loose.
> And yet I confess with candour
> That no matter where else they roam
> If they roam towards me
> I enter into life.

Ezra Pound and Noel Stock

The swallow sings "Dawn,
Whither fadeth the dawn?"

So fades my happy night
My love in bed beside me.

Imagine my joy at his whisper:
"I'll never leave you," he said.
"Your hand in mine we'll stroll
In every beautiful path."
Moreover he lets the world know
That I am first among his women
And my heart grieves no longer.

Ezra Pound and Noel Stock

Pleasant Songs

I

O flowers of Mekhmekh, give us peace!
For you I will follow my heart's dictation.

When you embrace me
So bright is the light that shines from you
I need balm for my eyes.

Knowing for certain that you love me
I nestle at your side.

My heart is sure that among all
Men you are the main one for me.

The whole world shines.
I wish we could go on sleeping together,
Like this, to the end of eternity.

II

So small are the flowers of Seamu
Whoever looks at them feels a giant.

I am first among your loves,
Like a freshly sprinkled garden of grass
and perfumed flowers.

Pleasant is the channel you have dug
In the freshness of the north wind.

Tranquil our paths
When your hand rests on mine in joy.

Your voice gives life, like nectar.

To see you is more than food or drink.

III

There are flowers of Zait in the garden.
I cut and bind flowers for you,
Making a garland,
And when you get drunk
And lie down to sleep it off,
I am the one who bathes the dust from your feet.

Ezra Pound and Noel Stock

The pomegranate speaks:
My leaves are like your teeth
My fruit like your breasts.
I, the most beautiful of fruits,
Am present in all weathers, all seasons,
As the lover stays forever with the beloved,
Drunk on "shedeh" and wine.

All the trees lose their leaves, all
Trees but the pomegranate.
I alone in all the garden lose not my beauty,
I remain straight.
When my leaves fall,
New leaves are budding.

First among fruits
I demand that my position be acknowledged,
I will not take second place.
And if I receive such an insult again
You will never hear the end of it.

.   .   .   .   .

With lotus in bloom
And lotus in bud,
And oil and sweet myrrh of every kind,
You will be among the contented
For the rose pavilion is highly thought of
And well looked after.

.   .   .   .   .

There he is!
Let us go up and embrace him
And keep him here all day long.

Ezra Pound and Noel Stock

I find my love fishing
His feet in the shallows.

We have breakfast together
And drink beer.

I offer him the magic of my thighs
He is caught in the spell.

Ezra Pound and Noel Stock

I wish to paint my eyes,
so if I see you, my eyes will glisten.
When I approach you and see your love,
you are richest in my heart.
How pleasant this hour is!
May it extend for me to eternity.
Since I have lain with you
you have lifted my heart high.

WB

Hebrew

ANCIENT HEBREW

The biblical selections represent poems specifically and traditionally attributed to women. The songs of Deborah and of Hannah are in the grand manner of biblical poetry and form the basis of the lament tradition in the New Testament. The Song of Songs is a fragmentary love idyll. No single work has been more central to the love tradition of Western poetry, from the *jarchas* of Spain and women's songs of medieval Portugal to the love lexicon of the mystics. The original lyrics probably had no religious meaning, but their inclusion in the canon was justified by treating this collection of impassioned folk songs as an allegory of the love of God for Israel, in rabbinic tradition, and of the love of Christ for his Church by early Christian writers. In his "Spiritual Canticle," Saint John of the Cross used the more heretical allegory of the individual soul joining with God. The Jews originally gave the speaker the names of King Solomon, the Shulamite, the Brothers, and the Chorus of the Daughters of Jerusalem in order to be able to keep the work within the holy canon, though apparently the work was collected centuries after the reign of King Solomon.

Hannah's Thanksgiving (Samuel 2:1–10)

And Hannah prayed, and said,

> "My heart rejoiceth in the Lord,
> Mine horn is exalted in the Lord:
> My mouth is enlarged over mine enemies;
> Because I rejoice in thy salvation.
> There is none holy as the Lord:
> For there is none beside thee:
> Neither is there any rock like our God.
> Talk no more so exceeding proudly;
> Let not arrogancy come out of your mouth:

For the Lord is a God of knowledge,
And by him actions are weighed.
The bows of the mighty men are broken,
And they that stumbled are girded with strength.
They that were full have hired out themselves for bread;
And they that were hungry ceased:
So that the barren hath borne seven;
And she that hath many children is waxed feeble.
The Lord killeth, and maketh alive:
He bringeth down to the grave, and bringeth up.
The Lord maketh poor, and maketh rich:
He bringeth low, and lifteth up.
He raiseth up the poor out of the dust,
And lifteth up the beggar from the dunghill,
To set them among princes,
And to make them inherit the throne of glory:
For the pillars of the earth are the Lord's,
And he hath set the world upon them.
He will keep the feet of his saints,
And the wicked shall be silent in darkness;
For by strength shall no man prevail.
The adversaries of the Lord shall be broken to pieces;
Out of heaven shall he thunder upon them:
The Lord shall judge the ends of the earth;
And he shall give strength unto his king,
And exalt the horn of his anointed."

The Song of Deborah   (Judges 5:1–31)

Then sang Deborah and Barak the son of Abinoam on that day,
    saying,

"Praise ye the Lord for the avenging of Israel,
When the people willingly offered themselves.
Hear, O ye kings; give ear, O ye princes;
I, even I, will sing unto the Lord;
I will sing praise to the Lord God of Israel.

Lord, when thou wentest out of Seir,
When thou marchedst out of the field of Edom,
The earth trembled, and the heavens dropped,
The clouds also dropped water.
The mountains melted from before the Lord,
Even that Sinai from before the Lord God of Israel.

In the days of Shamgar the son of Anath,
In the days of Jael, the highways were unoccupied,
And the travellers walked through byways.
The inhabitants of the villages ceased, they ceased in Israel,
Until that I Deborah arose,
That I arose a mother in Israel. They chose new gods;
Then was war in the gates:
Was there a shield or spear seen
Among forty thousand in Israel?
My heart is toward the governors of Israel,
That offered themselves willingly among the people.
Bless ye the Lord.
Speak, ye that ride on white asses,
Ye that sit in judgment, and walk by the way.
They that are delivered from the noise of archers
In the places of drawing water,
There shall they rehearse the righteous acts of the Lord,
Even the righteous acts toward the inhabitants of his villages
        in Israel:
Then shall the people of the Lord go down to the gates.

Awake, awake, Deborah:
Awake, awake, utter a song:
Arise, Barak, and lead thy captivity captive, thou son of
        Abinoam.
Out of Ephraim was there a root of them against Amalek;
After thee, Benjamin, among thy people;
Out of Machir came down governors,
And out of Zebulun they that handle the pen of the writer.
And the princes of Issachar were with Deborah;
Even Issachar, and also Barak;
He was sent on foot into the valley.
For the divisions of Reuben
There were great thoughts of heart.

Why abodest thou among the sheepfolds,
To hear the bleatings of the flocks?

For the divisions of Reuben
There were great searchings of heart.
Gilead abode beyond Jordan:
And why did Dan remain in ships?
Asher continued on the sea shore,
And abode in his breaches.
Zebulun and Naphtali were a people that jeoparded their
      lives unto the death
In the high places of the field.

The kings came and fought,
Then fought the kings of Canaan
In Taanach by the waters of Megiddo;
They took no gain of money.
They fought from heaven;
The stars in their courses fought against Sisera.
The river of Kishon swept them away,
That ancient river, the river Kishon.
O my soul, thou hast trodden down strength.
Then were the horsehoofs broken
By the means of the prancings, the prancings of their mighty
      ones.

'Curse ye Meroz,' said the angel of the Lord,
'Curse ye bitterly the inhabitants thereof;
Because they came not to the help of the Lord,
To the help of the Lord against the mighty.'

Blessed above women shall Jael be,
The wife of Heber the Kenite,
Blessed shall she be above women in the tent.
He asked water, and she gave him milk;
She brought forth butter in a lordly dish.
She put her hand to the nail,
And her right hand to the workmen's hammer;
And with the hammer she smote Sisera, she smote off his
      head,
When she had pierced and stricken through his temples.
At her feet he bowed, he fell, he lay down:

At her feet he bowed, he fell:
Where he bowed, there he fell down dead.

The mother of Sisera looked out at a window,
And cried through the lattice,
'Why is his chariot so long in coming?
Why tarry the wheels of his chariots?'
Her wise ladies answered her,
Yea, she returned answer to herself,
'Have they not sped? have they not divided the prey;
To every man a damsel or two;
To Sisera a prey of divers colours,
A prey of divers colours of needlework,
Of divers colours of needlework on both sides, meet for the
      necks of them that take the spoil?'

So let all thine enemies perish, O Lord:
But let them that love him be as the sun when he goeth forth
      in his might."

from **Song of Songs (The Shulamite)**

I

The voice of my darling
comes. O hear him
leaping on the mountains,
dancing on the hills!
My love is like a gazelle
or a young stag.
Here he is standing
behind our wall,
gazing from the window,
peering through the grille.
My love answers and speaks to me:
"Rise, my love, my beautÿ,
and come away.
Winter is past,

the rains are over and gone.
Flowers appear on the land,
the time of the nightingale has come.
The voice of the turtledove
is heard in our land.
The fig tree is heavy with small green figs,
and grapevines are in bloom,
pouring out fragrance.
Rise, my love, my beauty,
and come away.
My dove, you are in the crevices of the rock,
in the recess of the cliffs.
Let me see your face,
let me hear your voice,
for sweet is your voice
and your face is beautiful."

II

In my bed at night
I looked for him whom my soul loves
and could not find him.
"I will rise and wander in the city,
in the streets and marketplaces
I will look for him whom my soul loves,"
yet I could not find him.
The watchmen who go about the city
found me. I said:
"Have you seen him whom my soul loves?"
I barely left them
when I found him whom my soul loves.
I seized him and would not.let him go
until I took him to my mother's house,
to the room of her who conceived me.

O daughters of Jerusalem,
I have made you swear
by the gazelles and by the deer of the hills
not to wake, not to wake my love
before the hour is ripe.

III

I sleep but my heart is awake,
my lover's voice is knocking:
"Open, let me in, my sister, my darling,
my dove, my perfect one,
for my head is filled with dew,
my hair is wet with drops of night."

I have taken off my garments.
How can I put them on?
I have washed my feet.
How can I dirty them now?
My lover's hand showed at the door
and in me I burned for him.
I rose to open to my love,
my hands dripped with myrrh,
my fingers with myrrh flowing
over the handle of the bolt.
I opened to my love
but my love had gone, had vanished.

When he spoke my soul had vanished.
I looked for him and could not find him.
I called. He did not answer.
The watchmen who go about the city
found me.
They beat me, they wounded me,
they stripped me of my mantle,
those guardians of the walls!

I beg you, daughters of Jerusalem,
if you find my love
what will you tell him?
Say I am sick with love.

IV

My love has gone down to his garden,
to the bed of spices,
to feed his sheep in the orchards,

to gather lilies,
I am my lover's and my lover is mine.
He feeds his flock among the lilies.

V

I am my lover's and he desires me.
Come, my darling,
let us go out into the fields
and spend the night in villages.
Let us wake early and go to the vineyards
and see if the vine is in blossom,
if the new grape bud is open
and the pomegranates in bloom.

There I will give you my love.
The mandrakes will spray aroma
and over our door will be precious fruit,
new and old,
which I have saved for you, my darling.

VI

Set me as a seal on your heart,
as a seal on your arm,
for love is strong as death,
jealousy is cruel as the grave.
Its flashes are flashes of fire,
a flame of God.
Many waters cannot drown it.
If a man measured love
by all the wealth of his house,
he would be utterly scorned.

VII

My love is white and ruddy,
one in ten thousand.
His head is like the finest gold,
his locks are wavy palm leaves,
black as a raven.

His eyes, doves by the small rivers;
bathed in milk
they are deeply set.
His cheeks are a bed of spices
fragrant.
His lips are lilies
dripping myrrh.
His arms are round gold
wet with beryl.
His belly is bright ivory
starred with sapphires.
His thighs are pillars of marble
in sockets of fine gold.
His appearance is like Lebanon,
excellent as the cedars.
His mouth is sweet,
all of him is pleasant.
This is my love and this is my friend,
O daughters of Jerusalem.

WB

MODERN HEBREW

Leah Goldberg

Leah Goldberg (1911–1970).   Born in Lithuania, she was educated in Kovno and at the University of Bonn. After emigrating to Palestine in 1935, she was a professor of comparative literature at Hebrew University, Jerusalem. In addition to writing a novel and a play, she was well known as a translator of European literature and as an author of children's books.

from Nameless Journey

II

My room is so small
that the days sneak in, humiliated.

I, too, live that way,
in the smell of smoke and apples.
At night the neighbors turn on lights
on the other side of the yard.
They shine quietly
through the branches of the tall birch,
through the windows facing me.
At night sometimes it is difficult to remember
that once
somewhere
there was my own window.

III

These have been weeks when no one
calls me by name, and this is very simple:
The parrot in the kitchen of my house
has not yet learned it.
People the breadth of the city
don't know it.
It has no voice, no sound or note.
Days, I go without a name
in the street whose name I know.
I sit for hours without a name
before the tree whose name I know.
Sometimes I think without a name
of him whose name I don't know.

Ramah Commanday

Of Myself

My life is engraved on my poems
as rings show the age of a tree,
as my years are the wrinkles of my forehead.

II

I have no bitter words
to release my delusions—
My images are clear as stained-glass windows;

Through them
one can see
How light in the sky is changing,
and how my love fell
like a dead bird.

III

It is simple:
There was snow in one country
and thorns in another;
And a star in the window of an airplane
at night,
from above the many lands.

IV

And they came to me,
commanded me to sing,
and they said: We are words,
I surrendered;
I sang them.
And yet there was a bridge between them
with lamps on the other side.
The man did not approach,
so I said he never came.

V

The hours of humiliation,
hours of grandeur
hours of pain;
They are not necessary,
For there stands an ancient covenant
between myself and the silence—
And there is a road to buried dreams
from a place beyond words.

Ramah Commanday

Our Backs Are to the Cypress

Our backs are to the cypress.
We are hiding the mountains behind our houses.
We are ashamed to see the star.
We hurry to the commotion of the streets
so that our hearts won't be confused
by open spaces.

And so we live
in closed rooms,
in streets belted by telephone and telegraph wires.
It is so far from all that we loved innocently.
On the other side of ourselves, we live
in our times.

Ramah Commanday

Dahlia Ravikovitch

Dahlia Ravikovitch (1936–). Born near Tel Aviv in Israel, she was raised on a kibbutz and studied at Hebrew University. Her first volume in Hebrew, *The Love of an Orange* (1959), established her as a distinct, modern voice among younger poets. Her collection of poems *A Dress of Fire* (1979) was published by the Sheep Meadow Press.

Poem of Explanations

Some people know how to love,
for others it's just not right.
Some people kiss in the street,
others find it unpleasant
and not only in the street.
I think it's a talent like any other,
perhaps that's an advantage.
Like the rose of Sharon
with a gift for blooming,
like the hyacinth that chooses its colors.
A rose or a hyacinth in bloom
can blind you.
I mean no offense: of course
there are others.

Hummingbirds are the most beautiful of birds,
but if you like
you can go to the sparrow.
Even so, I keep telling myself,
I'm not a bird of paradise,
I'm not a three-legged ram,
I'm not an apple that never ripens.

Chana Bloch

The Everlasting Forests

The everlasting forests won't last forever
if lightning strikes them.
Rumors reach us a long way off
about the earth's
tremors.
The dream of the Yellow River no longer beguiles me
for there's nothing in it but water
and that goes down in the end to one of the seas.

The imagination has no bounds
but when you stop to think
how is the Black Sea different from the Caspian Sea?
A man of thirty is no child,
stops hoping for miracles, is not seduced
by the heart's noise.
He won't lose himself even when the sun goes down,
when the marvelous sea darkens and swallows its sharks.

But rumors keep returning, there's no way
to stop them.
They draw each other around the world
as the wind draws the waves.
First they bear you up like Ophelia
then they sweep you away into the depths
and all the dreams of your childhood, all your
imaginings
won't pull you out again from the waters.

Chana Bloch

Neo-Aramaic

PERSIA

Traditional Song

A folk poem (undated).   It is reported in Irene Garbell, *The Jewish Neo-Aramaic Dialect of Persian Azerbaijan*. This version is reworked by Jerome Rothenberg.

Young Woman's neo-aramaic jewish persian Blues

would write a letter with
                    my scissors mouth
                                        (would say)
how you were once a big
                    butter & egg man
                                        just a beggar now
still would I kill
                    myself for you
                                        you in your soldier suit
be down to meet you
                    in a taxi
                                        honey
God's up in heaven
                    he can get you
                                        all that you need
the while your momma
                    dies from it
                                        because you wouldn't
let it just be

                              Jerome Rothenberg

Greek

ANCIENT GREEK

Sappho

Sappho (7th–6th century B.C.).   Born on the island of Lesbos (hence Lesbian) in Eressos or the capital Mytilene. She was married and had a daughter, Kleis, to whom she wrote several poems. Other love poems were written to women friends. In an epigram in the Greek anthology, Plato writes: "Some say nine Muses—but count again./ Behold the tenth: Sappho of Lesbos." From these words attributed to Plato has come the custom of referring to outstanding women poets as the "tenth Muse," a title bestowed on Sor Juana Inés de la Cruz, Louise Labé, Alfonsina Storni, Gabriela Mistral, etc. Sappho was considered the most important lyric poet of Western antiquity. Catullus, writing in sapphics, imitated her forms and addressed his main love poems to Lesbia. It was common for Greek and Latin writers to know the entire canon of Sappho's poems by heart. Her work survived and was constantly recopied until nearly A.D. 1000, when a wrathful church destroyed whatever it could find. In 1073 her writings were publicly burned in Rome and Constantinople by order of Pope Gregory VII. Most of her poems have survived either as fragments in mutilated papyrus, largely found at Crocodilopolis in the Fayum in Egypt, or in quotations by ancient writers. One poem exists in its entirety, the "Prayer to Aphrodite," in *Literary Composition* by Dionysius of Halicarnassus. An equally famous poem, "To me he seems like a god," has been translated by poets from Catullus to William Carlos Williams. Sappho wrote with accuracy, involvement, and jarring detachment about herself, her friends, and the politics of tyranny and exile.

> To me he seems like a god
> as he sits facing you and
> hears you near as you speak
> softly and laugh

All the poems by Sappho, Praxilla, Telesilla, Anyte, and Korinna presented here have been translated by WB and are from his *Greek Lyric Poetry*.

in a sweet echo that jolts
the heart in my ribs. For now
as I look at you my voice
is empty and

can say nothing as my tongue
cracks and slender fire is quick
under my skin. My eyes are dead
to light, my ears

pound, and sweat pours over me.
I convulse, paler than grass,
and feel my mind slip as I
go close to death

[but must suffer all, being poor.]

✍

Come, holy tortoise shell,
my lyre, and become a poem.

✍

My mother always said
that in her youth she was
exceedingly in fashion

wearing a purple ribbon
looped in her hair. But
the girl whose hair is yellower

than torchlight need wear no
colorful ribbons from Sardis—
but a garland of fresh flowers.

✍

Some say cavalry and others claim
infantry or a fleet of long oars
is the supreme sight on the black earth.
I say it is

the one you love. And easily proved.
Did not Helen who far surpassed all
mortals in beauty desert the best
of men, her kin,

and sail off to Troy and forget
her daughter and dear kinsmen? Merely
the Kyprian's gaze made her bend and led
her from her path;

these things remind me now
of Anaktoria who is far,
and I
for one

would rather see her warm supple step
and the sparkle of her face than watch
all the dazzling chariots and armored
hoplites of Lydia.

～∽～

Like a mountain whirlwind
punishing the oak trees,
love shattered my heart.

～∽～

I could not hope
to touch the sky
with my two arms.

～∽～

The glow and beauty of the stars
are nothing near the splendid moon
when in her roundness she burns silver
about the world.

～∽～

In gold sandals
dawn like a thief
fell upon me.

～∽

My Atthis, although our dear Anaktoria
lives in distant Sardis,
she thinks of us constantly, and

of the life we shared in days when for her
you were a splendid goddess,
and your singing gave her deep joy.

Now she shines among Lydian women as
when the red-fingered moon
rises after sunset, erasing

stars around her, and pouring light equally
across the salt sea
and over densely flowered fields;

and lucent dew spreads on the earth to quicken
roses and fragile thyme
and the sweet-blooming honey-lotus.

Now while our darling wanders she thinks of
lovely Atthis's love,
and longing sinks deep in her breast.

She cries loudly for us to come! We hear,
for the night's many tongues
carry her cry across the sea.

∽∽

"Sappho, if you do not come out,
I swear, I will love you no more.

O rise and free your lovely strength
from the bed and shine upon us.
Lift off your Chian nightgown, and

like a pure lily by a spring,
bathe in the water. Our Kleïs
will bring a saffron blouse and violet

tunic from your chest. We will place
a clean mantle on you, and crown
your hair with flowers. So come, darling,

with your beauty that maddens us,
and you, Praxinoa, roast the nuts
for our breakfast. One of the gods

is good to us, for on this day
Sappho, most beautiful of women,
will come with us to the white city

of Mytilene, like a mother
among her daughters." Dearest Atthis,
can you now forget all those days?*

↬

Honestly I wish I were dead!
Although she too cried bitterly

when she left, and said to me,
"Ah, what a nightmare it is now.
Sappho, I swear I go unwillingly."

And I answered, "Go, and be happy.
But remember me, for surely you
know how we worshiped you. If not,

then I want to remind you of all
the exquisite days
we two shared; how

you took garlands of violets
and roses, and when by my side
you tied them round you in soft bands,

* The speaker may be Atthis, whose words Sappho is quoting.

and you took many flowers
and flung them in loops
about your sapling throat,

how the air was rich in a scent
of queenly spices made of myrrh
you rubbed smoothly on your limbs,

and on soft beds, gently, our desire
for delicate girls
was satisfied,

and how there was no dance and no
holy shrine
we two did not share,

no sound,
no
grove.''

∽∿∽

Love—bittersweet, irrepressible—
loosens my limbs and I tremble.

Yet, Atthis, you despise my being.
To chase Andromeda, you leave me.

∽∿∽

Then I said to the elegant ladies:
"How you will remember when you are old
the glorious things we did in our youth!

We did many pure and beautiful things.
Now that you are leaving the city,
love's sharp pain encircles my heart.''

∽∿∽

On your dazzling throne, Aphrodite,
sly eternal daughter of Zeus,
I beg you: do not crush me
with grief

but come to me now—as once
you heard my far cry, and yielded,
slipping from your
father's house

to yoke the birds to your gold
chariot, and came. Handsome sparrows
brought you swiftly to
the dark earth,

their wings whipping the middle sky.
Happy, with deathless lips, you smiled:
"What is wrong, Sappho, why have
you called me?

What does your mad heart desire?
Whom shall I make love you,
who is turning her back
on you?

Let her run away, soon she'll chase you;
refuse your gifts, soon she'll give them.
She will love you, though
unwillingly."

Then come to me now and free me
from fearful agony. Labor
for my mad heart, and be
my ally.

⮑

Leave Krete and come to this holy temple
where the graceful grove of apple trees
circles an altar smoking with frank-
incense.

Here roses leave shadows on the ground
and cold springs babble through apple branches
where shuddering leaves pour down pro-
found sleep.

In our meadow where horses graze
and wild flowers of spring blossom,
anise shoots fill the air with a-
roma.

And here, Aphrodite, pour
heavenly nectar into gold cups
and fill them gracefully with sud-
den joy.

❧

Mother darling, I cannot work the loom
for sweet Kypris has almost crushed me,
broken me with love for a slender boy.

❧

Like a sweet apple reddening on the high
tip of the topmost branch and forgotten
by the pickers—no, beyond their reach.

Like a hyacinth crushed in the mountains
by shepherds; lying trampled on the earth
yet blooming purple.

❧

All the while, believe me, I prayed
our night would last twice as long.

Andromache's Wedding

Kypros!
A herald came.
Idaos. Racing powerfully.

Of the rest of Asia. Imperishable glory! (He said:)
"From holy Thebes and the waters of Plakia,
graceful Andromache coming with the navy
over the salt sea. They come with armbands of gold

and purple gowns and odd trinkets of rare design
and countless silver jars and ivory pins."
So he spoke. And Priam sprang to his feet

and the glowing news went from friend to friend
through the wide city. Instantly the sons of Ilios
hitched the mules to their finely wheeled chariots,
and a throng of wives and slender-ankled girls
climbed inside. Priam's daughters rode alone,
while young men led their horses under the cars.
Greatly.
Charioteers.

Like gods.
Holy.
They all set out for Ilium
in the confusion of sweet flutes and crashing cymbals,

and women sang a loud heavenly song
whose wonderful echo
touched the sky.
Everywhere in the streets.
Bowls and chalices.

Myrrh and cassia and incense rode on the wind.
Old women sang happily
and all the men sang out with thrilling force,
calling on Paean, great archer, lord of the lyre,
and sang of Hektor and Andromache like gods.

∞·∞
You came. And you did well to come.
I longed for you and you brought fire
to my heart, which burns high for you.

Welcome, darling, be blessed three times
for all the hours of our separation.

ঔঔ
O Gongyla, my darling rose,
put on your milk-white gown. I want
you to come back quickly. For my
desire feeds on

your beauty. Each time I see your gown
I am made weak and happy. I too
blamed the Kyprian. Now I pray
she will not seek

revenge, but may she soon allow
you, Gongyla, to come to me
again: you whom of all women
I most desire.

ঔঔ
I have no embroidered headband
for you, Kleis, and no idea
where to find one while Myrsilos

rules in Mytilene. The bright
ribbon reminds me of those days
when our enemies were in exile.

ঔঔ
Here are fine gifts, children,
O friend, singer on the clear tortoise lyre,

all my flesh is wrinkled with age,
my black hair has faded to white,

my legs can no longer carry me,
once nimble like a fawn's,

but what can I do?
It cannot be undone,

no more than can pink-armed Dawn
not end in darkness on earth,

or keep her love for Tithonos,
who must waste away;

yet I love refinement, and beauty and light
are for me the same as desire for the sun.

~~~

O dream from the blackness,
come when I am sleeping.

Sweet is the god but still I am
in agony and far from my strength,

for I had hopes to share
something of the happy ones,

nor was I so foolish
as to scorn pleasant toys.

Now may I have
all these things.

~~~

You lay in wait
behind a laurel tree,

and everything
was pleasant:

you a woman
wanderer like me.

I barely heard you,
my darling;

you came in your
trim garments,

and suddenly: beauty
of your garments.

∿

Hesperos, you bring home all the bright dawn disperses,
bring home the sheep,
bring home the goat, bring the child home to its mother.

∿

Hermes came to me in a dream. I said
—My master, I am altogether lost,
and my many riches do not console me.
I care only
        to die, and to watch the dewy lotus
along the banks of Acheron, river of Hell.

∿

If my nipples were to drip milk
and my womb still carry a child,
I would enter this marriage bed
           intrepidly,

but age dries my flesh with a thousand
wrinkles, and love is in no hurry
to seize my body with the gifts
           of pleasant pain.

Yet, let us sing praises to her
who wears the scent of violets
           on her young breasts.

∿

It would be wrong for us. It is not right
for mourning to enter a home of poetry.*

---

* To her daughter when Sappho was dying.

⚬⚬⚬
Someone, I tell you,
will remember us.

We are oppressed by
fears of oblivion

yet are always saved
by judgment of good men.

⚬⚬⚬
Now in my
heart I
see clearly

a beautiful
face
shining,

etched
by love.

⚬⚬⚬
Andromeda
forgot,

and I too
blamed you,

yet Sappho,
I loved you.

In Kypros I am Queen
and to you a power

as sun of fire
is a glory to all.

Even in Hades
I am with you.

Praxilla

Praxilla (ca. 450 B.C.).   Praxilla was from the Argolid and wrote abundantly in diverse meters. What has survived is largely quotations of ancient critics who cited the "nonsense" in poetry. So her images and their startling, fresh sensuality have been preserved as exempla to support such statements as Zenobios's "Only a simpleton would put cucumbers and the like on a par with the sun and the moon."

You gaze at me teasingly through the window:
a virgin face—and below—a woman's thighs.

Most beautiful of things I leave is sunlight;
then come glazing stars and the moon's face;
then ripe cucumbers and apples and pears.

Telesilla

Telesilla (5th century B.C.).   A poet from Argos, she was also a military leader and heroine. Plutarch writes in *Feminine Virtue*, "No less renowned than these collective deeds is the battle in which the Spartan king Kleomenes was driven from Argos with his men by the poet Telesilla."

O Artemis and your virgin girls,
come to us.
Run swiftly to escape
the rape of the hunter Alpheus.

Anyte

Anyte (ca. 290 B.C.).   Anyte was a poet from Arkadia whose work has come down to us largely through the *Greek Anthology*. The earlier compiler of the *Greek* or *Palatine Anthology* Meleagros speaks of "the many lilies of Anyte" in his proem to the anthology (*anthos:* flower; *legein:* to collect). Her poems, usually in epigrammatic quatrains, speak in clear detail of nature and people in nature.

Lounge in the shade of the luxuriant laurel's
beautiful foliage. And now drink sweet water
from the cold spring so that your limbs weary
with summer toil will find rest in the west wind.

◦◦◦

Alive, this man was Manes, a common slave.
Dead, even great Darius is not his peer.

◦◦◦

I am Hermes.* I stand in the crossroads by a windy
    belt of trees near the gray shore of the sea
where the weary traveler may rest: here a fountain
    bubbles forth a cold and stainless water.

Korinna

Korinna (ca. late 3rd century B.C.).   Daughter of Acheloodoros and Hipokrateia, the Boiotian poet was a pupil of Myrtis. She defeated Pindar five times in poetry competitions. Her works included narrative choral lyrics for an audience of women. Aelianus wrote of her; "When Pindar the poet competed at Thebes he ran into ignorant judges, and was defeated five times by Korinna. To show the judges' bad taste, Pindar called Korinna a pig." Plutarch wrote in praise of Korinna, "When Pindar was still young and proud of his mastery of the language, Korinna censured him for his poor taste" (*Glory of Athens*).

I Korinna am here to sing the courage
of heroes and heroines in old myths.
To Tanagra's daughters in their white robes
I sing. And all the city is delighted
with the clean water of my plaintive voice.

◦◦◦

Kithairon sang of cunning Kronos
and sacred Rheia who stole her son
Zeus, mighty among immortals.

Then the Muses asked the gods to put
their ballot stones in the gold
urn. All stood up and Kithairon won

the greater part. Hermes shouted loud,
at once proclaiming sweet victory.
The gods adorned his brow with flowers,

* On a statue in an orchard.

and Kithairon rejoiced. But Helikon
was stunned with bitter rage, and tore
a massive boulder from the mountain.

Insanely he shouted and lobbed the rock
down on thousands of mortals below!

ॐ

When he sailed into the harbor
his ship became a snorting horse.

Hermes ravished the white city

while the wind like a nightingale
sang with its whirling war axe.

ॐ

Although I was her pupil,

even I reproach Myrtis
of the crystalline voice.

She was a mere woman poet
yet she challenged Pindar.

ॐ

Will you sleep forever,
Korinna?
There was a time
when you were not a loafer.

BIBLICAL GREEK (KOINÉ)

Mary, mother of Jesus

Mary, mother of Jesus.　　The "Magnificat" is the Latin title from the Vulgate of this song attributed in Luke to Mary. The poem exists in Greek and, like the gospel itself, had a Hebrew original, now lost. The hymn, like the songs of Deborah and of Hannah, is in the tradition of Old Testament poetry, in this instance in parallelistic stanzas found in the psalms, Ecclesiastes, and elsewhere.

The Magnificat　(Luke 1:46–56)

My soul magnifies the Lord
and my spirit is joyful in God my savior,

who looked upon his servant
in her low station.

As of now
all generations will call me blessed.

In his power he did wondrous things for me
and his name is holy.

His mercy goes from generation to generation,
to those who fear him.

He showed the strength of his arm
and scattered those who are proud in the mind of their heart.

He toppled monarchs from their thrones
and raised the poor to their feet.

He filled the hungry with good foods
and sent the rich away empty.

He helped Israel, his servant and child,
and remembered mercy

as he told our fathers,
Abraham and his seed, forever.

WB

BYZANTINE GREEK

Kassia

Kassia (ca. 840).   Kassia is the one woman poet who has come down to us from
Byzantine Greek. Her "Mary Magdalene" is chanted during Holy Week in the Eastern
Orthodox Church.

Mary Magdalene

Lord, this woman who fell into many sins
   perceives the God in you,
   joins the women bringing you myrrh,
   crying she brings myrrh   before your tomb.
"O what a night   what a night I've had!
   Extravagant frenzy   in a moonless gloom,
   craving the body.
Accept this spring of tears,
   you who empty seawater   from the clouds.
Bend to the pain   in my heart, you
   who made the sky bend   to your secret incarnation
   which emptied the heavens.
I will kiss your feet, wash them,
   dry them with the hair of my head, those feet whose steps
Eve heard at dusk
   in Paradise   and hid in terror.
Savior of souls   who will trace the plethora
   of my sins or the knowable chasm of your judgments?
Do not overlook me, your slave,
   in your measureless mercy."

AB, WB, and Elene Kolb

MODERN GREEK

Moirologia

Moirologia (of uncertain date).   These are traditional funeral songs that derive from the rich tradition of popular Greek poetry. A blend of Greek myth and Christian themes, they depict peasant life with harsh, often colorful realism.

Traditional Funeral Songs

What can I send you under the earth,
my darling eyes?
An apple? It would rot.
A quince would mold. If I sent grapes
they would shrivel,
a rose would be bare.
I send the tears caught in my bandana.

WB and Elene Kolb

Funeral Lament (Kommos) from Epiros

See the young man I've laid out.
   —snakes have eaten me—
   See the cypress tree.
      O!

He doesn't move, he doesn't sway.
   —kill me, my people—
   He doesn't walk with bravado.
      O!

Who cut your roots?
   —my soul!—
   Who burnt the treetops?
      O!

What have you done to me, hero?
   —snakes have eaten me—

What have you done, my soul?
   O!

Is it autumn?
   —I say the truth—
Winter?
   O!

Now spring comes.
   —my little child—
Now summer.
   O!

Branches bloom.
   —listen, child—
The wildflowers in the field.
   O!

Birds return.
   —my darling eyes—
The swallows of spring
   O!

It is Easter Sunday.
   —snakes have eaten me—
Christ is risen.
   O!

The young wear red,
   —my young hero—
the old men black.
   O!

But you, my hero
   —O my hero—
are in the ground
   O!

Open your eyes!

Elene Kolb

Eleni Vakalo

Eleni Vakalo (1921–).   Born in Athens, she studied archaeology in Athens and esthetics in Paris. The author of many books of poetry, she writes of urban life, of traditional families and political figures, with wit, irony, and surreal vividness.

My Father's Eye

My father had a glass eye.

On Sundays when he stayed at home he would take other eyes out of his pocket, polish them with the edge of his sleeve and then call my mother to make her choice. My mother would giggle.

In the mornings my father was well satisfied. He would toss the eye in his hand before he wore it and would say it was a good eye. But I did not want to believe him.

I would throw a dark shawl over my shoulders as though I were cold but this was that I might spy on him. At least one day I saw him weeping. There was no difference at all from a real eye.

This poem
Is not to be read
By those who do not love me
Not even
By those
Who will not know me
If they do not believe I existed
Like themselves

After this episode with my father
I became suspicious even of those who had real eyes.

Kimon Friar

Lydia Stephanou

Lydia Stephanou (1927–).   Born in Athens, Lydia Stephanou has lived abroad (Bulgaria, Australia, and the Middle East) for extended periods. Her poems are at once mythological and introspective. In addition to creating a substantial body of poetry, Stephanou is a distinguished literary critic who has published important volumes on poetic theory.

A "Case of Assault"

I did not know where you kept your heart
How far away so that you would not have to listen;
Perhaps in the box of the tobacconist
Who made the rounds of the coffee bars
With dark glasses much older than his eyes—
Or even deeper
Under the roots of that single tree we met
Along the asphalt road,
The motors spitting sparks in the shadow
Like fireflies that once filled the night.
The buses led us
Correctly
From death to death
As we lost more and more of our flesh each time.
—The day I loved you the bells rang
And the troops rolled by
Changing their long body continuously before us
Changing the sun into copper and bronze
Roses that tore the skin.
Your blood spurted,
Pellucid,
And I rushed to touch it
Before its source brimmed out of your eyes
And pierced the earth for the first time
—I did not know—
That very moment I lost you amid the crowd
I did not know—how blood
Returns again into the depths of the earth.
—A hubbub all around us, the lines breaking,
Everyone celebrating his own destruction.

Girls cut their hair short with bayonets
Others hugged the legs of horses and others
Climbed naked on the armored cars
Their legs boosted by the snow's height.
I stood there, for I did not want to kill you
And someone threw me down on my back, like all women.
—I never learned where you kept your heart.
You retained an undivided silence.

Kimon Friar

Lina Kasdaglis

Lina Kasdaglis (1928–).   Born in Corinth, Lina Kasdaglis now lives in Athens. She has published two books of her own poems and has translated books by Mauriac, Gide, and Steinbeck into modern Greek. She also writes children's literature.

Traffic Lights

What are you doing here in this strange world that goes on and off,
green lights—red lights,
green lights—red lights.

You don't manage to make the green lights
as you run in pursuit of lost time.
A moment, a moment in the darkness—
the red lights go on again.

What are you doing on this narrow island in the street?
Your love beckons from the far shore,
beckons and vanishes without waiting for you.
Your child has gone ahead, you call but he can't hear you—
again the red lights go on.

Whoever built a house became a window,
a large window to let the exhaust fumes in,
a naked window that lights up and goes out, lights up and goes out,
and never sleeps the sleep of the just.

What are you doing in this world that doesn't know coolness and mist,
the light rain, the sudden storm, the breath of God,
what are you doing in the forest that has no leaves,
gathering plastic flowers and shapeless words under the tree trunks—
Programming, Public Relations, Expansion of Labor Enterprise.

Green lights—red lights.
The red lights go on again
but you haven't made it across and never will.

Edmund Keeley and Mary Keeley

Nana Issaia

Nana Issaia (1934–).   Born in Athens, a painter and poet, she has had several one-woman shows and has published four collections of poems. Her poetry has appeared in many British and American magazines, and she has translated Sylvia Plath into modern Greek.

Sacrifice

Darkness reigned
no way for you to wake up again
the night had no solution.

As you were lying there
I sacrificed your standing erect
(but to what?)
as my daily life
took over the room.

Helle Tzalopoulou Barnstone

Dream

It's a madman, I said
he will go through my dream
he will come out the other end
yet no one has left
he is still inside.

Helle Tzalopoulou Barnstone

Eva Mylonás

Eva Mylonás (1936–).   Born in Athens, Eva Mylonás studied law there and French literature at the Sorbonne. Her first book, *Voyage*, was published in 1970; *Clear Metal* appeared in 1975. She has also published two collections of translated prose poems, *20 Prose Poems by Rimbaud* (1977) and *20 Prose Poems by Baudelaire* (1978).

Holidays

During the holidays
I received seven invitations to commit suicide
with the knives of strangers at my back
I drink fruit juice to my health
My luminous landscapes
my disobedient slaves
and the graves of my friends
are all so far behind me
The colors of lovers
the glimmering of hair
and the afternoon
are all so dark
During the holidays
they gave me a bright green dress
a live dress made of golden beetles
I wore my chlorophyll dress
Long rows of rotted leaves
beads
half-truths
are all so far behind me
that no connection no past exists
no remembrance exists
nor the sentiments of skeletons
I have no continuity
                    coherence
                       conventions.

                                        Kimon Friar

Jenny Mastoraki

Jenny Mastoraki (1949–).   Born in Athens, Mastoraki (also Mastorakis), a poet of intense conciseness and brutal satire bordering on the grotesque, is a powerful figure among modern Greek poets.

Then they paraded Pompey's urn
simply and soberly
on the backs of royal elephants.
They lifted it aboard with pulleys
in the port of Haifa,
and the stevedores still brag
how they debauched with him
down by the wharfs.

Nikos Germanakos

The Wooden Horse then said
no I refuse to see the press
and they said why not and he said
he knew nothing about the killing,
and anyway he himself always ate
lightly in the evenings
and once in his younger days
he'd worked as a pony on a merry-go-round.

Nikos Germanakos

The Crusaders
knew the Holy Places
only from postcards and tourist guides.
So, they set off
with banners, tents,
tools and sandwiches,
just like a school excursion.
One day, Baldwin's mistress
received a Polaroid snapshot
of some monument or other.
Her beau was marked with an arrow,
one among a dozen heads.
They brought it off—though it was a fluke,
to tell the truth.

The papers of the period
spoke of bloodless operations.

Nikos Germanakos

The Vandals

Now they're pillaging the last coast.
In the activities of the Vandals
there was always a certain faith
that history would ultimately justify
the Dorians

Nikos Germanakos

Prometheus

Nights bring you the fever
of a Roman triumph.
The legionnaire, the goddess, the demagogue—
a slave whispers your name in his ear—
the hetaera with the redskin cheeks,
the bath attendant.
Just before the ceiling opens
and they all die, smothered in flowers,
you, having discovered fire,
hastily trade your liver.

Nikos Germanakos

The Death of a Warrior

The death of a warrior
should be slow and studied
like the distilled
transport of an adolescent
who becomes a man when he first makes love.
On his tomb place
two large question marks
for life and for death
and a traffic sign
that forbids
the passing of parades.

Kimon Friar

Latin

CLASSICAL LATIN

Sulpicia

Sulpicia (1st century B.C.). Only her name and the six short poems contained in the third book of Tibullus' poetry are known. The poems describe her passion for her lover Cerinthus, which may, like her own name, be a literary name. Sulpicia is the only Latin woman poet to have survived the Classical period, although educated women were known to paint and write poems, which suggests that women poets, unlike their Greek or Oriental counterparts, were not esteemed highly enough to have their works copied and preserved.

> At last love has come. I would be more ashamed
> to hide it in cloth than leave it naked.
> I prayed to the Muse and won. Venus dropped him
> in my arms, doing for me what she
> had promised. Let my joy be told, let those
> who have none tell it in a story.
> Personally, I would never send off words
> in sealed tablets for none to read.
> I delight in sinning and hate to compose a mask
> for gossip. We met. We are both worthy.

AB and WB

> Darling, I won't be your hot love
> as a few days ago
> I thought I was, if in all my youth
> I ever did anything
> so stupid, which I regret more,

as yesterday
when I left you alone in the night
    to conceal my fire.

AB and WB

It's nice that though you are casual about me
    you keep me from stumbling into a mess.
Your toga and a hustling whore mean more
    to you than Sulpicia, Servius's daughter.
Friends worry about me and are upset that somehow
    I might tumble into bed with a nobody.

AB and WB

My hated birthday is here, and I must go
    to the awful country without Cerinthus.
What is sweeter than Rome? Is a farmhouse
    a place for a girl? Stuck in Arezzo
with its icy river and fields? Friend Messalla,
    don't worry. Trips are often poorly timed.
They drag me there. I leave my soul and heart here
    and, being forced, I cannot be myself.

AB and WB

Do you have a sweet thought, Cerinthus,
    for your girl?
Fever shakes my thin body. Unless
    I thought
it was your wish, I would not choose
    to win
over my sad disease. Why should I
    elude death
if when I am sick, your heart
    is calm?

AB and WB

Have you heard? The troubles
of the road
have vanished from your girl's
sad spirit?
I shall be in Rome for
my birthday.
Let that day be enjoyed
by us both.
It came from nowhere,
luckily for you.

                                    AB and WB

MEDIEVAL LATIN

Anonymous

Anonymous, from the *Cambridge Songs* (ca. 1000).   This *planctus* (lament) is the best-known surviving woman's lament from the Latin Middle Ages.

from the Cambridge Songs

Wind is thin,
sun warm,
the earth overflows
with good things.

Spring is purple
jewelry;
flowers on the ground,
green in the forest.

Quadrupeds shine
and wander. Birds
nest. On blossoming
branches they cry joy!

My eyes see, my ears
hear so much, and
I am thrilled.
Yet I swallow sighs.

Sitting here alone,
I turn pale. When strong
enough to lift my head,
I hear and see nothing.

Spring, hear me.
Despite green woods,
blossoms and seed,
my spirit rots.

WB

Anonymous

Anonymous, from the *Carmina Burana* (ca. 1200).   This ballad is similar to other pregnancy songs found in Middle English and other European languages.

from the Carmina Burana

I loved
secretly,
but now
the pain!
My belly
is huge,
and birth
is near.

Mother yelled,
Father slapped
me. Both
fumed. I'm
alone in
this room,
and can't
play outside.

Neighbors
look at me
as at a
monster. They
stare, poke each
other, and
clam up till
I walk by.

They always
point at me
with fingers.
I'm a wonder.
They wink
obscenely.
They damn me
for one sin.

Why am I
talking?
I'm gossip
in every mouth.
Pain grows
and now
my friend
is gone.

He ran off
for good,
back to France.
Without him
I hurt,
almost die.
I cry
for myself.

WB

The Languages of India

SANSKRIT

Sanskrit poets.   Unlike Chinese authors, whose dates of birth and death are usually known to the year, Indian authors, as contemporary historians lament, were revered, but except for major writers little is known about biography and chronology.

Vidya

Vidya (ca. 659).   Also written as Vijja and Vijjaka, Vidya has been identified as a queen, the wife of Candraditya (a son of Pulakesin II) from the Nerur.

> Friends,
> you are lucky you can talk
> about what you did as lovers:
> the tricks, laughter, the words,
> the ecstasy.
> After my darling put his hand on the knot
> of my dress,
> I swear I remember nothing.
>
> *WB*

> Please keep an eye on my house for a few moments,
> good wife and neighbor.
> My child's father despises the well water,
> which is tasteless,
> so I'm going to the river,
> alone,
> to its bank dark with tamala trees

and its dwarf forest of sugar cane
with their sharp and broken stalks,
which may scratch my breasts.

WB

Sila

Sila (between 700 and 1050).   Sila appears in Vidyakara's anthology of classical
Sanskrit poetry.

My husband is the same man
who first pierced me.
We knew long evenings wet with the moon.
Wind from the hills of Vindhya
was heavy with fresh jasmine.
I am the same woman
yet I long for the stream and its reeds
which knew us happy. Which knew us
graceful
in endless evenings of making love.

WB

Mahodahi

Mahodahi (between 700 and 1050).   Mahodahi appears in Vidyakara's anthology
of classical Sanskrit poetry.

On the holy day of your going out to war,
the sky is black with dust
which the chisel of your horses' feet
ground from the earth.
The sun's charioteer is lost,
his steeds rock from horizon to horizon,
stumbling off track,
and the sun on its longer voyage
is melancholy.

WB

Vallana

Vallana (between 900 and 1100).   Vallana appears in Vidyakara's anthology of classical Sanskrit poetry.

> After he stripped off my clothes,
> unable to cover my breasts with my thin arms
> I clung to his chest as to my robe.
> But when his hand crept below my hips,
> who could save me from plunging into a sea of shame
> but the love god
> who teaches us how to faint?

WB

Marula

Marula (ca. 1156).   Marula is thought to have been a contemporary of the Kalacuri king Bhijjala, who came to the throne at Kalyan in 1156. Tradition has it that she was an ascetic, but this is uncertain.

Meeting after Separation

> When I said "You have grown thin,"
> She came and clung to me.
> "Your clothes are bedraggled," I said
> And she hung down her head.
> When I said "I can hardly see you,"
> Her big breasts heaved, and she wept.
> When I embraced her
> She was troubled with indescribable love
> And in an instant the doe-eyed girl
> Was completely merged in my heart.

Tambimuttu and G. V. Vaidya

CLASSICAL TAMIL

Okkur Macatti

Okkur Macatti (between 1st and 3rd centuries).   A classical Tamil woman poet.

What Her Girlfriends Said to Her

Come, let's go climb on that jasmine-mantled rock
and look

> if it is only the evening cowbells
> of the grass-fed contented herds
> returning with the bulls

> or the bells of his chariot
> driving back through the wet sand of the
>   forest ways,
> his heart full of the triumph of a job
>   well done
> with young archers driving by his side.

A. K. Ramanujan

Kaccipettu Nannakaiyar

Kaccipettu Nannakaiyar (between 1st and 3rd centuries).   A classical Tamil woman
poet.

What She Said

My lover capable of terrible lies
at night lay close to me
in a dream
that lied like truth.

I woke up, still deceived,
and caressed the bed
thinking it my lover.

It's terrible. I grow lean
in loneliness,
like a water lily
gnawed by a beetle.

A. K. Ramanujan

Andal

Andal (ca. 10th century).   The daughter of a priest, Andal developed an intense
love for the god Krishna. According to legend, on reaching the age of marriage she
became the wife of Krishna.

Cuckoo, noisy among the Shenbaka flowers,
honey on your beak,
the god who holds a white conch shell
in his left hand
is not yet revealed to me
but he is in my heart and I suffer.
Sing,
but not too loudly, so he will come.

WB

O people who live in the world,
do you hear what we will do for our god?
We will sing to him, praise him who made
the ocean of milk his bed.
We will not use ghee nor drink milk,
we will not paint our eyes after our morning bath,
we will not wear flowers,
we will do good things,
use good words,
give away our possessions and live for him.

WB

To Krishna Haunting the Hills

Is it true that black birds infinitely dispersed
wake the dawn,
sing to the god
and welcome the sun?
They sing words of the great god whose bed
is the banyan leaf,
who lives on hills robed with the jungle.

WB

KANNADA

Mahādēvi

Mahādēvi (12th century).   Born in Udutadi, India, Mahādēvi was initiated into
Siva worship at the age of ten, which she considered the real moment of her birth. Siva
at the Udutadi temple was Mallikarjuna, or the Lord White as Jasmine, an epithet that
appears in her poems. She was apparently married to the local king, Kausika. Conflict
between divine and earthly love is shown in the poem beginning "husband inside,/
lover outside./ I can't manage them both." She left Kausika to live the life of a saint.
She threw away her clothing, a last concession to the male world, in a gesture of social
defiance, and wandered, god-intoxicated, thereafter covered only by her tresses. (See
her poem beginning "You can confiscate/ money in hand;/ can you confiscate/ the
body's glory?") Her poems express three forms of love: love in separation, love
forbidden, and love in union. According to legend she died into "oneness with Siva"
when she was still in her twenties, in a brief bright burning.

Riding the blue sapphire mountains
wearing moonstone for slippers
blowing long horns
O Siva
when shall I
crush you on my pitcher breasts?

O lord white as jasmine
when do I join you
stripped of body's shame
and heart's modesty?

                                        A. K. Ramanujan

Other men are thorn
under the smooth leaf.
I cannot touch them,
go near them, nor trust them,
nor speak to them confidences.

Mother,
because they all have thorns
in their chests,

                I cannot take
any man in my arms but my lord

        white as jasmine.

                                        A. K. Ramanujan

Would a circling surface vulture
    know such depths of sky
    as the moon would know?

would a weed on the riverbank
    know such depths of water
    as the lotus would know?

would a fly darting nearby
    know the smell of flowers
    as the bee would know?

O lord white as jasmine
    only you would know

the way of your devotees:
how would these,

these
   mosquitoes
   on the buffalo's hide?

                   A. K. Ramanujan

People,
male and female,
blush when a cloth covering their shame
comes loose.
         When the lord of lives
lives drowned without a face
in the world, how can you be modest?

When all the world is the eye of the lord,
onlooking everywhere, what can you
cover and conceal?

                   A. K. Ramanujan

Honnamma

Honnamma (late 17th century).   Commanded by her king to write him a poem, Honnamma wrote this poem on ideal wifehood.

Wasn't your mother a woman?
Who took care of you in your house,
a man?
Idiots!
Why do you vomit insults, screaming
"woman, woman!"
What special virtue is there in a son
or perdition in a daughter?
Here and in the other world
happiness

comes to a person, not a gender.
A crude man is nothing.
A noble daughter is blessed forever.

                                                    WB

MARATHI

Mukta Bai

Mukta Bai (13th century).   In her childhood she and her brothers and sisters survived abandonment by begging. Her poems are philosophical and religiously intellectual.

Although he has no form
my eyes saw him
and his glory shines in my mind,
which knows his secret
inner form
invented by the soul.
What is beyond the mind,
has no boundary.
In it our senses end.
Mukta says: Words cannot contain him,
yet in him all words are.

                                                    WB

I live where darkness
is not,
where I am happy.
I am not troubled by coming and going
and am beyond all vision,
above all spheres.
His spirit lives in my soul.
Mukta says: He is my heart's
only home.

                                                    WB

Jana Bai

Jana Bai (14th century?)   Jana Bai was the servant of the poet Namdev. Many of her poems speak of devotion to Namdev.

> She was my staff and I am blind.
> Where is she concealed?
> In what strange forests do you pause,
> my doe,
> while I your dumb fawn wander lost,
> looking for you?
> Without you, what is there?
> How can I stay alive?
> Let me find my mother, Vithoba!
> Your servant Jana pours out her prayer
> before the saints.

WB

PALI

Sumangala's Mother

Sumangala's Mother.   Only the language Pali is known.

> A free woman. At last free!
> Free from slavery in the kitchen
> where I walked back and forth stained
> and squalid among cooking pots.
> My brutal husband ranked me lower
> than the shade he sat in.
> Purged of anger and the body's hunger,
> I live in meditation
> in my own shade from a broad tree.
> I am at ease.

WB

HINDI

Mira Bai

Mira Bai (1498–1573).   Mira Bai is said to have been born in Merta, raised by her grandfather, and married at 18 to the Prince of Mewar. She was a rebel in thought, poetry, and religion, and after her husband's death, the local king attempted to poison her. She fled and lived in places sacred to Krishna, the god whom her poems address. She died in Dwarka.

Mira Bai is the best known Indian woman poet. Her poems are in Hindi, but appear from an early period in translation in other Indian languages. Her tone is at once humorous, daring, religious, ecstatic. As in the Western mystical tradition, her love for God is personal and erotic. Her "dancing" before God, as the whirling of the dervishes, the quaking of Quakers, the babbling of the Spanish mystics, is an example of extreme, defiant individualism and transcendental elation.

> Friend, how can I meet my lord?
> My love came
> and vanished from my courtyard
> while I was sleeping.
> I will tear my sari,
> wear faded red robes
> and live as an ascetic.
> I will break my bracelets,
> tangle my hair
> and wash away the mascara
> on my eyelashes.
> This separation is torture
> day and night.
> Peace never comes.
> Mira says: Lord Hari, god of permanence,
> when we come together,
> let us never again be torn apart.
>
>   *WB and Usha Nilsson*

> Friend, don't be angry.
> I'm going to see the holy men.

Shyam lives in my heart.
I hunger for no one else.
While others sleep pleasantly,
my eyes are awake.
People who do not worship Shyam
are ignorant and mad.
While the Dark One is in me,
I don't sleep.
I won't drink pond water
in the rain season.
Hari is the spring for my thirst.
He is shaped in delicate dark colors.
I look for his face.
Mira is desolate because you are not
with her.
Take her to you.

WB and Usha Nilsson

Mira is dancing with bells tied
on her ankles.
People say Mira has gone mad.

Her mother-in-law is upset
at the ruined family honor.

The king sends her a cup of poison.
Laughing, she drinks it
for her drink is Hari's beautiful face.

She has offered her body and her soul
at Hari's feet.
She drinks the honey of her vision.
Only he
is her ultimate protector.

WB and Usha Nilsson

Rana, I know you gave me poison
but I came through
as gold left in a fire
emerges bright as a dozen suns.
Opinion and family name
I throw away like water.
You should hide, Rana.
I am a powerless mad woman.
Krishna's arrow in my heart
destroys my reason.
I hug the lotus feet of holy men,
give them body and soul.
Mira's lord knows she is his servant.

WB and Usha Nilsson

I can't break with the Dark One.
Like leaves in the autumn
I turn sallow.
People say jaundice.
My father called the doctor who held
my hand, took the pulse.
He doesn't know it's my heart
that's wrong.
Away from her lover, Mira is in agony.
Lord, come. Let her see you.

WB and Usha Nilsson

Rana, why do you treat me
as your enemy?
You are like karil in the brush,
thorny aphylla of the desert.
I abandon the palace and its balconies,
have gone away from your city.
The mark on my forehead and my mascara
are gone.
I've chosen saffron robes

(of one who has forsaken the world).
Mira has her lord Girdhar,
who turns poison into nectar.

WB and Usha Nilsson

Hari, look at me a while.
I look at you
but your eyes are not on me.
Your heart is dead.
My hope is in your glance,
no other place.
I stand begging you
till morning.
Mira's Hari is imperishable.
Her life is his.

WB and Usha Nilsson

My eyes are thirsty
for you.
All day
I watch the road,
my eyes in pain.
The koel bird on the branch
sings,
also painful to me.
People gossip
and laugh at me.
But Mira is sold to Hari.
She is his slave for many lives.

WB and Usha Nilsson.

My love is in my house,
I watched the road for years
but never saw him.

I put out the worship plate,
gave away gems.
After this, he sent word.
My dark lover has come,
joy is on my limbs.
Hari is an ocean,
my eyes touch him.
Mira is an ocean of joy.
She takes him inside.

WB and Usha Nilsson

Yogi, don't go away.
I'm at your feet, your slave.
The way of love is strange.
Lead me to it.
I will build a pyre of sandalwood
for you to light.
When I am ashes,
smear them on your body.
Mira says: Lord Girdhar Nagar,
let our fires unite.

WB and Usha Nilsson

Hari helps his people.
Draupadi,
when your cousin tried to strip you naked
before the crowd,
he saved you by making your sari endless.
He became a man-lion for his disciple
and freed a drowning elephant,
sending it to heaven.
Mira says: Prince Girdhar,
help me.

WB and Usha Nilsson

I don't sleep. All night
I am watching for my love.
Friends offer
wise words.
I reject them.
Without him I can't rest,
but my heart is not angry.
My limbs are weak,
my lips call to him.
This pain of separation
cannot be understood.
I am like the rainbird calling for clouds,
like fish craving water.
Mira is lost,
her senses are dead.

WB and Usha Nilsson

At the Holi festival of color
I play with Shyam.
Red gulal powder
makes clouds red.
Long syringes
spray drops of color.
My pitcher is filled with saffron
and unguents of sandal, chova, and musk.
Mira belongs to Girdhar Nagar,
a slave at his feet.

WB and Usha Nilsson

Wake, child
with the flute.
Night is gone. It is dawn.
Every house has opened its doors.
As the milkgirls churn the cheese
their bracelets clamor.
Get up, child. It is dawn.

Outside the door are gods and men.
the boys with their cows,
noisy, shout: Jai!
The men with cattle offer the god
butter and bread.
Handsome Girdhar, Mira's lord,
saves those who come to be saved.

WB and Usha Nilsson

Let me see you.
I repeat:
be kind.
In the month of Jeth
birds are sad and waterless.
In Asarh peacocks and rainbirds
call for clouds.
Rain in Savan.
My friends celebrate the festival of Tij.
Rivers overflow in Bhadon.
Your distance hurts me.
In Ashwin
mother-of-pearl drinks from the star Swati.
In Kartik people worship gods.
You are my one god.
Agahan is cold.
Come quickly. Care for me.
In Paush frost blankets the earth.
You are not here.
Spring comes in Magh.
Everyone sings.
People play Holi in Phagun.
Banraj trees burn me.
My desire grows stronger in Chait.
Let me see you.
In Baishakh, Banraj trees bloom,
the koel bird sings.
It is the month

for consulting astrologers and priests.
Mira, alone, is desolate.
When will she see you?
She spends her days looking for crows.

WB and Usha Nilsson

TELUGU

Kshetrayya

Kshetrayya (17th century).   Only the language is known.

Dancing-Girl's Song

My heart's friend, will you tell me who this mischievous youngster
      is?
As I lay in bed he came to me, and with his bow shot me with a
      shower of softest flowers,
And so the unrest in my heart!
The young fellow boldly crashed into my house in daylight,
Held me very tight for a moment only,
Bit my lip, and ran off with the speed of an arrow.

My heart's friend, does he think I am his for life?
He came and I could not resist his great commanding Voice—
He set my heart floating on the honey stream of his words,
With his amorous kiss he burnt my lips,
And left me utterly alone, and unfulfilled.
Is it nothing more than his butter-stealing boyishness?*
Or does he think I'm like easy shepherdesses he ill-uses to his
      heart's content?

He came to me as if he had bought me for a wife,
Forced the clothing off my breasts,

* As a boy Lord Krishna stole some butter for a prank.

And held them, O so tight, in great hands
And told me not to be annoyed,
And then without pity, slipped away.
O my heart's own friend, this is not a place for poor young girls
    like me;
The old and young look on alike, and will not stop his tricks.
There is no one in this wide world to whom I can by right
    complain.
The playful youngster with cloud-blue skin and garment of yellow
    silk,
Boasted to me he rules the hearts of sixteen thousand
    shepherdesses,
And walked proudly away,
Leaving me in a daze of shameless desire.

Tambimuttu and R. Appalaswamy

KASHMIRI

Lal Ded

Lal Ded (16th century?)   Lal Ded is a poet of the *dhakti* school (poetry of devotion) whose search is for union with God.

I drag a boat over the ocean
with a solid rope.
Will God hear?
Will he take me all the way?
Like water in goblets of unbaked clay
I drip out slowly,
and dry.
My soul whirls. Dizzy. Let me
discover my home.

WB

I came by the way
but didn't go back by the way.
I was still on the riverbank
with its crazy bridges.
Day failed me.
I looked in my pocket
for money. Not a cowry shell.
How can I pay for the ferry?

WB

Impermanence

For a moment I saw a surging river.
For a moment I saw no bridge to cross it.
For a moment I saw a bush: all flowers.
For a moment I saw neither rose nor thorn.

For a moment I saw a cooking fire.
For a moment I saw no house nor smoke.
For a moment I saw no begging Brahmans.
For a moment I saw the aunt of a potter's wife.

WB

Persian

INDIA

Princess Zeb-un-Nissa

Princess Zeb-un-Nissa (1638–1702).   A patron of poets and scholars, and a deeply religious woman, she was later imprisoned by her father, perhaps for complicity in a rebellion by her brother.

> Though I am Laila of the Persian romance,
> my heart loves like ferocious Majnun.
> I want to go to the desert
> but modesty is chains on my feet.
> A nightingale came to the flower garden
> because she was my pupil.
> I am an expert in things of love.
> Even the moth is my disciple.
>
>   *WB*

Empress Nur Jahan

Empress Nur Jahan (?–1646).   Although born into a poor family and abandoned as a child, eventually she married Jehangir, a powerful emperor.

> The moon of Id came
> like a curved knife on the face
> of the firmament.
> The wine shop key was lost
> and is found at last.

My eyes have one job: to cry.
Since I have no hands or feet
what other work do I have?

WB

Your love turned my body
into water.
My eye-paint dripped into the eyes
of foamy water.
Morning wind in the garden
opens blossoms.
The key to my locked spirit is
your laughing mouth.

WB

IRAN

Forugh Farrokhzad

Forugh Farrokhzad (1935–1967).   Born in Teheran, Iran, Farrokhzad is considered the outstanding contemporary poet in the Middle East. She was also a filmmaker and critic. At the height of her creative career she was killed in an automobile accident.

On Earth

I never wanted to be a star
in the sky's mirage,
a select soul
or an unspeaking friend of angels.
I never left the earth
or took up with stars.

I stand on the earth
and my body like a plant
absorbs wind, sun, and water
to stay alive.

I'm looking out the window.
I'm an echo,
not eternal,
and look for nothing but a song's echo.
In the wailing chant is joy
and better than the plain silence of pain.
I look for no refuge
in the dew on the lily of my body.

People walking by have written memories
with a black line of love
on the walls of my life's cottage.
Arrows are in my heart,
the candle is upside down.
What are left are quiet dots of faded colors
in puzzling words of madness.

Every lip against my lips
conceived a star
and floated on the night river of my memories.
What good is a star?

Girdhard Tikku

I'm Sad

I'm sad
I'm sad

I go to the veranda and feel with my fingers
The taut skin of the night

No one will introduce me
To the sun
No one will take me to the feast of the sparrows

Keep in mind the flight
The bird is to die

Reza Baraheni

Once More

I'll greet the sun once more—
that stream running in me
those clouds unfurling my thoughts
pangs of the growing poplar grove
through seasons of drought
crows flying with me
offering the scent
of their fields at night
my mother who showed me my old age
in the mirror where she lived
and the earth, swollen with greening seeds,
lusting to make me again—
I'll greet them all

I'll come   I'll come   I'll come
my hair trailing its underground scents
my eyes heavy variations of darkness
herbs in my hands culled in those woods beyond the wall

I'll come   I'll come   I'll come
and the gate will be all love
and those who love
and that girl waiting there still
in the gate of love—I'll greet them all once more

> *Jascha Kessler with Amin Banani*

In the land of dwarfs,
criteria of measurement
always trod the axis of zero.
Why should I stop?
I obey the four elements
and the work of forming my heart's laws
is not the affair of the parochial blind
                              governors.

What have I to do with the long wails of fear
of the generic bestial organ?
What to me is the humble march of the worm
                              in the vacuity of flesh?
The bloody ruin of flowers
                         has committed me to live.
Bloody race of flowers, do you know?

                              Girdhard Tikku

Turkish

BAYATI

Bayati, Azerbaijani contemporary oral song (undated).   Azerbaijani is the Turkish dialect of the eleven million Turks in Iran. Each song has four parts (lines) of seven syllables. The songs dealing with death are often sung by professional mourners, *moshgars,* at the graveyard.

Love Songs

White cups white
mist on the mountains.
I remember
your black moustache.

Reza Baraheni and Zahra-Soltan Shokoohtaezeh

Your handkerchief should be blue,
a lover a good match.
With a handsome lover
you can stand pain.

Reza Baraheni and Zahra-Soltan Shokoohtaezeh

I am a bunch of red roses.
You hurt me
like the helpless nightingale
you locked in a cage.

Reza Baraheni and Zahra-Soltan Shokoohtaezeh

Our roofs are adjacent,
our balconies neighbors.
You see me from there,
I see you from here.
Let our enemies go blind.

Reza Baraheni and Zahra-Soltan Shokoohtaezeh

Stars in the sky are as big
as coins.
The door of my house
is on your way.
Come once in the morning
and once in the evening,
and those who see us
will think we are lovers.

Reza Baraheni and Zahra-Soltan Shokoohtaezeh

Death Songs

I'll keep your shirt white,
will wash and keep it unwrinkled.
If you come through my door,
I'll keep you as my guest.

Reza Baraheni and Zahra-Soltan Shokoohtaezeh

Leave the window open.
I want to see who is coming.
How can they bury in a grave
someone who died from love?

Reza Baraheni and Zahra-Soltan Shokoohtaezeh

I'm the snow on mountains,
I don't melt in the sun.
Bury me in the shade.
I'm young. I won't rot.

Reza Baraheni and Zahra-Soltan Shokoohtaezeh

Arabic

IRAQ

Rabi'a the Mystic

Rabi'a the Mystic (712–801).   Born in Basra (now in Iraq), her full name is
Rabi'a al-'Adawiyya. A celibate mystic, who wrote prose as well as poetry, and was
later canonized as an Islamic saint, she was a *zahid* (ascetic) and lived in seclusion in
the desert. Many miracles were attributed to her; for example, once when she needed
seasoning for her food, a peeled onion dropped from a bird's mouth directly into her
frying pan. Fire was a central symbol in her poems and in her spiritual life. She was
called "that woman on fire with love."

> O my Lord, if I worship you from fear of Hell
> burn me in Hell.
> If I worship you from hope of Paradise,
> exclude me from that place.
> But if I worship you for your own sake,
> do not withhold from me your eternal beauty.
>
> *WB*

> O my Lord, the stars glitter and eyes of men are closed,
> kings have shut their doors
> and each lover is alone with his love.
> Here, I am alone with you.
>
> *WB*

Al-Khirniq

Al-Khirniq (late 6th century).   Al-Khirniq's brother, the poet Tarafa, had satirized the king of Hira who sent Tarafa to an executioner with a sealed letter containing his death warrant. Most of Al-Khirniq's poems concern the death of her husband, Bishr ibn 'Amr, who was killed on Mount Qudab by a neighboring tribe.

Lament after Her Husband Bishr's Murder

You vilify me, but I rise above grief
when your blame choked me with saliva.

O I swear my sorrow for Bishr! He died
for the tribe, without a friend.

Good 'Alqama ibn Bishr! His soul oozed
from his throat, as the palm trunk

bends to fire. Death seized him pouring
out time . . . how many bones scattered on

Mt. Qulab: good men, companions of kings,
who sat pouring out cups of wine.

Their skulls were split, their noses mutilated
and rooted out. I could not

swallow my saliva. The others sat like women,
with their kohl washed

from their eyes. Bishr's death crushed them.
How could they recover from the sword?

WB

ARABIA

Al-Khansa

Al-Khansa (575–646).   Born in Mecca or Medina, Arabia, Al-Khansa was a member of a rich and powerful family, and was related to other important poets, including Zuhair ibn Abu Sulma. Her full name was Tumadir bint Amr ibn al Harith ibn al Sharid. Almost all her poems deal with the death of her two brothers Sakhr and Muawiya whom she laments with Homeric, epical strength. They were killed in a tribal battle before the coming of Islam. Later Al-Khansa evidently converted to Islam. She is a fiercely strong poet—earthy, wildly imaginative, using desert and tribal details to produce shocking, poignant images. She is the major woman poet in Arabic.

Elegy for Her Brother Sakhr

Cry out for Sakhr when a dove with necklaces
mourns gray in the valley.

When warriors put on light woven armor,
swords are the color of smooth salt

and bows groan and wail,
and bending spears are wet.

Giving, not weak,
brave like the predatory wood lion

of Bisha, he battles for friends
and kinsmen, who are like the lion,

whom he defends whether of the village
or wanderers on the desert.

When the wind howled his people were happy
as a wind of dust blew under a freezing cloud.

WB

On Her Brother Sakhr

No day was sad as the day Sakhr
left me. Sweet and forever bitter.

Sakhr was our lord, our chief.
In the winter Sakhr made a feast

and led us when we rode.
Sakhr killed when we were hungry.

Sakhr was our guide
like a mountain whose top is fire.

Firm, perfect face, and pious,
he kindled wars on the morning of fear.

He bore flags, saved our blood, was
witness for assemblies, an army for armies,

sacrificer of camels, a refuge for the oppressed,
liberator of prisoners, mender of bones.

I say there was no one like him in the world.

WB

The Night

My eye cried and woke me.
The night was pain.

WB

In Death's Field

In death's field, in morning distress,
every brother cries for you

in the field:
a fountain in the desert, protector

of their wealth.
When men fear a drought,

you are a night shower.
Waters fall on your grave.

I wished only
to pour rain as drink in the desert.

You and death have one shirt.
My passion scorns

all other solace.
A spirit went

on morning's track to the edge of day.
O striker of knights on the battle day,

your sword on the field of heat,
your camel swam through the dust,

short-haired like a wolf.
You attacked as their hero defender

until they turned from sacred relics . . .
If this age perished with you,

it was washed with rain,
and every tribe is a journey to ruin

and every treaty is erased by time.

WB

Sleepless

I was sleepless, I was awake all night
as if my eyes exuded pus.

I watched the stars, though I was not their shepherd,
and veiled my body in ragged cloth,

for I heard—it was black news—
the messenger's report:

"Sakhr is in the earth,
between wood and stones."

Go, may Allah receive you, as a man
of justice and revenge.

Your heart was free,
its roots were not weak.

Like a spearhead your shape shines in the night,
strong, firm, the son of free men.

I lament our tribe's hero. Death took you
and the others.

As long as the ringdove cries, I'll mourn you,
as stars light the midnight traveler.

I'll not make peace with the enemy
till their food kettles turn white . . .

They washed the shame from you,
your blood's sweat poured out purified,

and war rode a humpbacked herd,
bareback.

Defender in battle,
you ripped the spearmen, tooth and nail,

until thousands saw you
blind to fear. They were amazed

as your stomach burst, punctured above the nipples,
spurting the foam of your heart's blood.

WB

On Her Brother

My brother was not a camel driver,
a coward, shallow-hearted like a beast.

His sword glittered like a pool
under roaming night clouds.

He ran faster
than any of his men.

What good is life—even if he were happy—
since he ran out of time?

Each man whose family was happy in him
will visit his grave.

You saw a knight
on a horse running with its tail floating

in the wind, a brown warrior wrapped
in a coat of thin iron.

When they overtook him they shouted
like shepherds at daybreak.

WB

Rain to the Tribe

O eye, weep for a rider
skillful in jousting,

possessing strength and respect.
Just as death seizes him

we see him in the desert
guarding his troops

like a lion hidden in its cave.
He protects angrily,

scattering his iron-armored men over the earth
like dust in the noses of mangled warriors.

He dyes his spearhead against spears,
his madness burns.

When a bird flies out of the sticks
toward him, he catches it with his teeth.

What a handsome man in battle!
Late at night amid shouting,

our chief is lamented
in our babbling grief.

Who will rise from the desert? Who will save us
after my mother's son is buried?

WB and Tony Nawfal

Laila Akhyaliyya

Laila Akhyaliyya (late 7th century).   Born in Uqail, in present-day Iraq, Laila was married to a man named Sawwar, but her great love was for Tauba, probably a robber chief, who met a violent death, and her poems lament his death. Like Al-Khansa's poems, her work is characterized by intensity of feeling matched by a candid and often violent depiction of reality.

Lamenting Tauba

At Tauba's death I swore
I would not cry
I swore by Him who turns the spheres.

If a man has not lived shamefully,
there is no shame in dying.

No person, however safe in life, escapes
the tomb.
Only time is immortal.
No life is favored,
nor corpse reborn.
Every youth passes through destruction
to Allah.

All my dear friends, though eager to live long,
depart in disorder
while spheres spin around them.

I swear I won't stop crying for you
while one dove on a branch mourns
or birds fly.

                                                    WB

Laila Boasting

We are the Akhail. Our youth persists
until the enemy
creeps to us with the cane of praise.
Spears wept in fear

when we lost our hero
and revealed our friend to be an ocean.
The sword knew we were its brothers
in thirst
when it cut bones.
Our lungs are strong
when we wail with the first knives
of dawn.

WB

Camel

My camel kneels at Ibn Marwan's door
and groans three times in birth pangs.
Men circle her each night
with torches lighting the hills.
A leader and a youth bring companion armor
and words bright as Yemen cloth.
But crude milking injured her.
Now softly, on the slopes of Thadaq,
she's given dry food.
Then quickly to water, on good hoofs,
fast, her body lean.
Her summer offspring is unweaned
but day already smells of autumn.

WB

MOROCCO AND NORTHWEST AFRICA

Ancient Songs of the Women of Fez

Ancient Songs of the Women of Fez (undated).   These old traditional songs were collected in our century by Mohammed el Fasi in Fez, Morocco. They are in quatrains (*roubai* as in the *Rubayat* of Omar Khayyam) and are normally sung by a chorus of women.

I want to be in a garden with my love,
empty. Not even a gardener.
I want to be in a bath with my love,
empty. Not even a masseur,
and I'll bring him all the hot and cold water
he wishes.
Even his sweat I'll collect and put in flasks
so it will make me alive.
The day I am blind from crying,
I will paint my eyes with tears instead of khol.

WB

I see a man who is dull
and boring like no one else.

He is heavier than massive mountains.
When he laughs he shakes the plains of Gharb,
when he cries the coastal cities tremble.

To look at an ugly man
gives me a headache.

WB

My passion is like turbulence at the head
of waters
where boiling rivers sweep away a granite mill.

The sultan of love came to camp in my heart.
I welcomed him
and devised ecstatic nights with him,
but he debated with me and ordered me to satisfy
his every wild quirk.

But he has an untender heart.
I beg him.
He is iron and gives me neither freedom
nor the joy of union.
What causes my passion? Is love a joke?

WB

I want to be with my love in a garden
surrounded by pavilions with lovely cushions.
In its center are fountains and water
jetting up like milk.
The nightingale glorifies the orchard
and its seven-colored pears
with songs.

A young man goes from room to room,
gracefully.

The jasmine drops its branches.

Sitting by my friend,
I will be healed.

WB

A Rapier of Treason

My heart is an oil lamp
and the heart of him I love is the wick.
His oil consists of gentleness
and malice is the dart he cleans it with.

I'd like my love to be like the mast
holding a banner.

If my love walked as silently as
a tumbling goat,
I'd notice it.

I notice that my love now looks at me
crookedly.

Worse, the man is a rapier of treason.
Don't trust him.

Being intelligent, I measure him
by his mere look.

WB

haufi (traditional songs)

haufi (traditional women's songs of Algeria, undated).   These old songs, with many
variants, were recorded in our century by Mostefa Lacheraf. They deal with many
themes, including humor, frustrated and fulfilled love, social criticism, and the desert
and garden landscapes of Algeria.

Be happy for me, girls,
my mother-in-law is dead!
In the morning I found her
stiff, her mouth shut.
Yet I won't believe it
till I see the grass
waving on her tomb.

WB

The Languages of Africa

The source for all traditional African poems is *African Poetry* (1966), compiled and edited by Ulli Beier, by far the most sensitive and well translated of existing collections of traditional African poetry. As Beier points out, "Most translations of African poetry have been made by anthropologists, who were naturally more interested in the religious or sociological significance of the poems than in their literary merit." The poems have the universal qualities of the best oral poetry, some of them virtually indistinguishable from the most ancient Egyptian traditional poems that have survived in hieroglyphic texts.

BAGIRMI

Traditional

Love Song

I painted my eyes with black antimony
I girded myself with amulets.

I will satisfy my desire,
you my slender boy.
I walk behind the wall.
I have covered my bosom.
I shall knead coloured clay
I shall paint the house of my friend,
O my slender boy.
I shall take my piece of silver
I will buy silk.
I will gird myself with amulets
I will satisfy my desire
the horn of antimony in my hand,
Oh my slender boy!

H. Gaden

NYASA

Traditional

Song

Mother Mother shave me
let us go and see the bird
with the bright red beak.
Let's go to the bush Mother
to the small bush.
Let's brush off our hair
each other's hair.
Let us leave a guide-bone
for the goats that graze
that graze in my little field.
The little field I cultivate
I cultivate with a hoe
I bought in the European's home
the home where moss grows.
We shall bring forth a child
and we shall name him
and we shall name him *darkness*.

Ulli Beier

YORUBA (NIGERIA)

Traditional

Three Friends

I had three friends.
One asked me to sleep on the mat.
One asked me to sleep on the ground.
One asked me to sleep on his breast.

I decided to sleep on his breast.
I saw myself carried on a river.
I saw the king of the river and the king of the sun.
There in that country I saw palm trees
so weighed down with fruit
that the trees bent under the fruit,
and the fruit killed it.

Ulli Beier

HOTTENTOT (SOUTH AFRICA)

Traditional

Song of the Lioness for her Cub

Fear the one
who has sharp weapons
who wears a tassel of leopard tail,
he who has white dogs—
O son of the short-haired lioness!
My short-eared child,
son of the lioness who devours raw flesh,
you flesh-eater!
Son of the lioness whose nostrils are red with
    the bleeding prey,
you with the bloodred nostrils!
Son of the lioness who drinks water from the swamp,
You water-drinker!

Thomas Hahn

AMHARIC (ETHIOPIA)

Traditional

Song to a Lover

His trousers are wind,
his buttons hail.

He's a lump of Shoa earth,
at Gonda he is nothing.

A hyena with meat in its mouth,
dragged by a piece of leather.

Water in a glass, by the fire,
thrown into the heat.

A horse untouchable as mist,
a flooding brook.

No good for anything,
for anyone.

Why am I in love
with him?

WB

AFRIKAANS (SOUTH AFRICA)

Ingrid Jonker

Ingrid Jonker (1933–1965). Born in South Africa, she traveled extensively in Europe. She espoused the cause of the poor and blacks, which led to many personal difficulties with government authorities and with her father. She died by suicide.

Time of Waiting in Amsterdam

I can only say I have waited for you
through western nights
at bus stops
in lanes
by canals
on airfields
and the gallows of tears

And then you came
through the forlorn cities of Europe
I recognized you
I set out the table for you
with wine with bread with mercy
but imperturbably you turned your back
you detached your sex laid it down on the table
and without speaking a word
with your own smile
abandoned the world

Jack Cope and William Plomer

This Journey

This journey that obliterates your image
torn blood-angel thrown to the dogs
this landscape is deserted as my forehead
Wound of the roses

How I wanted to see you walk without chains
I longed to see your face open and free
your broken face dead and dry as the mud
Wound of the earth

In the nights of absence without eyes
I cried to see a real star in your hand
I cried to see the blue sky and to hear
One word from life

Bitter angel untrue with a flame in your mouth
under your armpits I have placed two swallows
and drawn a secret cross on your face
For the man

of whom you reminded me once

Jack Cope and William Plomer

I Am with Those

I am with those
who abuse sex
because the individual doesn't count
with those who get drunk
against the abyss of the brain
against the illusion that life
once was good or had beauty or sense
against the garden parties of falsehood
against the silence that beats into the temples
with those who poor and old
race against death the atom-bomb of the days
and in shacks count the last
flies on the walls
with those stupefied in institutions
shocked with electric currents
through the cataracts of the senses
with those who have been deprived of their hearts
like the light out of the robot of safety

with those coloured, african dispossessed
with those who murder
because every death confirms anew
the lie of life

And please forget
about justice it doesn't exist
about brotherhood it's deceit
about love it has no right

Jack Cope and William Plomer

Chinese

The Book of Songs

The Book of Songs (7th century B.C.).   *The Book of Songs* in Chinese is *Shih Ching* (song-word scripture), also known in the West as the 305 Confucian Odes; however, there is no reason to suppose that Confucius himself collected the songs. The poems' characteristic technique of parallelism occurs in popular poetry in many cultures, including biblical psalms and Romance popular song, especially the *leixapren* in Portuguese. Waley compares the poems to Japanese and even the Polish popular song: "They have cut the little oak, they have hewn it;/ It is no longer green./ They have taken away my lover./ Have taken him to the wars." *The Book of Songs* is one of the Five Confucian Classics. Ezra Pound translated it in its entirety, although the version is largely doggerel in contrast to his earlier, pioneer translations in *Cathay* (1915). It is thought that the poems of the *Shih Ching* were composed from the twelfth to the seventh century B.C., but their present form was established in the seventh century B.C. in the Chou dynasty.

A very handsome gentleman
Waited for me in the lane;
I am sorry I did not go with him.

A very splendid gentleman
Waited for me in the hall;
I am sorry I did not keep company with him.

I am wearing my unlined coat, my coat all of brocade.
I am wearing my unlined skirt, my skirt all of brocade!
Oh, sir, oh my lord,
Take me with you in your coach!

I am wearing my unlined skirt, my skirt all of brocade.
And my unlined coat, my coat all of brocade.

Oh, sir, oh my lord,
Take me with you in your coach!

Arthur Waley

Widow's Lament

The cloth-plant grew till it covered the thorn bush;
The bindweed spread over the wilds.
My lovely one is here no more.
With whom? No, I sit alone.

The cloth-plant grew till it covered the brambles;
The bindweed spread across the borders of the field.
My lovely one is here no more.
With whom? No, I lie down alone.

The horn* pillow so beautiful,
The worked coverlet so bright!
My lovely one is here no more.
With whom? No, alone I watch till dawn.

Summer days, winter nights—
Year after year of them must pass
Till I go to him where he dwells.
Winter nights, summer days—
Year after year of them must pass
Till I go to his home.

Arthur Waley

---

* A pillow of wood, inlaid with horn.

Cho Wen-chün

Cho Wen-chün (179?–117? B.C.).   According to legend, Cho Wen-chün (also written Chuo Wen-chün) eloped with the poet Ssu-ma Hsiang-ju and they set up a wine shop together. Her husband sold love poems to other ladies for a living. To persuade him to give up a concubine, she wrote ''Song of Snow-White Heads.'

Song of Snow-White Heads

Our love was pure
As the snow on the mountains:
White as a moon
Between the clouds—
They're telling me
Your thoughts are double;
That's why I've come
To break it off.
To-day we'll drink
A cup of wine.
To-morrow we'll part
Beside the Canal:
Walking about,
Beside the Canal,
Where its branches divide
East and west.
Alas and alas,
And again alas.
So must a girl
Cry when she's married,
If she find not a man
Of single heart,
Who will not leave her
Till her hair is white.

Arthur Waley

Hsi-chün

Hsi-chün (ca. 105 B.C.).   Arthur Waley adds the following note about Hsi-chün: "About the year 105 B.C. a Chinese lady named Hsi-chün was sent, for political reasons, to be the wife of a central Asian nomad king, K'un Mo, king of the Wu-sun. When she got there, she found her husband old and decrepit. He only saw her once or twice a year, when they drank a cup of wine together. They could not converse, as they had no language in common."

Lament of Hsi-Chün

My people have married me
In a far corner of Earth;
Sent me away to a strange land,
To the king of the Wu-sun.
A tent is my house,
Of felt are my walls;
Raw flesh my food
With mare's milk to drink.
Always thinking of my own country,
My heart sad within.
Would I were a yellow stork
And could fly to my old home!

Arthur Waley

Ch'in Chia's wife

Ch'in Chia's wife (1st century B.C.).   When Ch'in Chia was summoned to go to the capital at a time his wife was ill, he wrote her three poems instead of saying good-bye. She in turn sent him this reply.

Ch'in Chia's Wife's Reply

My poor body is alas unworthy:
I was ill when first you brought me home.
Limp and weary in the house—
Time passed and I got no better.
We could hardly ever see each other:
I could not serve you as I ought.
Then you received the Imperial Mandate:

You were ordered to go far away to the City.
Long, long must be our parting:
I was not destined to tell you my thoughts.
I stood on tiptoe gazing into the distance,
Interminably gazing at the road that had taken you.
With thoughts of you my mind is obsessed:
In my dreams I see the light of your face.
Now you are started on your long journey
Each day brings you further from me.
Oh that I had a bird's wings
And high flying could follow you.
Long I sob and long I cry:
The tears fall down and wet my skirt.

Arthur Waley

Lady Pan

Lady Pan (ca. 48–6 B.C.).   Pan Chieh-yu is the title bestowed on an imperial concubine of second rank. When a former slave girl, Chao Fei-yen, became the emperor Ch'eng's favorite concubine, the emperor disposed of Lady Pan, who was said to have written this poem on a fan. The emperor was so moved that he pardoned her from false accusations and rewarded her with much gold, whereupon she left the harem and wrote a considerable body of poetry. Unfortunately, only this poem survives, and its authorship is uncertain. It is the first of many poems written by deserted courtesans and was imitated many times in later centuries.

A Present from the Emperor's New Concubine

I took a piece of the rare cloth of Ch'i,
White silk glowing and pure as frost on snow,
And made you a fan of harmony and joy,
As flawlessly round as the full moon.
Carry it always, nestled in your sleeve.
Wave it and it will make a cooling breeze.
I hope, that when Autumn comes back
And the North wind drives away the heat,
You will not store it away amongst old gifts
And forget it, long before it is worn out.

Kenneth Rexroth

Anonymous

Anonymous Poems (ca. 206 B.C. to A.D. 220).   These anonymous poems are uniform in the use of five-word lines and are characterized by extreme economy and directness of language. They are thought to have been written by specific diverse writers during the late Han period. They had an enormous influence on later Chinese poetry.

from Nineteen Old Poems

A bright moon illumines the night-prospect;
The house-cricket chirrups on the eastern wall.
The Handle of the Pole-star points to the Beginning of Winter;
The host of stars is scattered over the sky.
The white dew wets the moor-grasses—
With sudden swiftness the times and seasons change.
The autumn cicada sings among the trees,
The swallows, alas, whither are they gone?
Once I had a same-house friend,
He took flight and rose high away.
He did not remember how once we went hand in hand,
But left me like footsteps behind one in the dust.
In the South is the Winnowing-fan and the Pole-star in the North,
And a Herd-boy* whose ox has never borne the yoke.
A friend who is not firm as a great rock
Is of no profit and idly bears the name.

Arthur Waley

Cold, cold the year draws to its end,
The mole-cricket makes a doleful chirping.
The chill wind increases its violence.
My wandering love has no coat to cover him.
He gave his embroidered furs to the Lady of Lo,
But from me his bedfellow he is quite estranged.
Sleeping alone in the depth of the long night
In a dream I thought I saw the light of his face.
My dear one thought of our old joys together,

* Herdboy is a star; here, a friend who is not a real friend.

He came in his chariot and gave me the front reins.
I wanted so to prolong our play and laughter,
To hold his hand and go back with him in his coach.
But when he had come he would not stay long
Nor stop to go with me to the Inner Chamber.
Truly without the falcon's wings to carry me
How can I rival the flying wind's swiftness?
I go and lean at the gate and think of my grief,
My falling tears wet the double gates.

Arthur Waley

At the beginning of winter a cold spirit comes,
The North Wind blows—chill, chill.
My sorrows being many, I know the length of the nights.
Raising my head I look at the stars in their places.
On the fifteenth day the bright moon is full,
On the twentieth day the "toad and hare" wane.*
A stranger came to me from a distant land
And brought me a single scroll with writing on it;
At the top of the scroll was written "Do not forget,"
At the bottom was written "Good-bye for ever."
I put the letter away in the folds of my dress,
For three years the writing did not fade.
How with an undivided heart I loved you
I fear that you will never know or guess.

Arthur Waley

---

*The "toad and hare" correspond to our "man in the moon." The waning of the moon symbolizes the waning of the lower's affection.

Yüeh-fu shih

Yüeh-fu shih, or Music Bureau poems (1st century).   The Music Bureau was established by Emperor Wu in 120 B.C., with the primary function of providing music and songs for ceremonies at court. There was a great variety of musical compositions. While the music of the formal poems has been lost, the words of about one hundred Han folk poems have been preserved. Most are in lines of varying length, but many have a regular form of five words (characters) per line, with rhymes on the even lines, which became a standard for later poetry.

I think of him
Who lives south of the big sea
What to send him as a gift?
Two pearls worked into a tortoise-shell pin
Intertwined with jade
I heard he is unfaithful
I angrily break and burn it
Break and burn it
And let the wind blow away its ashes
From now on
No thought of him
No more—the end of him
Cocks crow; dogs bark
My brother and wife would then know
Alas! alas!
Autumn winds whistle. Bird-of-morning-wind sings
When the east brightens, I then would know. . . .

Wai-lim Yip

Ts'ai Yen

Ts'ai Yen (162?–239?).   A daughter of the famous scholar and poet Ts'ai I, and widowed around 192, Ts'ai Yen was soon captured by Huns and taken north to the Tatar land, where she remained for twelve years. She bore two sons to a Hun chieftain and was at last ransomed back to China. Her joy at returning home was also grief because she was obliged to leave her two sons. Ts'ai Yen is the first important woman poet in China about whom we have information, although the attribution of the well-known poems to her is uncertain.

From 18 Verses Sung to a Tatar Reed Whistle

I

I was born in a time of peace,
But later the mandate of Heaven
Was withdrawn from the Han Dynasty.

Heaven was pitiless.
It sent down confusion and separation.
Earth was pitiless.
It brought me to birth in such a time.
War was everywhere. Every road was dangerous.
Soldiers and civilians everywhere
Fleeing death and suffering.
Smoke and dust clouds obscured the land
Overrun by the ruthless Tatar bands.
Our people lost their will power and integrity.
I can never learn the ways of the barbarians.
I am daily subject to violence and insult.
I sing one stanza to my lute and a Tatar horn.
But no one knows my agony and grief.

II

A Tatar chief forced me to become his wife,
And took me far away to Heaven's edge.
Ten thousand clouds and mountains
Bar my road home,
And whirlwinds of dust and sand

Blow for a thousand miles.
Men here are as savage as giant vipers,
And strut about in armor, snapping their bows.
As I sing the second stanza I almost break the lutestrings.
Will broken, heart broken, I sing to myself.

VII

The sun sets. The wind moans.
The noise of the Tatar camp rises all around me.
The sorrow of my heart is beyond expression,
But who could I tell it to anyway?
Far across the desert plains,
The beacon fires of the Tatar garrisons
Gleam for ten thousand miles.
It is the custom here to kill the old and weak
And adore the young and vigorous.
They wander seeking new pasture,
And camp for a while behind earth walls.
Cattle and sheep cover the prairie,
Swarming like bees or ants.
When the grass and water are used up,
They mount their horses and drive on their cattle.
The seventh stanza sings of my wandering.
How I hate to live this way!

XIII

I never believed that in my broken life
The day would come when
Suddenly I could return home.
I embrace and caress my Tatar sons.
Tears wet our clothes.
An envoy from the Han Court
Has come to bring me back,
With four stallions that can run without stopping.
Who can measure the grief of my sons?
They thought I would live and die with them.
Now it is I who must depart.

Sorrow for my boys dims the sun for me.
If we had wings we could fly away together.
I cannot move my feet,
For each step is a step away from them.
My soul is overwhelmed.
As their figures vanish in the distance
Only my love remains.
The thirteenth stanza—
I pick the strings rapidly
But the melody is sad.
No one can know
The sorrow which tears my bowels.

Kenneth Rexroth and Ling Chung

Tzu Yeh

Tzu Yeh (3rd–6th century).   A collection of short, popular songs, often love lyrics, these were attributed at one time to a woman poet of this name, but this notion is now rejected since they appear to have been written by many authors over a period of three hundred years. Some 124 Tzu Yeh songs have been preserved. They are from southern China in the areas of Soochow and Nanking.

Tzu Yeh Songs

At the time when blossoms
Fall from the cherry-tree:
On a day when yellow birds
Hovered in the branches—
You said you must stop,
Because your horse was tired:
I said I must go,
Because my silkworms were hungry.

Arthur Waley

All night I could not sleep
Because of the moonlight on my bed.
I kept on hearing a voice calling:
Out of Nowhere, Nothing answered "yes."

Arthur Waley

I will carry my coat and not put on my belt;
With unpainted eyebrows I will stand at the front window.
My tiresome petticoat keeps on flapping about;
If it opens a little, I shall blame the spring wind.

Arthur Waley

I heard my love was going to Yang-chou
And went with him as far as Ch'u-shan.
For a moment when you held me fast in your outstretched arms
I thought the river stood still and did not flow.

Arthur Waley

Chao Luan-luan

Chao Luan-luan (8th century?).   She was an elegant courtesan in the T'ang capital of
Ch'ang An.

Slender Fingers

Slender, delicate, soft jade,
Fresh peeled spring onions—
They are always hidden in emerald
Sleeves of perfumed silk.
Yesterday on the lute strings
All their nails were painted scarlet.

Kenneth Rexroth and Ling Chung

Anonymous Palace Women

(ca. 700)
(ca. 730)
(ca. 790)

Parting Is Hard

Parting is hard, I'll tell you twice.
Fallen petals in the wind make me sad again.

When you came, the plum bloomed through the snow.
When you left, the willows were in their spring glory.

Time and seasons hasten the traveler,
there is good weather again on the homeward road.

The world of cares is already far behind:
In a murky dream, I see your face again.

Geoffrey Waters

There is a soldier on a battlefield.
The numbing cold is freezing him to death.

I am making him this coat with my own hands,
who knows if he will get it?

I add each stitch to it with kindness,
tenderly fill it with down.

In this life we've already missed our chance to meet.
I hope we can be together in the next.

Geoffrey Waters

Written On a Leaf

Since I entered the inner rooms
I haven't seen the spring.

I write this poem on a fallen leaf
and send it out to a wandering man.

Geoffrey Waters

Hsüeh T'ao

Hsüeh T'ao (768–831).   Daughter of a government official in Ch'ang An, Hsüeh
T'ao was said to have become a "singing girl" at the age of ten. While still young, she
was recommended to be "collator," or "singing girl," at the imperial court. Evidently,
she served eleven regional commanders of Shu (modern Szechwan), and her precosity,
beauty, and talent were legendary. The *Chin River Collection* of her poems is said to
have contained five hundred lyrics, but these were lost by the beginning of the Ming
dynasty (1368). Ninety poems have come down to us. Hsüeh T'ao and Yü Hsüan-chi are
the leading women poets of the T'ang dynasty (618–907).

Spring-Gazing Song

Blossoms crowd the branches: too beautiful to endure.
Thinking of you, I break into bloom again.
One morning soon, my tears will mist the mirror.
I see the future, and I will not see.

Carolyn Kizer

Weaving Love-Knots

Daily the wind-flowers age, and so do I.
Happiness, long-deferred, is deferred again.
Of sand and ocean, the horizon line
Lies in the middle distance of the dream.
Because our lives cannot be woven together,
My fingers plait the same grasses, over and over.

Carolyn Kizer

Weaving Love-Knots 2

Two hearts: two blades of grass I braid together.
He is gone, who knew the music of my soul.

Autumn in the heart, as the links are broken.
                    Now he is gone, I break my lute.
But Spring hums everywhere: the nesting birds
Are stammering out their sympathy for me.

Carolyn Kizer

Yü Hsüan-chi

Yü Hsüan-chi (ca. 843–868).   Born in Ch'ang An, in her short life she was a highly cultivated literary courtesan, a concubine, a Taoist nun, and finally a criminal arrested for beating her maid to death. Although she was executed, it is virtually certain that the charge was trumped up; her poet friends tried unsuccessfully to save her. As a prostitute in Ch'ang An, she met Li Yi, whom she addresses in her poems. He purchased her freedom from the brothel and took her as his concubine. When he later abandoned her, she became a Taoist nun and followed a life of asceticism. Living in great poverty, she began to take lovers again, and until her frame-up and execution, she was a courtesan–nun–poet, careers which in other cultures and times would seem utterly contradictory. Although her poems are learned and rely naturally on symbolic images, they are never cluttered with historical and mythical allusions which, when poorly handled, are an impediment in many Chinese poems. She wrote as a woman dependent on men—resentful of this condition, yet philosophically above it all. Her poetry has a clarity and subdued passion that render her fifty-odd poems among the most personally intense, poignant, and fully realized poems in the Chinese language.

For Hidden Mist Pavilion

Spring flowers and autumn moon enter poems.
Bright days and clear nights are fit for idle gods.

Raised in vain the pearl screen, never lowered.
Long ago, I moved my couch to face the mountain.

Geoffrey Waters

Selling Ruined Peonies

Sigh, in the wind fall flowers, their petals dance.
Their secret fragrance dies in spring's decay.

Too costly: no one bought them.
Too sweet for butterflies.

If these red blooms had grown in a palace
Would they now be stained by dew and dust?

If they grew now in a forbidden garden
Princes would covet what they could not buy.

Geoffrey Waters

For a Neighbor Girl

Afraid of the sun, I hide behind my sleeve.
Gloomy in spring, lazy I rise and dress.

To find a rare jewel is easy.
To get a good man is harder.

Secret tears on the pillow,
Torn heart in the open flower.

If I can catch a glimpse of Sung Yü,
Why bother with the boy next door?

Geoffrey Waters

At the End of Spring

Deep lane, poor families; I have few friends.
He stayed behind only in my dream.

Fragrant silk scents the breeze: whose party?
A song comes carried in the wind: from where?

Drums in the street wake me at dawn.
In the courtyard, magpies mourn a spoiled spring.

How do we get the life we want?
I am a loosed boat floating a thousand miles.

Geoffrey Waters

To the Minister Liu

The Board of War has quelled the mutiny:
Songs fill the streets again.

Now there are spring rains on Fen River.
Flowers on the banks of the Chin.

The jails are long locked and empty,
Spears dusty.

Scholars and monks watch Midnight sing,
We travelers are drunk, on scarlet cushions.

Pen and inkstone close at hand,
Odes and *History* surround my seat;

For now, in happy times like these,
Even small talents live at ease.

Geoffrey Waters

Answering Li Ying Who Showed Me His Poems About Summer Fishing

Though we lived in the same lane,
A whole year we didn't meet,

Until his tender phrases touched this aging girl.
I broke a new cinnamon branch.

The Tao nature cheats ice and snow.
The enlightened heart laughs at summer silks.

Footsteps climb the River of Clouds,
Lost beyond roads in a sea of mist.

Geoffrey Waters

Rhyming a Friend's Poem

What can melt a traveler's grief?
Opening your letter I see the words in your fine hand.

Rain sprinkles a thousand peaks,
Tartar winds bleach ten thousand leaves.

Morning, word by word, I see the light blue jade;
Evening, page by page, I hum beneath my quilt.

I hide this letter in a scented box,
And when I'm sad, I take it out again.

Geoffrey Waters

For Kuo Hsiang

Morning and evening, drunk and singing,
Again this spring I think of you.

I watch a messenger in the rain,
Sad behind my window.

I roll up my pearl screen to see the mountains
And new grass is new sorrow.

Since we parted at the feast
Have you charmed them all again?

Geoffrey Waters

Poem to the Tune "Riverbank Willows"

Kingfisher blue along a tangled bank.
Mist drifts in a far tower.

Shadows creep across autumn water.
Flowers fall around fishermen's heads.

Fish hide in old roots.
Twigs catch on pleasure boats.

Then: the wind's whistle on a rainy night
Invades my dream. I awake to grief.

Geoffrey Waters

Rhyming with a Friend

Noisy politicians confuse the world
I sing to the moon alone.

Why did he write down elegant thoughts
And knock at my bushy gate with rhymes of jade?

I can't sing of white flowers as Hsieh did then.
Deep in the side lane, I'm wrong to follow Yen.

I didn't waste hope that we would meet:
Thready moss grows on the high hill between us.

Geoffrey Waters

To Tzu-an

Parting, a thousand cups won't wash away the sorrow.
Separation is a hundred knots I can't untie.

After a thaw, orchids bloom, spring returns,
Willows catch on pleasure boats again.

We meet and part, like the clouds, never fixed.
I've learned that love is like the river.

We won't meet again this spring,
But I can't rest yet, winesick in Jade Tower.

Geoffrey Waters

Telling My Feelings

Sad music from vermilion strings.
How can I hold it in?

Early I knew the lover's touch,
Before I was elegant, refined.

Gleaming, gleaming the peach and plum:
What harm if scholars seek them?

Green, green the pine and cinnamon:
The world respects them.

Clear moon on moss steps,
Deep in the bamboo yard, a song.

Outside the gate, red leaves on the ground
Wait for him. Why sweep them now?

Geoffrey Waters

Sent to Wen T'ing-Yün on a Winter Night

Thinking hard, hunting rhymes, humming by my lamp,
Awake all night, I fear the cold quilt.

In a courtyard full of leaves, sad winds rise.
Through my curtain, a wretched moon sinks.

I hoped we'd be together. Instead: apart.
But life's changes are nothing to a sage's heart.

Hunting a perch in the dark paulownia grove,
Wheeling, evening sparrows wail and sob.

Geoffrey Waters

Spring Thoughts Sent to Tzu-an

The mountain road is steep, the stone steps are dangerous;
The hard climb hurts me less than thoughts of you.

Ice melts in a far stream: your voice in its sad tune.
Snow on cold peaks like jade reminds me of you.

Don't listen to the singers, springsick with wine.
Don't call your guests to play chess at night.

Like pine or stone our promise stays,
So I can wait for paired wings to join.

I walk alone in the cold end of winter.
Perhaps we'll meet when the moon is round.

What can I give my absent man?
In the pure light, my tears fall: a poem.

Geoffrey Waters

Elegy for the Wife of a Friend

I remember you in young peaches like jade.
Windblown willows, your arched eyebrows.

When a pearl returns to the dragon's cave, who can see it?
Though the bird has flown, your mirror stayed behind.

After the dream, sad nights of rain and mist.
How can I sing, senseless and bitter?

The sun falls into West Mountain, the moon rises in the east.
From mourning, there is no relief.

Geoffrey Waters

Boudoir Lament

With a handful of weeds I weep in the slanting sun
To hear a neighbor's husband coming home.

When you left, the first southern swans were flying north.
This morning northern geese go south.

Spring comes, fall goes, love stays.
Fall goes, spring comes, messages are rare.

My scarlet door is closed, he doesn't knock;
Only the sound of washboards through silk curtains.

Geoffrey Waters

Letting My Feelings Out

Relaxed, nothing to do,
I travel alone in dancing light:

Clouds break, moon on water,
Adrift in a loosed boat.

I hear a lute from Hsiao Liang Temple,
A song from Yü Liang's Tower.

Clumps of bamboo are my companions
And stones my friends.

Swallows and sparrows follow me,
I need no silver nor gold.

I fill the cup with the green spring wine;
Under the moon, subtle music.

By the clear pond around my steps
I pull my hairpin out and let the bright stream flow.

In bed reading,
Half-drunk, I get up and comb my hair.

Geoffrey Waters

Regretful Thoughts

I

Fallen leaves are scattered by evening rain.
I sing and brush red strings alone.

Unmoved by heartless friends,
I go within, beyond the bitter sea.

Outside my gate rumble rich men's carts.
By my pillow Taoist books are rolled.

Now in simple cottons, no more a guest of clouds,
No more green water and blue hills.

II

Too much pain to sigh alone:
How can I face the windy courtyard filled with the autumn moon?

In dark rooms, I hear the watch sound,
Every night, by my lamp, hair turning white.

Geoffrey Waters

Staying in the Mountains in Summer

I've moved here to the Immortal's place:
Flowers everywhere we didn't plant before.

The courtyard trees are bent like clothes-horses.
At the feast, winecups float in a new spring.

Dark balcony. Path through deep bamboo.
Long summer dress. Confusion of books.

I sing in the moonlight and ride a painted boat,
Trusting the wind to blow me home again.

Geoffrey Waters

Li Ch'ing-chao

Li Ch'ing-chao (1084?–ca. 1151).   From Li-ch'eng (modern Tsi-nan) in Shantung Province, Li Ch'ing-chao was born into a literary family and married Chao Ming-ch'eng, a man of letters, who like herself was an antiquarian, book collector, and calligrapher. Together, as an ideal literary couple, they assembled a very large collection of bronzes, seals, manuscripts, and paintings. In 1127, when the Chin Tartars invaded Sung China, they were forced to flee from their home and most of their collection in ten buildings was destroyed. Two years later, in 1129, her husband left to take a new post in Che-chiang. En route he took sick and died. Thereafter, she attempted to retrieve what was left of their collection and continued to write poems, now not of early happiness but of loss and loneliness. Although she was a prolific writer—some six volumes of lyrics—only about fifty poems have survived. Always in control, her poems have the emotional authority of complete candor and exact observation. Nature, things, and feelings—a season, a window, sadness—are skillfully depicted and mingled in poems of extraordinary quality. Like her T'ang precursor Yü Hsüan-chi, she was a major poet.

How many evenings in the arbor by the river,
when flushed with wine we'd lose our way back.
The mood passed away, returning late by boat
we'd stray off into a spot thick with lotus,
and thrashing through
and thrashing through
startle a shoreful of herons by the lake.

Eugene Eoyang

Read down right to left

Rattan
bed,
paper
netting.
I wake
from morning
sleep.

I can't
reach
the end
of saying:
I've no
happy
thoughts.

Incense
flickers
on,
off.
The jade
burner
is cold,

a companion.
to
my feelings,
which
are
water.

I play
three times
with
the flute,
astonishing
a
plum's
heart.

How
I
feel
spring's
ache!

Slender
wind
and
thin
rain,
tapping
tapping.

Down
come
a
thousand
lines
of
tears.

The pipe
playing
jade
man
is gone.
Empty
tower.

My chest
is
broken.
On whom
can I
lean?

I
break off
a
twig.
On the
earth
and in
heaven,

there's
no one
person
to send
it to.

WB and Sun Chu-chin

Read down, right to left

Warm
rain,
sunny
wind
start
to break
the chill.

Willows
like eyes,
plums
like cheeks.

I
already
feel
spring's
heart
throbbing.

Wine
and poems.
Whom
can
I share

them
with?

Tears
dissolve
my makeup.
My gold
hairpin
is heavy.

I try on
a light
spring
robe,
threaded
with

gold,
and
lean
against
a hill
of pillows.

The hill
damages
the gold
phoenix
pin.

Alone
I hug
dense
pain,
with no

good dreams.

Late
at night,
still
I
play,
trimming
the wick.

WB and Sun Chu-chin

Read down, right to left

Sky
links
cloud
waves,
links
dawn
fog.

The star
river
is about
to turn.
A thousand
sails
dance.

As
if
in dream
my soul
returns
to god's
home,

hearing

heaven's
voice,

eagerly
asking:
Where
am I
going
back
to?

I
say:
The road
is long,
the day
near
dusk;

in writing
poems,
people-
startling
words
come
invisibly.

Ninety
thousand
miles
of wind,
the huge
peng bird
takes off.

Wind,

don't
stop.

The frail
boat
is to
reach
the three
holy
mountains.

WB and Sun Chu-chin

Read down, right to left

Are you	Last
blind!	night
I	thin
say.	rain,
	gusty
By now	wind.
they're	
fat	Dense
green	sleep
and skimpy	doesn't
red.	fade
	a wine
	hangover.
	I'm talking
	to her
	who
	rolled up
	the curtains.
	O,
	she says,
	the geraniums
	are
	still
	the same

WB and Sun Chu-chin

Two Springs

Spring has come to the Pass.
Once more the new grass is kingfisher green.
The pink buds of the peach trees
Are still unopened little balls.
The clouds are milk-white jade
Bordered and spotted with green jade.
No dust stirs.
In a dream that was too easy to read,
I have already drained and broken
The cup of Spring.
Flower shadows lie heavy
On the translucent curtains.
The full, transparent moon
Rises in the orange twilight.
Three times in two years
My lord has gone away to the East.
Today he returns.
And my joy is already
Greater than the Spring.

Kenneth Rexroth

Year after year I have watched
My jade mirror. Now my rouge
And creams sicken me. One more
Year that he has not come back.
My flesh shakes when a letter
Comes from South of the River.
I cannot drink wine since he left.
But the Autumn has drunk up all my tears.
I have lost my mind, far off
In the jungle mists of the South.
The gates of Heaven are nearer
Than the body of my beloved.

Kenneth Rexroth

Clear Bright

From the slopes of the mountain
From north to south
The fields are covered with tombs.
On the Feast of Clear Bright
They make sacrifices at every grave.
Bloody tears, sobs like horns,
Voices like screech owls.
After sunset the foxes come back
To their beds under the mounds,
And men and girls come,
And on top of the graves
Make love by lantern light.
My friend, while you're alive
And have wine, use it to get drunk.
There'll be no second helpings
When you get to the Nine Springs.

Kenneth Rexroth

I let the incense grow cold
In the burner. My brocade
Bed covers are tumbled as
The waves of the sea. Idle
Since I got up, I neglect
My hair. My toilet table
Is unopened. I leave the
Curtains down until the sun shines
Over the curtain rings.
This separation prostrates me.
The distance terrifies me.
I long to talk to him once more.
Down the years there will be only
Silence between us forever now.
I am emaciated, but
Not with sickness, not with wine,
Not with Autumn.
It is all over now forever.

I sing over and over
The song, "Goodbye Forever."
I keep forgetting the words.
My mind is far off in Wu Ling.
My body is a prisoner
In this room above the misty
River, the jade green river,
That is the only companion
of my endless days. I stare
Down the river, far off, into
The distance. I stare far away.
My eyes find only my own sorrow.

Kenneth Rexroth

Red lotus incense fades on
The jewelled curtain. Autumn
Comes again. Gently I open
My silk dress and float alone
On the orchid boat. Who can
Take a letter beyond the clouds?
Only the wild geese come back
And write their ideograms
On the sky under the full
Moon that floods the West Chamber.
Flowers, after their kind, flutter
And scatter. Water after
Its nature, when spilt, at last
Gathers again in one place.
Creatures of the same species
Long for each other. But we
Are far apart and I have
Grown learned in sorrow.
Nothing can make it dissolve
And go away. One moment,
It is on my eyebrows.
The next, it weighs on my heart.

Kenneth Rexroth

Light mist, then dense fog—
A day endless as my sorrow.
Rare incense smoke curls from the
Mouth of the gold animal.
Once more it is the Ninth Day
Of the Ninth Month. I lie restless
On my brocade pillow, under
The gauze curtains, until, past
Midnight, a chill seeps into me.
In the East Enclosed Garden
We got drunk one evening.
The wine's secret perfume has never
Left my sleeves. No one else notices,
But it carries my soul away.
Now when the West wind flaps the screens,
I am more frail than the orchid petals.

Kenneth Rexroth

A Weary Song to a Slow Sad Tune

Search. Search. Seek. Seek.
Cold. Cold. Clear. Clear.
Sorrow. Sorrow. Pain. Pain.
Hot flashes. Sudden chills.
Stabbing pains. Slow agonies.
I drink two cups, then three bowls,
Of clear wine until I can't
Stand up against a gust of wind.
Wild geese fly over head.
They wrench my heart.
They were our friends in the old days.
Gold chrysanthemums litter
The ground, pile up, faded, dead.
This season I could not bear
To pick them. All alone,
Motionless at my window,
I watch the gathering shadows.
Fine rain sifts through the *wu t'ung* trees,

And drips, drop by drop, through the dusk.
What can I ever do now?
How can I drive off this word—
Hopelessness?

Kenneth Rexroth

melting in thin mist and heavy clouds
the long day passes
camphor snorts from the golden beast, the censer
mid-autumn festival
last night the first cold breezes
to chill my pillow and my drapes

by eastern hedge at dusk I pour out wine
a secret fragrance fills my sleeves
don't ask me to resist its spell
the west wind curls my curtain
I'm paler, thinner than the yellow flower

J. P. Seaton

Anonymous Courtesan

This poem has frequently been attributed to Li Ch'ing-chao.

After kicking on the swing,
Lasciviously, I get up and rouge my palms.
Thick dew on a frail flower,
Perspiration soaks my thin dress.
A new guest enters.
My stockings come down
And my hairpins fall out.
Embarrassed, I run away,
And lean flirtatiously against the door,
Tasting a green plum.

Kenneth Rexroth and Ling Chung

Chu Shu-chen

Chu Shu-chen (ca. 1200).   Although Chu Shu-chen's reputation in Chinese is high and many of her poems have survived, virtually nothing is known of her life other than what may be derived from the poems. Her parents burned her poems after her death—many spoke of unhappy marriage—but copies were preserved by friends. Wei Chung-kung is said to have published his copies of her poems in 1182. She wrote in the *shih* and *tzu* verse forms, and was very conscious of her role as poet, as the lines "I write poems, change and correct them,/ And finally throw them away" indicate. Almost every line in her poetry (these quoted lines being an exception) brings in an observation of nature or objects in her room or garden. Her poems are among the most beautiful of the Sung dynasty.

Stormy Night in Autumn

Like a flight of arrows the wind
Pierces my curtain. The cold rain
Roars like the drum of the nightwatch.
My breasts are freezing. Huddled
In my folded quilt, I cannot sleep.
My tears flow without stopping.
The bamboos outside my window
Sob like the broken heart of Autumn.
Rain beats on the painted tiles.
This night will never end. Freezing,
Alone in the dark, I am
Going mad, counting my sorrows.
My heart pounds as if it would break.
Inside my body, thin as a
Stem of bamboo, my bowels
Twist and knot. How will I ever
Escape from this torture? Outside
My window now I hear the rain
Rattle on the banana trees.
Each beaten leaf contains
Ten thousand pains.

Kenneth Rexroth

Lost

Last year at the Feast of Lanterns,
The flower stalls were bright as day.
When the moon rose over the willows,
I walked in the moonlight with my beloved.
Another year—the same holiday—
The moon and the lanterns have not changed.
My lover is lost, I cannot find him,
And I wipe away my tears with my sleeve.

Kenneth Rexroth

The Old Anguish

Sheltered from the Spring wind by
A silver screen, I doze in my
Folded quilt, cold and alone.
I start awake at the cry
Of a bird—my dream is gone.
The same sorrow, the same headache
Return. Thick shadows of flowers
Darken the filigree lattice.
Incense coils over the screen
And spirals past my pillow.
The oriole is not to blame
For a broken dream of a
Bygone Spring. I sit with my
Old anguish as the evening fades.

Kenneth Rexroth

Alone

I raise the curtains and go out
To watch the moon. Leaning on the
Balcony, I breathe the evening
Wind from the west, heavy with the
Odors of decaying Autumn.

The rose jade of the river
Blends with the green jade of the void.
Hidden in the grass a cricket chirps.
Hidden in the sky storks cry out.
I turn over and over in
My heart the memories of
Other days. Tonight as always
There is no one to share my thoughts.

Kenneth Rexroth

Morning

I get up. I am sick of
Rouging my cheeks. My face in
The mirror disgusts me. My
Thin shoulders are bowed with
hopelessness. Tears of loneliness
Well up in my eyes. Wearily
I open my toilet table.
I arch and paint my eyebrows
And steam my heavy braids.
My maid is so stupid that she
Offers me plum blossoms for my hair.

Kenneth Rexroth

Sorrow

The white moon gleams through scudding
Clouds in the cold sky of the Ninth
Month. The white frost weighs down the
Leaves and the branches bend low
Over the freezing water.
All alone I sit by my
Window. The crushing burden
Of the passing days never

Grows lighter for an instant.
I write poems, change and correct them,
And finally throw them away.
Gold chrysanthemums wither
Along the balcony. Hard
Cries of migrating storks fall
Heavily from the icy sky.
All alone by my window
Hidden in my empty room,
All alone, I burn incense,
And dream in the smoke, all alone.

Kenneth Rexroth

Wang Ch'ing-hui

Wang Ch'ing-hui (13th century?).   This is one of many poems written by women
captured in war. One tradition suggests that Wang Ch'ing-hui was director of ceremonies
of the women's quarters of the imperial palace in Hang-chou, capital of Southern Sung,
when Kublai Khan's army of Mongols captured the city. The poem is also sometimes
attributed to another woman, Chang Ch'un-ying.

Now the lotuses in the imperial lake
Must look entirely different from the old days.
I remember when I received the gracious
Rain and dew, in the Emperor's golden bed
In the jade palace, and my fame spread
Like orchid incense among the queens and concubines.
I blushed like a lotus blossom
Whenever I was summoned to my Lord's side.
Suddenly, one day, war drums on horseback
Came like thunder, tearing off the sky,
And all the glorious flowery days were gone forever.
Generals scattered like dragons and tigers.
Courtiers fled like clouds in the storm.
To whom can I tell
My everlasting sorrow for the dead?
I look out on the mountains and rivers of this fastness,
And my tears mingle with blood on my sleeves.

I wake in a posthouse from dreams of dust and dirt.
Fleeing in the dawn, our palace carts
Roll through the mountain pass
Under the setting moon.
I pray to Ch'ang-O,
The girl who fled for refuge to the moon,
And ask her to permit me
To follow her to safety.

Kenneth Rexroth and Ling Chung

Chao Li-hua

Chao Li-hua (Ming dynasty, 1368–1644).   No information on Chao Li-hua, other
than that she was a Ming poet, has survived.

Farewell

my boat goes west, yours east
heaven's a wind for both journeys
from here the clouds and mountains
the horizon's vague
a thousand miles
my heart, a dark swan
confused in that vastness

J. P. Seaton

Huang O

Huang O (1498–1569).   The daughter of an official at the Ming court, Huang O
married the poet Yang Shen. Although the government in the sixteenth century did not
impede the dissemination of erotic novels like the *Chin P'ing Mei*, erotic poetry by
women who were not courtesans was not expected. Thus, Huang O's sexually allusive
poetry was unusual for her time. The poems stand apart from the lyrics of others in their
dominant themes of fulfillment, happiness, and physical pleasure, expressed in rich yet
delicate imagery.

A Farewell to
a Southern Melody

The day will come when I will
Share once more the quilts
And pillows I am storing
Away. Once more I will shyly
Let you undress me and gently
Unlock my sealed jewel.
I can never describe the
Ten thousand beautiful sensual
Ways we will make love.

Kenneth Rexroth and Ling Chung

Every morning I get up
Beautiful as the Goddess
Of Love in Enchanted Mountain.
Every night I go to bed
Seductive as Yang Kuei-fei,
The imperial concubine.
My slender waist and thighs
Are exhausted and weak
From a night of cloud dancing.
But my eyes are still lewd,
And my cheeks are flushed.
My old wet nurse combs
My cloud-like hair.
My lover, fragrant as incense,
Adjusts my jade hairpins, and
Draws on my silk stockings
Over my feet and legs
Perfumed with orchids;
And once again we fall over
Overwhelmed with passion.

Kenneth Rexroth and Ling Chung

You held my lotus blossom
In your lips and played with the
Pistil. We took one piece of
Magic rhinoceros horn
And could not sleep all night long.
All night the cock's gorgeous crest
Stood erect. All night the bee
Clung trembling to the flower
Stamens. Oh my sweet perfumed
Jewel! I will allow only
My Lord to possess my sacred
Lotus pond, and every night
You can make blossom in me
Flowers of fire.

Kenneth Rexroth and Ling Chung

Wang Wei

Wang Wei (17th century).   An orphan who grew up to be a courtesan poet in Yang Chou, Wang Wei married twice and became a priestess, calling herself "The Taoist Master in the Straw Coat." She is said to have traveled through the waterways of central China carrying her library in her small boat. Like Wang Wei the T'ang poet and painter (whose name is written with a different character for Wei), she too is primarily known as a nature poet.

Seeking a Mooring

A leaf floats in endless space.
A cold wind tears the clouds.
The water flows westward.
The tide pushes upstream.
Beyond the moonlit reeds,
In village after village, I hear
The sound of fullers' mallets
Beating the wet clothing
In preparation for winter.
Everywhere crickets cry
In the autumn frost.

A traveller's thoughts in the night
Wander in a thousand miles of dreams.
The sound of a bell cannot disperse
The sorrows that come
In the fifth hour of night.
What place will I remember
From all this journey?
Only still bands of desolate mist
And a single fishing boat.

Kenneth Rexroth and Ling Chung

Sun Yün-feng

Sun Yün-feng (1764–1814).   Born in Che-chiang, Sun Yün-feng was the daughter of an official, Sung Chia-lo, and married the scholar Ch'en. She was known as a favorite student of the Ch'ing dynasty poet Yüan Mei.

On the Road Through Chang-te

On the last year's trip I enjoyed this place.
I am glad to come back here today.
The fish market is deep in blue shadows.
I can see the smoke for tea rising
From the thatched inn.
The sands of the river beaches
Merge with the white moon.
Along the shore the willows
Wait for their Spring green.
Lines of a poem run through my mind.
I order the carriage to stop for a while.

Kenneth Rexroth and Ling Chung

The Trail Up Wu Gorge

The trail climbs in zig-zags
High above spiralling whirlpools.
Swift waters break against sheer rocks.

On the evening breeze comes the sound
Of a boy playing his flute,
Riding home on the back of an ox.
The last drops of rain mingle
With the cloud of my horse's breath.
New grass grows on the ancient ramparts.
On the abandoned monuments
The old inscriptions are lost in time.
I am bound on a journey without end,
And can not bear the song of the cuckoo.

Kenneth Rexroth and Ling Chung

Wu Tsao

Wu Tsao (19th century).   Wu Tsao was the daughter and wife of merchants, with
whom she had little understanding. Her friends were women, and she wrote to women
lovers and to courtesans. She may be considered China's major Lesbian poet. Her poems
read with fluent intimacy, with grace and psychological intelligence. Some of her poems
reflect philosophically on the past, on China's great poets, and on the misty temporality of
present conditions and memory.

For the Courtesan Ch'ing Lin

On your slender body
Your jade and coral girdle ornaments chime
Like those of a celestial companion
Come from the Green Jade City of Heaven.
One smile from you when we meet,
And I become speechless and forget every word.
For too long you have gathered flowers,
And leaned against the bamboos,
Your green sleeves growing cold,
In your deserted valley:
I can visualize you all alone,
A girl harboring her cryptic thoughts.

You glow like a perfumed lamp
In the gathering shadows.
We play wine games
And recite each other's poems.

Then you sing, "Remembering South of the River"
With its heartbreaking verses. Then
We paint each other's beautiful eyebrows.
I want to possess you completely—
Your jade body
And your promised heart.
It is Spring.
Vast mists cover the Five Lakes.
My dear, let me buy a red painted boat
And carry you away.

Kenneth Rexroth and Ling Chung

Bitter rain in my courtyard
In the decline of Autumn,
I only have vague poetic feelings
That I cannot bring together.
They diffuse into the dark clouds
And the red leaves.
After the yellow sunset
The cold moon rises
Out of the gloomy mist.
I will not let down the blinds
Of spotted bamboo from their silver hook.
Tonight my dreams will follow the wind,
Suffering the cold,
To the jasper tower of your beautiful flesh.

Kenneth Rexroth and Ling Chung

**In the Home of the Scholar Wu Su-chiang From Hsin-an, I
Saw Two Psalteries of the Late Sung General Hsieh Fang-tê**

Half of our borders, rivers and mountains were gone,
With their Spring orioles and blossoms.
Your former career was only a painful memory.
You watched the melancholy moon set
Over an abandoned temple in the wilderness.

You could no longer see the beacon fires of Sung,
So you lived disguised as a fortune teller,
In a kiosk on a bridge, and no one knew you.
You who had a will of iron,
And held back the billowing flood of the world,
All by yourself in a besieged city.
You chanted Tu Fu's songs of homesickness,
You chose death to preserve your integrity.
At the end of the years of hiding
On these slopes amongst the tea bushes
Haunted by the cuckoos crying as if in pain,
You left behind two psalteries
Of tung wood and these ancient songs,
And went to death, a handful of yellow dust,
But deserving a royal grave.
Now as I play them I can imagine
Dragons dancing in the depths
And the moss on the shore burning red.

Kenneth Rexroth and Ling Chung

Ch'iu Chin

Ch'iu Chin (1879–1907).   The daughter of a lawyer and local official, Ch'iu Chin
went to Japan to study after her early marriage and the birth of her first child. There she
joined Sun Yat-sen's revolutionary party and became a leader. Back in China in 1906 she
founded a newspaper for women in Shanghai. She also taught in a school which served as
secret headquarters for the revolutionary army. She was arrested by the Manchu
government, which used her poems as evidence against her in her trial, and was beheaded
on July 15, 1907, five years before the overthrow of the Manchu dynasty. Although her
poems have a political import, like the poems of Mao Tse-tung, their form and allusions
are classical.

How many wise men and heroes
Have survived the dust and dirt of the world?
How many beautiful women have been heroines?
There were the noble and famous women generals
Ch'in Liang-yu and Shen Yü-yin.

Though tears stained their dresses
Their hearts were full of blood.
The wild strokes of their swords
Whistled like dragons and sobbed with pain.

The perfume of freedom burns my mind
With grief for my country.
When will we ever be cleansed?
Comrades, I say to you,
Spare no effort, struggle unceasingly,
That at last peace may come to our people.
And jewelled dresses and deformed feet
Will be abandoned.
And one day, all under heaven
Will see beautiful free women,
Blooming like fields of flowers,
And bearing brilliant and noble human beings.

Kenneth Rexroth and Ling Chung

Ping Hsin

Ping Hsin (1902–).   Born in Fu-chien, the daughter of a naval officer, Ping Hsin's real name is Hsieh Wang-ying. Ping Hsin means "Ice Heart." She was educated both in her father's library and later in Peking. She graduated from Yenching University in 1923, and during 1923–1926 attended Wellesley College, where she obtained her M.A. She returned to teach at Yenching. In 1951 she and her husband Wu Wen-tsao, a sociologist, returned to the mainland, where until the Cultural Revolution in 1964 she was active in many literary organizations. Fond of Tagore, she wrote *The Star* in 1921, which she claimed was not poetry. Although she also claimed in 1932 that she did not understand "modern poetry," her publications launched her as a leading modern Chinese poet.

from Spring Waters

In shaping the snow into blossoms—
The north wind is tender after all.

All beings are deceived by light and shadow.
Beyond the horizon—
When did the moon ever wax and wane?

In this hazy world,
I have forgotten the first word,
Nor will I ever know the last.

Kai-yu Hsu

The orphan boat of my heart
Crosses the unsteady, undulant
Ocean of Time.

Kenneth Rexroth and Ling Chung

The commonplace puddle
Reflects the setting sun
And becomes the Sea of Gold.

Kenneth Rexroth and Ling Chung

Li Chü

Li Chü (mid-20th century).   Li Chü is a member of a farm commune in Honan
Province.

Harvesting Wheat for the Public Share

It is a year of good harvest
The wheat is brought to the threshing yard.
The second sister crushes it.
The elder sister threshes it.
The third sister winnows it
Very carefully and throws away the husks.
The golden grain piles high in the yard.
Round, round wheat, better than pomegranate seeds.
Bite it with your teeth, it goes "go-pou!"
The first pile of wheat is really lovely.
After we have dried it in the sun,
And cleaned it,
We will turn it in as the public share.

Kenneth Rexroth and Ling Chung

Japanese

Empress Iwa no Hime

Empress Iwa no Hime (?–347). **She was empress consort of Emperor Nintoku, and** in 314 was proclaimed empress.

Longing for the Emperor

My Lord has departed
And the time has grown long.
Shall I search the mountains,
Going forth to meet you,
Or wait for you here?

No! I would not live,
Longing for you.
On the mountain crag, rather,
Rock-root as my pillow,
Dead would I lie.

Yet even if it be so
I shall wait for my Lord
Till on my black hair—
Trailing fine in the breeze—
The dawn's frost shall fall.

In the autumn field,
Over the rice ears,
The morning mist trails,
Vanishing somewhere. . . .
Can my love fade too?

Geoffrey Bownas and Anthony Thwaite

Princess Oku

Princess Oku (661–701).   The daughter of Emperor Temmu and the sister of Prince Otsu, she served as a vestal at the Ise Shrine.

How will you cross
the autumn mountain
alone?
It was hard
for us,
even when we went
together.

WB

A Court Lady

A Court Lady (?–671).   She waited on Emperor Tenji.

On the Death of Emperor Tenji

I am of this world,
Unfit to touch a god.
Separated from his spirit,
In the morning I grieve my Lord:
Sundered from his soul,
I long for my Lord.
Would he were jade
I might coil on my arm!
Would he were a robe
I might never put off!
I saw my Lord,
The one I love,
Last night . . . in sleep.

Geoffrey Bownas and Anthony Thwaite

Woman of Suminoe

Woman of Suminoe (ca. 699).   This poem is from the *Manyōshū*, or "Collection of Ten Thousand Leaves," the oldest and greatest anthology in the Japanese language. Compiled in the middle of the eighth century, it contains material of a much earlier date. There are about 4,500 poems in the *Manyōshū*, in a variety of forms.

> How I wish I had known
> beforehand of this journey
> you would make, my lord:
> with the red clay from the banks
> I would have dyed a robe for you!

Kenneth Yasuda

Anonymous

Anonymous (ca. 733).   This poem, addressed by a mother to her son as he is about to depart for a position in a far embassy, is from the *Manyōshū*.

Mother's Song

> If snow falls on the far field
> where travelers
> spend the night,
> I ask you, cranes,
> to warm my child in your wings.

WB

Anonymous

Anonymous (8th century).   Azuma-uta, or songs of the Eastlands, were adopted by the noble families, who had them sung by a chorus with orchestral and dance accompaniment. A *tanka* version of a work song is presented here. Rice was polished by pounding it with a large mallet.

> Even though my hands
> are rough from much rice-pounding,

on this night again
my master's son will clasp them
with a heavy, broken, sigh.

Kenneth Yasuda

Young Woman of Harima

Young Woman of Harima (ca. 715–719).   This poem is addressed to an official
who, between 715 and 719, left to assume a post in the capital. Boxwood combs were
highly valued then (as now) in Japan. The poem is from the *Manyōshū*.

If you go away,
why should I adorn myself?
From my toilet case
I shall not think of taking
even my comb of boxwood.

Kenneth Yasuda

Lady Ōtomo of Sakanone

Lady Ōtomo of Sakanone (ca. 8th century).   Lady Ōtomo was the youngest sister of
Tabito, governor, councillor of state, and poet. Her daughter married her nephew,
Otomo no Yakamochi, another well-known poet. Lady Ōtomo followed her brother
from place to place according to his official duties, and belonged to one of the powerful
political and literary clans in Japan, in Sakanone, the present Ikoma district.

Sent from the Capital to Her Elder Daughter

More than the gems
Locked away and treasured
In his comb-box
By the God of the Sea,
I prize you, my daughter.
But we are of this world
And such is its way!
Summoned by your man,
Obedient, you journeyed
To the far-off land of Koshi.

Since we parted,
Like a spreading vine,
Your eyebrows, pencil-arched,
Like waves about to break,
Have flitted before my eyes,
Bobbling like tiny boats.
Such is my yearning for you
That this body, time-riddled,
May well not bear the strain.

Had I only known
My longing would be so great,
Like a clear mirror
I'd have looked on you—
Not missing a day,
Not even an hour.

Geoffrey Bownas and Anthony Thwaite

My brother has on
a thin robe.
O Sao wind, don't blow hard
till he is home.

WB

Unknown love
is bitter
as a virgin lily
on the summer
meadow,
blooming in bushes.

WB

Lady Kasa

Lady Kasa (mid to late 8th century).   Little is known of her life, but twenty-nine *tanka* poems are preserved in the *Manyōshū,* and six of these are addressed to the poet Otomo Yakamochi.

> I dreamed I held
> a sword against my flesh.
> What does it mean?
> It means I shall see you soon.

> *Kenneth Rexroth*

> I love and fear him
> Steadily as the surf
> Roars on the coast at Ise

> *Kenneth Rexroth*

Ono no Komachi

Ono no Komachi (834–880).   A legendary beauty of Japan, her father was Yoshisada, lord of Dewa. She is the central figure in three Noh plays, and myth has it that she died an old, ugly beggar. Her poems have the verbal complexity typical of the *Kokinshū* anthology, and unusual erotic directness.

> Doesn't he realize
> that I am not
> like the swaying kelp
> in the surf,
> where the seaweed gatherer
> can come as often as he wants.

> *Kenneth Rexroth and Ikuko Atsumi*

> A thing which fades
> With no outward sign—

Is the flower
Of the heart of man
In this world!

Arthur Waley

So lonely am I
My body is a floating weed
Severed at the roots.
Were there water to entice me,
I would follow it, I think.

Donald Keene

The color of the flowers
has faded
while I contemplated it,
as my body
passed through the world.

Kenneth Rexroth

Lady Ise

Lady Ise (875?–938?).   Along with Ono no Komachi, Lady Ise is considered a representative poet of the *Kokinshū* ("A Collection of Ancient and Modern Poems"), the first imperial anthology of verses in tenth-century Japan (completed in 905). Her father, Tsugukage, belonged to the northern branch of the Fujiwara family, and served as governor of Ise and, later, Yamato provinces. Known as Lady Ise, she served as a lady-in-waiting for Emperor Uda's consort Onshi (872–907), and was active as an important literary celebrity throughout her life at court. Except for a short period at the end of her love affair with Fujiwara no Nakahira, Onshi's older brother, she spent her adult life at court. She was one of Emperor Uda's favorites and bore him an imperial prince. In 899, the emperor retired into priesthood and Empress Onshi moved her quarters to the palace in Shichijō, where Lady Ise continued to serve. Later her relationship with Prince Atsuyoshi, Emperor Uda's fourth son, resulted in the birth of a daughter. Not much is known about Lady Ise's later years.

   The inclusion of so many poems (173) by a woman in the twenty-one imperial anthologies was unprecedented in Lady Ise's time. She was further honored by being chosen to participate in the Teiji-in poetry match sponsored by Emperor Uda in 913. She is distinguished as one of the Thirty-six Poetic Geniuses of Japan.

Hanging from the branches of a green
willow tree,
the spring rain
is a
thread of pearls.

WB

Seeing the Returning Geese

Lightly forsaking
the Spring mist as it rises,
the wild geese are setting off.
Have they learned to live
in a flowerless country?

Etsuko Terasaki with Irma Brandeis

Seeing the Plum Blossoms by the River

If again in the Spring
I take the flowing river
for a bed of flowers,
I will only wet my sleeve*
in impervious waters.

Etsuko Terasaki with Irma Brandeis

When the fifth month comes,
Hototogisu,†
what if your voice has grown hoarse?
It is now I long to hear you,
before the summer begins.

Etsuko Terasaki with Irma Brandeis

---

* Traditionally the wet sleeve signified weeping.
† Japanese cuckoo, not resembling the Western cuckoo; it often sings plaintively at dusk.

A flower of waves
blossoms in the distance
and ripples shoreward
as though a breeze had quickened
the sea and set it blooming.

Etsuko Terasaki with Irma Brandeis

Near a Waterfall at Ryūmon

Hidden immortal,
whose garment has no break nor seam,
if you have gone from us
what mountain princess is this
displaying to us her white robes?

Etsuko Terasaki with Irma Brandeis

Because we suspected
the pillow would say "I know,"
we slept without it.
Nevertheless my name
is being bandied like dust.

Etsuko Terasaki with Irma Brandeis

Even in my dreams
I must no longer meet you.
Each day more clearly
my mirror offers
a face I am ashamed to show.

Etsuko Terasaki with Irma Brandeis

Like a ravaged sea
this bed.
Were I to smooth it,

the sleeve I pressed to it
would float back moist with foam.

Etsuko Terasaki with Irma Brandeis

Correspondence:
when I have sad thoughts
even the moon's face
embroidered on my sleeve
is wet with tears.

Etsuko Terasaki with Irma Brandeis

On Seeing the Field Being Singed

My body is like
a field wasted by winter.
If only
I, like the field burnt-over,
awaited the return of Spring!

Etsuko Terasaki with Irma Brandeis

News of the palace
comes to me only through voice
of streams and mountains.
Not enough! Let me see it
once again—and as it was.

Etsuko Terasaki with Irma Brandeis

They are rebuilding
the old bridge, the Nagara,
in Tsu province.
Soon there will be nothing left
with which to compare myself.

Etsuko Terasaki with Irma Brandeis

If it is you, there
in the light boat on the pond,
I long to beg you
"Do not go; linger a while
among us here in this place."

Etsuko Terasaki with Irma Brandeis

Elegy: Ise Lamenting the Death of Empress Onshi

The waves surge higher still
far off:
within the palace
Ise the diver
who has long lived there
feels her home-ship
swept away,
nothing left to cling to;
grief overcomes her.
Our tears are like
scarlet-tinged
autumn rain.
And like the maple leaves
of autumn, when the members
of the household
have scattered
in their own ways,
uncertainty
fills the air.
We who stayed behind
are like the pampas flowers
in a garden without a keeper.
We huddle together
and beckon to the sky:
the first wild geese of the season
cry out as they fly off,
indifferent to us.

Etsuko Terasaki with Irma Brandeis

Anonymous

(10th century?)

With every note
of the mountain temple
sunset bell
how sad to hear
day turn dark

WB

Izumi Shikibu

Izumi Shikibu, or Lady Izumi (10th–11th century).   Izumi was the daughter of Oe no Masamune and the wife of Tachibana no Michisada, the lord of Izumi. She was the mistress of Prince Tametaka and also of his brother Prince Atsumichi, and a contemporary of Murasaki. Her masterpiece in Japanese prose is her diary in the form of correspondence. In the diary were poems by Izumi Shikibu to and from her lover the prince, which are recorded as being sent back and forth; hence the form of epistolary diary. These poems are among the finest in the Japanese language, in which conciseness, clarity, and erotic as well as philosophical reflection find their quintessential expression. There is great variety of theme—humor, defiance, authority—in her many poems. In addition to the diary poems, many other sequences of poems have been preserved.

from The Diary of Izumi Shikibu

From darkness
I go onto the road
of darkness.
Moon, shine on me from far
over the mountain edge.

WB

On nights when hail
falls noisily
on bamboo leaves,
I completely hate
to sleep alone.

WB

Someone else
looked at the sky
with the same rapture
when the moon
crossed the dawn.

WB

I left my hills,
struggled along a dark
worldly way,
for I still hunger
to be with you again.

WB

You told me it was
because of me
you gazed at the moon.
I've come to see
if this is true.

WB

Since that night
I cannot know myself.
I go to unheard of places
and sleep recklessly
on a strange bed.

WB

You wear the face
of someone awake
in the icy air,
seeing the moon we saw
in our night of no sleep.

WB

Orange leaves are gone,
ripped away by cold night
and winter rain.
If only yesterday we'd gone
to see the mountains!

WB

I wish you would come
to me right now. How can
I brave the scandal:
go to you
and say I love you?

WB

When you broke from me
I thought I let the thread
of my life break,
yet now, for you,
I don't want to die.

WB

If you have no time
to come, I'll go.
I want to learn the way
of writing poems
as a way to you.

WB

If you love me,
come. The road
I live on
is not forbidden
by impetuous gods.

WB

On this winter night
my eyes were closed
with ice.
I wore out the darkness
until lazy dawn.

                                        WB

Here in this world
I won't live
one minute more,
where pain is rank
like black bamboo.

                                        WB

Lady Sagami

Lady Sagami (ca. 1000).   Lady-in-waiting to Princess Yūshi, she married Oe no Kinyori, Lord of Sagami, who divorced her when she became a lover of Fujiwara no Sadayori.

In the gathering dew
low leaves of the lespedeza
are cold.
On the autumn moor
young deer cry.

                                        WB

Akazome Emon

Akazome Emon (?–1027).   Was the daughter of Taira no Kanemori, a poet and statesman, and the wife of Oe no Masahira, as well as a lady-in-waiting at the court. Akazome belonged to a famous circle of women poets contemporary with Murasaki.

I, who cut off my sorrows
like a woodcutter,

should spend my life in the mountains.
Why do I still long
for the floating world?

Kenneth Rexroth and Ikuko Atsumi

Murasaki Shikibu

Murasaki Shikibu (974–1031).   The author of *Genji Monogatari (The Tale of Genji)*, one of the world's major novels, predating the novel in China, Murasaki came from a family of literary people, the Fujiwara clan. The reputation of her novel, in classic translation by Arthur Waley, tends to overshadow her poetry, but many beautiful poems are included in it. Kenneth Rexroth considers the first two poems here as pivotal to the longer work. Murasaki Shikibu also wrote poems in Chinese.

from The Tale of Genji

Lady Murasaki says:

The troubled waters
are frozen fast.
Under clear heaven
moonlight and shadow
ebb and flow.

Answered by Prince Genji:

The memories of long love
gather like drifting snow,
poignant as the mandarin ducks
who float side by side in sleep.

Kenneth Rexroth and Ikuko Atsumi

Someone passes,
And while I wonder
If it is he,
The midnight moon
Is covered with clouds.

Kenneth Rexroth

Ise Tayū

Ise Tayū (11th century).   Ise Tayū was the daughter of Onakatomi no Sukechika, chief priest of the Ise Shrine.

> The clear water of the imperial pond
> has been transparent for so many generations
> that every water plant at the bottom can be recognized.
> Just so, I am grateful to be singled out though I am of low birth.

> *Kenneth Rexroth and Ikuko Atsumi*

Ryōjin Hishō

Ryōjin Hishō (1179?).   This is a collection of songs in twenty books gathered by Emperor Go-Shirakawa (1127–1192) containing Buddhist hymns, Shintō chants, folk and traditional songs. Most of the poems are in *Imayō* form, with four lines of twelve syllables each (seven plus five). Often the poems are written by court dancers, "singing girls," and prostitutes.

> May the man who gained my trust yet did not come
> Turn to a devil, sprouting triple horns.
> Then he would find himself shunned by mankind.

> May he become a bird of the water-paddy
> With frost and snow and hailstones raining down.
> Then he would find his feet were frozen fast.

> May he become the duckweed on the pond.
> Then he would sway and shiver as he walked.

> *Geoffrey Bownas and Anthony Thwaite*

Lady Horikawa

Lady Horikawa (12th century).   An attendant to the Empress Dowager Taiken.

> Will he always love me?
> I cannot read his heart.

This morning my thoughts
Are as disordered
As my black hair.

Kenneth Rexroth

Princess Shikishi

Princess Shikishi (?–1201).   Princess Shikishi was the third daughter of Emperor
Go-Shirakawa, one of the "Three Talented Women," a princess of the Kamo Shrine in
Kyoto, and later a Buddhist nun.

The blossoms have fallen.
I stare blankly at a world
Bereft of color:
In the wide vacant sky
The spring rains are falling

Donald Keene

Chiyo

Chiyo (1703–1775).   Chiyo is considered the most important woman haiku com-
poser in the classical period.

After a long winter, giving
each other nothing, we collide
with blossoms in our hands.

David Ray

Don't dress for it.
The moon will transfigure—
those darling rags.

David Ray

Hardly Spring, with ice
still upon the rocks, and yet
the kisses are bitter.

David Ray

Once my parents were older
than I, still children,
same cicadas.

David Ray

Yosano Akiko

Yosano Akiko (1878–1942).   Yosano Akiko was an important figure in the modern
tanka movement, and part of the Myōjō (morningstar) movement, a romantic tendency
in the twentieth century. The *tanka* consists of five lines: the first and third lines contain
five syllables; the second, fourth, and fifth contain seven each.

You never touch
This soft skin
Surging with hot blood.
Are you not bored,
Expounding the Way?

Geoffrey Bownas and Anthony Thwaite

Spring is short:
Why ever should it
Be thought immortal?
I grope for
my full breasts with my hands.

Geoffrey Bownas and Anthony Thwaite

Mitsuhashi Takajo

Mitsuhashi Takajo (1899–1972).   Beginning as a disciple of Yosano Akiko, she lived a religious, ascetic life.

The hair ornament of the sun
has sunk
into the legendary sea.

Kenneth Rexroth and Ikuko Atsumi

Nagase Kiyoko

Nagase Kiyoko (1906–). She was born in Okayama Prefecture, and her poems deal with the complexities of family relationships.

Mother

I am always aware of my mother,
ominous, threatening,
a pain in the depths of my consciousness.
My mother is like a shell,
so easily broken.
Yet the fact that I was born
bearing my mother's shadow
cannot be changed.
She is like a cherished, bitter dream
my nerves cannot forget
even after I awake.
She prevents all freedom of movement.
If I move she quickly breaks,
and the splinters stab me.

Kenneth Rexroth and Ikuko Atsumi

Fumi Saitō

Fumi Saitō (1909–).   The daughter of an army general who wrote *tanka* poetry Fumi Saitō has lived most of her life in Nagano in the mountains. She has published many books of *tanka* poems, for which she has received much acclaim.

The palm of the hand
is not aware of dying as
without compulsion
it becomes cold and hardened
and only slightly shrunken.

Edith Marcombe Shiffert and Yuki Sawa

Kiyoko Tsuda

Kiyoko Tsuda (1920–).   Born in Nara, the ancient capital of Japan, she studied with
Takako Hashimoto and now teaches in the city of Osaka.

To be a mistress
is enough to tame me and
I cut a watermelon.

Edith Marcombe Shiffert and Yuki Sawa

Tada Chimako

Tada Chimako (1930–).   Tada Chimako is one of the most educated and sophisti-
cated of contemporary writers, highly knowledgeable in Western literature, philosophy,
and literary criticism. She has translated St. Jean Perse and Lévi-Strauss into Japanese,
and now lives in Kobe.

Mirror

My mirror is always a little taller than I am.
It laughs a little later than I laugh.
I blush like a boiled crab,
and cut off a projection of myself with my nail scissors.

When I let my lips approach the mirror,
it blurs, and I vanish beyond my sighs,
as a nobleman disappears behind his crest,
and a blackguard behind his tatoo.

My mirror is the cemetery of smiles.
Traveler, when you come to Lakaidaimon,

tell them that there stands here a grave,
painted white with heavy makeup,
with only wind blowing in the mirror.

Kenneth Rexroth and Ikuko Atsumi

Shiraishi Kazuko

Shiraishi Kazuko (1931–).   Born in Vancouver, she came to Japan when seven years
old. Probably Japan's leading contemporary poet, she also writes magazine columns and
prose fiction, and often appears on television.

Phallus

for Sumiko's birthday

God exists, though he doesn't exist
And, humorous as he is,
He resembles a certain kind of man.

This time,
Bringing a gigantic phallus,
He joined the picnic
above the horizon of my dream.
By the way
I regret
I didn't give Sumiko something for her birthday:
But at least I would now wish
To implant the seeds of that God-brought phallus
In the thin, small, charming voice of Sumiko
At the other end of the telephone.

Forgive me, Sumiko,
But the phallus shooting up day by day
Now grows in the heart of the cosmos
And, like a damaged bus, cannot be moved.
Therefore
If you want to see
The beautiful sky with its bright star-spangle

Or some man other than this God-brought phallus,
A man who dashes out in a car
Along the highway with a hot girl,
Then you must really
Hang out of the bus window
And peep about.

When the phallus
Begins to move and comes to the side of the cosmos
It commands a most splendid view. In such a time,
Dear Sumiko,
The loneliness of the way in which the starred night shines
And the curious coldness of midnoon
Thrill me to the marrow.
What is seen is seen whole-heartedly. No man
But goes mad.
Because a phallus has neither name nor personality
And is timeless,
It sometimes leaves its traces
On the tumbled air
When someone passes by
Carrying it uproariously like a portable shrine.
In that hum of voices
One hears the expansion of savage
Disturbance, the imprecations
Of semen not yet ruled by God. Sometimes
God is apt to be absent:
He seems to go somewhere else
Leaving debts or a phallus behind him.

Now
The phallus abandoned by God
Comes this way
Being young and gay
And full of clumsy confidence
It, surprisingly, resembles the shadow
Of an experienced smile.

The phallus seems to grow beyond all numeration,
And, beyond counting, comes this way.
It is in fact in the singular. It comes alone.
Seen from whatever horizon,
It has neither face nor words.
I would like to give you, Sumiko,
Such a thing for your birthday.

When therewith your whole life is enswaddled,
You will become invisible to yourself.
Occasionally you will turn into the will of the very phallus
And wander endlessly.
I would wish to catch in my arms,
Endlessly,
One such as you.

Ikuko Atsumi

Sachiko Yoshihara

Sachiko Yoshihara (1932–).   Sachiko Yoshihara was awarded the Muro Saisei Prize
in 1964 for her first book of poetry, *Litanies of Infancy.* Her most recent volume,
Hirugao, appeared in 1973.

Madness

Eyes shut tight
I hear my brains go splat and scatter
like dry tea-leaves.

I must kill
one lovely languid serpent after another.

A horse lies dangling upside down   and a moon rising
Mary with a child in her arms   weeps with red eyes—
now watch me whittle my finger away
and paint red characters.

One streak of white hair   many streaks of white hair
I am not to blame   it's the dreams the paper that are to blame

A car crashes into another car   slowly   undersea.
Whittling my finger   sharpening it like a pencil
let me write in red   O Mary   what words do you want me to
                                                    write down?

Darkness comes rushing on me   with waves   with fever
a knife comes flying to me   with a cat   O burst the window!

Pitiful
O everything   each and everyone so pitiful.

James Kirkup and Shozo Tokunaga

Takako U. Lento

Takako U. Lento (1941–).   She publishes poetry under her maiden name, but her translations appear under the name of Takako Uchino Lento. She was a member of the International Writing Program at the University of Iowa, and her poems have appeared widely in American periodicals.

Glass

They were dancing as if
swimming among the rocks.
We stood by the wall,
drinking beer
out of the green-labeled can.
We talked about
shadow plays, operas and
how your friend's father witnessed
Caruso break a goblet
by his forceful voice.
I laughed,
wishing I could break
the thin but inevitable glass
between me and your world.

Kanai Mieko

Kanai Mieko (1947–).   Born in Takasai, a city sixty miles from Tokyo, by the age of twenty she was winning literary awards. The title poem of her book *The House of Madam Juju,* here included, refers to the famous "Madam Juju" line of Japanese cosmetics, and to its widely advertised warning to women over twenty-five to preserve their skins by "rhythmical massage" with Madam Juju's creams. The poem also alludes to the Beatles' song "Strawberry Fields Forever." Young women are often called "strawberry" in colloquial Japanese.

The House of Madam Juju

Turning, following the arrows through
the slimy passages of the city's intestines
to the house of Madam Juju
above the revolving dome of the sea.
A wind blows up out of the subways and underground
arcades smelling of rich soup
a wind with just a hint of late autumn
as you slide your cracked lips along
the burning naked body of Madam Juju.
How skillfully you suck
mulberry facets from deep in marble.
And young women drip liquid on
the strawberry fields above the revolving sea.
The young women pant and claw
in Madam Juju's soft embrace,
their blue-tinted eyes shut, moaning
they drop tears of ecstasy
and exchange saliva with the obscene Madam.
The red stain of crushed strawberries
is drying on the back of your shirt.
The sun and blissful clouds above the strawberry fields
brighten in the afterflow of thought
and will disappear over the flaccid horizon.
      But strawberry fields forever
      Strawberry fields, yes, forever
Madam Juju wipes up the young ladies' liquid
with her whip while the sun trembles down.
You disappear through the gate

of the whiplashing Madam Juju.
Tender screams!
Your hips twitch continually
under Madam Juju's stinging blows
in a recital of tireless, eternal convulsions
forever, spastically repeating words of love.
As she raises her whip Madam Juju
encourages you, gently, almost singing

> *Shoot every arrow!*
> *Take careful aim*
> *The violence of words of love*
> *That awful violence ah*
> *A single shaft of love*

The gland of night writhes like an acrobat
over the strawberry field horizon
to the house of Madam Juju.
The whipping party starts at dusk
as the rhythmical movements of the young women
lay waste to the strawberry fields.
It will go on forever.
You won't find satisfaction
even if you climb to the morning star.

Christopher Drake

Provençal

Countess Beatritz de Die

Countess Beatritz de Die (born ca. 1140).   Little is known for certain of her life, including who her husband and family were. We know she was a trobairitz, one of the women troubadors. Evidently she was a countess, and by popular tradition "Beatritz." A medieval Provençal account of her life reads: "The Countess of Dia was the wife of En Guillen de Poitiers, a lady beautiful and good. And she fell in love with En Raimbaut d'Orange, and wrote many good *chansons* in his honor." Five poems are extant.

Lately I've felt a grave concern
over a knight who caused me pain.
For every age I want to make it plain
how this love vanquished me. I burn,
knowing I have been doublecrossed
only because I'd not make love
with him! Dressed or naked I think of
my immense error, and I am lost.

How I would love to hold my knight
a whole night in my naked arms!
I'd give him crazy joy—that harms
no one—a cushion of delight.
For I am happier with him
than Floris was with Blancaflor.
I gave my heart to him, and more:
my mind, my life, my eyes that brim

with light. My handsome, graceful friend,
when will I have you in my power?
If I could lie with you one hour,
one night, kiss you tenderly blind,

know then I would do any deed
to have you in my husband's place.
But one condition you must face:
you must obey my every need.

WB

Anonymous

Anonymous (12th century).   Nothing is known of these three women. The poem is
clearly allegorical, bitterly humorous, and wittily parodies a religious homelitic
convention.

My Lady Carenza of the lovely body,
please offer sisters your profound advice,
and since you know what's best, tell us precise-
ly what to do. You know. Your ways embody
all ways of woman. Please say: shall I wed
someone we know? Or stay a virgin? I've said
that would be good. But having kids. What for?
To me a marriage seems a painful bore.

Lady Carenza, I'd like to have a man,
but what a penance when you have a clan
of brats. Your tits hang halfway to the ground;
your belly is discomfited and round.

My lady Iselda and my Lady Alais,
you have youth, beauty; your skin a fresh color
and you know courtly manners; you have valor
beyond all other women in your place.
Hear me. And for the best seed from a cod,
marry the Crown of Knowledge, who is GOD.
And you will bear the fruit in glorious sons,
saving your chastity like married nuns.

My Lady Iselda and my Lady Alais,
remember me and may my light erase
all fears. Please ask the king of glory, when
you enter heaven, to join us once again.

WB

French

FRANCE

Anonymous Songs (12th–13th centuries).   Simplicity, lyrical directness, poignancy, and angry humor characterize the following rondeau and motet.

I walk in loneliness through the greenwood
　　for I have none to go with me.
Since I have lost my friend by not being good
I walk in loneliness through the greenwood.
I'll send him word and make it understood
　　that I will be good company.
I walk in loneliness through the greenwood
　　for I have none to go with me.

WB

I am a young girl, gay,
　　graceful, not yet
　　in my fifteenth year.
My breasts have now begun to sway
　　and swell,
　　I should be set
　　for love and hear
　　its lovely bell.
But I am in an awful prison!
　　God curse the villain,
that wicked sinner who put me
　　in a nunnery.
I cannot stand religious life.
God, but I'm far too young!
In my belly I feel sweetly stung.
God curse the man who saddled me
　　as Jesus' wife.

WB

Marie de France

Marie de France (ca. 1155–1189).   Marie de France wrote in the second half of the twelfth century, which is all we know for certain. The dates usually given refer to the ascension to the throne of Henry II, to whom she addressed her poems. She was perhaps the daughter of Geoffrey Plantagenet and therefore half-sister to Henry II. Although born in France, she probably did all her writing in England, where she was Abbess of Shaftesbury. Marie de France is the greatest woman poet of medieval Europe. She wrote *lais*, narrative poems of love and adventure, using prevalent medieval legends as her source. Although the poems are narrative, the lines read with the grace and lyrical flow of skillful song. She takes advantage of narrative technique in order to create suspense, drama, and often exquisitely poignant climactic scenes.

The Nightingale

The story I shall tell today
Was taken from a Breton lay
Called Laustic in Brittany,
Which, in proper French would be
Rossignol. They'd call the tale
in English lands *The Nightingale.*

There was, near Saint Malo, a town
Of some importance and renown.
Two barons who could well afford
Houses suited to a lord
Gave the city its good name
By their benevolence and fame.
Only one of them had married.
His wife was beautiful indeed
And courteous as she was fair,
A lady who was well aware
Of all that custom and rank required.
The younger baron was much admired,
Being, among his peers, foremost
In valor, and a gracious host.
He never refused a tournament,
And what he owned he gladly spent.
He loved his neighbor's wife. She knew
That all she heard of him was true,

And so she was inclined to be
Persuaded when she heard his plea.
Soon she had yielded all her heart
To his real merit and, in part,
Because he lived not far away.
Fearful that they might betray
The love that they had come to share,
They always took the greatest care
Not to let anyone detect
Anything that might be suspect.
And it was easy enough to hide;
Their houses were almost side by side
With nothing between the two at all
Except a single high stone wall.
The baron's wife need only go
And stand beside her bedroom window
Whenever she wished to see her friend.
They would talk for hours on end
Across the wall, and often threw
Presents through the window too.
They were much happier than before,
And would have asked for nothing more;
But lovers can't be satisfied
When love's true pleasure is denied.
The lady was watched too carefully
As soon as her friend was known to be
At home. But still they had the delight
Of seeing each other day or night
And talking to their heart's content.
The strictest guard could not prevent
The lady from looking out her window;
What she saw there no one could know.
Nothing came to interfere
With their true love until one year
In the season when the summer grows
Green in all the woods and meadows,
When birds to show their pleasure cling
To flower tops and sweetly sing.
Then those who were in love before

Do, in love's service, even more.
The baron, in truth, was all intent
On love; the messages he sent
Across the wall had such replies
From his lady's lips and from her eyes,
He knew that she felt just the same.
Now she very often came
To her window lighted by the moon,
Leaving her husband's side as soon
As she knew that he was fast asleep.
Wrapped in a cloak, she went to keep
Watch with her lover, sure that he
Would be waiting for her faithfully.
To see each other was, despite
Their endless longing, great delight.
She went so often and remained
So long, her husband soon complained,
Insisting that she must reply
To where she went at night and why.
"I'll tell you, my lord," the lady answered;
"Anyone who has ever heard
The nightingale singing will admit
No joy on earth compares with it.
That music just outside my window
Gives me such pleasure that I know
I cannot go to sleep until
The sweet voice in the night is still."

The baron only answered her
With a malicious raging laughter.
He wrought a plan that could not fail
To overcome the nightingale.
The household servants all were set
To making traps of cord or net;
Then, throughout the orchard, these
Were fixed to hazel and chestnut trees,
And all the branches rimmed with glue
So that the bird could not slip through.
It was not long before they brought

The nightingale who had been caught
Alive. The baron, well content,
Took the bird to his wife's apartment.
"Where are you, lady? Come talk to me!"
He cried, "I've something for you to see!
Look! Here is the bird whose song
Has kept you from your sleep so long.
Your nights will be more peaceful when
He can't awaken you again!"

She heard with sorrow and with dread
Everything her husband said,
Then asked him for the bird, and he
Killed it out of cruelty;
Vile, with his two hands he wrung
Its neck, and when he finished, flung
The body at his wife. The red
drops of blood ran down and spread
Over the bodice of her dress.
He left her alone with her distress.
Weeping, she held the bird and thought
With bitter rage of those who brought
The nightingale to death, betrayed
By all the hidden traps they laid.
"Alas!" she cried. "They had destroyed
The one great pleasure I enjoyed.
Now I can no longer go
And see my love outside my window
At night the way I used to do!
One thing certainly is true:
He'll think that I no longer care.
Somehow he must be made aware
Of what has happened. It will be clear
Then why I cannot appear."

And so she began at once to write
On a piece of gold-embroidered samite.
When it couldn't hold another word

She wrapped it around the little bird.
Then she called someone in her service
Whom she could entrust with this,
Bidding him take without delay
Her message to her chevalier.
Thus he came to understand
Everything, just as she planned.
The servant brought the little bird;
And when the chevalier had heard
All that he so grieved to know,
His courteous answer was not slow.
He ordered made a little case,
Not of iron or any base
Metal, but fine gold embossed
With jewels—he did not count the cost.
The cover was not too long or wide.
He placed the nightingale inside
And had the casket sealed with care!
He carried it with him everywhere.
Stories like this can't be controlled,
And it was very promptly told.
Breton poets rhymed the tale,
Calling it *The Nightingale.*

Patricia Terry

Honeysuckle (Chevrefoil)

This lay, a favorite of mine,
Was named for the honeysuckle vine
And written to commemorate
The incident which I'll relate.
Many times I've had the chance
To hear or read the old romance
Of Tristan and the queen who were
So true to love and to each other,
And who, because of love, were tried
So terribly until they died.

Tristan, by King Mark's command,
Was exiled back to his own land
When, furious, the king had seen
The love he bore Iseut, the queen.
He stayed in South Wales for a year
And all that time did not appear
At court. But then, in his despair,
He couldn't bring himself to care
What might happen if he went back—
It was better to risk death than lack
The one thing that counted in his eyes.
This shouldn't cause anyone surprise—
Every lover grieves and broods that way
If he is true and far away
From the lady who has won his heart,
And that's why Tristan had to start
For Cornwall. Whatever that could mean
At least he was sure to see the queen.
He went through the forest all alone
So that his plan would not be known,
Until, at vespers, it seemed all right
To seek some shelter for the night.
From poor peasants whom he met
He took what lodging he could get,
And asked if they knew anything
About the intentions of the king.
They told him that by King Mark's decree
The barons who owed him fealty
Had all been summoned forth to ride
To Tintagel where at Whitsuntide
The king intended to hold his court.
There would be feasting and good sport.
The queen was going to be there too.

Tristan was overjoyed. He knew
That for the journey she would make
There was just one road the queen could take.
As soon as the king was on his way
Tristan went into the woods to stay

Close to the road where he could meet
The queen as she passed by with her suite.
Meanwhile, he cut down and squared
A hazel branch. When it was pared,
He signed it, using his knife to write,
And placed the signal well in sight.
The queen would never fail to notice,
Expecting such a sign as this—
They had used it in another case
To indicate a meeting place—
And so the message would be clear;
She'd know her friend was somewhere near.

Earlier, he had sent a letter.
This is what he wrote to her:
In the forest where he had to hide
He waited a long time to decide
How best to find her, where and when
They could see each other once again.
He could no longer live that way,
Cut off from all he loved, for they
Were like the honeysuckle vine
Which around a hazel tree will twine,
Holding the trunk as in a fist
And climbing until its tendrils twist
Around the top and hold it fast.
Together tree and vine will last.
But then, if anyone should pry
The vine away, they both will die.
"Dearest, we're like that vine and tree;
I'll die without you, you without me."

The queen, as she rode along the way,
Was waiting for something to betray
The presence of her friend, and spied
The hazelstick upon a hillside.
She knew what its inscription meant;
And calling the chevaliers, present
To be her escort, she expressed

A wish to stop for a while and rest.
Promptly, on hearing what she said.
All the queen's company dismounted
And waited there while she withdrew
Alone, except for one she knew
Would keep her secret, the faithful maid
Brangene. After a while they strayed
Off the road and into the forest.
There was the one the queen loved best
In all the world, waiting for her.
Great was their joy at being together,
With time to talk once more at leisure.
The queen told him Mark's displeasure
Had changed to grief at having exiled
Tristan; they'd soon be reconciled.
The king was sure he'd been deceived
By slander he shouldn't have believed.
But when it was time for her to go,
Both of them wept in bitter sorrow.
Tristan went back to Wales and waited
Until he had been reinstated.

Because he wanted to express
The overwhelming happiness
He knew in the forest where they met,
And at the queen's desire, he set
To music the letter he had sent
Explaining what his signal meant.
And so it was remembered long
After their time in Tristan's song.
"Gotelef" in English, which became
"Honeysuckle," translates the name
"Chevrefoil." Here I've related
Just what the lay commemorated.

Patricia Terry

The Two Lovers

There came from Normandy an old
Story that was often told
Of how because two children tried
To win the right to love, they died.
A Breton lay preserves their fame;
The Two Lovers is its name.

As proof of the story, you can see
In the country we call Normandy
A mountain marvelously high
On top of which the children lie.
Close to the mountain, on one side,
There is a city, once the pride
Of Pître, named as was that land
By the king whose wise command
Had built it. Honoring his will
The city is called Pître still,
And people even now are living
In the dominions of that king.
The valley of Pître that we know
Remains as it was so long ago.

The king had just one child, a daughter
Gentle and fair; he turned to her
For comfort when her mother died,
And kept her always at his side.
People began to be aware
That the king might never have an heir;
To hear them openly complain
Caused him to suffer bitter pain.
With craft to meet his need he planned
How none should win his daughter's hand
And yet the king be free from blame.
He ordered heralds to proclaim
Near and far to everyone
How the princess could be won.
The king would let his child be married,
But first the princess must be carried

Up the high mountain near the town
Before her suitor set her down.
As soon as they heard about the test,
Suitors hastened to request
A chance to win the promised bride.
But none, no matter how he tried,
Could ever get beyond half way
Before exhaustion made him lay
His burden and his hopes to rest;
All were defeated in their quest.
The princess found herself a prize
To which no one dared lift his eyes.

In that country lived a youth,
The son of a count, and in all truth
Noble, courteous, and fair.
To be the best knight anywhere
Was what he wanted most to do.
Living much at court, he knew
And loved the princess. Eloquent,
He tried to make her heart consent
To trust his own, to have her learn
From love to love him in return.
She knew his valor, his gentle ways,
And that he had won her father's praise,
And so she said that she would be
His love, for which he thanked her humbly.
Often they would talk together,
Taking great care, although they were
So much in love, never to show
Their feelings, and let no one know.
But having to hide their love, they grieved.
The boy was prudent; he believed
Whatever the cost they must refuse
To venture all too soon and lose.
But very great was his distress.
One day it drove him to confess
How much he suffered to his friend,
Pleading with her to put an end
To their unhappiness and run

Away with him. That seemed the one
Way possible—he could no longer
Live in torment there with her,
But surely, if he asked for her hand
In marriage, the king's love would stand
Between them: he would not agree
To lose his daughter willingly
Unless the suitor, to win his bride
Carried her up the mountainside.

"I know too well," she said, "dear friend,
How that trial would have to end—
You are not strong enough to win.
But there is no good either in
Running away. I couldn't forgive
Myself if I should ever give
My father such good cause to grieve.
I love him too much, I couldn't leave
Knowing his rage and suffering.
I think there is only one thing
To do: I have an aunt I know
Could help, but you would have to go
To Salerno—she has lived there more
Than thirty years. She's famous for
Her learning, and rich; for every kind
Of sickness she knows how to find
Medicine in roots and plants:
Surely this is our only chance.
If you agree I'll write a letter
For you to take and give to her,
And you can tell our story too.
She will know how to counsel you
And give you some kind of medicine
To make you strong enough to win.
Then you can come back to this land,
And ask my father for my hand.
He'll say that you are young and foolish,
And that he will grant your wish,

According to his own decree,
Only if you can carry me
All the way up to the top
Of the mountain, and you do not stop."
For the prudent counsel that he heard
The boy gave joyful thanks, and answered
That he would, that very day,
With her consent, be on his way.

He went to his own home, and hurried
To assemble all that he would need,
Gold enough and fine clothing,
Pack horses, palfreys, summoning
Those of his men he trusted most
To travel with him to the coast.
Once in Salerno, he visited
The princess' aunt; when she had read
The letter from beginning to end,
She decided first to recommend
He stay with her a while. And so
She learned all that there was to know.
She gave him medicines to build
His strength, and by her arts distilled
A philter that would meet his need.
As soon as he drank it, however wearied
He might be, no matter how great
His burden, he would not feel the weight
Because of the power that had flown
From his lips to veins and bone.
She sent him back then to his trial;
He carried the philter in a phial.

When he reached his home, the boy,
Confident and full of joy,
Wasted no time at all, but went
To ask the king if he'd consent
To give him the princess for his bride
When he carried her up the mountainside.
The king felt no need to refuse;

He thought the boy would surely lose,
That it was madness to imagine
Someone of his age could win
Where so many wise and valiant men
Had tried and every one was beaten.
The king then willingly proclaimed
The contest would be held, and named
A date. He summoned every friend,
Every vassal to attend
The ceremony. At his command
They gathered from throughout the land
To see the youth put to the trial
Of climbing up the mountain while
Holding in his arms the princess.
She, by eating less and less,
Prepared in the most useful way
She could for the appointed day.

Finally, when everyone
Arrived, the contest was begun.
In a meadow near the Seine,
First the boy appeared, and then
The king, who led his daughter through
The crowd assembled there to do
Them honor. The young princess wore
Only a shift and nothing more.
Holding her in his arms, the boy
Believed that nothing could destroy
Their hopes; he had the little phial
Which she would carry for a while.

However sure the outcome seems,
I fear he'll go to such extremes
That the medicine will go to waste.

He reached the halfway point in haste,
Far too happy to remember
More than that he was close to her.
She felt his strength would not allow
Much more. "Please drink the philter now!"

She said, "Dear friend, you cannot hide
Your weariness!" The boy replied,
"Dearest, my heart is very strong;
I will not stop to drink as long
As I can manage three steps more—
Nothing can change my mind before!
We would be seen by all the crowd,
And, if they should shout aloud,
I'd lose my balance. They're too near;
I won't take time to drink right here."

Two thirds of the way up to the top
He stumbled, and nearly let her drop.
Time and again the girl would plead,
"Here is the medicine you need!"
But trying, in pain, to reach the peak,
He didn't even hear her speak.
Exhausted, he went on until
He fell at the top, and then lay still;
His heart cracked open in his breast.
Thinking him worn out by his conquest,
The maiden came to kneel beside
Her friend, and once again she tried
To bring him comfort with the philter.
But now he could not answer her.

Thus, as I have told, he died
There upon the mountainside.
Crying aloud her grief, the girl
Picked up the phial again to hurl
The philter down. And it was worth
Much to that well watered earth
And to the region all around,
For afterwards the people found
Powerful herbs that flourished there.

The maiden, in her great despair,
Lay down beside her friend, alone
With sorrow she had never known,
Now that he was lost forever.

So she held him close to her
Tightly in her arms, and still
Kissing his eyes and mouth until
Her grief became a sword inside
Her heart. And so the maiden died
Who was so lovely, and so wise.

Those waiting began to realize
The children should long since have returned.
When they climbed the peak, and learned
The truth, the king, in horror, fainted.
When he could speak, he mourned the dead,
And all the people shared his sorrow.
They did not let the children go
For three days. A marble coffin
Holding them both was buried in
The place that would forever tell
The story. Then they said farewell.

"Two Lovers" is the name they gave
The mountain that was now a grave.
It all happened just this way
In truth and in a Breton lay.

Patricia Terry

Anonymous

The Song of the Ill-Married (*chanson de mal-mariée*) (14th–15th century).   The
story in this poem appears in Latin and other romance languages: the wife regrets her
unhappy marriage to a jealous, worthless husband, and she thinks of ways to outwit
him with a better man.

Song of the Ill-Married

In an orchard a little fountain flows,
Shadowless ripples over white stones,

There a king's daughter, her head bowed low,
Remembers her sweet love and her sorrows.
    Alas, Count Guy, my friend!
Without you I'll never know joy again.

Count Guy, my love, how cruel is my fate!
The old man my father gave me for a mate
Keeps me in his house and locks every gate,
Nor can I leave it early or late;
    Alas, Count Guy, my friend!
Without you I'll never know joy again.

The cruel husband hears her, and soon
Appears in the orchard, his belt removes,
And belts her until she is so badly bruised
She falls at his feet in a deathlike swoon.
    Alas, Count Guy, my friend!
Without you I'll never know joy again.

The lady arose from her faint to pray
That God in pity her grief allay,
"Let me not be forgotten! Oh, may
I see my love before vespers today."
    Alas, Count Guy, my friend!
Without you I'll never know joy again.

And Our Lord listened to her lament;
Her lover consoled the chatelaine.
Beneath a great tree whose branches bend,
Many tears for their love have fallen.
    Alas, Count Guy, my friend!
Without you I'll never know joy again.

Patricia Terry

Christine de Pisan

Christine de Pisan (1363–1430).   Born in Venice, the daughter of Thomas Pisani, a physician and astrologer to Charles V of France, at fifteen she married Étienne de

Castel. Widowed ten years later, she suffered many hardships to support herself and three children. A staunch defender of women, she replied eloquently to attacks by Jean de Meun and wrote a treatise on the education of women. In part she supported herself through her writing, the first French woman to do so. Her last days were spent in a convent. Her poems are addressed to men; frequently, however, using the diction of courtly love, she assumes a male voice and addresses a woman lover in her poems.

Christine to Her Son

Son, of great fortune have I none
To make you rich: instead of gold,
Though, certain lessons I would bring
Up, if you'll give them a hearing.

From first youth, innocent and pure,
Learn to know what people are,
And so, by seeing what they're like,
Protect yourself from gross mistake.

Upon the destitute take pity,
Poor creatures you will naked see,
Give them assistance as you may!
Bearing in mind you too will die.

Love him who is a friend to you
And watch out for your enemy:
No one can have too many friends,
There is no minor enemy.

What serves the Lord do not discard
For a world overmuch enslaved:
The worldly go to meet their fate
And the enduring soul holds out.

Barbara Howes

I'll always dress in black and rave
for I have been dismissed by her.

Now nothing startles me. You were
my lady, I your rightful slave.

I'll never know her villa, save
in mournful dream. My visions blur.
I'll always dress in black and rave.

I will not stay when you behave
harshly, insult me like a cur,
for things have changed. I won't concur
and won't reveal my sorrow, save
I'll always dress in black and rave.

WB

I am a widow, robed in black, alone:
my face is sad and I am plainly dressed.
Dark is my daily life. I am distressed,
for bitter mourning dries me to the bone.

Of course I feel dejected, dead like stone,
in tears, silenced, in every way depressed.
I am a widow, robed in black, alone.

For I have lost the one who makes me own
the memory of pain with which I am obsessed.
Gone are the days of joy I once possessed.
With poison herbs my hard terrain is sewn.
I am a widow, robed in black, alone.

WB

Alone am I, and alone I wish to be;
Alone my sweet love has left me.
Alone am I, without friend or mate,
Alone am I, mournful and angry.
Alone am I, listless I wait,

Alone am I, stranded far away.
Alone am I, without my lover late.

Alone, by the window or the door,
Alone, in a hidden corner.
Alone, feeding only on my tears,
Alone, here I calmly mourn.
Alone. Nothing pleases me.
Alone, closed in my room,
Alone, my lover's death decrees.

I am alone, wherever I may be,
I am alone, whether I rest or flee.
I am alone, more than anything alive,
I am alone, kept from company.
I am alone, cruelly deprived,
I am alone, often full of tears,
I am alone, now my love has died.

Noble listeners, my anguish is begun,
Alone am I, menaced by mourning,
Alone am I, dyed deeper than dark brown,
Alone am I, my love no longer living.

Julie Allen

Louise Labé

Louise Labé (1525–1566).   Louise Labé was born in Lyons, a cultural center second only to Paris. Clement Marot and Maurice Scève were in her circle. As a young woman she was an extraordinary horsewoman and archer, "la belle Amazone," and her early biographers report that she fought on horseback in the ranks of the dauphin (Henry II) in the expedition against the Spanish and participated in jousts performed in Lyons in honor of Henry II's visit there. She was married to a ropemaker, Ennemond Perrin, and was called "La belle Cordière." In her rich salon, not only Scève, but other important poets, such as Claude Taillemont, Pontus de Tyard, and Pernette du Guillet, were regular guests. One poet, Olivier de Magny, was passing through Lyons and fell in love with Louise. She in turn received him and her love became a passion. Love is the central theme of her sonnets. When de Magny had to proceed to Rome, the absence haunted her. Finally she tired of waiting and developed a friendship with Claude de Rubys, a Lyonnese lawyer. When Olivier returned and discovered his loss, he wrote an insulting poem about Louise and her husband, which, ironically, is the main work for which he is still known. Labé broke with Rubys, retired to the country, and died a few years later. Louise Labé wrote the first of her twenty-four sonnets in Italian, the remainder in French. Of course, she followed Petrarchan form and conventions, but her poems are anything but the artificial exercises which characterize most contemporary Petrarchan imitators. The poems do not disappear weakly in Platonic idealizations or expected paradoxes. Except for a few poems at the beginning of the sequence, her sonnets speak with extraordinary candor of particular moments, in which she also embraces a world of associations from tournaments and cities to forests and mythological figures. Ecstasy, despair, anger, contempt pervade her poems. She is in bed and in a forest, on her lover's chest and on a mountain in the cosmos—naturally, forcefully, convincingly. She constantly wakes to her own self-deceptions and psychologically points out the lies and hopes of love: "How can I breathe one tranquil breath/ when my eye fights my heart with deadly light?" When she is angered against a man who has praised and left her, she writes: "Your brutal goal was to make *me* a slave/ beneath the ruse of being served by you./ Pardon me, friend, and for once hear me through:/ I am outraged with anger and I rave." In the end she tells her jealous ladies, "Don't blame me, ladies, if I've loved. No sneers/ if I have felt a thousand torches burn." No one has written more intelligently, forcefully, and lyrically about the good and the sorrow of love.

I*

Not Ulysses, no, nor any other man
however astute his mind, ever longed for
that holy face shaded with grace, honor,
respect, more than I sigh for you. Nor can
I turn my gaze, Love, from your handsome eyes,
which wound me deeply in my innocent chest;
and though I have food, warmth, and tenderest
relief, without your hand all my hope dies.
O terrible fate! Suffering the scorpion to feast
on me, I seek protection from the pain
of poison by appealing to the beast
that stings me. Though I beg the sun at dawn
to kill the hurt, if it burns up the stain
of sweet desire, I'll die when it is gone.

WB

* Written in Italian.

II

O handsome chestnut eyes, evasive gaze,
O fiery sighs and falling tears, O night
obscurely black through which I wait for light
for nothing, O clear dawn of futile days!
O lamentations, O obstinate desires,
O wasted time, O grief scattered about,
O thousand deaths, O thousand nets throughout
my life among the worst insidious fires,
O laughing lips, brow, hair, arms, hands, and fingers,
O funereal lute, viol, bow, and voice!
A woman's heart always has a burned mark.
I sob because of you. Your fire lingers
in every place my seared heart would rejoice,
except in you who keep no single spark.

WB

III

O interminable desires, O futile hope,
depressing sighs and now familiar tears
engendering in me many rivers, spheres
of rain whose source and fountain are my grop-
ing eyes. O cruelty, inhumanity,
commiserating glance of heavenly rays,
O chilled heart, early passions. These days
I ask, can you still swell my agony?
Let Love again try out his bow and pierce
me with new fire and stab me with new darts.
Let him exact revenge the worst he can.
I am so torn in every limb, no man
can cut another wound in me, no fierce
monstrous attack can find unsuffering parts.

WB

IV

From that first flash when awful Love took flame
to poison me, steeping it in my chest,
it burns with holy fury, without rest,
and not a single day has seen it tame.
With all the horror it imposed, the tale
and threat of devastation at each breath
and each thought looming over me with death,
my fiery heart could not be stunned or fail.
However much Love tries to batter us,
our force congeals at every impetus,
becoming fresh with each attacking prong.
Yet Love does not assail without a plan,
for it despises gods as well as man
and so appears more dreadful to the strong.

WB

V

White Venus limpid wandering in the sky,
hear my voice. It sings to you. Its cares grow
while your high face makes the firmament glow.
It is weary, filled with worry. Now my eye
will be more tender, straining to stay awake,
and it will cry more tears and it will stare
at you. My pillow will be drenched. Your car-
ing eye is certain witness to my ache.
But people have a feeble spirit. They need
to lie down, fade away, and deeply feed
on sleep. I suffer now in the sun's light
and when I'm almost broken, pierced, and when
abandoned in my lonely bed, it's then
I must scream out my misery through the night.

AB and WB

VI

The coming of that limpid Star is twice
or three times blessed, and happiest are they
who have the honor of his dazzling ray.
Let her one day receive his paradise,
let her be free to brag that as he dips
to kiss the most exquisite florid lawn,
the keenest fragrance ever seen by Dawn,
he also lingers slowly on her lips!
I am the only one for such reward,
for all the tears and time lost and abhorred.
And when I see him I will act, and he
will glow with happiness. I'll use my eyes
to spread a power on my handsome prize
and quickly have my own great victory.

WB

VII

We see each living thing finally die
when the fine soul leaves the body's chart.
I am the body, you the better part.
Where are you soul I love and sanctify?
Do not leave me too long in misery.
If you would save me, then do not be late
nor let your body linger in that state.
Give it the half it worships tenderly.
And act, dear Friend, so that our loving union,
our world, will have no danger in its place,
no bitterness and only friendly grace,
no stain of harshness in our white communion.
Then your good beauty I will calmly greet,
formerly cruel, but now immensely sweet.

WB

VIII

I live, I die, I burn myself and drown.
I am extremely hot in suffering cold:
my life is soft and hardness uncontrolled.
When I am happy, then I ache and frown.
Suddenly I am laughing while I cry
and in my pleasure I endure deep grief:
my joy remains and slips out like a thief.
Suddenly I am blooming and turn dry.
So Love inconstantly leads me in vain
and when I think my sorrow has no end
unthinkingly I find I have no pain.
But when it seems that joy is in my reign
and an ecstatic hour is mine to spend,
He comes and I, in ancient grief, descend.

WB

IX

As soon as I lie down in my soft bed,
trying to vanish into wanted sleep,
my sad feelings overcome me and sweep,
me out toward you to whom I'm wildly led.
When I suppose that on my tender breasts
I hold the darling face I longly tried
to find, for whom openly I have sighed,
I break, I sob, and then my soul protests.
O gentle sleep, O night of ecstasy!
Pleasure, repose, immense tranquility!
Let each night be an agent that will tie
me to my dream. And yet, if my poor soul
truly is doomed to play a loveless role,
arrange, at least, for it to have its lie.

WB

X

When I perceive your blond and graceful head
crowned with green laurel, making your lute sigh,
you could compel the rocks and trees to fly
with you, and when I see you garlanded
with ten thousand virtues, each in place,
and at the peak of honor, beyond all
a man desires of fame, supreme and tall—
to you my maddened heart whispers its case:
"With all those virtues raising you above
the rest, each one of which makes you esteemed,
could they not just as well cause you to love?
So adding virtue many times redeemed,
you might be known for being kind to me;
for burning with my love in sympathy."

WB

XI

O eyes clear with beauty, O tender gaze,
small gardens filled with amorous blossoms where
felonious darts of Love spin through the air,
where my eyes glare and blanken in dead glaze.
O criminal heart, O granite cruelty,
you hold me now viciously in your power,
I cry so many weary tears, and hour
on hour my heart suffers a burning sea.
Although my eyes have sudden pleasure stored
from drinking in the eyes of him my lord,
heart, the more you look, darker is your night,
the more you languish, closer is your death.
Tell me, how can I breathe one tranquil breath
when my eye fights my heart with deadly light?

WB

XII

Lute, companion of my calamity,
unblamable witness of my sighs, ver-
itable assessor of my gray despair,
often you have shared your lament with me.
So many tears have fallen constantly
on you, that when you are to sing a rare
and happy sound, you hide it unaware,
converting the white song to agony
And if I want to force you to rejoice,
you silence me by loosening a string.
But when my gentle sighs enter your being,
then you approve of my unhappy voice
and my hurt makes me cheerful like a friend
and from sweet pain I hope for a sweet end.

AB and WB

XIII

If I could linger on his lovely chest
happy, soaring with him for whom I see
myself die, if envy did not keep me
from living my brief days with him, and best,
if holding me he'd say: "My dear friend,
let us enjoy each other and be sure
that no rainburst or seas or seastorm lure
us to separation before our lives end,"
if, while my arms were sleeping on the nape
of his neck like ivy circling a tree,
death came, jealous of our carefree rapport
as tenderly he kissed me more and more,
into his lips my soul would then escape
and, more than alive, I'd die in ecstasy.

AB and WB

XIV

Although I cry and though my eyes still shed
tears for the seasons I once spent with you,
and while my voice—suppressing sobs, subdu-
ing sighs—still rings out vaguely spirited,
while my hand can still pluck the supple string
of the exquisite Lute to sing your grace
and while my arms care only to embrace
your lovely body and to share your being,
while this is true I have no wish to die.
But when I feel my eyes begin to spin,
my voice is broken and my fingers lack
all power, then waiting in my mortal skin
my spirit has no lover's glow, and I
pray death to make my brightest day turn black.

WB

XV

To honor the return of sparkling sun
the gentle zephyr winds of dawn awake,
and out of sleep the earth and water shake
supplely in the day. Night has kept the one
from flowering in a bed of brilliant hues
and stilled the other, the loquacious brooks.
Now birds and trees perform their books
of wonder, passersby hear wondrous news
and are less sad. The nymphs play in the mass
of last moonrays, and dancing bend the grass.
Zephyr of the morning, strike me and bring
me light, renew me with your potency!
Please make my secret sun return to me
and I'll be iridescent, blossoming.

WB

XVI

After an age when thunderbolts and hail
ravaged the peaks of the Caucasian ridge,
the clear day came quivering like a wide bridge
of rays. When Phoibos on his earthly trail
is done, and wanders to the ocean floor
his sister climbs, her crown pointed with light;
after the Parthian struggles from the fight,
fleeing, he must unbend the bow he wore.
There was a time you cried and I consoled,
although you did not trust my cautious flame.
But now you have enraged the fire in me,
consuming me as you wanted me to be.
You drowned your fire in water and became—
more than I ever was—perfectly cold.

WB

XVII

I flee the city, temples, and each place
where you took pleasure in your own lament,
where you used every forceful argument
to make me yield what I could not replace.
Games, masques, tournaments bore me and I sigh
and dream no beauty that is not of you.
And so I try to kill my passion too,
forcing another image to my eye,
hoping to break away from tender thought.
Deep in the woods I found a lonely trail,
and after wandering in a maze I sought
to put you wholly out of mind. I fail.
Only outside my body can I live
or else in exile like a fugitive.

WB

XVIII

Kiss me again, rekiss me, kiss me more,
give me your most consuming, tasty one,
give me your sensual kiss, a savory one,
I'll give you back four burning at the core.
Are you up in arms? Well, I'll give you ten
erotic kisses for your appetite
and we will mingle kisses and excite
our bodies with an easy joy again.
Then we will live a double life, and each
of us will be alone and yet will blend
our love. Love, please allow a little madness:
I'm always hurt and live with temperate speech,
veiling these days in which I find no gladness
if I can't leave myself and find my friend.

WB

XIX

After having slain very many beasts
Diana went into the thickest wood
and in the coolness, near her nymphs, she stood
a while as I was walking in a feast
of mindless reverie. Then suddenly:
"O worried nymph," I heard a voice call out,
"What are you doing here, wandering about
far from Diana?" And she looked at me
without my bow or quiver. Then she cried,
"Who took your bow and arrows?" But I sighed:
"I shot my arrows at a stranger, and
hurled the bow too, trying to reach his heart.
He gazed at me and took them in his hand,
shot a hundred times, tearing me apart."

WB

XX

I was foretold that on a certain day
I would fall fatally in love with one

whose face had been described to me. Though none
had painted him, I knew him by the first ray
of light. And seeing him enthralled with me,
I felt compassion for his mournful state
and forced my heart to work so ardently
that I loved him the same. We share our fate.
Who would have ever dreamed that something born
of destiny and heaven could be bad?
But when I see the misty landscape mad
with punishing winds, storm, unrelenting strife,
I think that powers out of hell have torn
the world and schemed the shipwreck of my life.

WB

XXI

What grandeur makes a man seem venerable?
What hair? What color of his skin? What size?
What kind of glance is best? What honeyed eyes?
Who stabs a wound that is incurable?
What song is proper for a man to sing?
And who in singing pain perceives it well?
What makes a lute sound sweet and amiable?
What natural qualities are flattering?
I tell you nothing, for I feel unsure;
moreover, love has made my judgment poor
but one fact I am deadly certain of:
all the world's beauty that may cause alarm
and all of art contriving nature's charm
could never fill me with a wilder love.

WB

XXII

O blazing Sun, how happy you are there
where you can always see your lover's face,

and you who have Endymion's embrace:
the sister pampered by his tender care.
Mars looks at Venus, Mercury can stare
freely through the sky, glide from place to place,
and Jupiter recalls the happy pace
of many old adventures hot and rare.
Just think of Heaven's awesome harmony
binding those holy spirits into one.
But should they lose what they love distantly
their power and order all would be undone:
those stars would wander dumbly and insane
and struggle fitfully, like me, in vain.

                                                                    WB

XXIII

What good is it to me if long ago
you eloquently praised my golden hair,
compared my eyes and beauty to the flare
of two suns where, you say, love bent the bow,
sending the darts that needled you with grief?
Where are your tears that faded in the ground?
Your death? by which your constant love is bound
in oaths and honor now beyond belief?
Your brutal goal was to make *me* a slave
beneath the ruse of being served by you.
Pardon me, friend, and for once hear me through:
I am outraged with anger and I rave.
Yet I am sure, wherever you have gone,
your martyrdom is hard as my black dawn.

                                                                    WB

XXIV

Don't blame me, ladies, if I've loved. No sneers
if I have felt a thousand torches burn,

a thousand wounds, a thousand daggers turn
in me, if I have burnt my life with tears.
Especially, leave my good name alone.
If I have failed, my hurt is very plain.
Don't sharpen razors to increase my pain,
but know that love, whom none of you have known,
needing no Vulcan to excuse your flame,
nor beautiful Adonis for your shame,
can make you fall in love and anywhere.
You will have fewer chances for relief,
your passion will be stronger and more rare,
and so beware of a more shattering grief.

WB

Marceline Desbordes-Valmore

Marceline Desbordes-Valmore (1786–1859).   Brought up in poverty, she became
an actress, married an actor, and then toured France with him for twenty years. Her
poems speak of an unhappy love affair, childhood, and escape. Verlaine included her in
his *Poètes maudits,* 1884. Her poems rarely escape the clichés of late romantic poetry.
"The Roses of Sa'adi" is one of her best known and finest poems.

The Roses of Sa'adi

I wanted this morning to bring you a gift of roses,
But I took so many in my wide belt
The tightened knots could not contain them all

And burst asunder. The roses taking wing
In the wind were all blown out to sea,
Following the water, never to return;

The waves were red with them as if aflame.
This evening my dress bears their perfume still:
You may take from it now their fragrant souvenir.

Barbara Howes

Marguerite Burnat-Provins

Marguerite Burnat-Provins (1872–1952).   Of Flemish and Spanish ancestry,
Burnat-Provins was born in Arras, married in Switzerland, and lived a nomadic life in
many countries. Jean Héritier described her prose poems "as the most admirable in
French literature." They are exuberantly erotic and romantic. Her many volumes
include *Tableaux valaisans* (1903), *Le livre pour toi* (1908), *Cantique d'été* (1910),
Poèmes de la boule de verre (1917), *Poèmes du scorpion* (1921), and *Choix de poèmes*
(1933).

The fruits you give me are more savory than others,
their aroma brings me something of you.

I ate them again on your mouth, where I recaptured
their flavor, with provoking kisses, in the perfumed juice
of blue plums.

You held my hands and our lips were fresher than the
centers of fruit bursting with ripeness; hard nuts cracked
between our teeth; your eyes were laughing, but suddenly
they grew dark, and you bit the ripe raspberries at the tips
of my inflamed breasts.

If one day you must tear my heart to pieces, Sylvius,
as you rend apart the blond pulp that summer lavishes on us,
don't bother to sharpen the blade that sparkles on the wall
in the house, take it with your bare teeth, tear it out and
let my blood pour out of my open heart, more sparkling than
the bright blood that swells through the currants.

Cassia Berman

You told me: "I am not worthy of you." And you hid
your face from me.

But my kiss found it, and slipped lightly over your
sweet golden temples where magic lies asleep.

What do you know about yourself? Nothing.

You know nothing of the charm and freshness that play
around your beauty.

You know nothing of your laughter, similar to that of
fountains.

You've never seen the shining nimbus that circles your
head during times I wish were fatal, they give me so much
happiness.

You've never seen your eyes where the whole sky catches
fire and dies in the pleasure of my caresses.

You don't hear the words which dissolve my soul and lead
it toward paradise.

You don't know anything, so shut up.

Cassia Berman

Sylvius, your hands near my mouth are heady flowers
that intoxicate me, and I take your strong fingers between
my teeth like the alder branches that, laughing, I break.

But you disdain this childish game that leaves no
traces, and shake your head.

If you only knew how I would like to bite into your
heart and drink your life very very slowly, without raising
my head.

Cassia Berman

Thérèse Plantier

Thérèse Plantier (1911–).   Born in Nîmes, she began an association with the
postwar Paris surrealists, but she returned to the southern France of her youth and now
lives in the village of Faucon. She has contributed to the journal *La Brèche*, and
translates contemporary British poets. Among her volumes are *Chemin d'eau* (1963),
Jusqu'à ce que l'enfer gêle (1974), and *La loi du silence* (1975).

Doors

They unfold before the sky
I escape from these doors
into my vast night
without you,
you alone, restless,
half-charred

on your island splashed
with the squeezed juice of animals,
you come apart through your own powers
you sink under your own weight
in the middle of a black concrete clearing
where octopus trees move away
each tree replaced by a smoking door
by a blinker
a circular house
punctuated by innumerable incinerations.

WB and Elene Kolb

Overdue Balance Sheet

Forgot to mail my letter to my friend Death
lost my pocketbook
took a lot of turns too sharply to the left
caught cold caught hot caught tepid caught fire caught nothing
skidded on an ice patch
had to chase from one place to another
parked
screwed up (got control in time)
hit the jackpot in matters of sheer idiocy
buried a cat I wrapped in the morning paper
was ashamed
was brave
was down and out
talked too much heard too much
tore my life to shreds
burned a hole in my pantsuit with a cigarette
and all at once caught sight of night.

Maxine Kumin and Judith Kumin

Joyce Mansour

Joyce Mansour (1928–).   Born in London of Egyptian parents, she lives in France but has also lived in Egypt. She is a leading member of the present surrealist movement in France, and her books include *Rapaces* (1960), *Carré blanc* (1965), and *Phallus et momies* (1969).

Seated on her bed legs spread open
A bowl before her
Looking for food but seeing nothing
A woman with eyelids eaten by flies
Moaned
The flies came in through the window
Left by the door
Went into her bowl
Red eyes black flies
Eaten by a woman
Who saw nothing

WB

Last night I saw your corpse
You were moist and naked in my arms
I saw your skull
I saw your bones tossed by the morning sea
Onto white sand under a hesitant sun
Crabs fought for your flesh
Nothing was left of your bloated breasts
Yet that's how I preferred you
my flower

WB

Yvonne Caroutch

Yvonne Caroutch (1937–).   Born in Paris of Mongolian parents, she is married to the writer Frederick Tristan. She has traveled extensively in Europe, Latin America, Turkey, the USSR, and the Near and Far East, and lived for a long time in Venice where she translated the poems of Dino Campana, Montale, and Ungaretti. Her own work was first recognized in 1954 when her volume of poems *Soifs* was hailed, along with Françoise Sagan's *Bonjour tristesse,* as one of the two literary events of the year. In 1974 she received the Cocteau Prize for *La voie du coeur de verre.* She has written a play, a novella, and short stories. Her books include *Soifs* (1954), *Les veilleurs endormis* (1955), *Lieux probables* (1968), and *La voie du coeur de verre* (1972).

When we are two drunk suns
in the quiet of the figs
when clammy night crumbles far
over dead cities
when we hear
the compact cry of hidden seeds
under the thickness of the earth
we will make a great fire of mint
to announce the wedding
of the rivers' dark souls
and our multiple thirsts.

WB and Elene Kolb

Night opens like an almond
Suns explode on the walls
Stars of healthy flesh
hang from our chests
Wounds drill into sand
The wild grass of our gaze
descends down to the heart
But in our blood we keep
the smell of rain in a forest
In our cold beds we pursue
the endless fall of silences.

Elene Kolb

Child of silence and shadow
you lay in great beds
of wild nettles and mint
You dreamt on the immense river
devoured by a flame of moon
Your hands flowed into the wind
of oceans and forests
Where are your nights lost angel
Dawn Listen to the blood too heavy
throbbing in the castings of steel
Do you feel the fear entering you

like a knife into your chest
You pass through our lands
vessel lost in the mists
You don't see the sun shining
like the first morning on earth

David Cloutier

I come to you with the vertigoes of the source
numbed into stone
Standing up to death entwined in the grasses
we penetrate into an empire without contours
wide open to our disproportion
Silence holds its breath
in the midst of a motionless wind
and the riotings of mirrors
High walls patiently conquered by our rites
keep watch over our movements
We are monotonous stars
astonished insects in worlds of feathers

David Cloutier

The limb of forests rises up
behind the foliage stirring
Ghost people gravitate beneath the bark
assail your castles of nutmeg
Sublime thorn planted in scarlet time
Winged heel of the starry arcanum
House of sulfur and mercury
held spellbound by a feather
increased by what weight
on the scales of dreams
Logic at the triple stage
of this bleeding communion

It made the white rose of winds revolve
Nothing can ever cloud
its incorruptible retina

David Cloutier

Anne-Marie Albiach

Anne-Marie Albiach (1937–).   Albiach lives in Paris and is associated with recent French literary theory and experimental poetry. A semiotician, she is a member of the editorial board of *Siècle à mains*. She has translated Louis Zukofsky's *'A'–9*. In her explanatory note on the poem *Etat*, Rosemarie Waldrop notes that *Etat* is "the epic of the imagination. . . . if Anne-Marie rejects rationality, she quite obviously writes with full intelligence. . . . Etat is a beautiful, important work." Her books are *Flammigère* (1967) and *Etat* (1971).

he accepts the circle, speech and so
resolves himself
is reabsorbed into a higher equation

IRREDUCIBLE GEOMETER

Not to be seized by swallowing
our, the polygonal
form
His Entry holds it in our view

Recapitulation:
last movement
doubled

Also something of this trajectory
in the stance

that oversteps expression

formulae
the one for place

Keith Waldrop

Marie-Françoise Prager

Marie-Françoise Prager (20th century).   Born of French parents in Amsterdam, she now lives in Italy, under medical treatment. Although her poetry remained for a long time unpublished, it was not unrecognized. Before 1966, when her first volume, *Narcoses,* was published, Gaston Bachelard, Roland Barthes, and Jean Rousselot had all expressed their admiration for her poetry. Prager has contributed to the journal *Esprit,* and has published two books of poems: *Narcoses* (1966) and *Rien ne se perd* (1970).

> I'll act out a weird dream
> hobble like a broken bird
> howl a name over and over like a hyena
> flare an open wing like a fan to a half-eaten moon
> choose a grain from the sands of your closed lips
> and retrace my steps and always
> come back in half shadows
> damned by the wing I have left
> I am the sign who names you.

> *WB and Elene Kolb*

BELGIUM

Anne-Marie Kegels

Anne-Marie Kegels (1912–).   Anne-Marie Kegels was born in Belgium where she currently lives. Her many awards include the Prix Renée Vivien, Paris (1953), Prix Gerard de Nerval, Paris (1955), Prix Félix Denayer, Brussels (1962), Chevalier de l'Ordre de Léopold II (1968). She is a member of the Academy of Luxembourg and of the Société de Gens de Lettres de France. Her books include *Nothing but Living* (1953), *Songs of Deaf Joy* (1955), *High Vine* (1962), *Twelve Poems for a Year* (1967), *Adverse Light* (1970), and *The Roads Are on Fire* (1973).

> When I strip,
> stop walking
> and drop into sleep
> —before I'm at the bottom
> of unmoving waters—

I think of you
restless,
journeying.

WB

I write to make you suffer,
To dance life before you.
Now watch me bend at the waist.
Do you see how summer holds me?
I run from you. My heart gallops.
My blood saunters before your eyes.
I vow: let this poem
be the asp, diminutive,
but biting you.

WB

Nocturnal Heart

Master of blood I am yours.
O tireless captain
upright on the plains of sand,
at night, at night I hear you
march toward a doubtful sea
with footsteps falsely restrained
—at that time I touch my breath,
I search for you with my bare wrist,
I defend you against the seaweed,
the salt, the wakened fish,
we faint under a wave,
people tell of two that are drowned,
of a fog mowing the beach.

Midnight descends, covers my lips,
keeps me from calling for help.
We float, forgotten by day.

W. S. Merwin

SWITZERLAND

Monique Laederach

Monique Laederach (1938–).   Monique Laederach was born in Les Brenets, Switzerland. Her poems have appeared in many French and Swiss magazines and anthologies. Her books are *Penelope* (1970), *The Tin, The Stream* (1970), and *Ballad of the Famished Clowns in Their Den* (1974).

from Penelope

(Leaving the island, she believes, to go to the child.
She herself is like an island.
But on the last step, what she treads
is a spongy artificial turf, like the islands
of memory, unreal islands.
For a man rises. Young. With the face
of Telemachus, doubly bound to his father by love
and resemblance. With a stature already hardened
by the demand of muscles. His voice: a man's.
"This place isn't for you," he says. "I am
their host.")

Charles Guenther

from Penelope

And so I speak
in place of that primordial cry,
and the day stands in my memory like a land
without trees, without dust—
Lost is the proud insubordination, my virtue
of silence; lost is the piercing flight
into the sun; the inverted dawn
inside me is reborn only in a dream,
and I have nothing left to drink but water
brought to me at the half-light through the bars,
in a broken bowl.

Charles Guenther

Claude Maillard

Christmas Mass for a Little Atheist Jesus

you
my bell-clapper
me
your bell
and us both
resonant pealing chiming
making the faithful hasten forth
getting them down on their knees
to pray to us
to believe in us
moisten your fingers in holy water
at the sway of the censer
murmur your ritual words
vobiscum
we are the pipes of great organs
the stained-glass windows of ex-cathedrals
the club feet that you kiss
at the midnight mass
we stay in the crèche
to keep warm
warm in the straw
and the shepherds come
how lovely they are in their cloaks of animal fur
we forgive us our venial sins
you say to me
vow to me
I answer you
amen

Maxine Kumin and Judith Kumin

Denise Jallais

Denise Jallais (20th century).   Denise Jallais is an editor for *Elle* magazine, and
presently lives in Geneva, Switzerland.

Lullaby for My Dead Child

You shouldn't be afraid of the dark
Or of worms
Besides
Now you can play with the rain
And see the grass come up

You shouldn't put dirt in your mouth
And sit still waiting for me
Besides
We've given you some flowers
To console you for being little
And dead.

Maxine Kumin and Judith Kumin

CANADA

Anne Hébert

Anne Hébert (1916–).   Born and raised in Sainte Catherine, a village twenty miles from Quebec, Anne Hébert was educated at home because of a childhood disease which made her an invalid for many years. Her reputation was established with the publication of *Le tombeau des rois* (The Tomb of the Kings) in 1953. She has also written extensively for film, television, and the theater. Her novel *Kaouraska* was recently made into a film. Her most common subject is a woman in a bizarre domestic setting, repressed and sad. The scene appears normal, but on closer inspection it takes on a surreal, even hallucinatory quality. Her volumes of poems are *Dreams in Suspension* (1942), *The Tomb of the Kings* (1953), and *Poems* (1960).

Bread Is Born

How do you make bread talk, this old treasure all wrapped
up in its strictures like a winter tree, anchored so that
its nakedness is set off against the see-through day?

If I lock myself up in the darkroom of my mind's eye
with this everlasting name stamped there, and if I importune
the old flat syllable to yield its shifting images

what I hear are a thousand blind and bitter animals thumping
against the door, a servile pack of hounds, slack and sub-
missive in their mangy pelts, who've been chomping on words
like grass since the dawn of time.

But a clean sweep of space stretches out for the poet,
an open field of wilderness and want, while on the far
side of the horizon time breaks open and the taste of
bread, salt, water sprouts like flat blue stones under the
sea. It's always like this, the age-old hunger.

Suddenly the hunger flows forth, it kneels on the ground,
it plants its round heart there in the shape of deep sleep.

O that long first night, face pressed against the cracked
earth, listening, taking the blood's pulse, all dream
banished, all movement arrested, all attention swelling to
love's tip.

The raw stubble pokes out of the land. An underground
source tells its green head of hair to break through.
The earth's belly bares its flowers and fruits in the
great noon sun.

The sky dusts itself blue; our stained hands flush with
the fields are like great fresh poppies.
All the shapes and colors that are called up from the
earth rise on the upbeat like a visible exhaled breath.

The land throbs and bleats. Its wool grows white under
the summer's jarring glare, the sour cicada song.

The millstones with their porous rough grains have the
muffled ardor of huge looking glasses condemned to reflect
nothing.

All they can do is serve in the shadows, be heavy and
dark, hard and grating so as to shatter the heart of
the harvest, grind it to dust, to a stifling dry downpour.

It makes living flowers of these odd, pointy beach shells.
The seafaring sun crystallizes them in a bright spray. The
kernels open at once for us, singing, giving up their true,
well-crafted forms.

After that, we will sleek the milky dough, make it lie out
in its flat torpor, becalmed, still lacking breath where
it sleeps like a little pond.

And what if by chance the wind should rise? What if
our souls should give themselves up entirely? What if
their nights were clotted with roots, what if great holes
were bored in their days?

Even so, this bitter teaspoonful will outlast us, will
outlast all those who come after us. Crushed like October
leaves to release their musky smell, it will thrive in the
guise of yeast.

In the reek of roasted flesh, on the blackened stone, in
the midst of all this disorderly feasting, see how a pure
ancient act shines forth in the primal night. See how
that slow ripening of crust and dough heart begins while
Patience sits on the rim of the fire.

And nothing may touch its silence until morning.

Under the ashes which unmake themselves like a bed, watch
the round loaves and the square loaves puff up. Feel their
deep animal heat and the elusive heart perfectly centered
like a captive bird.

Oh, we live again! Day begins again at the skyline!
God can be born in His turn, a pale child to be put on

the cross in his season. Our work has already risen
brown and pungent with good smell.

We offer Him some bread for his hunger.

And in time we will sleep, heavy creatures, witness to
the festival and the drunkenness that morning catches us
in. And daylight straddles the world.

Maxine Kumin

The Great Fountains

Better not go to these deep woods
for great fountains
sleep in their depths.

Better not wake the great fountains
A false sleep closes their salty eyelids
No dream invents the blossoms
underwater white and rare.

The days around them
and the lean and chanting trees
sink no image into them.

Water in these dark woods
is so pure and uniquely fluid
and hallowed in this flowing source
a sea profession where I gaze.

O tears inside me
in the hollow of this grave space
where erect columns oversee
my old patience
keep intact
eternal solitude water solitude.

WB

Crown of Happiness

Death, become a shewolf
A stone corpse on the burnt horizon

Dream tiny smoke from a village
a hundred houses smoking back to back

Swimmers, swim in a storyless night
smelling of seaweed and ocean

Your facial light
wakens
the life of a feature
love of a breath

Day begins again
Night crosses the line of waters
Dawn's outspread wings
dazzle the earth

Joy at arm's length
The poem on the summit of a high head
Crown of happiness

WB

The Offended

The needy were lined up by order of famine
The traitors were examined by order of anger
The masters were judged by order of clear conscience
The humbled were questioned by order of offence
The crucified were considered by order of wounds
In this extreme misery the dumb took the lead
A dumb populace massed on the barricades
Their desire for speech was so urgent
that the Word came to meet them through the streets
The load they put on it was so heavy

that the cry FIRE burst from its heart
as its speech.

                                                    WB

The Skinny Girl

I am a skinny girl
And I have beautiful bones.

I treat them carefully
And with strange pity.

I polish them endlessly
Like old metals.

Jewels and flowers
Are out of season.

One day I'll grab my love
And make a silver reliquary of him.

I'll hang myself
In place of his absent heart.

Teeming space, who is this feverless guest
Suddenly inside you?

You walk,
You move.
Your every gesture
Decorates the death inside with terror.

I receive your trembling
Like a gift.

And sometimes
Paralyzed on your chest,

I half open
My liquid eyeballs

And weird and childlike dreams
Sir
Like green water.

WB

The Alchemy of Day

Let no girl wait on you on that day when you bind your wild
wounds, bloody beast, to the black pine's low branches.

Don't tell the girls around the rusty fire, don't warn the girls
with violet hearts.

All seven of them will appear in your room carrying blue pities in
quiet amphorae hoisted on their hair.

They'll slide along the thread of their mauve shadows like the back
of underwater flames in a quiet processional frieze along the four
winds of your walls.

Don't warn the girls with green felt feet cut out of antique rugs
reserved for the slow unrolling of sacred sorrows, soft meadow
mowed by the sun, silent and thick grass without the cry's stark
space,

Nor the hidden strong vibration of an underground love like the
excessive passion of the sea when its song starts to sail.

The first girl alerted will gather her sisters one by one and tell
them softly about the wounded love moored in the leaves of your
open veins.

The darkest of those appointed sisters will bring you balsam just
blossomed out of bitter hearts, old desecrated cellars, flower beds
of medicine and midnight diagnoses,

While the slowest will remake her face with burnt tears like a lovely stone brought to light by patient and precise excavations.

There she is, delegating a girl of salt to bring you gorgeous baskets of her bright harvest. On the way she weighs your tears like dew plucked off a sinking garden with the tips of fingernails.

See, the one called Veronica folds large pine sheets and dreams of trapping a tortured face in her veils unrolled like bright mirrors of water.*

The feverish girl stuck with brass thorns hurries now that night, risen to its full height, stirs its ripe palms like black sunflowers.

Soon she'll place her hands tightly over your eyes like a living oyster where death meditates, centuries of perfect dreams, the white blood of a hard pearl.

Oh you trembling in the wind, the beauty of your face hoisted on the masts of the four seasons,

You grating with sand, annointed with pure oils, naked in certain miracles of agile color and powerful water,

Beware of the silent coming of chalk compassions with faces of mixed clays.

Poise the green against the blue, and, possessor of power, don't be afraid of ochre and purple, let the world rush out bound to the world like an arrow to its arc,

Let the alerted gift ripen its strange alchemy in impetuous traffic,

Utter wild things in the sun, name everything facing the tumult of the great crumbling and irritated dead.

The walls of broken blue glass break like circles of water in the sea,

* The legendary Veronica wiped the bleeding face of Jesus on the way to Calvary; the image of His face is supposed to have appeared on the veil or handkerchief she used.

And the heart's very center designs its own supple fence.

Called for a second time, day rises in words like huge poppies
exploding on their stems.

A. Poulin, Jr.

Our Hands in the Garden

We got this idea
To plant our hands in the garden.

Branches of ten fingers
Saplings of bones
Cherished rock garden.

All day long
We waited for the red bird
And the fresh leaves
Of our polished nails.

No bird
Nor spring
Was trapped in the lair of our severed hands.

For just one flower
One small star of color
The swoop of calm wings

Just one pure note
Repeated three times

We'll need another season
And our hands must melt like water.

A. Poulin, Jr.

The Tomb of the Kings

My heart is on my fist
like a blind falcon.

The taciturn bird clutching my fingers.
A lamp swollen with wine and blood,
I go down
Toward the tomb of the kings
Astonished
Scarcely born.

What thread of Ariadne leads me
Along the deaf labyrinths?
The echoing steps are swallowed one by one.

(In what dream
Was this child tied by the ankle
Like a spellbound slave?)

The author of the dream
Squeezes the thread
And naked steps come
One by one
Like the first drops of rain
On the floor of wells.

The smell already moves in bloated storms
Oozes under doorsills
Into rooms, secret and round,
Where confined beds are stiffly erect.

The motionless desire of effigies moves me.
Astounded I watch
Black bones
Shining blue incrusted stones

A few tragedies, patiently carved out
On the chests of kings, are displayed

As if they were jewels
And are offered to us
Without tears or regrets.

In a single row:
Incense smoke, dry rice cake.
And my quivering flesh:
Ritual and submissive offering.

The gold mask on my absent face
Purple flowers like the pupils of my eyes,
Love's shadow paints me in small precise lines
And my bird breathes
And sobs strangely

A long shudder
Like the wind catching tree after tree
Stirs seven great ebony pharaohs
In their solemn ornate coverings.

It's only the depth of death that survives,
Simulating the last torment
Looking for appeasement
And its eternity
In a light tinkling of bracelets,
Vain ring games of other places
Around the sacrificial flesh.

They sleep and drink,
Avid for the fraternal source of evil in me;
Seven times I've known the vise of bones
And the dry hand that looks through the heart to break it.

Livid and glutted on a horrible dream
My limbs unraveled
The dead outside me, assassinated,
What reflection of dawn wanders here?
Why does this bird tremble

And turn its punctured eyeballs
Toward the morning?

AB and WB

Life in the Castle

It is an ancestral castle
With no tables or fire
With no dust or rug.

The perverse spell of this place
Is wholly in its shiny mirrors.

The only possible thing to do here
Is to look at oneself day and night.

Toss your image into the hard fountains
Your hardest image no shadow no color.

See, these mirrors are deep
Like closets
Some corpse always lives there under the silver
Immediately covers your image
And sticks to you like seaweed.

It adjusts to you, skinny and naked,
And simulates love in a slow bitter shiver.

AB and WB

LEBANON

Nadia Tuéni

Nadia Tuéni (1935–).   Born in Beirut, Lebanon, Tuéni was educated in French
schools in Lebanon and Greece and at the Université Saint Joseph in Beirut, where she
received a law degree. She has been a journalist for *An Nahar*, and composed the story

and scenario for *Faramane*, a drama produced for the 1970 International Baalbeck Festival. In 1973, she received the Prix de l'Académie Française. Her works include *Blond Texts* (1963) and *Dreamers of the Earth* (1975).

Nothing but a man
let's execute him against the door.
The morning of taking him away was robed
    with the freshness of water;
it would be best to finish him off
    against a door of blue wood.
His knees were knees of water
a forehead of oak under the rain.
He told me: "I would like to talk
of this flower dying according to the curve
    of a thought,
of oblivion it offers in the shelter of
    the sun,
and of multiplied love". . .
Enough.
We shot him against the light
and let hatred rise like baked bread.
Maybe I'll weep for him.
It was simple in the deep earth
and brief.

WB

Would you come back if I said the earth
    was at the tip of my fingers
like a charred branch already cooled?
birds often die deep in your blond hair
they adopt the sea as a vice
because of its sonorous seaweed
and runways coming undone
too late to be born each second
on their knees before the faces whose every color
    is a holy wafer

like a throat seized by cattle who devour a sunray
would you come back if I said the earth
     was at the tip of my fingers?

                                           WB

Vénus Khoury-Gata

Vénus Khoury-Gata (1937–).   Born in Babda, Lebanon, Khoury-Gata was
educated in Arab schools and studied at the Université Saint Joseph, Beirut. Since
1972 she has lived in Paris. In addition to her poems, she has published a novel, *The
Maladjusted* (1972). Her volumes of poems include *Unfinished Faces* (1965), *Stagnant
Lands* (1967), and *South of Silence* (1975).

The autumn made colors burn
In the noise of swift wings
We spoke about winters inscribed on waiting lists
Of migratory birds who bang their wings like shutters
Then grow heavy calling the earth.

The autumn confused its colors
Your eyes were tired of being dead
We spoke of the great trees that wander
     without moving

Of the remoteness of crowds
Of your last dull scream

I spoke to you peacefully under a layer of summer
Horizontal like stagnating planets
and now they have asked me to draw you
I sketch you with quivering leaves

                                           WB

your cheeks flat on the sand
and winds can't reach you
your waist is anchored there

my mouth is only a sandbox
and grains of words grind under my teeth
                         like stardust

get up
even dead I'll stand you erect against my masts
and you'll see her in her immense nakedness
loving the sea

in her last spasm
curse the sea

get up
only men erect bind heavens to the earth

WB

EGYPT

Andrée Chedid

Andrée Chedid (1921–).   Born in Egypt, Chedid is a well-known contemporary French poet. In addition to many volumes of poetry, Chedid has published novels, essays, and plays, one of which is in the repertory cycle of the Comédie-Française. Among her works are *Contre chant* (1969), *Cérémonial de la violence* (1976), and *Fraternité de la parole* (1976).

What Are We Playing At?

What else can we do
but garden our shadows
while far away
the universe burns and vanishes?

What else can we do
but visit with time
while nearby
time times us to death?

What else can we do
but stop at the horizon
while far away
and nearby—

the real collision.

Samuel Hazo and Mirene Ghossem

Catalan

Anonymous

Anonymous ballad (16th century).   Catalan is the language spoken in Barcelona, the province of Catalonia, and the Balearic Islands. During the Middle Ages, Catalan and Provençal were almost the same language, and the literature of Catalonia was similar to the lyricism of Provençal courtly love poems. However, Catalonia produced major poets in the fifteenth century, Ausias March and Ramon Llull, as well as the first European novel in vernacular, *Tirant lo blanc*, which gave it a distinctive, diverse, and important literature. "The Corpse-Keeper" is an anonymous *romance* (ballad) in the Spanish tradition of popular ballads.

The Corpse-Keeper

    Seven years I have kept him, dead
And hidden in my chamber
I change the shirt on him
Every holiday of the year.
I have anointed his face
With roses and white wine.
I have watched his bones laid bare
Of their white white flesh.
Alas, what can I do,
Wretch, in my disgrace?
Should I tell my father
He would say it is my lover;
Should I tell my mother
I would have no peace after;
Should I tell my sister
She knows nothing of love;
Should I tell my brother
He is the man to kill me;
Should I tell the constable

He would have me punished.
Better for me to say nothing,
To endure it and hold my tongue.
One day at my balcony,
Looking from my window,
I saw a huntsman passing
Who hunts in our crags.
—Huntsman, good huntsman,
One word, hear me:
Will you bury a dead boy?
You will be rewarded.
And not in worthless coppers
But in gold and silver.—
Going down the stairs
Two thousand kisses I gave him:
—Farewell, delight of my life,
Farewell, delight of my soul;
It will not be long
Before I come and visit you.

W. S. Merwin

Two Gifts

When I was a girl
I had many lovers.
Now that I'm big,
I only have two:
one a fancy tailor,
the other a weaver.
What can I do?
Both want my love.
Spring is coming
with many flowers,
carnations, roses,
violets of all colors.
I'll go to my father's
garden, pick a few,
give the tailor flowers
and the weaver my love.
If they don't want them,
God rid me of both.

WB

Spanish

SPAIN

Hispano-Arabic jarchas

Hispano-Arabic *jarchas* (1000–1300).   The *jarcha* was written in Islamic Spain by Arabs and Jews as the ending or refrain of a longer composition, the *muwassaha*, which was written in classical Arabic or Hebrew. The *muwassaha* called for a last stanza in the vulgar tongue, hence the *jarcha* in Spanish. These are the first lyrics we have in a modern romance tongue. Although the poems were written in Spanish, the script was Arabic or Hebrew. The poems are often specifically sensual, and rich in color and imagery. These qualities were not usually found in European medieval poetry, or for that matter in later Spanish poetry, until Federico García Lorca (1898–1936) consciously drew on the Arabic tradition, even giving his last book an Arabic title, *Diván del Tamarit* (1936).

I will make love
with you,
but only if you hold me
so my earrings
touch the jewelry
on my ankles.

WB

If you really care for me
like a good lover,
kiss this string of pearls
and kiss
my small mouth of cherries.

WB

Anonymous Ballad

Spanish Ballad (15th–16th centuries).   The ballad (*romance*) is a narrative poem, epico-lyric in character, written in octosyllabic, assonant-rhyming couplets. The ballad is at the heart of the oral tradition of popular Spanish poetry, which has persisted through all periods of Spanish literature. Because of its swift narration the ballad is the basic verse form for Spanish poetic drama. Collections of ballads in ballad books (*romanceros*) appear in Spanish in the sixteenth century, although the oral tradition goes back at least to the twelfth century. One of the key books of modern Spanish poetry is Federico García Lorca's *Gypsy Ballad Book (El romancero gitano)*, 1928.

Ballad of the Cool Fountain

Fountain, coolest fountain,
Cool fountain of love,
Where all the sweet birds come
For comforting—but one,
A widow turtledove,
Sadly sorrowing.
At once the nightingale,
That wicked bird, came by
And spoke these honied words:
"My lady, if you will,
I shall be your slave,"
"You are my enemy:
Begone, you are not true!
Green boughs no longer rest me,
Nor any budding grove.
Clear springs, when there are such,
Turn muddy at my touch.
I want no spouse to love
Nor any children either.
I forego that pleasure
And their comfort too.
No, leave me: you are false
And wicked—vile, untrue!
I'll never be your mistress!
I'll never marry you!"

Edwin Honig

Morisco Ballad

Morisco Ballad (15th–16th centuries).   An anonymous ballad written in Spanish about Moors. (From 711 until 1492 southern Spain was occupied by the Moors; *Morisco* means "young Moor.")

A Lovely Young Moor

I was the Moor Moraima,
a Moor young and lovely.
A Christian came to my door,
intent on doing me in.
He spoke to me in Arabic
like one who knows it well.
"Open the door for me, Moor,
if Allah's to keep you safe."
"How can I open for you,
not knowing who you are?"
"I am Mazote the Moor,
a brother of your mother,
and I've killed a Christian.
The mayor's men are coming.
If you keep me out, my love,
you'll see them kill me here."
My God, when I heard this
I got up and dressed in
my short Morisco blouse
(couldn't find my brocade),
and went toward the door,
which I opened all the way.

WB

Jewish Ballad

Jewish Ballad (15th–16th centuries).   One of the classifications of medieval ballads are the *romances judíos,* Jewish ballads, which appear in Spanish or in Ladino, the Spanish of the exiled Jews who fled to Holland, Greece, Turkey, and other Mediterranean countries after the 1492 expulsion from Spain.

Mother, I want to go,
I want to go away.
The herbs of the fields
I'll eat for my bread;
tears from my eyes
I'll drink for water.
Right out in the fields
I'll build myself a hut,
with strong walls outside.
The inside I'll burn black.
With my fingernails
I'll dig up the earth.
With blood from my veins
I'll mix the building mud.
With sighs from my soul
I'll dry it out.
Any man walking by
I'll welcome in,
let him tell me his troubles
and I will tell him mine.
If his are really worse,
I'll listen patiently.
If mine are really worse,
with my hands I'll kill myself.

                                        WB

Anonymous Songs

Anonymous Songs (15th–16th centuries).   The first important songbook (*canci-onero*) containing popular songs as well as learned poems is the *General Songbook* (*Cancionero general*) by Hernando del Castillo, published in 1511. The first examples of Spanish song are the Mozarabic *jarchas* of Islamic Spain. Spanish medieval song is one of the finest achievements of the poetry of Spain. The beauty and strength of the anonymous ballads have distracted us from the qualities of the old songbooks, which in many ways have a greater emotional range than the ballads, from playful humor and satire to poignant dreams. Unlike the ballads, they are in a variety of meters. Many popular songs have been set by classical Spanish composers, and modern poets from

Antonio Machado to García Lorca and Rafael Alberti have written poems in the manner of Spanish popular song.

> The bee-keeper kissed me.
> By the taste of honey I knew it was he.

> *W. S. Merwin*

> There in the flower garden
> I will die.
> Among the rose bushes
> they will kill me.
> I was on my way,
> mother, to cut some roses;
> there in the flower garden
> I found my love.
> There in the flower garden
> they will kill me.

> *WB*

> Come at dawn, good friend,
> come at dawn.

> Friend whom I most cared for,
> come at dawn of day.

> Friend whom I most loved,
> come at light of dawn.

> Come at light of day,
> bring no friend along.

> Come at light of dawn,
> and bring no good friend.

> *WB*

Under the oak tree, oak tree,
under the oak tree.

I was on my way, mother,
to a pilgrimage.
To be more devout
I took no companion
under the oak tree.

To be more devout
I took no companion.
I took another road,
left the one I knew
under the oak tree.

Soon I was lost
on a small mountain,
and fell into sleep
at the foot of an oak
under the oak tree.

In the middle of night
I woke—what a plight!—
and was in the arms
of him I loved most
under the oak tree.

It hurt me, grieved me
that it was dawning.
I was enjoying
him I loved most
under the oak tree.

Very blessed be
every pilgrimage
under the oak tree.

WB

Dress me in green,
it's a good color,
like the parrot
of the king my lord;
dress me in green
for its beauty,
like the pear
when it grows ripe.

WB

Rose and grape, pear and bean
are bad to keep.

I awoke, mother,
at the cold dawn;
I went to pick the rose,
the rose in bloom.
They are bad to keep.

I awoke, mother,
at the bright dawn;
I went to cut the rose,
the rose in seed.
They are bad to keep.

I went to pick the rose,
the rose in bloom;
when I reached the garden
it had been picked.
They are bad to keep.

I went to cut the rose,
the rose in seed;
when I reached the garden
it had been cut.
They are bad to keep.

Rose and grape, pear and bean
are bad to keep.

WB

Since the night is dark
and the road so short,
friend, why don't you come?

Midnight is gone,
and he who troubles me
doesn't come.
My fate keeps him away.
I am very unlucky.
I am abandoned
and ache greatly.
Friend, why don't you come?

WB

Kiss me and hug me,
my husband,
and in the morning I'll give you
a big clean shirt.

I never saw a man alive
so dead,
who acts asleep
awake.
Go on, husband, get some blood
in your arms
and in the morning I'll give you
a big clean shirt.

WB

Stop! Don't touch me,
my love,
your hands are cold.

I trust you if you come
this freezing night;
if you don't keep your word
you've lost your mind.

Don't touch me where it's wrong,
my love,
your hands are cold.

WB

Though I am dark
I was born white.
I lost my color
tending the flock.

WB

When the birds sang
my love fell asleep;
O God, who can
come and ask him
what he dreamed?

WB

Since I'm a girl
I want fun.
It won't help God
for me to be a nun.
Since I'm a girl
with long hair,
they want to dump me
in a convent.
It won't help God
for me to be a nun.
Since I'm a girl,
I want fun.
It won't help God
for me to be a nun.

WB

I don't want to be a nun.
No.
I am a girl waking to love.
Leave me happy and daring
with my love.
I am a girl in pain.
No!

WB

Florencia del Pinar

Florencia del Pinar (late 15th century).   Three poems by Florencia del Pinar appear
in early sixteenth-century *cancioneros* (songbooks), in the *Cancionero del British
Museum,* the *Cancionero Costantina,* and the *Cancionero general of Hernando del
Castillo* (1511). We know nothing of her life other than that she had a brother, also
named Pinar, who was a poet. The critic Manuel Alvar wrote. "She deserves special
praise for her passionate grace and for the innovation of certain themes."

Another Song of the Same Woman, to Some Partridges, Sent to Her Alive

These birds were born
singing for joy;
such softness imprisoned
gives me such sorrow—
yet no one weeps for me.

They cry that they flew
fearless of capture
and those whom they shunned
were those who seized them:
their names write my life
which goes on, losing joy;
such softness imprisoned
give me such sorrow—
yet no one weeps for me.

Julie Allen

Rosalía de Castro

Rosalía de Castro (1837–1885).   Born an illegitimate child in Santiago de
Compostela, she was brought up secretly by a peasant woman and "adopted" when she
was nine by her real mother. Then she was given an exceptional private education. Of
importance was a family servant, La Choina, who taught her Galician folk songs. She
was later to write her own songs in Galician (*gallego*), the dialect of northwest Spain
which during medieval times was the same as Portuguese (*gallego-portugués*) and in
which there was a flourishing tradition of song. She married a Galician historian,
Manual Murgia, a dwarf, with whom she had five children before they separated.
Thereafter her life was one of poverty, isolation, and finally an early death from cancer.
Rosalía's poems begin with nature, which is an analogue of her own feelings, yet a
nature that has a detailed appearance. Her brooks, winds, gray rainclouds, grassy
mountains are real—at least as much as the "real toad in an imaginary garden."
Sometimes she is sentimental, a characteristic of her period; more often she is harsh,
self-critical, dark in her pessimism, dramatic and profound. Her language is sonorous.
She wrote in both Spanish and Galician. Her work is contained in *Collected Works*,
edited by García Martí (1944).

They say that plants don't talk, nor do
    brooks or birds,
nor the wave with its chatter, nor stars
    with their shine.
They say it but it's not true, for whenever
    I walk by
they whisper and yell about me
                    "There goes the crazy woman dreaming
of life's endless spring and of fields
and soon, very soon, her hair
    will be gray.
She sees the shaking, terrified frost
    cover the meadow."
There are gray hairs in my head; there is frost
    on the meadows,
but I go on dreaming—a poor, incurable
    sleepwalker—
of life's endless spring that is receding
and the perennial freshness of fields
    and souls,

although fields dry and souls burn up.
Stars and brooks and flowers! Don't gossip about
   my dreams:
without them how could I admire you? How could
   I live?

                              AB and WB

   Now all that sound of laughter, sound of singing,
going, coming, happy stir!
that talk of *Know what happened? What's about to?*
the breathless *Have you heard?*
all of that bright vitality, so restless,
of boys and girls
—too much to bear. I begged
"Please leave me. Don't return."

   So one by one they left me, left in silence
this way or that. Alone.
Beads of a broken rosary rolled and scattered
across the floor.
And as they left, the brush of footsteps moving
away, went softly eddying round me, so
softly who'd ever heard
such lonely tones?
No, not the last farewell
the living give their hollow dead below.

   And finally left alone here, so alone
I heard the restless fly buzz to and fro,
heard the rat gnaw, his purpose one thing only,
heard the thin sticks aglow
hiss on the hearth, the fire protest, consuming
raw logs of greener oak.
I dream they're talking to me, dream I listen,
I know I've no other folk,

and so I urge them one and all, heart skipping,
"Don't you leave. Don't you go."

All's well with me. No grieving.
This solitude's my home.

John Frederick Nims (from Galician)

Gloria Fuertes

Gloria Fuertes (1918–).   Born in Madrid, Gloria Fuertes has worked as an editor, librarian, and teacher. She spent three years in the United States at various universities, where she taught Spanish literature. Her first book was published in 1954, *Anthology of Poetics and Poems of the Slums*. In her poems she is concerned with daily life, lesbian love, and human rights in a society which until very recently was extremely repressive. She has been widely translated and is a leading contemporary Spanish poet. Her books include *Pirulí* (1955), *I Advise Drinking Thread* (1954), *With Neither Bullet or Poison or Blade* (1965), and *Selected Poetry* (1970).

Interior Landscape

Like a madwoman and almost alone,
I take some food out to the country,
a thorn and foliage omelette
and a wine bag, while
I pull out a mulberry flute and play
a very green song of hope;
I see female turtledoves loving like male
    turtledoves,
a heron crossing the river
and through my thought crosses
a wingless "what is it to me?"

WB

Human Geography

Look at my continent containing
arms, legs, and an unmeasured torso,
my feet are small, my hands tiny,
my eyes deep, my breasts pretty good,
I have a lake under my forehead
which at times spills over through the sockets
where it bathes the pupils of my eyes,
when crying gets into my legs
and my volcanoes quake in dance.

In the north I'm bordered by doubt
in the east by the other
in the west an Open Heart
and Castilian soil in the south.

Inside my continent there is content,
the united states of my body,
the state of pain at night,
the state of laughter in the soul—
state of the spinster all day long.

At noon I have earthquakes
if the wind of a letter doesn't reach me;
fire is furious and wipes out
the wheat harvest of my chest.
The forest of my poorly combed hair
stiffens when a river of blood
runs through the continent;
and not having sinned it pardons me.

The sea around me changes;
it's called Great Sea or Sea of People;
at times it shakes my sides,
at times it hugs me gently;
it depends on breezes or weather,
on heaven and cyclones maybe;

the fact is I'm an island
known to submerge or merge
in the waters of the human ocean
vulgarly known as the mob.

I've finished my lesson in geography.

Look at my contained continent.

WB

Julia Uceda

Julia Uceda (1925–).   Born in Sevilla, Julia Uceda taught at Michigan State
University from 1966 to 1973, when she returned to Spain. She publishes regularly in
various Spanish and American journals. Her books include *Butterfly in Ashes* (1959),
Strange Childhood (1962), *Without Much Hope* (1966), *Poems of Cherry Lane*
(1968), and *Bells of Sansueña* (1977).

Time Reminded Me

To remember is not always to go back to what was,
for memory holds seaweed dragging up
wonders,
alien objects that never floated.
A light racing through chasms
lights up earlier years I've never lived,
which I recall like yesterday.
About 1900
I was strolling in a Paris park . . . it was
enveloped in fog.
My dress was the same color as the mist.
The light was the same as now
after seventy years.
Now the brief storm is over
and through the pane I see people walk by
near this window so near the clouds.
A time that is not mine
seems to rain inside my eyes.

WB

2976

They've opened up a road in the jungle and found
a dark palace. Now almost humus.
Boots thunder in the rooms. Echoes and birds
fly up from another time. Light maddens them. Winds
flooding the dry lungs of the room
loosen ponderous curtains which fall swishing
to the floor.
When armchairs are touched by a future astonished heart
they dissolve in their own ashes;
worms pile dust upon dust,
digging the marrow out of mahogany and silks,
eating rugs and mirrors. Roses
in the rugs collapse under footsteps. Nothing.

WB

MEXICO

Sor Juana Inés de la Cruz

Sor Juana Inés de la Cruz (1648/51–1695).   Born in the Mexican village of San Miguel de Nepantla, Juana de Asbaje y Ramirez, an illegitimate child, was apparently the daughter of a Spaniard and a Mexican woman. She was to become the first and the most important literary figure in the New World.

As a young girl she was precocious in reading, writing, and literary composition. She was taken to the viceroy's court in Mexico City, where she learned Latin and became immersed in other studies. One delightful story of her life, probably true, is of the oral examination she undertook at thirteen before forty leading professors and authorities on science, philosophy, mathematics, literature, theology, and music: she responded brilliantly to their queries.

In 1669 she joined the order of St. Jerome. As a nun Sor Juana found the time and means to devote herself to science and letters. She possessed a sober, inquiring mind, unsurpassed in the New World, along with the best scientific instruments available at that time. The importance of her scientific writing should not be underestimated. She turned to literature with the same clarity of mind. Her love poems brought a reprimand from the bishop of Puebla; this led to her famous defense of her intellectual life, the *Reply to Sister Filotea*. She strongly defended women's rights in all personal and social areas. Soon after this incident, however, she sold her library of some four thousand volumes, abandoned her studies, and went to work among the poor of the provinces, where she died attending the sick during an epidemic.

Sor Juana wrote scientific and theological studies, plays, and poems. Her long composition *First Dream*, which uses the poetic devices of Góngora, is the most sustained philosophical poem in the Golden Age of Spanish literature. Her famous poem beginning "Foolish men" is an angry, ironic description of the inferior role imposed upon women; her "Self-Portrait" sonnet bitterly upturns polite *carpe diem* platitudes of so many poems about time. As she regards a painting of herself (which hangs today in the Museum of Fine Arts in Mexico City), she rips away masks of flattery and self-deception. "Self-Portrait" is Sor Juana at her best: unrelenting candor, disarming strength, accurate psychological perception, and sonorous, haunting diction. Sor Juana is the last high moment of the Spanish Golden Age and the first poetic figure of the New World. Her works are collected in a volume edited in 1965 by Antonio Castro Leal.

She Attempts to Refute the Praises That Truth, Which She Calls Passion, Inscribed on a Portrait of the Poet

What you see here is a colorful illusion,
an art bragging of its beauty and skill,
which in fake syllogisms of color will
pervert the mind in delicate delusion;
here where the flatteries of paint engage
to vitiate the horrors of the years,
where a softening of harsh time appears
to triumph over oblivion and age,
all is a vain, careful device of dress,
it is a slender flower in the gale,
it is a futile port for doom reserved,
it is foolish labor that can only fail:
it is a wasting zeal and, well observed,
is corpse, is dust, is shade, is nothingness.

WB

In Which She Satisfies a Fear with the Rhetoric of Tears

This afternoon, my love, speaking to you
since I could see that in your face and walk

I failed in coming close to you with talk,
I wanted you to see my heart. Love, who
supported me in what I longed to do,
conquered the impossible to attain.
Amid my tears that were poured out by pain,
my heart became distilled, was broken through.
Enough, my love. Don't be so stiff. Don't let
maddening jealousies and arrogance
haunt you or let your quiet be upset
by foolish shadows: false signs of a man's
presence; for now you see my heart which met
your touch—and so is shattered in your hands.

AB and WB

She Proves the Inconsistency of the Desires and Criticism of Men Who Accuse Women of What They Themselves Cause

Foolish men who accuse
women unreasonably,
you blame yet never see
you cause what you abuse.

You crawl before her, sad,
begging for a quick cure;
why ask her to be pure
when you have made her bad?

You combat her resistance
and then with gravity,
you call frivolity
the fruit of your intents.

In one heroic breath
your reason fails, like a wild
bogeyman made up by a child
who then is scared to death.

With idiotic pride
you hope to find your prize:
a regal whore like Thaïs
and Lucretia for a bride.

Has anyone ever seen
a stranger moral fervor:
you who dirty the mirror
regret it is not clean?

You treat favor and disdain
with the same shallow mock-
ing voice: love you and you squawk,
demur and you complain.

No answer at her door
will be a proper part:
say no—she has no heart,
say yes—and she's a whore.

Two levels to your game
in which *you* are the fool:
one you blame as cruel,
one who yields, you shame.

How can one not be bad
the way your love pretends
to be? Say no and she offends.
Consent and you are mad.

With all the fury and pain
your whims cause her, it's good
for her who has withstood
you. Now go and complain!

You let her grief take flight
and free her with new wings.
Then after sordid things
you say she's not upright.

Who is at fault in all
this errant passion? She
who falls for his pleas, or he
who pleads for her to fall?

Whose guilt is greater in
this raw erotic play?
The girl who sins for pay
or man who pays for sin?

So why be shocked or taunt
her for the steps you take?
Care for her as you make
her, or shape her as you want,

but do not come with pleas
and later throw them in
her face, screaming of sin
when you were at her knees.

You fight us from our birth
with weapons of arrogance.
Between promise and pleading stance,
you are devil, flesh, and earth.

AB and WB

from **First Dream**

But Venus first
with her fair gentle morning-star
shone through the dayspring,
and old Tithonus' beauteous spouse
—Amazon in radiance clad—
armed against the night,
fair though martial
and though plaintive brave,
showed her lovely brow

crowned with morning glimmers,
tender yet intrepid harbinger
of the fierce luminary
that came, mustering his van
of tiro gleams
and his rearward
of stouter veteran lights
against her, usurping tyrant
of day's empire, who,
girt with gloom's black bays
sways with dread nocturnal sceptre
the shades,
herself by them appalled.
But the fair forerunner,
herald of the bright sun,
scarce flew her banner in the orient sky,
calling all the sweet if warlike
clarions of the birds to arms,
their featly artless
sonorous bugles,
when the doomed tyrant, trembling,
distraught with dread misgiving,
striving the while
to launch her vaunted might, opposing
the shield of her funereal cloak
in vain to the unerring
shafts of light
with the rash unavailing
valiance of despair,
sensible of her faintness to withstand,
prone already to commit to flight,
more than to might, the means of her salvation,
wound her raucous horn,
summoning her black battalions
to orderly retreat.
Forthwith she was assailed
with nearer plenitude of rays
that streaked the highest pitch

of the world's lofty towers.
The sun in truth, its circuit closed, drew near,
limning with gold on sapphire blue a thousand
times a thousand points and gleaming scarves,
and from its luminous circumference
innumerable rays of pure light streamed,
scoring the sky's cerulean plain,
and serried fell on her who was but now
the baneful tyrant of their empire.
She, flying in headlong rout,
mid her own horrors stumbling,
trampling on her shade,
strove, with her now blindly fleeing host
of shadows harried by the overtaking light,
to gain the western verge which loomed at last
before her impetuous course.
Then, by her very downfall vivified,
plunging in ever more precipitant ruin,
with renewed rebellion she resolves,
in that part of the globe
forsaken by the day,
to wear the crown,
what time upon our hemisphere the sun
the radiance of his fair golden tresses shed,
with equable diffusion of just light
apportioning to visible things their colours
and still restoring
to outward sense its full efficacy,
committing to surer light
the world illuminated and myself awake.

Samuel Beckett

Rosario Castellanos

Rosario Castellanos (1925–1974).   Born in Mexico City, Castellanos was raised in Comitán, a small town on the Guatemalan border, where much of the population was Indian. Thus Indians are a main subject of her novels. She attended the University of

Mexico and later taught there, but she lived mainly from her novels and other writing, the first Mexican woman to do so. In the tradition that saw Octavio Paz ambassador to India and Carlos Fuentes ambassador to France, Rosario Castellanos was appointed Mexican ambassador to Israel. In an accident recalling the death of the American poet Thomas Merton in Burma, she was killed in Jerusalem from a faulty electrical connection in her hotel room. She was better known as a novelist, but her poems have great power and mastery. Among her works are *Of the Sterile Vigil, The Ransom of the World*, and *Presentation in the Temple*.

Three Poems

I

What is weaker than a god? It groans hungry
     and smells out
its victim's blood,
eating sacrifices, and looks for the entrails
of what it created in order to sink
its hundred rapacious teeth in them.

(A god. Or certain men who have a destiny.)

Each morning it wakes
and the world is newly freshly devoured.

II

The great fish's eyes never shut.
It doesn't sleep. It always stares (at whom? where?)
in its bright and soundless universe.

Once its heart, beating
near a thorn, says: I want.

And the great devouring fish,
weighs down and dyes the water with its rage,
and moves with nerves of lightning,
can do nothing, not even shut its eyes.

It stares beyond the glass.

III

O cloud that wants to be the sky's arrow
or God's halo or lightning's fist!

Each wind alters its form and it vanishes,
and each gust drags it about and tricks it.

Unraveling rag, dirty fleece,
with no entrails, no force, nothing, cloud.

WB

Isabel Fraire

Isabel Fraire (1936–).   Born in Mexico City, Isabel Fraire studied philosophy at
the Autonomous National University of Mexico. Her first book of poems was published
in 1959, and in 1960 she joined the editorial board of the influential Mexican journal
Revista Mexicana de literatura. In addition to the publication of her own poetry,
reviews, and critical articles, Fraire has translated various American poets into Spanish.
Her translations of Pound's *Cantos* have appeared in many Mexican journals. Her
works include *15 Poems of Isabel Fraire* (1959) and *Only This Light* (1969).

if night takes the form of a whale and
        devours everything obliterating the image from memory
and you fall in time losing even
        the track of your name
        leaving in space traces
            of shadow over shadow
eyeless night keeps silent
        silence without hearing
        it is only an enormous scar
and everything insists on persistent movement
            useless withered leaves
                in a blind well

then
a sequence of nothingness
the end and beginning

are tied and untied by absent-minded fingers
  I spin and spin toward my death
  and I desire nothing
dreams have been erased from my eyes
  the world from my hands

  balancing on a stain of earth
seizing my death in a root

I write
  night takes the form of a whale
    that devours everything
      endlessly

Thomas Hoeksema

PUERTO RICO

Julia de Burgos

Julia de Burgos (1914–1953).   Born in 1914 in Carolina, Puerto Rico, the eldest
of thirteen children, Julia de Burgos attended the University of Puerto Rico and taught
school in Naranjito. After the publication of her first book in 1938, she taught at the
University of Havana, and then, in 1940, moved to New York where she spent her
remaining years. Her short life was tormented and chaotic, fraught with poverty and
alcoholism. The harsh tone of her often self-demeaning verses reveals unusual force.
Her works include *Poem in Twenty Furrows* (1938) and *Collected Works* (1961).

To Julia de Burgos

The people are saying that I am your enemy,
  That in poetry I give you to the world.

  They lie, Julia de Burgos. They lie, Julia de Burgos.
The voice that rises in my verses is not your voice: it is my voice;
For you are the clothing and I am the essence;
Between us lies the deepest abyss.

You are the bloodless doll of social lies
And I the virile spark of human truth;

You are the honey of courtly hypocrisy; not I—
I bare my heart in all my poems.

You, like your world, are selfish; not I—
I gamble everything to be what I am.

You are only the serious lady. Señora. Doña Julia.
Not I. I am life. I am strength. I am woman.

You belong to your husband, your master. Not I:
I belong to nobody or to all, for to all, to all
I give myself in my pure feelings and thoughts.

You curl your hair and paint your face. Not I:
I am curled by the wind, painted by the sun.

You are the lady of the house, resigned, submissive,
Tied to the bigotry of men. Not I:
I am Rocinante, bolting free, wildly
Snuffling the horizons of the justice of God.

Grace Schulman

Poem to My Death

Confronting a longing
To die with my very self, abandoned and alone,
On the densest rock of a deserted island.
At that moment, a final yearning for carnations,
On the landscape, a tragic horizon of stone.

My eyes filled with graves of stars,
My passion spread out, exhausted, dispersed,
My fingers like children watching a cloud fade,
My reason mobbed with enormous sheets.

My pale affections returning to silence
—Even love, consumed brother in my path!—
My name untangling, yellow in the branches,
And my hands, twitching to give me to the grass.

To rise to the final, the whole minute,
And to offer myself to the fields,
Then to bend the leaf of my ordinary flesh
And fall unsmiling, without witness to inertia.

Let nobody dishonor my death with sobs
Or wrap me forever in plain earth
For in a moment of freedom I may freely
Demand the one liberty of this planet.

With what mad joy will my bones begin
To see airholes in my brown flesh
And I, giving myself, giving myself fiercely and boldly
To the elements: in solitude breaking my chains!

Who will detain me with useless dreams
When my soul begins to fulfill its task
Making of my sleep a rich dough
For the frail worm that knocks at my door?

Smaller and smaller my worn-out humility
At every instant greater and easier the surrender
Perhaps my chest will turn to begin a flower bud
Maybe my lips will feed lilies.

What shall I be called when all that remains
Is my memory of myself on the rock of the deserted island?
A carnation wedged between my shadow and the wind,
Death's child and mine: My name will be poet.

Grace Schulman

Nothing

Since life is nothing in your philosophy,
let's drink to the fact of not being our bodies.

Let's drink to the nothing of your sensual lips,
which are sensual zeros in your blue kisses:
like all blue a chimerical lie
of white oceans and white firmaments.

Let's drink to the touchable decoy bird
sinking and rising in your carnal desire:
like all flesh, lightning, spark,
in the truth, unending lie of the universe.

Let's drink to nothing, the perfect nothing
of your soul, that races its lie on a wild colt:
like all nothing, perfect nothing, it's not even
seen for a second in sudden dazzle.

Let's drink to us, to them, to no one;
to our always nothing of our never bodies;
to everyone at least; to everyone so much nothing,
to bodiless shadows of the living who are dead.

We come from not being and march toward not being:
nothing between two nothings, zero between two zeros,
and since between two nothings nothing can be,
let's drink to the splendor of not being our bodies.

AB and WB

Elsa Tió

Elsa Tió (1950–).   In 1958, a girl of eight published a book of poems with an
introduction by Juan Ramón Jiménez, the Spanish Nobel Prize laureate poet. Playful,
ingenious, her volume of poems was a shock of freshness. More recently, she has
published a new collection of poems which fulfills the promise of her precocious
publication.

I am furious with myself
for this waste
useless like a blindman before a mirror
like the watch on a corpse's wrist.
I only see land without peasants or songs
before my lost things,
a huge slab of cement and stone
as a tomb for seeds
a kidnapped leaf for a somnambulist wind
and a tree as a coffin for some crushed wings.
I've tried to make out the wind's tracks
of what's going on
bleeding, weeping, and dying.
I only see time's scar.

                                        WB

Rosario Ferré

Rosario Ferré (20th century).   Born in Ponce, Puerto Rico, she majored in English
and Latin American literature and is the founder and director of one of the important
literary journals in Latin America, *Zona de carga y descarga,* which publicizes new
Puerto Rican literature. Her first book, *The Pandora Papers,* is a combination of
fourteen stories and six narrative poems. The poems are wild, surreal, and shocking,
with unreserved energy. Her father is the governor of Puerto Rico.

I Hear You've Let Go

                            I hear you've let go
                              now listen
when you walk down the street
everyone points a finger at your craning head
as if they wanted to floor you
just squeeze the trigger and bop!
your forehead crunches like a beer can

don't say hello to anyone
don't comb your hair or shine your shoes

cross the street on your own arm
shake your own hand, stiffen your neck
and watch out

                    there goes the looney, they say
you wobble by, your head dusty
like a wooden saint sticking up in a parade
its feet nailed to worm-eaten boards,
gazing far off
don't let your flesh blossom
let yourself be chewed up

               I hear you've finally let go
               listen carefully
rope yourself to a mast
tie yourself to the Polestar
don't take down the old planks
don't pry the oars out of their locks
nail your best eye to the star
keep the faith
don't wink too often
sleep quietly on your fists
don't worry about remembering
shut your glass-cutting teeth
cage your tongue
don't swallow anything

                   I hear you've let go, friend
                   the time has come
                   now cut the cord
                   climb the wind
                   toughen your heart

                                        WB

EL SALVADOR

Claribel Alegría

Claribel Alegría (20th century).   One of the leading poets of El Salvador, Claribel
Alegría has published a novel in addition to her many volumes of poetry. Alegría

produces political poems of the highest quality, devoid of facile rhetoric and artless polemic, sensitive, yet at the same time powerful statements of third world anger. She also writes highly imaginative and accomplished personal poems. Her volumes of poetry include *Vigils* (1953), *Guest of My Time* (1961), and *Long Distance Call* (1966–1969).

Search

If my torch goes out it will be dark.
Dark like behind the eyes.
My trip with no way back
and this tunnel, my tomb.
A tunnel like a mother's stomach.
Her identical architecture.
Her climate of signs and penumbra.
Through this labyrinth until finding it.
Through this stomach where rivers are born.
I won't fear the crest of winters again,
nor the fallen jawbone.
In shadowy sanctuaries
they are building castles with my shells,
with dead butterflies and with leaves.

Someone waits in ambush.
He rips the dagger from my fingers
and turns it against me.
The two of us face each other down.
My hand glimmering.
His coat envelops me.
The same forehead.
Suddenly my eyes are drugged.
I thought he would be shaped like a serpent,
would be an insect.
Suddenly myself.
Will I make a tomb out of the tunnel?
Wind waits outside.
My disguises, my veils,
lie there, destroyed.

Will I be alone until death?
Each morning I will know it.

AB and WB

Loneliness and July Ninth

It has no wings.
It's small,
gray,
deformed.
It hides in leaves,
under headlamps.
It assaults
while one is walking casually
with the night,
with the chiaroscuro geometry
of the buildings.
It sees my eyes.
They have become ruthless,
scrutinizers,
eyes of opium,
glass eyes
of an animal crushed on the road.
Don't talk to me about streetcars
or theater halls
with posters.
A night reaches out to me,
that is thicker,
more encompassing.
One day I will die
in an absurd place.
I don't want to know
about tobacco stands
where old people stand around
with bluish hands.

AB and WB

Small Country

Behind you
a riot of pallid orphans,
children with protruding bellies,
mendicant mothers
exhibiting their kids
full of flies,
tricky beggars
who pour their life
onto a clotted, scabby leg
and filthy bandages.
I stop and yell:
"The sky is falling!"
"Dear friends,"
the fat lady comments,
shuffling her cards,
"have you heard the latest?
They say the sky is falling."
At three in the afternoon
the board meeting starts.
I rise and say:
"Gentlemen,
there's only one item
on the agenda today.
The sky is falling."
The manager is upset.
"I propose," he exclaims,
"the construction of a vault
under the earth.
We must protect our archives,
our valuables."
The sentry reports the order
to the barracks.
"Have the troops fall out
in combat fatigues,"
screeches the general.
"Raise your rifles and bayonets,
hold up the sky."

The day is overcast.
A normal quota of events
takes place.
Butchers sell 3/4s
to the housewives
and charge them for a kilo,
fat old maids vent their hatred
in classrooms,
Don Juans
peacock with their pals
while maids
ruin the meal
and contemplate abortion.
Soon the small tree by the café
will issue red cherries;
sugar cane, honey,
marching cotton
and meaty clouds
will turn into Cadillacs
on a casino night
upon renting a suite in Cannes.
I sit down at the table of intellectuals.
"What can we do?" I ask.
"The sky is falling."
An old radical smiles.
He saw it coming twenty years ago.
"And if it's true,"
an angry student asks,
"what will we do?"
With a gesture appropriate
to the historical significance,
he pulls out a pen
and on the tablecloth
begins to compose a manifesto
by intellectuals and artists.
I don't go out for days.
The sky is not falling.
The politicians have said so,

the directors,
the generals,
even the beggars confirm it.
For every young lord
there's a knocked-up maid,
holding her own.
For every fat matron,
someone tubercular picking cotton,
for every politician
a blindman with a white cane.
Everything is licit, right.
My terror, infantile.
The public show
of anxiety
is bad for people,
is rotten for business,
scares children.
Tomorrow I'll go to the market.
The psychiatrist prescribed it.
I'll be in a position
to offer ten centavos to a beggar
and to feel compassion.

AB and WB

PERU

Blanca Varela

Blanca Varela (1926–).   Born in Lima, Blanca Varela has lived in both Paris and New York. In Lima she directs the Fondo de Cultura bookstore. When her first book, *This Port Exists,* appeared in 1959, Octavio Paz praised the work of a poet who, with the simplest words, turned ordinary observations into magical reality. A thread of ironic surrealism, characteristic of many French and Latin American poets, runs through her work, but her individual voice goes beyond any school. In more recent books, her poems have become longer, more powerful and complex, yet they have lost none of the early clarity. Entirely devoid of easy rhetoric, each poem is a careful work of art, an important object of the imagination. Her books are *This Port Exists* (1959), *Daylight* (1963), and *Waltzes and Other False Confessions* (1972).

Before the Pacific

Yellow blood on the dunes.
A day in ruins.

Something was looking upward.
Not long ago
someone was trying to fly.
Sown in the sand:
dark noon in the fig grove;
an absurd smile of salt
in brown foam on the beach.

Stars come. Powerful, filled
with secrets and on time.
Impassive and heavenly Venus
drops a ray of oblivion.

In free air,
a day in ruins,
messy beds of the afternoon.

Things talk among themselves,
move toward each other.
The wind perceives and orders.

WB

Nobody will open the door for you.
Keep banging on it.
On the other side is music. No. It's
    the phone.
You're wrong.
It's a noise of machines, electric panting,
    hissing, lashes.
No. It's music.
No. Someone is crying very slowly.
No. It's a stabbing siren, a huge, steep tongue
    licking the empty, colorless sky.

No. It's fire.
All wealth, miseries, all men,
    all
things fade at hot noon.
You're alone, on the other side.
They don't want to let you in.
Look, again, climb, yell. Useless.
I know it's the small, transparent, coiled,
    meaningless worm.
With your tiny mortal eyes, turn the apple
    over, measure it
with your muddy stomach and heat its impregnable
    plumpness.
You, small worm, worm-mouth, worm-hate, master
    of death and
life. You can't go in. They say.

                           WB

The Things I Say Are True

A star crashes in a small plaza and a bird loses its eyes
and falls. Gathered around it, men weep and see the new
season arrive. The river flows and sweeps along in its cold,
confused arms the dark material accumulated by years and
years behind the windows.

A horse dies and his soul flies to heaven smiling with
its big wooden teeth stained by the dew. Later, amidst
the angels, he will sprout black, silky wings for scaring flies.

All is perfect. Being shut up in a small hotel room,
being injured, cast aside and impotent, while outside
the rain falls softly, unexpectedly.

What is it that is coming, that leaps from above and bathes
the leaves with blood and fills the streets with gilded rubbish?

I know I am sick with a heavy illness, filled with a bitter
water, with an inclement fever that whistles and frightens
all who hear it. My friends have left me, my parrot now is
dead, and I cannot prevent people or animals from fleeing
the terrible black radiance my steps leave in the streets.
I must have lunch alone forever. Terrible.

Donald Yates

Lucia Fox

Lucia Fox (1930-).   Peruvian poet, Lucia Fox teaches at Michigan State
University.

Dream of the Forgotten Lover

That man entered through my eyes
and left I dare not mention how. . . .
But now there seems to remain no trace of him
in my body. The effects have passed
like a fever, and I hardly think of him
when he returns sick from Japan
in my dream.
So united in bed, so close on our walks,
and now a postcard
painted in the windowpane by my dream.
　　　　Is it possible to sacrifice?
　　　　Is it a sacrifice to sleep in flamingo feathers?
　　　　Patience stretches out unbelievably,
　　　　developed while drinking—unlike Socrates—
　　　　a cup of tea.
　　　　The feeling
　　　　is a little like when the Tarot cards by chance
　　　　turn up the Hanged Man.

R. Maghan

ARGENTINA

Alfonsina Storni

Alfonsina Storni (1892–1938).   Born in Sala Capriasca, Switzerland, of Italian-Swiss parents, Alfonsina Storni lived in Argentina from the age of four. After the death of her father, she held various jobs to help support her family, and worked as an actress, touring Argentina for a year. She received a teacher's diploma in 1910 and taught elementary school in San Juan, Argentina. During this year she published her first poems, and at the end of the school term, moved to Buenos Aires. In 1912 her illegitimate son was born. She supported herself and her son in Buenos Aires as a journalist and held teaching positions in state schools. She was awarded various prizes and in 1923 was named professor of literature at the Normal School of Modern Languages. In 1935 she underwent cancer surgery for a breast tumor. In 1938 the cancer recurred and on October 25 Alfonsina Storni drowned herself in the ocean at Mar del Plata. Storni developed from commonplace sentimental poems with expected clichés to a poetry of surprise, ironic strength, and gloomy vision. Her works include *The Disquiet of the Rosebush* (1916), *Selected Poems* (1940), and *Poetry* (1948).

My Sister

It's ten. Evening. The room is in half light.
My sister's sleeping, her hand on her chest; although
her face is very white, her bed entirely white,
the light, as if knowing, almost doesn't show.

She sinks into the bed the way pinkish fruit
does, into the deep mattress of soft grass.
Wind brushes her breasts, lifts them resolute-
ly chaste, measuring seconds as they pass.

I cover her tenderly with the white spread
and keep her lovely hands safe from the air.
On tiptoes I close all the doors near her bed,
leave the windows open, pull the curtain, prepare

for night. A lot of noise outside. Enough to drown
in: quarreling men, women with the juiciest
gossip. Hatred drifting upward, storekeepers shouting down
below. O voices, stop! Don't touch her nest.

Now my sister is weaving her silk cocoon
like a skillful worm. Her cocoon is a dream.
She weaves a pod with threads of a gold gleam.
Her life is spring. I am the summer afternoon.

She has only fifteen Octobers in her eyes
and so the eyes are bright, clear, and clean.
She thinks that storks from strange lands fly unseen,
leaving blond children with small red feet. Who tries

to come in? Is it you, now, the good wind?
You want to see her? Come in. But first cool
my forehead a second. Don't freeze the pool
of unwild dreams I sense in her. Undisciplined

they want to flood in and stay here, like you,
staring at that whiteness, at those tidy cheeks,
those fine circles under her eyes that speak
simplicity. Wind, you would see them and, falling to

your knees, cry. If you love her at all, be good
to her, for she will flee from wounding light.
Watch your word and intention. Her soul like wood
or wax is shaped, but rubbing makes a blight.

Be like that star which in the night stares at
her, whose eye is filtered through glassy thread.
That star rubs her eyelashes, turning like a cat
quiet in the sky, not to wake her in her bed.

Fly, if you can, among her snowy trees.
Pity her soul! She is immaculate.
Pity her soul! I know everything, but she's
like heaven and knows nothing. Which is her fate.

AB and WB

They've Come

Today my mother and sisters
came to see me.

I had been alone a long time
with my poems, my pride . . . almost nothing.

My sister—the oldest—is grown up,
is blondish. An elemental dream
goes through her eyes: I told the youngest
"Life is sweet. Everything bad comes to an end."

My mother smiled as those who understand souls
tend to do;
She placed two hands on my shoulders.
She's staring at me . . .
and tears spring from my eyes.

We ate together in the warmest room
of the house.
Spring sky . . . to see it
all the windows were opened.

And while we talked together quietly
of so much that is old and forgotten,
My sister—the youngest—interrupts:
"The swallows are flying by us."

AB and WB

Lighthouse in the Night

The sky a black sphere,
the sea a black disk.

The lighthouse opens
its solar fan on the coast.

Spinning endlessly at night,
whom is it searching for

when the mortal heart
looks for me in my chest?

Look at the black rock
where it is nailed down.

A crow digs endlessly
but no longer bleeds.

AB and WB

I Am Going to Sleep
(Suicide Poem)

Teeth of flowers, hairnet of dew,
hands of herbs, you, perfect wet nurse,
prepare the earthly sheets for me
and the down quilt of weeded moss.

I am going to sleep, my nurse, put me to bed.
Set a lamp at my headboard;
a constellation; whatever you like;
all are good: lower it a bit.

Leave me alone: you hear the buds breaking through . . .
a celestial foot rocks you from above
and a bird traces a pattern for you

so you'll forget . . . Thank you. Oh, one request:
if he telephones again
tell him not to keep trying, for I have left . . .

AB and WB

Martha Paley Francescato

Martha Paley Francescato (1934–).   Born in Buenos Aires, Martha Paley
Francescato taught in secondary schools and at the Instituto del Profesorado in Buenos
Aires until 1964. She received her Ph.D. from the University of Illinois in 1970,
where she taught literature, and is presently chairwoman of the Department of Spanish
and Portuguese at the University of Massachusetts at Amherst. Her "shaped" poems
are allied to concrete poetry, more specifically to the tradition beginning with
Apollonias of Rhodes through George Herbert's "Altars" and Apollinaire's "Rain."

Parody
to Octavio Paz

                    Earthworms
                   Its Fragments
          Earth   Bull
          Active   Passive
          No o   No i
          Eye   Blade
          Needle   Watch
          Door   Raceme
        Laughter   Port
          Ash   Fire
          Sail   Day
          Siesta   Dream
          Shaft   Wake
        she-bull   Manure
                   Earthworms
                Fragments excrements
          Your eye in my leaf In your leaf my eye
 Man one with leaf woman against the eye woman around the leaf
                 The eye in the leaf
                    Wombs

                                                            WB

```
                              S
                              e
                              m
                              e
                              n


                                a
                              r   y
                            g       f
                          l           i
                        o               l
                      p                   t
                                            h
                            damned


                      I               O
                      n               f



                      t               m
                      h               u
                      e               t
                      .               e
                      d
                      e               a
                      e               n
                      p               d



                      n               s
                      o               h
                      t               i
                      h               n
                      i               i
                      n               n
                      g               g
                            silences
                          tomb
                        forgotten
                       in the rock
                         burning
                          mouth
                        screamless
                       sterile tongue
            blurry                    dry
       yellow drizzle            porous stones
          mirrored                 calcined
           futile                    tough


                                            WB
```

CHILE

Gabriela Mistral

Gabriela Mistral (1889–1957).   Born Lucila Godoy y Alcayaga in Vicuna, Chile, Gabriela Mistral took her pen name from the Archangel Gabriel and the *mistral* wind that blows over the south of France. In 1914, while a provincial schoolteacher in Chile, she made public her first poems, "The Sonnets of Death," which won her the Chilean National Prize for Poetry. These poems, along with some fifty stories and poems published in 1917, established her as an important national writer. In 1922 the Mexican minister of education asked her to collaborate with him in a program of educational reform for the Indian adults and children living in rural areas. This project made her well known as an educator throughout Latin America. In 1945 Gabriela Mistral was awarded the Nobel Prize for Literature. The poet speaks of elemental things in her poems—of nature, death, childbirth. Although she had no children of her own, maternity is an obsessive preoccupation in her poems. In her lifetime she received every external form of recognition a poet can have. She was called the "Citizen of the Americas." Today her poetry is less esteemed and her reputation has diminished. Her works include *Desolation* (1922), *Tenderness* (1924), *Feeling* (1938), and *Lagar* (1954).

Sister

Today I saw a woman plowing a furrow. Her hips are
broad, like mine, for love, and she goes about her work
bent over the earth.

I caressed her waist; I brought her home with me. She
will drink rich milk from my own glass and bask in the
shade of my arbors growing pregnant with the pregnancy
of love. And if my own breasts be not generous, my son
will put his lips to hers, that are rich.

Langston Hughes

Midnight

Fineness of midnight.
I hear the nodes of the rosebush:
the sap pushes, raising the rose.

I hear
the burnt stripes of the Bengal
tiger: they don't let him sleep.

I hear
someone's poem
and in the night it swells in him
like the sand dune.

I hear
my mother asleep,
breathing for us both.
(I sleep inside her.
I'm five.)

I hear the Rhone
descending and carrying me like a father
blind in blind foam.

Then nothing.
I am falling
inside the walls of Arles
full of sun . . .

David Garrison

Drops of Gall

Don't sing: a song
always sticks to your
tongue: the song that was to be surrendered.

Don't kiss: the kiss
by a strange curse
always lingers where the heart doesn't reach.

Pray, pray, for it is pleasing, but know
that your greedy tongue won't say
the only Lord's Prayer to save you.

And don't call on death for mercy,
for in the flesh of immense whiteness
a live shred feels the rock
that smothers you
and the voracious worm upbraiding you.

David Garrison

Death Sonnet I

From the icy niche where men placed you
I lower your body to the sunny, poor earth.
They didn't know I too must sleep in it
and dream on the same pillow.

I place you in the sunny ground, with a
mother's sweet care for her napping child,
and the earth will be a soft cradle
when it receives your hurt childlike body.

I scatter bits of earth and rose dust,
and in the moon's airy and blue powder
what is left of you is a prisoner.

I leave singing my lovely revenge.
No hand will reach into the obscure depth
to argue with me over your handful of bones.

David Garrison

Dusk

I feel my heart melting
in the mildness like candles:
my veins are slow oil
and not wine,
and I feel my life fleeing
hushed and gentle like the gazelle.

David Garrison

Portuguese

PORTUGAL

Sor Violante do Céu

Sor Violante do Céu (1602?–1693). Born Violante Montesino in Lisbon, Portugal, Sor Violante entered the order of Our Lady of the Rosary in 1630. One of the most reknowned women of her time, she was the subject of many poems by seventeenth-century poets. Her play, *Saint Eufemia*, was performed before Phillip III of Spain. Her own poems show the influence of Góngora and *conceptismo*, and her major themes concern divine love, the brevity of life, and death. Her works are contained in *Collected Poems* (1646) and *Lusitanian Parnassus* (1733).

**Voice of a Dissipated Woman Inside a Tomb,
Talking to Another Woman Who Presumed to Enter
a Church with the Purpose of Being Seen and
Praised by Everyone, Who Sat Down Near a Sepulcher
Containing This Epitaph, Which Curiously Reads:**

You fool yourself and live a crazy day
or year, dizzy with adventures, and bent
solely on pleasures! Know the argument
of rigid doom and find a wiser way.
Consider that here, buried in the earth,
a dazzling and commended beauty lies,
and all live things are nothing, dust, and worth
less than the nothing of your life and lies.
Consider that when rigid death is come,
it laughs at beauty and discernment, and
what seems entirely certain fades in doubt.
Learn from this tomb what you will soon become,
and live more prudently till that command
is heard: the end which ends with no way out.

WB

Sophia de Mello Breyner Andresen

Sophia de Mello Breyner Andresen (1919–).   Born in Oporto, Mello Breyner Andresen was educated at Lisbon University. In addition to her own poems, she has published many books of stories, translations, and children's books. Wife of a newspaper director, she was a Socialist member of parliament in the first freely elected government after the years of dictatorship. Many of her poems depict Portugal's Algarve region, the white geometry of its village architecture, and the clean spacial planes of the coast and sea. Her works include *Poetry* (1944), *O Vagabond Christ* (1961), and *Selected Works* (1968).

Camoes and the Debt*

You'll go to the plaza. To ask
For the debt to be paid at a set date
This country kills you slowly
Country you shouted at and was deaf
Country you name and is unborn

In your name a scheme
Of insult neglect hot envy
And enemies who laugh off
Your unequaled adventure

Those you called never came
They were twisted in their own acts
The dead hand of patience
Locks the eyes on your face

You will go to the plaza patiently
They won't ask for your poem patiently
This country kills you slowly

WB and Nelson Cerqueira

*Camoes was Portugal's Renaissance epic poet, author of *Os Luziadas*.

The Three Marias:
Maria Isabel Barreno,
Maria Teresa Horta,
Maria Velho da Costa

The Three Marias—Maria Isabel Barreno (1939–), Maria Teresa Horta (1937–), and Maria Velho da Costa (1939–).   "*What* is in the book cannot be dissociated from *how* it evolved," the three Marias declared at the obscenity trial against their collaborative book *New Portuguese Letters* in 1972. The book, which became a milestone in the women's movement when the charges against the authors were dropped and the book was declared to be of literary merit, is the work of two writers and a third writer-editor of a Lisbon daily who were in their early thirties, all married and the mothers of sons. They began to meet regularly to discuss their role as women and as writers in the repressive Portuguese society. These discussions led them to begin a series of letters, modeled after a seventeenth-century Portuguese classic *Letters of a Portuguese Nun*, which resulted in the "notorious" *New Portuguese Letters* (1972).

Conversation between the Chevalier de Chamilly and Mariana Alcoforado in the Manner of a Song of Regret

—By your breasts
  senhora
  I remember you

—By your mouth holding them
  and the fear
  of losing them

—By your womb
  senhora
  I remember you

—By your copious milk
  and the warmth
  of being filled with it

—By your thighs
  senhora
  I remember you

—Once your possession
  they bitterly lament
  being forsaken by you

—By your arts
  senhora
  I remember you

—Deprived of you
  thanks to them
  and their hold over me

—By your moan
  senhora
  I remember you

—More a cry
  of pleasure
  than a moan of pain

—By your orgasm
  senhora
  I remember you

—The battlefield
  of your body
  the song of mine

—By your tongue
  senhora
  I remember you

—Sap in your mouth
  terror
  in your member

Helen R. Lane

Saddle and Cell

I argue
that where the body is concerned
no battleflag should be hoisted
on the flagpole gently planted
high between our thighs.

Be it dry burning torch, mast, or spilled must
the fissures it turns round in always bleed
yet that is not where the harm lies.

The male is exposed and his erectness
may be like a flower
his testicles tender bulbs of life (giving milky water)
and so humble that the hand
may gather them like fruits or sever them.

A man is strong only in that place
where shelter can be found   and completeness
and his uncertain verticality sustained.

To serve as sustenance is not to be devoured
and in the name of wholeness
may the mouth of a woman and her words
not become ravening jaws.

I argue
that the wedge and the hollow are imprinted on everything
the tender drop of sap inscribed in the tree's rough trunk and bark
the piercing pain of losing the breast one day soon
stamped upon its roundness.

And thus perhaps entering into collision/collusion with you
I oblige you to accept
this new seed that may burn like acid   our cause *per juris*
(a rose or tables of the law?)

To love another truly
be that person wedge or hollow

a fine rider or a cloistered house (a womb)
is to keep that beloved's other face
clasped in your hands.

Helen R. Lane

BRAZIL

Cecília Meireles

Cecília Meireles (1901–1964).   Born in Rio de Janeiro, Cecília Meireles worked as a primary school teacher, librarian, journalist, and professor of comparative literature. One of Brazil's major poets, Meireles was also a playwright, a translator of European and Indian writers into Portuguese, and a specialist in Brazilian folklore. Her volumes of poetry include *Spectres* (1919) and *Collected Works* (1958).

Ballad of the Ten Casino Dancers

Ten dancers glide
across a mirror floor.
They have thin gilt plaques on Egyptian bodies,
fingertips reddened, blue lids painted,
lift white veils naively scented,
bend yellow knees.

The ten dancers go
voiceless among customers,
hands above knives, teeth above roses,
little lamps befuddled by cigars.
Between the music and the movement flows
depravity, a flight of silken stairs.

The dancers now advance
like ten lost grasshoppers,
advance, recoil, avoiding glances
in the close room, and plucking at the din
they are so naked, you imagine
them clothed in the stuff of tears.

The ten dancers screen
their pupils under great green lashes.
Death passes tranquil as a belt around
their phosphorescent waists.
As who should bear a dead child to the ground
each bears her flesh that moves and scintillates.

Fat men watch in massive tedium
those cold, cold dancers,
pitiful serpents without appetite
who are children by daylight.
Ten anemic angels made of hollows,
melancholy embalms them.

Ten mummies in a band,
back and forth go the tired dancers.
Branch whose fragrant blossoms bend
blue, green, gold, white.
Ten mothers would weep at the sight
of those dancers hand in hand.

James Merrill

Henriqueta Lisboa

Henriqueta Lisboa (20th century).   Born in Lambari, Brazil, Henriqueta Lisboa
was a college professor in Belo Horizonte, where she now lives.

Minor Elegy

How do you recognize death?
Maybe she looks gray.
Does she give out calling cards, with her name
        correctly embossed?
Will she waylay us in the hall?

When she was in the neighborhood,
not even a curtain blew into

the window. Everything
was sober and precise. What a canyon
between someone on her list
and someone waiting for another visit.

"I came by and thought of you."

Calendar pages are thin.
Wind blows them in the air, looming with a date.
Now, later?
Like a violin cracking into silence
before the last chord.
A chaos of strings. A vein
out of order. Ordinary things.
Routine matters in the bottom drawer.
A trusting, hanging head.

Then the dubious smell
of flowers placed under circling flies.

WB and Nelson Cerqueira

Leila Miccolis

Leila Miccolis (1947–).   A contemporary Brazilian poet.

I wanted to see you,
thighs showing
(as I see hairs on your chest
through your silk shirt),
walking in the street
through whistles and goosing,
looking around
as if you see nothing.
As you sit down
you hike up your pants.
Your drawers match your tie.

WB and Nelson Cerqueira

Till Death Do Us Part

My desire for revenge, the bitterness,
repression of everything, goes
out of my mind
as I start to rub your loose organ
with the tip of my toes.

WB and Nelson Cerqueira

Maria Amália Fonte Boa

Maria Amália Fonte Boa (20th century).   A contemporary poet who follows the
school of concrete poetry, which has been very influential in Brazil.

Vitality

Abysmal corners will dis (be) located
Heavy clumps
                        virgin earth
on aerial roads of freedom

A huge breast STICKS (UP) HIGH
will grab iron/earth-belly
of my country

Y O U T H

milk leaps POWERFUL
                            luminous fountain
it will feed its prostituted
guts

R E S U R R E C T I O N

OF THIS FECUND EARTH
THROUGH THE BLOODY URINE OF BISON
a new race will be born
                        pure children
naked
            h u m a n   b e i n g s

NEW FLAGS
     AMAZON
NEW RIVERS
     MINES
will recompose a mutilated symphony
in its ruby veins

White immensity
         s t i c k y
                V I T A L
will split the nation
in four powers

Tropical head reigns
will dominate them (selves)
                UNDERSTANDING
                INTELLIGENCE
                WISDOM

PEACE
     PEACE
          PEACE
LOVELOVELOVELOVELOVELOVELOVE
seven gifts

Its reign will be
                diamond
                S U N

WB and Nelson Cerqueira

Two Tile Beaks

Small space
         N
      body O passes
         T
Winds
      wiiiinnnd   s
come to   poliiissssss   h
o o o o o o o o o o o
               o o o o o o o
Bird
I will reach   LIGHT
             wetness to open eyes
gulfpuke white
           c l o u d s
washed blue
        bluuuuuuuuuuuuuuu   e

WB and Nelson Cerqueira

Italian

Vittoria da Colonna

Vittoria da Colonna (1490–1547). A member of a noble family, Vittoria da Colonna is one of the most celebrated women of the Italian Renaissance. A member of an elite circle of artists, poets, and essayists, she was the subject of many poems and portraits, including those by her closest friend, Michaelangelo. Her own sonnets are mainly written to her husband, "the sun [she] worships and adores," and are rather conventional in their use of Neoplatonic imagery so prevalent in contemporary poetry.

> I live on this depraved and lonely cliff
> like a sad bird abhorring a green tree
> or plashing water; I move forcefully
> away from those I love, and I am stiff
> even before myself, so that my thoughts
> may rise and fly to him: sun I adore
> and worship. Though their wings could hurry more,
> they race only to him; the forest rots
> until the instant when they reach that place.
> Then deep in ecstasy, though brief, they feel
> a joy beyond all earthly joy. I reel,
> and yet if they could recreate his face
> as my mind, craving and consuming, would,
> then here perhaps I'd own the perfect good.

WB

As When Some Hungry Fledgling Hears and Sees

> As when some hungry fledgling hears and sees
>   His mother's wings beating around him, when
>   She brings him nourishment, from which loving
>   Both meal and her, he cheers up and rejoices,

And deep within the nest, chafes and worries
  With desire to follow her, even flying,
  And offers thanks with such a caroling
  His tongue seems loosed beyond its usual power;
So I, at times, when warm and living rays
  Come from the heavenly sun by which my heart
  Is fed, shine forth with such a lightening,
And I find my pen moves, urged on always
  By an inner love, as if it had no part
  In what I say: it is his praise I sing.

Barbara Howes

Gaspara Stampa

Gaspara Stampa (1523–1554).   Perhaps the most famous Italian victim of unhappy love aside from Juliet or Francesca, Gaspara Stampa fell in love with Collatino, conte di Collalto, and recorded her wild passion in a long series of fiery sonnets. Love for Gaspara Stampa is totally debilitating, an illness, a fever which literally killed her. Like Sappho and Catullus, she experiences physical symptoms from her love for Collatino, and these manifestations form the main imagery for her sonnets. Unlike Sappho, however, her poems are repetitive and, although the passion burns in a constant flame, the light bathing her courtly world and cosmos is as sad as it is dazzling.

At dawn of the day the Creator (for Whom
His own sphere was perfect bursting to unfold)
came to reveal Himself in human mold,
emanating from the virginal womb,
  then my illustrious lord (from whose dart
so many of my laments have since rained),
able to nestle in higher places, deigned
to make a nest and shelter of my heart.
  There I welcomed, with happy arms, such rare
and lofty fortune, of which (oh time's mischance!)
I was late made worthy by eternal care.
  From that day hence all thought, hope, and glance
I turned to him, him so gentle and fair:
sun that whirls and glares in a mad dance.

J. Vitiello

Often when alone I liken my lord
to the cosmos: his lovely brow the sun,
his eyes the stars, the sound of his words one
harmony, Lord Apollo's concord.
    The rains, the frost, the thunder claps, the hail
are signs of his rage when he is indignant;
the lulls and clear skies come when he, benignant,
chooses to rend and cast off his fury's veil.
    Spring and the budding forth of the flowers
come when he wills to make my hope bloom,
vowing to keep me forever in this state.
    Dreadful winter comes when, fickle as fate,
he threatens to change his mind and bring my doom,
leaving me despoiled of my glorious hours.

J. Vitiello

Women, whoever wishes to know my lord,
fix your gaze upon that sweet and natural presence,
youth by his years, sage by experience,
image of valor and glory in concord:
    with blond hair and color clear and bright,
stately profile and torso of a steed,
ultimately perfect in word and deed,
except, alas! in love, all lies and spite.
    And whoever wishes to know me, gaze nigh
on a woman, in deed and look a worm,
image of death and of the martyr's sty,
    abode of faith, ever constant and firm,
one who, though she weep and burn and sigh,
gets no pity, but just her lover's spurn.

J. Vitiello

Holy angels, in envy I cast no sigh
for your blessings and glories—infinite!—
and your beautitude—desiring! consummate!—
as you stand before our Lord on high,

for my delights, great beyond numbering,
cannot descend to any earthly guise
while, before me, serene, life-giving eyes
always inspire me to write and sing.

And, as in Heaven you enjoy from His face
solace and contentment as you gaze,
so here below endless beauty I embrace.

You surpass my rejoicing only in these ways:
your glory is eternal and fixed in space,
while mine can pass by in a few days.

J. Vitiello

When before those eyes, my life and light,
my beauty and fortune in the world, I stand,
the style, speech, passion, genius I command,
the thoughts, conceits, feelings I incite,

in all I'm overwhelmed, utterly spent,
like a deaf mute, virtually dazed,
all reverence, nothing but amazed
in that lovely light, I'm fixed and rent.

Enough, not a word can I intone
for that divine incubus never quits
sapping my strength, leaving my soul prone.

Oh Love, what strange and wonderful fits:
one sole thing, one beauty alone,
can give me life and deprive me of wits.

J. Vitiello

Ruth Domino

Ruth Domino (Tassoni) (1908–).   Born in Berlin of a Jewish mother, Ruth Domino obtained her Ph.D. in Vienna. She was a refugee in Paris and then came to the United States during World War II. While in America she taught and published fiction in the *New Yorker* and the *Kenyon Review*. Later she lived in Lausanne, Brussels, and London. She is now married to an Italian, lives in Bergamo, Italy, and writes in her third language, Italian. In 1976 she published her first book of poems in Calabria, *Suns of Solitude*, composed of poems written during the previous twelve years.

A Sparrow in the Dust

Every morning, in the dust
I chased a sparrow with my broom.
In the four corners
I found four feathers.

Every night my sparrow flew,
every night
from my breast he plucked
four beads of sleep.

Chasing him, I never saw him,
nor in the night when he came flying,
when he plucked four beads of sleep.
He was so quick!

I tried to spin his feathers of the morning
to cover me at night.
Feathers, you were too few
and the broom was breaking.

Now in the four corners
I hear his feathers rustling,
his beak knocks
for four beads of sleep,

knocks at my breast all night
until the bone will break.

Daniel Hoffman and Jerre Mongione

Maria Luisa Spaziani

Maria Luisa Spaziani (1924–).   Born in Turin, Spaziani now lives in Rome. She has written five books of poetry, including *The Eye of the Cyclone* (1970) and *Passage with Chains* (1977).

Journey in the Orient

Now in my Samarkand of blue enamels
the domes shine with icy winter lights.
The grain's scent sleeps; old men with gold teeth
pull turbans down over their ears.

The flies grant a respite to the bazaar donkeys,
I would no longer hear them bray their childish complaints.
Tamerlane's mulberry trees sleep, sleep,
the huge sextant of Ulugh Beg fails to pierce the fog.

I have truly traversed the route of the Pamir;
did my dancing body leave my shadow's imprint there?
Have I breathed the incense of the caravan trails
where Bibi Khanum, the ardent one, risked his head for a glance?

The kolkoz had one wall in common with the mosque,
the leader's discourse faded in the muezzin's cry.
I changed skin, spirit, aspect,
was nomad and fervent, seeking the traces of a god.

Now if I look at the ground I think Samarkand is down there,
separated by strata of clay, magma, and fire.
My Proserpine, inner inexpressible kernel,
point of the universe with no possible roads.

Maybe Samarkand is my own heart, the time zones
go off the rails if I try to reach it.
Samarkand goes in me; biting into fruit I illuminate it,
drinking water I nourish it, deep root.

Samarkand is the past, but so long past
that I find it sometimes in the doorway of my house,
dawn wind, star, archetype functioning in the dark,
collage with the Tartar's shout, and my mother who bakes the bread.

Edith Bruck

Edith Bruck (1932–).   Born in the Hungarian village of Tiszabércel, Bruck's entire family was deported to a concentration camp in Germany. Surviving the camp, she moved to Italy where she has lived and written for many years. Her publications include novels, stories, and poems.

Birth

Feeling the urge my mother
made for the privy at the far end of the courtyard
and strained strained with all her might
plagued by her painful constipation.
"It's like giving birth," she kept saying to herself
and strained strained harder
broad forehead dripping sweat
bluegreen eyes full of tears
veins swollen on the white neck
untouched by real or imitation jewels.
The kerchief slipped off
showing her dark hair;
with both hands she held onto the swollen belly with me inside.
To readjust her head-covering
like a good Orthodox Jew she let go of her belly
and kept straining straining.
The next thing was a cry a long-drawn-out wail:
my head almost grazed the pit full of excrement.
A busy neighbor woman
ran to her aid and that's how I was born.
According to the gypsies a lucky future was in store for me;
for my father I was another mouth to feed
for my mother an unavoidable calamity
that befalls poor religious couples who make love
as a gesture of peace after months of quarrels
for my five not seven brothers
(luckily two died young)
a real toy that squealed
sucked at the wrinkled nipples
clung to the skin of mama's empty breasts

a mother undernourished like the mothers
of Asia Africa India South
or North America of yesterday today and tomorrow . . .

Ruth Feldman and Brian Swann

You Hide

You hide in the ostrich egg
behind the Coptic parchment
among the rows of books
in your mother's closed mouth
in the portrait hanging in the living room
in the Etruscan urn in the hall
that will never hold your ashes.
You live in my mind when I work
think, sleep
inhabit my eyes
when I cry,
laugh, speak or am silent.
You're in my blood which circulates badly
you often make your presence felt
with a sharp pain in the liver
a headache
gut-ache
until you rise rise
toward my stomach
stopping at the height
of my throat,
I can't digest your presence
your absence makes me ill.
I vomit, hoping to feel better,
from the stimulus of birth
an emptiness is born
that never sleeps at night
wakes every morning.
Don't think about it everyone says:
I keep quiet lower my eyes
death winks at me.

Ruth Feldman and Brian Swann

Rossana Ombres

Rossana Ombres (20th century).   Born in Turin, Rossana Ombres now lives in Rome
and is the literary critic of the Turin newspaper *La Stampa*. In addition to her books of
poetry, Ombres published a novel, *Principessa Giacinta*, in 1970. Acclaimed by her
contemporaries Carlo Betocchi, Mario Luzi, and Eugene Montale as a vital force in
Italian literature, her books of poems include *Horizon Also You* (1956) and *The
Bestiary of Love* (1974).

Flower Ensnarer of Psalms

There is a flower blossoming out of season
resembling
in conformation
an ace of spades:
its hue a blade, its piercing scent
of nemesis impeding.

A thalamus, overflowing its border,
moans in rancor or in love,
swollen and brightly colored
like the hilt of an ace of spades.

One night a prophet
dreamt of it
and
saw it next morning:
it moaned aloud
close to his doorstep,
it was rooted in a heap of crumbling earth
like the rump of a running colt.

Few are given to see
the flower ensnarer of psalms:
blossoming when the season of flowers
is remote and forgotten
and only the holiest
hear it moan.

I. L. Salomon

German

GERMANY

Frau Ava

Frau Ava (ca. 1160).   This lyric is popularly attributed to the first German woman poet, Frau Ava of Melk; however, there is no solid evidence for this attribution. The lyric is attached to a young woman's letter, written in Latin to a cleric, and dealing with the Ciceronian ideal of friendship. The poem appears in a Bavarian manuscript dated about 1160.

> I am yours,
> you are mine.
> Of this we are certain.
> You are lodged
> in my heart,
> the small key
> is lost.
> You must stay there
> forever.

WB

Annette Von Droste-Hülshoff

Annette Von Droste-Hülshoff (1797–1848).   From a family of Westphalian nobility, Annette Von Droste-Hülshoff is often called Germany's greatest woman writer. Her poems are passionate, pessimistic, occasionally astringent, normally inflated. Critics comment on her poor eyesight to which they attribute, in part, her interesting and peculiar vision of nature.

The Last Day of the Year (New Year's Eve)

The year at its turn,
the whirring thread unrolls.

One hour more, the last today,
and what was living time is scrolls
of dust dropping into a grave.
I wait in stern

silence. O deep night!
Is there an open eye?
Time, your flowing passage shakes
these walls. I shiver, my
one need is to observe. Night wakes
in solitude. I light

my eyes to all
that I have done and thought.
All that was in my head and heart
now stands like sullen rot
at Heaven's door. Victory in part—
the rest a fall

into dark wind
whipping my house! Yes, this year
will shatter and ride on the wings
of storm; not breathe under the clear
light of stars like quiet things.
You, child of sin,

has there not been
a hollow, secret quiver each
day in your savage chest,
as the polar winds reach
across the stones, breaking, possessed
with slow and in-

sistent rage? Now my lamp
is about to die; the wick
greedily sucks the last drop of oil.
Is my life like smoke lick-
ing the oil? Will death's cave uncoil
before me black, damp?

My life breaks down
somewhere in the circle of
this year. Long have I known
decay. Yet my heart in love
glows under the huge stone
of passion. I frown,

sweating in deep
fear, my hands, forehead wet.
Why? Is there a moist star
burning through clouds? Is it
the star of love, with far
light, dim from fear, a steep

booming note. Do you hear?
Again! Song for the dead!
The bell shakes in its mouth.
O Lord, on my knees I spread
my arms, and from my drouth
beg mercy. Dead is the year!

WB

Else Lasker-Schüler

Else Lasker-Schüler (1869–1945).   Born in Elberfeld, she was an early German expressionist poet. She formed part of the expressionist circle which included Daubler, George Trakl, Karl Draus, Schickele, the painter Franz Marc, and others. When her work was banned by the Nazis, she fled to Switzerland, and later Jerusalem, where she died in 1945. While her early poetry deals mainly with love, religious themes enter her later work, which she expresses in an allegorical, often childlike manner. Among her masterpieces are those poems with biblical themes. Her poems appear in the *Collected Works* (10 vols.), 1920.

A Love Song

Come to me in the night—we shall sleep closely together.
I am so tired, lonely from being awake.
A strange bird already sang in the dark early morning,
As my dream still wrestled with itself and me.

Flowers open before all the springs
Taking on the color of your eyes. . . .

Come to me in the night on seven-starred shoes
And love shall be wrapped up until late in my tent.
Moons rise from the dusty trunk of heaven.

We shall make love quietly like two rare animals
In the high reeds behind this world.

Michael Gillespie

End of the World

There is a crying in the world,
As if the good Lord had died,
And the lead shadow, which falls down,
Suffers gravely.

Come, let us hide nearer each other . . .
Life lies in every heart
As in coffins.

You! let us kiss deeply—
A longing throbs against the planet
On which we must die.

WB and Michael Gillespie

Jacob

Jacob: a bull among his herd.
His stomping hoofs
struck sparks of fire from the earth.

He left his speckled brothers with a roar,
ran off across the river to the woods
and wrestled monkeys for their food.

He falls in fever, tired, riled
by the pain, his dislocated thigh:
his oxen face invents the smile.

Rosemarie Waldrop

Abraham and Isaac

Abraham built a town of sod
and leaves in Eden's landscape
and practiced talking to his God.

Angels stopped in at his hut;
Abraham knew
the print left by each winged foot.

Until one day they heard the cries
of tortured goats:
little Isaac played at sacrifice.

And God called: Abraham! He broke
shells from the sea and coral rock
to decorate the altar on the bluff

and carried Isaac there, bound, on his back
to give the Lord His due.
The Lord, however, said: This is enough.

Rosemarie Waldrop

Hagar and Ishmael

Abraham's children played with shells,
made them their toys, their boats,
and Isaac, when afraid, hugged Ishmael.

Then the two black swans sang a song
mourning for the bright world lost,
and Hagar, cast forth, had to steal her son

And shed her large tears with his small.
Their hearts gave off a sound like wells,
they hurried faster than an ostrich can.

The sun, implacable, burnt up the land,
the desert's yellow hide where Hagar fell.
With their white negro teeth they bit the sand.

Rosemarie Waldrop

Jacob and Esau

Rebecca's maid: a girl come from afar,
an angel, lovely, in a shift of roses,
and on her face she seemed to wear a star.

Her eyes modestly lowered to her feet,
her soft hands sorted golden lentils,
baked bread and pottage with the meat.

The brothers thrived near her. They could
not quarrel over the sweets
that her sweet lap offered as food.

So Esau leaves the land for good,
leaves home and birthright for this meal.
The cloak he wears around his shoulders is the woods.

Rosemarie Waldrop

Nelly Sachs

Nelly Sachs (1891–1970).   Born in Berlin, she hid from the Nazis during the
brief Third Reich. She escaped to Stockholm with other Jews in 1940, where she lived
for the rest of her life. The author of many collections of poems, she also wrote a series
of lays called *Scenic Poetry* and the verse play *Eli*. In 1966 she was awarded the Nobel
Prize for Literature. Her poems have been translated into the world's major languages.
Among her books are *In the Habitations of Death* (1947), *O the Chimneys*, selected
poems in English translation (1967), *The Seeker, and Other Poems* in English (1970).

But Perhaps

But perhaps
we
smoky with error
have still created a wandering universe
with the language of breath?

Again and again the fanfare
of beginning blown
the grain of sand coined at full speed
before it grew light again
above the embryo's
bud of birth?

And are again and again
encircled
in your domains
even when we do not remember night
and bite off with our teeth
the starry veins of words
from the depth of the sea.

And yet till your acre
behind the back of death.

Perhaps the detours of the Fall
are like meteors' secret desertions
but inscribed in the alphabet of storms
beside the rainbows—

But who knows
the degrees of making fertile
and how the green corn is bent
from soils eaten away
for the sucking mouths
of light.

Ruth and Matthew Mead

In the blue distance
where the red row of apple trees wanders
—rooted feet climbing the sky—
the longing is distilled
for all those who live in the valley.

The sun, lying by the roadside
with magic wands,
commands the travelers to halt.

They stand still
in the glassy nightmare
while the cricket scratches softly
at the invisible

and the stone dancing
changes its dust to music.

Ruth and Matthew Mead

White Serpent

White serpent
polar circle
wings in the granite
rose-colored sadness in blocks of ice
frontier zones around the secret
heart-throbbing miles of distance
wind-chains hanging from homesickness
flaming grenade of anger—

And the snail
with the ticking luggage of God's time.

Michael Hamburger

The Sleepwalker

The sleepwalker
circling upon his star

is awakened by
the white feather of morning—
the bloodstain on it reminds him—
startled, he drops
the moon—
the snowberry breaks
against the black agate of night
sullied with dream—

No spotless white on this earth—

Michael Hamburger

Line Like

Line like
living hair
drawn
deathnightobscured
from you
to me.
Reined in
outside
I bend
thirstily
to kiss the end of all distances.

Evening
throws the springboard
of night over the redness
lengthens your promontory
and hesitant I place my foot
on the trembling string
of my death already begun.

But such is love—

Michael Hamburger

In flight in escape
how grand the reception
on the way underway—

Wrapped
in the wind's shrouds
Feet
deep in the prayer of the sand
that never can utter amen
It has not the choice—
its way is from dorsal to wing
Ever over and on

The butterfly dying
again knows the ways of the sea
And this stone
inscribed by the fly
has pressed itself into my palm—

Instead of a home
I clutch the world's mutations.

Arthur Wensinger

The last one
to die here
will bear the kernel of the sun
between his lips—
will be the tempest in the final night
in the death throes of decay.

All the dreams
kindled in blood
will dart from his shoulders
jagged lightning from wings
stigma of pain
on the membrane of heaven.

Since the path of the Ark
was a tumbling down
down the highways of stars
the last one to die here
will be shod
with a flooded shoe

wherein a fish
with the homing sail of its dorsal fin
will speed its freight
dismal time
to its sodden grave.

Arthur Wensinger

Hilde Domin

Hilde Domin (1912–).   Born in Cologne, Hilde Domin studied law, sociology, and philosophy at Heidelberg, Berlin, Rome, and Florence. Among her teachers were Karl Jaspers and Karl Mannheim. From 1939 to 1954 she lived in England, Italy, South America, and the United States. Since 1961 she has lived in Heidelberg. Apart from four books of poetry, she has translated Ungaretti and Neruda, and written a novel, *Hier* (1966), and several studies of modern poetry. She has received numerous important awards, including the Ida Dehmel Prize (1968), the Meersburger Droste Prize (1971), and the Heinrich Heine Society Prize (1972). Among her books are *Nur eine Rose als Stütze* (1959), and *Ruckkehr der Schiffe* (1965).

Birthdays

I

She is dead

today is her birthday
that is the day
on which she
was disgorged
in that triangle
between her mother's legs

she
who disgorged me
between her legs

she is ashes

II

I always think
of the birth of a deer
how it sets its legs on the ground

III

I have forced nobody into the light
only words
words do not turn their heads
they get up
at once
and go

Tudor Morris

Martina Werner

Martina Werner (1929–).   Born in Cologne, Martina Werner lives today in Baden Baden. A journalist, she published her first volume of poems, *Monogramme,* in 1965.

Monogram 4

I

Mama
eats death
tastes like fish
      "ambulances disgust me"
      behind, charwomen in empty offices
                    twelve
      white virgins at Kreon's grave
      and the roofs white

with cement dust
(light feather in flight)

there are worse things
parents
on top of me
children
on top of me

. . . and at bedtime—go ahead say
what's so
bad about snow the
                heavy feathers the
                light claws

II

powermad for the infinite:
hands free of action
the curled tip of the wine leaf:
      not in humility
      not in humility
      in which cave
is it good to sleep—
      in this
      in this
  in my mother—there are
 no miracles
        except this
        except this
she remembers: two
crocks with
        blue forget-me-nots
        glaze cracked

Rosemarie Waldrop

Monogram 23

I

bled
holding on
to details "can't
look at blood" (I'm
                    glad
                my children have turned
                into Negroes Indians
            Jews) don't
want to trade in
my chips don't want don't want to
turns
the trumpet—
till the spittle
                runs out "the trees
bury
their roots from the sun"

II

new impressions
(can't be
used as ciphers) "this
fire
   not strong enough to glow"
new impressions:
shell of an egg
not at all fragile
(the dream in vain like death) not at all
                            fragile: in vain
this word
(my mother, sad bird)
                    in vain in vain
in
your mouth
I want to be laid to sleep
walk

at your
end

        in vain in vain the
        moment
        gone

                Rosemarie Waldrop

Monogram 29

signs of wear
          a
cardboard model in my head "can't
live without you" without
        mirror all
        lost oh look "no place
        to call
        my home no place"
bird of black bile
"a scarab of the sea" what
are you where d'you
come from lovely skin mis
tresses of oceans:
rejects the fruit cardboard model
        in my head where
nothing gives and nothing holds loosely
knit: these
        children play at Palau—re
        vealed your
        outline "the
        ordering of form alone . . .
no
way to recognize
        the trees
reproduce
more humanely

                Rosemarie Waldrop

Petra von Morstein

Petra von Morstein (1941–).   Born in Potsdam, she lives in Canada and teaches philosophy at the University of Calgary, Alberta. She has translated Ludwig Wittgenstein's *Blue and Brown Notebooks* into German. Her poems were published in *To All* (1969).

. . . 1968 . . .

nevertheless I prefer
in the morning rush
to let the water run
during
the news
and to make up my
face

Rosemarie Waldrop

Justice

I'm always
most surprised
when
after a trip
a plane trip especially
I meet
in a station
for example
at a movie
while windowshopping
someone I know

Now I've decided
to be just as
surprised
at the just as
fortuitous
encounters with strangers

even
if I only
pass them

Rosemarie Waldrop

For one who says he feels
as if he had to push
undigested
hours around in his mouth
after having
chewed each second
twenty-eight times.

if time
doesn't agree
with you,
if half-chewed seconds catch
in your throat
throw
out the clocks, as
I've done,
with a steady sound

Rosemarie Waldrop

Thing Poem

Moving out
I was given
a vase.

The notebook was bought
on the island
in the store there.

You found
the striped pebble
on the beach at Aber-Bach, in Wales.

With this pencil
I wrote
things nobody liked, not even I.

Please.
Take off these story tags.
I'd really like
a few things with
qualities of their own.

Rosemarie Waldrop

Anthology Poem

Yesterday I was
given flowers.

The fact that
I see their wilting
only when
I've gone out for a while
inhibits
my decisions.

At night
I don't need
to put out the light.

Rosemarie Waldrop

In the Case of Lobsters

There are
2 methods some put
the live lobster

in boiling
water for the best
taste
but
with a microphone
you can hear screams
of pain if
in the case of lobsters
one can speak of such a thing
as pain

Others
for humanitarian reasons
put it in cold
then bring to the boil

Rosemarie Waldrop

Karin Kiwus

Karin Kiwus (1942–).   Kiwus lives in Berlin. She has just published her first
book, *On Both Sides of the Present* (1976).

All Splendor on Earth

To demolish it
　　to demolish everything
　　　　to haul off
　　the whole heap of junk
and stuff it into the big cauldron

To cook up a small firm felt hat
　　as weather guard
　　　　as piss-pot
　　　　　　as feeding dish
　　　　　　　　as puking bag
　　as horn of plenty

To perch on a rock worn smooth
and lose all one's senses
to the nothing
to the sweet nothing

Almut McAuley

AUSTRIA

Ingeborg Bachmann

Ingeborg Bachmann (1926–1973).   Born in Klagenfurt, Austria, Ingeborg
Bachman grew up in a valley town in Carinthia. At the University of Vienna she
studied philosophy, writing a dissertation on Martin Heidegger. She worked for
newspapers, the radio, and lectured at several universities. She lived in many capital
cities of the world—Paris, Munich, London, New York—and died in Rome when a
burning cigarette ignited the mattress of her bed. A curious dreamlike imagery pervades
her poems. Her philosophical lyrics speak of disconnection, the unreality of love, and
despair. Arthur Wensinger has described her poems as "a nocturnal phantasmagoria
peopled with her own prophet-birds and visionary animals which seem immune to the
overwhelming feeling of the evanescence which is man's lot." Her poems are collected
in *Die gestundete Zeit* (1953), *Anrufung des Grossen Bären* (1956), and a final book
of her prose and poems, *Gedichte, Erzählungen, Hörspiel, Essays* (1964).

Out of the corpse-warm vestibule of heaven steps the sun.
It is not the immortals who are there
but the war dead, so we understand.

And splendor pays no heed to decay. Our Godhead,
History, has ordained us a grave
from which there is no resurrection.

Janice Orion

The Firstborn Land

To my firstborn land, in the south,
I went and found, improverished and naked
and up to the waist in the sea,
town and castle.

Trodden by dust into sleep,
I lay in the light
and over me, leaved by Ionian salt,
a tree skeleton hung.

There fell no cream from it.

There blooms no rosemary,
no bird
refreshes its song in the springs.

In my firstborn land, in the south,
the viper sprang at me
and in the light, the horror.

O close,
close your eyes!
Press your mouth to the bite!

And as I drank myself
and the earthquake gently rocked
my firstborn land
I was woken up to seeing.

There life fell to me.

There stone is not dead.
The wick flares up
should a glance light it.

Daniel Huws

You want the summer lightning, throw the knives,
and tear the warm veins open to the air;

blinding you, the last fireworks soar,
soundlessly springing from the open pulses;

madness, contempt, then the revenge,
and already the remorse and disavowal.

You still notice how your blades get blunt,
and at long last you feel how love ends:

with honest thunderstorms and pure breath,
And in the dream dungeon it shuts you up.

Where its golden hair hangs down
you reach for it, the ladder into nothingness.

A thousand and one nights high are the rungs.
The step off into emptiness is the last step.

And where you rebound are the old places,
and every place you give three drops of blood.

Out of your mind, you hold rootless locks.
The bell rings, and it is enough.

Daniel Huws

Days in White

These days I get up with the birches
and comb the wheat hair from my forehead
in front of a mirror of ice.

Mixed with my breath
the milk flakes.
So early it frosts up.

And where I breathe on the pane appears
drawn by a childish finger
once more your name, innocence!
After so long.

These days it doesn't pain me
that I'm able to forget
and have to remember.

I'm in love. To white-heat
I love and give thanks with angelic greetings.
I learnt them in flight.

These days I think of the albatross
with whom I soared
up and over
to an undescribed country.

There on the horizon,
brilliant in its destruction,
I'm aware of my fabulous continent
that dismissed me
in a shroud.

I'm alive and from afar I hear its swansong.

Daniel Huws

Curriculum Vitae

Long is the night,
long as the shame of the man
who can't manage to die, long
under the lamp post his naked
eye swung, and his eye, blind with the breath of gin
and the smell of a blonde girl's wet flesh
under his nails, oh God, long is the night.

My hair won't turn white,
for I dropped from a womb of machines,

Rose Red smeared tar on my forehead
and curls, they had
strangled her snow-white sister. But I,
the oldest, marched through a town
of ten hundred thousand souls, and my foot
stepped on a soul-louse under the leather sky from which
ten hundred thousand peace-pipes
were hanging, mutely. And often
I wish for angels' repose
and hunting grounds, sick
of the powerless cries
of my friends.

With wide-straddling legs and wings,
youth like some marsh grass shot up
over me, over ordure, over jasmine it went
on those towering nights with their square-
root dilemmas, breathing
the wisdom of death on my window each hour,
giving me wolf's milk, and pouring
old age's ridicule into my throat,
when I fell
over folios in sleep,
in a disconcerting dream
where I wasn't found worthy of thought,
playing with tassels
whose fringes were snakes.

And our mothers would also
dream of the future of their men,
they would see someone powerful,
revolutionary, withdrawn,
and mostly after prayers in the garden,
while bending over the burning weeds,
hand in hand with the howling child
of their love. Oh my gloomy father,
why were you always so silent then,
nor ever thought past tomorrow?

Forsaken in the fire fountains,
a night of crouching near a gun
that misses fire, so goddamn long
a night, under the refuse
of a jaundiced moon, whose light
stunk gall, there rumbled in the shadow
of a dream of power (why hide it now?)
the bobsled of our ornamented
past, and cut me down.
Not that I slept: awake
under the icy bones I trailed it
homeward, wrapped my arms and legs
in ivy and daubed the ruins
white with droppings from the sun.
I kept the holy festivals,
and only after prayers
did bread appear.

In a self-righteous decade
a man moves faster from one light
to another, from one country
to another, under the rainbow,
the compass points stuck in his heart,
towards the radius labeled the night.
Wide open. From the mountains
one sees oceans, in the oceans
mountains, and where the clouds line up
in pews, the swinging of the bells
of the one and only world. Which world
I was commanded not to know.

It happened on a Friday—
my life ran down with fasting,
the air oozed with vapors of lemon
and the fishbone stuck in my craw—
when out of the gutted fish, I lifted
a ring which, thrown away at the time
of my birth, fell in the river

of night, where it sank.
I threw it back to the night.

O if I had no fear of death!
If I had the word
(nor knew its loss)
if I had no thorns within my heart
(but battered out the sun)
If I had no greed within my mouth
(nor drank from the wild water)
if I waited without blinking
(nor saw the threads before me).
Must they drag the sky away?
Let the Earth not play me false,
but lay me long in stillness,
long in stillness, for Night
with its black snout to nose me,
and dream the next caress
of its devouring arms.

Jerome Rothenberg

Every Day

War is not declared any more,
but simply continued. The terrible
is an everyday thing. The hero
stays far from battles. The weakling
is moved into the firing lines.
The uniform of the day is patience,
its decoration the shabby star
of hope above the heart.

It is conferred
when nothing more happens,
when the drumfire stops,
when the enemy has become invisible,
and the shadow of eternal armament
darkens the sky.

It is conferred
for the deserting of flags,
for courage in the face of friends,
for the betrayal of despicable secrets
and disregard
of all commands.

                        Christopher Middleton

Dutch

Hadewijch

Hadewijch (13th century).   Little is known about the life of the greatest name in medieval Dutch literature, but Hadewijch was probably the head of a *beguinage,* that curious 13th-century phenomenon which produced some of the most interesting women's writing in the later Middle Ages. Her poems are complex mystical visions concerning the nature of divinity and divine love, and perhaps the most interesting one is a poem on the seven names of love.

Love has seven names.
Do you know what they are?
Rope, Light, Fire, Coal
make up its domain.

The others, also good,
more modest but alive:
Dew, Hell, the Living Water.
I name them here (for they
are in the Scriptures),
explaining every sign
for virtue and form.
I tell the truth in signs.
Love appears every day
for one who offers love.
That wisdom is enough.

Love is a ROPE, for it ties
and holds us in its yoke.

It can do all, nothing snaps it.
You who love must know.

The meaning of LIGHT
is known to those who
offer gifts to love,
approved or condemned.

The Scripture tells us
the symbol of COAL:
the one sublime gift
God gives the intimate soul.

Under the name of FIRE, luck,
bad luck, joy or no joy,
consumes. We are seized
by the same heat from both.

When everything is burnt
in its own violence, the DEW,
coming like a breeze, pauses
and brings the good.

LIVING WATER (its sixth name)
flows and ebbs
as my love grows
and disappears from sight.

HELL (I feel its torture)
damns, covering the world.
Nothing escapes. No one has grace
to see a way out.

Take care, you who wish
to deal with names
for love. Behind their sweetness
and wrath, nothing endures.
Nothing but wounds and kisses.

Though love appears far off,
you will move into its depth.

WB and Elene Kolb

Sister Bertken

Sister Bertken (1427?–1514).   Little is known of this late medieval Dutch nun's life other than that she spent fifty-seven years of her life in a Utrecht convent. Her poems are allegorical with obvious biblical allusions, particularly from the Song of Songs.

When I went into my garden, I found
only nettles and thorns.

The nettles and thorns I threw out.
I seeded some flowering plants.

I found someone who knew his work,
willing to help me in my task.

The tree was in such a hurry to climb,
I couldn't dig it out in time.

In my dilemma he had a remedy.
Alone he pulled up the tree.

Now I must ask advice from him
or he won't help me again.

However much I weed and clear,
the poison grass appears.

I'd like to seed lilies on this site
before the day is bright.

If my lover feeds it with dew,
it will richly bloom.

He loves among all flowers,
the lily in its white splendor.

Red roses unfurl.
In their calices burns the pearl.

Then the pearl is dressed in sun.
The strong heart looks on.

Jesus is the gardener's name.
I am his. One being, we are the same.

His love is sweetest breath,
beyond all things on earth.

WB

Judith Herzberg

Judith Herzberg (1934–).   The leading contemporary woman poet of her generation
in the Netherlands, Judith Herzberg shows affinities with Sylvia Plath and Adrienne
Rich in her poems.

Reunion

For years I had not seen such a town
or stood at the bottom of such stairs
as on that hot day, in black Sunday best
and shiny shoes. And at the top
I saw vaguely my strange mother
waiting to be kissed.

Soft cuddling that night after night
I'd conjured to creep from
the war into sleep
was behind us now. Too grown up,
too skinny and countrified, I took
it all back. Was this
really my mother?

Come up, she said,
winking to put me at ease,
but with both eyes at once.
I thought the right moment
had come for goodbyes we'd postponed,
but I did not know how
with difficult eyes.

Shirley Kaufman

Nearer

To know there are rhododendrons on the slopes of the Himalayas
is not enough. To see a green beetle crawl
on a shiny leaf see it fall off
in the shadow underneath to recognize the color of the earth
not once or twice
but year after year, not on the slopes of the Himalayas
but here with this grass, this earth
and thus to know a small part of a larger
land, so huge it might be called motherland
mother Russia, mother Europe.
And winters, when the clouds stop
in front of the window, flashes of a precise longing,
leaves, each vein in them.
Later to be able to say: this is me,
I come from this part of the country
instead of having like a nomad
the trek itself for a homeland, gravel
along the railway, for childhood smells
a breath of scorched earth, as stake
for a new start only the fact
that scorched earth can still be used.

Shirley Kaufman

Polish

Wislawa Szymborska

Wislawa Szymborska (1923–).   Szymborska is a leading contemporary Polish poet. Condemned for not following Stalinist critics, who rejected her "aesthetic" tendencies, Szymborska has developed as a poetic phenonemon, on a par with Zbigniew Herbert and the avant-garde Polish theater. She writes of herself that she "borrows words weighed down with pathos, and then tries to make them appear light." Her most recent book is *Every Incident* (1972).

I Am Too Near

I am too near to be dreamt of by him.
I do not fly over him, do not escape from him
under the roots of a tree. I am too near.
Not in my voice sings the fish in the net,
not from my finger rolls the ring.
I am too near. A big house is on fire
without me, calling for help. Too near
for a bell dangling from my hair to chime.
Too near to enter as a guest
before whom walls glide apart by themselves.
Never again will I die so lightly,
so much beyond my flesh, so inadvertently
as once in his dream. Too near.
I taste the sound, I see the glittering husk of this word
as I lie immobile in his embrace. He sleeps,
more accessible now to her, seen but once,
a cashier of a wandering circus with one lion,
than to me, who am at his side.
For her now in him a valley grows,
rusty-leaved, closed by a snowy mountain
in the dark blue air. I am too near

to fall to him from the sky. My scream
could wake him up. Poor thing
I am, limited to my shape,
I who was a birch, who was a lizard,
who would come out of my cocoons
shimmering the colors of my skins. Who possessed
the grace of disappearing from astonished eyes,
which is a wealth of wealths. I am near,
too near for him to dream of me.
I slide my arm from under the sleeper's head
and it is numb, full of swarming pins,
on the tip of each, waiting to be counted,
the fallen angels sit.

Czeslaw Milosz

Rumanian

Maria Banus

Maria Banus (1914–).　　　Born in Bucharest, Banus studied law and philology. Her first poem was published when she was fourteen. She translated poetry from German, Russian, Spanish, Turkish, and French, including poems by Goethe, Pushkin, Neruda, Hikmet, and Rimbaud. In addition to her poems, she has written plays and many articles. After the war she was one of the official Stalinist poets. Later, disenchanted, she embarked on a defiantly individual course, producing poems reminiscent of her best early work. Her volumes are *The Girl's Country* (1937), *Joy* (1947), *I Am Speaking to You, America!* (1955), *Metamorphosis* (1963), and *Anyone and Something* (1972).

Gift Hour

From moonwater, from mirror mist, a slender porcelain
body emerged.
A vase pale and heavy. Ponderous with raspberries
　　of blood.
How can you stand this sadness, my lover, my love?

Don't be late. Give me your ankle and forehead. Not
　　tomorrow.
Today my bedroom walls are fresh,
tender and concealed like the inside of bread.

Look, they still flash white and delicious at night:
my knees. Take them. They're yours. You don't see them,
shivering and full like two cups of milk.

WB and Matei Calinescu

Eighteen

Wet streets. It has rained drops big as silver coins,
gold in the sun.
My mind charges the world like a bull.
Today I am eighteen.

The good rain batters me with crazy thoughts.
Look. Drops are warm and slow
as when I was in a carriage, pinned tight
in diapers, drenched and unchanged for an hour.

Yes, it rained as tomorrow, in the past, always.
The heart scrapes through time, is one heart.
My temples beat stronger than temples of time.

Like a common bum I think of drinking life,
but I am burnt, even by the hot stream of its juices.
I am eighteen.

WB and Matei Calinescu

Magda Isanos

Magda Isanos (1916–1944).   One of the earlier Rumanian poets, whose premature
death silenced a highly developed voice, Isanos suffered from tuberculosis, which is
reflected in her neo-romantic, extremely sensitive poetry. Most of her work was published
posthumously: *The Sky of Mountains* (1945), *The Land of Light* (1946), and *Poems*
(1948).

Apricot Tree

This morning I woke
to an impatient scratching on the window,
the finger branches
of the apricot that bloomed in the night.

At first I didn't know him
amid the squandering of so much white and rose.
I thought an angel had swooped down
and broken her wing in the tree.

Could it not be the apricot? I thought.
Then annoyed that I was silent
it slashed my cheek with a blossoming branch.
Then I saw him,

the childhood friend I loved.

WB and Matei Calinescu

Veronica Porumbacu

Veronica Porumbacu (1921–1977).   Born in Bucharest and educated at the
University of Bucharest, Porumbacu translated extensively, mainly poetry by women,
and edited an anthology of world women poets. After practicing "committed" poetry in
the 1950s, she found her true voice—a mixture of childlike naiveté and subtle allegories.
She was killed in the March 1977 earthquake when the apartment house in which she
was living collapsed. Her volumes include *Dreams of Old Dokia* (1947), *Poems,
Retrospective Selection* (1962), and *Circle* (1971).

Of Autumn

In the night there was murder in the street.
Summer was killed.
At the window you could hear the wind yelling
in the garden.

The trees stopped talking.
Blood drips from the ivy on the walls.
King Herod of the Autumn massacred hundreds
of leaves with his words.

WB and Matei Calinescu

Nina Cassian

Nina Cassian (1924–).   Born in Galati, Cassian studied at the University of Bucharest and the Conservatory of Music, and is a composer and musician as well as a translator and poet. She has won prizes for her many books, including children's books. Her translations from the French and German include books by Molière, Heine, Becher, and Brecht. A former socialist realist, Cassian has become one of the most distinctive and perversely intelligent voices in contemporary Rumanian poetry. Her works include *On the Scale of One to One* (1947), *Outdoor Performance—A Monograph of Love* (1954), *Everyday Holidays* (1961), and *Outdoor Performance—Another Monograph of Love* (1974).

Like Gulliver

Like Gulliver pulling a hundred ships,
I draw you, my lovers, to the shore,
clumsy, in all colors, cunning with your
tiny swords and shooting from the hips.

Like Gulliver I spare you, even though
you hit my skull cruelly and hope it breaks.
I laugh at you through strings and snakes
of blood, my furious lovers with your tiny bows.

WB and Matei Calinescu

Knowledge

I've stitched my dress with continents,
bound the equator round my waist.
I waltz to a steady rhythm, bending slightly.

I can't stop my arms
plunging into galaxies,
gloved to elbows in adhesive gold;
I carry on my arms a star's vaccine.

With such greedy sight
my eyelids flutter in the breeze
like a strange enthusiastic plant.

No one fears me
except Error,
who is everywhere.

Michael Impey and Brian Swann

hills picking up the
moonlight like
huge sheep of stone
leaping heads huddled
in the hard freeze and sparkle

the moon then comes to me
builds me up
plasters me up
smashes my forehead
the moon

Stavros Deligiorgis

Ileana Malancioiu

Ileana Malancioiu (1940–).   Malancioiu is a highly unconventional talent, with images charged with sexual symbolism. Her volumes include *Beheaded Bird* (1964), *The Queen's Heart* (1971), and *Lilies for Miss Bride* (1973).

bear's blood

To heal you Hieronymus I had brought you
bear's blood I begged you
whispering you have a taste it will do you good
truly I believed
that night you would be healed

you wouldn't touch the blood
I felt like forcing it down your throat
it was thick it stayed around your lips
I would unstick it quietly and throw
it away to bring then one more pitcher of it

you'd spill it again and would scream my way
you cannot know Hieronymus how bad I felt
that night ought to have been different
your shattered bones gathered hastily in one spot
the bear's blood unable to heal them

Stavros Deligiorgis

Constanta Buzea

Constanta Buzea (1941–).   A delicate, withdrawn poet, with unusual metaphors and
a modern sensibility, Buzea represents the best of the younger poets in Rumania. Her
works include *From the Earth* (1963), *The Clouds* (1968), *Hills* (1970), and *Medicine
for the Angel* (1972).

I'm not here   never was

I am reminded of the vestment
I meant sometimes to throw
around the trees in winter

my son's asleep
and his sister quietly paces
over runners not to wake him

at the other end of the world I am torn
between the dusk at home
and the midnight all around

my nightmare
is full of pure sounds
as distinct as feuds

in vain

I am not here never was
I am only sick and on this earth

like a twig stuck into a snowman

Ana Blandiana

Ana Blandiana (1942–).   Born in Timisoara, Blandiana studied philosophy at Cluj
and was a magazine editor in Bucharest. She has traveled extensively in Europe and in
1973 spent a year at the International Writers Program at the University of Iowa. Her
poetry, as described by the Rumanian critic and poet Matei Calinescu, "has the strength
and subtle aroma of dry vermouth." She has done a book of interviews with her husband,
a journalist, and an interesting "antijournal." Her volumes include *The Third Mystery*
(1969), *Fifty Poems* (1970), and *October, November, December* (1972).

I need only fall asleep
to return
where only I believe I left
I and the dogs
who sense my approach
and fill the dream
with their rushing joy
I need only sleep
to smell almost impudic green
tall inviting grass to
sleep inside sleep
light fading inside light
inside the sensual omniscient
yelping of the dogs
on the very edge of your eyelashes
where the landscape is flattened out thin
and is all
yours

Stavros Deligiorgis

Gabriela Melinescu

Gabriela Melinescu (1942–).   Born in Bucharest, Melinescu graduated from the
Rumanian Faculty of Language and Literature and published her first book at the age of
twenty-three. Since then she has done many books of poems, a collection of fantasy
stories, and a book of children's literature. Presently she lives in Sweden and is married to
a Swedish publisher. She is also a painter. Her poetry is linguistically playful, intricate,
and lucidly sensuous. Her volumes include *Winter Ceremony* (1965), *The Abstract*

Beings (1966), *The Disease of Divine Origin* (1970), and *The Oath of Poverty,
Chastity and Submission* (1972).

time of fish dying

colors shifting
silver to yellow and
    I could say that much only
he has not been seen since
    not once

risking death
skirting poles and corners
hung with the yellow magnetic strip

but the fish had left
for the world of fishes
    and I can but say
he has not been seen since
    not once

Stavros Deligiorgis

Birth

Let us bring out those heavy dice
cut from elephant tusks.
Let us hammer them on the wet earth
till under the pounding they crack.
And good luck bursts out.
No one knows how it looks:
maybe it's a horrible beast
or steam hovering over neverness.
I sit on my knees. I illumine
the uncertain birth from ivory,
and elephants come squealing.
They hold up my temples with their tusks.

WB and Matei Calinescu

Hungarian

Anna Hajnal

Anna Hajnal (1907–1977).   Born in Gyepurüzes, in western Hungary, Anna Hajnal studied English in Vienna and was co-editor of a Budapest literary magazine in the mid-1930s. She translated Shakespeare and others in addition to publishing thirteen books of her own poems. She was a leading literary figure in Hungary.

Fear

I am afraid I may be Ilia
the wild duck mired in the oil.

What if, instead, I'm Algernon
the white mouse in the maze,

or Pompilius, the dog in the laboratory
with the cancer graft under his skin?

I am afraid. What if the bull calf
with the new moon marking his forehead

—the one chosen for slaughter—
is really who I am? I have a fear

that maybe I am Bonnie
the chimpanzee who died

in the solitude of the spacecraft . . .
But no, I know I'm Anna, and afraid,

for knowing this, I know I live
until the debt I owe for this is paid.

Daniel Hoffman

Half Past Four, October

Twilight. By now the genial sea of dusk
is lapping at the window. A rising tide
bears the plane-tree aloft and far away.
Above these undulations of the sky
on silky wings the wild goose floats unseen.
His cries we hear, and hear again
until the waves of dust rise over him,
but where will he be then? Where does he fly
southward with his strong companions?

How many planes and levels deep does dusk
hover in autumn? Deeper than the sea
where the wild saffron, purple sea-star blooms,
down to the cellar where the silken mole,
hardworking and secure, lives with his brood.
It seeps where the snake is drowsing amid dead leaves.

The dusk flows past us, turns on wings
noiseless as fins,
the owl, his eyes like bulbs, drifts by, a fish with ears;
the bat's wings wriggle like a slowly-swimming skate,
we grow sleepy too but cannot hang
head-downward from the plane tree's hollow all the winter long—
we know what would be good,
we live as best we can.

Daniel Hoffman

The Felled Plane Tree

Its trunk as of dead silver cast,
a statue, it lies,
within whose tufted crest ground-creeping
wind bubbles and sighs.
Its branches are lopped silver arms,
stubs that do not stir,
its tresses matted by the mud,
turned brown and grey.

Spirit high above it flies;
transparent vapor encircles
its many long-lashed
eyes, all shut.
Its lopped head dropped upon the earth,
giant tresses sprawling,
the smoke of dead breath rising,
in faded, soundless music calling;
rustling, whispering, it breathes,
voicing the vacant altitude's agony;
through changing shapes, the fallen tree
weeps silently from dead, fringed eyes.

William J. Smith

Ágnes Nemes Nagy

Ágnes Nemes Nagy (1922–).   Born in Budapest, Nemes Nagy studied Hungarian, Latin, and art history at the University of Budapest. She taught in a secondary school and was a staff member of an educational journal, before devoting her time exclusively to writing. She has translated Corneille, Racine, Molière, Brecht, Rilke, and other French, German, and English poets, and has written a book of essays on poetry and four books of her own poems.

I Carried Statues

I carried statues on the ship,
their enormous anonymous faces.
I carried statues on the ship
to the island, to take their places.
Between the ear and the nose
was an angle of ninety degrees,
for the rest their faces were blank.
I carried statues on the ship,
and in that way I sank.

Bruce Berlind

Bird

There's a bird perched on my shoulder,
twin-bird, bird born with me.
It's grown so large, grown so heavy,
each step I take is torture.

Dead weight, dead weight, dead weight on me.
I'd shove it off—it's tenacious,
it claws into my shoulder
like the roots of an oak tree.

An inch from my ear: the sound
of its horrible bird-heart throbbing.
If it flew off one day
I'd drop down to the ground.

Bruce Berlind

Words to a Song

The fruit on the trees is aging fast,
aging too is the fruit on the grass,
just like after death.

At the weekend houses twilight nears.
The season even changes its life,
and north and south have been man and wife
for 26 thousand years.

26 thousand years have passed,
the fruit on the trees is aging fast.
July: you can hear in the garden grass tick
the falling fruits' uneven spastic
extrasystolic beats.

Bruce Berlind

Ágnes Gergely

Ágnes Gergely (1933–).　　Born in Budapest, Gergely studied Hungarian and English at the University of Budapest. She has been a secondary schoolteacher, a producer for Hungarian radio, and a feature editor of a literary weekly. She is now editor of a Budapest publishing house. In 1973–1974 she spent six months at the International Writing Program at the University of Iowa. In addition to numerous translations, she has published four books of poems and three novels.

Crazed Man in Concentration Camp

All through the march, besides bag and blanket
he carried in his hands two packages of empty boxes,
and when the company halted for a couple of minutes
he laid the two packages of empty boxes neatly at each side,
being careful not to damage or break either of them,
the parcels were of
ornamental boxes
dovetailed by sizes each to each
and tied together with packing-cord,
the top box with a picture on it.
When the truck was about to start, the sergeant
shouted something in sergeant's language,
they sprang up suddenly,
and one of the boxes rolled down to the wheel,
the smallest one, the one with the picture:
"It's fallen," he said and made to go after it,
but the truck moved off
and his companions held his hands
while his hands held the two packages of boxes
and his tears trailed down his jacket.
"It's fallen," he said that evening in the queue—
and it meant nothing to him to be shot dead.

Edwin Morgan

Norwegian

Astrid Hjertenaes Andersen

Astrid Hjertenaes Andersen (1915–). Born in Norway, Andersen is one of the foremost postwar poets. She has published eight volumes of verse, and has studied and traveled extensively in the United States.

Before the sun goes down

I'll lay my wildflower hand
in your hand's white wicker basket

and bold–tender–shy I'll encircle you
as day and night would encircle
the trees of the day and night

and my kisses will live like birds on your shoulder

Nadia Christensen

Swedish

Sonja Åkesson

Sonja Åkesson (1926–1977).   Born in Buttle, Gotland, Sweden, Åkesson has published prose and poetry. Her poems deal with everyday domestic situations, expressed in overheard everyday speech. She depicts the modern scene with satiric barbs against people, society, and government, in her major poem "Autobiography," from which a large excerpt is included here. Her books are *Situations* (1957), *Peace in the House* (1963), *Streetballads* (1969), and *Collected Poems: We Must Be Content and Thank God* (1967).

Autobiography
(reply to Ferlinghetti)
(1963)

I am leading a quiet life
on 83 A Queen's Street every day.
I blow my kids' noses and polish floors
and copper pots
and cook potatoes and sausage.

I am leading a quiet life
near the subway.
I am a Swede.
I was a Swedish girl.
I read the medical book under the blanket
and was a member of the Baptist
Junior League.
I dreamed of singing in the choir
and singing to the guitar
under the flames of the candles.
I dreamed of singing
to the guitar at the Lucia party.

I owned two records by Alice Babs
and a sports jacket, with a zipper,
that used to be Dad's pants.
I worked in a café
with mirrors and beer
and a pig-sty in the yard.
I can still sense the smell of rats
and raspberry frosting, and of cheese
from the owner who was also a milk tester.

I was a typical brat.
I dug tunnels under the snow.
I sat under a snowing apple tree
waiting for Doomsday.
I was caught in a migrant's shack
on my way home from Junior League.
I took a correspondence course in shorthand
and doodled cover girls
on the pad.
I was in a snowed-in car
picking up Baltic refugees.
Men with mushed-up lungs
crying for water.
A woman with her eye hanging
like a bloody egg down her cheek.
. . . .
I have seen silent children
in starving crowds
from the depths of a movie seat.
I have seen them.
I am a mother.
I was there.
But I did not suffer
enough.

I am a Swede.
I have a health insurance card.
I cry in my room.
I will die of cancer.

I am formed by circumstances.
I am carrying on a war with myself
as a rejected female.
And I have certain plans!
I have a daughter
who should have a future.
I might buy myself a burial plot.
I am only temporarily
a usable household utensil.
I never keep a promise.
I see an expectation
in my childish mirror
as if I should get to have a Christmas tree.

I am leading a quiet life
on 83 Queen's Street across the yard every day
looking at the walls.
I think of my sister
who carefully crochets pot holders
from my brother-in-law's
wound-up brain.
I think of my brother
who is a cannibal.
I fry my steaks.
I wash my hands.
I have heard the lonely cry
from the half-devoured in the wilderness.
I am the woman.
I was she.
But I did not suffer
enough.

I went inside and closed my door.
I sit in my comfortable chair.
I visit the staid department stores
where I buy my sterile
props of propriety.
I have written poems with thoughtful
pauses and punctuations.

I change bread into stones.
I feel as if I had my hands tied behind my back.
I feel as if I had a mute skin
tightened over my face
and fantasize about a small knife
between my teeth.

I have felt
how I vomited my throat
and how my tongue too slipped out
an unusable rag of skin.
Where do I find an instrument
for all my closed-in air?
I am a soiled shoe
in an overcrowded street.
I am a dog without a master
full of persistent love
among indifferent soiled shoes.

I see a similarity between me
and potatoes.
I have felt the rot from within
in the autumn rain.

I have heard married couples
on their custom-made foam rubber mattresses
complain about lost excitements.
I understand their disgust.
I have felt caresses
stick like chewing gum.
I doze by my little wading pool.
I wait
together with bored mothers.
And I watch their husbands
come rolling in their VW's
in their worn down wheel tracks.
They wear shiny nylon shirts
and small leather cushions behind.
They've got idiot-proof chronometers

and looks full of dead flesh
and I feel it
in my own gnawing face.

I am leading a quiet life
reading homages to existence
by someone who did not suffer enough.
I chew my own jokes.
I struggle with my tough skin.
I was the ugly duckling
who never changed into a swan.
Did I have a pair of wings then?
I feel the aftereffects of burns.
I pamper my poor hunchback.
I try to find my little knife
way back ruined by rust
and crushed by feet in the yellow grass.

Ingrid Claréus

Danish

Cecil Bødker

Cecil Bødker (1927–).   Born in Denmark, she was trained as a silversmith. In addition to four volumes of poems, she has written several novels and children's stories. She has won the Hans Christian Andersen Medal for her children's stories, which are now being published in English.

Calendar

One year there were too many
frogs
—and maybe mosquitoes.

People talked about the soil's
increased aquasity
and had it noted
in the calendar.

Last year it was the snails.

And the year before
roving
foxes.

Things will work out, people said:
they'll die off by themselves.
And people talked about mange
and prolonged sickness
starvation
stress
rabies—
it will all come to an end.

Just look at the foxes, people said.

One year there were mice
the next year there were none.
That was proof.

This year it is children.

People talk about the soil's
lack of aquasity
and the blighted grain
people talk about responsibility
and lack of responsibility
people talk—

For things will surely work out
by themselves.
Just look at the foxes

Just look at all the mice—
it goes into the calendar.

Next year it will be flies.

Nadia Christensen and Alexander Taylor

Self-Portrait

Weeds grow shamelessly
on my tongue
in the middle of a bed
of taste buds,
and among my hair's
mangrove roots
swamp-fish shoal
like fleeing silvergreen
shadowanimals.

My heart dangles
carefree
on its string
from my lower left rib,
if it gets broken,
I'll scatter it
like ashes on the top of my head,
—or perhaps
like gunpowder.

Nadia Christensen

Inger Christensen

Inger Christensen (1935–).   Born in Denmark, she is a teacher and the author of radio and television plays and two novels. She has published two books of poems and a poem of book length called *Poems from It*. This latter book has been reviewed as the most important book to appear in Scandinavia in the last decade.

Men's Voices

Men's voices in the darkness
—once in a temple—
men's voices in the sun
—I was once caryatid
number nine—
men's voices in the park
—I was a statue
naked, inviolate
with no other mirror
than fingers of air
moving from thought to thought
with no other sorrow
than the rustle of leaves—
men's voices in the park:
why have they wakened me?

Nadia Christensen

Estonian

Betti Alver

Betti Alver (1906–).   Alver is the leading woman poet in Estonia. Distinct from the popular Marie Under, whose late romantic voice dominated Estonian poetry for many years, Alver has developed a diction at once colloquial, half epic, allegorical, dealing with many subjects, from personal spiritual enclosures to social causes. Her irony, rippling with humor, extends from the everyday to the cosmic. Her tragi-comic treatment of spiritual life often takes on a science fiction imagination when heavenly beings invade the earth. She is married to the Estonian poet Heiti Talvik. Her volumes include *Dust and Fire* (1936) and *Starry Hour* (1936).

A Tailor Called Sorrow

Yesterday in drizzling rain
on the road,
depression came
with its scissors open.

He put unhappy shirts
around the necks
of children,
and stitched black markings
on the lives
of the others.

Around the red faces
the tailor called sorrow
let a cloth with death silk
in it
hang,
and mingled white basting thread
in their hair.

WB and Felix Oinas

The Painter in the Lion Cage

On the ground are my sketches of the contours
    of the restless beast.
My eyes glare like a drunk at the waving colors
    of its mane.
I mix the paints. Out of this cage
I won't get a single drawing.

If I am lucky enough to slip loose from its claws
I will think of it as an understanding friend,
yet never will be saved from the majestic brute
I drew myself.

WB and Felix Oinas

The Titans

Don't suppose that the weightless phantom
will disappear.
It is lurking in the other world like a huge angel
or beast,
waiting to return.

Passion floats away. Bile is vaporized
in a defenseless larva that is bleaching the soil.
We long.
But this is only an instant
in the circling of quick Bohemians.

Behind the circling planets the kingdom of giants
floats lucidly,
but in the legend
of the inquisitive child of man,
the Titans are back on earth, in prison.

If the earth blows up, they won't come here again,
exiled from heaven.

Yet some blazing hand will remake the chaos
of earth, people, and death.

WB and Felix Oinas

Iron Heaven

Today I saw a place no one has seen:
the Heaven of the damned.
No one—proud or worried—goes
unharassed by it.
It keeps going endlessly. No one
escapes. No drought
can kill the coagulated petals
of its flowers.
Its horror
is that what we did or longed
to do
is perfect there.
On its seas of glass no storm
ever ages,
no pestilence rots its vineyards.
Only the eternal, fixed form
is open
to our glance, everywhere.
My iron soul sobs and finds the gold
of Heaven.
Now, with no pride or worry,
it wants to shiver with the passion
of the earth
and feel its wings of weakness.

WB and Felix Oinas

Russian

Anna Akhmatova

Anna Akhmatova (1889–1966).   Born in Odessa, Akhmatova spent her first sixteen years at the imperial summer residence at Tsarskoe Selo near St. Petersburg. She went to law school in Kiev, and married the poet-critic Nikolai Gumilev in 1910. In Paris in 1911, the unknown painter Modigliani did sixteen portrait drawings of her. Her second book of poems, *Rosary* (1914), brought her fame. At this time, along with her husband and the poet Osip Mandelstamm, she became associated with *Acmeism,* a movment which strove for clarity after the vagueness of the then-fashionable symbolism. She was divorced in 1918.Three years later Gumilev was executed. After the publication of *Anno Domini* (1922), for the next eighteen years she was silenced as a poet—as were Pasternak and many of her contemporaries. She earned her living as a translator. She was living with the Mandelstamm family in 1934 when Osip Mandelstamm was arrested, to disappear in the camps, sharing the same fate as Isaac Babel. During the war, she was evacuated to Tashkent, but the political thaw permitted her to become a member of the Writer's Union and publish her own poems. Then in 1946 she was again bitterly attacked, expelled from the Union, and her son arrrested. After Stalin's death she was rehabilitated and her son was released. During her last years her work again began to appear in periodicals and she was restored to membership in the Writer's Union. In 1965 she was given an honorary degree by Oxford University. Most of her life she lived in Leningrad, and several poets, particularly Joseph Brodsky, were protégés within her circle. With Pasternak she was revered for her literary and spiritual integrity and courage. Her long poem "Requiem" combines personal sensibility and national consciousness in a great, yet controlled, lyrical statement.

Lot's Wife

The just man followed then his angel guide
Where he strode on the black highway, hulking and bright;
But a wild grief in his wife's bosom cried,
Look back, it is not too late for a last sight

Of the red towers of your native Sodom, the square
Where once you sang, the gardens you shall mourn,

And the tall house with empty windows where
You loved your husband and your babes were born.

She turned, and looking on the bitter view
Her eyes were welded shut by mortal pain;
Into transparent salt her body grew,
And her quick feet were rooted in the plain.

Who would waste tears upon her? Is she not
The least of our losses, this unhappy wife?
Yet in my heart she will not be forgot
Who, for a single glance, gave up her life.

Richard Wilbur

What's worse than this past century?
Dazed with sadness, anxiety,
it touches the darkest sore
and cannot heal.

Winter's sun still shines in the West,
the city roofs bright in its rays.
Here a white house aims upward its crosses,
ravens crying out, ravens flying in.

Barbara Einzig

He loved three things in life:
singing at vespers, white peacocks,
and worn-out maps of America.
He did not love tea with raspberries,
or feminine hysteria.
. . . And I was his wife.

Barbara Einzig

Summer Garden

Wishing for roses, I walk through the garden
Where the world's reddest rose leans from a wall,

Where the statues still remember me as a girl,
And I recall their gestures under the Neva's water.

In that expanding silence, among the tsarist lindens,
I mistake a ship's mast for a violin.

And the swan keeps swimming across the years,
Deeply in love with his disturbing double.

And death-deep is the sleep of the hundred
Thousand marches of enemies and friends,

And a procession of shadows moves without end
From the granite vase to the portals of the palace.

There I hear my white nights whispering of
A transcendent, secret love.

And the garden burns in pearl and jasper,
But the source of light is hidden in the leaves.

Stephen Stepanchev

Tashkent Breaks into Blossom

As if somebody ordered it
the city suddenly became bright—
it came into every court
in a white, light apparition.
Their breathing is more understandable than words,
in the burning blue sky
their reflection is doomed
to lie at the bottom of the ditch.

I will remember the roof of stars
in the radiance of eternal glory,
and the small rolls of bread
in the young hands
of dark-haired mothers.   1944

Richard McKane

How can you look at the Neva,
how can you stand on the bridges? . . .
No wonder people think I grieve:
his image will not let me go.
Black angels' wings can cut one down,
I count the days till Judgment Day.
The streets are stained with lurid fires,
bonfires of roses in the snow.   1914

Stanley Kunitz with Max Hayward

Your lynx-eyes, Asia,
spy on my discontent;
they lure into the light
my buried self,
something the silence spawned,
no more to be endured
than the noon sun in Termez.
Pre-memory floods the mind
like molten lava on the sands . . .
as if I were drinking my own tears
from the cupped palms of a stranger's hands.   1945

Stanley Kunitz with Max Hayward

REQUIEM 1935—1940

No, not under the vault of another sky,
not under the shelter of other wings.
I was with my people then,
there where my people were doomed to be.   1961

Instead of a Foreword

During the terrible years of Yezhovshchina* I spent seventeen
months in the prison queues in Leningrad. One day someone
recognized me. Then a woman with lips blue with cold who was
standing behind me, and of course had never heard of my name,
came out of the numbness which affected us all and whispered in my
ear—(we all spoke in whispers there):
  "Can you describe this?"
  I said, "I can!"
  Then something resembling a smile slipped over what had once
been her face.   1 April 1957
                                                        Leningrad

Dedication

The mountains bend before this grief,
the great river does not flow,
but the prison locks are strong
and behind them the convicts' holes,
and a deathly sadness.
For someone the fresh wind blows,
for someone the sunset basks . . .
We don't know, we are the same everywhere;
we only hear the repellent clank of keys,
the heavy steps of the soldiers.
We rose as though to early mass,
and went through the savage capital,

---

* 'Yezhovshchina': Yezhov was head of Stalin's secret police in the late 1930s and was himself
purged.

and we used to meet there, more lifeless than the dead,
the sun lower, the Neva mistier,
but in the distance hope still sings.
Condemned . . . Immediately the tears start,
one woman, already isolated from everyone else,
as though her life had been wrenched from her heart,
as though she had been smashed flat on her back,
still, she walks on . . . staggers . . . alone . . .
Where now are the chance friends
of my two hellish years?
What do they see in the Siberian blizzard,
what comes to them in the moon's circle?
I send them my farewell greeting.   March 1940

Introduction

It was a time when only the dead
smiled, happy in their peace.
And Leningrad dangled like a useless pendant
at the side of its prisons.
A time when, tortured out of their minds,
the convicted walked in regiments,
and the steam whistles sang
their short parting song.
Stars of death stood over us,
and innocent Russia squirmed
under the bloody boots,
under the wheels of Black Marias.

1*

They took you away at dawn,
I walked after you as though you were being borne out,
the children were crying in the dark room,
the candle swam by the ikon-stand.
The cold of the ikon on your lips.
Death sweat on your brow . . . Do not forget!

* This poem refers to the arrest of N. N. Punin, Anna Akhmatova's close friend.

I will howl by the Kremlin towers
like the wives of the Streltsy.*   1935

2

The quiet Don flows quietly,
the yellow moon goes into the house,

goes in with its cap askew,
the yellow moon sees the shadow.

This woman is sick,
this woman is alone,

husband in the grave, son in prison,
pray for me.

3

No, this is not me—someone else suffers.
I couldn't stand this: let black drapes
cover what happened,
and let them take away the street lights . . .
    Night.

4

If I could show you, the mocker,
everybody's favourite,
happy sinner of Tsarskoe Selo,
how your life will turn out:
you will stand at Kresty†
three hundredth in the line with your prison parcel,

*The Streltsy were a body of soldiers organized about 1550 by Ivan the Terrible. Their suppression enabled Peter I to establish a regular army. In 1698 Peter defeated them outside Moscow, executed 800 of them and disbanded the others.

†'Kresty': a prison built on the Vyborg side of Leningrad in 1893. It literally means 'Crosses' (referring to the layout of the buildings)—and the additional sense of 'standing before the cross' should be borne in mind; cf. parts 6 and 10.

and set fire to the new year ice
with your hot tears.
There the prison poplar sways,
silence—and how many
innocent lives are ending there . . .

5

For seventeen months I have been screaming,
calling you home.
I flung myself at the executioner's feet.
You are my son and my terror.
Everything is confused for ever,
and I can no longer tell
beast from man,
and how long I must wait for the execution.
Only the dusty flowers,
the clank of censers, and tracks
leading from somewhere to nowhere.
An enormous star
looks me straight in the eye
and threatens swift destruction.   1939

6

Weightless weeks fly by,
I will never grasp what happened.
How the white nights looked
at you, my son, in prison,
how they look again
with the burning eye of the hawk,
they speak of your tall cross,
they speak of death.   1939

7
Verdict

The stone wall fell
on my still living breast.
Never mind, I was prepared,
somehow I'll come to terms with it.

Today I have much work to do:
I must finally kill my memory,
I must, so my soul can turn to stone,
I must learn to live again.

Or else . . . The hot summer rustle,
like holiday time outside my window.
I have felt this coming for a long time,
this bright day and the empty house.   Summer 1939

8
To Death

You will come anyway—so why not now?
I am waiting for you—it's very difficult for me.
I have put out the light and opened the door
to you, so simple and wonderful.
Assume any shape you like,
burst in as a poison gas shell,
or creep up like a burglar with a heavy weight,
or poison me with typhus vapours.
Or come with a denunciation thought up by you
and known *ad nauseam* to everyone,
so that I may see over the blue cap*
the janitor's fear-whitened face.
I don't care now. The Yenisey rolls on,†
the Pole star shines.
And the blue lustre of loving eyes
conceals the final horror.   19 August 1939

9

Already madness has covered
half my soul with its wing,
and gives me strong liquor to drink,
and lures me to the black valley.

* 'the blue cap' and 'the janitor': an arrest.
† 'Yenisey': river in Siberia where many of the concentration camps were.

I realized that I must
hand victory to it,
as I listened to my delirium,
already alien to me.

It will not allow me to take
anything away with me
(however I beseech it,
however I pester it with prayer):

not the terrible eyes of my son,
the rock-like suffering,
not the day when the storm came,
not the prison visiting hour,

nor the sweet coolness of hands,
nor the uproar of the lime trees' shadows,
nor the distant, light sound—
the comfort of last words.   4 May 1940

10
Crucifixion

"Weep not for Me, Mother,
in the grave I have life."

I

The choir of angels glorified the great hour,
the heavens melted in flames.
He said to His Father: "Why hast Thou forsaken me?"
and to His Mother: "Oh, weep not for Me . . ."

II

Mary Magdalene smote her breast and wept,
the disciple whom He loved turned to stone,
but where the Mother stood in silence
nobody even dared look.   1940–43

Epilogue
I

I found out how faces droop,
how terror looks out from under the eyelids,
how suffering carves on cheeks
hard pages of cuneiform,
how curls ash-blond and black
turn silver overnight,
a smile fades on submissive lips,
fear trembles in a dry laugh.
I pray not for myself alone,
but for everyone who stood with me,
in the cruel cold, in the July heat,
under the blind, red wall.

II

The hour of remembrance has drawn close again.
I see you, hear you, feel you.

The one they hardly dragged to the window,
the one who no longer treads this earth,

the one who shook her beautiful head,
and said: "Coming here is like coming home."

I would like to call them all by name,
but this list was taken away and I can't remember.

For them I have woven a wide shroud
from the humble words I heard among them.

I remember them always, everywhere,
I will never forget them, whatever comes.

And if they gag my tormented mouth
with which one hundred million people cry,

then let them also remember me
on the eve of my remembrance day.

If they ever think of building
a memorial to me in this country,

I solemnly give my consent,
only with this condition: not to build it

near the sea where I was born;
my last tie with the sea is broken;

nor in Tsarsky Sad by the hallowed stump
where an inconsolable shadow seeks me,

but here, where I stood three hundred hours,
and they never unbolted the door for me.

Since even in blessed death I am terrified
that I will forget the thundering of the Black Marias,

forget how the hateful door slammed,
how an old woman howled like a wounded beast.

And let the melting snow stream
like tears from my motionless, bronze eyelids,

let the prison dove call in the distance
and the boats go quietly on the Neva.   March 1940

Richard McKane

Alone

No one can hurt me. They've tried to kill me
so many times that nobody scares me now.
I know what kind of people want me dead:
believers in love, political, dressed like the poor.

Nothing they can do is hidden from me.
This whitewashed ordinary room of mine
is Paradise, cut off, a plain white square
that overlooks the same street, the same people.
There's almost nothing in it—a few chairs,
bed, table, books, a red Persian prayer rug
with a cross in a yellow field in the middle.
It could be called a trap; maybe it is.
But what I feel
is gratitude—to those who put me here
and in their way hung doors, cemented brick, glazed windows:
may they never be ill or worried; may life pass them by.
I'm up this morning with the workers, I see
my old face in the mirror, bleached with anxiety,
and what I am is what the sun is—
itself free of itself daily
even when its last thin light goes out under the rim of the earth.
Everything's dark. Whenever I close my eyes.
Behind me,
much smaller than my head, abandoned, clear,
trees, miles away across a field, a road, one pinkish cloud,
live in the oval glass.
I tie one short ribbon in my gray hair
and step back—younger than the face I see—
nowhere, homeless, peaceful,
and talk to the voice inside me who talks to me.
Sometimes I sit here. Winds from a frozen sea
blow through my open windows. I don't get up, I
don't close them. I let that air touch me. I freeze.
Twilight or dawn, the same bright streaks of cloud.

A dove pecks wheat from my extended hand,
those infinite blank pages, placed on my writing stand . . .

some desolate urge lifts my right hand, guides me.
Much much older than I am, it comes down,
blue as an eyelid, godless, and I write.

                              version by Stephen Berg

Marina Tsvetayeva

Marina Tsvetayeva (1892–1941).   Born in Moscow, the daughter of an art history professor father at Moscow University, who founded what is now called the Pushkin Museum of Fine Arts, and a musician mother, Tsvetayeva spent part of her childhood in Tarusa, 150 miles from Moscow, a town which combined an intellectual community with peasant customs of old Russia. During the Revolution she sided with the White Army. She emigrated to Prague, then to Paris, and finally, finding exile intolerable, was persuaded by Pasternak to go back to the Soviet Union. At her return her husband was arrrested and shot. Later, her son was killed in the war. The poetry she wrote in exile could not at that time be published in Russia, and like Akhmatova and Pasternak, she was silenced. She was in the provincial town of Elabuga, harassed and destitute, when she hanged herself. Ilya Ehrenberg says of her, "She was a candid and sweet pagan, not from Greece but from Moscow where warm, living flesh lurks underneath the gilded vestments of the Byzantine icons." In his reminiscence *I Remember, I Remember,* speaking of the poets of modern Russia, Pasternak said simply, "She was the best of us." Her lines are usually short, jerky, with images of amazing strength. Her stanzas reach crescendos of intense, defiant passion and thought. Tsvetayeva is a major poet of our century. In recent years, she has been rehabilitated and, with Osip Mandelstamm, another victim of Stalinist days, is a model for contemporary writers. Her *Collected Poems* have recently appeared for the first time in Russia.

We Shall Not Escape Hell

We shall not escape Hell, my passionate
sisters, we shall drink black resins—
we who sang our praises to the Lord
with every one of our sinews, even the finest.

we did not lean over cradles or
spinning wheels at night, and now we are
carried off by an unsteady boat
under the skirts of a sleeveless cloak,

we dressed every morning in
fine Chinese silk, and we would
sing our paradisal songs at
the fire of the robbers' camp,

slovenly needlewomen (all
our sewing came apart), dancers,

players upon pipes: we have been
the queens of the whole world!

first scarcely covered by rags,
then with constellations in our hair, in
gaol and at feasts we have
bartered away heaven,

in starry nights, in the apple
orchards of Paradise.
—Gentle girls, my beloved sisters,
we shall certainly find ourselves in Hell!

Elaine Feinstein

. . . I'd like to live with you
In some small town,
In never-ending twilight
And the endless sound of bells.
And in the little town's hotel—
The thin chime
Of an antique clock,
Like little drops of time.
And sometimes, evenings, from some attic room,
A flute,
A flute-player by a window.
And huge tulips at the windows.
And if you didn't love me, I wouldn't even mind.

In the middle of a room, a great tile stove,
And a picture on every tile:
A heart, a sailboat, a rose.
And out beyond our only window,
Snow, snow, snow.

You'd lie about the way I like you: lazy,
Unconcerned, indifferent.
Once or twice the harsh crack
Of a match.

Your cigarette flares and then burns down,
And trembling, trembling at its tip
a short gray stump—the ash
You're too lazy to shake away—
And the cigarette flies into the fire.

Paul Schmidt

Ars

I was born with a song in my tongue—but would
not waste it for a phony chasuble or hood.

I dream—not in bed—but in full day, awake,
and can't live like you with chitchat of a snake.

I come from you, lyre, my lyre, and my voice
and chitchat are your swanlike curve and hiss.

I'm an ally of the laurel, the wind and dawn,
and would rather be happy: I am no nun,

and have a friend who is blond—maybe a rat,
but I stick with him when everything is bad.

I come from you, lyre, my lyre, and my voice
and chitchat are your swanlike curve and hiss.

They say to be a woman is a heavy fate.
I wouldn't know. I never take my weight.

I freely give—but never sell my goods to you,
and now that my fingernails are turning blue

my death rattle and eagle scream and wheeze,
lyre, my lyre, are your swanlike curve and hiss.

WB and Edward Brown

from **Poem of the End**

III

And now the riverbank. I cling
to water, it's dense and strong.
Hanging gardens. Oh Babylon,
I have found you at last.

I cling to this corpse-colored
strip of steel water
as a singer grips
her score, a blind man

Gropes for a wall . . . Can't you give?
No? I lean forward. Won't you hear?
I cling to this slaker of universal
thirst as a madman clutches

The edge of a roof . . . It's not the river
makes me shake: I'm a naiad, you know.
I can cling to rivers, to the hands
of a lover

Who's faithful. The dead are faithful.
Yes, but not to everyone they knew.
Death on my left side, you
on my right. You seem dead too.

A shaft of shrieking light.
Flaring laughter.
. . . you and I should . . . (I shake)
. . . let's be manly, can't we, and brave? . . .

V

I catch the movement of his lips
and I know he won't speak first.
. . . don't you love me . . . no, I do . . .
. . . you don't love me . . . but it's worn out,

Drunk up, worried to death . . .
(An eagle eye glancing at the place):
. . . for God's sake, is *this* a home? . . .
. . . home is in my heart . . . oh, that's poetry . . .

Love is bodies, blood and sweat,
a flower caked with my blood.
Do you think love is
a chat at a small table

For an hour or so and home alone?
The way these ladies and gentlemen do?
Love is—   . . . something sacred?
Dear, change that: *scarred*; scar

For scar—   . . . in front of waiters
and customers? (I, soundlessly:
"Love is a drawn bow:
a bow: then a bow: goodbye.")

Love is contact, connection.
We are all apart—mouths and lives.
(But I begged you then: knock wood!
Then, that secret moment, that

Hour high on a hill,
height of passion. *Memento!* Memory
is mist: love is throwing everything
into the fire. And always in vain.)

A shellfish smile, the mouth
is pale: not irony. Inventory.
. . . and above all it's sharing
a bed—   . . . don't you mean

A gulf between? The drumming
of his fingers. . . . let's not try to move
mountains. Love is—   . . . mine. You're mine.
I understand. And then what?

The drumming of his fingers
grows (the scaffold, the public square).
. . . let's go. (And I: let's die,
I had hoped. It's so much simpler.)

Too much tawdriness and cheap economy:
even the rhythm—railroads, hotel rooms—
. . . love is life.
. . . no, the ancients had another word

For it . . . So? A shred of handerchief
like a fish in my fist.
. . . shall we go? . . . which way are you going?
(The train tracks, poison, a bullet, who knows.

Death.) . . . I have no plans.
. . . life! Like a Roman commander,
An eagle-eyed glance at the remnant
of his troops.
                    . . . well then, goodbye.

VII

And now the riverbank. For the last time.
Ever. Our hands hang apart
like neighbors whom nonsense
has made spiteful. By the waters

I weep. I lick away the salt
mercuric silver without caring:
my tears can call no enormous
Solomon moon out of heaven.

A post. Could I pound my forehead
till blood comes? It would crack in dry bits.
Accomplice criminals, breathless
with fear. (What we killed was love.)

Stop it! Lovely, these two lovers
in the night. Apart? Off to bed with others?

. . . you know, the future is all up there
above us—I lean back, and look.

To bed! Like newlyweds, bedded in
brand-new sheets! We are all out of step,
out of time. Sadly: . . . take my arm.
We're not convicts in a prison walk.

A shock! His hand is like
his soul upon my arm. The shock
screams along feverish wires:
his hand has touched my soul!

He holds me. Rainbows everywhere!
Rainbow tears, bead curtain, bright
showers. I know this riverbank
will never end. A bridge, and

                            . . . well?

Here? (The hearse has arrived.)
Quiet eyes look up,
look up.   . . . couldn't we go home?
For the last time?

VIII

Our last bridge.
(I won't let his hand go.)
Final bridge,
last toll.

Dry land, and water.
Count. Count out my coins.
Charon's coin,
payment for Lethe.

Coin's shadow, in a shadowy
hand. These coins

don't clink. So,
into a shadowy hand,

The shadow of a coin.
Without gleam or chime.
Money. For them.
The dead are tired of poppies.

The bridge.

The happiest lovers
have no hope.
A bridge is like passion, all convention:
entirely *in-between.*

I nestle, warm:
a rib, I cling so close.
Not *up to,* not *against*
(moment of sight regained)

Not with arms or legs:
all bone and persistence.
Only my side is alive, oh
where it touches, presses close.

My life is in my side!
It is all ear and echo.
I stick like yolk
to white, an Eskimo

Nestling in his furs.
I cling. Siamese twins.
Only an ally?
Remember that woman?

Mother? Herself and all
forgotten to carry you
in exultant stillness?
She never held you closer.

You understand? We're grafted together.
We're one, lulled into one another.
I won't jump off, won't drown.
To dive would mean

Letting go your hand. I press
closer. You cannot tear me off.
A bridge is not a husband, only
a lover: totally over and gone.

And the bridge is behind us!
(We feed the river with bodies.)
I have stuck like a tick,
like ivy: tear me out

By the roots! Like a tick!
Shameless, inhuman,
to throw me away like a thing
when I've cared for no

Thing ever in all this swollen
world of things.
Say it's a dream,
say it's night, then comes morning,

An express train speeding to Rome!
Or Granada? I won't even know,
throwing off Mont Blancs
and Himalayas of blankets.

We are deep in a dark wood.
I warm you with my blood.
Listen to me as I lean against you!
Surely this is far more true

Than poetry. Are you warm through
and through? Tomorrow who'll warm you?
Say it's delirium! Tell me
there's no last bridge, will be

No end—

        . . . this is the end.

. . . here? His gesture is divine,
child-like. . . . no. I don't let go.
. . . only a little further, just
for the last time?

IX

—Past factory workshops, empty
and echoing—if only we called.
Here is a secret deeper than language:
wives keep it from husbands and widows

From their friends. It's for you.
The sinewy secret of maw and vent.
I am only an animal
someone has hurt in the gut.

It burns! You've stripped off my soul
with my skin. It escaped like steam
through some slit—absurd, notorious,
the heresy they call soul.

Pale Christian cancer,
only mist! Medicine that!
And it never existed, ever.
There was a body, it wanted to live.

Now it doesn't.

Forgive me! I didn't mean that.
My gutted insides cried. Condemned
prisoners must wait like this
to be shot in the morning,

Playing chess, their ironic glances
teasing the corridor's eye.

We are all chess pawns
and someone plays us, I

Wonder who? Kind gods? Or thieves?
A round eye looms
in the peephole. The red corridor
clangs. A slab slides.

The last cigarette: harsh.
Spit, it's over now, spit.
These chessboard paths
lead straight to a ditch

Full of blood. The secret eye
of a round dormer moon.
And I glance to the side:
. . . you seem already gone.

XI

To lose it all at once—
nothing neater.
Suburbs, the edge of town.
Here end our days

Our happiness (read: hatefulness)
days and the houses and us.

Emptied summer cottages. Like someone's
aging mother. I respect them.
I mean it's an *action*, emptying:
something hollow can't be emptied out.

(Empty a cottage bit by bit—
better burn it down!)

Only you mustn't flinch
when you reach the quick.
The edge of town, the edge of town,
a rip along a seam.

For—no more splendid
superfluous words—love is a seam.

A seam, not a sling, a seam, not a shield
(Oh, don't ask to be shielded!),
A seam—dead people are sewn to the ground
and I am sewn to you.

(Time will show what the seam was like:
a simple stitch or tripled.)

Cut as you like, my dear, you must tear
on a seam. Wave the pieces in the air!
It's good at least that you tore,
didn't just let it unravel,

That the broken basting shows a live red
vein, not something rotting away.

He cannot lose
who will only tear.
Suburbs, the edge of town:
divorce either way.

Suburbs put people to death
nowadays. A cold wind in the brain.

He cannot lose who leaves
at break of day.
I have stitched you a life together by night
out of whole cloth, never a fitting.

So don't reproach me. It just doesn't fit.
The edge of town: a rip along a seam.

Unfinished souls
seamed with scars.
Suburbs, the edge of town . . .
Violent is the sweep

Of suburbs. Can you hear the boot
of fate in this slippery clay?
Judge my quick hand, dear,
and the live tenacious thread,

However much it slips away.
The last streetlight.

Here? It's like conspiracy:
a furtive glance. The shifty eyes
of lower beings . . . couldn't we climb the hill?
For the last time?

XII

Rain. A heavy mane
in our eyes. Hills.
We have passed the suburbs,
we are out of town.

The town is there, but not
for us: only a stepmother.
There's nowhere further to go.
This is the end of the road.

A field. A fence.
Brother and sister we stand.
Life is a suburb,
build out of town.

Oh, it's a lost
cause, gentlemen,
it's suburbs everywhere.
Whatever became of the town?

The rain tears and rages.
We stand and tear apart.
In the last three months
this is all we've shared.

God even wanted
to borrow from Job.
It didn't work.
We're out of town.

Out of town. Understand?
Outside! Beyond the walls.
Life is a place where no one
can live: a Jewish quarter.

It's a hundred times better
being the Wandering Jew.
For all but reptiles
life is a Jewish

Pogrom. Only converts survive,
Judases of all faiths.
Go live in leper colonies,
in hell. Anywhere. Only leave

Life. Life wants converts
only, sheep for butchers.
I trample on my right-to-life
certificate.

Vengeance for the Star of David!
For jumbles of bodies!
Isn't it entrancing that the Jews
simply didn't want to live?

This ghetto of the Elect. A wall,
a ditch. Expect no mercy.
In this most Christian of worlds
all poets are Jews.

Paul Schmidt

Olga Berggolts

Olga Berggolts (1910–).   Born in Leningrad where she lived through Stalin's purges in the thirties, Berggolts was jailed for two years, her husband executed. Her second husband died of hunger during the German blockade of Leningrad in 1942. Her poems reflect war, love, suffering—all poignantly described. Her *Leningrad Notebook* is her most famous work.

To Song

Wake as you will, but wake in me,—
in the cold, in the voiceless depths of me.

I will not beg for words, but give
me a sign that you are still alive.

Not for long—just a moment of your time.
If not a verse, just a sigh, just a cry.

Just a whisper or just a moan.
Just the muffled clink of your chains.

Daniel Weissbort

Infidelity

Not waking, in my dreams, my dreams,
I saw you—you were alive.
You had endured all and come to me,
crossing the last frontier.

You were earth already, ashes, you
were my glory, my punishment.
But, in spite of life,
                              of death,
you rose from your thousand
                                        graves.

You passed through war hell, concentration camp,
through furnace, drunk with the flames,

through your own death you entered Leningrad,
came out of love for me.

You found my house, but I live now
not in our house, in another;
and a new husband shares my waking hours . . .
O how could you not have known?!

Like the master of the house, proudly you crossed
the threshold, stood there lovingly.
And I murmured: "God will rise again,"
and made the sign of the cross
over you—the unbeliever's cross, the cross
of despair, as black as pitch,
the cross that was made over each house
that winter, that winter in which

you died.
                 O my friend, forgive me
as I sigh. How long have I not known
where waking ends and the dream begins . . .

Daniel Weissbort

To My Sister

I dreamt of the old house
where I spent my childhood years,
and the heart, as before, finds
comfort, and love, and warmth.

I dreamt of Christmas, the tree,
and my sister laughing out loud,
from morning, the rosy windows
sparkle tenderly.

And in the evening gifts are given
and the pine needles smell of stories,

And golden stars risen
are scattered like cinder above the rooftop.

I know that our old house
is falling into disrepair.
Bare, despondent branches
knock against darkening panes.

And in the room with its old furniture,
a resentful captive, cooped up,
lives our father, lonely and weary—
he feels abandoned by us.

Why, oh why do I dream of the country
where the love's all consumed, all?
Maria, my friend, my sister,
speak my name, call to me, call . . .

Daniel Weissbort

Natalya Gorbanyevskaya

Natalya Gorbanyevskaya (1936–).   A 1964 graduate of Leningrad University, Gorbanyevskaya has worked as a technical editor and a translator. Only nine of her poems have appeared in authorized Soviet journals, although her poems have circulated privately and have been published abroad in many languages. She was one of the demonstrators in Red Square protesting against the Russian invasion of Czechoslovakia, but because of her infant child she was not tried with the other dissenters. In 1969 Gorbanyevskaya was arrested; in 1970 she was declared to be suffering from schizophrenia and placed in a Moscow insane asylum where she was given drug treatments. After various protests on her behalf, she was released in 1972.

This world
is amazingly flat.
The other—
nailed up airtight.
Not even a crack in the boards is left.
We've tried. We are masters.

Two
dimensions in this world.

But to me
three aren't enough.

I beat my head on the door
to break into the universe,
but find myself in someone's apartment.

Better to be a petty thief
than be shut in my own four walls
with no window.

I want to get out, to go into the "real world."

But the "real world"
is this theater.

The movie's running on the wide screen,
hopelessly flat, like fine linen.
You know how everything will turn out—
right on time, a boring ceremony.

These peaceful dreams
aren't ours.
We want what is strange—
for example, depth.

Depth.
Tell me—
what is it?
An ocean?
or maybe
someone's soul?
Everyone knows the human soul is a darkness.

So take your old knapsack,
let's go anywhere

to see
if we can't find a hole in the fence,
to look
for a world we didn't lose.

To bring up
out of the rotten wells
fragments of skylight,
dull clouds,
nothing spectacular.

Leave drama to talented movie stars.

Unfortunately,
we don't believe in it.

Barbara Einzig

And there is nothing at all—neither fear,
nor a stiffening before the executioner.
I lay my head upon the hollowed block,
as on a casual lover's shoulder.

Roll, curly head, over the planed boards,
mind you don't get a splinter in your parted lips—
the boards bruise your temples, the trumpets
sound solemnly in your ears;

the polished copper dazzles you,
the horses' manes toss—
O, what a day to die on!

Another day dawns sunless,

and in the semidark—either
through sleepiness, some ancient madness,
or new apocrypha—my lover's shoulder
still smells to me of pine shavings.

Daniel Weissbort

Not because of you, not because of me, just that
the earth was fire underfoot.

Not because of me, not because of you, just that
the summer, embracing both of us together,
put me so close to you
there could be no escape.

Yesterday's heat ebbed from the iron roofs
and by morning the close atmosphere was dissipated
but, from three windows, the fire rising
over the sleeping street did not abate.

At parting, tears did not flow
from a single scorched eye-socket,
and since then, like a naked torch,
I have been steeped in pitch.

Daniel Weissbort

Here, as in a painting, yellow noon burns,
like grief, the air itself is incorporeal,
and in the utter silence, a winged army,
the crows in Crow Park hover.

But the mouldering leaves of years past
cling to my elbows, to the palms
of my hands that reek of cigarettes,
and the bare shrubbery claws my tangled curls.

I have wandered so far from home,
like a plane from its aerodrome,
which in dense fog strays into the dark . . .
Am I living, dead, leaves or grass?

Daniel Weissbort

To I. Lavrentevaya

The train's french horn sighs, sheds a few tears,
an unattainable myth.
A match gleam trickles through the prison bars,
the whole world is eclipsed.

The horn takes wing, into the night it sweeps.
To flick through tracks
like notes. Oh how am I to reach you,
rainy platform!

Forsaken, sleepless, deserted,
deserted without me—
tatters of clouds like letters drift down
to your concrete,

and leaving a trail across the puddles
of stops, hooks, tails,
like treble clefs they resound after
the departed train.

13th July–10th September 1970
Butyrka Prison

Daniel Weissbort

Bella Akhmadulina

Bella Akhmadulina (1937–).   Born in Moscow of Tartar and Italian descent, Akhmadulina attended the Gorky Institute of Literature, from which she was expelled. She married the Poet Yevgeny Yevtushenko, from whom she was later divorced. She then was married to the short-story writer Yuri Nagibin, and more recently to Gennadi Mamlin, the children's writer. Her first collection of poems, *String* (1962), was strongly influenced by Akhmatova and was criticized by the government as "superfluous and too intimate." Although she was able to publish in magazines and almanacs, it was not until 1969 that her second volume, *Music Lessons,* appeared. She was not permitted to join the Writer's Union as a poet, but finally qualified as a translator and thereafter translated extensively from Georgian. Her long poem, "A Fairy Tale about the Rain," published in

Literary Georgia, is considered her most important work. A formal poet, she has all the freshness of daring free verse. In recent years, if she has moved closer to a Russian mentor it is to Marina Tsvetayeva. Yevtushenko says of her, "Bella Akhmadulina wants to tear away the garments of decorum from everything, to tear away everything from her own soul and place it, fearlessly naked and contemptuous, right before the slippery gaze of other people."

Silence

Who was it that took away my voice?
The black wound he left in my throat
Can't even cry.

March is at work under the snow
And the birds of my throat are dead,
Their gardens turning into dictionaries.

I beg my lips to sing.
I beg the lips of the snowfall,
Of the cliff and the bush to sing.

Between my lips, the round shape
Of the air in my mouth.
Because I can say nothing.

I'll try anything
For the trees in the snow.
I breathe. I swing my arms. I lie.

From this sudden silence,
Like death, that loved
The names of all words,
You raise me now in song.

Daniel Halpern

Goodbye

And in conclusion I'll say—
goodbye. Don't commit yourself to love.
I'm breaking down. Or going up
to a high degree of madness.

How did you love?—you tasted
disasters. That's not the question.
How did you love?—you ruined,
but you ruined so clumsily.

The cruelty of a mistake, oh, for
you there's no forgiveness. My body's alive,
and wanders, sees the world,
but everything's gone out of me.

My head still manages a little work.
But my hands fall slack,
and in a flock, obliquely,
my senses leave me.

Barbara Einzig

Autumn

Not working, not breathing,
the beehive sweetens and dies.
The autumn deepens, the soul
ripens and grows round;

drawn into the turning color of fruit,
cast out of the idle blossoms.
Work is long and dull in autumn,
the word is heavy.

More and more heavily, day by day,
nature weighs down the mind.

A laziness like wisdom
overshadows the mouth with silence.

Even a child, riding along,
cycling into white shafts of light,
suddenly will look up
with a pale, clear sadness.

Barbara Einzig

Winter

O, winter, your gesture,
cold and diligent.
Yes, in you an element
of delicate medicine.

How else could the trusting sickness,
out of darkness and anguish,
toward you suddenly
turn its hand?

O, dear one, be magical.
Touch my forehead again
with your healing kiss,
chill flake of snow.

A temptation, always stronger—
to confront deception with trust,
to look dogs in the eye,
to press my body against trees.

To be equal to a winter day
with its empty oval,
always to be within
its slightness of curve.

To reduce myself to nothing,
that I might call into being

not my shadow, but light,
direct, not blocked by me.

Barbara Einzig

Words Spoken by Pasternak during a Bombing*

In that ancient time—in eternity—
What was I then a cloud, a star?
Not wakened yet by love,
A mountain stone, clear like water?

Brought from eternity by desire
I was torn from the dark, I was born.
Now a man, I am a singing cupola,
Rounded and mysterious as a hull.

I have experience now, adept in the arts.
That day I cried out: Oh earth!
Give me shade, the smallest bush
Which will forgive and protect me!

There in the sky, implacably shines
The bombsight, so that I
May taste the helplessness of a dot,
Created by an avid perpendicular.

I am to my knees in doom, to my waist;
I struggle in quicksand, out of breath.
Oh, insane schoolboy, awake!
Do not draw this fateful line!

I am a man, and a precious nugget
Lies in my soul. Yet, I do not wish to gleam,
To glow—I am a mountain stone,
Soft and worn, and want to be invisible!

* This is based on an episode related by Pasternak in his wartime reminiscences.

The even roaring faded;
The bush exhaled and grew, and I breathed
Under it. The pitiless modern angel
Winged away, despising my insignificance.

Into this world of fresh smells,
Where things turn gold with light,
Where they sing and sparkle, I carried my body,
That intimate and fragile thing.

I cried, feeling close to all living things,
Sighing, pulsating, alive.
O my prayer, lowly yet so high,
I repeat your tender whisper.

Death, I have seen your blank,
Lonely features, I carried myself
Away from them like a strange child
Who vaguely resembled me.

I am not praying for my longevity!
But, as at that hour in gray silence,
For some human and flamelike unfolding
Which accidentally inhabited me.

It survived, and over the water
I stood for a long, long time, tired.
I wanted to be a cloud, a star,
A mountain stone—clear, like water.

Jean Valentine and Olga Carlisle

Small Aircraft

As if I didn't have enough
Bothering me, now I'm confused
By dreaming nightly
Of small airplanes. I don't understand it.

The planes don't care that I dream of them:
Now like chickens they peck seed
From my hand. Now like termites
They live in the walls of my house.

Or else they poke me
With their dumb noses: little fish
Move like this to a child's foot,
Tickling, making their feet laugh.

Sometimes they push and bump each other
Around my fire, blinded by the light.
They won't let me read and the noise
Of their wings excites me.

They have another trick: they come
To me like children in tears
And sit in my lap,
Crying, *Take us in your arms*.

You can drive them away, but they're right back,
Flying out of the polished darkness,
Looking from their eyes like sad dachshunds
As their long bodies float by.

Daniel Halpern

At Night

How can I call out? How can I shout?
In silence everything is fragile as glass.
Having laid its head on the receiver,
the telephone sleeps soundly.

I'll walk across the sleeping city
through a snowy side street.
I'll go up to your window,
quietly and tenderly.

I'll protect you from the street sounds
with the palms of my hands,
the streets ringing with drops of melting snow.
I'll put out the lamps to keep your eyes in sleep.
I'll command the spring to put the nightsounds in order.

So, what kind of person are you in sleep!
Your arms have grown so weak
Fatigue is concealed in the wrinkles of your eyes—
tomorrow I'll kiss them so no trace remains.

I'll watch over your sleep till dawn,
then leave in the clean snowy morning,
forgetting about my tracks in the snow,
through the dry leaves of last autumn.

Daniel Halpern with Albert Todd

The Sound of Rain

The sound of rain like a lute—
such strumming on the roof!
To the pedestrian in the Square of Arising
I say, *Be very kind!*

I tell a boy, *Be wild!*
Leaning to his curly head
I say, *Loosen the string,*
Free the green balloons!

On the street where the public chatters
I come upon a white dog—
with a compassionate look
the dog fixes me in its gaze.

And in a store I discover a miser
in the paleness of a face.
He admires a bottle of cologne,
but the price tag has him sweating.

I say to him, *Don't be a pig, cure yourself,*
Buy something expensive
and take it to someone you love.

But I'm not very successful.
Among the boys and girls,
the grownups who look like me,
an ice-cream cart rolls in.

And so, I walk at sunrise.
I notice the long shadows.
I notice the surprise
of people who look at me as I pass.

Daniel Halpern with Albert Todd

Sleepwalkers

The moon rises, a vengeance on anguish,
on my own arrogant privacy.
The hands of sleepwalkers,
of their own accord, rise, follow.

The ponderability of daily fatigue—
on wings consciousness runs wild,
transparent creations are flying,
they've heard the reflection of the moon.

It flickers cold, stingy,
not promising anything,
draws out of me distant art,
demands my agreement.

Can the torture and charm of its omens
be fought down, overcome,
can I make out of moonlight
a heavy, tangible object?

Barbara Einzig

The Names of Georgian Women

There on the sea sails wandered,
And unconcerned by the heat
Sycamores blossomed at leisure,
Leaves for streets in December.

The market sounds intermingled;
On naked heights above
Basalt and snow wove light
Into rainbow prisms.

A kiosk in the park by the seaside
Stood empty and white and silent;
The syllabled names of Georgian women
Seemed to smell of grapes;

They became a chirruping
Breezing out to sea,
Sailing out like a black swan
Strangely reaching his neck.

Then a woman called Lamara
Ran down to the water
Where she broke her heel on the pebbles
Tinting her lips with wine.

Medea's hair was dark and wet;
Arms wove the waterfall;
Drying, drops on skin turned golden,
Sparkling at odd moments.

Stronger even than oleanders
Embraced into a cluster,
The name of Ariadne floated
And dissolved upon the skyline.

Swaying and barely touching the shoreline
A float poised on the water—
Tisana! called a voice from a window—
Natella! a voice answered.

Stanley Noyes and Olga Carlisle

In the Emptied Rest Home

To fall, like an apple, no mind,
no memory! To lie
on the soft ground, blank as an apple,
to not feel this body.

An apple: muscles of moisture,
veins of color, all sorts of changes
crowding each other out.
The apple doesn't care.

Hopeless to care here,
it's war, whole gangs of orphans
run wild with real guns and knives,
and the water's rising.

And it's boring. I'm tired of looking at it
both ways, doctor and patient.
The same crackling heart, the same
tickling run of the molecules.

I'm ready to turn away,
but I don't turn away: I half stay,
the way you half listen to someone
whistling in the next apartment.

Solitude, distance. The snow keeps on rising
up on the roof. I'm too much alone,
it's as if there were two of us here,
the air in my lungs, the beat in my blood.

But my eyes can still see, my voice
squeaks, my pulse beats like a moth
in my closed hand: oh, thank God, my body,
little child, little mouse! Thank God

there's something alive in this house!
In the dead of winter, alone,
go on with your simple life, the life
of the black woods, the vegetable gardens, the sun.

Jean Valentine and Olga Carlisle

A Dream

It's all familiar,
the fall air, clear and sober,
the little house, the door half open,
the salty taste of our apples,

but a stranger is raking the garden.
He says he is the rightful owner now,
and asks me in. The brick floor, the blank
where the clock stood, that slant of light,

my rushed, uncertain steps,
my eyes that saw, and saw nothing,
your tender voices . . . but the gardener's wife
is standing there waiting.

"It's so foggy here! I lived here too, once,
a hundred years ago . . .
it's all the same, that same
smoky smell over the garden,

the dog's fur still wet on my fingers . . ."
"You don't say," the gardener answers,
cocking his head, coming closer.
Then he smiles, and asks,

"Isn't it you, though, that picture
up in the attic? Isn't it her,
with the long, old-fashioned curls?
But your eyes have changed

since those terrible old days
a hundred years ago,
when you died, alone in the house here,
poor, without work or friends."

Jean Valentine and Olga Carlisle

The Bride

Oh to be a bride
Brilliant in my curls
Under the white canopy
Of a modest veil!

How my hands tremble
Bound by my icy rings!
The glasses gather, brimming
With red compliments.

At last the world says yes;
It wishes me roses and sons.
My friends stand shyly at the door,
Carrying love gifts.

Chemises in cellophane,
Plates, flowers, lace . . .
They kiss my cheeks, they marvel
I'm to be a wife.

Soon my white gown
Is stained with wine like blood;
I feel both lucky and poor
As I sit, listening, at the table.

Terror and desire
Loom in the forward hours.
My mother, the darling, weeps—
Mama is like the weather.

. . . My rich, royal attire
I lay aside on the bed.
I find I am afraid
To look at you, to kiss you.

Loudly the chairs are set
Against the wall, eternity . . .
My love, what more can happen
To you and to me?

Stephen Stepanchev

Native American Languages

One of the major losses in the history of the Americas is the disappearance of virtually all written pre-Columbian literature. Unlike the sculptures and temples which were often saved by their obscure burial under sand or in a remote forest, few of the codices in Nahuatl (the language of the Aztecs) or Maya escaped the fire of the early *conquistadores* or the insistence of centuries of neglect. What has survived is largely oral poetry, recorded by early priests and more recently by scholars who have discovered ancient poems which still exist among the Nahuatl-speaking Indians of Mexico and the Quechuan Indians of Peru and Bolivia. In what is now the United States, the North American Indians did not evidently have an ancient script. Their oral tradition, however, preseved many poems which in recent years have been transcribed and translated. Among the most extraordinary artists of the Americas are the Eskimos. Their traditional design drawings and sculpture have the geometric purity of Cycladic art or Henry Moore. Similarly, their poems have a primordial power and clarity. Armand Schwerner's reexpressions of Hawaiian poetry are based on the transcriptions of anthropologists.

NAHUATL (AZTEC)

Anonymous

Poem to Ease Birth

in the house with the tortoise chair
    she will give birth to the pearl
        to the beautiful feather

in the house of the goddess who sits on a tortoise
    she will give birth to the necklace of pearls
        to the beautiful feathers we are

there she sits on the tortoise
   swelling to give us birth

on your way on your way
   child be on your way to me here
        you whom I made new

come here child   come be pearl
          be beautiful feather

               Anselm Hollo

QUECHUA (PERU)

Anonymous

My spouse, Chunaychunay,
Sweetly you carry me.

And what you say to me is sweet.
You, Wichiri,
Your cruel father
Stole from my mother
Her horses and saddled mules.

You wander by the river
With a blazing club
Abusing me because I am an orphan.
In the midst of many
Rags I sleep.
I live among miseries.

For your sake I will go.
Thus I sleep, I sleep.
Your net catches two abreast,
Rain, giver of water.

Oh Chunaychunay, brotherly heart,
Portion of the great feast
Which now will never return.
Do nothing to me, Putti,
For today my heart was brought to tears.

W. S. Merwin

PAMPA

Anonymous

When I was a good and quick little girl
they treated me like a treasure

oh heart!

Many suns and many moons I saw
time passes

oh heart!

How I have changed. I am not a girl now
I am very old

oh heart!

What is the use of grieving
if nobody will listen

oh heart!

W. S. Merwin

CHIPPEWA

Anonymous

Chippewa Love Song

A loon? No.
It was my lover's
splashing oar.

Why should I
be jealous?

Or weep?
I'm not going to die.

When I think of him,
I hurt.

Darling,
I've been waiting
long
for you to come.

               WB, adapted from Frances Desmore

APACHE

Anonymous

Puberty Rite Dance Song (Traditional)

I come
to the White Painted Woman.
I come
through her long life.

I come
through her blessing.
I come
through her good life.
I come through all her fruits.

Through the long life she gives
I come to her.

Through her holy truth
she goes about.

WB

PAPAGO

Anonymous

Owl Woman's Death Song

In the great night my heart will go out,
Toward me the darkness comes rattling.
In the great night my heart will go out.

Ruth Underhill

I'd run about
on the desert
me a young girl fierce to see
whatever I could. My heart
was not cool.

When there was no Coyote
I saw Coyote

then a spider
on the house-post, the central one,

stopped to look at me, just
ready to speak.
I made a song, about Coyote.
A shaman sang over me, to find out.
And when he spoke father said—No
one shaman in the house is enough—
my body already sheltered
the divining crystals, growing in my body.
The shaman bent over me he sucked them one by one
out of my breast
                    they were long
like the joint of my pinkie, white and moving like worms
o the shaman said See I've taken them out
before they got big
                    He made a hole in a giant cactus
and put them away, inside

                              Ruth Underhill

HAWAIIAN

Anonymous

Dirge

I make this dirge for you Miss Mary Binning I miss you
o my daughter the wind of Na'alehu used to scatter dust in our
       house
o my daughter at the Lau-hu cliff
I'm crying for missing you and let it be; I love you I see us
o my daughter at the cold Ka-puna spring our water, in the rain
that the Ha'ao hill undergoes
up the trail almost nobody knew, us alone o my daughter
I'm missing you my life turns
a shade greyer forever
it's over now, you on your road endlessly who used to shine so my
       darling,

now in the one direction, away, me still in these places,
on a walk, up a hill, next to the spring dampening me, bent
from this stone yearning

                  o precious
as pearls, in Waikapuna the sun warmed you I didn't know you
from the flowers

                                    Armand Schwerner

ESKIMO

Anonymous

Far inland
go my sad thoughts.
It is too much
never to leave this bench.
I want to wander
far inland.

I remember
hunting animals,
the good food.
It is too much
never to leave this bench.
I want to wander
far inland.

I hunted
like men. I carried
weapons, shot reindeer,
bull, cow, and calf,
killed them with my arrows
one evening
when almost winter

twilight fell
far inland.

I remember
how I struggled
inland
under the dropping sky
of snow.
The earth is white
far inland.

WB, adapted from Knud Rasmussen

Song of the Old Woman

all those heads those ears those eyes
around me
how long will the ears hear me?
and those eyes so long
will they look at me?
when those ears won't hear me anymore
when those eyes turn aside from my eyes
I'll eat no more raw liver with fat
and those eyes won't see me anymore
and my hair my hair will have disappeared

Armand Schwerner, adapted from Paul Emile Victor

Papuan

NEW GUINEA

These traditional women's songs from tribes of Papua New Guinea were translated by the Australian linguist Don Laycock and by students of the University of Papua and New Guinea, all under the direction of the folklorist Ulli Beier. They appear in a collection edited by Beier, *Words of Paradise: Poetry of Papua New Guinea.*

Buin Tribe

Lament for a Husband

O my hornbill husband, you have a bad smell,
and when Kaaeko comes and smells you
he will take you to Panirai, and your spirit
   will enter a pig.
He'll make you like a curly-tailed pig,
and at dawn you will cry for food.
You will sing out for yams,
the food of the living.

Don Laycock

Elema Tribe

Oh moon, oh moon!
Who is your mother?
White crescent!
If she frowns at you
bad harvest befalls you.
If she does not—
your mouth will be full.
She gave me charms
for women of any age.
She gave me these two secrets—
but don't ask why.

Mari Marase

Boiken Tribe

Song for a Girl on Her First Menstruation

Hold, hold it tight,
grasp the black crayfish,

hold, hold it tight.
Grab the white eel,
Sisirik, Miampa lumbo
grasp the black crayfish
Kayame Parilumpo
kill the white eel.

Joe Prentuo

Welsh

Gwerfyl Mechain

Gwerfyl Mechain (ca. 1460–1500).   Very little is known of the life of Gwerfyl
Mechain, other than what may be surmised from her texts.

In the Snowfall

Tiny snow of the stunningly cold black day
is white flour,
is flesh of the earth,
cold lamb fleece on the mountain
a platter and awful-tasting cold feathers.
Tiny snow is softness dropped to trick
and overwhelm me.

Snow on the ice hill is blinding my eyes,
soaking my clothes, my skin.
O God! Bless God!
I had no hope of getting home.

WB

Lady of the Ferry Inn

Who am I? I am a lady faithful to the ways
of the Ferry Inn.
I run a tavern and cheat no one.
The moon in its robes of snow clouds
welcomes you
and your silver coins.

Before the men who drink here, I offer
a perfect world.
I want nothing more.
I walk among men, faultlessly,
sing intimate songs
and pour the mead.

WB

Anglo-Saxon

Anonymous Woman

"Wulf and Eadwacer" (ca. 800).   This anonymous poem is the earliest extant
Anglo-Saxon women's song. Written in the Late West Saxon dialect in the Exeter Book
manuscript, this poem continually baffled scholars trying to locate its setting. Perhaps
taken from an incident in the *Volsungasaga* or other Germanic legends, or from the
Viking tales mentioned in the *Jomsvikingasaga,* the lament of this desolate, unknown
woman, with its brutal realism and unsentimental pathos, is an awesome beginning to the
history of English language women's poetry.

Wulf and Eadwacer

His being gone is a gift to my people.
They will destroy him if he comes near,
but I welcomed him.

Wulf is on one island, I on another.
The island is safe, surrounded by fens.
Angry warriors are on that island.
They will destroy him if he comes near,
but I welcomed him.

I wait despairing while my Wulf wanders.
When it rained, I sat and cried.
When the brave man hugged me,
I was happy, it was loathsome.

Wulf, my Wulf, waiting for you,
for your seldom coming has made me sick.
I'm not starving but my mind is hungry

Eadwacer, do you hear? A wolf carries off
our wretched whelp to the woods.

What was never bound is easily broken:
our song together.

WB and Elene Kolb

Anonymous Woman

"The Wife's Lament" (ca. 900).   Like "Wulf and Eadwacer," "The Wife's Lament" is an anonymous woman's song written in the Late West Saxon dialect and found in the Exeter Book manuscript. Sometimes thought to be the companion piece to "The Husband's Message," another poem in the same manuscript, "The Wife's Lament" is a brilliant example not only of a woman's song but also of exile songs that were so prevalent in early medieval poetry. "The Wife's Lament," along with "The Wanderer" and "The Seafarer" in Anglo-Saxon, and numerous German exile laments, is a poignant, lyrical portrait of isolation and solitude.

The Wife's Lament

I make this song sadly about myself,
about my life. I a woman say
I've been unhappy since I grew up,
yet no old pain like now
for now I know dark exile.
First my lord left his people,
went over the rolling waves. I had dawn sorrow,
wondering in what land my lord was.
Then I went out into friendless exile
to remedy my grief. Then men
of my husband's tribe began to plot
secretly to drive us apart,
hugely far in the world's kingdom.
I lived loathsomely with longing.
My lord commanded me to take a hut here
in a land where I have few friends,
few good friends, so my mind is sad.
When will I find the man matched to me,
wretched, sad-minded,
hiding his mood, thinking of murder?
Before, we were happy and swore
that only death could rip us apart,

nothing else. But this is turned round,
as if our friendship
never was. Far and near I must
suffer my love's anger.
That man drove me out to live in the woods
under an oak tree, in a cave.
This cave is old, I despair.
The valleys are dim, the dunes tall,
the village overgrown with bitter thorns,
and joyless houses. Often my lord's wrathful
going seizes me. There are friends on earth
living in love, lying in bed,
while I go alone at dawn
under the oak, through the cave.
There I must sit each long summer day,
weeping abundantly over my exile
and troubles. So I can't rest
from my worried mind, nor the longings
which hold me for life.
May that man always have darkness
in his heart. He will seem
happy, but his chest will ache,
a throng of sorrow. Let him find joy
off by himself. Let him be banished
on a far land. My love sits
under a stone slope rimed with storms,
a lord weary in mind, soaked with water
in a dreary room. My lord endures
much mind-sadness. Often he remembers
a joyful floor. Grief for them
who wait longing for love.

WB and Elene Kolb

English

ENGLAND, UNITED STATES,
CANADA, AUSTRALIA

Mary Sidney Herbert, Countess of Pembroke

Mary Sidney Herbert, Countess of Pembroke (1561–1621).   The daughter of Sir
Henry Sidney, lord deputy of Ireland, and Lady Sidney, sister to the earl of Leicester,
Herbert's father was one of King Edward's principal gentlemen of the privy chamber.
Her brother was Sir Philip Sidney. She was educated by tutors. At the age of sixteen
she became the countess of Pembroke. A patron of the arts, she entertained a literary
circle whose members included Thomas Kyd, Samuel Daniel, and, perhaps, Shake-
speare. She edited and published Sir Philip Sidney's *Arcadia*. Although she was
overshadowed by her brother, she was well known and respected as a poet.

Psalm 58: Si Vere Utique

And call ye this to utter what is just,
   You that of justice hold the sov'reign throne?
And call ye this to yield, O sons of dust,
   To wronged brethren ev'ry man his own?
O no: it is your long malicious will
   Now to the world to make by practice known,
With whose oppression you the balance fill,
   Just to your selves, indiff'rent else to none.

But what could they, who ev'n in birth declined,
· From truth and right to lies and injuries?
To show the venom of their cank'red mind
   The adder's image scarcely can suffice;

Nay scarce the aspic may with them contend,
    On whom the charmer all in vain applies
His skillfull'st spells: aye missing of his end,
    While she self-deaf, and unaffected lies.

Lord crack their teeth, Lord crush these lion's jaws,
    So let them sink as water in the sand:
When deadly bow their aiming fury draws,
    Shiver the shaft ere past the shooter's hand.
So make them melt as the dishoused snail
    Or as the Embryo, whose vital band
Breaks ere it holds, and formless eyes do fail
    To see the sun, though brought to lightful land.

O let their brood, a brood of springing thorns,
    Be by untimely rooting overthrown
Ere bushes waxed, they push with pricking horns,
    As fruits yet green are oft by tempest blown.
The good with gladness this revenge shall see,
    And bathe his feet in blood of wicked one
While all shall say: the just rewarded be,
    There is a God that carves to each his own.

Emilia Lanier

Emilia Lanier (1569–1645).   Born Emilia Bassano, Lanier was the illegitimate daughter of Baptista Bassano, musician to the Queen, and Margaret Johnson. Although her father died when she was young, she evidently received an extensive education. In his recent book, *The Poems of Shakespeare's Dark Lady,* A. L. Rowse demonstrates that Sonnets 127 through 152, those to the so-called Dark Lady, were addressed to Emilia, who was then married to Alphonso Lanier, also a musician to the Queen. Emilia Lanier was offended by Shakespeare's depiction of her in the sonnets. As an accomplished poet, her long work *Salve Deus Rex Judaeorum* (1611) is a dexterous work of historical and biblical events in which she reveals and argues the virtue of Eve, Deborah, Judith, Esther, Susanna, as well as Cleopatra with whom she had full sympathy. Her work, recognized only now with the publication of Rowse's edition of her collected poems, is compelling both artistically and for its original, independent, and lucid thought.

Eves Apologie

Till now your indiscretion sets us free
And makes our former fault much less appeare;
Our Mother *Eve*, who tasted of the Tree,
Giving to *Adam* what shee held most deare,
Was simply good, and had no powre to see,
The after-comming harme did not appeare:
      The subtile Serpent that our Sex betraide,
      Before our fall so sure a plot had laide.

That undiscerning Ignorance perceav'd
No guile, or craft that was by him intended;
For had she knowne, of what we were bereav'd,
To his request she had not condiscended.
But she (poore soule) by cunning was deceav'd,
No hurt therein her harmelesse Heart intended:
      For she alleadg'd Gods word, which he denies,
      That they should die, but even as Gods, be wise.

But surely *Adam* can not be excusde,
Her fault though great, yet hee was most too blame;
What Weaknesse offered, Strength might have refusde,
Being Lord of all, the greater was his shame:
Although the Serpents craft had her abusde,
Gods holy word ought all his actions frame,
      For he was Lord and King of all the earth,
      Before poore *Eve* had either life or breath.

Who being fram'd by Gods eternall hand,
The perfect'st man that ever breath'd on earth;
And from Gods mouth receiv'd that strait command,
The breach whereof he knew was present death:
Yea having powre to rule both Sea and Land,
Yet with one Apple wonne to loose that breath
      Which God had breathed in his beauteous face,
      Bringing us all in danger and disgrace.

And then to lay the fault on Patience backe,
That we (poore women) must endure it all;

We know right well he did discretion lacke,
Beeing not perswaded thereunto at all;
If *Eve* did erre, it was for knowledge sake,
The fruit being faire perswaded him to fall:
    No subtill Serpents falshood did betray him,
    If he would eate it, who had powre to stay him?

Not *Eve,* whose fault was onely too much love,
Which made her give this present to her Deare,
That what shee tasted, he likewise might prove,
Whereby his knowledge might become more cleare;
He never sought her weakenesse to reprove,
With those sharpe words, which he of God did heare:
    Yet Men will boast of Knowledge, which he tooke
    From *Eves* fair hand, as from a learned Booke.

If any Evill did in her remaine,
Beeing made of him, he was the ground of all;
If one of many Worlds could lay a staine
Upon our Sexe, and worke so great a fall
To wretched Man, by Satans subtill traine;
What will so fowle a fault amongst you all?
    Her weakenesse did the Serpents words obay,
    But you in malice Gods deare Sonne betray.

Whom, if unjustly you condemne to die,
Her sinne was small, to what you doe commit:
All mortal sinnes that doe for vengeance crie,
Are not to be compared unto it:
If many worlds would altogether trie,
By all their sinnes the wrath of God to get;
    This sinne of yours, surmounts them all as farre
    As doth the Sunne, another little starre.

Then let us have our Libertie againe,
And challendge to your selves no Sov'raigntie;
You came not in the world without our paine,
Make that a barre against your crueltie;
Your fault being greater, why should you disdaine

Our beeing your equals, free from tyranny?
    If one weake woman simply did offend,
        This sinne of yours, hath no excuse, nor end.

Anne Bradstreet

Anne Bradstreet (1612?–1672).   Born in Lincolnshire, England, Anne Bradstreet
arrived on John Winthrop's ship *Arabella* in 1630, a member of one of the founding
families of the Massachussetts Bay Colony. Living in various towns in Massachussetts,
she and her husband Simon Bradstreet (who was to become governor seven years after
Anne's death) settled in the house in North Andover where the last four of her eight
children were born, and the locale of one of her most moving poems, "On the Burning
of Our House," composed in 1666. Bradstreet's poems combine personal detail and
events—the births and deaths of her children, the illnesses from which she constantly
suffered, her relationship with her husband, and her domestic duties—Puritan allegory,
classical mythological allusions, and metaphysical conceit reminiscent of her compatriot
Edward Taylor and of the John Donne of the longer poems. In addition to her role as
the first American poet, Bradstreet's poems and life form the basis for one of America's
finest modern long poems, the fifty-seven stanzas of John Berryman's *Homage to
Mistress Bradstreet* (1956).

The Prologue

I

To sing of wars, of captains, and of kings,
Of cities founded, commonwealths begun,
For my mean pen are too superior things:
Or how they all, or each their dates have run
Let poets and historians set these forth,
My obscure lines shall not so dim their worth.

II

But when my wond'ring eyes and envious heart
Great Bartas' sugared lines do but read o'er,
Fool I do grudge the Muses did not part
'Twixt him and me that overfluent store;
A Bartas can do what a Bartas will
But simple I according to my skill.

III

From schoolboy's tongue no rhet'ric we expect,
Nor yet a sweet consort from broken strings,
Nor perfect beauty where's a main defect:
My foolish, broken, blemished Muse so sings,
And this to mend, alas, no art is able,
'Cause nature made it so irreparable.

IV

Nor can I, like that fluent sweet tongued Greek,
Who lisped at first, in future times speak plain.
By art he gladly found what he did seek,
A full requital of his striving pain.
Art can do much, but this maxim's most sure:
A weak or wounded brain admits no cure.

V

I am obnoxious to each carping tongue
Who says my hand a needle better fits,
A poet's pen all scorn I should thus wrong,
For such despite they cast on female wits:
If what I do prove well, it won't advance,
They'll say it's stol'n, or else it was by chance.

VI

But sure the antique Greeks were far more mild
Else of our sex, why feigned they those nine
And poesy made Calliope's own child;
So 'mongst the rest they placed the arts divine:
But this weak knot they will full soon untie,
The Greeks did nought, but play the fools and lie.

VII

Let Greeks be Greeks, and women what they are
Men have precedency and still excel,
It is but vain unjustly to wage war;
Men can do best, and women know it well.

Preeminence in all and each is yours;
Yet grant some small acknowledgement of ours.

VIII

And oh ye high flown quills that soar the skies,
And ever with your prey still catch your praise,
If e'er you deign these lowly lines your eyes,
Give thyme or parsley wreath, I ask no bays;
This mean and unrefined ore of mine
Will make your glist'ring gold but more to shine.

To My Dear and Loving Husband

If ever two were one, then surely we.
If ever man were loved by wife, then thee;
If ever wife was happy in a man,
Compare with me, ye women, if you can.
I prize thy love more than whole mines of gold
Or all the riches that the East doth hold.
My love is such that rivers cannot quench,
Nor ought but love from thee, give recompense.
Thy love is such I can no way repay,
The heavens reward thee manifold, I pray.
Then while we live, in love let's so persevere
That when we live no more, we may live ever.

Before the Birth of One of Her Children

All things within this fading world hath end,
Adversity doth still our joys attend;
No ties so strong, no friends so dear and sweet,
But with death's parting blow is sure to meet.
The sentence past is most irrevocable,
A common thing, yet oh, inevitable.
How soon, my Dear, death may my steps attend,
How soon't may be thy lot to lose thy friend,
We both are ignorant, yet love bids me
These farewell lines to recommend to thee,

That when that knot's untied that made us one,
I may seem thine, who in effect am none.
And if I see not half my days that's due,
What nature would, God grant to yours and you;
The many faults that well you know I have
Let be interred in my oblivious grave;
If any worth or virtue were in me,
Let that live freshly in thy memory
And when thou feel'st no grief, as I no harms,
Yet love thy dead, who long lay in thine arms.
And when thy loss shall be repaid with gains
Look to my little babes, my dear remains.
And if thou love thyself, or loved'st me,
These O protect from step-dame's injury.
And if chance to thine eyes shall bring this verse,
With some sad sighs honour my absent hearse;
And kiss this paper for thy love's dear sake,
Who with salt tears this last farewell did take.

In Reference to Her Children, 23. June, 1656

I had eight birds hatcht in one nest.
Four Cocks there were, and Hens the rest,
I nurst them up with pain and care,
Nor cost, nor labour did I spare,
Till at the last they felt their wing,
Mounted the Trees, and learn'd to sing;
Chief of the Brood then took his flight,
To Regions far, and left me quite:
My mournful chirps I after send,
Till he return, or I do end,
Leave not thy nest, thy Dam and Sire,
Fly back and sing amidst this Quire.
My second bird did take her flight,
And with her mate flew out of sight;
Southward they both their course did bend,
And Seasons twain they there did spend
Till after blown by *Southern* gales,

They *Norward* steer'd with filled sayles,
A prettier bird was no where seen,
Along the Beach among the treen.
I have a third of colour white,
On whom I plac'd no small delight;
Coupled with mate loving and true,
Hath also bid her Dam adieu:
And where *Aurora* first appears,
She now hath percht, to spend her years;
One to the Academy flew
To chat among that learned crew;
Ambition moves still in his breast
That he might chant above the rest,
Striving for more than to do well,
That nightingales he might excell.
My fifth, whose down is yet scarce gone
Is 'mongst the shrubs and bushes flown,
And as his wings increase in strength,
On higher boughs he'l pearch at length.
My other three, still with me nest,
Untill they'r grown, then as the rest,
Or here or there, they'l take their flight,
As is ordain'd, so shall they light.
If birds could weep, then would my tears
Let others know what are my fears
Lest this my brood some harm should catch,
And be surpriz'd for want of watch,
Whilst pecking corn, and void of care
They fall un'wares in Fowlers snare:
Or whilst on trees they sit and sing,
Some untoward boy at them do fling:
Or whilst allur'd with bell and glass,
The net be spread, and caught, alas.
Or least by Lime-twigs they be foyl'd,
Or by some greedy hawks be spoyl'd.
O would my young, ye saw my breast,
And knew what thoughts there sadly rest,
Great was my pain when I you bred,

Great was my care, when I you fed,
Long did I keep you soft and warm,
And with my wings kept off all harm,
My cares are more, and fears than ever,
My throbs such now, as 'fore were never:
Alas my birds, you wisdome want,
Of perils you are ignorant,
Oft times in grass, on trees, in flight,
Sore accidents on you may light.
O to your safety have an eye,
So happy may you live and die:
Mean while my dayes in tunes Ile spend,
Till my weak layes with me shall end.
In shady woods I'le sit and sing,
And things that past, to mind I'le bring.
Once young and pleasant, as are you,
But former toyes (no joyes) adieu.
My age I will not once lament,
But sing, my time so near is spent.
And from the top bough take my flight,
Into a country beyond sight,
Where old ones, instantly grow young,
And there with Seraphims set song:
No seasons cold, nor storms they see;
But spring lasts to eternity,
When each of you shall in your nest
Among your young ones take your rest,
In chirping language, oft them tell,
You had a Dam that lov'd you well,
That did what could be done for young,
And nurst you up till you were strong,
And 'fore she once would let you fly,
She shew'd you joy and misery;
Taught what was good, and what was ill,
What would save life, and what would kill.
Thus gone, amongst you I may live,
And dead, yet speak, and counsel give:
Farewel my birds, farewel adieu,
I happy am, if well with you.

In Memory of My Dear Grandchild Anne Bradstreet
Who Deceased June 20, 1669,
Being Three Years and Seven Months Old

With troubled heart and trembling hand I write,
The heavens have changed to sorrow my delight.
How oft with disappointment have I met,
When I on fading things my hopes have set?
Experience might 'fore this have made me wise,
To value things according to their price.
Was ever stable joy yet found below?
Or perfect bliss without mixture of woe?
I knew she was but as a withering flower,
That's here today, perhaps gone in an hour;
Like as a bubble, or the brittle glass,
Or like a shadow turning as it was.
More fool then I to look on that was lent
As if mine own, when thus impermanent.
Farewell dear child, thou ne'er shall come to me,
But yet a while, and I shall go to thee;
Mean time my throbbing heart's cheered up with this:
Thou with thy Saviour art in endless bliss.

Here Follows Some Verses upon the Burning of Our House
July 10th, 1666. Copied Out of a Loose Paper

In silent night when rest I took
For sorrow near I did not look
I wakened was with thund'ring noise
And pieteous shrieks of dreadful voice.
That fearful sound of "Fire!" and "Fire!"
Let no man know is my desire.
I, starting up, the light did spy,
And to my God my heart did cry
To strengthen me in my distress
And not to leave me succorless.
Then, coming out, beheld a space
The flame consume my dwelling place.
And when I could no longer look,

I blest His name that gave and took,
That laid my goods now in the dust.
Yea, so it was, and so 'twas just.
It was His own, it was not mine,
Far be it that I should repine;
He might of all justly bereft
But yet sufficient for us left.
When by the ruins oft I past
My sorrowing eyes aside did cast,
And here and there the places spy
Where oft I sat and long did lie:
Here stood that trunk, and there that chest,
There lay that store I counted best.
My pleasant things in ashes lie,
And them behold no more shall I.
Under thy roof no guest shall sit,
Nor at thy table eat a bit.
No pleasant tale shall e'er be told,
Nor things recounted done of old.
No candle e'er shall shine in thee,
No bridegroom's voice e'er heard shall be.
In silence ever shall thou lie,
Adieu, Adieu, all's vanity.
Then straight I 'gin my heart to chide,
And did thy wealth on earth abide?
Didst fix thy hope on mold'ring dust?
The arm of flesh didst make thy trust?
Raise up thy thoughts above the sky
That dunghill mists away may fly.
Thou hast an house on high erect,
Framed by that mighty Architect,
With glory richly furnished,
Stands permanent though this be fled.
It's purchased and paid for too
By Him who hath enough to do.
A price so vast as is unknown
Yet by His gift is made thine own;
There's wealth enough, I need no more,

Farewell, my pelf, farewell my store.
The world no longer let me love,
My hope and treasure lies above.

The Author to Her Book

Thou ill-form'd offspring of my feeble brain,
Who after birth did'st by my side remain,
Till snatcht from thence by friends, less wise than true
Who thee abroad, expos'd to publick view;
Made thee in raggs, halting to th' press to trudg,
Where errors were not lessened (all may judg)
At thy return my blushing was not small,
My rambling brat (in print) should mother call,
I cast thee by as one unfit for light,
Thy Visage was so irksome in my sight;
Yet being mine own, at length affection would
Thy blemishes amend, if so I could:
I wash'd thy face, but more defects I saw,
And rubbing off a spot, still made a flaw.
I stretcht thy joynts to make thee even feet,
Yet still thou run'st more hobling than is meet;
In better dress to trim thee was my mind,
But nought save home-spun Cloth, i'th' house I find.
In this array, 'mongst Vulgars mayst thou roam
In Criticks hands, beware thou dost not come;
And take thy way where yet thou art not known,
If for thy Father askt, say, thou hadst none:
And for thy Mother, she alas is poor,
Which caus'd her thus to send thee out of door.

Katherine Philips

Katherine Philips (1631–1664).   The daughter of a merchant, educated at
boarding school, at seventeen she married a Welshman, referred to as "Antenor" in
her poems. Known as "The Matchless Orinda," she was a successful literary lady who
gained fame when in 1650 she published poems on Henry Vaughan's poems. Vaughan
was in the literary circle the "Society of Friendship" that Orinda established, which

included Abraham Cowley, Jeremy Taylor, and William Cartwright. She was also known as the translator of Corneille's play *Pompée*. She died in a smallpox epidemic.

Against Love

Hence Cupid! with your cheating toys,
Your real griefs, and painted joys,
Your pleasure which itself destroys.
Lovers like men in fevers burn and rave,
And only what will injure them do crave.
Men's weakness makes love so severe,
They give him power by their fear,
And make the shackles which they wear.

Who to another does his heart submit,
Makes his own idol, and then worships it.
Him whose heart is all his own,
Peace and liberty does crown,
He apprehends no killing frown.
He feels no raptures which are joys diseased,
And is not much transported, but still pleased.

Aphra Behn

Aphra Behn (1640–1689).   Born in Kent, the daughter of a barber and a lady's maid, Aphra Behn's early history is unclear; one commentator described it as "obscure and probably improper." It is believed that she spent her childhood in Surinam, Guiana. She returned to England when she was eighteen and married a merchant, who died early in their marriage. When she was twenty-six she went to Antwerp as a spy for Charles II. She was known as "the Incomparable" for her skill in espionage. She fell out of favor, however, possibly over money, and soon afterward was sent to debtors prison. After her release she decided to make money by writing. She was the first woman in history to support herself in this manner. She wrote poems, histories, novels, and seventeen plays, and enjoyed great success, especially for her play *The Rover*, a picaresque drama, and for *Oroonoko, or the History of the Royal Slave*, a novel. She was one of the most famous and unconventional women writers in England before the nineteenth century.

When you Love, or speak of it,
   Make no serious matter on't,
'Twill make but subject for her wit
   And gain her scorn in lieu of Grant.
Sneeking, whining, dull Grimasses
   Pale the Appetite, they'd move;
Only Boys and formal Asses
   Thus are Ridicul'd by Love.

While you make a Mystery
   Of your Love and awful flame;
Young and tender Hearts will fly,
   Frighted at the very name;
Always brisk and gayly court,
   Make Love your pleasure not your pain,
'Tis by wanton play and sport
   Heedless Virgins you will gain.

Not to sigh and to be tender,
   Not to talk and prattle Love,
Is a Life no good can render,
   And insipidly does move:
Unconcern do's Life destroy,
   Which, without Love, can know no Joy.

Life, without adoring Beauty,
   Will be useless all the day;
Love's a part of Human Duty,
   And 'tis Pleasure to obey.
In vain the Gods did Life bestow,
   Where kinder Love has nought to do.

What is Life, but soft desires,
   And that Soul, that is not made
To entertain what Love inspires,
   Oh thou dull immortal Shade?
Thou'dst better part with Flesh and Blood,
   Than be, where Life's not understood.

Love's Witness

Slight unpremeditated Words are borne
   By every common Wind into the Air;
Carelessly utter'd, die as soon as born,
   And in one instant give both Hope and Fear:
Breathing all Contraries with the same Wind
According to the Caprice of the Mind.

But *Billetdoux* are constant Witnesses,
   Substantial Records to Eternity;
Just Evidences, who the Truth confess,
   On which the Lover safely may rely;
They're serious Thoughts, digested and resolv'd;
And last, when Words are into Clouds devolv'd.

Anne Killigrew

Anne Killigrew (1660–1685).   The daughter of Dr. Henry Killigrew, she came from a theatrical family. Her uncles, Sir William and Thomas, and her cousins, Charles and Thomas Killigrew, were playwrights. Her father, a royalist and theologian, became chaplain to the duke of York, and later, master of the Savoy. Anne became maid of honor to the duchess of York, Mary of Modena. Anne Finch, countess of Winchelsea, was also a member of the household. Anne Killigrew's poems were praised by John Dryden, who wrote, "Art she had none, yet wanted none:/For Nature did Want that supply." Killigrew wrote about the life of the court, the duchess who was unpopular and caused her pain, poetic theory, and about her painting, another talent she possessed. She died of smallpox at the age of twenty-five.

On Death

Tell me though safest End of all our Woe,
Why wreched Mortals do avoid thee so:
Thou gentle drier o' th' afflicted Tears,
Thou noble ender of the Coward's Fears;
Thou sweet Repose to Lover's sad dispaire,
Thou Calm t' Ambitions rough Tempestous Care.
If in regard of Bliss thou wert a Curse,
And then the Joys of Paradise art worse;

Yet after Man from his first Station fell,
and God from *Eden Adam* did expel,
Thou wert no more an Evil, but Relief;
The Balm and Cure to ev'ry Humane Grief:
Through thee (what Man had forfeited before)
He now enjoys, and ne'r can loose it more.
No subtile Serpents, in the Grave betray,
Worms on the Body there, not Soul do prey;
No Vice there Tempts, no Terrors there afright,
No Coz'ning Sin affords a false delight:
No vain Contentions do that Peace annoy,
No fierce Alarms break the lasting Joy.

Ah since from thee so many Blessings flow,
Such real Good as Life can never know;
Come when thou wilt, in thy afrighting'st Dress,
Thy Shape shall never make thy Welcome less.
Thou mayst to You, but ne'er to Fear give Birth,
Thou Best, as well as Certain'st thing on Earth.
Fly thee? May Travellers then fly their Rest,
And hungry Infants fly the profer'd Brest.
No, those that faint and tremble at thy Name,
Fly from their Good on a mistaken Fame.
Thus Childish fear did Israel of old
From Plenty and the Promis'd Land with-hold;
They fancy'd Giants, and refus'd to go,
When *Canaan* did with Milk and Honey flow.

A Farewel to Worldly Joyes

Farewel to Unsubstantial Joyes,
Ye Gilded Nothings, Gaudy Toyes,
Too long ye have my Soul misled,
Too long with Aiery Diet fed:
But now my Heart ye shall no more
Deceive, as you have heretofore:
for when I hear such *Sirens* sing,
Like *Ithica's* fore-warned King,

With prudent Resolution I
Will so my Will and Fancy tye,
That stronger to the Mast not he,
Than I to Reason bound will be:
And though your Witchcrafts strike my Ear,
Unhurt, like him, your Charms I'll hear.

Lady Mary Wortley Montagu

Lady Mary Wortley Montagu (1684–1763).   A member of the ruling class, her father was the duke of Kingston. She was well known as a poet and better known as a brilliant and satirical letter writer. When she was pressured into marrying a man of her father's choice, a nobleman, she and Edward Wortley Montagu eloped. After her marriage, however, it appeared she was bored in their country home: "I cannot help gratifying myself in saying something, yet I dare not say half I think of your delightful letter. . . . 'Tis impossible to send an equivalent out of this stupid town, as it would be to return a present of fruits of Provence out of Lapland. We have no news, no trade, no sun. . . ." Later she went east to Turkey, and upon her return to England introduced the Turkish practice of innoculation against smallpox. She and Alexander Pope were close friends, but their friendship ended bitterly. He claimed that the cause of their disagreement was a pair of borrowed sheets which she returned unwashed, but she claimed that it was an incident in which he made advances and she, "in spite of her utmost endeavors to be angry or look grave," responded with an excessive fit of laughter. Pope wrote what she considered libelous things against her. Finally, she left England without her husband and lived on the Continent.

The Lady's Resolve

Whilst thirst of praise and vain desire of fame,
In every age, is every woman's aim;
With courtship pleas'd, of silly toasters proud,
Fond of a train, and happy in a crowd;
On each proud fop bestowing some kind glance,
Each conquest owing to some loose advance;
While vain coquets affect to be pursued,
And think they're virtuous, if not grossly lewd:
Let this great maxim be my virtue's guide;
In part she is to blame that has been try'd—
He comes too near, that comes to be deny'd.

On the Death of Mrs. Bowes

Hail, happy bride, for thou art truly blest!
Three months of rapture, crown'd with endless rest.
Merit like yours was Heav'n's peculiar care,
You lov'd—yet tasted happiness sincere.
To you the sweets of love were only shown,
The sure succeeding bitter dregs unknown;
You had not yet the fatal change deplor'd,
The tender lover for th' imperious lord:
Nor felt the pain that jealous fondness brings:
Nor felt, that coldness from possession springs.
Above your sex, distinguish'd in your fate,
You trusted—yet experienc'd no deceit;
Soft were your hours, and wing'd with pleasure flew;
No vain repentance gave a sigh to you:
And if superior bliss Heaven can bestow,
With fellow-angels you enjoy it now.

Charlotte Smith

Charlotte Smith (1749–1806).   Born in London of a wealthy family, at sixteen
she married Benjamin Smith. Her husband was an extravagant man, constantly in debt.
At one point he was obliged to serve a six-month term in debtor's prison, most of
which she spent with him. She wrote novels, poems, letters, children's books, and did
translations in order to support her ten children. Sir Walter Scott admired her novels
and wrote a long critique of them.

from Montalbert

Swift fleet the billowy clouds along the sky,
    Earth seems to shudder at the storm aghast;
While only beings as forlorn as I,
    Court the chill horrors of the howling blast.
Even round yon crumbling walls, in search of food,
    The ravenous owl foregoes his evening flight,
And in his cave, within the deepest wood,
    The fox eludes the tempest of the night.

But to my heart congenial is the gloom
   Which hides me from a world I wish to shun:
That scene where ruin saps the mouldering tomb
   Suits with the sadness of a wretch undone.
Nor is the deepest shade, the keenest air,
Black as my fate, or cold as my despair.

Phillis Wheatley

Phillis Wheatley (ca. 1752–1784).   Phillis Wheatley was the first American woman and the first black writer to publish a book in North America. In 1761 at the age of eight she was brought from West Africa to Boston on the slave ship *Phillis*. The well-to-do merchant John Wheatley purchased her for his wife, Susanna. The Wheatleys were members of the New South Congregational Church and devout Christians and their daughter Mary became Phillis's friend and tutor in religion. Through Mary and by her own motivation, Phillis became as learned in the classics as any Bostonian woman of her time. She began writing poetry at the age of twelve.

In 1773 the Wheatleys' son Nathaniel took Phillis to London where arrangements were made for the publication of her book, *Poems on Various Subjects, Religious and Moral*. Although the book was reviewed in England and in Scotland, by the time it was published she had been called back to Boston to attend the ailing Mrs. Wheatley, who died several months later. By then Phillis Wheatley's work was known among some of the most prominent families of the revolutionary period. In October 1775 she sent a poem to George Washington, which led to a personal visit with him at his headquarters in Cambridge. Later, her book was in the libraries of several of the signers of the Declaration of Independence and of the Constitution.

Around the time of her book's publication, John Wheatley freed her. But during the war, her freedom did not bring about a personal renaissance. As Julian D. Mason, Jr., editor of a recent volume of her collected poems, points out, the period of her remarkable public success was over:

> when the war unsettled her residence and her life in general, though she continued writing, this woman, who had been exchanging poems with Royal Navy personnel . . . would publish no more poems over the nine years before 1784, during which period her life departed further and further from the encouragement and security she had known . . . since her arrival in Boston as a child slave.

In 1778 she married John Peters, a free man, and had three children. Little is known of their life other than what Mason tells us: "what began as a marriage which was financially and otherwise comfortable deteriorated." She had three children but they did not survive her. When she died in Boston at the age of thirty-one, her third child was buried with her. Notices appeared widely in New England newspapers that a poet "who was known to the world for celebrated anonymous poems" had died. By 1778, John and Mary Wheatley, and nearly half the people who signed the "Letter to the Publick" that prefaced her book, were all dead.

Wheatley is an eighteenth-century poet and her medium is the neoclassical heroic couplet of Pope, Dryden, and Swift. Her great mythological source is Homer—and to a lesser extent the Latin poets—yet while she will evoke "wise Apollo," the major figures in her poems are biblical patriarchs and heroes whom she treats with Homeric descriptions. Although she was classically educated and even spent time in London as a littérateur, there is no suggestion of Milton in her work, a natural ally who also gave his biblical figures the dimensions of Greek mythological heroes. Mason speculates how her work might have developed had she lived beyond her thirty-first year and come to terms with Milton and absorbed a wider range of Romantic influences. But like Sylvia Plath, who also died in the early stages of her career, Wheatley ultimately wrote about what was closest to her—her friends, and especially the friends who died.

In this era when early deaths from natural or violent causes were common, poets often wrote in the elegiac form. As in the work of Anne Bradstreet, virtually half of Wheatley's poems were elegies. Also like Bradstreet, Wheatley is grateful to God for her mortality, while wistfully recalling love for the deceased, at once affirming and subverting the harsh justice of death. Erlene Stetson, in her *Black Sister: Poetry by Black American Women, 1746–1980,* says of Wheatley's formal strengths and her subject matter: "The strength of her poetics lies in the mastery, skill, perception, and black female consciousness that she fuses with these [neoclassical] conventional models." As for Wheatley's preoccupation with the sorrow of illness and death, Stetson comments:

> Wheatley wrote many vivid poems on the deaths of women and children, and she paid particular attention to the suffering of mothers. These poems particularize the emotion of loss, and they imply the importance of women's experience, which was largely ignored in her time. Wheatley made the death of a woman in a hurricane or the death of an infant as significant as that of a public figure. Her poems teach women how to survive the loss of husbands, sisters, brothers, fathers, and especially children.

One example of resignation and a return to heaven in grace is her poem "To a Gentleman and Lady on the Death of the Lady's Brother and Sister, and a Child of the Name Avis, Aged One Year":

> Resign thy friends to that Almighty hand,
> Which gave them life, and bow to his command;
> Thine Avis give without a murm'ring heart,
> Though half thy soul be fated to depart.

To shining guards consign thine infant care
To waft triumphant through the seas of air:
Her soul enlarg'd to heav'nly pleasure springs,
She feeds on truths and uncreated things.

Just as Bradstreet also protests the notion that she should be scorned for her sex, Wheatley protests the notion that she should be scorned for her race, for being Ethiopic and "black as Cain." In "On Being Brought from Africa to America" she writes:

Some view our sable race with scornful eye,
"Their colour is a diabolic die."
Remember, Christians, Negroes, black as Cain,
May be refin'd, and join th' angelic train.

One might draw a parallel between William Blake, the social poet of London, and Phillis Wheatley, who as the first African-American poet was also the first literary conscience of the slave. Blake rebukes God and Church for human misery, and in "The Little Black Boy" he writes: "And I am black, but O! my soul is white." With no little irony, he concludes that only after death will the boy find justice: i.e., "When I from black and he from white cloud free, / And round the tent of God like lambs we joy," he will one day, in angelic form, be kissed and loved by both the English boy and by God. So too Phillis Wheatley, two decades before Blake, scolds white Christians for their lack of Christian love, for their "scornful eye" against her "sable race," and steadfastly places her faith in redemption after life, when she will join "the angelic train."

The poems and letters of Phillis Wheatley are collected in *The Poems of Phillis Wheatley*, revised and enlarged edition, edited with an introduction by Julian D. Mason, Jr. (Chapel Hill, N.C.: University of North Carolina Press, 1989).

On Being Brought from Africa to America.

'Twas mercy brought me from my *Pagan* land,
Taught my benighted soul to understand
That there's a God, that there's a *Saviour* too:
Once I redemption neither sought nor knew.
Some view our sable race with scornful eye,
"Their colour is a diabolic die."
Remember, *Christians, Negros,* black as *Cain,*
May be refin'd, and join th' angelic train.

To a Lady on the Death of Her Husband.

Grim monarch! see, depriv'd of vital breath,
A young physician in the dust of death:
Dost thou go on incessant to destroy,
Our griefs to double, and lay waste our joy?
Enough thou never yet wast known to say,
Though millions die, the vassals of thy sway:
Nor youth, nor science, nor the ties of love,
Nor aught on earth thy flinty heart can move.
The friend, the spouse from his dire dart to save,
In vain we ask the sovereign of the grave.
Fair mourner, there see thy lov'd *Leonard* laid,
And o'er him spread the deep impervious shade;
Clos'd are his eyes, and heavy fetters keep
His senses bound in never-waking sleep,
Till time shall cease, till many a starry world
Shall fall from heav'n, in dire confusion hurl'd,
Till nature in her final wreck shall lie,
And her last groan shall rend the azure sky:
Not, not till then his active soul shall claim
His body, a divine immortal frame.

   But see the softly-stealing tears apace
Pursue each other down the mourner's face;
But cease thy tears, bid ev'ry sigh depart,
And cast the load of anguish from thine heart:
From the cold shell of his great soul arise,
And look beyond, thou native of the skies;
There fix thy view, where fleeter than the wind
Thy *Leonard* mounts, and leaves the earth behind.
Thyself prepare to pass the vale of night
To join for ever on the hills of light:
To thine embrace his joyful spirit moves
To thee, the partner of his earthly loves;
He welcomes thee to pleasures more refin'd,
And better suited to th' immortal mind.

To the Right Honourable William, Earl of Dartmouth, His Majesty's Principal Secretary of State for North-America, &C.

Hail, happy day, when, smiling like the morn,
Fair *Freedom* rose *New-England* to adorn:
The northern clime beneath her genial ray,
Dartmouth, congratulates thy blissful sway:
Elate with hope her race no longer mourns,
Each soul expands, each grateful bosom burns,
While in thine hand with pleasure we behold
The silken reins, and *Freedom's* charms unfold.
Long lost to realms beneath the northern skies
She shines supreme, while hated *faction* dies:
Soon as appear'd the *Goddess* long desir'd,
Sick at the view, she lanquish'd and expir'd;
Thus from the splendors of the morning light
The owl in sadness seeks the caves of night.

No more, *America,* in mournful strain
Of wrongs, and grievance unredress'd complain, }
No longer shalt thou dread the iron chain,
Which wanton *Tyranny* with lawless hand
Had made, and with it meant t' enslave the land.

Should you, my lord, while you peruse my song,
Wonder from whence my love of *Freedom* sprung,
Whence flow these wishes for the common good,
By feeling hearts alone best understood,
I, young in life, by seeming cruel fate
Was snatch'd from *Afric's* fancy'd happy seat:
What pangs excruciating must molest,
What sorrows labour in my parent's breast?
Steel'd was that soul and by no misery mov'd
That from a father seiz'd his babe belov'd:
Such, such my case. And can I then but pray
Others may never feel tyrannic sway?

For favours past, great Sir, our thanks are due,
And thee we ask thy favours to renew,

Since in thy pow'r, as in thy will before,
To sooth the griefs, which thou did'st once deplore.
May heav'nly grace the sacred sanction give
To all thy works, and thou for ever live
Not only on the wings of fleeting *Fame,*
Though praise immortal crowns the patriot's name,
But to conduct to heav'n's refulgent fane,
May fiery coursers sweep th' ethereal plain,
And bear thee upwards to that blest abode,
Where, like the prophet, thou shalt find thy God.

To a Gentleman and Lady on the Death of the Lady's Brother and Sister, and a Child of the Name *Avis,* Aged One Year.

On *Death's* domain intent I fix my eyes,
Where human nature in vast ruin lies:
With pensive mind I search the drear abode,
Where the great conqu'ror has his spoils, bestow'd;
There there the offspring of six thousand years
In endless numbers to my view appears:
Whole kingdoms in his gloomy den are thrust,
And nations mix with their primeval dust:
Insatiate still he gluts the ample tomb;
His is the present, his the age to come.
See here a brother, here a sister spread,
And a sweet daughter mingled with the dead.

But, *Madam,* let your grief be laid aside,
And let the fountain of your tears be dry'd,
In vain they flow to wet the dusty plain,
Your sighs are wafted to the skies in vain,
Your pains they witness, but they can no more,
While *Death* reigns tyrant o'er this mortal shore.

The glowing stars and silver queen of light
At last must perish in the gloom of night:
Resign thy friends to that Almighty hand,
Which gave them life, and bow to his command;

Thine *Avis* give without a murm'ring heart,
Though half thy soul be fated to depart.
To shining guards consign thine infant care
To waft triumphant through the seas of air:
Her soul enlarg'd to heav'nly pleasure springs,
She feeds on truth and uncreated things.
Methinks I hear her in the realms above,
And leaning forward with a filial love,
Invite you there to share immortal bliss
Unknown, untasted in a state like this.
With tow'ring hopes, and growing grace arise,
And seek beatitude beyond the skies.

To S. M., a Young *African* Painter, on Seeing His Works.

To show the lab'ring bosom's deep intent,
And thought in living characters to paint,
When first thy pencil did those beauties give,
And breathing figures learnt from thee to live,
How did those prospects give my soul delight,
A new creation rushing on my sight?
Still, wond'rous youth! each noble path pursue,
On deathless glories fix thine ardent view:
Still may the painter's and the poet's fire
To aid thy pencil, and thy verse conspire!
And may the charms of each seraphic theme
Conduct thy footsteps to immortal fame!
High to the blissful wonders of the skies
Elate thy soul, and raise thy wishful eyes.
Thrice happy, when exalted to survey
That splendid city, crown'd with endless day,
Whose twice six gates on radiant hinges ring:
Celestial *Salem* blooms in endless spring.

Calm and serene thy moments glide along,
And may the muse inspire each future song!
Still, with the sweets of contemplation bless'd,
May peace with balmy wings your soul invest!
But when these shades of time are chas'd away,

And darkness ends in everlasting day,
On what seraphic pinions shall we move,
And view the landscapes in the realms above?
There shall thy tongue in heav'nly murmurs flow,
And there my muse with heav'nly transport glow:
No more to tell of *Damon's* tender sighs,
Or rising radiance of *Aurora's* eyes,
For nobler themes demand a nobler strain,
And purer language on th' ethereal plain.
Cease, gentle muse! the solemn gloom of night
Now seals the fair creation from my sight.

Elizabeth Barrett Browning

Elizabeth Barrett Browning (1806–1861).   Born at Durham, she was educated by
tutors. At the age of twelve she wrote an epic in four parts, *The Battle of Marathon*,
which her father had published. She was a semi-invalid and stayed inside her father's
house at Wimpole Street until she eloped with Robert Browning. Her father never
forgave her for marrying; he believed "She should have been thinking of another
world." The Brownings went to Italy where Elizabeth Barrett miraculously recovered,
and in 1849 gave birth to a son, Robert. Except for occasional trips, the Brownings
stayed at Casa Guidi, in Florence, writing and entertaining friends (among them,
Margaret Fuller, Nathaniel Hawthorne, Julia Ward Howe, Harriet Martineau,
William Wetmore Story, Hiram Powers, and Walter Savage Landor) until Elizabeth
Barrett died. She enjoyed great success for her *Sonnets from the Portuguese* (1850)
and for *Aurora Leigh* (1857). She was a champion of the Italian struggle for freedom
from Austria, women's rights, and the abolition of child labor and slavery.

When our two souls stand up erect and strong,
Face to face, silent, drawing nigh and nigher,
Until the lengthening wings break into fire
At either curvèd point,—what bitter wrong
Can the earth do to us, that we should not long
Be here contented? Think. In mounting higher,
The angels would press us on and aspire
To drop some golden orb of perfect song
Into our deep, dear silence. Let us stay
Rather on earth, Belovèd—where the unfit

Contrarious moods of men recoil away
And isolate pure spirits, and permit
A place to stand and love in for a day,
With darkness and the death-hour rounding it.

To George Sand

I. A Desire

Thou large-brained woman and large-hearted man,
Self-called George Sand! whose soul, amid the lions
Of thy tumultuous senses, moans defiance,
And answers roar for roar, as spirits can!
I would some mild miraculous thunder ran
Above the applauded circus, in appliance
Of thine own nobler nature's strength and science,
Drawing two pinions, white as wings of swan,
From thy strong shoulders, to amaze the place
With holier light! that thou to woman's claim,
And man's, mightst join beside the angel's grace
Of a pure genius sanctified from blame,—
Till child and maiden pressed to thine embrace,
To kiss upon thy lips a stainless fame.

II. A Recognition

True genius, but true woman! dost deny
Thy woman's nature with a manly scorn,
And break away the gauds and armlets worn
By weaker women in captivity?
Ah, vain denial! that revolted cry
Is sobbed in by a woman's voice forlorn!—
Thy woman's hair, my sister, all unshorn,
Floats back dishevelled strength in agony,
Disproving thy man's name! and while before
The world thou burnest in a poet-fire,
We see thy woman-heart beat evermore
Through the large flame. Beat purer, heart, and higher,
Till God unsex thee on the heavenly shore,
Where unincarnate spirits purely aspire.

Emily Brontë

Emily Brontë (1818–1848).   Emily Brontë was the daughter of an Irish clergyman, Patrick Brunty, who changed his name on coming to England to study at Cambridge. Emily's older sister Charlotte Brontë (1816–1855) was the author of *Jane Eyre,* Emily of *Wuthering Heights.* Together with her younger sister Anne (1820–1849) and Charlotte, she made up an imaginary country, called Gondal, and composed countless poems and legends about it. Fanny Elizabeth Ratchford revealed in *The Bronte's Web of Childhood* (1941) that much of the imagery and many of the personages of the Brontë sisters' poems derive not from autobiography but from the invented life of their childhood reveries. Life itself on the moors of her father's curacy at Haworth was bleak. Most of her education was at home. She attended a Clergy Daughters' School, studied briefly in Brussels, and taught at a seminary for girls. Most of her life was on the moors, in the dark home at Haworth, which attracted her despite the severe climate which very much contributed to her early death from consumption. Her poems, like her famous novel, are wild yet stark, Gothically imaginative yet harshly real. Her one collection of poems during her lifetime appeared with poems of her two sisters under the names of Currer, Ellis, and Acton Bell in order to disguise the authorship by women. Published at their own expense, it sold two copies.

Remembrance

Cold in the earth, and the deep snow piled above thee!
Far, far removed, cold in the dreary grave!
Have I forgot, my Only Love, to love thee,
Severed at last by Time's all-wearing wave?

Now, when alone, do my thoughts no longer hover
Over the mountains on Angora's shore;
Resting their wings where heath and fern-leaves cover
That noble heart for ever, ever more?

Cold in the earth, and fifteen wild Decembers
From those brown hills have melted into spring—
Faithful indeed is the spirit that remembers
After such years of change and suffering!

Sweet Love of youth, forgive if I forgot thee
While the World's tide is bearing me along:
Sterner desires and darker hopes beset me,
Hopes which obscure but cannot do thee wrong.

No other Sun has lightened up my heaven;
No other Star has ever shone for me;
All my life's bliss from thy dear life was given—
All my life's bliss is in the grave with thee.

But when the days of golden dreams had perished
And even Despair was powerless to destroy,
Then did I learn how existence could be cherished,
Strengthened and fed without the aid of joy;

Then did I check the tears of useless passion,
Weaned my young soul from yearning after thine;
Sternly denied its burning wish to hasten
Down to that tomb already more than mine!

And even yet, I dare not let it languish,
Dare not indulge in Memory's rapturous pain;
Once drinking deep of that divinest anguish,
How could I seek the empty world again?

Upon Her Soothing Breast

Upon her soothing breast
She lulled her little child;
A winter sunset in the west,
A dreary glory smiled.

Christina Rossetti

Christina Rossetti (1830–1894).   Christina Rossetti was born in London, the daughter of Gabriel Rosetti, an Italian poet and political refugee who was a professor at King's College. Her brothers, pre-Raphaelites like herself, were the editor of *The Germ*, William Michael Rossetti, and the poet and painter Dante Gabriel Rossetti. All three contributed to the magazine. Christina was Dante Gabriel's favorite model in paintings of the Virgin. She was a devout Anglican who renounced pleasure, saying "I cannot possibly use the word 'happy' without meaning something beyond this present life." At thirty she fell in love with Charles Cayley, and although she remained devoted to him for the rest of her life, she refused to marry him because he was not devout enough. *Goblin Market,* for which she is best known, was published in 1862; *The*

Prince's Progress and Other Poems in 1866. Both were well received, but she never enjoyed the success of her brother. Though she became a recluse in later life, she entertained many friends, among them Lewis Carroll. She wrote prolifically, producing prose, children's books, and hundreds of devotional verses and hymns.

In Progress

Ten years ago it seemed impossible
 That she should ever grow so calm as this,
 With self-remembrance in her warmest kiss
And dim dried eyes like an exhausted well.
Slow-speaking when she had some fact to tell,
 Silent with long-unbroken silences,
 Centred in self yet not unpleased to please,
Gravely monotonous like a passing bell.
Mindful of drudging daily common things,
 Patient at pastime, patient at her work,
  Wearied perhaps but strenuous certainly.
  Sometimes I fancy we may one day see
 Her head shoot forth seven stars from where they lurk
And her eyes lightnings and her shoulders wings.

The World

By day she woos me, soft, exceeding fair:
 But all night as the moon so changeth she;
 Loathsome and foul with hideous leprosy,
And subtle serpents gliding in her hair.
By days she woos me to the outer air,
 Ripe fruits, sweet flowers, and full satiety:
 But thro' the night a beast she grins at me,
A very monster void of love and prayer.
By day she stands a lie: by night she stands
 In all the naked horror of the truth,
With pushing horns and clawed and clutching hands.
Is this a friend indeed, that I should sell
 My soul to her, give her my life and youth,
Till my feet, cloven too, take hold on hell?

Emily Dickinson

Emily Dickinson (1830–1886) was born and died in Amherst, Massachusetts. She was the daughter of Edward and Emily Norcross Dickinson. Her older brother was Austin; her younger sister, Lavinia. She came from a long line of Puritans. Her ancestor, Nathaniel Dickinson, came to America in 1630, with the Great Migration led by John Winthrop. Her grandfather, Samuel Fowler Dickinson, founded the evangelical and orthodox Amherst College in reaction to liberal Harvard. Like her grandfather, her father, Edward, and her brother, Austin, who were lawyers, were at the center of Amherst's civic and religious activities. Both served in the role of treasurer at the college. Edward was a member of the U.S. House of Representatives. He brought the railroad to Amherst (recall Emily's famous "I like to see it lap the Miles"). Austin supervised the construction and landscaping of the Dickinson's First Congregational Church. Austin's wife, Susan, was also a prominent social figure, and the couple entertained many speakers and scholars who visited Amherst, including Emerson, who ate and slept in their home.

Emily Dickinson attended Amherst Academy and Mount Holyoke Female Seminary, which, like Amherst College, was an evangelical institution. Dickinson reveled in her studies—"I love this Seminary," she wrote—but since religion was the basis of education there, the pressure on her to convert was profound. She wrote of herself mockingly, "I am one of the bad ones." After a year she withdrew, and at eighteen her formal education was over. During the Awakening (1845–46) and the Great Revival (1850), two periods of religious revival in the Amherst area, Dickinson remained the only member of her family who did not convert through a profession of faith. She wrote a friend, "How lonely this world is growing. . . . Christ is calling everyone here, all my companions have answered, even my darling Vinnie believes she loves, and trusts him, and I am standing alone in rebellion." The isolation in these words, which remained with her her whole life, seem to presage her later withdrawal from society.

Dickinson read widely. She was influenced by the Bible and Shakespeare, as well as by the popular, sentimental writers of the nineteenth century. The prosody of the Protestant hymns also informs her poems. She mentioned Keats and Robert Browning and Elizabeth Barrett Browning in an introductory letter to Higginson. She kept a portrait of George Eliot in her bedroom, where she began to write the first of the nearly eighteen hundred poems, which were to be her "center": "Each Life Converges to some Centre." Although it is not known exactly when she began to write poetry, her handwriting dates the earliest of her poems in the late 1850s. The period of her greatest poetic activity was from 1860 to 1865. If the dating of her poetry is correct, it indicates that Dickinson wrote approximately one poem a day in the year 1862. That year, encouraged by his essay "Letter to a Young Contributor," she wrote to Thomas Wentworth Higginson, editor of *The Atlantic Monthly:* "Are you too deeply occupied to say if my Verse is alive?" Though Higginson remained her lifelong friend and correspondent (he read a eulogy at her funeral), he failed to recognize her genius. Her innovative poetry was not regular in rhyme, meter, and the thematic structure that nineteenth century literary convention required, and he discouraged her from publication.

In the early 1860s Dickinson wrote some of her most famous and despairing poetry. Critics have speculated that during these years she had suffered a terrible disappointment in love, which led to an emotional crisis. Though much of the earlier Dickinson criticism focuses on whom the poet loved, there is no solid evidence that a man was at the heart of her despair. In her groundbreaking feminist essay "Vesuvius at Home: The Power of Emily Dickinson," Adrienne Rich points out, "The women and men in her life she equally converted into metaphor. The masculine pronoun in her poems can refer simultaneously to many aspects of the 'masculine' in the patriarchal world . . . it is far too limiting to trace that 'He' to some specific lover."

Dickinson herself was concerned that her words be representative, not confessional or autobiographical. Thus, she wrote to Higginson: "When I state myself, as Representative of the Verse—it does not mean—me—but a 'supposed' person." Dickinson, whose poetry and letters have an elusive literal level, claims for herself, no less than Walt Whitman, the authority to be an Emersonian representative poet.

In the late 1860s Dickinson began her withdrawal from society. She was known in Amherst as "the Myth," the eccentric poet who always wore white and who never left the grounds of the Homestead. This myth has persisted more than a hundred years after the poet's death. It must be remembered, however, that her withdrawal was not complete. She continued to carry on an extensive correspondence with her family and friends, many of whom were well-known literary figures. Since she often enclosed poems in her letters, her correspondence served as a kind of self-publication.

She chose readers for her poetry well. In addition to Higginson, who was a reformer, Dickinson carried on correspondences with Samuel Bowles, popular author and editor of *The Springfield Republican*; Dr. Josiah Holland; Charles Wadsworth, a renowned reformist preacher; and Helen Hunt Jackson, a popular poet and novelist. Critics speculate that Dickinson was in love with either Wadsworth or Bowles, who published, anonymously, the few Dickinson poems that did appear in print during her lifetime.

By aligning herself with several of the most progressive religious stylists of the day, Emily Dickinson was launching a silent but major rebellion against the doctrinal tradition valued by her father. Helen Hunt Jackson, one of the few people Dickinson consented to see face to face in the 1880s, was one of the rare people who saw that Dickinson's genius lay partly in what was unusual to the nineteenth-century poetic sensibilities. She chastised her: "You are a great poet—and it is wrong to the day you live in, that you will not sing aloud. When you are what men call dead, you will be sorry you were so stingy." Jackson even asked to be her reclusive friend's literary executor, but she died before Dickinson.

In addition to her relationships with correspondents, Dickinson discovered romantic love toward the end of her life. She and Judge Otis Phillips Lord had a mutual, passionate relationship: "I feel like wasting my Cheek on your hand tonight—" she wrote him, "Will you accept the squander—Lay up Treasures immediately." Lord died in 1884. Her father had died in 1874; her mother and Charles Wadsworth in 1882. Her nephew, Gilbert, died tragically in 1883 at the age of eight. Her grief over these deaths is believed to have hastened Emily's own death. Death on May 15, 1886, from Bright's disease, was the last in a series of deaths whose nature she had observed, terribly understood, and recorded in her astonishing poems. Contrary to the mythology about her withdrawal and her renunciation, Dickinson was worldly. She could not accept death as a release from the suffering on Earth, as heavenly reward. The loss of loved ones was too profound; love was, as she wrote in a poem to Otis Lord, "The joyful little Deity/We are not scourged to serve."

While she was alive, Emily had sewn together many of her poems into fascicles. Lavinia Dickinson discovered them and was determined to publish these "volumes" after Emily's death. She enlisted the help of Mabel Loomis Todd and Thomas Wentworth Higginson. Todd transcribed the poems, and she and Higginson smoothed out the rhymes, regularized the meter, substituted more conventional metaphors, and sometimes deleted entire stanzas, for which Higginson has been much maligned. Yet the readers for Roberts Brothers, the publishers of the first edition of Dickinson's work, regarded the changes as "absolutely necessary." Many reviewers reiterated this opinion, declaring that the poetry had "a startling disregard for poetic laws." One of the dissenting opinions, however, came from the powerful William Dean Howells, who praised its innovation: "If nothing else should come out of our life but this strange poetry we should feel that in the work of Emily Dickinson, America, or New England rather, had made a distinctive addition to the literature of the world, and should not be left out of any record of it."

It was not until 1955 that Thomas H. Johnson restored the original texts (several critics question his methods, however). Today, unfortunately, the poems are often printed in their altered form; since the doctored versions are now in the public domain, they may be printed without cost. The most public distortion of her poetry is the use of the bowdlerized texts in the scenario of *The Belle of Amherst.*

Dickinson's universe, the world of Amherst and her home, is deceptively small. She imagined places that she knew from almanacs and maps, and she humorously followed a train—with Whitman she was among the first to bring the machine into poetry—through a distant countryside. But often she reflectively observed both repressive external circumstances and the boundaries of the soul, whose immortality she imagined and hoped for—but doubted.

Emily Dickinson's poems appear in a three-volume variorum edition, *The Poems of Emily Dickinson;* in a reader's edition, *The Complete Poems of Emily Dickinson;* and in a selection, *Final Harvest,* all edited by Thomas H. Johnson. Johnson also edited Dickinson's letters, which are themselves great literary achievements. The fascicle manuscripts are reproduced in R. W. Franklin's *The Manuscript Books of Emily Dickinson.*

> There's a certain Slant of light,
> Winter Afternoons—
> That oppresses, like the Heft
> Of Cathedral Tunes—
>
> Heavenly Hurt, it gives us—
> We can find no scar,

But internal difference,
Where the Meanings, are—

None may teach it—Any—
'Tis the Seal Despair—
An imperial affliction
Sent us of the Air—

When it comes, the Landscape listens—
Shadows—hold their breath—
When it goes, 'tis like the Distance
On the look of Death—

◦◦◦

I felt a Funeral, in my Brain,
And Mourners to and fro
Kept treading—treading—till it seemed
That Sense was breaking through—

And when they all were seated,
A Service, like a Drum—
Kept beating—beating—till I thought
My Mind was going numb—

And then I heard them lift a Box
And creak across my Soul
With those same Boots of Lead, again,
Then Space—began to toll,

As all the Heavens were a Bell,
And Being, but an Ear,
And I, and Silence, some strange Race
Wrecked, solitary, here—

And then a Plank in Reason, broke,
And I dropped down, and down—
And hit a World, at every plunge,
And Finished knowing—then—

❧

I'm Nobody! Who are you?
Are you—Nobody—Too?
Then there's a pair of us?
Don't tell! they'd advertise—you know!

How dreary—to be—Somebody!
How public—like a Frog—
To tell one's name—the livelong June—
To an admiring Bog!

❧

The Soul selects her own Society—
Then—shuts the Door—
To her divine Majority—
Present no more—

Unmoved—she notes the Chariots—pausing—
At her low Gate—
Unmoved—an Emperor be kneeling
Upon her Mat—

I've known her—from an ample nation—
Choose One—
Then—close the Valves of her attention—
Like Stone—

❧

'Tis not that Dying hurts us so—
'Tis living—hurts us more—
But Dying—is a different way—
A Kind behind the Door—

The Southern Custom—of the Bird—
That ere the Frosts are due—

Accepts a better Latitude—
We—are the Birds—that stay.

The Shiverers round Farmers' doors—
For whose reluctant Crumb—
We stipulate—till pitying Snows
Persuade our Feathers Home.

After great pain, a formal feeling comes—
The Nerves sit ceremonious, like Tombs—
The stiff Heart questions was it He, that bore,
And Yesterday, or Centuries Before?

The Feet, mechanical, go round—
Of Ground, or Air, or Ought—
A Wooden way
Regardless grown,
A Quartz contentment, like a stone—

This is the Hour of Lead—
Remembered, if outlived,
As Freezing persons, recollect the Snow—
First—Chill—then Stupor—then the letting go—

Of Course—I prayed—
And did God Care?
He cared as much as on the Air
A Bird—had stamped her foot—
And cried "Give Me"—
My Reason—Life—
I had not had—but for Yourself—
'Twere better Charity
To leave me in the Atom's Tomb—
Merry, and Nought, and gay, and numb—
Than this smart Misery.

~~~

There is a Languor of the Life
More imminent than Pain—
'Tis Pain's Successor—When the Soul
Has suffered all it can—

A Drowsiness—diffuses—
A Dimness like a Fog
Envelops Consciousness—
As Mists—obliterate a Crag.

The Surgeon—does not blanch—at pain—
His Habit—is severe—
But tell him that it ceased to feel—
The Creature lying there—

And he will tell you—skill is late—
A Mightier than He—
Has ministered before Him—
There's no Vitality.

~~~

Much Madness is divinest Sense—
To a discerning Eye—
Much Sense—the starkest Madness—
'Tis the Majority
In this, as All, prevail—
Assent—and you are sane—
Demur—you're straightway dangerous—
And handled with a Chain—

~~~

I died for Beauty—but was scarce
Adjusted in the Tomb
When One who died for Truth, was lain
In an adjoining Room—

He questioned softly "Why I failed"?
"For Beauty", I replied—

"And I—for Truth—Themself are One—
We Brethren, are", He said—

And so, as Kinsmen, met a Night—
We talked between the Rooms—
Until the Moss had reached our lips—
And covered up—our names—

I heard a Fly buzz—when I died—
The Stillness in the Room
Was like the Stillness in the Air—
Between the Heaves of Storm—

The Eyes around—had wrung them dry—
And Breaths were gathering firm
For that last Onset—when the King
Be witnessed—in the Room—

I willed my Keepsakes—Signed away
What portion of me be
Assignable—and then it was
There interposed a Fly—

With Blue—uncertain stumbling Buzz—
Between the light—and me—
And then the Windows failed—and then
I could not see to see—

I saw no Way—The Heavens were stitched—
I felt the Columns close—
The Earth reversed her Hemispheres—
I touched the Universe—

And back it slid—and I alone—
A Speck upon a Ball—
Went out upon Circumference—
Beyond the Dip of Bell—

⟨ornament⟩

We dream—it is good we are dreaming—
It would hurt us—were we awake—
But since it is playing—kill us,
And we are playing—shriek—

What harm? Men die—externally—
It is a truth—of Blood—
But we—are dying in Drama—
And Drama—is never dead—

Cautious—We jar each other—
And either—open the eyes—
Lest the Phantasm—prove the Mistake—
And the livid Surprise

Cool us to Shafts of Granite—
With just an Age—and Name—
And perhaps a phrase in Egyptian—
It's prudenter—to dream—

⟨ornament⟩

I've seen a Dying Eye
Run round and round a Room—
In search of Something—as it seemed—
Then Cloudier become—
And then—obscure with Fog—
And then—be soldered down
Without disclosing what it be
'Twere blessed to have seen—

⟨ornament⟩

I like to see it lap the Miles—
And lick the Valleys up—
And stop to feed itself at Tanks—
And then—prodigious step

Around a Pile of Mountains—
And supercilious peer
In Shanties—by the sides of Roads—
And then a Quarry pare

To fit its Ribs and crawl between
Complaining all the while
In horrid—hooting stanza—
Then chase itself down Hill—

And neigh like Boanerges—
Then—punctual as a Star
Stop—docile and omnipotent
At its own stable door—

~~

one

There is a pain—so utter—
It swallows substance up—
Then covers the Abyss with Trance—
So Memory can step
Around—across—upon it—
As one within a Swoon—
Goes safely—where an open eye—
Would drop Him—Bone by Bone.

~~

To make a prairie it takes a clover and one bee,
One clover, and a bee.
And revery.
The revery alone will do,
If bees are few.

~~

My life closed twice before its close—
It yet remains to see
If Immortality unveil
A third event to me

So huge, so hopeless to conceive
As these that twice befell.
Parting is all we know of heaven,
And all we need of hell.

The last Night that She lived
It was a Common Night
Except the Dying—this to Us
Made Nature different

We noticed smallest things—
Things overlooked before
By this great light upon our Minds
Italicized—as 'twere.

As We went out and in
Between Her final Room
And Rooms where Those to be alive
Tomorrow were, a Blame

That Others could exist
While She must finish quite
A Jealousy for Her arose
So nearly infinite—

We waited while She passed—
It was a narrow time—
Too jostled were Our Souls to speak
At length the notice came.

She mentioned, and forgot—
Then lightly as a Reed
Bent to the Water, struggled scarce—
Consented, and was dead—

And We—We placed the Hair—
And drew the Head erect—

And then an awful leisure was
Belief to regulate—

❧

A narrow Fellow in the Grass
Occasionally rides—
You may have met Him—did you not
His notice sudden is—

The Grass divides as with a Comb—
A spotted shaft is seen—
And then it closes at your feet
And opens further on—

He likes a Boggy Acre
A Floor too cool for Corn—
Yet when a Boy, and Barefoot—
I more than once at Noon

Have passed, I thought, a Whip lash
Unbraiding in the Sun
When stooping to secure it
it wrinkled, and was gone—

Several of Nature's People
I know, and they know me—
I feel for them a transport
of cordiality—

But never met this Fellow
Attended, or alone
Without a tighter breathing
And Zero at the Bone—

❧

A Light exists in Spring
Not present on the Year
At any other period—
When March is scarcely here

A Color stands abroad
On Solitary Fields
That Science cannot overtake
But Human Nature feels.

It waits upon the Lawn,
It shows the furthest Tree
Upon the furthest Slope you know
It almost speaks to you.

Then as Horizons step
Or Noons report away
Without the Formula of sound
It passes and we stay—

A quality of loss
Affecting our Content
As Trade had suddenly encroached
Upon a Sacrament.

∾

Because I could not stop for Death—
He kindly stopped for me—
The Carriage held but just Ourselves—
And Immortality.

We slowly drove—He knew no haste
And I had put away
My labor and my leisure too,
For His Civility—

We passed the School, where Children strove
At Recess—in the Ring—
We passed the Fields of Grazing Grain—
We passed the Setting Sun—

Or rather—He passed Us—
The Dews drew quivering and chill—
For only Gossamer, my Gown—
My Tippet—only Tulle—

We paused before a House that seemed
A Swelling of the Ground—
The Roof was scarcely visible—
The Cornice—in the Ground—

Since then—'tis Centuries—and yet
Feels shorter than the Day
I first surmised the Horses' Heads
Were toward Eternity—

There is a morn by men unseen—
Whose maids upon remoter green
Keep their Seraphic May—
And all day long, with dance and game,
And gambol I may never name—
Employ their holiday.

Here to light measure, move the feet
Which walk no more the village street—
Nor by the wood are found—
Here are the birds that sought the sun
When last year's distaff idle hung
And summer's brows were bound.

Ne'er saw I such a wondrous scene—
Ne'er such a ring on such a green—
Nor so serene array—
As if the stars some summer night
Should swing their cups of Chrysolite—
And revel till the day—

Like thee to dance—like thee to sing—
People upon the mystic green—
I ask, each new May Morn.
I wait thy far, fantastic bells—
Announcing me in other dells—
Unto the different dawn!

Come slowly—Eden!
Lips unused to Thee—
Bashful—sip thy Jessamines—
As the fainting Bee—

Reaching late his flower,
Round her chamber hums—
Counts his nectars—
Enters—and is lost in Balms.

Wild Nights—Wild Nights!
Were I with thee
Wild Nights should be
Our luxury!

Futile—the Winds—
To a Heart in port—
Done with the Compass—
Done with the Chart!

Rowing in Eden—
Ah, the Sea!
Might I but moor—Tonight—
In Thee!

This is my letter to the World
That never wrote to Me—
The simple News that Nature told—
With tender Majesty

Her Message is committed
To Hands I cannot see—
For love of Her—Sweet—countrymen—
Judge tenderly—of Me

৶৹৹

Dare you see a Soul *at the White Heat?*
Then crouch within the door—
Red—is the Fire's common tint—
But when the vivid Ore
Has vanquished Flame's conditions,
It quivers from the Forge
Without a color, but the light
Of unanointed Blaze.
Least Village has its Blacksmith
Whose Anvil's even ring
Stands symbol for the finer Forge
That soundless tugs—within—
Refining these impatient Ores
With Hammer, and with Blaze
Until the Designated Light
Repudiate the Forge—

৶৹৹

I would not paint—a picture—
I'd rather be the One
Its bright impossibility
To dwell—delicious—on—
And wonder how the fingers feel
Whose rare—celestial—stir—
Evokes so sweet a Torment—
Such sumptuous—Despair—

I would not talk, like Cornets—
I'd rather be the One
Raised softly to the Ceilings—
And out, and easy on—
Through Villages of Ether—
Myself endued Balloon
By but a lip of Metal—
The pier to my Pontoon—

Nor would I be a Poet—
It's finer—own the Ear—

Enamored—impotent—content—
The License to revere,
A privilege so awful
What would the Dower be,
Had I the Art to stun myself
With Bolts of Melody!

      ∽∽

Mine—by the Right of the White Election!
Mine—by the Royal Seal!
Mine—by the Sign in the Scarlet prison—
Bars—cannot conceal!

Mine—here—in Vision—and in Veto!
Mine—by the Grave's Repeal—
Titled—Confirmed—
Delirious Charter!
Mine—long as Ages steal!

      ∽∽

I reckon—when I count at all—
First—Poets—Then the Sun—
Then Summer—Then the Heaven of God—
And then—the List is done—

But, looking back—the First so seems
To Comprehend the Whole—
The Others look a needless Show—
So I write—Poets—All—

Their Summer—lasts a Solid Year—
They can afford a Sun
The East—would deem extravagant—
And if the Further Heaven—

Be Beautiful as they prepare
For Those who worship Them—
It is too difficult a Grace—
To justify the Dream—

~∞~

They shut me up in Prose—
As when a little Girl
They put me in the Closet—
Because they liked me "still"—

Still! Could themself have peeped—
And seen my Brain—go round—
They might as wise have lodged a Bird
For Treason—in the Pound—

Himself has but to will
And easy as a Star
Abolish his Captivity—
And laugh—No more have I—

~∞~

Me from Myself—to banish—
Had I Art—
Impregnable my Fortress
Unto All Heart—

But since Myself—assault Me—
How have I peace
Except by subjugating
Consciousness?

And since We're mutual Monarch
How this be
Except by Abdication—
Me—of Me?

~∞~

I dwell in Possibility—
A fairer House than Prose—
More numerous of Windows—
Superior—for Doors—

Of Chambers as the Cedars—
Impregnable of Eye—
And for an Everlasting Roof
The Gambrels of the Sky—

Of Visitors—the fairest—
For Occupation—This—
The spreading wide my narrow Hands
To gather Paradise—

⁀ഊ⁀

One need not be a Chamber—to be Haunted—
One need not be a House—
The Brain has Corridors—surpassing
Material Place—

Far safer, of a Midnight Meeting
External Ghost
Than its interior Confronting—
That Cooler Host.

Far safer, through an Abbey gallop,
The Stones a'chase—
Than Unarmed, one's a'self encounter—
In lonesome Place—

Ourself behind ourself, concealed—
Should startle most—
Assassin hid in our Apartment
Be Horror's least.

The Body—borrows a Revolver—
He bolts the Door—
O'erlooking a superior spectre—
Or More—

∽∽

Publication—is the Auction
Of the Mind of Man—
Poverty—be justifying
For so foul a thing

Possibly—but We—would rather
From Our Garret go
White—Unto the White Creator—
Than invest—Our Snow—

Thought belong to Him who gave it—
Then—to Him Who bear
Its Corporeal illustration—Sell
The Royal Air—

In the Parcel—Be the Merchant
Of the Heavenly Grace—
But reduce no Human Spirit
To Disgrace of Price—

∽∽

Sweet Mountains—Ye tell Me no lie—
Never deny Me—Never fly—
Those same unvarying Eyes
Turn on Me—when I fail—or feign,
Or take the Royal names in vain—
Their far—slow—Violet Gaze—

My Strong Madonnas—Cherish still—
The Wayward Nun—beneath the Hill—
Whose service—is to You—
Her latest Worship—When the Day
Fades from the Firmament away—
To lift Her Brows on You—

∽∽

She rose to His Requirement—dropt
The Playthings of Her Life

To take the honorable Work
Of Woman, and of Wife—

If ought She missed in Her new Day,
Of Amplitude, or Awe—
Or first Prospective—Or the Gold
In using, wear away,

It lay unmentioned—as the Sea
Develop Pearl, and Weed,
But only to Himself—be known
The Fathoms they abide—

∽∽

My Life had stood—a Loaded Gun—
In Corners—till a Day
The Owner passed—identified—
And carried Me away—

And now We roam in Sovereign Woods—
And now We hunt the Doe—
And every time I speak for Him—
The Mountains straight reply—

And do I smile, such cordial light
Upon the Valley glow—
It is as a Vesuvian face
Had let its pleasure through—

And when at Night—Our good Day done—
I guard My Master's Head—
'Tis better than the Eider-Duck's
Deep Pillow—to have shared—

To foe of His—I'm deadly foe—
None stir the second time—
On whom I lay a Yellow Eye—
Or an emphatic Thumb—

Though I than He—may longer live
He longer must—than I—
For I have but the power to kill,
Without—the power to die—

∞

Perception of an object costs
Precise the Object's loss—
Perception in itself a Gain
Replying to its Price—

The Object Absolute—is nought—
Perception sets it fair
And then upbraids a Perfectness
That situates so far—

∞

Title divine—is mine!
The Wife—without the Sign!
Acute Degree—conferred on me—
Empress of Calvary!
Royal—all but the Crown!
Betrothed—without the swoon
God sends us Women—
When you—hold—Garnet to Garnet—
Gold—to Gold—
Born—Bridalled—Shrouded—
In a Day—
Tri Victory
"My Husband"—women say—
Stroking the Melody—
Is *this*—the way?

∞

A Word made Flesh is seldom
And tremblingly partook
Nor then perhaps reported
But have I not mistook
Each one of us has tasted

With ecstasies of stealth
The very food debated
To our specific strength—

A Word that breathes distinctly
Has not the power to die
Cohesive as the Spirit
It may expire if He—
"Made Flesh and dwelt among us"
Could condescension be
Like this consent of Language
This loved Philology.

Ada

Ada (fl. 1836–1855).   We know nothing about Ada other than that Ada is proba-
bly a nom de plume, that she called herself a woman of color, and that she contributed
poems regularly against slavery in William Lloyd Garrison's *The Liberator.* The poem
we include, "Lines: Suggested on Reading 'An Appeal to Christian Women of the
South' by A. E. Grimké," is one of the major feminist documents after the work of Sor
Juana Ines and Anne Bradstreet. It was published under Ada's name in the October
29, 1836, issue of *The Liberator.*

"Lines" is written in Miltonic blank verse, with skillful enjambment. The rhetoric
is high and impeccable. Its concerns are those which feminist voices today most fully
explore. As Bradstreet angrily states about the woman writer: "I am obnoxious to each
carping tongue / Who says my hand a needle better fits" (from the "Prologue"), in
her exclamation Ada takes up not only the cause of the woman writer, which goes
beyond "the woof our sex is weaving," and, most compellingly, states that the woman
writer should use her pen to free her people: "To swell the rolling tide of sympathy /
. . . champions of a fettered race, / Now laboring arduous in the moral field. . . . The
pen is ours to wield."

Ada champions the causes of the committed woman writer. As she calls on God to
help, as she exhorts him to act, her lines have lofty theological reference, alluding to
the biblical story of Jacob wrestling with God. She will not let her Father go until he
joins her and other women writers to take heed and free the oppressed: "Father of
love, we join, / To wrestle with thy presence, as of old / Did Israel, and will not let
thee go / Until them bless. The cause is thine. . . .''

In the same masterful poem, she equates motherhood, the agony of childbirth, and
woman's love for child with a force which even slavery cannot erase: "Yes, this is
woman's work,? Her own appropriate sphere . . . / Oh! slavery, with all its withering
power, / Can never wholly quench the flame of love, / . . . In breasts maternal."

Finally, Ada again calls on God to join in, indeed demands his fiat, and prophesies that then, victorious, woman's voice will be heard and the "Accursed thing" of the auctioneer's hammer will be removed:

> Then, long as mothers' hearts are breaking
> Beneath the hammer of the auctioneer,
> And ruthless Avarice tears asunder bonds,
> That the fiat of the Almighty joined,
> So long should woman's melting voice be heard,
> In intercession strong and deep, that this
> Accursed thing, this Achan in our camp,
> May be removed.

Ada's poetry anticipated the work of Harriet Beecher Stowe by a decade and a half; Stowe also used the authority of God to justify *Uncle Tom's Cabin* (1851)—the first American novel to sell over a million copies—claiming: "God wrote it." Like Stowe, Ada regards it as a woman's "appropriate sphere" through Christian love to guide American society away from slavery. Her means is the powerful poem. Nothing is known of the woman; all that remains is the voice.

Lines

Suggested on Reading "An Appeal to Christian Women of the South," by A. E. Grimké.

> My spirit leans in joyousness tow'rd thine,
> My gifted sister, as with gladdened heart
> My vision flies along thy "speaking pages."
> Well hast thou toiled in Mercy's sacred course;
> And thus another strong and lasting thread
> Is added to the woof our sex is weaving,
> With skill and industry, for Freedom's garb.
> Precious the privilege to labor here,
> Worthy the lofty mind and handy-work
> Of Chapman, Chandler, Child and Grimké too.
> There is much in woman's influence, ay much,
> To swell the rolling tide of sympathy,
> And are those champions of a fettered race,
> Now laboring arduous in the moral field.
> One may not "cry aloud" as they are bid,
> And lift our voices in the *public* ear;

Nor yet be mute. The pen is ours to wield,
The heart to will, and hands to execute.
And more the gracious promise gives to all
Ask, says the saviour, and ye shall receive.
In concert then, Father of love, we join,
To wrestle with thy presence, as of old
Did Israel, and will not let thee go
Until them bless. The cause is thine—for 'tis
Thy guiltless poor who are oppressed, on whom
The sun of Freedom may not cast his beams,
Nor dew of heavenly knowledge e'er descend.
And for their fearless advocates we ask
The wisdom of the serpent—above all,
Our heavenly Father, clothe, oh clothe them with
The dove-like spirit of thine own dear Son.
Then are they safe; tho' persecution's waves
Dash o'er their backs, and furious winds assail—
Still they are safe.
                    Yes, this is woman's work,
Her own appropriate sphere; and nought should drive
Her from the mercy seat, till mercy's work be finished.
                 Whose is that wail, piercing the ear
Of night, with agony too deep for words
To give birth? 'Tis woman's—she of Ramab—
Another Rachel, weeping for her babes,
And will not be consoled, for they are not.
Oh! slavery, with all its withering power,
Can never wholly quench the flame of love,
Nor dry the stream of tenderness that flows
In breasts maternal. A *mother's love*! deep grows
That plant of Heaven, fast by the well of life,
And nought can pluck it thence till woman cease
To be. Then, long as mothers' hearts are breaking
Beneath the hammer of the auctioneer,
And ruthless Avarice tears asunder bonds,
That the fiat of the Almighty joined,
So long should woman's melting voice be heard,
In intercession strong and deep, that this
Accused thing, this Achan in our camp,
May be removed.

Mary Elizabeth Coleridge

Mary Elizabeth Coleridge (1861–1907).   Coleridge grew up in a literary household from which she never lived away. Her father entertained Browning and Tennyson. Committed to helping working women, she lectured at the Working Women's College and taught in their homes. Essays in periodicals and several successful novels were published in her lifetime, but Coleridge never allowed her verse to be published under her own name, only anonymously or under a Greek pseudonym meaning "The Wanderer." Her collected poems appeared posthumously.

The Other Side of a Mirror

I sat before my glass one day,
    And conjured up a vision bare,
Unlike the aspects glad and gay,
    That erst were found reflected there—
The vision of a woman, wild
    With more than womanly despair.

Her hair stood back on either side
    A face bereft of loveliness.
It had no envy now to hide.
    What once no man on earth could guess.
It formed the thorny aureole
    Of hard unsanctified distress.

Her lips were open—not a sound
    Came through the parted lines of red.
Whate'er it was, the hideous wound
    In silence and in secret bled.
No sigh relieved her speechless woe,
    She had no voice to speak her dread.

And in her lurid eyes there shone
    The dying flame of life's desire,
Made mad because its hope was gone,
    And kindled at the leaping fire
Of jealously, and fierce revenge,
    And strength that could not change nor tire.

Shade of a shadow in the glass,
   O set the crystal surface free!
Pass—as the fairer visions pass—
   Nor ever more return, to be
The ghost of a distracted hour,
    That heard me whisper, "I am she!"

Amy Lowell

Amy Lowell (1874–1925).   Amy Lowell was born in Brookline, Massachusetts, of a distinguished New England family: James Russell Lowell was a cousin of her grandfather, and Abbott Lawrence Lowell, her brother, was president of Harvard. Her first book, *A Dome of Many-Colored Glass* (1912), was conventional and highly influenced by the English romantics. It was not until her second book, *Sword Blades and Poppy Seed* (1914), that Lowell exhibited her revolutionary style. She was the first to employ "polyphonic prose" in English, mixing formal verse and free forms. The focus of the Imagist movement shifted from Erza Pound to Amy Lowell, which caused Pound to quip that the Imagists had become the "Amygists." In addition to her innovations in American poetic style, her translations from the Japanese and Chinese with Florence Ayscough (*Fin-Flower Tablets,* 1921) introduced Oriental poetry to the English-speaking literary world. Poetry in Chinese and Japanese is characterized by the predominance of images, usually in clear color planes. Such qualities found their way into Amy Lowell's poetry. Perceptions of everyday life mark her poetry and contrast with the prevalent romantic diction of contemporaries. Beneath the colorful and intimate details, in her best poems pathos reigns. Her other volumes of poetry are: *Men, Women, and Ghosts* (1916). *Can Grande's Castle* (1918), *Pictures of the Floating World* (1919), and three posthumous volumes, *What's O'Clock* (1925), which was awarded the Pulitzer Prize, *East Wind,* and *Ballads for Sale* (1927). Her critical works were: *Six French Poets* (1915), *Tendencies in Modern American Poetry* (1917), *A Critical Fable,* which was a sequel to James Russell Lowell's *A Fable for Critics,* and *John Keats,* a biography.

Patterns

I walk down the garden paths,
And all the daffodils
Are blowing, and the bright blue squills.
I walk down the patterned garden paths
In my stiff, brocaded gown.

With my powdered hair and jewelled fan,
I too am a rare
Pattern. As I wander down
The garden paths.

My dress is richly figured,
And the train
Makes a pink and silver stain
On the gravel, and the thrift
Of the borders,
Just a plate of current fashion
Tripping by in high-heeled, ribboned shoes.
Not a softness anywhere about me,
Only whalebone and brocade.
And I sink on a seat in the shade
Of a lime tree. For my passion
Wars against the stiff brocade.
The daffodils and squills
Flutter in the breeze
As they please.
And I weep;
For the lime tree is in blossom
And one small flower has dropped upon my bosom.

And the plashing of waterdrops
In the marble fountain
comes down the garden paths.
The dripping never stops.
Underneath my stiffened gown
Is the softness of a woman bathing in a marble basin,
A basin in the midst of hedges grown
So thick, she cannot see her lover hiding,
But she guesses he is near,
And the sliding of the water
Seems the stroking of a dear
Hand upon her.
What is Summer in a fine brocaded gown!
I should like to see it lying in a heap upon the ground.
All the pink and silver crumpled up on the ground.

I would be the pink and silver as I ran along the paths.
And he would stumble after,
Bewildered by my laughter.
I should see the sun flashing from his sword-hilt and buckles on his
    shoes.
I would choose
To lead him in a maze along the patterned paths.
A bright and laughing maze for my heavy-booted lover.
Till he caught me in the shade,
And the buttons of his waistcoat bruised my body as he clasped me,
Aching, melting, unafraid.
With the shadows of the leaves and the sundrops.
And the plopping of the waterdrops,
All about us in the open afternoon—
I am very like to swoon
With the weight of this brocade,
For the sun sifts through the shade.

Underneath the fallen blossom
In my bosom,
Is a letter I have hid.
It was brought to me this morning by a rider from the Duke.
"Madam, we regret to inform you that Lord Hartwell
Died in action Thursday se'nnight."
As I read it in the white, morning sunlight,
The letters squirmed like snakes.
"Any answer, Madam," said my footman.
"No," I told him.
"See that the messenger takes some refreshment.
No, no answer."
And I walked into the garden,
Up and down the patterned paths,
In my stiff, correct brocade.
The blue and yellow flowers stood up proudly in the sun,
Each one.
I stood upright too,
Held rigid to the pattern
By the stiffness of my gown.
Up and down I walked.
Up and down.

In a month he would have been my husband.
In a month, here, underneath this lime,
We would have broken the pattern;
He for me, and I for him,
He as Colonel, I as Lady,
On this shady seat.
He had a whim
That sunlight carried blessing.
And I answered, "It shall be as you have said."
Now he is dead.

In Summer and in Winter I shall walk
Up and down
The patterned garden paths
In my stiff, brocaded gown.
The squills and daffodils
Will give place to pillard roses, and to asters, and to snow.
I shall go
Up and down
In my gown.
Gorgeously arrayed,
Boned and stayed.
And the softness of my body will be guarded from embrace
By each button, hook, and lace.
For the man who should loose me is dead,
Fighting with the Duke in Flanders,
In a pattern called a war.
Christ! What are patterns for?

Grotesque

Why do the lilies goggle their tongues at me
When I pluck them;
And writhe, and twist,
And strangle themselves against my fingers,
So that I can hardly weave the garland
For your hair?
Why do they shriek your name

And spit at me
When I would cluster them?
Must I kill them
To make them lie still,
And send you a wreath of lolling corpses
To turn putrid and soft
On your forehead
While you dance?

From One Who Stays

How empty seems the town now you are gone!
   A wilderness of sad streets, where gaunt walls
   Hide nothing to desire; sunshine falls
Eery, distorted, as it long had shone
On white, dead faces tombed in halls of stone.
   The whir of motors, stricken through with calls
   Of playing boys, floats up at intervals;
But all these noises blur to one long moan.
   What quest is worth pursuing? And how strange
That other men still go accustomed ways!
I hate their interest in the things they do.
   A spectre-horde repeating without change.

Carrefour

O you,
Who came upon me once
Stretched under apple-trees just after bathing,
Why did you not strangle me before speaking
Rather than fill me with the wild white honey of your words
And then leave me to the mercy
Of the forest bees?

Proportion

In the sky there is a moon and stars,
And in my garden there are yellow moths
Fluttering about a white azalea bush.

Wind and Silver

Greatly shining,
The Autumn moon floats in the thin sky;
And the fish-ponds shake their backs and flash their dragon scales
As she passes over them.

The Taxi

When I go away from you
The world beats dead
Like a slackened drum.
I call out for you against the jutted stars
And shout into the ridges of the wind.
Streets coming fast,
One after the other,
Wedge you away from me,
And the lamps of the city prick my eyes
So that I can no longer see your face.
Why should I leave you,
To wound myself upon the sharp edges of the night?

The Fisherman's Wife

When I am alone,
The wind in the pine-trees
Is like the shuffling of waves
Upon the wooden sides of a boat.

from Dreams in War Time

I dug a grave under an oak-tree.
With infinite care, I stamped my spade
Into the heavy grass.
The sod sucked it,
And I drew it out with effort,
Watching the steel run liquid in the moonlight

As it became clear.
I stooped, and dug, and never turned,
For behind me,
On the dried leaves,
My own face lay like a white pebble,
Waiting.

Mina Loy

Mina Loy (1882–1966).   Born Mina Gertrude Lowy in London, Mina Loy was the daughter of Sigmund Lowry, a Jewish tailor of Hungarian background. Poet, playwright, painter, sculptor, model, and commercially successful fashion designer, Loy was one of the major figures of the modernist movement in both literature and the visual arts. After emigrating to Paris in 1905, she met Gertrude Stein and through her salon became acquainted with Apollinaire, Picasso, and Rousseau. In 1906 her paintings were singled out in the *Gazette des Beaux Arts* review of the exhibit at the Salon d'Automne in which Fauvism was born. At twenty-three she was elected a member of the Salon d'Automne. When she wasn't living at the residences in Paris, Florence, London, Paris, and Mexico, she was in the Alfred Stieglitz circle in New York from 1916 to 1918, and became a close friend of Marcel Duchamp and William Carlos Williams. In 1917 she was profiled as the prototypical "Modern Woman" in the *New York Evening Sun.*

These were heady years for Loy. Her poetry was praised by Ezra Pound in *The Little Review* and Ivor Winters in "The Dial." T. S. Eliot lauded both Mina Loy and Marianne Moore in *The Egoist,* where their poems appeared. Roger L. Conover, editor of Loy's collected poems, *The Last Lunar Baedeker* (1982), points out the significance of Loy's contribution to that issue, "At the Door of the House," to Eliot's oeuvre, noting that "its imagery and phrasing are cues to the Tarot passage of *The Waste Land* published five years later" in the 1922 issue of "The Dial" in which *The Waste Land* first appeared. In fact, *The Waste Land* is permeated with the exotic symbolism, the satiric puns, and modernist collage conversations characteristic of Loy's poetry.

In an age of frivolous yet scorching literary anti-Semitism, her extraordinary "automythology" *Anglo-Mongrels and the Rose* (1923–1925) was a response to the shallow bigotry of the time. In her "Feminist Manifesto" (ca. 1914) Loy advises women: "Leave off looking to men to find out what you are not. See within yourselves to find out what you are." She asserts that "men and women are enemies," mutually parasitic and exploited, and that the "only point at which the interests merge is the sexual embrace." Alicia Ostriker writes that Loy became

the first woman poet to examine female sexual experience with a combination of scandalous candor and formal rigor. Her "Parturition" . . . moves toward a definition of female libido, a "lascivious revelation." Her "Love Songs," contemporary with J. Alfred Prufrock's, unsentimentally . . . conclude with a sardonic salute to "Love . . . the preeminent littérateur," which dismisses not simply an individual lover but an entire tradition of poetry as mere male posturing.

After extensive travels, Loy settled in Paris in 1923, living in the same building as Djuna Barnes, who served briefly as her agent, and appearing regularly at Gertrude Stein's salon. At the time, Peggy Guggenheim Vail arranged exhibits of her paper cutouts in New York (years before Matisse was to bring that medium to world attention). Loy herself became an agent for preeminent Parisian artists who were also her friends, including Henri Cartier-Bresson, Georges Braque, Salvador Dali, Max Ernst, Juan Gris, Arshile Gorky, and René Magritte.

She married Stephen Haweis in 1903. Their first daughter, Oda, died on her first birthday. In 1907 their daughter Joella was born, followed in 1909 by a son, Giles. But the marriage was troubled and ended in an angry divorce. Her great romance was with boxer, writer, and creator of hoaxes Arthur Craven, whom she met at a lecture he gave, "The Independent Artists in France and America" (during which he undressed and was arrested). They were married in Mexico. When Loy became pregnant, they decided to return to Europe. Loy sailed ahead via Buenos Aires, and Craven was never seen again. Their daughter, Fabi, was born in London. In 1921 Haweis kidnapped Giles, and in 1923 the boy died.

Though Loy was pivotal in the early history of Anglo-American poetry, and praise for her work abounded—Yvor Winters predicted that she and Williams would be the two most influential poets of the future—after 1936, when she came to America, where she would spend the last thirty years of her life, whatever influence she had in literary and art circles seemed to vanish. In New York she still had contact with some friends, particularly Djuna Barnes and Joseph Cornell. But her real friends were the "Angel-Bums" in the Bowery of Manhattan, where she lived. A Christian Scientist since 1909, she sought Christian purity in social and material poverty during the forties, proclaiming that "owning things and knowing people meant absolutely nothing." She was, Conover writes,

engaged in a metaphorical quest to find Christ in the Bowery . . . She writes a series of destitution poems which as a group comprise her best late work. She now scavenges back alleys and abandoned lots for trash . . . Out of discarded remnants and materially bland elements she assembled montages of street scenes and framed nativities of Bowery anonyms into scenes of divine grace. Twenty years after losing the Poet-Boxer, she reanimates his essence in the Angel-Bum.

Conover asks the essential question: "How could an entire generation of poets and critics save a few umbrageous guerrillas come of age without paying the slightest attention to one of the most pivotal voices in the American Free Verse Movement?" Paradoxically, though she seems to have been well known in Paris, from early on she tended toward reticence and withdrawal. Conover recounts:

She wrote under an elaborate system of anagrammatically and numerologically derived pseudonyms . . . a rumour was circulating around Paris in the Twenties—that Mina Loy was in fact not a real person at all, but a forged persona, a hoax of critics . . . Loy turned up at Natalie Barney's salon in order to convince guests of her existence. "I assure you I am indeed a live being. But it is necessary to stay very unknown . . . To maintain my incognito the hazard I chose was—poet."

Like Emily Dickinson, Loy chose isolation and obscurity, albeit ambivalently. Some attribute her obscurity to the difficulty of her poems. Pound arrogantly claimed: "She is readable, by me that is." But William Carlos Williams had perhaps the clearest vision of the poet and her life. Cut off from her for nearly thirty years, he was asked by a publisher to write an introduction, and with characteristic straightforwardness wrote:

Mina Loy was endowed from birth with a first-rate intelligence and a sensibility which has plagued her all her life facing a shoddy world. When she puts a word down on paper it is clean; that forces her fellows to shy away from it because they are not clean and will be contaminated by her cleanliness. Therefore she has not been a successful writer and couldn't care less. But it has hurt chances of being known.

In 1953 she moved to Aspen, Colorado, where her two daughters lived. By then she was a recluse from the literary world, seeking neither publication nor fame. As revealed in one of her last poems, "Letters of the Unliving," Loy was perfectly aware of her choice to go on writing, with or without an audience. Emily Dickinson's skepticism about that "shapeless friend" immortality is amplified by Loy:

> The present implies presence
> thus
> unauthorized by the present
> these letters are left authorless—
> have lost all origin
> since the inscribing hand
> lost life.

Yet the last lines of the poem are puzzling. While she bleakly predicts the oblivion of her person and her words, she does so paradoxically—with more poetry. Ophelia's youthful beauty and madness survive, although she is older now, and comatose:

Leave me
my final illiteracy
of memory's languor—
my preference
to drift in lenient coma
an older Ophelia
on Lethe

When she died in 1966, Mina Loy's disappearance was seemingly complete.

Poe

a lyric elixir of death
embalms
the spindle spirits of your hour glass loves
on moon spun nights

sets
icicled canopy
for corpses of poesy
with roses and northern lights

where frozen nightingales in ilex aisles
sing burial rites

Gertrude Stein

Curie
of the laboratory
of vocabulary
she crushed
the tonnage
of consciousness
congealed to phrases
to extract
a radium of the word

Three Moments in Paris

1. One O'Clock at Night

Though you have never possessed me
I have belonged to you since the beginning of time
And sleepily I sit on your chair beside you
Leaning against your shoulder
And your careless arm across my back gesticulates
As your indisputable male voice   roars
Through my brain and my body
Arguing "Dynamic Decomposition"
Of which I understand nothing
Sleepily
And the only less male voice of your brother
     pugilist of the intellect
Booms   as it seems to me   so sleepy
Across an interval of a thousand miles
An interim of a thousand years
But you who make more noise than any man
     in the world when you clear your throat
Deafening   wake me
And I catch the thread of the argument
Immediately assuming my personal mental
     attitude
And cease to be a woman

Beautiful halfhour of being a mere woman
The animal woman
Understanding nothing of man
But mastery   and the security of imparted
     physical heat
Indifferent to cerebral gymnastics
Or regarding them as the self-indulgent
     play of children
Or the thunder of alien gods
But you wake me up
Anyhow   who am I that I should criticize
     your theories of "Plastic Velocity"

"Let us go home   she is tired   and
     wants to go to bed."

2. Café du Néant

Little tapers lighted   leaning diagonally
Stuck in coffin tables of the Café du Néant
Leaning to the breath of baited bodies
Like young poplars fringing the Loire

Eyes that are full of love
And eyes that are full of kohl
Projecting light across the fulsome ambiente
Trailing the rest of the animal behind them
Telling of tales without words
And lies of no consequence
One way or another

The young lovers hermetically buttoned up in black
To black cravat
To the blue powder edge dusting the yellow throat
What color could have been your bodies
When last you put them away

Nostalgic youth
Holding your mistress's pricked finger
In the indifferent flame of the taper
Synthetic symbol of   LIFE
In this factitious chamber of   DEATH
The woman
As usual
Is smiling   as bravely
As it is given to her to be   brave
While the brandy cherries
In winking glasses
Are decomposing
Harmoniously

With the flesh of spectators
And at a given spot

There is one
Who
Having the concentric lighting focussed precisely upon her
Prophetically blossoms in perfect putrefaction
Yet   there are cabs outside the door.

3. Magasins du Louvre

All the virgin eyes in the world are made of glass

Long lines of boxes
Of dolls
Propped against banisters
Walls and pillars
Huddled on shelves
And composite babies with arms extended
Hang from the ceiling
Beckoning
Smiling
In a profound silence
Which the shop walker left trailing behind him
When he ambled to the further end of the gallery
To annoy the shop girl

All the virgin eyes in the world are made of glass
They alone have the effrontery to
Stare through the human soul
    seeing nothing
Between parted fringes

One cocotte wears a bowler hat and a sham camellia
And one an iridescent boa
For there are two of them
Passing
And the solicitous mouth of one is straight
The other curved to a static smile

They see the dolls
And for a moment their eyes relax
To a flicker of elements unconditionally primeval
And now averted
Seek each other's   surreptitiously
To know if the other has seen
While mine are inextricably entangled with the
     pattern on the carpet
As eyes are apt to be
In their shame
Having surprised a gesture that is ultimately intimate

All the virgin eyes in the world are made of glass.

At the Door of the House

A thousand women's eyes
Riveted to the unrealizable
Scatter the washstand of the cardteller
Defiled marble of Carrara
On which she spreads
Color picture maps of destiny
In the corner
Of an inconducive bedroom

"Impassioned
Doubly impassioned
Sad
You see these three cards
But here is the Double Victory
And there is an elderly lady
Ill   in whom you are concerned
This   is the Devil
And these two skeletons
Are mortifications
You   are going to make a journey

At evening   about love
Here is the Man of the Heart

Turning his shoulders to a lady
Covered with tears   about matrimony

At the door of your house
There is a letter   about an affair
And a bed   and a table
And this ace of spades turned upside-down
'With respect'
Means   that some man
Has   well you know
Intentions   little honorable

Here you are   covered with tears
For a deception
The Man of the Heart
Is in thoughtfulness for a letter
He will make a journey at evening
And really   lady
I should say
It will not be long before you see him
For there he is at the door of the house

And look
Here you are
    And here he is
    In life and thought
At the door of the house"

Muddled among the analine brightness of the Tauro Cards
The wheels with wings
The rows on rows of goblets
    Passionate magneta blossoms
Hermits   —bring luck—
Moons   Prison-fortresses
Cudgels
A man cut in half
    Means a deception
And the nude woman
    Stands for the world

Those eyes

Of Petronilla Lucia Letizia
   Felicita
Filomena Amalia
Orsola Geltrude Caterina Delfina
Zita Bibiana   Tarsilla
Eufemia,
Looking for the little love-tale
That never came true
At the door of the house

Parturition

I am the centre
Of a circle of pain
Exceeding its boundaries in every direction
The business of the bland sun
Has no affair with me
In my congested cosmos of agony
From which there is no escape
On infinitely prolonged nerve-vibrations
Or in contraction
To the pinpoint nucleus of being
Locate an irritation   without
It is   within
Within
It is without.
The sensitized area
Is identical   with the extensity
Of intension

I am the false quantity
In the harmony of physiological potentiality
To which
Gaining self-control
I should be consonant
In time

Pain is no stronger than the resisting force
Pain calls up in me
The struggle is equal

The open window is full of a voice
A fashionable portrait painter
Running upstairs to a woman's apartment
Sings
    "All the girls are tid'ly did'ly
    All the girls are nice
    Whether they wear their hair in curls
    Or—"
At the back of the thoughts to which I permit crystallization
The conception   Brute
Why?
    The irresponsibility of the male
Leaves woman her superior Inferiority.

He is running upstairs
I am climbing a distorted mountain of agony
Incidentally with the exhaustion of control
I reach the summit
And gradually subside into anticipation of
Repose
Which never comes.
For another mountain is growing up
Which   goaded by the unavoidable
I must traverse
Traversing myself

Something in the delirium of night hours
Confuses while intensifying sensibility
Blurring spatial contours
So aiding elusion of the circumscribed
That the gurgling of a crucified wild beast
Comes from so far away
And the foam on the stretched muscles of a mouth
Is no part of myself
There is a climax in sensibility

When pain surpassing itself
Becomes exotic
And the ego succeeds in unifying the positive and
   negative poles of sensation
Uniting the opposing and resisting forces
In lascivious revelation

Relaxation
Negation of myself as a unit
    Vacuum interlude
I should have been emptied of life
Giving life
For consciousness in crises   races
Through the subliminal deposits of evolutionary processes

Have I not
Somewhere
Scrutinized
A dead white feathered moth
Laying eggs?

A moment
Being realization
Can
Vitalized by cosmic initiation
Furnish an adequate apology
For the objective
Agglomeration of activities
Of a life
LIFE
A leap with nature
Into the essence
Of unpredicted Maternity
Against my thigh
Touch of infinitesimal motion
Scarcely perceptible
Undulation
Warmth   moisture

Stir of incipient life
Precipitating into me
The contents of the universe
Mother I am
Identical
With infinite Maternity
  Indivisible
  Acutely
  I am absorbed
  Into
The was-is-ever-shall-be
Of cosmic reproductivity

Rises from the subconscious
Impression of a cat
With blind kittens
Among her legs
Same undulating life-stir
I am that cat

Rises from the subconscious
Impression of small animal carcass
Covered with blue bottles
—Epicurean—
And through the insects
Waves that same undulation of living
Death
Life
I am knowing
All about
  Unfolding

The next morning
Each woman-of-the-people
Tiptoeing the red pile of the carpet
Doing hushed service
Each woman-of-the-people
Wearing a halo
A ludicrous little halo
Of which she is sublimely unaware

I once heard in church
God made them

From: Love Songs to Joannes

Spawn of Fantasies
Sitting the appraisable
Pig Cupid
His rosy snout
Rooting erotic garbage
"Once upon a time"
Pulls a weed
White star-topped
Among wild oats
Sown in mucous-membrane

I would
An eye in a Bengal light
Eternity in a skyrocket
Constellations in an ocean
Whose rivers run no fresher
Than a trickle of saliva

There are   suspect places

I must live in my lantern
Trimming subliminal flicker
Virginal   to the bellows
Of experience

                    Coloured glass

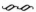

The skin-sack
In which a wanton duality
Packed
All the completions

Of my infructuous impulses
Something the shape of a man
To the casual vulgarity of the merely observant
More of a clock-work mechanism
Running down against time
To which I am not paced

My fingertips are numb
from fretting your hair
A God's doormat
On the threshold of your mind

∽∽

We might have coupled
In the bedridden monopoly of a moment
Or broken flesh with one another
At the profane communion table
Where wine is spilled on promiscuous lips

We might have given birth to a butterfly
With the daily news
Printed in blood on its wings

∽∽

. . .
And Time would be set back

∽∽

The wind stuffs the scum of the white street
Into my lungs and my nostrils
Exhilarated birds
Prolonging flight into the night
Never reaching——

∽∽

I am the jealous storehouse of the candle-ends
That lit your adolescent learning

Behind God's eyes
There might
Be other lights

✺

Dear one   at your mercy
Our Universe
Is only
A colourless onion
You derobe
Sheath by sheath
      Remaining
A disheartening odor
About your nervy hands

✺

Today
Everlasting passing apparent imperceptible
To you
I bring the nascent virginity of
—Myself—for the moment

No love   or the other thing
Only the impact of lighted bodies
Knocking sparks off each other
In chaos

✺

Seldom   Trying for Love
Fantasy dealt them out as gods
Two or three men   looked only human
But you alone
Superhuman   apparently
I had to be caught in the weak eddy
Of your drivelling humanity
            To love you most

∾

We might have lived together
In the lights of the Arno
Or gone apple stealing under the sea
Or played
Hide and seek in love and cobwebs
And a lullaby on a tin pan

And talked till there were no more tongues
To talk with
And never have known any better

∾

I don't care
Where the legs of the legs of the furniture are walking to
Or what is hidden in the shadows they stride
Or what would look at me
If the shutters were not shut

Red   a warm colour on the battlefield
Heavy on my knees as a counterpane
Count counter
I counted   the fringe of the towel
Till two tassels clinging together
Let the square room fall away
From a round vacuum
Dilating with my breath

∾

Let Joy go solace-winged
To flutter whom she may concern

∾

Green things grow
Salads

For the cerebral
Forager's revival

Upon bossed bellies
Of mountains
Rolling in the sun
And flowered flummery
Breaks
To my silly shoes

In ways without you
I go
Gracelessly
As things go

✿

Shedding our petty pruderies
From slit eyes
We sidle up
To Nature
       that irate pornographist

✿

The prig of passion
To your professorial paucity

Protoplasm was raving mad
Evolving us

✿

Love—the preeminent littérateur

Photo after Pogrom

Arrangement by rage
of human rubble
the false-eternal statues of the slain
until they putrify:

Tossed on a pile of dead,
one woman,

her body hacked to utter beauty,
oddly, by murder,

attains the absolute smile
of dispossession:
the marble pause before the extinct haven.

Death's drear
erasure of fear,
the unassumed
composure,

the purposeless peace
sealing the faces
of corpses.

Corpses are virgin.

An Old Woman

The past has come apart
events are vagueing
the future is a seedless pod
the present   pain.

Not even pain has that precision
with which it struck in youth.

Years like moths
erode internal organs
hanging or falling
in a spoiled closet.

Does your mirror bedevil you?
Or is the impossible
possible to senility?

How could the erstwhile
agile and slim self—
that narrow silhouette—
come to contain
this huge incognito—
this bulbous stranger—
only to be exorcised by death?

Dilation has entirely dominated
your long reality.

Letters of the Unliving

The present implies presence
thus
unauthorized by the present
these letters are left authorless—
have lost all origin
since the inscribing hand
lost life.

The hoarseness of the past
croaks
from creased leaves
covered with unwritten writing
since death's erasure
of the writer—
erased the lover

Well-chosen and so ill-relinquished
the husband heartsease—
acme of communion—

made euphonious
our esoteric universe.

Ego's oasis now's
the sole companion.

My body and my reason
you left to the drought of your dying:
the longing and the lack
of a racked creature
shouting
to an unanswering hiatus
"reunite us!"

till slyly
patience creeps up on passion
and the elation of youth
dwindles out of season.

Agony
ends in an equal grave
with ecstasy.

An uneasy mist
rises from this calligraphy of recollection
documenting a terror of dementia.

This package of ago
creaks with the horror of echo.

The bloom of love
decoyed
to decay by the finger
of Hazard the swindler—
deathly handler who leaves
no post-mortem mask
but a callous earth.

Posing the extreme enigma
in my Bewilderness
can your face excelling Adonis
have ceased to be
or ever have had existence?

With you no longer the addresser
there is no addressee
to dally with defunct reality.

Can one who still has being
be inexistent?

I am become
dumb
in answer
to your dead language of amor.

Diminuendo
of life's imposture
implies no possible retrial
by my present self—
my cloud-corpse
beshadowing your shroud.

The one I was with you:
inhumed in chasms.
No creator
reconstrues scar-tissue
to shine as birth-star.

But to my sub-cerebral surprise
at last on blasé sorrow
dawns an iota of disgust
for life's intemperance:

"As once you were"

Withhold your ghostly reference
to the sweet once were we.

Leave me
my final illiteracy
of memory's languor—

my preference
to drift in lenient coma
an older Ophelia
on Lethe.

Elinor Wylie

Elinor Wylie (1885–1928).   Wylie was born in Somerville, New Jersey. Her
grandfather was governor of Pennsylvania and she was raised in a socially prominent
family in Washington, D.C. She eloped with Philip Hichborn, and later eloped with
Horace Wylie. Her last marriage—in a short, flamboyant life—was to the writer
William Rose Benét. Talented in several arts, she was torn between painting and writing.
She wrote eight novels and books of poetry. Her first book, *Incidental Numbers* (1912),
was published privately in England. The first of her books to bring her recognition was
Nets to Catch the Wind (1921). Her other volumes of poetry include: *Black Armour*
(1923), *Trivial Breath* (1928), *Angels and Earthly Creatures* (1929), and *Collected
Poems of Elinor Wylie* (1932).

Sanctuary

This is the bricklayer; hear the thud
Of his heavy load dumped down on stone.
His lustrous bricks are brighter than blood,
His smoking mortar whiter than bone.

Set each sharp-edged, fire-bitten brick
Straight by the plumb-line's shivering length;
Make my marvelous wall so thick
Dead nor living may shake its strength.

Full as a crystal cup with drink
Is my cell with dreams, and quiet, and cool. . . .
Stop, old man! You must leave a chink;
How can I breathe? *You can't, you fool!*

The Eagle and the Mole

Avoid the reeking herd,
Shun the polluted flock,

Live like that stoic bird,
The eagle of the rock.

The huddled warmth of crowds
Begets and fosters hate;
he keeps, above the clouds,
His cliff inviolate.

When flocks are folded warm,
And herds to shelter run,
He sails above the storm,
He stares into the sun.

If in the eagle's track
Your sinews cannot leap,
Avoid the lathered pack,
Turn from the steaming sheep.

If you would keep your soul
From spotted sight or sound,
Live like the velvet mole;
Go burrow underground.

And there hold intercourse
With roots of trees and stones,
With rivers at their source,
And disembodied bones.

Prophecy

I shall lie hidden in a hut
    In the middle of an alder wood,
With the back door blind and bolted shut,
    And the front door locked for good.

I shall lie folded like a saint.
    Lapped in a scented linen sheet,

On a bedstead striped with bright-blue paint,
   Narrow and cold and neat.

The midnight will be glassy black
   Behind the panes, with wind about
To set his mouth against a crack
   And blow the candle out.

⚮

Down to the Puritan marrow of my bones
There's something in this richness that I hate.
I love the look, austere, immaculate,
Of landscapes drawn in pearly monotones.
There's something in my very blood that owns
Bare hills, cold silver on a sky of slate,
A thread of water, churned to milky spate
Streaming through slanted pastures fenced with stones.

I love those skies, thin blue or snowy gray,
Those fields sparse-planted, rendering meagre sheaves
That spring, briefer than apple-blossom's breath,
Summer, so much too beautiful to stay,
Swift autumn, like a bonfire of leaves,
And sleepy winter, like the sleep of death.

H.D.

H.D. (1886–1961). Hilda Doolittle was born in Bethlehem, Pennsylvania. She attended Bryn Mawr College and was a classicist all her life. In 1911 she went to England and never returned to America. With Ezra Pound, she was an early Imagist, and while she abandoned the movement formally, she held closer to its tenets of clarity, precision, and brevity than any other member of the group. She admired Sappho's fragments—her own poems have the intimacy and classical purity of Sapphic lines—and many of her poems were actually expansions of phrases of the poet from Lesbos. She wrote a play, novels, and essays, and translated Greek drama. In the last years of her life her poetry received much critical appreciation after a lapse of interest in her work. Early in life she signed her published works simply "H.D.," by which she was known to friends and readers. Her volumes of poetry include *Sea Garden* (1916),

Hymen (1921), Heliodora and Other Poems (1924), Red Roses for the Bronze (1932), Hermetic Definition (1972), Helen in Egypt (1961). The Walls Do Not Fall (1944), Tribute to the Angels (1945), and The Flowering of the Rod (1946) appeared as Trilogy in 1972. Her Selected Poems appeared in 1957, and her Collected Poems, 1912–1944, edited by Louis Martz, in 1983. Tribute to Freud (1956) records her psychoanalysis with Freud, and End to Torment her relationship with Ezra Pound. She also wrote three autobiographical novels: The Gift, which evokes her childhood, HERmioné, and Bid Me to Live, in which her estranged husband Richard Aldington, Ezra Pound, Amy Lowell, and D. H. and Frieda Lawrence appear as thinly disguised characters.

Pear Tree

Silver dust,
lifted from the earth,
higher than my arms reach,
you have mounted,
O, silver,
higher than my arms reach,
you front us with great mass;

no flower ever opened
so staunch a white leaf,
no flower ever parted silver
from such rare silver;

O, white pear,
your flower-tufts
thick on the branch
bring summer and ripe fruits
in their purple hearts.

Helen

All Greece hates
the still eyes in the white face,
the lustre as of olives
where she stands,
and the white hands.

All Greece reviles
the wan face when she smiles,
hating it deeper still
when it grows wan and white,
remembering past enchantments
and past ills.

Greece sees, unmoved,
God's daughter, born of love,
the beauty of cool feet
and slenderest knees,
could love indeed the maid,
only if she were laid,
white ash amid funereal cypresses.

Evadne

I first tasted under Apollo's lips,
love and love sweetness,
I, Evadne;
my hair is made of crisp violets
or hyacinth which the wind combs back
across some rock shelf;
I, Evadne,
was made of the god of light.

His hair was crisp to my mouth,
as the flower of the crocus,
across my cheek,
cool as the silver-cress
on Erotos bank;
between my chin and throat,
his mouth slipped over and over.

Still between my arm and shoulder,
I feel the brush of his hair,
and my hands keep the gold they took,
as they wandered over and over,
that great arm-full of yellow flowers.

The Moon in Your Hands

If you take the moon in your hands
and turn it round
(heavy, slightly tarnished platter)
you're there;

if you pull dry sea-weed from the sand
and turn it round,
and wonder at the underside's bright amber,
your eyes

look out as they did here,
(you don't remember)
when my soul turned round,

perceiving the other-side of everything,
mullein-leaf, dogwood-leaf, moth-wing
and dandelion-seed under the ground.

We have seen how the most amiable,
under physical stress.

become wolves, jackals,
mongrel curs;

we know further that hunger
may make hyenas of the best of us;

let us, therefore (though we do not forget
Love, the Creator,

her chariot and white doves),
entreat Hest,

Aset, Isis, the great enchantress,
in her attribute of Serqet,

the original great-mother,
who drove

harnessed scorpions
before her.

Invisible, indivisible Spirit,
how is it you come so near,

how is it that we dare
approach the high-altar?

we crossed the charred portico,
passed through a frame—doorless—

entered a shrine; like a ghost,
we entered a house through a wall;

then still not knowing
whether (like the wall)

we were there or not-there,
we saw the tree flowering;

it was an ordinary tree
in an old garden-square.

Heliodora

He and I sought together,
over the spattered table,
rhymes and flowers,
gifts for a name.

He said, among others,
"I will bring"
(and the phrase was just and good,
but not as good as mine,)
"the narcissus that loves the rain."

We strove for a name,
while the light of the lamps burnt thin
and the outer dawn came in,
a ghost, the last at the feast
or the first,
to sit within
with the two that remained
to quibble in flowers and verse
over a girl's name.

He said, "the rain-loving,"
I said, "the narcissus, drunk,
drunk with the rain,"
yet I had lost
for he said,
"the rose, the lover's gift,
is loved-of-love,"
he said it,
"loved-of-love";

I waited, even as he spoke,
to see the room filled with a light,
as when in winter,
the embers catch in a wind
when a room is dank;
so it would be filled, I thought,
our room with a light
when he said,
(and he said it first),
"the rose, the lover's delight,
is loved-of-love,"
but the light was the same.

Then he caught,
seeing the fire in my eyes,
my fire, my fever, perhaps,
for he leaned
with the purple wine
stained on his sleeve,

and said this:
"did you ever think
a girl's mouth,
caught in a kiss,
is a lily that laughs?"

I had not.
I saw it now
as men must see it forever afterwards;
no poet could write again,
"the red-lily,
a girl's laugh caught in a kiss";
it was his to pour in the vat
from which all poets dip and quaff,
for poets are brothers in this.

So I saw the fire in his eyes,
it was almost my fire,
(he was younger,)
I saw the face so white,
my heart beat,
it was almost my phrase;
I said, "surprise the muses,
take them by surprise;
it is late,
rather it is dawn-rise,
those ladies sleep, the nine,
our own king's mistresses."

A name to rhyme,
flowers to bring to a name,
what was one girl faint and shy,
with eyes like the myrtle,
(I said: "her underlids
are rather like myrtle,")
to vie with the nine?

Let him take the name,
he had the rhymes,

"the rose, loved-of-love,
the lily, a mouth that laughs,"
he had the gift,
"the scented crocus,
the purple hyacinth,"
what was one girl to the nine?

He said:
"I will make her a wreath;"
he said:
"I will write it thus:
I will bring you the lily that laughs,
I will twine
with soft narcissus, the myrtle,
sweet crocus, white violet,
the purple hyacinth, and last,
the rose, loved-of-love,
that these may drip on your hair
the less soft flowers,
may mingle sweet with the sweet
of Heliodora's locks,
myrrh-curled."

(He wrote "myrrh-curled,"
I think, the first.)

I said:
"they sleep, the nine,"
when he shouted swift and passionate:
"*that* for the nine!
above the hills,
the sun is about to wake,
and to-day white violets
shine beside white lilies
adrift on the mountain side;
to-day the narcissus opens
that loves the rain."

I watched him to the door,
catching his robe
as the wine-bowl crashed to the floor,
spilling a few wet lees,
(ah, his "purple hyacinth!")
I saw him out of the door,
I thought:
there will never be a poet
in all the centuries after this,
who will dare write,
after my friend's verse,
"a girl's mouth
is a lily kissed."

from Tribute to the Angel

I can not invent it,
I said it was agate,

I said, it lived, it gave—
fragrance—was near enough

to explain that quality
for which there is no name;

I do not want to name it,
I want to watch its faint

heart-beat, pulse-beat
as it quivers, I do not want

to talk about it,
I want to minimize thought,

concentrate on it
till I shrink,

dematerialize
and am drawn into it.

from The Flowering of the Rod

It was easy to see that he was not an ordinary
    merchant;
she saw that certainly—he was an ambassador;

there was hardly anyone you could trust
with this precious merchandise,

though the jars were sealed,
the fragrance got out somehow,

and the rumour was bruited about,
even if you yourself managed to keep out

of the ordinary haunts of the merchants;
some said, this distillation, this attar

lasted literally forever, had so lasted—
though no one could of course, actually know

what was or was-not in those alabaster boxes
of the Princesses of the Hyksos Kings,

there were unguent jars, certainly;
but who would open them?

they had charms wrought upon them,
there were sigils and painted figures on all the jars;

no one dismantled the tombs,
that would be wickedness—but this he knew,

his own people for centuries and centuries,
had whispered the secret of the sacred processes of
    distillation;

it was never written, not even in symbols, for this
    they knew—
no secret was safe with a woman.

Edith Sitwell

Edith Sitwell (1887–1964).   Dame Edith was born in Scarbourough, Yorkshire, the daughter of Sir George and Lady Ida Sitwell and the granddaughter of the earl of Landesbourough. With her brothers, Osbert and Sacheverell, she was in the aristocratic avant-garde of English literary life. She recited *Façade* through a megaphone to William Watson's music while hiding behind a screen on which a woman's enormous wide-open mouth was painted. In her life and her verse she ridiculed prevailing proprieties. Her poems dazzle and jingle: "Jane, Jane/ Tall as a crane/ The morning light creeks down again." During World War II she wrote moving, patriotic poems and was created dame commander of the British Empire by Queen Elizabeth II. She edited "Wheels," an anthology whose modernity created an outrage, and also wrote fiction, criticism, and history. Dame Edith's many volumes of poetry include *The Mother and Other Poems* (1915), *Clown's Houses* (1918), *The Wooden Pegasus* (1920), *Façade* (1922), *Bucolic Comedies* (1923), *The Sleeping Beauty* (1924), *Troy Park* (1925), *Rustic Elegies* (1927), *Gold Coast and Other Poems* (1930), *Street Song* (1942), *The Song of the Cold* (1948), and *Gardeners and Astronomers* (1953).

Sir Beelzebub

WHEN
Sir
Beelzebub called for his syllabub in the hotel in Hell
        Where Proserpine first fell,
Blue as the gendarmerie were the waves of the sea,

    (Rocking and shocking the bar-maid).

Nobody comes to give him his rum but the
Rim of the sky hippopotamus-glum

Enhances the chances to bless with a benison
Alfred Lord Tennyson crossing the bar laid
With cold vegetation from pale deputations
Of temperance workers (all signed In Memoriam)
Hoping with glory to trip up the Laureate's feet,

(Moving in classical meters). . . .

Like Balaclava, the lava came down from the
Roof, and the sea's blue wooden gendarmerie
Took them in charge while Beelzebub roared for his rum.

. . . None of them come!

Still Falls the Rain
The Raids, 1940. Night and Dawn

Still falls the Rain—
Dark as the world of man, black as our loss—
Blind as the nineteen hundred and forty nails
Upon the Cross.

Still falls the Rain
With a sound like the pulse of the heart that is changed to the
      hammer-beat
In the Potter's Field, and the sound of the impious feet
On the Tomb:
          Still falls the Rain

In the Field of Blood where the small hopes breed and the human
      brain
Nurtures its greed, that worm with the brow of Cain.

Still falls the Rain
At the feet of the Starved Man hung upon the Cross.
Christ that each day, each night, nails there, have mercy on us—
On Dives and on Lazarus:
Under the rain the sore and the gold are as one.

Still falls the Rain—
Still falls the blood from the Starved Man's wounded Side:
He bears in His Heart all wounds,—those of the light that died,
The last faint spark
In the self-murdered heart, the wounds of the sad uncomprehending
    dark,

The wounds of the baited bear,—
The blind and weeping bear whom the keepers beat
On his helpless flesh . . . the tears of the hunted hare.

Still falls the Rain—
Then—O Ile leape up to my God:who pulles me doune—
See, see where Christ's blood streames in the firmament:
It flows from the Brow we nailed upon the tree
Deep to the dying, to the thirsting heart
That holds the fires of the world,—dark-smirched with pain
As Caesar's laurel crown.

Then sounds the voice of One who like the heart of man
Was once a child who among beasts has lain—
"Still do I love, still shed my innocent light, my Blood, for thee."

Marianne Moore

Marianne Moore (1887–1972). Born in St. Louis, Missouri, she received her B.A. from Bryn Mawr College. A teacher of stenography, typing, bookkeeping, and commercial law at the Carlisle Indian School, she worked at the New York Public Library, and edited "The Dial" from 1925 to 1929. Her first volume of poetry, *Poems,* was published in 1921 when two of her friends, one of whom was H.D., "pirated" her work. In 1924 she received the Dial Award "for distinguished services to poetry" for her volume *Observations*. In 1951 her *Collected Poems,* with an introduction by T. S. Eliot, received the Bollingen Prize, the National Book Award, and the Pulitzer Prize. Her volumes include *Poems* (1921), *Observations* (1924), *Selected Poems* (1935), *The Pangolin, and Other Verse* (1936), *What Are Years?* (1941), *Nevertheless* (1944), *Collected Poems* (1951), *O To Be a Dragon* (1959), *Tell Me, Tell Me* (1966), *The Complete Poems of Marianne Moore* (1967). Her translations are *The Fables of La Fontaine* (1954) and

Adalbert Stifter's *Rock Crystal: A Christmas Tale;* her criticism, *Predilections* (1955) and *The Complete Prose of Marianne Moore* (1986). In each of her collections Moore deleted poems and extensively revised others. Characteristically, she begins her *Complete Poems* with the epigraph "Omissions are not accidents," and condenses the poem "Poetry" into an aphorism: "I, too, dislike it. / Reading it, however, with a perfect contempt for it, one discovers in / it, after all, a place for the genuine" (the long version of the poem appears in that volume's notes).

  Her attention to minute detail, strict syllabic meter, quotations, and personal associations creates a unique style and reveals a vision of curiosity. Along with the other moderns—H.D., Amy Lowell, Loy, Pound, Eliot, and Williams—she revolutionized poetry. Although all the moderns appropriated texts for use in their poems, Moore does so to a far greater extent, observing that hers is a "hybrid method of composition." Bonnie Costello writes: "Probably no other poet kept such careful track of the world as it is mediated by the printed word." In fact, Moore's notebooks are not personal reflections, but compilations of the works of others. Costello goes on to surmise: "For Moore, a poem is *not* a functional utterance; rather it is an ordering of language. The poet's function is not to say something, so much as to creatively order and reimagine our sayings." It is not surprising, then, that Moore copied into her notebook: "A good stealer is *ipso facto* a good inventor."

Poetry

  I, too, dislike it: there are things that are important beyond all this
          fiddle.
    Reading it, however, with a perfect contempt for it, one discovers
            in
      it, after all, a place for the genuine.
          Hands that can grasp, eyes
        that can dilate, hair that can rise
            if it must, these things are important not because a

    high-sounding interpretation can be put upon them but because they
            are
        useful. When they become so derivative as to become
            unintelligible,
      the same thing may be said for all of us, that we
          do not admire what
        we cannot understand: the bat
            holding on upside down or in quest of something to

eat, elephants pushing, a wild horse talking a roll, a tireless wolf
          under
   a tree, the immovable critic twitching his skin like a horse that
          feels a flea, the base-
   ball fan, the statistician—
          nor is it valid
             to discriminate against "business documents and

school-books;" all these phenomena are important. One must make
          a distinction
   however: when dragged into prominence by half poets, the result
          is not poetry,
   nor till the poets among us can be
          "literalists of
          the imagination"—above
             insolence and triviality and can present

for inspection, imaginary gardens with real toads in them, shall we
          have
   it. In the meantime, if you demand on the one hand,
   the raw material of poetry in
          all its rawness and
          that which is on the other hand
             genuine, then you are interested in poetry.

The Steeple-Jack

Dürer would have seen a reason for living
          in a town like this, with eight stranded whales
   to look at; with the sweet sea air coming into your house
   on a fine day, from water etched
          with waves as formal as the scales
   on a fish.

One by one in two's and three's, the seagulls keep
          flying back and forth over the town clock,
   or sailing around the lighthouse without moving their wings—
   rising steadily with a slight
          quiver of the body—or flock
   mewing where

a sea the purple of the peacock's neck is
    paled to greenish azure as Dürer changed
the pine green of the Tyrol to peacock blue and guinea
gray. You can see a twenty-five-
    pound lobster; and fish nets arranged
to dry. The

whirlwind fife-and-drum of the storm bends the salt
    marsh grass, disturbs stars in the sky and the
star on the steeple; it is a privilege to see so
much confusion. Disguised by what
    might seem the opposite, the sea-
side flowers and

trees are favored by the fog so that you have
    the tropics at first hand: the trumpet vine,
foxglove, giant snapdragon, a salpiglossis that has
spots and stripes; morning-glories, gourds,
    or moon-vines trained on fishing twine
at the back door:

cattails, flags, blueberries and spiderwort,
    striped grass, lichens, sunflowers, asters, daisies—
yellow and crab-claw ragged sailors with green bracts—toad-plant,
petunias, ferns; pink lilies, blue
    ones, tigers; poppies; black sweet-peas.
The climate

is not right for the banyan, frangipani, or
    jack-fruit trees; or for exotic serpent
life. Ring lizard and snakeskin for the foot, if you see fit;
but here they've cats, not cobras, to
    keep down the rats. The diffident
little newt

with white pin-dots on black horizontal spaced-
    out bands lives here; yet there is nothing that
ambition can buy or take away. The college student

named Ambrose sits on the hillside
    with his not-native books and hat
and sees boats

at sea progress white and rigid as if in
    a groove. Liking an elegance of which
the source is not bravado, he knows by heart the antique
sugar-bowl shaped summerhouse of
    interlacing slats, and the pitch
of the church

spire, not true, from which a man in scarlet lets
    down a rope as a spider spins a thread;
he might be part of a novel, but on the sidewalk a
sign says C. J. Poole, Steeple-Jack,
    in black and white; and one in red
and white says

Danger. The church portico has four fluted
    columns, each a single piece of stone, made
modester by whitewash. This would be a fit haven for
waifs, children, animals, prisoners,
    and presidents who have repaid
sin-driven

senators by not thinking about them. The
    place has a schoolhouse, a post-office in a
store, fish-houses, hen-houses, a three-masted
    schooner on
the stocks. The hero, the student,
    the steeple-jack, each in his way,
is at home.

It could not be dangerous to be living
    in a town like this, of simple people,
who have a steeple-jack placing danger signs by the church
while he is gilding the solid-
    pointed star, which on a steeple
stands for hope.

Marriage

This institution,
perhaps one should say enterprise
out of respect for which
one says one need not change one's mind
about a thing one has believed in,
requiring public promises
of one's intention
to fulfil a private obligation:
I wonder what Adam and Eve
think of it by this time,
this fire-gilt steel
alive with goldenness;
how bright it shows—
"of circular traditions and impostures,
committing many spoils,"
requiring all one's criminal ingenuity
to avoid!
Psychology which explains everything
explains nothing,
and we are still in doubt.
Eve: beautiful woman—
I have seen her
when she was so handsome
she gave me a start,
able to write simultaneously
in three languages—
English, German and French—
and talk in the meantime;
equally positive in demanding a commotion
and in stipulating quiet:
"*I* should like to be alone";
to which the visitor replies,
"I should like to be alone;
why not be alone together?"
Below the incandescent stars
below the incandescent fruit,
the strange experience of beauty;
its existence is too much;
it tears one to pieces

and each fresh wave of consciousness
is poison.
"See her, see her in this common world,"
the central flaw
in that first crystal-fine experiment,
this amalgamation which can never be more
than an interesting impossibility,
describing it
as "that strange paradise
unlike flesh, stones,
gold or stately buildings,
the choicest piece of my life:
the heart rising
in its estate of peace
as a boat rises
with the rising of the water";
constrained in speaking of the serpent—
shed snakeskin in the history of politeness
not to be returned to again—
that invaluable accident
exonerating Adam.
And he has beauty also;
it's distressing—the O thou
to whom from whom,
without whom nothing—Adam;
"something feline,
something colubrine"—how true!
a crouching mythological monster
in that Persian miniature of emerald mines,
raw silk—ivory white, snow white,
oyster white and six others—
that paddock full of leopards and giraffes—
long lemon-yellow bodies
sown with trapezoids of blue.
Alive with words,
vibrating like a cymbal
touched before it has been struck,
he has prophesied correctly—
the industrious waterfall,
"the speedy stream

which violently bears all before it,
at one time silent as the air
and now as powerful as the wind."
"Treading chasms
on the uncertain footing of a spear,"
forgetting that there is in woman
a quality of mind
which as an instinctive manifestation
is unsafe,
he goes on speaking
in a formal customary strain,
of "past states, the present state,
seals, promises,
the evil one suffered,
the good one enjoys,
hell, heaven,
everything convenient
to promote one's joy."
In him a state of mind
perceives what it was not
intended that he should;
"he experiences a solemn joy
in seeing that he has become an idol."
Plagued by the nightingale
in the new leaves,
with its silence—
not its silence but its silences,
he says of it:
"It clothes me with a shirt of fire."
"He dares not clap his hands
to make it go on
lest it should fly off;
if he does nothing, it will sleep;
if he cries out, it will not understand."
Unnerved by the nightingale
and dazzled by the apple,
impelled by "the illusion of a fire
effectual to extinguish fire,"
compared with which
the shining of the earth
is but deformity—a fire

"as high as deep
as bright as broad
as long as life itself,"
he stumbles over marriage,
"a very trivial object indeed"
to have destroyed the attitude
in which he stood—
the ease of the philosopher
unfathered by a woman.
Unhelpful Hymen!
a kind of overgrown cupid
reduced to insignificance
by the mechanical advertising
parading as involuntary comment,
by that experiment of Adam's
with ways out but no way in—
the ritual of marriage,
augmenting all its lavishness;
its fiddle-head ferns,
lotus flowers, opuntias, white dromedaries,
its hippopotamus—
nose and mouth combined
in one magnificent hopper—
its snake and the potent apple.
He tells us
that "for love that will
gaze an eagle blind,
that is with Hercules
climbing the trees
in the garden of the Hesperides,
from forty-five to seventy
is the best age,"
commending it
as a fine art, as an experiment,
a duty or as merely recreation.
One must not call him ruffian
nor friction a calamity—
the fight to be affectionate:
"no truth can be fully known
until it has been tried
by the tooth of disputation."

The blue panther with black eyes,
the basalt panther with blue eyes,
entirely graceful—
one must give them the path—
the black obsidian Diana
who "darkeneth her countenance
as a bear doth,"
the spiked hand
that has an affection for one
and proves it to the bone,
impatient to assure you
that impatience is the mark of independence,
not of bondage.
"Married people often look that way"—
"seldom and cold, up and down,
mixed and malarial
with a good day and a bad."
We Occidentals are so unemotional,
self lost, the irony preserved
in "the Ahasuerus *tête-à-tête* banquet"
with its small orchids like snakes' tongues,
with its "good monster, lead the way,"
with little laughter
and munificence of humor
in that quixotic atmosphere of frankness
in which "four o'clock does not exist,
but at five o'clock
the ladies in their imperious humility
are ready to receive you";
in which experience attests
that men have power
and sometimes one is made to feel it.
He says, "What monarch would not blush
to have a wife
with hair like a shaving-brush?"
The fact of woman
is "not the sound of the flute
but very poison."
She says, "Men are monopolists
of 'stars, garters, buttons
and other shining baubles'—

unfit to be the guardians
of another person's happiness."
He says, "These mummies
must be handled carefully—
'the crumbs from a lion's meal,
a couple of shins and the bit of an ear';
turn to the letter M
and you will find
that 'a wife is a coffin,'
that severe object
with the pleasing geometry
stipulating space not people,
refusing to be buried
and uniquely disappointing,
revengefully wrought in the attitude
of an adoring child
to a distinguished parent."
She says, "This butterfly,
this waterfly, this nomad
that has 'proposed
to settle on my hand for life'—
What can one do with it?
There must have been more time
in Shakespeare's day
to sit and watch a play.
You know so many artists who are fools."
He says, "You know so many fools
who are not artists."
The fact forgot
that "some have merely rights
while some have obligations,"
he loves himself so much,
he can permit himself
no rival in that love.
She loves herself so much,
she cannot see herself enough—
a statuette of ivory on ivory,
the logical last touch
to an expansive splendor
earned as wages for work done:
one is not rich but poor

when one can always seem so right.
What can one do for them—
these savages
condemned to disaffect
all those who are not visionaries
alert to undertake the silly task
of making people noble?
This model of petrine fidelity
who "leaves her peaceful husband
only because she has seen enough of him"—
that orator reminding you,
"I am yours to command."
"Everything to do with love is mystery;
it is more than a day's work
to investigate this science."
One sees that it is rare—
that striking grasp of opposites
opposed each to the other, not to unity,
which in cycloid inclusiveness
has dwarfed the demonstration
of Columbus with the egg—
a triumph of simplicity—
that charitive Euroclydon
of frightening disinterestedness
which the world hates,
admitting:

    "I am such a cow,
    if I had a sorrow
    I should feel it a long time;
    I am not one of those
    who have a great sorrow
    in the morning
    and a great joy at noon";

which says: "I have encountered it
among those unpretentious
protégés of wisdom,
where seeming to parade
as the debater and the Roman,
the statesmanship

of an archaic Daniel Webster
persists to their simplicity of temper
as the essence of the matter:

   'Liberty and union
   now and forever';

   the Book on the writing-table;
   the hand in the breast-pocket."

Statements that took my fancy which I tried to arrange plausibly.

Lines 14–15: *"Of circular traditions . . ."* Francis Bacon.
Lines 25–28: *Write simultaneously.* "Miss A_____ will write simultaneously in three languages, English, German, and French, talking in the meantime. [She] takes advantage of her abilities in everyday life, writing her letters simultaneously with both hands; namely, the first, third, and fifth words with her left and the second, fourth, and sixth with her right hand. While generally writing outward, she is able as well to write inward with both hands." "Multiple Consciousness or Reflex Action of Unaccustomed Range," *Scientific American,* January 1922.
Line 42: *"See her, see her in this common world."* "George Shock."
Lines 48–55: *"That strange paradise, unlike flesh, stones . . ."* Richard Baxter, *The Saints' Everlasting Rest.*
Lines 65–66: "We were puzzled and we were fascinated, as if by something feline, by something colubrine." Philip Littell, reviewing Santayana's *Poems* in *The New Republic,* March 21, 1923.
Lines 83–84: *"Treading chasms . . ."* Hazlitt: "Essay on Burke's Style."
Lines 91–97: *"Past states . . ."* Richard Baxter.
Lines 101–102: *"He experiences a solemn joy."* "A Travers Champs," by Anatole France in *Filles et Garçons* (Hachette): *"Le petit Jean comprend qu'el est beau et cette idée le pénétre d'un respect profond de lui-même. . . . Il goûte une joie pieuse à se sentir devenu une idole."*
Line 108: *"It clothes me with a shirt of fire."* Hagop Boghossian in a poem, "The Nightingale."
Lines 109–113: *"He dares not clap his hands . . ."* Edward Thomas, *Feminine Influence on the Poets* (Martin Secker, 1910).
Lines 116–117, 121–123: *"Illusion of a fire . . . ," "as high as deep . . ."* Richard Baxter.
Line 125: "Marriage is a law, and the worst of all laws . . . a very trivial object indeed." Godwin.
Lines 146–152: *"For love that will gaze an eagle blind . . ."* Anthony Trollope, *Barchester Towers.*
Lines 159–161: *"No truth can be fully known . . ."* Robert of Sorbonne.
Lines 167–168: *"Darkeneth her countenance as a bear doth."* Ecclesiasticus.
Lines 175: *"Married people often look that way."* C. Bertram Hartmann.
Lines 176–178: "Seldom and cold . . ." Richard Baxter.

Line 181: "Ahasuerus' *tête-à-tête* banquet." George Adam Smith, *Expositor's Bible.*

Line 183: *"Good monster, lead the way." The Tempest.*

Lines 187–190: *"Four o'clock does not exist . . ."* Comtesse de Noailles, "Le Thé," *Femina,* December 1921. *"Dans leur impérieuse humilité elles jouent instinctivement leurs rôles sur le globe."*

Lines 194–196: *"What monarch . . ."* From "The Rape of the Lock," a parody by Mary Frances Nearing, with suggestions by M. Moore.

Lines 198–199: *"The sound of the flute . . ."* A. Mitram Rihbany, *The Syrian Christ* (Houghton, Mifflin, 1916). Silence of women—"to an Oriental, this is as poetry set to music."

Lines 200–204: *"Men are monopolists . . ."* Miss M. Carey Thomas, Founder's address, Mount Holyoke, 1921: "Men practically reserve for themselves stately funerals, splendid monuments, memorial statues, membership in academies, medals, titles, honorary degrees, stars, garters, ribbons, buttons and other shining baubles, so valueless in themselves and yet so infinitely desirable because they are symbols of recognition by their fellow-craftsmen of difficult work well done."

Lines 207–208: *"The crumbs from a lion's meal . . .":* Amos iii, 12. Translation by George Adam Smith, *Expositor's Bible.*

Line 211: *"A wife is a coffin."* Ezra Pound.

Line 223: *"Settle on my hand."* Charles Reade, *Christie Johnston.*

Lines 232–233: "Asiatics have rights; Europeans have obligations." Edmund Burke.

Lines 252–253: *"Leaves her peaceful husband . . ."* Simone Puget, advertisement entitled "Change of Fashion," *English Review,* June 1914: "Thus proceed pretty dolls when they leave their old home to renovate their frame, and dear others who may abandon their peaceful husband only because they have seen enough of him."

Lines 256–258: *"Everything to do with love is mystery . . ."* F. C. Tilney, *Fables of La Fontaine,* "Love and Folly," Book XII, No. 14.

Lines 286–287: *"Liberty and Union . . ."* Daniel Webster (statue with inscription, Central Park, New York City).

The Paper Nautilus

For authorities whose hopes
are shaped by mercenaries?
　　Writers entrapped by
　　teatime fame and by
commuters' comforts? Not for these
　　the paper nautilus
　　constructs her thin glass shell.

Giving her perishable
souvenir of hope, a dull
　　white outside and smooth-

edged inner surface
glossy as the sea, the watchful
   maker of it guards it
   day and night; she scarcely

   eats until the eggs are hatched.
Buried eight-fold in her eight
   arms, for she is in
   a sense a devil-
fish, her glass ram's horn-cradled freight
   is hid but is not crushed;
   as Hercules, bitten

   by a crab loyal to the hydra,
was hindered to succeed,
   the intensively
   watched eggs coming from
the shell free it when they are freed,—
   leaving its wasp-nest flaws
   of white on white, and close-

   laid Ionic chiton-folds
like the lines in the mane of
   a Parthenon horse,
   round which the arms had
wound themselves as if they knew love
   is the only fortress
   strong enough to trust to.

"Avec Ardeur"

Dear Ezra, who knows what cadence is.

   I've been thinking—mean, cogitating:

Make a fuss
and be tedious.

I'm annoyed?
Yes; am. I avoid

"adore"
and "bore";

am, I
say, by

the word
(bore) bored.

I refuse
to use

"divine"
to mean

something
pleasing:

"terrific color"
for some horror.

Though flat
myself, I'd say that

"Atlas"
(pressed glass)

looks best
embossed.

I refuse
to use

"enchant,"
"dement";

even "fright-
ful plight"
(however justified)

or "frivol-
ous fool"
(however suitable).

I've escaped?
am still trapped

by these
word diseases.

Without pauses,
the phrases

lack lyric
force, unlike

Attic
Alcaic,

or freak
calico-Greek.

This is not verse
of course.

I'm sure of this;

Nothing mundane is divine;
Nothing divine is mundane.

A Grave

Man looking into the sea,
taking the view from those who have as much right to it as
                                        you have to it yourself,
it is human nature to stand in the middle of a thing,
but you cannot stand in the middle of this;
the sea has nothing to give but a well excavated grave.
The firs stand in a procession, each with an emerald turkey-
                                        foot at the top,
reserved as their contours, saying nothing;
repression, however, is not the most obvious characteristic of
                                        the sea;
the sea is a collector, quick to return a rapacious look.
There are others besides you who have worn that look—
whose expression is no longer a protest; the fish no longer
                                        investigate them
for their bones have not lasted:
men lower nets, unconscious of the fact that they are
                                        desecrating a grave,
and row quickly away—the blades of the oars
moving together like the feet of water-spiders as if there were
                                        no such thing as death.
The wrinkles progress among themselves in a phalanx—
                                beautiful under networks of foam,
and fade breathlessly while the sea rustles in and out of the
                                        seaweed;
the birds swim through the air at top speed, emitting cat-calls
                                        as heretofore—
the tortoise-shell scourges about the feet of the cliffs, in motion
                                        beneath them;
and the ocean, under the pulsation of lighthouses and noise of
                                        bell-buoys,
advances as usual, looking as if it were not that ocean in
                                which dropped things are bound to sink—
in which if they turn and twist, it is neither with volition nor
                                        conciousness.

Critics and Connoisseurs

There is a great amount of poetry in unconscious
    fastidiousness. Certain Ming
        products, imperial floor-coverings of coach-
    wheel yellow, are well enough in their way but I have seen
                                    something
        that I like better—a
            mere childish attempt to make an imperfectly bal-
                lasted animal stand up,
            similar determination to make a pup
                eat his meat from the plate.

I remember a swan under the willows in Oxford,
    with flamingo-colored, maple-
        leaflike feet. It reconnoitered like a battle-
    ship. Disbelief and conscious fastidiousness were
        ingredients in its
            disinclination to move. Finally its hardihood was
                not proof against its
            proclivity to more fully appraise such bits
                of food as the stream

bore counter to it; it made away with what I gave it
    to eat. I have seen this swan and
        I have seen you; I have seen ambition without
    understanding in a variety of forms. Happening to stand
        by an ant-hill, I have
            seen a fastidious ant carrying a stick north, south,
                east, west, till it turned on
            itself, struck out from the flower-bed into the lawn,
            and returned to the point

from which it had started. Then abandoning the stick as
useless and overtaxing its
        jaws with a particle of whitewash—pill-like but
heavy, it again went through the same course of procedure.
        What is
        there in being able
            to say that one has dominated the stream in an attitude
                            of self-defense;

in proving that one has had the experience
of carrying a stick?

Silence

My father used to say,
"Superior people never make long visits,
have to be shown Longfellow's grave
or the glass flowers at Harvard.
Self-reliant like the cat—
that takes its prey to privacy,
the mouse's limp tail hanging like a shoelace from its mouth—
they sometimes enjoy solitude,
and can be robbed of speech
by speech which has delighted them.
The deepest feeling always shows itself in silence;
not in silence, but restraint."
Nor was he insincere in saying, "Make my house your inn."
Inns are not residences.

Edna St. Vincent Millay

Edna St. Vincent Millay (1892–1950).   Born in Rockland, Maine, she received
her A.B. from Vassar College. She went to live in Greenwich Village, where she
supported herself by translating songs, writing stories under pseudonyms, writing
poetry, and working with the Provincetown Players as both actress and playwright.
Her poetry was popular; her style traditionally romantic and at the same time reflected
unconventional, shocking ideas. In *A Few Figs from Thistles* (1920), she declared the
right of women to be as promiscuous as men. In 1922 her poem "The Harp Weaver"
(from *The Harp Weaver and Other Poems,* 1924) received the Pulitzer Prize. She is
best-known for *Fatal Interview* (1931), a collection of love sonnets. She wrote ten
volumes of poetry, and also plays. Other volumes of poetry include *Renascence* (1917),
Second April (1921), *The Buck in the Snow and Other Poems* (1928), *Wine from These
Grapes* (1934), *Conversation at Midnight* (1937), *Huntsman, What Quarry?* (1939),
Make Bright the Arrows (1940), and *The Murder of Lidice* (1942).

Spring

To what purpose, April, do you return again?
Beauty is not enough.
You can no longer quiet me with the redress

Of little leaves opening stickily.
I know what I know.
The sun is hot on my neck as I observe
The spikes of the crocus.
The smell of the earth is good.
It is apparent that there is no death.
But what does that signify?
Not only under ground are the brains of men
Eaten by maggots.

Life in itself
Is nothing
An empty cup, a flight of uncarpeted stairs,
It is not enough that yearly, down this hill,
April
Comes like an idiot, babbling and strewing flowers.

Sonnet to Gath

Country of hunchbacks!—where the strong, straight spine
Jeered at by crooked children, makes his way
Through by-streets at the kindest hour of day,
Till he deplore his stature, and incline
To measure manhood with a gibbous line;
Till out of loneliness, being flawed with clay,
He stoop into his neighbor's house and say,
"Your roof is low for me—the fault is mine."

Dust in an urn long since, dispersed and dead
Is great Apollo; and the happier he;
Since who amongst you all would lift a head
At a god's radiance on the mean door-tree,
Saving to run and hide your dates and bread,
And cluck your children in about your knee?

Oh, oh, you will be sorry for that word!
Give back my book and take my kiss instead.
Was it my enemy or my friend I heard,

"What a big book for a such little head!"
Come, I will show you now my newest hat,
And you may watch me purse my mouth and prink!
Oh, I shall love you still, and all of that.
I never again shall tell you what I think.
I shall be sweet and crafty, soft and sly;
You will not catch me reading any more:
I shall be called a wife to pattern by;
And some day when you knock and push the door,
Some sane day, not too bright and not too stormy,
I shall be gone, and you may whistle for me.

Louise Bogan

Louise Bogan (1897–1970).   Born in Livermore Falls, Maine, Louise Bogan attended the Girl's Latin School in Boston and the Western College for Women in Oxford, Ohio. She lived in New York City, where she was an editor and critic for the *New Yorker.* She held the chair of poetry at the Library of Congress, and received the Bollingen Prize and an award from the Academy of American Poets. Her books include: *Body of This Death* (1923), *Dark Summer* (1929), *The Sleeping Fury* (1937), *The Blue Estuaries: Poems 1923–1968* (1968), and a highly acclaimed book of criticism, *Achievement in American Poetry* (1951).

Medusa

I had come to the house, in a cave of trees,
Facing a sheer sky.
Everything moved,—a bell hung ready to strike,
Sun and reflection wheeled by.

When the bare eyes were before me
And the hissing hair,
Held up at a window, seen through a door.
The stiff bald eyes, the serpents on the forehead
Formed in the air.

This is a dead scene forever now.
Nothing will ever stir.
The end will never brighten it more than this,
Nor the rain blur.

The water will always fall, and will not fall,
And the tipped bell make no sound.
The grass will always be growing for hay
Deep on the ground.

And I shall stand here like a shadow
Under the great balanced day,
My eyes on the yellow dust, that was lifting in the wind,
And does not drift away.

Women

Women have no wilderness in them,
They are provident instead,
Content in the tight hot cell of their hearts
To eat dusty bread.

They do not see cattle cropping red winter grass,
They do not hear
Snow water going down under culverts
Shallow and clear.

They wait, when they should turn to journeys,
They stiffen, when they should bend.
They use against themselves that benevolence
To which no man is friend.

They cannot think of so many crops to a field
Or of clean wood cleft by an axe.
Their love is an eager meaninglessness
Too tense, or too lax.

They hear in every whisper that speaks to them
A shout and a cry.
As like as not, when they take life over their door-sills
They should let it go by.

Stevie Smith

Stevie Smith (1902–1971).   Born in Hull, Yorkshire, England, Smith worked in a publishing house and did broadcasts for the BBC. She illustrated all her collections of poetry with line drawings. Her poems are full of inner rhymes and assonances, and are reminiscent of nursery rhymes. Muriel Rukeyser called her "our acrobat of simplicity." She received the Cholmondely Award and the Queen's Gold Medal for Poetry. Her titles include *Selected Poems* (1962) and *Work It Out for Yourself,* a novel.

The Weak Monk

The monk sat in his den,
He took the mighty pen
And wrote "Of God and Men."

One day the thought struck him
It was not according to Catholic doctrine;
His blood ran dim.

He wrote till he was ninety years old,
Then he shut the book with a clasp of gold
And buried it under the sheep fold.

He'd enjoyed it so much, he loved to plod,
And he thought he'd a right to expect that God
Would rescue his book alive from the sod.

Of course it rotted in the snow and rain;
No one will ever know now what he wrote of God and men.
For this the monk is to blame.

I Remember

It was my bridal night I remember,
An old man of seventy-three
I lay with my young bride in my arms,
A girl with t.b.
It was wartime, and overhead
The Germans were making a particularly heavy raid on
    Hampstead.

What rendered the confusion worse, perversely
Our bombers had chosen that moment to set out for Germany.
Harry, do they ever collide?
I do not think it has ever happened,
Oh my bride, my bride.

Lorine Niedecker

Lorine Niedecker (1903–1970). Born in Fort Atkinson, Wisconsin, she said of her childhood: "I spent my childhood outdoors—redwings, blackbirds, willows, maples, boats, fishing (the smell of tarred nets), twittering and squawking noises from the marsh." She was educated at Beloit College, then worked as a writer and research editor for the WPA State Guide and as a script writer for WHA Radio in Madison, Wisconsin. Disenchanted with the city, she lived for the next twenty years on Black Hawk Island on Lake Koshkonong, earning her living by cleaning the kitchen and scrubbing floors in a local hospital. In her poem that begins "Old Mother turns blue and from us," she records her mother's dying words: "Wash the floors, Lorine, wash clothes! Weed!" In 1951 she married Albert Millen, a Milwaukee housepainter, and moved with him to an apartment in the poorest section of Milwaukee. In 1969 she returned to Black Hawk Island and built a two-and-a-half-room cabin, where she expected to live and write for many years. She died suddenly in 1970.

Cid Corman, her literary executor, calls Niedecker's poetry "quiet music." It received high praise from Kenneth Rexroth, Robert Duncan, Robert Creeley, and James Laughlin, among others. In 1931 Niedecker initiated a lifelong correspondence with Louis Zukofsky after reading the "Objectivist" issue of *Poetry* which he edited. He would later include her in his *Objectivist Anthology.* William Carlos Williams once wrote to her of her poetry: "It is good poetry. It is difficult and warm. It has a life to it." Basil Bunting averred: "No one is so subtle with so few words." Her books include: *New Goose* (1946), *My Friend Tree* (1970), *North Central* (1968), *T & G: The Collected Poems* (1969), *My Life by Water* (1970), *Blue Chicory* (1976), *The Granite Pail: The Selected Poems of Lorine Niedecker* (1985), *From This Condensery: The Complete Writing of Lorine Niedecker,* edited by Robert J. Berthoff (1985), and *Between Your House and Mine: The Letters of Lorine Niedecker to Cid Corman, 1960–1970* (1986).

In the tradition of Pound and Williams, Niedecker was a master of the condensed poem, of the image that illumines and quietly explodes with sound and meaning. But she was also a master of the difficult form of the long poem, and her long poems and sequences are among the most successful of the century. Like García Lorca's sequences in *El cante jondo,* Niedecker's long poems have, from part to part, a cumulative power, informing each stanza with authority and narrative drama. In "Thomas Jefferson" she re-creates the public and domestic Jefferson. In "Darwin" she humanizes the man and his discovery of a theory and of a territory—a mythological place whose rocks, sea, and beasts, like her primordial Wisconsin island, becomes its own speculative Eden. Niedecker's poetry was influenced by the poets whom she most admired, including the Chinese Tang poets, Whitman, and of course her fellow Objectivists, Cid Corman and William Carlos Williams.

My friend tree
I sawed you down
but I must attend
an older friend
the sun

⁓⁓

Well, spring overflows the land,
floods floor, pump, wash machine
of the woman moored to this low shore by deafness.

　　Good-bye to lilacs by the door
　　and all I planted for the eye.
　　If I could hear—too much talk in the world,
　　too much wind washing, washing
　　good black dirt away.

Her hair is high.
Big blind ears.

　　I've wasted my whole life in water.
　　My man's got nothing but leaky boats.
　　My daughter, writer, sits and floats.

⁓⁓

Old Mother turns blue and from us,
　　"Don't let my head drop to the earth.
I'm blind and deaf." Death from the heart,
　　a thimble in her purse.

"It's a long day since last night.
　　Give me space. I need
floors. Wash the floors, Lorine!—
　　wash clothes! Weed!"

⁓⁓

What horror to awake at night
and in the dimness see the light.
　　　　Time is white

      mosquitoes bite
I've spent my life on nothing.

The thought that stings. How are you, Nothing,
sitting around with Something's wife.
        Buzz and burn
          is all I learn
I've spent my life on nothing.

I'm pillowed and padded, pale and puffing
lifting household stuffing—
        carpets, dishes
         benches, fishes
I've spent my life in nothing.

⚬⚬

I knew a clean man
but he was not for me.
Now I sew green aprons
over covered seats. He

wades the muddy water fishing,
falls in, dries his last pay-check
in the sun, smooths it out
in *Leaves of Grass.* He's
the one for me.

⚬⚬

In the great snowfall before the bomb
colored yule tree lights
windows, the only glow for contemplation
along this road

I worked the print shop
right down among em
the folk from whom all poetry flows
and dreadfully much else.

I was Blondie
I carried my bundles of hog feeder price lists

down by Larry the Lug,
I'd never get anywhere
because I'd never had suction,
pull, you know, favor, drag,
well-oiled protection.

I heard their rehashed radio barbs—
more barbarous among hirelings
as higher-ups grow more corrupt.
But what vitality! The women hold jobs—
clean house, cook, raise children, bowl
and go to church.

What would they say if they knew
I sit for two months on six lines
of poetry?

࿊

Swept snow, Li Po,
by dawn's 40-watt moon
to the road that hies to office
away from home.

Tended my brown little stove
as one would a cow—she gives heat.
Spring—marsh frog-clatter peace
                    breaks out.

࿊

New-sawed
clean-smelling house
sweet cedar pink
            flesh tint
I love you

࿊

Popcorn-can cover
screwed to the wall
over a hole

      so the cold
can't mouse in

    ∽ᐤ
Get a load
    of April's
          fabulous

frog rattle—
    lowland freight cars
        in the night

    ∽ᐤ
Now in one year
    a book published
        and plumbing—
took a lifetime
     to weep
        a deep
            trickle

    ∽ᐤ
In Leonardo's light
we questioned

the sun does not love
My hat

attained
the weight falls

I am at rest
You too

hold a doctorate
in Warmth

    ∽ᐤ
As praiseworthy

The power of breathing (Epictetus)
while we sleep. Add:
to move the parts of the body
without sound

and to float
on a smooth green stream
in a silent boat

⁓
As I paint the street

I melt the houses
to point up the turreted cupola
I make hoopla

of the low tavern's neon cross—
very like a cross from here—
I honor the huge blue distant dome
valid somehow to the fellow falling high

⁓
Some float off on chocolate bars
and some on drink

Harmless, happy, soft of heart

This bottle may breed
a new race
              no war
              and let birds live

Myself, I gripped my melting container
the night I heard the wild
wet rat, muskrat
grind his frogs and mice
the other side of a thin door
in the flood

∽∾

Poet's Work

Grandfather
  advised me:
      Learn a trade

I learned
  to sit at desk
      and condense

No layoff
  from this
      condensery

∽∾

To My Pressure Pump

I've been free
          with less
              and clean
I plumbed for principles

Now I'm jet-bound
by faucet   shower
heater   valve
ring seal   service

cost to my little
  humming
        water
            bird

∽∾

Alcoholic dream
that ran him
          out from home
                  to return
leaning

like the house
in this old part

of town leaves him
grieving:
why

do I hurt you
whom I love?
Your ear
is cold!—here,
drink

∽

Consider at the outset:
to be thin for thought
or thick cream blossomy

Many things are better
flavored with bacon

Sweet Life, My love:
didn't you ever try
this delicacy—the marrow
in the bone?

And don't be afraid
to pour wine over cabbage

∽

Hear
wher her snow-grave is
the *You*
ah you
of mourning doves

Tradition

I

The chemist creates
the brazen
approximation:
Life
  Thy will be done
  Sun

II

Time to garden
  before I
  die—
to meet
  my compost maker
  the caretaker
of the cemetery

∽⌒

Easter Greeting

I suppose there is nothing
so good as human
immediacy

I do not speak loosely
of handshake
   which is

   of the mind
or lilies—stand closer—
smell

∽∞

Laundromat

Once again a public wedding
a casual, sudsy
social affair
at the tubs

After all, ecstasy
can't be constant

∽∞

I married

in the world's black night
for warmth
                if not repose.
                At the close—
someone.

I hid with him
from the long range guns.
                We lay leg
                in the cupboard, head
in closet.

A slit of light
at no bird dawn—
                Untaught
                I thought
he drank

too much.
I say
                I married
                and lived unburied.
I thought—

∽∾

Foreclosure

Tell 'em to take my bare walls down
my cement abutments
their parties thereof
and clause of claws

Leave me the land
Scratch out: the land

May prose and property both die out
and leave me peace

∽∾

Darwin

I

His holy
    slowly
        mulled over
  matter

not all 'delirium
    of delight'
        as were the forests
  of Brazil

'Species are not
    (it is like confessing
        a murder)
  immutable'

He was often becalmed
    in this Port Desire by illness
        or rested from species
  at billiard table

As to Man
　　'I believe Man . . .
　　　　in the same predicament
　　with other animals'

II

Cordilleras to climb—Andean
　　peaks 'tossed about
　　　　like the crust
　　of a broken pie'

Icy wind
　　Higher, harder
　　　　Chileans advised eat onions
　　for shortness of breath

Heavy on him:
　　Andes miners carried up
　　　　great loads—not allowed
　　to stop for breath

Fossil bones near Santa Fe
　　Spider-bite-scauld
　　　　Fever
　　Tended by an old woman

'Dear Susan . . .
　　I am ravenous
　　　　for the sound
　　of the pianoforte'

III

FitzRoy blinked—
　　sea-shells on mountain tops!
　　　　The laws of change
　　rode the seas

without the good captain
    who could not concede
        land could rise from the sea
  until—before his eyes

earthquake—
    Talcahuana Bay drained out—
        all-water wall
  up from the ocean

—six seconds—
    demolished the town
        The will of God?
  Let us pray

And now the Galàpagos Islands—
    hideous black lava
        The shore so hot
  it burned their feet

through their boots
    Reptile life
        Melville here later
  said the chief sound was a hiss

A thousand turtle monsters
    drive together to the water
        Blood-bright crabs hunt ticks
  on lizards' backs

Flightless cormorants
    Cold-sea creatures—
        penguins, seals
  here in tropical waters

Hell for FitzRoy
    but for Darwin Paradise Puzzle
        with the jig-saw gists
  beginning to fit

IV

Years . . . balancing
   probabilities
      I am ill, he said
and books are slow work

Studied pigeons
   barnacles, earthworms
      Extracted seeds
from bird dung

Brought home Drosera—
   saw insects trapped
      by its tentacles—the fact
that a plant should secrete

an acid acutely akin
   to the digestive fluid
      of an animal! Years
till he published

He wrote Lyell: Don't forget
   to send me the carcass
      of your half-bred African cat
should it die

V

I remember, he said
   those tropical nights at sea—
      we sat and talked
on the booms

Tierra del Fuego's
   shining glaciers translucent
      blue clear down
(almost) to the indigo sea

(By the way Carlyle
    thought it was most ridiculous
        anyone should care
  whether a glacier

moved a little quicker
    or a little slower
        or moved at all)
  Darwin

sailed out
    of Good Success Bay
        to carcass-
conclusions—

the universe
    not built by brute force
        but designed by laws
  The details left

to the working of chance
    'Let each man hope
        and believe
  what he can'

Kathleen Raine

Kathleen Raine (1909-). Born in England, she was educated at Girton College, Cambridge, and later taught there. Her first volume of poetry, *Stone and Flower,* appeared in 1934, her *Collected Poems* (which includes three other previous volumes) in 1956. She is a nature poet who believes that nature's images mirror "eternal reality." She also wrote a volume of criticism, *Aspects of English Literature.*

The Wilderness

I came too late to the hills: they were swept bare
Winters before I was born of song and story,
Of spell or speech with power of oracle or invocation,

The great ash long dead by a roofless house, its branches rotten,
The voice of the crows an inarticulate cry,
And from the wells and springs the holy water ebbed away.

A child I ran in the wind on a withered moor
Crying out after those great presences who were not there,
Long lost in the forgetfulness of the forgotten.

Only the archaic forms themselves could tell!
In sacred speech of hoodie on gray stone, or hawk in air,
Of Eden where the lonely rowan bends over the dark pool.

Yet I have glimpsed the bright mountain behind the mountain,
Knowledge under the leaves, tasted the bitter berries red,
Drunk water cold and clear from an inexhaustible hidden fountain.

Elizabeth Bishop

Elizabeth Bishop (1911–1979).   Elizabeth Bishop's poetry has been described as
intensely visual, exotic, and musical, yet understated. This paradox of the wild and the
muted reflects what Helen Vendler calls "the continuing vibration of her work
between the two frequencies—the domestic and the strange. In another poet the
alternation might seem a debate, but Bishop drifts rather than divides, gazes rather
than chooses. Though the exotic is frequent in her poems of travel, it is not only the
exotic that is strange and not only the local that is domestic."

Bishop was born in Worcester, Massachusetts. Her father died when she was eight
months old, and her mother was hospitalized for mental illness shortly thereafter. She
was raised by her paternal and maternal grandparents in New England and Nova
Scotia, and did not attend school regularly until she enrolled at Walnut Hill School at
sixteen. At Vassar College, together with Mary McCarthy and several others, she
started a literary magazine, *Con Spirito.* When T. S. Eliot visited the college, Bishop
interviewed him for the magazine. In 1934 Vassar's librarian, Fanny Borden, intro-
duced her to Marianne Moore after Bishop could not find a copy of Moore's book
Observations in the library. The two became lifelong friends.

In 1954 she wrote to Moore: "When I began to read your poetry at college I think
it immediately opened up my eyes to the possibility of the subject matter I could use
and might never have thought of using if it hadn't been for you.—(I might not have
written any poems at all, I suppose.)" In addition to Moore, her other most notable
close friend and literary conspirator was Robert Lowell. By her accounting she was
also strongly influenced by George Herbert, Gerald Manley Hopkins, hymns, and
nursery rhymes.

Bishop lived in Brazil from 1951 to 1966 with her friend Lota Costellat de Macedo
Soares. During this period she turned her attention to translation, even as she con-

tinued to write her own poetry. She translated Carlos Drummond de Andrade and other poets from the Portuguese; Max Jacob from the French; she later translated Octavio Paz from the Spanish when the two were both living in Cambridge. She also translated *The Diary of "Helena Morley"* (1957), the actual diary a girl kept between the ages of twelve and fifteen. Bishop was co-editor of *An Anthology of Twentieth-Century Brazilian Poetry* (1972) and wrote a book about Brazil, *Brazil*, which was published against her wishes in 1962. Translation was one of her "questions of travel." In fact, one of her translations, of Paz's "Objects & Apparitions," appeared in her last volume of poetry, *Geography III* (1976). The book contains only ten poems; thus, the order of the poems is crucial. Just as Bishop's translation echoes and comments on Paz's Spanish, so does his poem echo and comment on the other poems of the collection, particularly "The End of March," which precedes it. *The Complete Poems 1927–1979*, published posthumously, relegates "Objects & Apparitions" to the "Translations" section at the end of the volume, thereby violating the sequence and the complex, powerful structure of *Geography III*.

When Bishop returned to the United States, she taught at the University of Washington and then, from 1969 to 1977, at Harvard. Later in 1977 she taught at NYU; in 1979, the year of her death, she assumed a post at MIT. Her other books are *North & South* (1946); *Poems: North & South—A Cold Spring* (1955), which won the Pulitzer Prize; *Questions of Travel* (1965); *The Complete Poems* (1969), which won the National Book Award; and *The Collected Prose* (1984). *Geography III* received the Poetry Award of the National Book Critics Circle. In her lifetime Bishop never allowed her poems to be published in women's anthologies precisely, she reckoned, because of "feminist principles." She wrote: "Undoubtedly gender does play an important part in the making of any art, but art is art and to separate writings, paintings, musical compositions, etc., into two sexes is to emphasize values in them that are *not* art."

The Fish

I caught a tremendous fish
and held him beside the boat
half out of water, with my hook
fast in a corner of his mouth.
He didn't fight.
He hadn't fought at all.
He hung a grunting weight,
battered and venerable
and homely. Here and there
his brown skin hung in strips
like ancient wallpaper,
and its pattern of darker brown
was like wallpaper:
shapes like full-blown roses

stained and lost through age.
He was speckled with barnacles,
fine rosettes of lime,
and infested
with tiny white sea-lice,
and underneath two or three
rags of green weed hung down.
While his gills were breathing in
the terrible oxygen
—the frightening gills,
fresh and crisp with blood,
that can cut so badly—
I thought of the coarse white flesh
packed in like feathers,
the big bones and the little bones,
the dramatic reds and blacks
of his shiny entrails,
and the pink swim-bladder
like a big peony.
I looked into his eyes
which were far larger than mine
but shallower, and yellowed,
the irises backed and packed
with tarnished tinfoil
seen through the lenses
of old scratched isinglass.
They shifted a little, but not
to return my stare.
—It was more like the tipping
of an object toward the light.
I admired his sullen face,
the mechanism of his jaw,
and then I saw
that from his lower lip
—if you could call it a lip—
grim, wet, and weaponlike,
hung five old pieces of fish-line,
or four and a wire leader
with the swivel still attached,
with all their five big hooks
grown firmly in his mouth.

A green line, frayed at the end
where he broke it, two heavier lines,
and a fine black thread
still crimped from the strain and snap
when it broke and he got away.
Like medals with their ribbons
frayed and wavering,
a five-haired beard of wisdom
trailing from his aching jaw.
I stared and stared
and victory filled up
the little rented boat,
from the pool of bilge
where oil had spread a rainbow
around the rusted engine
to the bailer rusted orange,
the sun-cracked thwarts,
the oarlocks on their strings,
the gunnels—until everything
was rainbow, rainbow, rainbow!
And I let the fish go.

The Imaginary Iceberg

We'd rather have the iceberg than the ship,
although it meant the end of travel.
Although it stood stock-still like cloudy rock
and all the sea were moving marble.
We'd rather have the iceberg than the ship;
we'd rather own this breathing plain of snow
though the ship's sails were laid upon the sea
as the snow lies undissolved upon the water.
O solemn, floating field,
are you aware an iceberg takes repose
with you, and when it wakes may pasture on your snows?

This is a scene a sailor'd give his eyes for.
The ship's ignored. The iceberg rises
and sinks again; its glassy pinnacles
correct elliptics in the sky.

This is a scene where he who treads the boards
is artlessly rhetorical. The curtain
is light enough to rise on finest ropes
that airy twists of snow provide.
The wits of these white peaks
spar with the sun. Its weight the iceberg dares
upon a shifting stage and stands and stares.

This iceberg cuts its facets from within.
Like jewelry from a grave
it saves itself perpetually and adorns
only itself, perhaps the snows
which so surprise us lying on the sea.
Good-bye, we say, good-bye, the ship steers off
where waves give in to one another's waves
and clouds run in a warmer sky.
Icebergs behoove the soul
(both being self-made from elements least visible)
to see them so: fleshed, fair, erected indivisible.

Insomnia

The moon in the bureau mirror
looks out a million miles
(and perhaps with pride, at herself,
but she never, never smiles)
far and away beyond sleep, or
perhaps she's a daytime sleeper.

By the Universe deserted,
she'd tell it to go to hell,
and she'd find a body of water,
or a mirror, on which to dwell.
So wrap up care in a cobweb
and drop it down the well

into that world inverted
where left is always right,
where the shadows are really the body,

where we stay awake all night,
where the heavens are shallow as the sea
is now deep, and you love me.

At the Fishhouses

Although it is a cold evening,
down by one of the fishhouses
an old man sits netting,
his net, in the gloaming almost invisible,
a dark purple-brown,
and his shuttle worn and polished.
The air smells so strong of codfish
it makes one's nose run and one's eyes water.
The five fishhouses have steeply peaked roofs
and narrow, cleated gangplanks slant up
to storerooms in the gables
for the wheelbarrows to be pushed up and down on.
All is silver: the heavy surface of the sea,
swelling slowly as if considering spilling over,
is opaque, but the silver of the benches,
the lobster pots, and masts, scattered
among the wild jagged rocks,
is of an apparent translucence
like the small old buildings with an emerald moss
growing on their shoreward walls.
The big fish tubs are completely lined
with layers of beautiful herring scales
and the wheelbarrows are similarly plastered
with creamy iridescent coats of mail,
with small iridescent flies crawling on them.
Up on the little slope behind the houses,
set in the sparse bright sprinkle of grass,
is an ancient wooden capstan,
cracked, with two long bleached handles
and some melancholy stains, like dried blood,
where the ironwork has rusted.
The old man accepts a Lucky Strike.
He was a friend of my grandfather.
We talk of the decline in the population

and of codfish and herring
while he waits for a herring boat to come in.
There are sequins on his vest and on his thumb.
He has scraped the scales, the principal beauty,
from unnumbered fish with that black old knife,
the blade of which is almost worn away.

Down at the water's edge, at the place
where they haul up the boats, up the long ramp
descending into the water, thin silver
tree trunks are laid horizontally
across the gray stones, down and down
at intervals of four or five feet.

Cold dark deep and absolutely clear,
element bearable to no mortal,
to fish and to seals . . . One seal particularly
I have seen here evening after evening.
He was curious about me. He was interested in music;
like me a believer in total immersion,
so I used to sing him Baptist hymns.
I also sang "A Mighty Fortress Is Our God."
He stood up in the water and regarded me
steadily, moving his head a little.
Then he would disappear, then suddenly emerge
almost in the same spot, with a sort of shrug
as if it were against his better judgment.
Cold dark deep and absolutely clear,
the clear gray icy water . . . Back, behind us,
the dignified tall firs begin.
Bluish, associating with their shadows,
a million Christmas trees stand
waiting for Christmas. The water seems suspended
above the rounded gray and blue-gray stones.
I have seen it over and over, the same sea, the same,
slightly, indifferently swinging above the stones,
icily free above the stones,
above the stones and then the world.
If you should dip your hand in,
your wrist would ache immediately,

your bones would begin to ache and your hand would burn
as if the water were a transmutation of fire
that feeds on stones and burns with a dark gray flame.
If you tasted it, it would first taste bitter,
then briny, then surely burn your tongue.
It is like what we imagine knowledge to be:
dark, salt, clear, moving, utterly free,
drawn from the cold hard mouth
of the world, derived from the rocky breasts
forever, flowing and drawn, and since
our knowledge is historical, flowing, and flown.

Invitation to Miss Marianne Moore

From Brooklyn, over the Brooklyn Bridge, on this fine morning,
    please come flying.
In a cloud of fiery pale chemicals,
    please come flying,
to the rapid rolling of thousands of small blue drums
descending out of the mackerel sky
over the glittering grandstand of harbor-water,
    please come flying.

Whistles, pennants and smoke are blowing. The ships
are signaling cordially with multitudes of flags
rising and falling like birds all over the harbor.
Enter: two rivers, gracefully bearing
countless little pellucid jellies
in cut-glass epergnes dragging with silver chains.
The flight is safe; the weather is all arranged.
The waves are running in verses this fine morning.
    Please come flying.

Come with the pointed toe of each black shoe
trailing a sapphire highlight,
with a black capeful of butterfly wings and bon-mots,
with heaven knows how many angels all riding
on the broad black brim of your hat,
    please come flying.

Bearing a musical inaudible abacus,
a slight censorious frown, and blue ribbons,
    please come flying.
Facts and skyscrapers glint in the tide; Manhattan
is all awash with morals this fine morning,
    so please come flying.

Mounting the sky with natural heroism,
above the accidents, above the malignant movies,
the taxicabs and injustices at large,
while horns are resounding in your beautiful ears
that simultaneously listen to
a soft uninvented music, fit for the musk deer,
    please come flying.

For whom the grim museums will behave
like courteous male bower-birds,
for whom the agreeable lions lie in wait
on the steps of the Public Library,
eager to rise and follow through the doors
up into the reading rooms,
    please come flying.
We can sit down and weep; we can go shopping,
or play at a game of constantly being wrong
with a priceless set of vocabularies,
or we can bravely deplore, but please
    please come flying.

With dynasties of negative constructions
darkening and dying around you,
with grammar that suddenly turns and shines
like flocks of sandpipers flying,
    please come flying.

Come like a light in the white mackerel sky,
come like a daytime comet
with a long unnebulous train of words,
from Brooklyn, over the Brooklyn Bridge, on this fine morning,
    please come flying.

Sestina

September rain falls on the house.
In the failing light, the old grandmother
sits in the kitchen with the child
beside the Little Marvel Stove,
reading the jokes from the almanac,
laughing and talking to hide her tears.

She thinks that her equinoctial tears
and the rain that beats on the roof of the house
were both foretold by the almanac,
but only known to a grandmother.
The iron kettle sings on the stove.
She cuts some bread and says to the child,

It's time for tea now; but the child
is watching the teakettle's small hard tears
dance like mad on the hot black stove,
the way the rain must dance on the house.
Tidying up, the old grandmother
hangs up the clever almanac

on its string. Birdlike, the almanac
hovers half open above the child,
hovers above the old grandmother
and her teacup full of dark brown tears.
She shivers and says she thinks the house
feels chilly, and puts more wood in the stove.

It was to be, says the Marvel Stove.
I know what I know, says the almanac.
With crayons the child draws a rigid house
and a winding pathway. Then the child
puts in a man with buttons like tears
and shows it proudly to the grandmother.

But secretly, while the grandmother
busies herself about the stove,
the little moons fall down like tears

from between the pages of the almanac
into the flower bed the child
has carefully placed in the front of the house.

Time to plant tears, says the almanac.
The grandmother sings to the marvellous stove
and the child draws another inscrutable house.

In the Waiting Room

In Worcester, Massachusetts,
I went with Aunt Consuelo
to keep her dentist's appointment
and sat and waited for her
in the dentist's waiting room.
It was winter. It got dark
early. The waiting room
was full of grown-up people,
arctics and overcoats,
lamps and magazines.
My aunt was inside
what seemed like a long time
and while I waited I read
the *National Geographic*
(I could read) and carefully
studied the photographs:
the inside of a volcano,
black, and full of ashes;
then it was spilling over
in rivulets of fire.
Osa and Martin Johnson
dressed in riding breeches,
laced boots, and pith helmets.
A dead man slung on a pole
—"Long Pig," the caption said.
Babies with pointed heads
wound round and round with string;
black, naked women with necks
wound round and round with wire

like the necks of light bulbs.
Their breasts were horrifying.
I read it right straight through.
I was too shy to stop.
And then I looked at the cover:
the yellow margins, the date.

Suddenly, from inside,
came an *oh!* of pain
—Aunt Consuelo's voice—
not very loud or long.
I wasn't at all surprised;
even then I knew she was
a foolish, timid woman.
I might have been embarrassed,
but wasn't. What took me
completely by surprise
was that it was *me:*
my voice, in my mouth.
Without thinking at all
I was my foolish aunt,
I—we—were falling, falling,
our eyes glued to the cover
of the *National Geographic,*
February, 1918.

I said to myself: three days
and you'll be seven years old.
I was saying it to stop
the sensation of falling off
the round, turning world
into cold, blue-black space.
But I felt: you are an *I,*
you are an *Elizabeth,*
you are one of *them.*
Why should you be one, too?
I scarcely dared to look
to see what it was I was.
I gave a sidelong glance
—I couldn't look any higher—

at shadowy gray knees,
trousers and skirts and boots
and different pairs of hands
lying under the lamps.
I knew that nothing stranger
had ever happened, that nothing
stranger could ever happen.

Why should I be my aunt,
or me, or anyone?
What similarities—
boots, hands, the family voice
I felt in my throat, or even
the *National Geographic*
and those awful hanging breasts—
held us all together
or made us all just one?
How—I didn't know any
word for it—how "unlikely" . . .
How had I come to be here,
like them, and overhear
a cry of pain that could have
got loud and worse but hadn't?

The waiting room was bright
and too hot. It was sliding
beneath a big black wave,
another, and another.

Then I was back in it.
The War was on. Outside,
in Worcester, Massachusetts,
were night and slush and cold,
and it was still the fifth
of February, 1918.

Crusoe in England

A new volcano has erupted,
the papers say, and last week I was reading
where some ship saw an island being born:
at first a breath of steam, ten miles away;
and then a black fleck—basalt, probably—
rose in the mate's binoculars
and caught on the horizon like a fly.
They named it. But my poor old island's still
un-rediscovered, un-renamable.
None of the books has ever got it right.

Well, I had fifty-two
miserable, small volcanoes I could climb
with a few slithery strides—
volcanoes dead as ash heaps.
I used to sit on the edge of the highest one
and count the others standing up,
naked and leaden, with their heads blown off.
I'd think that if they were the size
I thought volcanoes should be, then I had
become a giant;
and if I had become a giant,
I couldn't bear to think what size
the goats and turtles were,
or the gulls, or the overlapping rollers
—a glittering hexagon of rollers
closing and closing in, but never quite,
glittering and glittering, though the sky
was mostly overcast.

My island seemed to be
a sort of cloud-dump. All the hemisphere's
left-over clouds arrived and hung
above the craters—their parched throats
were hot to touch.
Was that why it rained so much?
And why sometimes the whole place hissed?
The turtles lumbered by, high-domed,
hissing like teakettles.

(And I'd have given years, or taken a few,
for any sort of kettle, of course.)
The folds of lava, running out to sea,
would hiss. I'd turn. And then they'd prove
to be more turtles.
The beaches were all lava, variegated,
black, red, and white, and gray;
the marbled colors made a fine display.
And I had waterspouts. Oh,
half a dozen at a time, far out,
they'd come and go, advancing and retreating,
their heads in cloud, their feet in moving patches
of scuffed-up white.
Glass chimneys, flexible, attenuated,
sacerdotal beings of glass . . . I watched
the water spiral up in them like smoke.
Beautiful, yes, but not much company.

I often gave way to self-pity.
"Do I deserve this? I suppose I must.
I wouldn't be here otherwise. Was there
a moment when I actually chose this?
I don't remember, but there could have been."
What's wrong about self-pity, anyway?
With my legs dangling down familiarly
over a crater's edge, I told myself
"Pity should begin at home." So the more
pity I felt, the more I felt at home.

The sun set in the sea; the same odd sun
rose from the sea,
and there was one of it and one of me.
The island had one kind of everything:
one tree snail, a bright violet-blue
with a thin shell, crept over everything,
over the one variety of tree,
a sooty, scrub affair.
Snail shells lay under these in drifts
and, at a distance,
you'd swear that they were beds of irises.

There was one kind of berry, a dark red.
I tried it, one by one, and hours apart.
Sub-acid, and not bad, no ill effects;
and so I made home-brew. I'd drink
the awful, fizzy, stinging stuff
that went straight to my head
and play my home-made flute
(I think it had the weirdest scale on earth)
and, dizzy, whoop and dance among the goats.
Home-made, home-made! But aren't we all?
I felt a deep affection for
the smallest of my island industries.
No, not exactly, since the smallest was
a miserable philosophy.

Because I didn't know enough.
Why didn't I know enough of something?
Greek drama or astronomy? The books
I'd read were full of blanks;
the poems—well, I tried
reciting to my iris-beds,
"They flash upon that inward eye,
which is the bliss . . ." The bliss of what?
One of the first things that I did
when I got back was look it up.

The island smelled of goat and guano.
The goats were white, so were the gulls,
and both too tame, or else they thought
I was a goat, too, or a gull.
Baa, baa, baa and *shriek, shriek, shriek,*
baa . . . shriek . . . baa . . . I still can't shake
them from my ears; they're hurting now.
The questioning shrieks, the equivocal replies
over a ground of hissing rain
and hissing, ambulating turtles
got on my nerves.

When all the gulls flew up at once, they sounded
like a big tree in a strong wind, its leaves.

I'd shut my eyes and think about a tree,
an oak, say, with real shade, somewhere.
I'd heard of cattle getting island-sick.
I thought the goats were.
One billy-goat would stand on the volcano
I'd christened *Mont d'Espoir* or *Mount Despair*
(I'd time enough to play with names),
and bleat and bleat, and sniff the air.
I'd grab his beard and look at him.
His pupils, horizontal, narrowed up
and expressed nothing, or a little malice.
I got so tired of the very colors!
One day I dyed a baby goat bright red
with my red berries, just to see
something a little different.
And then his mother wouldn't recognize him.

Dreams were the worst. Of course I dreamed of food
and love, but they were pleasant rather
than otherwise. But then I'd dream of things
like slitting a baby's throat, mistaking it
for a baby goat. I'd have
nightmares of other islands
stretching away from mine, infinities
of islands, islands spawning islands,
like frogs' eggs turning into polliwogs
of islands, knowing that I had to live
on each and every one, eventually,
for ages, registering their flora,
their fauna, their geography.

Just when I thought I couldn't stand it
another minute longer, Friday came.
(Accounts of that have everything all wrong.)
Friday was nice.
Friday was nice, and we were friends.
If only he had been a woman!
I wanted to propagate my kind,
and so did he, I think, poor boy.
He'd pet the baby goats sometimes,

and race with them, or carry one around.
—Pretty to watch; he had a pretty body.

And then one day they came and took us off.

Now I live here, another island,
that doesn't seem like one, but who decides?
My blood was full of them; my brain
bred islands. But that archipelago
has petered out. I'm old.
I'm bored, too, drinking my real tea,
surrounded by uninteresting lumber.
The knife there on the shelf—
it reeked of meaning, like a crucifix.
It lived. How many years did I
beg it, implore it, not to break?
I knew each nick and scratch by heart,
the bluish blade, the broken tip,
the lines of wood-grain on the handle . . .
Now it won't look at me at all.
The living soul has dribbled away.
My eyes rest on it and pass on.

The local museum's asked me to
leave everything to them:
the flute, the knife, the shrivelled shoes,
my shedding goatskin trousers
(moths have got in the fur),
the parasol that took me such a time
remembering the way the ribs should go.
It still will work but, folded up,
looks like a plucked and skinny fowl.
How can anyone want such things?
—And Friday, my dear Friday, died of measles
seventeen years ago come March.

The Moose

For Grace Bulmer Bowers

From narrow provinces
of fish and bread and tea,
home of the long tides
where the bay leaves the sea
twice a day and takes
the herrings long rides,

where if the river
enters or retreats
in a wall of brown foam
depends on if it meets
the bay coming in,
the bay not at home;

where, silted red,
sometimes the sun sets
facing a red sea,
and others, veins the flats'
lavender, rich mud
in burning rivulets;

on red, gravelly roads,
down rows of sugar maples,
past clapboard farmhouses
and neat, clapboard churches,
bleached, ridged as clamshells,
past twin silver birches,

through late afternoon
a bus journeys west,
the windshield flashing pink,
pink glancing off of metal,
brushing the dented flank
of blue, beat-up enamel;

down hollows, up rises,
and waits, patient, while

a lone traveller gives
kisses and embraces
to seven relatives
and a collie supervises.

Goodbye to the elms,
to the farm, to the dog.
The bus starts. The light
grows richer; the fog,
shifting, salty, thin,
comes closing in.

Its cold, round crystals
form and slide and settle
in the white hens' feathers,
in gray glazed cabbages,
on the cabbage roses
and lupins like apostles;

the sweet peas cling
to their wet white string
on the whitewashed fences;
bumblebees creep
inside the foxgloves,
and evening commences.

One stop at Bass River.
Then the Economies—
Lower, Middle, Upper;
Five Islands, Five Houses,
where a woman shakes a tablecloth
out after supper.

A pale flickering. Gone.
The Tantramar marshes
and the smell of salt hay.
An iron bridge trembles
and a loose plank rattles
but doesn't give way.

On the left, a red light
swims through the dark:
a ship's port lantern.
Two rubber boots show,
illuminated, solemn.
A dog gives one bark.

A woman climbs in
with two market bags,
brisk, freckled, elderly.
"A grand night. Yes, sir,
all the way to Boston."
She regards us amicably.

Moonlight as we enter
the New Brunswick woods,
hairy, scratchy, splintery;
moonlight and mist
caught in them like lamb's wool
on bushes in a pasture.

The passengers lie back.
Snores. Some long sighs.
A dreamy divagation
begins in the night,
a gentle, auditory,
slow hallucination. . . .

In the creakings and noises,
an old conversation
—not concerning us,
but recognizable, somewhere,
back in the bus:
Grandparents' voices

uninterruptedly
talking, in Eternity:
names being mentioned,
things cleared up finally;

what he said, what she said,
who got pensioned;

deaths, deaths and sicknesses;
the year he remarried;
the year (something) happened.
She died in childbirth.
That was the son lost
when the schooner foundered.

He took to drink. Yes.
She went to the bad.
When Amos began to pray
even in the store and
finally the family had
to put him away.

"Yes . . ." that peculiar
affirmative. "Yes . . ."
A sharp, indrawn breath,
half groan, half acceptance,
that means "Life's like that.
We know *it* (also death)."

Talking the way they talked
in the old featherbed,
peacefully, on and on,
dim lamplight in the hall,
down in the kitchen, the dog
tucked in her shawl.

Now, it's all right now
even to fall asleep
just as on all those nights.
—Suddenly the bus driver
stops with a jolt,
turns off his lights.

A moose has come out of
the impenetrable wood
and stands there, looms, rather,
in the middle of the road.
It approaches; it sniffs at
the bus's hot hood.

Towering, antlerless,
high as a church,
homely as a house
(or, safe as houses).
A man's voice assures us
"Perfectly harmless. . . ."

Some of the passengers
exclaim in whispers,
childishly, softly,
"Sure are big creatures."
"It's awful plain."
"Look! It's a she!"

Taking her time,
she looks the bus over,
grand, otherworldly.
Why, why do we feel
(we all feel) this sweet
sensation of joy?

"Curious creatures,"
says our quiet driver,
rolling his *r*'s.
"Look at that, would you."
Then he shifts gears.
For a moment longer,

by craning backward,
the moose can be seen
on the moonlit macadam;
then there's a dim

smell of moose, an acrid
smell of gasoline.

Josephine Miles

Josephine Miles (1911–1985).   Born in Chicago Josephine Miles moved with her
family to California when she was a child. She studied at UCLA and Berkeley, and was
a professor at Berkeley until her retirement. Although she suffered since early child-
hood from crippling arthritis, requiring a wheelchair, she taught, gave readings, and
lectured publicly until the end of her life. Miles had a political and poetic ear, and her
fresh observations come through with humor and irony, as well as an understated
pathos rendering her poems profound and memorable. She published more than ten
volumes of poetry, including her *Collected Poems* (1983). Her important critical works
include *The Vocabulary of Poetry: Three Studies* (1946), *Ralph Waldo Emerson* (1964),
and *Poetry and Change: Donne, Milton, Wordsworth and the Equilibrium of the Present*
(1974).

Memorial Day

After noon, in the plaza, cries, shrill yells, running and breaking,
Students look desperately
Out of the open windows. We have to be there.
A rifle waves in the window,
Tear gas gusts in, no one to help
In the furtherance of this class in Milton's epics.
Well let's meet tomorrow at my house.
OK, we'll bring the wholegrain wheat-germ raisin bread.
Up in the office floors, out in the square,
Gas of a new kind in experimentation.
I choke and cry the tears they call for.
    So I say, and now we are munching
Crunchies in the front yard,
And finishing the patristic part of Book VII,
Papers are due after the weekend,
Please go home and work there,
And tell your parents the story of these weeks.
Even if they believe in the war you're protesting,
They will believe you too. Tell them
The sorts of pressures, absences of aid,
Losses of understanding you are working under.
They say they've already tried: I get my dad on the phone
And he says You can't tell me.

Give me Mom, and my mom says
You can't tell me. Stay out of trouble.
The army helicopter
In its regular rounds of surveillance drops down low—
Our twenty figures in a courtyard may mean trouble.
Couldn't we pick these flowers to throw at them?
All these camellias overgrown and wasting?

Before

Earlier, what I remember: a small
Flame of arthritis in the midst of fields
In the Euclidean Sunday mustard fields
And the mud fields of the potted palm,
In Jackie's airy room,
And at the fire station
All the brass
And all of us
Feeding the gulls.
A fresh salt breeze and foam
Around a plaster leg.
Away from the chloroform intern, joy
Of the long journey when I ran
Free of the plaster, and got back
Down those long hills, spent out.
Where had I been, oh tell me.
And where
Under those vast sunny
Apricot trees in the front yard?
Go tell Aunt Rhodie the old gray goose is dead.

If You Will

Shall I pull the curtains against the coming night?
No, there is still a fine sun in the tree tops; let them be.
All right; now it is darker; shall I now
Close out the dark? You will close out the light.
All right; how quick the dark comes. But see how the moon
Floods as it floods the earth even this room.

Moonlight, it's time to sleep, shall I draw now
Curtains against the cold? It's summer weather.
Shall I? Yes, if you will; the light will pass.
It is your life that stands beyond the glass.

Doll

Though the willows bent down to shelter us where we played
House in the sandy acres, though our dolls,
Especially Lillian, weathered all the action,
I kept getting so much earlier home to rest
That medical consultation led to cast
From head to toe. It was a surprise for my parents
And so for me also, and I railed
Flat out in the back seat on the long trip home
In which three tires blew on our trusty Mitchell.
Home, in a slight roughhouse of my brothers,
It turned out Lillian had been knocked to the floor and broken
Across the face. Good, said my mother
In her John Deweyan constructive way,
Now you and Lillian can be mended together.
We made a special trip to the doll hospital
To pick her up. But, They can't fix her after all, my father said,
You'll just have to tend her with her broken cheek.
I was very willing. We opened the box, and she lay
In shards mixed among tissue paper. Only her eyes
Set loose on a metal stick so they would open
And close, opened and closed, and I grew seasick.

A friend of the family sent me a kewpie doll.
Later Miss Babcox the sitter,
After many repetitious card games,
Said, We must talk about bad things.
Let me tell you
Some of the bad things I have known in my life.
She did not ask me mine, I could not have told her.
Among the bad things in my life, she said,
Have been many good people, good but without troubles;
Her various stories tended
To end with transmigrations of one sort or another,

Dishonest riches to honest poverty; kings and queens
To Indians over an adequate space of time.
Take this cat coming along here, she said,
A glossy black cat whom she fed her wages in salmon,
He is a wise one, about to become a person.
Come to think of it, possibly Lillian
Is about to become a cat.
She will have different eyes then, I said.
Obviously. Slanted, and what is more,
Able to see in the dark.

Muriel Rukeyser

Muriel Rukeyser (1913–1980).   Born in New York City, she was educated at Ethical Culture and the Fieldston School, Vassar College, and Columbia. She also went to Roosevelt Aviation School, and shortly afterward wrote her volume of poems *Theory of Flight* (1935). She was awarded a Guggenheim Fellowship, the National Institute Award, and a fellowship from the American Council of Learned Societies. On the board of directors of the Teacher's-Writer's Collaborative and a member of the National Institute of Arts and Letters, she wrote prose and children's books, and illustrated her book *Come Back, Paul* (1955). Her political activism began in college when she was involved in civil rights. Her books of poetry include: *U.S.1* (1938), *A Turning Wing* (1939), *The Soul and Body of John Brown* (1940), *Beast in View* (1944), *The Green Wave* (1948), *Body of Waking* (1958), *The Speed of Darkness* (1968), *The Traces of Thomas Hariot* (1971), *Breaking Open* (1973), *The Gates* (1976), and *The Collected Poems* (1978).

Eyes of Night-Time

On the roads at night I saw the glitter of eyes:
My dark around me let shine one ray; that black
allowed their eyes   :   spangles in the cat's, air in
    the moth's eye shine,
mosaic of the fly, ruby-eyed beetle, the eyes that never weep,
the horned toad sitting and its tear of blood,
fighters and prisoners in the forest, people
aware in this almost total dark, with the difference,
the one broad fact of light.

Eyes on the road at night, sides of a road like rhyme;
the floor of the illumined shadow sea
and shallows with their assembling flash and show

of sight, root, holdfast, eyes of the brittle stars.
And your eyes in the shadowy red room,
scent of the forest entering, various time

calling and the light of wood along the ceiling
and over us birds calling and their circuit eyes.
And in our bodies the eyes of the dead and the living
giving us gifts at hand, the glitter of all their eyes.

Darkness Music

The days grow and the stars cross over
And my wild bed turns slowly among the stars.

This Morning

Waking this morning,
a violent woman in the violent day
laughing.
                    Past the line of memory
along the long body of your life
in which move childhood, youth, your lifetime of touch,
eyes, lips, chest, belly, sex, legs, to the waves of the sheet.
I look past the little plant
on the city windowsill
to the tall towers bookshapes, crushed together in greed,
the river flashing flowing corroded,
the intricate harbor and the sea, the wars, the moon the planets
                    all who people space
in the sun visible invisible.
African violets in the light
breathing, in a breathing universe. I want strong peace, and
     delight,
the wild good.
I want to make my touch poems:
to find my morning, to find you entire
alive moving among the anti-touch people.

             I say across the waves of the air to you:
today once more

I will try to be non-violent
one more day
this morning, waking the world away
in the violent day.

Ruth Stone

Ruth Stone (1915-).   Born in Roanoke, Virginia, she grew up in Indianapolis and
attended the University of Illinois. Later she worked as an assistant to the literary and
dramatic editor of the *Indianapolis Star.* She married Walter Stone, a poet and profes-
sor of English at Vassar. In 1958, while they were in England, he died. She became
an editor at Wesleyan University Press, and subsequently a professor at Wellesley,
Brandeis, the University of Wisconsin, the University of California at Irvine, Indiana
University, and more recently at the University of Virginia. She has been a fellow at
the Radcliffe Institute and a Pulitzer nominee, has won the Shelley Award from the
Poetry Society of America, and twice has been a Guggenheim Fellow. She raised her
three daughters in Vermont, where she lives when not teaching, and whose landscape
and severe winters often enter her poems. A poet of immaculate diction, pathos, and
humor, her insights are always fresh and profound. Her highly personal poetry, often
of specific people and places, is emotionally intense but totally devoid of sentimental-
ity. Her books of poetry are *In an Iridescent Time* (1951), *Topography and Other Poems*
(1970), and *Cheap* (1972).

Room

Someone in the next apartment
Walks slowly back to a room abutting mine.
I am on this side, sitting.
It is uncomfortable trying to be quiet.
For weeks coming in here to change my clothes,
I think, are my clothes too daring?
And the sound of water rushing in
Filling a tub in the other room
Makes a loud continuity,
As though many people might be living here,
Twining their arms about me,
Passing me in the hall,
Making tender jokes.
Sunlight enters the room near the ceiling.
And shadows of leaves letting go
Flash in downward slants
Falling inside the room
To sink through the floor.

And I think
Is this the way it will be?
And I listen
With my ear against the plaster.

Liberation

We ladies sense it is the cuckoo builds no nest;
To float the flower on the pond and hide the stem,
That's to be as we are. God gives us recompense.
Within the nursery one may smack and kiss
As among giggling nuns. The business is,
Secure the man when young and then repent
Amid his willows and his streams. Sweet lioness,
The sorcerer says in ugly dreams you have
No bloodless sorrow. Whose bones attest to this?
We ache, we grow fat, we are oppressed.
Metamorphosis deceives our innocence.
Morning after morning slips
The spider with her web across our lips.

Dénouement

You intimidated me. I was thrown into hell without a trial.
Guilty by default. It was clear the murdered one was dead.
There were only two of us. But no one came to lead me away.
A hundred eyes looked in and saw me on fire.
We loved him, they said. Then they forgot.
After many years I knew who it was who had died.
Murderer, I whispered, you tricked me.

Whose Scene?

I crawl up the couch leg feeling
Your blond hair, your bloomy skin.
What do I want from you, giant?
I am afraid. But I laugh; I enjoy.

You fabricate. The words and music tremble
And thunder my thin blood.
The air is heated; odor of indian oil.
Trussed bed where bodies grapple; arms, legs,
Breasts, balls; the giants copulating.
I crawl up a wall and open my wings
And flutter down in borrowed ecstasy.

But then not open ended as it ought to be;
The beer, the refrigerator, the dull
Sequel shrinks to five rooms
In a treeless suburb. And cockroach that I am,
I go behind the baseboard to fornicate and spread
Myself, ancient as the ovulum and sperm.

Codicil

I am still bitter about the last place we stayed.
The bed was really too small for both of us.
In that same rooming house
Walls were lined with filing cases,
Drawers of bird's eggs packed in cotton.
The landlady described them.
As widow of the ornithologist,
Actually he was a postal clerk,
She was proprietor of the remains.
Had accompanied him on his holidays
Collecting eggs. Yes,
He would send her up the tree
And when she faltered he would shout,
"Put it in your mouth. Put it in your mouth."
It was nasty, she said,
Closing a drawer with her knee.
Faintly blue, freckled, mauve, taupe,
Chalk white eggs.
As we turned the second flight of stairs
Toward a mattress unfit for two,
Her voice would echo up the well,
Something about an electric kettle
At the foot of our bed.

Eggs, eggs, eggs in secret muted shapes in my head;
Hundreds of unborn wizened eggs.
I think about them when I think of you.

Dark Conclusions

Like cutting the dry rot out of a potato,
There is nothing left in a moment but the skin
And a little milky juice. How awful to slice it open
And find the center fustating, malevolent.

On the Mountain

Still in October, the woodcock,
Silent in the gold leaves,
Waits for the last breath of summer.
In the wet grass a firefly signals like Betelgeuse
Across the darkness; late lover,
Saving his flash for the death-boom
In the Northern lights.
On this ridge the nights flicker and fall with the Orionids.
Here on the ground I look up
Into the white haze of the universe.
The summer is in me like a readiness for flight,
And I search among the signs
For the flare, polestar, pulley toward the edge.

The Talking Fish

My love's eyes are red as the sargasso
With lights behind the iris like a cephalopod's.
The weeds move slowly, November's diatoms
Stain the soft stagnant belly of the sea.
Mountains, atolls, coral reefs,
Do you desire me? Am I among the jellyfish of your griefs?
I comb my sorrows singing; any doomed sailor can hear
The rising and falling bell and begin to wish

For home. There is no choice among the voices
Of love. Even a carp sings.

Years Later

Years later my eyes clear up
and the blood veil turns into a net.
Through hexagonal holes, sections
of your arms appear, or the fingers
of your right hand, our innocent obsessions,
your eyebrows, individual hair follicles
or the Mongol pockets of fat
along your high arrogant cheeks.
These parts of you are clear
and reasonable and finally tell me
that it is your skeleton I crave;
the way the bones of your feet,
fitted like the wing sockets of angels,
came toward me in time over the long
plateaus of ice, their delicate mouse-like tread
printed in tracks of snow over my mind.

Winter

The ten o'clock train to New York;
coaches like loaves of bread powdered with snow.
Steam wheezes between the couplings.
Stripped to plywood, the station's cement standing room
imitates a Russian novel. It is now that I remember you.
Your profile becomes the carved handle of a letter knife.
Your heavy-lidded eyes slip under the seal of my widowhood.
It is another raw winter. Stray cats are suffering.
Starlings crowd the edges of chimneys.
It is a drab misery that urges me to remember you.
I think about the subjugation of women and horses.
Brutal exposure. Weather that forces, that strips.
In our time we met in ornate stations
arching up with nineteenth century optimism.
I remember you running beside the train waving goodbye.

I can produce a facsimile of you standing
behind a column of polished oak to surprise me.
Am I going toward you or away from you on this train?
Discarded junk of other minds is strewn beside the tracks.
Mounds of rusting wire. Grotesque pop-art of dead motors.
Senile warehouses. The train passes a station.
Fresh people standing on the platform;
their faces expecting something.
I feel their entire histories ravish me.

Repetition of Words and Weather

A basket of dirty clothes
spills all day long
down the mountain
beating the rocks
with a horrible washer-woman's cry.
Now two riders go by
horseback on the dirt road.
Young women talking of antique latches,
blind to the dirty linen,
smells of urine, bedsores,
bowels of old women
left on their backs,
fat and lye,
lies of doctoring men.
Strange weather mid-summer
is summer spent.
I open a book of poems.
All lies on the psalter, I say,
the dead are silent.
The riders come back
chatting like birds.
What would I not give
to return that way.
Their horses trot in a break
of sunlight over the road.
And I think, what's done is done.
It won't be changed with words.

Gwendolyn Brooks

Gwendolyn Brooks (1917–).   Born in Topeka, Kansas, Gwendolyn Brooks grew up in Chicago, where at the age of seven she began to write poetry. She graduated from Wilson Junior College, and in the forties attended a poetry workshop at Southside Community Art Center. With Inez Cunningham Stark, a rich Chicago socialite and a reader for *Poetry* magazine, Brooks studied modernism. She modeled herself on the writers of the Harlem Renaissance, writing poetry that combined the traditional forms of English poetry with African-American idiom, jazz, and blues. In 1949, she was awarded a Pulitzer Prize for *Annie Allen,* her second volume of poetry, making her the first African-American poet so honored. She is poet laureate of the state of Illinois.

In 1967 Brooks attended the second Black Writers' Conference. There she was inspired to direct her poetry toward a black audience and to become a political activist. She has said about her work:

My aim, in my next future, is to write poems that will somehow successfully "call" all black people: black people in taverns, black people in alleys, black people in gutters, schools, offices, factories, prisons, the consulate; I wish to reach black people in mines, on farms, on thrones; *not* always to "teach"—I shall wish often to entertain, to illumine.

Brooks's volumes of poetry include *A Street in Bronzeville* (1945), *Annie Allen* (1949), *Bronzeville Boys and Girls* (1956), *The Bean Eaters* (1960), *Selected Poems* (1963), *In the Mecca* (1968), *Riot* (1969), *Family Pictures* (1970), *The World of Gwendolyn Brooks* (1971), *Aloneness* (1972), *Beckonings* (1975), and *To Disembark* (1981). She has written ten novels, and an autobiography, *Report from Part One* (1972).

Jessie Mitchell's Mother

Into her mother's bedroom to wash the ballooning body.
"My mother is jelly-hearted and she has a brain of jelly:
Sweet, quiver-soft, irrelevant. Not essential.
Only a habit would cry if she should die.
A pleasant sort of fool without the least iron. . . .
Are you better, mother, do you think it will come today?"
The stretched yellow rag that was Jessie Mitchell's mother
Reviewed her. Young, and so thin, and so straight.
So straight! as if nothing could ever bend her.
But poor men would bend her, and doing things with poor men,
Being much in bed, and babies would bend her over,
And the rest of things in life that were for poor women,
Coming to them grinning and pretty with intent to bend and to
    kill.
Comparisons shattered her heart, ate at her bulwarks:

The shabby and the bright: she, almost hating her daughter,
Crept into an old sly refuge: "Jessie's black
And her way will be black, and jerkier even than mine.
Mine, in fact, because I was lovely, had flowers
Tucked in the jerks, flowers were here and there. . . ."
She revived for the moment settled and dried-up triumphs,

Forced perfume into old petals, pulled up the droop,
Refueled
Triumphant long-exhaled breaths.
Her exquisite yellow youth . . .

my dreams, my works, must wait till after hell

I hold my honey and I store my bread
In little jars and cabinets of my will.
I label clearly, and each latch and lid
I bid, Be firm till I return from hell.
I am very hungry. I am incomplete.
And none can tell when I may dine again.
No man can give me any word but Wait,
The puny light. I keep eyes pointed in;
Hoping that, when the devil days of my hurt
Drag out to their last dregs and I resume
On such legs as are left me, in such heart
As I can manage, remember to go home,
My taste will not have turned insensitive
To honey and bread old purity could love.

kitchenette building

We are things of dry hours and the involuntary plan,
Grayed in, and gray. "Dream" makes a giddy sound, not
   strong
Like "rent," "feeding a wife," "satisfying a man."

But could a dream send up through onion fumes
Its white and violet, fight with fried potatoes

And yesterday's garbage ripening in the hall,
Flutter, or sing an aria down these rooms

Even if we were willing to let it in,
Had time to warm it, keep it very clean,
Anticipate a message, let it begin?

We wonder. But not well! not for a minute!
Since Number Five is out of the bathroom now,
We think of lukewarm water, hope to get in it.

A Sunset of the City

Kathleen Eileen

Already I am no longer looked at with lechery or love.
My daughters and sons have put me away with marbles and dolls,
Are gone from the house.
My husband and lovers are pleasant or somewhat polite
And night is night.

It is a real chill out,
The genuine thing.
I am not deceived, I do not think it is still summer
Because sun stays and birds continue to sing.

It is summer-gone that I see, it is summer-gone.
The sweet flowers indrying and dying down,
The grasses forgetting their blaze and consenting to brown.

It is a real chill out. The fall crisp comes.

We Real Cool

The Pool Players. Seven at the Golden Shovel.

We real cool. We
Left school. We

Lurk late. We
Strike straight. We

Sing sin. We
Thin gin. We

Jazz June. We
Die soon.

Boy Breaking Glass

To Marc Crawford from Whom the Commission

Whose broken window is a cry of art
(success, that winks aware
as elegance, as a treasonable faith)
is raw: is sonic: is old-eyed première.
Our beautiful flaw and terrible ornament.
Our barbarous and metal little man.

"I shall create! If not a note, a hole.
If not an overture, a desecration."

Full of pepper and light
and Salt and night and cargoes.

"Don't go down the plank
if you see there's no extension.
Each to his grief, each to
his loneliness and fidgety revenge.

Nobody knew where I was and now I am no longer there."

The only sanity is a cup of tea.
The music is in minors.

Each one other
is having different weather.

"It was you, it was you who threw away my name!
And this is everything I have for me."

Who has not Congress, lobster, love, luau,
the Regency Room, the Statue of Liberty,
runs. A sloppy amalgamation.
A mistake.
A cliff.
A hymn, a snare, and an exceeding sun.

May Swenson

May Swenson (1919–).   Born in Logan, Utah, she earned her B.A. from the
University of Utah. She has received a Guggenheim Fellowship, a Ford Foundation
Poet-Playwright Grant, an Amy Lowell Poetry Travelling Scholarship, a Rockefeller
Scholarship, and a Robert Frost Fellowship, and was elected to membership in the
National Institute of Arts and Letters. Her volumes of poetry include *A Cage of Spines*
(1958), *To Mix with Time* (1963), *Half Sun Half Sleep* (1967), and *Iconographs*.

Women

Women	Or they
should be	should be
pedestals	little horses
moving	those wooden
pedestals	sweet
moving	oldfashioned
to the	painted
motions	rocking
of men	horses

the gladdest things in the toyroom

The	feelingly
pegs	and then
of their	unfeelingly
ears	To be
so familiar	joyfully
and dear	ridden
to the trusting	rockingly
fists	ridden until

To be chafed	the restored

egos dismount and the legs stride away

Immobile	willing
sweetlipped	to be set
sturdy	into motion
and smiling	Women
women	should be
should always	pedestals
be waiting	to men

Amy Clampitt

Amy Clampitt (1920–).   Born and raised in New Providence, Iowa, Amy Clampitt was graduated and awarded an honorary doctorate from Grinnell College. She has received a Guggenheim Fellowship and an award from the Academy of American Poets, and is a member of the National Institute of Arts and Letters. Her first volume of poetry, *The Kingfisher* (1983), was nominated for the National Book Critics Circle Award. Her other books are *What the Light Was Like* (1985), *Archaic Figure* (1987), and *Westward* (1990).

In Clampitt, observation, lexicon, and drama coalesce in stubbornly learned poems reflecting a tradition of earlier major poets—Keats, Hopkins, Stevens, Marianne Moore—their lives and their music. Clampitt writes that in *Archaic Figure,* from which we selected "Archaic Figure" and "Margaret Fuller, 1947," "A central concern is with the experience of women, as individuals and as a part of history."

A Baroque Sunburst

struck through such a dome
as might await a groaning Michelangelo,
finding only alders and barnacles
and herring gulls at their usual squabbles,
sheds on the cove's voluted
silver the aloof skin tones
of a Crivelli angel: a region,
a weather and a point of view
as yet unsettled, save for the lighthouse
like a Venetian campanile, from whose nightlong
reflected angelus you might suppose
the coast of Maine had Europe
on the brain or in its bones, as though
it were a kind of sickness.

Archaic Figure

Headless in East Berlin, no goddess
but a named mere girl (Ornithe, "Little Bird")
out of the rubble, six centuries underneath
    the plinth of what we quaintly call

Our Time, informs the foaming underside
of linden boulevards in bloom, sweet hide
laid open onto—sterile as an operating table,
    past the closed incision of the Wall—

the treeless reach of Alexanderplatz,
paved counterpart of the interior flatland,
halfway across the globe, we'd left behind:
    projection, factor, yield, the quantifiable

latitude; malls, runways, blacktop; tressed
cornsilk and alfalfa, drawn milk of the humdrum
nurture there were those of us who ran away from
    toward another, earlier, bonier

one, another middle of the earth, yearned-for stepmotherland of
    Hölderlin and Goethe:
sunlight and grief, the cypress and the
    crucifix, the vivid poverty

of terraced slopes, of bread, wine, olives,
fig and pomegranate shade we stumbled into,
strolling the sad northern drizzle, in
    the uprooted Turks' quasi-bazaar,

as here, among uprooted artifacts, we've come
upon this shape's just-lifted pleats, her
chitoned stillness the cold chrism of a time
    that saw—or so to us it seems—

with unexampled clarity to the black core
of what we are, of everything we were to be,

have since become. Who stands there headless.
    Barbar, she would have called us all.

Margaret Fuller, 1847

In this her thirty-seventh year, the Italy
she'd discerned already smoldering,
through some queer geological contortion,
beneath a New World crust, abruptly ceased
to be a metaphor. She was in Rome,
and from her lodgings on the Corso
she watched as things began to happen:
the torchlit procession to the Quirinal,
the flung-out embrace of Pio Nono
from his balcony seeming (at least)
to give the upheaval in the streets his blessing.

By September, in Florence, in Milan,
more demonstrations: that second spring
she'd once despaired of, the kernel
lying dormant in the husk no longer,
the shattered chrysalis, the tidal
concourse in the streets and through the bloodstream
one and the same. Angelo Ossoli, whom
she'd met by chance—the faintly scandalous
perennial adventure that awaits a woman,
of whatever age or status, in such a place—
was now her lover. Without the cause he'd drawn

her into—a mutilated Italy made whole,
at peace within, left to itself at last,
the hated foreign uniforms gone home—
she'd once again have kept her head,
perhaps: remained unconscionably chaste,
seen the admirer she'd somehow led on
pull back bewildered as, her self-esteem
gone numb, she worked at being noble.
Not now. Not in this place. The furnace
that had scathed her solitude burned with the torches,
glowed in the votive banks lit by the faithful.

The two of them went frequently to Mass;
on long excursions into the countryside
inhaled the reek of grapes still on the vine,
observed the harvest. The violets and roses
that still bloomed made her bedroom sweet
all through November. "I have not been so well,"
she wrote her mother, "since I was a child, nor
so happy ever." *Nor so happy ever.* Short of money,
she lived now in one room, on fruit, bread,
a little wine; saw few acquaintances,
dissembled, as she'd so often done, even with those.

The mild days shrank. A season ended.
Nor so happy ever. In mid-December
a cold, steady rain began. Increasingly
the high-walled towers along the Corso
shut out the daylight. *Since I was a child:*
then there had been terror
in the night, as now: she'd wake
alone to find herself back in Nantasket,
where she'd dreamed her mother dead,
re-dreamed her best friend's body lying
on hard sand, until the waves reclaimed it,

drowned. Brave metaphor of tides became,
lodged in that sullen dark, a heaving
succubus of mud. The street-corner
flower vendors disappeared.
Lamplit all day, the stale cul-de-sac
she could not leave now stank of charcoal
and the chamber pot. Migraine, a vengeful
ever-since-childhood doppelgänger,
returned, with a new kind of nausea:
the body so little of her life had ever
found sweetness in, life for its own inexorable

purposes took over. "A strange lilting lean
old maid," Carlyle had called her—though
not nearly such a bore as he'd expected.
What would Carlyle, what would straitlaced

Horace Greeley, what would fastidious
Nathaniel Hawthorne, what would all Concord,
all New England and her own mother
say now? An actuality more fraught
than any nightmare: terrors of the sea,
of childbirth, the massive, slow,
unending heave of human trouble.

Injustice. Ridicule. What did she *do?*
it would be asked (as though that mattered).
Gave birth. Lived through a revolution.
Nursed its wounded. Saw it run aground.
Published a book or two.
And drowned.

Mary Ellen Solt

Mary Ellen Solt (1920–)   She was born in Gilmore City, Iowa. As a critic Solt has
written extensively about her friend William Carlos Williams; as a poet, she is a
pioneer theorist, anthologist, and poet of the international concrete movement—no
one has contributed more to the diffusion of concrete poetry in the United States and
abroad. She is the editor of *Concrete Poetry: A World View* (1968), the most comprehen-
sive anthology of concrete poetry and theory. Her poems reveal far-reaching interests,
from moon rocketry to semiotics. As a sensitive observer of nature and people, her
impeccably crafted poems unite verbal and visual arts in unique creations. In addition
to publications, her poems have been exhibited at La Galérie Denise Davy, Paris;
Galérie Nächst, Vienna; Instituto Torculato di Tella, Buenos Aires; La Bienale de
Venezia; the Jewish Museum, New York; the Museum of Modern Art, New York;
Geijutsu Seikatsu Gallery, Tokyo; Stedeliji Museum, Amsterdam; Galleria Chiara,
Brescia, Italy; and Riviera-Reymont Gallery, Warsaw. Her books are *Flowers in Con-
crete* (1966), *Concrete Poetry: A World View* (1968), *The Peoplemover* (1968), *A Trilogy
of Rain* (1970), *Marriage* (1976), *A Demonstration Poem* (1978), and *Words and Spaces*
(1957–1977).

Notes on the Poems:
"Moonshot Sonnet" (1964). The poem was found on the moon photos in the *New
York Times.* When the scientists' symbols were simply copied, there were fourteen
"lines" with five "accents." Design: Mary Ellen Solt. Drawings: Timothy Mayer.
"Wild Crab" (from *Flowers in Concrete,* 1966). Design: Mary Ellen Solt. Typography:
John Dearstyne.
"Forsythia" (from *Flowers in Concrete,* 1966). The image is made from the letters of the
word and their equivalents in the Morse Code. Design: Mary Ellen Solt. Typography:
John Dearstyne.

"rain down" (from *A Trilogy of Rain*, 1970). Design: Mary Ellen Solt. Typography: A. Doyle Moore.

"Marriage" (1976) is a semiotic (code) poem. Its meaning is conveyed initially by the visual image, which is meant to suggest such domestic objects as wallpaper, quilts, rugs. But beyond this, the poem attempts, through literal and metaphorical meanings, to express the complexity of marriage. The complete poem consists of eight sets of signs. Presented here are the first four sets, which deal with the more basic biological and domestic facets of marriage. The remaining four sets are concerned with "Relationships," "Moods," "Dimensions," and "Conclusions." Signs drawn by Sheryl Nelson. Design: Mary Ellen Solt. Typography: A. Doyle Moore and Susan Solt.

Moonshot Sonnet

Wild Crab

Wind, Intrudes, Lifting Day
Cantabile, cantabile

Forsythia

rain down rain down rain down rain down rain **dow n** rai n b o w
rain down rain down rain down rain down rain **dow n** rai n b o w
rain down rain down rain down rain down rain **dow n** rai n b o w
rain down rain down rain down rain down rain **dow n** rai n b o w
rain down rain down rain down rain down rain **dow n** rai n b o w
rain down rain down rain down rain down rain **dow n** rai n b o w
rain down rain down rain down rain down rain **dow n** rai n b o w
rain down rain down rain down rain down rain **dow n** rai n b o w
rain down rain down rain down rain down rain **dow n** rai n b o w
rain down rain down rain down rain down rain **dow n** rai n b o w
rain down rain down rain down rain down rain **dow n** rai n b o w
rain down rain down rain down rain down rain **dow n** rai n b o w
rain down rain down rain down rain down rain **dow n** rai n b o w
rain down rain down rain down rain down rain **dow n** rai n b o w
rain down rain down rain down rain down rain **dow n** rai n b o w
rain down rain down rain down rain down rain **dow n** rai n b o w
rain down rain down rain down rain down rain **dow n** rai n b o w
rain down rain down rain down rain down rain **dow n** rai n b o w
rain down rain down rain down rain down rain **dow n** rai n b o w
rain down rain down rain down rain down rain **dow n** rai n b o w
rain down rain down rain down rain down rain **dow n** rai n b o w
rain down rain down rain down rain down rain **dow n** rai n b o w
rain down rain down rain down rain down rain **dow n** rai n b o w
rain down rain down rain down rain down rain **dow n** rai n b o w
rain down rain down rain down rain down rain **dow n** rai n b o w
rain down rain down rain down rain down rain **dow n** rai n b o w

Marriage

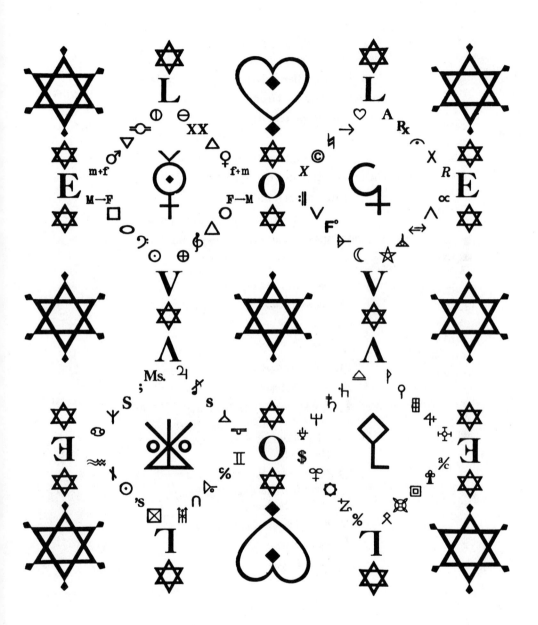

MARRIAGE

A code poem derived from the universal language
of signs and symbols used from primitive times
to the present day:
the alphabet
astrology   astronomy   botany
chemistry   commerce   engineering
mathematics   medicine
meteorology   music   physics
punctuation   runes   zoology   &c.

◆ *dot:secrecy   origin of all signs*

◇ *diamond   female anatomical symbol*

♡ *heart*

♡ *composite symbol*

✡ *perfect marriage*

✡ *composite symbol*

L *length(terrestrial)   lambert:unit of brightness   right angle:meeting of the celestial(vertical) and the terrestrial (horizontal)*

O *oxygen   ocean   blood type of husband and wife   October(unofficial): husband's birth month*

V *potential energy   velocity   volume*

E *earth   excellent*

LEO *husband's name*

I Pairings

⚥ *sun (old oriental symbol) source of all life*

⊕ *active male element saltpeter*

⊖ *passive female element earth (with equator)*
salt element: water

♂ *male male flower*

♀ *female female flower planet Venus*
mirror of Venus

▽ *male element: water*

△ *female wisdom godhead element: fire*

□ *male*

○ *female new moon unborn child God*
eternity element : fire

𝄞 *treble clef*

𝄢 *bass clef*

☉ *sun open eye of God element: air*

⊕ *earth creation: male plus female*
sun cross element: earth

⋍ *equivalent*

△ *finite difference*

◯ *whole note*

XX *double strength*

m+f = f+m *commutative law*

M—F *male implies female*

F—M *female implies male*

II Conjugations

♃ *Ceres : goddess of earth's fertility*

♡ *love*

© *copyright*

⇌ *reversible reaction*

F° *degrees of heat warmth*

⌒ *hold*

♮ *natural*

:‖ *repeat*

V *up-bow*

∧ *down-bow*

A *first class vessel*

X *kiss the unknown takes (chess)*

∝ *varies as*

→ *give*

Rₓ *take*

X *reactance*

R *resistance*

☾ *the moon's phases*

⊢ *man & woman united: procreation*

⚢ *pregnant woman*

☆ *the five senses happy homecoming*

III Family

✳ *family: man with wife and children*

S *Solt school sulfur combustible elements*

s *plural stem sire son sister series*

's *contraction: us is has possessive*

ᚾ *(rune: nied) necessity thraldom*

Υ *man*

△ *woman*

▷ᵒ *woman bears child*

☉ *moment of birth: awakening of inner*
     life in body

♎ *Libra: astrological sign of father*

♋ *Cancer: astrological sign of mother*

♊ *Gemini: astrological sign of daughter*

♒ *Aquarius: astrological sign of daughter*

♃ *planet Jupiter: name of family cat*

Ms. *female of undefined status: name of family dog*

% *in care of*

; *related and continuing*

∩ *intersection: shared in common*

⊠ *simple activity*

♪ *appoggiatura: grace note*

♯♯ *unity*

IV Home

⚲ *key*

△ *house*

ᚹ *(rune: wynn) comfort*

▣ *orderliness*

✿ *disorder*

ｈ *chair*

♀ *frying pan*

⊣⊢ *fork*

✛ *olive oil*

♆ *vinegar*

▦ *water*

4+ *borax*

♀ *wood*

♀ *glass*

⚴ *lime*

♄ *tree*

$ *money*

⅌ *account*

% *mortgage*

ᛉ *(rune: ogal) possession*

⊠ *to exorcise evil spirits*

Shirley Kaufman

Shirley Kaufman (1923–).   Born in Seattle, Washington, she won the Academy of
American Poets prize while studying for her M.A. at San Francisco State College. Her
book *The Floor Keeps Turning* (1970) won the U.S. Award of the International Poetry
Forum and was a National Council of the Arts selection. Her most recent volume,
Looking at Henry Moore's Elephant Skull Etchings in Jerusalem During the War (1977), is
a series of sixteen poems accompanied by Moore's etchings. The accurate depiction of
clean spaces, suggesting primordial forces, is a perfect marriage with the etchings of
Henry Moore. She lives in Israel. Her other titles include *Gold Country,* and *Selected
Poems of Abba Kovner* (translations from the Hebrew).

from Looking at Henry Moore's Elephant Skull Etchings in Jerusalem During the War

VI

There are caverns
under our feet
with rivers running deep in them.

They hide
in the sides of cliffs
at Rosh Hanikra
where the sea breaks in.

There is a way to enter
if you remember
where you came from

how to breathe under water
make love in a trap.

X

We are going down a long slide
into the secret chamber
we bought our tickets for the ride

the passage is narrow
and we can't find ourselves
in the trick mirrors

we lie down in the foetal position
back to back
each of us in his own eye socket

marvelous holes
the mind looked out of
filling with dust.

XV

I see bodies in the morning kneel
over graves and bodies under them
the skin burned off
their bones laid out in all the cold
tunnels under the world.

There is a photograph in the next room
of a dead child
withered against its mother
between the dry beans of her breasts

there is no blood
under the shrunk skin

their skulls are already visible.

Denise Levertov

Denise Levertov (1923–).   Born in Ilford, Essex, England, Denise Levertov
served as a nurse during World War II, and immigrated to the United States in 1948.
She has been a Guggenheim Fellow, poetry editor of *The Nation,* an associate scholar
at the Radcliffe Institute, and has recently retired from Tufts University, where she was
a full professor. Her books include the volumes of poetry *The Double Image* (1946),
Here and Now (1957), *Overland to the Islands* (1958), *With Eyes at the Backs of Our Heads*
(1959), *The Jacob's Ladder* (1961), *O Taste and See* (1964), *The Sorrow Dance* (1967),
Relearning the Alphabet (1970), *To Stay Alive* (1971), *Footprints* (1972), *The Freeing of
the Dust* (1975), *Life in the Forest* (1978), *Collected Earlier Poems 1940–1960* (1979),
Candles in Babylon (1982), *Poems 1960–1967* (1983), *Oblique Prayers* (1984), *Poems
1968–1972* (1987); two works of prose, *The Poet in the World* (1973) and *Light Up the
Cave* (1981); and two translations, *In Praise of Krishna: Songs from the Bengali* (with
Edward C. Dimmrock, Jr., 1968) and *Guillevic/Selected Poems* (1969).
    Her opposition to the Vietnam War and her political activism are reflected in her

poems of the late sixties. Her more recent poetry, however, though still informed by a political consciousness, is more introspective. In the essay "The Nature of Poetry" she writes:

> The didactic has a place in poetry, but only when it is inseparable from the intuitive . . . the poetry of political anguish is at its best both didactic and lyrical.
>
> In our time, a political poetry untinged with anguish . . . is unimaginable.
>
> Yet—because it creates autonomous structures that are imbued with life and which stir the life of those who experience them—poetry is, in process and in being, intrinsically affirmative.

Adam's Complaint

Some people,
no matter what you give them,
still want the moon.

The bread,
the salt,
white meat and dark,
still hungry.

The marriage bed
and the cradle,
still empty arms.

You give them land,
their own earth under their feet,
still they take to the roads.

And water: dig them the deepest well,
still it's not deep enough
to drink the moon from.

Overheard over S.E. Asia

"White phosphorous, white phosphorous,
mechanical snow,

where are you falling?"
"I am falling impartially on roads and roofs,
on bamboo thickets, on people.
My name recalls rich seas on rainy nights,
each drop that hits the surface eliciting
luminous response from a million algae.
My name is a whisper of sequins. Ha!
Each of them is a disk of fire,
I am the snow that burns.
                              I fall
wherever men send me to fall—
but I prefer flesh, so smooth, so dense:
I decorate it in black, and seek
the bone."

The Roamer

The world comes back to me
eager and hungry, and often
too tired to wag its tail,

a dog with wanderlust
back from South Boston or the Reservoir.

Keeps coming back,
brought by triumphant strangers
who don't understand he knows the way well.
Faint jingle of collartag breaking
my sleep, he arrives
and patiently scratches himself on the front steps.
I let in blue
daybreak,
in rushes the world,

visible dog concocted
of phantasmagoric atoms.

Nudges my hand with wet nose,
flumps down, deeply sighing,

smelling of muddy streams, of thrown-away treasures,
of some exotic news, not blood, not flowers,
and not his own fur—
                    unable
except by olifact
to tell me anything.
                    Where have I been
without the world? Why am I glad
he wolfs his food and gathers
strength for the next journey?

To Antonio Machado

Here in the mountain woods
a furious small fountain
is channelled through pipes of hollow sapling
into a great wooden vat bevelled with moss,
and thence brims over into a concrete cistern
and from the cistern quietly
in modest rills
into the meadow where cows graze
and fringed wild carnations, white and sweet,
grow by the path.
Machado,
        old man,
                dead man,
        I wish you were here alive
to drink of the cold, earthtasting, faithful spring,
to receive the many voices
of this one brook,
to see its dances
of fury and gentleness,
to write the austere poem
you would have known in it.

Brunnenburg, 1971

Stepping Westward

What is green in me
darkens, muscadine.

If woman is inconstant,
good, I am faithful to

ebb and flow, I fall
in season and now

is a time of ripening.
If her part

is to be true,
a north star,

good, I hold steady
in the black sky

and vanish by day,
yet burn there

in blue or above
quilts of cloud.

There is no savor
more sweet, more salt

than to be glad to be
what, woman,

and who, myself,
I am, a shadow

that grows longer as the sun
moves, drawn out

on a thread of wonder.
If I bear burdens

they begin to be remembered
as gifts, goods, a basket

of bread that hurts
my shoulders but closes me

in fragrance. I can
eat as I go.

Jane Cooper

Jane Cooper (1924–).   Jane Cooper grew up in Jacksonville, Florida, and Prince-
ton, New Jersey. In 1968 she received the Lamont Award of the Academy of Ameri-
can Poets for her first book, *The Weather of Six Mornings.* In 1974 she published *Maps
& Windows.* She was co-recipient of the Shelley Award from the Poetry Society of
America in 1978. *Scaffolding: New and Selected Poems* appeared in 1984. "Nothing has
been Used in the Manufacture of This Poetry that Could Have been Used in the
Manufacture of Bread," her autobiographical essay included in *Scaffolding,* explores
the difficulties of being a woman writer in a literary atmosphere dominated by men,
which fosters "a dichotomy between 'woman' and 'poet.'" About the poems in
Scaffolding, Grace Paley wrote, "They have about them a deep patience for the whole
truth, a waiting in quietness for tremor and explosion."

In the House of the Dying

So once again, hearing the tired aunts
whisper together under the kitchen globe,
I turn away; I am not one of them.

At the sink I watch the water cover my hands
in a sheath of light. Upstairs she lies alone
dreaming of autumn nights when her children were born.

On the steps between us grows in a hush of waiting
the impossible silence between two generations.
The aunts buzz on like flies around a bulb.

I am dressed like them. Standing with my back turned
I wash the dishes in the same easy way.
Only at birth and death do I utterly fail.

For death is my old friend who waits on the stairs.
Whenever I pass I nod to him like the newsman
who is there every day; for them he is the priest.

While the birth of love is so terrible to me
I feel unworthy of the commonest marriage.
Upstairs she lies, washed through by the two miracles.

Carolyn Kizer

Carolyn Kizer (1925–).   Born in Spokane, Washington, she attended Sarah Law-
rence College and Columbia University. Vachel Lindsay (who lived with her family),
Stanley Kunitz, and Theodore Roethke were her mentors. In 1957 she founded *Poetry
Northwest*. In 1966 she became the first director of the Literary Program for the
National Endowment for the Arts. When President Nixon dismissed Roger Stevens,
the chairman of the Endowment and the Council on the Arts, she resigned from her
post. She has also been poet-in-residence at the U.S. Embassy in Pakistan and directed
the Graduate Writing Program at Columbia University. Kizer lived in China and has
translated from the Chinese; the influence of Chinese poetry can be seen in her work,
especially in her "Chinese imitations." Of her feminist stance, Kizer writes: I am a
premature Women's Liberationist. I was writing poems on the subject ten years before
it became fashionable, and a great many people, then, didn't understand what the hell
the fuss was about." Her volumes of poetry are *The Ungrateful Garden* (1960), *Knock
upon Silence* (1965), and *Midnight Was My Cry* (1971). She also writes fiction.

The Intruder

My mother—preferring the strange to the tame:
Dove-note, bone marrow, deer dung,
Frog's belly distended with finny young,
Leaf-mould wilderness, hare-bell, toadstool,
Odd, small snakes roving through the leaves,
Metallic beetles rambling over stones: all
Wild and natural!—flashed out her instinctive love,
    and quick, she
Picked up the fluttering, bleeding bat the cat laid at her feet,
And held the little horror to the mirror, where

He gazed on himself, and shrieked like an old screen door
    far off.

Depended from her pinched thumb, each wing
Came clattering down like a small black shutter.
Still tranquil, she began, "It's rather sweet. . . ."
The soft mouse body, the hard feral glint
In the caught eyes. Then we saw,
And recoiled: lice, pallid, yellow,
Nested within the wing-pits, cosily sucked and snoozed.
The thing dropped from her hands, and with its thud,
Swiftly, the cat, with a clean careful mouth
Closed on the soiled webs, growling, took them out
    to the back stoop.

But still, dark blood, a sticky puddle on the floor
Remained, of all my mother's tender, wounding passion
For a whole wild, lost, betrayed and secret life
Among its dens and burrows, its clean stones,
Whose denizens can turn upon the world
With spitting tongue, an odor, talon, claw,
To sting or soil benevolence, alien
As our clumsy traps, our random scatter of shot.
She swept to the kitchen. Turning on the tap,
She washed and washed the pity from her hands.

Through a Glass Eye, Lightly

In the laboratory waiting room
containing
one television actor with a teary face
trying a contact lens;
two muscular victims of industrial accidents;
several vain women—I was one of them—
came Deborah, four, to pick up her glass eye.

It was a long day:
Deborah waiting for the blood-vessels
painted
on her iris to dry.

Her mother said that, holding Deborah
when she was born,
"First I inspected her, from toes to navel,
then stopped at her head. . . ."
We wondered why
the inspection hadn't gone the other way.
"Looking into her eye
was like looking into a volcano:

"Her vacant pupil
went whirling down, down to the foundation
of the world . . .
When she was three months old they took it out.
She giggled when she went under
the anaesthetic.
Forty-five minutes later she came back
happy! . . .
The gas wore off, she found the hole in her face
(you know, it never bled?),
stayed happy, even when I went to pieces.
She's five, in June.

"Deborah, you get right down
from there, or I'll have to slap!"
Laughing, Deborah climbed into the lap
of one vain lady, who
had been discontented with her own beauty.
Now she held on to Deborah, looked her steadily
in the empty eye.

Lines to Accompany Flowers for Eve

who took heroin, then sleeping pills
and who lies in a New York hospital

The florist was told, cyclamen or azalea;
White in either case, for you are pale
As they are, "blooming early and profusely"
Though the azalea grows in sandier soil

Needing less care; while cyclamen's fleshy tubers
Are adored, yes, rooted out by some.
One flourishes in aridness, while the other
Feeds the love which devours.

But what has flung you here for salvaging
From a city's dereliction, this New York?
A world against whose finger-and-breath marked windows
These weak flares may be set.
Our only bulwark is the frailest cover:
Lovers touch from terror of being alone.
The urban surface: tough and granular,
Poor ground for the affections to take root.

Left to our own devices, we devise
Such curious deaths, comas or mutilations!

You may buy peace, white, in sugary tincture,
No way of knowing its strength, or your own,
Until you lie quite still, your perfect limbs
In meditation: the spirit rouses, flutters
Like a handkerchief at a cell window, signalling
Self-amazed, its willingness to endure.

The thing to cling to is the sense of expectation.
Who knows what may occur in the next breath?
In the pallor of another morning we neither
Anticipated or wanted! Eve, waken to flowers
Unforeseen, from someone you don't even know.
Azalea or cyclamen . . . we live in wonder,
Blaze in a cycle of passion and apprehension
Though once we lay and waited for a death.

Maxine Kumin

Maxine Kumin (1925–).   Born in Philadelphia, she received her B.A. and M.A. from Radcliffe. In 1973 her book of poetry *Up Country* received the Pulitzer Prize. She was awarded the William Marion Reedy Award from the Poetry Society of America, the Lowell Mason Palmer Award, and a grant from the National Council on the Arts and Humanities, and was a scholar at the Radcliffe Institute for Independent Study. She also writes novels and children's books. Her volumes of poetry include *The Privilege* (1964), *The Nightmare Factory* (1970), and *House, Bridge, Fountain, Gate* (1975).

The Hermit Has a Visitor

Once he puts out the light
moth wings on the window screen slow
and drop away like film lapping the spool
after the home movie runs out.

He lies curled like a lima bean
still holding back its cotyledon.
Night is a honeycomb.
Night is the fur on a blue plum.
And then she sings. She raises the juice.
She is a needle, he the cloth.
She is an A string, he the rosewood.
She is the thin whine at concert pitch.

She has the eggs and he the blood
and after she is a small
red stain on the wall
he will itch.

Together

The water closing
over us and the
going down is all.
Gills are given.
We convert in a
town of broken hulls
and green doubloons.
O you dead pirates
hear us! There is
no salvage. All
you know is the color
of warm caramel. All
is salt. See how
our eyes have migrated
to the uphill side?
Now we are new round
mouths and no spines

letting the water cover.
It happens over
and over, me in
your body and you
in mine.

Dolores Kendrick

Dolores Kendrick (1927–).   Dolores Kendrick lives in New Hampshire where
she teaches at Phillips Academy at Exeter. Author of earlier books, *Through the Ceiling*
and *Now Is the Thing to Praise,* she has recently published *The Women of Plums: Poems
in the Voices of Slave Women* (1989) with William Morrow. Strong, polished, largely
neglected despite her immense historical and intellectual breadth, she is an important
voice in American poetry.

Canticle of a Black Lady

dying asks a question: she gives an answer

Done. Every ounce of it. Fly winds to sea-rocks and break
a round of prayer upon their backs.

Turtles, take notice! You may walk with your eyes upright.
Beasts in the forest, part the noon with your cries.
Stretch your bones into the sun, embrace Amen as you eat
     the air.

It is done! Said. Pronounced. Motioned. Spoken.
     Astonished.
The men of oranges have shed their skins and their flesh is
     puffed
upon weeds. The women of plums are sweet and black.
     Their flesh
is moist with tears of joy! Their dreams are skins the color
     of dusk.
Their ripe dreams bitten into leave a sour sweetness in the
     membranes of the mouth.

The children of quince quiver in the womb; their eyes are
     dowries,
their tongues, soft songs.

And the Bride comes forth carrying peacocks upon her
  fingers, bearing roses in her hair. She comes forth
  beyond the wedding-day and speaks
  I will and *Amen.*

Leah: in Freedom

I run away
      I keep runnin' away
           they won't let me alone
                  they won't let me bear
my misery to the river
      and out
          over the sky
             or even
                under the trees
in moles' holes
      and wolves' caves
          and blackberry patches
             with my feet
skiddin' and bleedin'
      on the thorns
          and then it rains
             on my run
as quick as my momma's voice
      on the slippery road
           to freedom.
They catch me
      all the time they catch me
          and bring me back
and whip me
      till I'm blind and deaf
          and dumb,
  and put me in the cabin
          where the blood soak my back
like scaldin' water
      and take me out to the fields
and whip me some more.

      Oh! the sky is so big!
      Ain't it?

The trees are so tall!
Ain't they?

The river's so wide!
Ain't it?

Don't you hear?
Cain't you hear

all that callin', Leah?
Leah's gotta go!

And I run again
    all twenty-three years of me
             all white and black of me
all the angels in me
       and the wings
            growing out of my armpits
flapping against my thighs
         makin' me move
            when I can't,
when I don't want to,
        when my back is so sore
            and painful
that every flight
    makes my wings stick to my side sometimes
            and keep me slow
and earthbound;
    all my momma in me.
           So soon they catch me again
and beat me again.
      That was the last time for that.
            I lay here
on the hard floor on my back
    only place that's soft:
           guess it's the flesh,
the wounds that do it,
      guess it's the salt, too.
           So much pain
it don't pain no more,

only the want of freedom pains,

only the fear
of dyin' before I'm free.

Yesterday they took out

one of my front teeth
to identify me

in case I 'scape again

and now when I ain't doin'
the housework

they put me in an iron collar.

Three days they gives me
three days I got for my wings

to heal

but they's bent and dirty
and tattered, need washin'

they's not the same

don't round themselves right
somehow.

I can see the roots of trees now,

don't see the tops no more.
The mole and me

we's on our own.

These days I go

to my mistress' room
sew her clothes and cloaks

though the wounds be still breakin'
through my shawl

and I be sore.

She got lots of holes

under her armpits
of her dresses:

that makes me shiver,

think of my momma.
Mistress say, "good mawnin', Leah"

(won't look at me)
and tell me about faith

and Jesus.

Lucy Sleeps with Master Muford

He come
in the night,
it be dark,
no moon.

He do some
funny things
to me
(weren't mischief)
then he die
in my arms.

Anne Sexton

Anne Sexton (1928–1974).   Born in Newton, Massachusetts, she was educated at Garland Junior College and studied with Robert Lowell at Boston University. She was a scholar at the Radcliffe Institute and won the Pulitzer Prize for her volume *Live or Die* in 1967. She received the Robert Frost Fellowship at the Vermont Bread Loaf Writers' Conference, a Ford Foundation grant, an Academy of Arts and Letters Traveling Fellowship, and three honorary Doctor of Arts and Letters degrees. A poet of diversity, she writes about motherhood, marriage, love; she did a bestiary and a well-crafted book of "transformations" of fairy tales. Her poetry reflects a struggle within herself, as well as a view of the world in which all horror and beauty are seen at once and often intermingled: "I would like to think that no one would die anymore/ if we all believed in daisies/but the worms know better, don't they?" Ultimately, Sexton's poetry centers on "The awful rowing toward God," on perfection and death. In 1974 she commited suicide. Her volumes include *To Bedlam and Part Way Back* (1960), *All My Pretty Ones* (1962), *Love Poems* (1969), *Transformations* (1971), *The Book of Folly* (1972), *The Death Notebooks* (1974), *The Awful Rowing Toward God* (1974), *45 Mercy Street* (1976), and *Words for Dr. Y.* (1978).

Rowing

A story, a story!
(Let it go. Let it come.)
I was stamped out like a Plymouth fender
into this world.
First came the crib
with its glacial bars.
Then dolls
and the devotion to their plastic mouths.
Then there was school,

the little straight rows of chairs,
blotting my name over and over,
but undersea all the time,
a stranger whose elbows wouldn't work.
Then there was life
with its cruel houses
and people who seldom touched—
though touch is all—
but I grew,
like a pig in a trenchcoat I grew,
and then there were many strange apparitions,
the nagging rain, the sun turning into poison
and all of that, saws working through my heart,
but I grew, I grew,
and God was there like an island I had not rowed to,
still ignorant of Him, my arms and my legs worked,
and I grew, I grew,
I wore rubies and bought tomatoes
and now, in my middle age,
about nineteen in the head I'd say,
I am rowing, I am rowing
though the oarlocks stick and are rusty
and the sea blinks and rolls
like a worried eyeball,
but I am rowing, I am rowing,
though the wind pushes me back
and I know that that island will not be perfect,
it will have the flaws of life,
the absurdities of the dinner table,
but there will be a door
and I will open it
and I will get rid of the rat inside of me,
the gnawing pestilential rat.
God will take it with his two hands
and embrace it.

As the African says:
This is my tale which I have told,
if it be sweet, if it be not sweet,
take somewhere else and let some return to me.
This story ends with me still rowing.

The Risk

When a daughter tries suicide
and the chimney falls down like a drunk
and the dog chews her tail off
and the kitchen blows up its shiny kettle
and the vacuum cleaner swallows its bag
and the toilet washes itself in tears
and the bathroom scales weigh in the ghost
of the grandmother and the windows,
those sky pieces, ride out like boats
and the grass rolls down the driveway
and the mother lies down on her marriage bed
and eats up her heart like two eggs.

The Fury of Flowers and Worms

Let the flowers make a journey
on Monday so that I can see
ten daisies in a blue vase
with perhaps one red ant
crawling to the gold center.
A bit of the field on my table,
close to the worms
who struggle blindly,
moving deep into their slime,
moving deep into God's abdomen,
moving like oil through water,
sliding through the good brown.

The daisies grow wild
like popcorn.
They are God's promise to the field.
How happy I am daisies, to love you.
How happy you are to be loved
and found magical, like a secret
from the sluggish field.
If all the world picked daisies
wars would end, the common cold would stop,
unemployment would end, the monetary market
would hold steady and no money would float.

Listen world,
if you'd just take the time to pick
the white fingers, the penny heart,
all would be well.
They are so unexpected.
They are as good as salt.
If someone had brought them
to van Gogh's room daily
his ear would have stayed on.
I would like to think that no one would die anymore
if we all believed in daisies
but the worms know better, don't they?
They slide into the ear of a corpse
and listen to his great sigh.

That Day

This is the desk I sit at
and this is the desk where I love you too much
and this is the typewriter that sits before me
where yesterday only your body sat before me
with its shoulders gathered in like a Greek chorus,
with its tongue like a king making up rules as he goes,
with its tongue quite openly like a cat lapping milk,
with its tongue—both of us coiled in its slippery life.
That was yesterday, that day.

That was the day of your tongue,
your tongue that came from your lips,
two openers, half animals, half birds
caught in the doorway of your heart.
That was the day I followed the king's rules,
passing by your red veins and your blue veins,
my hands down the backbone, down quick like a firepole,
hands between legs where you display your inner knowledge,
where diamond mines are buried and come forth to bury,
come forth more sudden than some reconstructed city.
It is complete within seconds, that monument.
The blood runs underground yet brings forth a tower.

A multitude should gather for such an edifice.
For a miracle one stands in line and throws confetti.
Surely The Press is here looking for headlines.
Surely someone should carry a banner on the sidewalk.
If a bridge is constructed doesn't the mayor cut a ribbon?
If a phenomenon arrives shouldn't the Magi come bearing gifts?
Yesterday was the day I bore gifts for your gift
and came from the valley to meet you on the pavement.
That was yesterday, that day.

That was the day of your face,
your face after love, close to the pillow, a lullaby.
Half asleep beside me letting the old fashioned rocker stop,
our breath became one, became a child-breath together,
while my fingers drew little o's on your shut eyes,
while my fingers drew little smiles on your mouth,
while I drew I LOVE YOU on your chest and its drummer
and whispered, "Wake up!" and you mumbled in your sleep,
"Sh. We're driving to Cape Cod. We're heading for the Bourne
Bridge. We're circling around the Bourne Circle." Bourne!
Then I knew you in your dream and prayed of our time
that I would be pierced and you would take root in me
and that I might bring forth your born, might bear
the you or the ghost of you in my little household.
Yesterday I did not want to be borrowed
but this is the typewriter that sits before me
and love is where yesterday is at.

The Child Bearers

Jean, death comes close to us all,
flapping its awful wings at us
and the gluey wings crawl up our nose.
Our children tremble in their teen-age cribs,
whirling off on a thumb or a motorcycle,
mine pushed into gnawing a stilbestrol cancer
I passed on like hemophilia,
or yours in the seventh grade, with her spleen
smacked in by the balance beam.

And we, mothers, crumpled, and flyspotted
with bringing them this far
can do nothing now but pray.

Let us put your three children
and my two children,
ages ranging from eleven to twenty-one,
and send them in a large air net up to God,
with many stamps, *real* air mail,
and huge signs attached:
SPECIAL HANDLING
DO NOT STAPLE, FOLD OR MUTILATE!
And perhaps He will notice
and pass a psalm over them
for keeping safe for a whole,
for a whole God-damned life-span.

And not even a muddled angel will
peek down at us in our foxhole.
And He will not have time
to send down an eyedropper of prayer for us,
the mothering thing of us,
as we drop into the soup
and drown
in the worry festering inside us,
lest our children
go so fast
they go.

Adrienne Rich

Adrienne Rich (1929–).   Born in Baltimore, she received her B.A. from Radcliffe College. *A Change of World* (1951), her first book, was published by the Yale Series of Younger Poets. She has been awarded two Guggenheim Fellowships, an Amy Lowell Poetry Travelling Scholarship, and a grant from the National Institute of Arts and Letters. Her volume of poems, *Diving into the Wreck* (1973), received the National Book Award. Other titles include *The Diamond Cutters* (1955), *Snapshots of a Daughter-in-law* (1963), *Necessities of Life* (1966), *Leaflets* (1969), *The Will to Change* (1971), *The Dream of a Common Language* (1978), *On Lies, Secrets, and Silence—Selected Prose, 1966–1978* (1979), and *Of Woman Born,* a study of motherhood.

"I Am in Danger—Sir—"

"Half-cracked" to Higginson, living,
afterward famous in garbled versions,
your hoard of dazzling scraps a battlefield,
now your old snood

mothballed at Harvard
and you in your variorum monument
equivocal to the end—
who are you?

Gardening the day-lily,
wiping the wine-glass stems,
your thought pulsed on behind
a forehead battered paper-thin,

you, woman, masculine
in single-mindedness,
for whom the word was more
than a symptom—

a condition of being.
Till the air buzzing with spoiled language
sang in your ears
of Perjury

and in your half-cracked way you chose
silence for entertainment,
chose to have it out at last
on your own premises.

1964

Diving into the Wreck

First having read the book of myths,
and loaded the camera,

and checked the edge of the knife-blade,
I put on
the body-armor of black rubber
the absurd flippers
the grave and awkward mask.
I am having to do this
not like Cousteau with his
assiduous team
aboard the sun-flooded schooner
but here alone.

There is a ladder.
The ladder is always there
hanging innocently
close to the side of the schooner.
We know what it is for,
we who have used it.
Otherwise
it's a piece of maritime floss
some sundry equipment.

I go down.
Rung after rung and still
the oxygen immerses me
the blue light
the clear atoms
of our human air.
I go down.
My flippers cripple me,
I crawl like an insect down the ladder
and there is no one
to tell me when the ocean
will begin.

First the air is blue and then
it is bluer and then green and then
black I am blacking out and yet
my mask is powerful
it pumps my blood with power
the sea is another story

the sea is not a question of power
I have to learn alone
to turn my body without force
in the deep element.

And now: it is easy to forget
what I came for
among so many who have always
lived here
swaying their crenellated fans
between the reefs
and besides
you breathe differently down here.

I came to explore the wreck.
The words are purposes.
The words are maps.
I came to see the damage that was done
and the treasures that prevail.
I stroke the beam of my lamp
slowly along the flank
of something more permanent
than fish or weed
the thing I came for:
the wreck and not the story of the wreck
the thing itself and not the myth
the drowned face always staring
toward the sun
the evidence of damage
worn by salt and sway into this threadbare beauty
the ribs of the disaster
curving their assertion
among the tentative haunters.

This is the place.
And I am here, the mermaid whose dark hair
streams black, the merman in his armored body
We circle silently
about the wreck
we dive into the hold.

I am she: I am he
whose drowned face sleeps with open eyes
whose breasts still bear the stress
whose silver, copper, vermeil cargo lies
obscurely inside barrels
half-wedged and left to rot
we are the half-destroyed instruments
that once held to a course
the water-eaten log
the fouled compass

We are, I am, you are
by cowardice or courage
the one who find our way
back to this scene
carrying a knife, a camera
a book of myths
in which
our names do not appear.

1972

Moving in Winter

Their life, collapsed like unplayed cards,
is carried piecemeal through the snow:
Headboard and footboard now, the bed
where she has lain desiring him
where overhead his sleep will build
its canopy to smother her once more;
their table, by four elbows worn
evening after evening while the wax runs down;
mirrors grey with reflecting them,
bureaus coffining from the cold
things that can shuffle in a drawer,
carpets rolled up around those echoes
which, shaken out, take wing and breed
new altercations, the old silences.

Peeling Onions

Only to have a grief
equal to all these tears!

There's not a sob in my chest.
Dry-hearted as Peer Gynt

I pare away, no hero,
merely a cook.

Crying was labor, once
when I'd good cause.
Walking, I felt my eyes like wounds
raw in my head,
so postal-clerks, I thought, must stare.
A dog's look, a cat's, burnt to my brain—
yet all that stayed
stuff in my lungs like smog.

These old tears in the chopping-bowl.

from Twenty-One Love Poems

II

I wake up in your bed. I know I have been dreaming.
Much earlier, the alarm broke us from each other,
you've been at your desk for hours. I know what I dreamed:
our friend the poet comes into my room
where I've been writing for days,
drafts, carbons, poems are scattered everywhere,
and I want to show her one poem
which is the poem of my life. But I hesitate,
and wake. You've kissed my hair
to wake me. *I dreamed you were a poem,*
I say, *a poem I wanted to show someone . . .*
and I laugh and fall dreaming again
of the desire to show you to everyone I love,

to move openly together
in the pull of gravity, which is not simple,
which carries the feathered grass a long way down the upbreathing
air.

IV

I come home from you through the early light of spring
flashing off ordinary walls, the Pez Dorado,
the Discount Wares, the shoe-store. . . . I'm lugging my sack
of groceries, I dash for the elevator
where a man, taut, elderly, carefully composed
lets the door almost close on me.—*For god's sake hold it!*
I croak at him.—*Hysterical,* —he breathes my way.
I let myself into the kitchen, unload my bundles,
make coffee, open the window, put on Nina Simone
singing *Here comes the sun.* . . . I open the mail,
drinking delicious coffee, delicious music,
my body still both light and heavy with you. The mail
lets fall a Xerox of something written by a man
aged 27, a hostage, tortured in prison:
My genitals have been the object of such a sadistic display
they keep me constantly awake with the pain . . .
Do whatever you can to survive.
You know, I think that men love wars . . .
And my incurable anger, my unmendable wounds
break open further with tears, I am crying helplessly,
and they still control the world, and you are not in my arms.

XI

Every peak is a crater. This is the law of volcanoes,
making them eternally and visibly female.
No height without depth, without a burning core,
though our straw soles shred on the hardened lava.
I want to travel with you to every sacred mountain
smoking within like the sibyl stooped over his tripod,
I want to reach for your hand as we scale the path,
to feel your arteries glowing in my clasp,
never failing to note the small, jewel-like flower

unfamiliar to us, nameless till we rename her,
that clings to the slowly altering rock—
that detail outside ourselves that brings us to ourselves,
was here before us, knew we would come, and sees beyond us.

(The Floating Poem, Unnumbered)

Whatever happens with us, your body
will haunt mine—tender, delicate
your lovemaking, like the half-curled frond
of the fiddlehead fern in forests
just washed by sun. Your traveled, generous thighs
between which my whole face has come and come—
the innocence and wisdom of the place my tongue has found
     there—
the live, insatiate dance of your nipples in my mouth—
your touch on me, firm, protective, searching
me out, your strong tongue and slender fingers
reaching where I had been waiting years for you
in my rose-wet cave—whatever happens, this is.

XX

That conversation we were always on the edge
of having, runs on in my head,
at night the Hudson trembles in New Jersey light
polluted water yet reflecting even
sometimes the moon
and I discern a woman
I loved, drowning in secrets, fear wound round her throat
and choking her like hair. And this is she
with whom I tried to speak, whose hurt, expressive head
turning aside from pain, is dragged down deeper
where it cannot hear me,
and soon I shall know I was talking to my own soul.

Final Notations

it will not be simple, it will not be long
it will take little time, it will take all your thought
it will take all your heart, it will take all your breath
it will be short, it will not be simple

it will touch through your ribs, it will take all your heart
it will not be long, it will occupy your thought
as a city is occupied, as a bed is occupied
it will take all your flesh, it will not be simple

You are coming into us who cannot withstand you
you are coming into us who never wanted to withstand you
you are taking parts of us into places never planned
you are going far away with pieces of our lives

it will be short, it will take all your breath
it will not be simple, it will become your will

1991

Sylvia Plath

Sylvia Plath (1932–1963).   Born in Boston, Plath went to Smith College and enjoyed early success, publishing her poems in many magazines. She was a guest editor of *Mademoiselle,* an experience which forms the basis of her novel *The Bell Jar.* She went to Newnham College, Cambridge, as a Fulbright scholar, where she met the English poet Ted Hughes, whom she later married. The couple returned to America, where Plath taught at Smith for a year. They returned to England where their two children were born. Her first volume of poems, *The Colossus,* was published in England in 1960. From the beginning, her poems show a classical and desperate clarity, although the images themselves, startling and brutal, crowd elliptically in both her closed and open forms.

In 1962 Plath and Hughes separated. She moved from Devon to London, cared for her children and continued to write poetry. On February 11, 1963, she died by her own hand.

While in Boston she had informally attended Robert Lowell's poetry workshop at Boston University. In the foreword to her posthumous collection *Ariel,* Lowell praised her effusively but, perhaps as a reflection of the times, felt it necessary to excuse her for being a woman poet:

In these poems, written in the last months of her life and often rushed out at a rate of two or three a day, Sylvia Plath becomes herself, becomes something imaginary, newly, wildly and subtly created—hardly a person at all, or a woman, certainly not another "poetess," but one of those super-real, hypnotic, great, classical heroines. This character is feminine, rather than female, though most everything we customarily think of as feminine is turned on its head.

Plath's *Collected Poems* edited by Hughes, appeared in 1982, almost twenty years after her death. Hughes also edited *Johnny Panic and the Bible of Dreams and Other Prose Writings* (1978) and, with Frances McCullough, *The Journals of Sylvia Plath.* Plath's mother, Aurelia Schober Plath, edited *Letters Home: Correspondence 1950–1963.*

In a passionate indictment of Ted Hughes's intrusive and self-protective editing of the work and literal destruction of some of Plath's poems, Marjorie Perloff asserts:

But the attic was soon invaded, the dangerous notebooks were destroyed, and the poems that were permitted to enter the literary world had to get past the Censor. The words of the dead woman, to paraphrase W. H. Auden, were modified in the guts of the living.

Daddy

You do not do, you do not do
Any more, black shoe
In which I have lived like a foot
For thirty years, poor and white,
Barely daring to breathe or Achoo.

Daddy, I have had to kill you.
You died before I had time—
Marble-heavy, a bag full of God,
Ghastly statue with one grey toe
Big as a Frisco seal

And a head in the freakish Atlantic
Where it pours bean green over blue
In the waters off beautiful Nauset.
I used to pray to recover you.
Ach, du.

In the German tongue, in the Polish town
Scraped flat by the roller

Of wars, wars, wars.
But the name of the town is common.
My Polack friend

Says there are a dozen or two.
So I never could tell where you
Put your foot, your root,
I never could talk to you.
The tongue stuck in my jaw.

It stuck in a barb wire snare.
Ich, ich, ich, ich,
I could hardly speak.
I thought every German was you.
And the language obscene.
An engine, an engine
Chuffing me off like a Jew.
A Jew to Dachau, Auschwitz, Belsen.
I began to talk like a Jew.
I think I may well be a Jew.

The snows of the Tyrol, the clear beer of Vienna
Are not very pure or true.
With my gypsy ancestress and my weird luck
And my Taroc pack and my Taroc pack
I may be a bit of a Jew.

I have always been scared of *you,*
With your Luftwaffe, your gobbledygoo.
And your neat moustache
And your Aryan eye, bright blue.
Panzer-man, panzer-man, O You—

Not God but a swastika
So black no sky could squeak through.
Every woman adores a Fascist,
The boot in the face, the brute
Brute heart of a brute like you.

You stand at the blackboard, daddy,
In the picture I have of you,

A cleft in your chin instead of your foot
But no less a devil for that, no not
Any less the black man who

Bit my pretty red heart in two.
I was ten when they buried you.
At twenty I tried to die
And get back, back, back to you.
I thought even the bones would do.

But they pulled me out of the sack,
And they stuck me together with glue.
And then I knew what to do.
I made a model of you,
A man in black with a Meinkampf look
And a love of the rack and the screw.
And I said I do, I do.
So daddy, I'm finally through.
The black telephone's off at the root,
The voices just can't worm through.

If I've killed one man, I've killed two—
The vampire who said he was you
And drank my blood for a year,
Seven years, if you want to know.
Daddy, you can lie back now.

There's a stake in your fat black heart
And the villagers never liked you.
They are dancing and stamping on you.
They always *knew* it was you.
Daddy, daddy, you bastard, I'm through.

Morning Song

love set you going like a fat gold watch.
the midwife slapped your footsoles, and your bald cry
took its place among the elements.

our voices echo, magnifying your arrival. new statue.
in a drafty museum, your nakedness
shadows our safety. we stand round blankly as walls.

i'm no more your mother
than the cloud that distils a mirror to reflect its own slow
effacement at the wind's hand.

all night your moth-breath
flickers among the flat pink roses. i wake to listen;
a far sea moves in my ear.

one cry, and i stumble from bed, cow-heavy and floral
in my victorian nightgown.
your mouth opens clear as a cat's. the window square
whitens and swallows its dull stars. and now you try
your handful of notes;
the clear vowels rise like balloons.

The Eye-mote

Blameless as daylight I stood looking
At a field of horses, necks bent, manes blown,
Tails streaming against the green
Backdrop of sycamores. Sun was striking
White chapel pinnacles over the roofs,
Holding the horses, the clouds, the leaves

Steadily rooted though they were all flowing
Away to the left like reeds in a sea
When the splinter flew in and stuck my eye,
Needling it dark. Then I was seeing
A melding of shapes in a hot rain:
Horses warped on the altering green,

Outlandish as double-humped camels or unicorns,
Grazing at the margins of a bad monochrome,
Beasts of oasis, a better time.

Abrading my lid, the small grain burns:
Red cinder around which I myself,
Horses, planets and spires revolve.

Neither tears nor the easing flush
Of eyebaths can unseat the speck:
It sticks, and it has stuck a week.
I wear the present itch for flesh,
Blind to what will be and what was.
I dream that I am Oedipus.

What I want back is what I was
Before the bed, before the knife,
Before the brooch-pin and the salve
Fixed me in this parenthesis;
Horses fluent in the wind,
A place, a time gone out of mind.

The Moon and the Yew Tree

This is the light of the mind, cold and planetary.
The trees of the mind are black. The light is blue.
The grasses unload their griefs on my feet as if I were God,
Prickling my ankles and murmuring of their humility.
Fumy, spiritous mists inhabit this place.
Separated from my house by a row of headstones.
I simply cannot see where there is to get to.

The moon is no door. It is a face in its own right,
White as a knuckle and terribly upset.
It drags the sea after it like a dark crime; it is quiet
With the O-gape of complete despair. I live here.
Twice on Sunday, the bells startle the sky——
Eight great tongues affirming the Resurrection.
At the end, they soberly bong out their names.

The yew tree points up. It has a Gothic shape.
The eyes lift after it and find the moon.
The moon is my mother. She is not sweet like Mary.

Her blue garments unloose small bats and owls.
How I would like to believe in tenderness——
The face of the effigy, gentled by candles,
Bending, on me in particular, its mild eyes.

I have fallen a long way. Clouds are flowering
Blue and mystical over the face of the stars.
Inside the church, the saints will be all blue,
Floating on their delicate feet over the cold pews,
Their hands and faces stiff with holiness.
The moon sees nothing of this. She is bald and wild.
And the message of the yew tree is blackness—blackness and
    silence.

Crossing the Water

Black lake, black boat, two black, cut-paper people.
Where do the black trees go that drink here?
Their shadows must cover Canada.

A little light is filtering from the water flowers.
Their leaves do not wish us to hurry:
They are round and flat and full of dark advice.

Cold worlds shake from the oar.
The spirit of blackness is in us, it is in the fishes.
A snag is lifting a valedictory, pale hand;

Stars open among the lilies.
Are you not blinded by such expressionless sirens?
This is the silence of astounded souls.

The Arrival of the Bee Box

I ordered this, this clean wood box
Square as a chair and almost too heavy to lift.
I would say it was the coffin of a midget

Or a square baby
Were there not such a din in it.

The box is locked, it is dangerous.
I have to live with it overnight
And I can't keep away from it.
There are no windows, so I can't see what is in there.
There is only a little grid, no exit.

I put my eye to the grid.
It is dark, dark,
With the swarmy feeling of African hands
Minute and shrunk for export,
Black on black, angrily clambering.

How can I let them out?
It is the noise that appalls me most of all,
The unintelligible syllables.
It is like a Roman mob,
Small, taken one by one, but my god, together!

I lay my ear to furious Latin.
I am not a Caesar.
I have simply ordered a box of maniacs.
They can be sent back.
They can die, I need feed them nothing, I am the owner.

I wonder how hungry they are.
I wonder if they would forget me
If I just undid the locks and stood back and turned into a tree.
There is the laburnum, its blond colonnades,
And the petticoats of the cherry.

They might ignore me immediately
In my moon suit and funeral veil.
I am no source of honey
So why should they turn on me?
Tomorrow I will be sweet God, I will set them free.

The box is only temporary.

Poppies in October

Even the sun-clouds this morning cannot manage such skirts.
Nor the woman in the ambulance
Whose red heart blooms through her coat so astoundingly——

A gift, a love gift
Uttterly unasked for
By a sky

Palely and flamily
Igniting its carbon monoxides, by eyes
Dulled to a halt under bowlers.

O my God, what am I
That these late mouths should cry open
In a forest of frost, in a dawn of cornflowers.

Lady Lazarus

I have done it again.
One year in every ten
I manage it——

A sort of walking miracle, my skin
Bright as a Nazi lampshade,
My right foot

A paperweight,
My face a featureless, fine
Jew linen.

Peel off the napkin
O my enemy.
Do I terrify?——

The nose, the eye pits, the full set of teeth?
The sour breath
Will vanish in a day.

Soon, soon the flesh
The grave cave ate will be
At home on me

And I a smiling woman.
I am only thirty.
And like the cat I have nine times to die.

This is Number Three.
What a trash
To annihilate each decade.

What a million filaments.
The peanut-crunching crowd
Shoves in to see

Them unwrap me hand and foot——
The big strip tease.
Gentlemen, ladies

These are my hands
My knees.
I may be skin and bone,

Nevertheless, I am the same, identical woman.
The first time it happened I was ten.
It was an accident.

The second time I meant
To last it out and not come back at all.
I rocked shut

As a seashell.
They had to call and call
And pick the worms off me like sticky pearls.

Dying
Is an art, like everything else.
I do it exceptionally well.

I do it so it feels like hell.
I do it so it feels real.
I guess you could say I've a call.

It's easy enough to do it in a cell.
It's easy enough to do it and stay put.
It's the theatrical

Comeback in broad day
To the same place, the same face, the same brute
Amused shout:

"A miracle!"
That knocks me out.
There is a charge

For the eyeing of my scars, there is a charge
For the hearing of my heart——
It really goes.

And there is a charge, a very large charge
For a word or a touch
Or a bit of blood

Or a piece of my hair or my clothes.
So, so, Herr Doktor.
So, Herr Enemy.

I am your opus,
I am your valuable,
The pure gold baby

That melts to a shriek.
I turn and burn.
Do not think I underestimate your great concern.

Ash, ash——
You poke and stir.
Flesh, bone, there is nothing there——

A cake of soap,
A wedding ring,
A gold filling.

Herr God, Herr Lucifer
Beware
Beware.

Out of the ash
I rise with my red hair
And I eat men like air.

Sheep in Fog

The hills step off into whiteness.
People or stars
Regard me sadly, I disappoint them.

The train leaves a line of breath.
O slow
Horse the color of rust,

Hooves, dolorous bells——
All morning the
Morning has been blackening,

A flower left out.
My bones hold a stillness, the far
Fields melt my heart.

They threaten
To let me through to a heaven
Starless and fatherless, a dark water.

Edge

The woman is perfected.
Her dead

Body wears the smile of accomplishment,
The illusion of a Greek necessity

Flows in the scrolls of her toga,
Her bare

Feet seem to be saying:
We have come so far, it is over.

Each dead child coiled, a white serpent,
One at each little

Pitcher of milk, now empty.
She has folded

Them back into her body as petals
Of a rose close when the garden

Stiffens and odors bleed
From the sweet, deep throats of the night flower.

The moon has nothing to be sad about,
Staring from her hood of bone.

She is used to this sort of thing.
Her blacks crackle and drag.

Audre Lorde

Audre Lorde (1934–).   Born in New York City, and educated at Hunter College
(B.A.) and at Columbia University (M.L.S.), she worked as a librarian for a while, then
began teaching creative writing. Now she lives on Staten Island and is a professor of
English at Hunter College. Her many volumes of poetry include *Coal* (1976), *The
Black Unicorn* (1978), in which she uses African mythology to create her own mythol-
ogy of self, *Chosen Poems: Old and New* (1982), and *Our Dead Behind Us* (1986), all from
Norton. Her two autobiographical works are *The Cancer Journal* (1980) and her
fictionalized "biomythography," *Zami: A New Spelling of My Name* (1982).

    She has also written a book of essays, *Sister Outsider: Essays and Speeches* (1984). Lorde
has said, "When I say myself, I mean not only the Audre who inhabits my body but
all those feisty, incorrigible black women who insist on standing up and saying, 'I am
and you cannot wipe me out no matter how irritating I am, how much you fear what

I might represent.' " In her essay "The Transformation of Silence into Language and Action," Lorde writes that she is "a black woman warrior poet doing my work." Her work is the reclamation of "language which has been made to work against us." Her words "bridge some of the differences between us, for it is not difference which immobilizes us, but silence."

Coal

is the total black, being spoken
from the earth's inside.
There are many kinds of open
how a diamond comes into a knot of flame
how sound comes into words, coloured
by who pays what for speaking.

Some words are open like a diamond
on glass windows
singing out within the crash of sun
Then there are words like stapled wagers
in a perforated book—buy and sign and tear apart—
and come whatever wills all chances
the stub remains
an ill-pulled tooth with a ragged edge.
Some words live in my throat
breeding like adders. Others know sun
seeking like gypsies over my tongue
to explode through my lips
like young sparrows bursting from shell.
Some words
bedevil me.

Love is a word, another kind of open.
As the diamond comes into a knot of flame
I am Black because I come from the earth's inside
Now take my word for jewel in the open light.

From the House of Yemanjá

My mother had two faces and a frying pot
where she cooked up her daughters

into girls
before she fixed our dinner.
My mother had two faces
and a broken pot
where she hid out a perfect daughter
who was not me
I am the sun and moon and forever hungry
for her eyes.

I bear two women upon my back
one dark and rich and hidden
in the ivory hungers of the other
mother
pale as a witch
yet steady and familiar
brings me bread and terror
in my sleep
her breasts are huge exciting anchors
in the midnight storm.

All this has been
before
in my mother's bed
time has no sense
I have no brothers
and my sisters are cruel.

Mother I need
mother I need
mother I need your blackness now
as the august earth needs rain.

I am
the sun and moon and forever hungry
the sharpened edge
where day and night shall meet
and not be
one.

Jean Valentine

Jean Valentine (1934–).   Jean Valentine's collections of poetry include *Dream Barker and Other Poems,* with a foreword by Dudley Fitts (1965), *Pilgrims* (1969), *Ordinary Things* (1974), *The Messenger* (1979), and *Home Deep Blue* (1989). She received Guggenheim and Rockefeller Foundation fellowships, and awards from the National Endowment for the Arts. She lives in New York City and teaches at Sarah Lawrence College and the Poetry Center of the 92nd Street YM-YWHA.

Foraging

1. The Room

Why did you keep finding me where I was?
Your seeking, your cage:
oh, your animus against breasts, shadowed eyelids
yet like holding your breath, holding Love.

Love, you said,
come in. Love, let me in.
Everyone else was asleep.
Look at me, you said.

The luminous room.
Eve formalized.

A kiss: my fear and
my love,

not here yet,
but for here.

2. The Luminous Room

What it felt like:
first it was the kiss.
Look at me, he said.
And then it was the floor,
the boards. He went slow, he'd
pull and pull and pull at my leaf thirst.
Or running backwards he'd wind the kite-string lace

down out of me so the hot slow wind
would almost touch me . . . No . . . then Jesus God,
the first room: sky, and trees,
but water: blue blue blue bloom bloom.
It was the feeling of terrible scarcity
and then it was the boards
and then it was the luminous room.

The One You Wanted to Be Is the One You Are

She saying, You don't have to do anything,
you don't even have to be, you Only who are,
you nobody from nowhere,
without one sin or one good quality,
without one book, without one word,
without even a comb, you!
The one you wanted to be
is the one you are. Come play . . .

And he saying,
Look at me!
I don't know how . . .

Their breath like a tree's breath. Their silence
like a deer's silence. Tolstoy
wrote about this: all misunderstanding.

The Free Abandonment Blues

Now I don't have to leave this place not for anybody
No I don't have to go out of this wooden house not to oblige
    anybody
Once I would have lifted clean out of my own place to please
    somebody

The blue-robed man who said You want to be loved, love me
The man in the blue robe who said I give, in order that you will
    give to me

I remember you my old blue-robed man, but you know this just
   can not be

Now if I want to warm myself I look up at the blue sky
Now I look to a number of people here and also to the round blue
   sky
To feel the sun, your free mouth on my mouth, not the fire that is
   gone by

I don't wear any clothes nowadays or say that I am me
I don't wear the right clothes in the closet or explain how I am me
I come as I go translucent oh what you get is what you see

The woman said:
They held her in their arms and knew that she would save them
They brought her into their houses and into their hands to save
   them
But secretly they knew so certainly that no one would ever have
   them

And she said,
Listen, it's only a little time longer to wait
When you have taken this path you need just a little more time to
   wait
Maybe not today the amazing loveliness but it won't be long for us
   to wait

Mary Oliver

Mary Oliver (1935–).   Born in Cleveland, Ohio, and graduated from Vassar
College, Mary Oliver has taught and been poet-in-residence at several colleges. She
lives in Provincetown, Massachusetts, where she teaches at the Fine Arts Work
Center. She won the 1984 Pulitzer Prize for *American Primitive* (1983). Her other
books include *No Voyage and Other Poems* (1965), *The River Styx, Ohio and Other Poems*
(1972), *Twelve Moons* (1979), and *Dream Work* (1968). She has received grants from
the John Simon Guggenheim Foundation and from the Artists Foundation of
Boston, Massachusetts. Oliver is a fine and musical observer of nature. Her rare
exuberance makes her poetry read, as Stanley Kunitz says, "like a blessing."

John Chapman

He wore a tin pot for a hat, in which
he cooked his supper
toward evening
in the Ohio forests. He wore
a sackcloth shirt and walked
barefoot on feet crooked as roots. And everywhere he went
the apple trees sprang up behind him lovely
as young girls.

No Indian or settler or wild beast
ever harmed him, and he for his part honored
everything, all God's creatures! thought little,
on a rainy night,
of sharing the shelter of a hollow log touching
flesh with any creatures there: snakes,
raccoon possibly, or some great slab of bear.

Mrs. Price, late of Richland County,
at whose parents' house he sometimes lingered,
recalled: he spoke
only once of women and his gray eyes
brittled into ice. "Some
are deceivers," he whispered, and she felt
the pain of it, remembered it
into her old age.

Well, the trees he planted or gave away
prospered, and he became
the good legend, you do
what you can if you can; whatever

the secret, and the pain,

there's a decision: to die,
or to live, to go on
caring about something. In spring, in Ohio,
in the forests that are left you can still find
sign of him: patches
of cold white fire.

The Honey Tree

And so at last I climbed
the honey tree, ate
chunks of pure light, ate
the bodies of bees that could not
get out of my way, ate
the dark hair of the leaves,
the rippling bark,
the heartwood. Such
frenzy! But joy does that,
I'm told, in the beginning.
Later, maybe,
I'll come here only
sometimes and with a
middling hunger. But now
I climb like a snake,
I clamber like a bear to
the nuzzling place, to the light
salvaged by the thighs
of bees and racked up
in the body of the tree.
Oh, anyone can see
how I love myself at last!
how I love the world! climbing
by day or night
in the wind, in the leaves, kneeling
at the secret rip, the cords
of my body stretching
and singing in the
heaven of appetite.

Jayne Cortez

Jayne Cortez (1936–).   Jayne Cortez was born in Arizona, grew up in Los Angeles, and is currently living in New York City. She has been published in numerous magazines and anthologies and has lectured and read poetry throughout the United States and West Africa. Her publications include *Piss-stained Stairs and the Monkey Man's Wares* (1969), *Sacrifications* (1973), *Mouth on Paper* (1977), and a recording *Celebrations and Solitudes, The Poetry of Jayne Cortez.*

I Am New York City

i am new york city
here is my brain of hot sauce
my tobacco teeth my
    mattress of bedbug tongue
legs apart   hand on chin
    war on the roof   insults
pointed fingers   pushcarts
    my contraceptives all

look at my pelvis blushing

i am new york city of blood
police and fried pies
    i rub my docks red with grenadine
and jelly madness in a flow of tokay
my huge skull of pigeons
my seance of peeping toms
my plaited ovaries excuse me
this is my grime my thigh of
steelspoons and toothpicks
    i imitate no one
i am new york city
of the brown spit and soft tomatoes
    give me my confetti of flesh
my marquee of false nipples
    my sideshow of open beaks
in my nose of soot
    in my ox bled eyes
in my ear of saturday night specials

i eat ha ha   hee hee and ho ho

i am new york city
never-change-never-sleep-never-melt
    my shoes are incognito
cadavers grow from my goatee
    look i sparkle with shit with wishbones
my nickname is glue-me

Take my face of stink bombs
my star spangle banner of hot dogs
take my beer-can junta
my reptilian ass of footprints
and approach me through life
approach me through death
approach me through my widows peak
through my split ends my asthmatic laugh
approach me through my wash rag
half ankle   half elbow
massage me with your camphor tears
salute the patina and concrete
of my rat tail wig
face up   face down
piss into the bite of our handshake

i am new york city
    my skillet-head friend
my fat-bellied comrade
    citizens
        break wind with me.

So Long

My man loved me so much
he wanted to kill me
cause he loved me so good
he wanted to die
cause he loved me without sorrow
so sad without tears
he loved me to kill to die to cry
so much he wanted to scream
cause i loved him too much i
drank his tears
loved him too much
i ate his strength
loved him too much i stole his joy
i loved him to drink to eat to steal
cause we loved so much
so good to love to love

so long to love
so long

Marge Piercy

Marge Piercy (1936–).   Born in Detroit but now living in Wellfleet, Massachu-
setts, Piercy is a novelist as well as a poet. Her volumes of poetry include *Breaking
Camp* (1968), *Hard Loving* (1969), *To Be of Use* (1973), and *Living in the Open* (1976).

Song of the Fucked Duck

In using there are always two.
The manipulator dances with a partner who cons herself.
There are lies that glow so brightly we consent
to give a finger and then an arm
to let them burn.
I was dazzled by the crowd where everyone called my name.
Now I stand outside the funhouse exit, down the slide
reading my guidebook of Marx in Esperanto
and if I don't know anymore which way means forward
down is where my head is, next to my feet
with a pocketful of words and plastic tokens.
Form follows function, says the organizer
and turns himself into a paperclip,
into a vacuum cleaner,
into a machinegun.
Function follows analysis
but the forebrain
is only an owl in the tree of self.
One third of life we prowl in the grottos of sleep
where neglected worms ripen into dragons
where the spoilt pencil swells into an oak
and the cows of our early sins are called home chewing their cuds
and turning the sad faces of our childhood upon us.
Come back and scrub the floor, the stain is still there,
come back with your brush and kneel down
scrub and scrub again
it will never be clean.
Fantasy unacted sours the brain.
Buried desires sprout like mushrooms on the chin of the morning.
The will to be totally rational

is the will to be made out of glass and steel:
and to use others as if they were glass and steel.
We can see clearly no farther
than our hands can touch.

The cockroach knows as much as you know about living.
We trust with our hands and our eyes and our bellies.
The cunt accepts.
The teeth and back reject.
What we have to give each other:
dumb and mysterious as water swirling.
Always in the long corridors of the psyche
doors are opening and doors are slamming shut.
We rise each day to give birth or to murder
selves that go through our hands like tiny fish.
You said: I am the organizer, and took and used.
You wrapped your head in theory like yards of gauze

and touched others only as tools that fit to your task
and if the tool broke you seized another.
Arrogance is not a revolutionary virtue.
The manipulator liberates only
the mad bulldozers of the ego to level the ground.
I was a tool that screamed in the hand.
I have been loving you so long and hard and mean
and the taste of you is part of my tongue
and your face is burnt into my eyelids
and I could build you with my fingers out of dust
and now it is over.
Whether we want or not
our roots go down to strange waters,
we are creatures of the seasons and the earth.
You always had a reason and you have them still
rattling like dried leaves on a stunted tree.

June Jordan

June Jordan (1936–).   Born in Harlem, the daughter of Jamaican immigrants, she
was educated at Barnard College and the University of Chicago. She taught at Sarah
Lawrence College, City College, Yale University, and Connecticut College, and was
cofounder of the Voice of Children Workshop for Black and Puerto Rican Teenagers.

She has also worked in film. Her poems and essays have been widely published, and she edited the anthologies *Soulscript* and *The Voice of the Children.* Her volumes include *Look at Me, Some Changes,* and *New Days* (poetry); *Fannie Lou Hammer* (biography); *Dry Victories* (history); and *His Own Where,* a highly acclaimed novel.

For My Mother

for my mother
I would write a list
of promises so solid
loafing fish and onions
okra palm tree coconut
and Khus-Khus paradise
would
hard among the mongoose
enemies delight
a neo-moon-night trick
prosperity
for my father
I would decorate a doorway
weaving women into the daytime
of his travel also
season the snow to rice and peas
to peppery pearls on a flowering
platter drunkards stilt
at breakfast bacchanalia
swaying swift or stubborn
coral rocks
regenerate

for my only love
I would stop the silence

one of these days

won't come too soon
when the blank
familias blank
will fold away

a highly inflammable
balloon eclipsed by seminal
and nubile

loving

Lucille Clifton

Lucille Clifton (1936–).   Lucille Clifton was born in Depew, New York, and educated at the State University of New York at Fredonia and at Howard University. She has taught widely in American colleges and universities. She now teaches at the University of California, Santa Cruz. She has received many awards and distinctions as a poet: the Juniper Prize for poetry, and Emmy Award from the American Academy of Television Arts and Sciences, and fellowships from the National Endowment for the Arts. A prolific author of poetry and fiction for children, she is also the author of *Generations of Americans: A Memoir* (1976). Her volumes of poetry include *Good Times* (1969), *Good News about the Earth* (1972), *An Ordinary Woman* (1974), and *Two-Headed Woman* (1980).

Clifton draws from a large range of personal and public experience and history, but she offers us a distillation in her utterly personal style. She performs an amazing balancing linguistic feat: her speech is at once black idiom, the history of poetry, and her own voice, each word and phrase crafted with evocative care. Her poems, of domestic drama, biblical re-creation, or defiant prayer, expand with each rereading. Indeed, she wastes no words in her powerful portraits, and makes her readers "wild/ with the damn wonder of it."

Miss Rosie

when i watch you
wrapped up like garbage
sitting, surrounded by the smell
of too old potato peels
or
when i watch you
in your old man's shoes
with the little toe cut out
sitting, waiting for your mind
like next week's grocery
i say
when i watch you
you wet brown bag of a woman
who used to be the best looking gal in georgia
used to be called the Georgia Rose

i stand up
through your destruction
i stand up

∽っ∽

if i stand in my window
naked in my own house
and press my breasts
against my windowpane
like black birds pushing against glass
because i am somebody
in a New Thing

and if the man come to stop me
in my own house
naked in my own window
saying i have offended him
i have offended his

Gods

let him watch my black body
push against my own glass
let him discover self
let him run naked through the streets
crying
praying in tongues

The Lost Baby Poem

the time i dropped your almost body down
down to meet the waters under the city
and run one with the sewage to the sea
what did i know about waters rushing back
what did i know about drowning
or being drowned

you would have been born into winter
in the year of the disconnected gas

and no car   we would have made the thin
walk over genesee hill into the canada wind
to watch you slip like ice into strangers' hands
you would have fallen naked as snow into winter
if you were here i could tell you these
and some other things

if i am ever less than a mountain
for your definite brothers and sisters
let the rivers pour over my head
let the sea take me for a spiller
of seas   let black men call me stranger
always   for your never named sake

She Understands Me

it is all blood and breaking,
blood and breaking. the thing
drops out of its box squalling
into the light. they are both squalling,
animal and cage. her bars lie wet, open
and empty and she has made herself again
out of flesh out of dictionaries,
she is always emptying and it is all
the same wound the same blood the same breaking.

Cutting Greens

curling them around
i hold their bodies in obscene embrace
thinking of everything but kinship.
collards and kale
strain against each strange other
away from my kissmaking hand and
the iron bedpot.
the pot is black,
the cutting board is black,
my hand,

and just for a minute
the greens roll black under the knife,
and the kitchen twists dark on its spine
and i taste in my natural appetite
the bond of live things everywhere.

Homage to My Hips

these hips are big hips
they need space to
move around in.
they don't fit into little
petty places. these hips
are free hips.
they don't like to be held back.
these hips have never been enslaved,
they go where they want to go
they do what they want to do.
these hips are mighty hips.
these hips are magic hips.
i have known them
to put a spell on a man and
spin him like a top!

there is a girl inside.
she is randy as a wolf.
she will not walk away
and leave these bones
to an old woman.

she is a green tree
in a forest of kindling.
she is a green girl
in a used poet.

she has waited
patient as a nun
for the second coming,

when she can break through gray hairs
into blossom

and her lovers will harvest
honey and thyme
and the woods will be wild
with the damn wonder of it.

I Once Knew a Man

i once knew a man who had wild horses killed.
when he told about it
the words came galloping out of his mouth
and shook themselves and headed off in
every damn direction. his tongue
was wild and wide and spinning when he talked
and the people he looked at closed their eyes
and tore the skins off their backs as they walked away
and stopped eating meat.
there was no holding him once he got started;
he had had wild horses killed one time and
they rode him to his grave.

Anna Speaks of the Childhood of Mary Her Daughter

we rise up early and
we work. work is the medicine
for dreams.
          that dream
i am having again;
she washed in light,
whole world bowed to its knees,
she on a hill looking up,
face all long tears.
          and shall i give her up
to dreaming then? i fight this thing.
all day we scrubbing   scrubbing.

How He Is Coming Then

like a pot turned on the straw
nuzzled by cows and an old man
dressed like a father. like a loaf
a poor baker sets in the haystack to cool.
like a shepherd who hears in his herding
his mother whisper   my son   my son.

Holy Night

joseph, i afraid of stars,
their brilliant seeing.
so many eyes. such light.
joseph, i cannot still these limbs,
i hands keep moving toward i breasts,
so many stars. so bright.
joseph, is wind burning from east
joseph, i shine, oh joseph,   oh
illuminated night.

Island Mary

after the all been done and i
one old creature carried on
another creature's back, i wonder
could i have fought these thing?
surrounded by no son of mine save
old men calling Mother like in the tale
the astrologer tell, i wonder
could i have walk away when voices
singing in my sleep? i one old woman.
always i seem to worrying now for
another young girl asleep
in the plain evening.
what song around her ear?
what star still choosing?

Sandra M. Gilbert

Sandra M. Gilbert (1936–).   In addition to publishing three books of poems, *In the Fourth World, Emily's Bread,* and *Blood Pressure,* Sandra M. Gilbert is one of our foremost feminist critics. Her groundbreaking book *The Madwoman in the Attic: The Woman Writer and the 19th Century Imagination,* co-written with Susan Gubar, came out in 1980. With Gubar she also co-wrote *No Man's Land: The Place of the Woman Writer in the 20th Century,* and co-edited *Shakespeare's Sister: Feminist Essays on Women Poets* and *The Norton Anthology of Literature by Women: The Tradition in English.*

She received her doctorate from Columbia University, and has taught at Indiana University and Princeton University. She teaches at the University of California at Davis and lives in Berkeley with her husband. Gilbert's poems, Alicia Ostriker writes, "are tasty, bitter, delicious, rotted in earth like her Sicilian grandmother's garden, exploring twentieth century love in all its thwarted and soaring branches."

My Grandmother in Paris

Paris. 1900. A sky of corrugated iron. Snow and mud.
Beggars like heaps of debris on street corners.
Women with pink cheeks melting in doorways.
Splashes of laughter, church bells, creaking boots.
Puccini's Paris, Paris of *La Bohème,* Paris
of garrets and prisons, Paris of sweet fevers, Paris

of phlegm and sweat, ivory breasts, skylights, *opéra:*
Paris of Wagner and Rilke, Paris of delicious
nineteenth-century melancholy, Paris where streetlights
glisten through the winter twilight
like pomegranates in hell.
                    Twilight.

My grandmother walks in the Bois de Boulogne
under frosted chestnuts. She's twelve years old,
a roundfaced girl just come from Russia,
her hair in skinny braids
like strange embroidery around her head.
She's on her way to the house of the Russian priest

where her mother cooks and cleans
but she watches, wondering, as carriages plunge
through the slush of the Bois, their lamps

leaping like goblin heads, their blanketed horses
clopping docile as cows through all the Paris noise.
Baudelaire is dead, Rimbaud dead in Africa, Gertrude Stein

thinking in Baltimore, Picasso painting in Barcelona.
My grandmother has learned three words of French:
allo, comment, combien. Amedée, the boy she's
going to marry four years from now,
is in Nice with his sister Eugénie,
who will die next year at nineteen,

and his sister Rosette, who will die at forty.
My grandmother is still tired from last week.
She stops to sit on a low wall beside the road
and begins to shape a tiny angel out of crumbs of snow.
From a passing *fiacre* a young clerk off to the *opéra*
sees her round pink face suspended like a small balloon

in the blue air.
                    What is she thinking
as she pats a cold celestial head and frozen wings?
Is she remembering the awful trainride
across Europe, the bonfires at the Polish border, the shouts
as the engine chuffed into Berlin? No. She rises,

makes her angel into a snowball and tosses it at a tree.
She's thinking of Russia, of her grandmother back in the room
in Rostov-on-the-Don, of the ice like silver on the river
all winter and long into spring, of the black fields
outside town and the old stories of Baba Yaga and the tales
she has also heard of the redhaired cossack

said to be her own father.
                    She walks faster.
It's late and cold. Her mother will worry.
The fat priest will be cross. Paris
grows around her like an enigmatic alphabet.
Even the trees are different here. No firs, no birches!
As she walks, Baba Yaga's house on chicken legs
steps delicately away across snowy meadows

and her father the cossack, with his furry animal head, fierce teeth,
                    red beard,
gallops into glacial distances.
(Does she suspect that from now on
she'll never really know any language again?)

Tomorrow the priest will be sixty. To celebrate
he'll buy a Swiss cane at the Galéries Lafayette.
                                    In seventy years
my grandmother will twirl that cane and dance a twostep
among the eucalyptuses above San Francisco Bay,
singing me the song about the lost princess of the Volga

while, far below, the cold Pacific
glitters like an ice field.

Diane Wakoski

Diane Wakoski (1937–).   Born in Whittier, California, and educated at the University of California, Berkeley, Diane Wakoski moved to New York City in the sixties, where she worked in a bookstore and taught junior high school. Now she is writer-in-residence at Michigan State University.

   She has published many collections of poetry, among them, *The Motorcycle Betrayer Poems* (1971), *Dancing on the Grave of a Son of a Bitch* (1973), *Waiting for the King of Spain* (1976), *Spending Christmas with the Man from Receiving at Sears* (1977), *Cap of Darkness* (1980), *The Magician's Feast Letters* (1982), *The Collected Greed* (1984), *The Rings of Saturn* (1986), *Emerald Ice: Selected Poems 1962–1987* (1988); *Trilogy: Coins and Coffins; Discrepancies and Apparitions, The George Washington Poems* (1974) and *The Man Who Shook Hands* (1978). Her book of criticism is *Toward a New Poetry,* in the Poets on Poetry series from the University of Michigan Press (1980).

Belly Dancer

Can these movements which move themselves
be the substance of my attraction?
Where does this thin green silk come from that covers
    my body?
Surely any woman wearing such fabrics
would move her body just to feel them touching every
    part of her.

Yet most of the women frown, or look away, or laugh stiffly.
They are afraid of these materials and these movements

in some way.
The psychologists would say they are afraid of
    themselves, somehow.
Perhaps awakening too much desire—
that their men could never satisfy?

So they keep themselves laced and·buttoned and made up
in hopes that the framework will keep them stiff enough
    not to feel
the whole register.
In hopes that they will not have to experience that
    unquenchable desire for rhythm and contact.

If a snake glided across this floor
most of them would faint or shrink away.
Yet that movement could be their own.
That smooth movement frightens them—
awakening ancestors and relatives to the tips of the
    arms and toes.

So my bare feet
and my thin green silks
my bells and finger cymbals
offend them—frighten their old-young bodies.
While the men simper and leer—
glad for the vicarious experience and exercise.
They do not realize how I scorn them:
or how I dance for their frightened,
unawakened, sweet
women.

Blue Monday

Blue of the heaps of beads poured into her breasts
and clacking together in her elbows;
blue of the silk
that covers lily-town at night;
blue of her teeth
that bite cold toast

and shatter on the streets;
blue of the dyed flower petals with gold stamens
hanging like tongues
over the fence of her dress
at the opera/ opals clasped under her lips
and the moon breaking over her head a
gush of blood-red lizards.

Blue Monday. Monday at 3:00 and
Monday at 5:00. Monday at 7:30 and
Monday at 10:00. Monday passed under the rippling
California fountain. Monday alone
a shark in the cold blue waters.

    You are dead: wound round like a paisley shawl.
    I cannot shake you out of the sheets. Your name
    is still wedged in every corner of the sofa.

    Monday is the first of the week,
    and I think of you all week.
    I beg Monday not to come
    so that I will not think of you
    all week.

You paint my body blue. On the balcony
in the soft muddy night, you paint me
with bat wings and the crystal
the crystal
the crystal
the crystal in your arm cuts away
the night, folds back ebony whale skin
and my face, the blue of new rifles,
and my neck, the blue of Egypt,
and my breast, the blue of sand,
and my arms, bass-blue,
and my stomach, arsenic;

there is electricity dripping from me like cream;
there is love dripping from me I cannot use—like acacia or
jacaranda—fallen blue and gold flowers, crushed into the street.

Love passed me in a blue business suit
and fedora.

How do I reconcile these images with our cool president,
George Washington, walking the streets? Every bone
in my body is ivory and has the word, "America"
carved on it, but
my head takes me away from furniture and pewter
to the sun tugging at my nipples and trying to squeeze
under my toes.
The sun appeared in the shape of a man and he had
a ring made of sun around his little finger.
"It will burn up your hand," I said.
But he made motions in the air and passed by.
The moon appeared in the shape of a young negro boy,
and he had a ring made of dew around his little finger.
"You'll lose it," I said,
but he touched my face,
not losing a drop and passed away. Then I saw
Alexander Hamilton, whom I loved,
and he had a ring on his little finger,
but he wouldn't touch me.
And Lorca had rings around both little fingers,
and suddenly everyone I knew appeared,
and they all had rings on their little fingers,
and I was the only one in the world left without any
rings
on any
of my fingers whatsoever.
And worst of all,
there was George Washington
walking down the senate aisles
with a ring on his little finger—managing
the world,
managing *my* world.
This is what I mean—you wear a ring on your
little finger
and you manage the world
and I am ringless
ringless . . .

I cannot stand the man who wears
a ring
on his little finger;

not even if it is you.

Kathleen Spivack

Kathleen Spivack (1938–).   Spivack is a fellow at the Radcliffe Institute. Her
poems have appeared in many magazines, among them *Poetry,* the *New Yorker,* and the
Atlantic Monthly, as well as in numerous anthologies. She has taught the Advanced
Poetry Workshop at the Radcliffe Graduate Center. Her volumes of poetry include
Flying Inland (1973) and *The Jane Poems* (1974).

Dust

she wanted rain
as release from her longing

she wanted rain
sluicing her breasts after love

when the great thirst
filling, leaf-brown, swept

and she sobbed, o yes,
and the water beat down

and bent her. she wanted
violence, over-abundance

flowing in gullies
up over the lip.

she wanted rain
easing her like a child

while the trees, eager,
thrust out their roots:

the earth drank.
she wanted the dank

smell of wry dust,
soaked after storms. she

sought virulent summer-
green satisfactions.

Love U.S.A.

love in the peaceful u.s.a.
draw the shades down   draw
our light limbs together

and let us love gently
as if
that's still possible

not heaving and struggling
like
in the movies

with bosomy gasps as
the man
takes her over—

I'll tame you my
vixen as
he rips

off her clothes:
she sighs
aaaahhhhh.   Not

like young re-
volutionaries
shouting and fucking

sweating out power
more
power in bed

fighting the
system by
freeing your body

till you are a
cipher in
some weird class struggle.   No   love

me   lie down and
close out the country
and close out

tradition
and turn off the
tv

and let the newspapers
pile up on
the doorstep

and kick in the
radio   see how the
rhetoric dribbles away

and for once let's be
lyrical
like in the

poems
let's
pretend.

Grace Schulman

Grace Schulman (1939–).   Born in New York City, Grace Schulman is poetry
editor of *The Nation,* director of the Poetry Center of the 92nd Street YM-YWHA,

and assistant professor of English at Baruch College. In 1975 she received the Lucille Medwick Memorial Award from the P.E.N. American Center in recognition of her many activities as poet, critic, and translator. Her work has appeared in leading magazines. She has published one volume of poems, *Burn Down the Icons* (1976).

Burial of a Fisherman in Hydra

The day time failed began as usual.
Seeing the sun strike mica on the rocks,
I raced down terraces, past white
Sea houses casting black trapezoids
To watch the nightboat stagger in.
No nightboat, but a strange gray cutter
Moved into the harbor, bringing a fisherman
Who died in Athens, in a hospital.
There was a priest, a brilliant procession
Balancing scalloped crosses; the bells
Brawled; his women were black birds
Ridding the pier of swimmers and fishermen.
Suddenly, as though we knew him well,
The people stood in a silent chorus
Until the last cross-bearer disappeared
Among the listed saint-heads in the chapel.
Shadows that had been knives on the ground
Grew as on a sundial, measuring
The light; we followed in suppliance,
Night crowding every gutter of the rock.
In another time we might have mourned
Fallen heroes, carried in from sea
But in the imagination of the living
The fall from glory is the fall from being.
Night comes; that is the mystery of day.

Margaret Atwood

Margaret Atwood (1939–).   Atwood was born in Canada. Her volume of poetry, *The Circle Game,* received the Governor-General's Award in 1966. Her poems have appeared in many magazines, among them, *Poetry,* the *New Yorker,* and the *Atlantic Monthly.* Her volumes include *The Animals in That Country* (1968), *The Journals of Susanna Moodie* (1970), *Procedures for Underground* (1970), *Power Politics* (1971), *You Are Happy* (1974), and *Selected Poems* (1976) (poetry); *Surfacing, The Edible Woman,* and *Lady Oracle* (novels); and *Survival: A Thematic Guide to Canadian Literature* (criticism).

Dream 2: Brian the Still-Hunter

The man I saw in the forest
used to come to our house
every morning, never said anything;
I learned from the neighbours later
he once tried to cut his throat.

I found him at the end of the path
sitting on a fallen tree
cleaning his gun.

There was no wind;
around us the leaves rustled.

He said to me:
I kill because I have to

but every time I aim, I feel
my skin grow fur
my head heavy with antlers
and during the stretched instant
the bullet glides on its thread of speed
my soul runs innocent as hooves.

Is God just to his creatures?

I die more often than many.

He looked up and I saw
the white scar made by the hunting knife
around his neck.

When I woke
I remembered: he has been gone
twenty years and not heard from.

Habitation

Marriage is not
a house or even a tent

it is before that, and colder:

the edge of the forest, the edge
of the desert
                the unpainted stairs
at the back where we squat
outside, eating popcorn

the edge of the receding glacier

where painfully and with wonder
at having survived even
this far

we are learning to make fire

Daguerreotype Taken in Old Age

I know I change
have changed

but whose is this vapid face
pitted and vast, rotund
suspended in empty paper
as though in a telescope

the granular moon

I rise from my chair
pulling against gravity
I turn away
and go out into the garden

I revolve among the vegetables,
my head ponderous
reflecting the sun
in shadows from the pocked ravines
cut in my cheeks, my eye-
sockets 2 craters

among the paths
I orbit
the apple trees
white white spinning
stars around me

I am being
eaten away by light

Elegy for the Giant Tortoises

Let others pray for the passenger pigeon,
the dodo, the whooping crane, the eskimo:
everyone must specialize

I will confine myself to a meditation
upon the giant tortoises
withering finally on a remote island.

I concentrate in subway stations,
in parks, I can't quite see them,
they move to the peripheries of my eyes

but on the last day they will be there;
already the event
like a wave travelling shapes vision:

on the road where I stand they will materialize,
plodding past me in a straggling line
awkward without water

their small heads pondering
from side to side, their useless armour
sadder than tanks and history,

in their closed gaze ocean and sunlight paralysed,
lumbering up the steps, under the archways
toward the square glass altars

where the brittle gods are kept,
the relics of what we have destroyed,
our holy and obsolete symbols.

Death of a Young Son by Drowning

He, who navigated with success
the dangerous river of his own birth
once more set forth

on a voyage of discovery
into the land I floated on
but could not touch to claim.

His feet slid on the bank,
the currents took him;
he swirled with ice and trees in the swollen water

and plunged into distant regions,
his head a bathysphere;
through his eyes' thin glass bubbles

he looked out, reckless adventurer
on a landscape stranger than Uranus
we have all been to and some remember.

There was an accident; the air locked,
he was hung in the river like a heart.
They retrieved the swamped body,

cairn of my plans and future charts,
with poles and hooks
from among the nudging logs.

It was spring, the sun kept shining, the new grass
leapt to solidity;
my hands glistened with details.

After the long trip I was tired of waves.
My foot hit rock. The dreamed sails
collapsed, ragged.

I planted him in this county
like a flag.

Anne Winters

Anne Winters (1939–).   Anne Winters grew up in New York City, was educated
at New York University (B.A.) and Columbia University (M.A.), and has taught at the
Massachusetts Institute of Technology and the University of California, Davis, and is
now working toward a Ph.D. at the University of California, Berkeley. She is currently
a visiting Assistant Professor at Northwestern University. She has won several awards
and fellowships, most recently an Ingram Merrill grant and a National Endowment for
the Arts Fellowship. Winters is a poet, translator, and essayist. Her languages are
French, German, Italian, Latin, Ancient Greek, and Hebrew. She has written the
books *The Key to the City* (1985), nominated for the National Book Critics Circle
Award for Poetry, and *Salamander: Selected Poems of Robert Marteau* (1979), which won
Poetry magazine's Jacob Glatstein Memorial Prize.

With Adrienne Rich, Jean Valentine, Frank Bidart, and Alan Williamson she
attended Robert Lowell's "office hours," an informal and unofficial workshop, at-
tended occasionally by Elizabeth Bishop. Robert Pinsky writes that "Winters's mas-
tery of an extreme, packed formal alertness is part of a characteristically American
response to shifting, undetermined manners, form and idioms, to heroic structures and
appalling lives and deaths. . . . I like the visible speed and intelligence."

Night Wash

All seas are seas in the moon to these
lonely and full of light.
High above laundries and rooftops
the pinstriped silhouettes speak nightmare

as do the faces full of fire and orange peel.
Every citizen knows what's the trouble: *America's longest river is—*
   New York; that's what they say, and I say so.

Wonderful thing, electricity,
all these neons and nylons spun dry by a dime
in the Fifth Street Laundromat. The city
must be flying a thousand kites tonight
with its thousands of different keys.
—Sir, excuse me, *sir?*
Excuse me interfering, but you don't want
to put that in—it's got a rubber backing, see? Oh, not at all . . .

Piles of workshirts, piles of leopard underthings,
it's like fishing upside down all night long, and then the moon
   rises
like armfuls of thready sleeves. Her voice
rising and falling, her boys folded sideways asleep on the bench:
—Listen, that old West Indian cleaning lady?
Ask anyone here, she never has change.
Come on, she's too wise . . .

Down in the Tombs
the prisoner's knuckles climb like stripes
of paint in the light. He dreams he hears
the voice of a pig he used to slop for his uncles.
It pokes its head
through the bars and says
"Have you brought any beet greens?"

—You can never leave them alone at night. Like today
the stitching overseer says to me
If you can't keep the rhythm missus . . .
I says to him fire
me all you want, I don't take that shit
off anybody. That was a scare though—
you can't always get back on a day shift.

In the moonlight
the city rides serenely enough, its thousand light moorings

the hunted news in their eyes. Even the rivers
are tidal, as sailors and bankers know.
The glass bank of the Chase Manhattan stands dark
over the Harbor. One last
light slowly moving around the top floor.

—No washing machines in the basement, that's
what's the trouble. The laundry would dry overnight
on the roof, in the wind. Well a month ago
you know, some big boys took this twelveyearold
little Spanish girl up there. Then they killed her, they
threw her, six stories down. Listen, the stone age or something
running around on those roofs. So this cop said to me
Your street is the bottom, he actually
said that to me. So what could I say—that it's great?

On the folding table the same
gestures repeat, smoothing and folding
the same ancient shirt. Or the old West Indian cleaning lady
pretending to finger her pockets for change. At midnight she'll
    prop
her grey spaghetti mop and glide toward you
in her black cotton trousers, her black
lavender face tilted up. Very clearly
she says to the world in dream-language
I mean to live.

Elizabeth Near and Far

The Stethoscope

Like Halley's comet, bending on its tail,
you curl beneath the black cup on my skin:
I guess at limbs in half-eclipse, obscure
and fluent as a distant telegram.
Unworldly, small, sealed orders, darkroom heat,
soon among the signals pulsed, the static whoosh, arrives
in distant thuds your rapider than human
heartbeat—sex unknowable—bud eyes—

Yet of our world you only know the tree
you lie beneath, its root your belly, fronds
and villi falling in the sunken lake
of capillaries, bubbles, breathing bonds . . .
I sigh. And somewhere you incline your vast
night-sighted brow—your jointed, swimming hands—

Linda Gregg

Linda Gregg (1942–).   Born in Suffern, New York, Gregg grew up in northern
California and was educated at San Francisco State University. Among the places she
has taught are the University of Tucson, the College of Marin Poetry Center, the Napa
Valley Poetry Conference. She has been awarded fellowships from the Guggenheim
Foundation and the National Endowment for the Arts. She has written the books *Too
Bright to See* (1981) and *Alma* (1985).

In her essay, "Not Understanding," Gregg writes,

> There is something in poetry which . . . cannot be studied scientifically. Can
> only be approached, can only be honored . . . We must remember there is a
> kind of safety in trusting the unknown. There are things beyond the border
> which are invisible, but if we are patient and listen hard, we can sometimes
> hear them.

Linda Gregg's poetry—influenced by Li Po and by Greek literature and landscape—
guides us over the border, into the ineffable.

With a Blessing Rather Than Love Said Nietzsche

The square stone room makes a shape in the air
to rest inside. A form for holding what is loved
beyond naming. With gratitude and reverence
as Nietzsche. We have other ways,
other places. Like figs left on the stone shelf
above the patio as a gift.
You go out and return with fruit you've picked
and I make jam for our crepes and yogurt
and we eat. It is still morning and we look
at each other even though we have known each other
for years. You take me on your lap
in the chair by the open window and pull off
the shirts over our heads so we can feel the air
and embrace and kiss high up on the mountain
in the shaded room by the screen window
where the air comes in and keeps touching us

and we are happy beyond saying, beyond
any sounds even. Less than nothing and deeper.

Balancing Everything

When I lie in bed thinking of those years, I often
remember the ships. On the Aegean especially.
Especially at night among the islands or going
to Athens. The beauty of the moon and stillness.
How hard those journeys sometimes were.
The powerful smell of vomit and urine, sweetened
coffee and crude oil when the ship struggled
against the wind. I think of the night
we were going to die in the storm trying to reach
the passenger liner. Huge waves smashing
over our little boat. Jack screaming at the captain
because he hit me in his fear. Old Greek women
hiding their heads in my lap. Like a miracle.
I talked to them with the few words I knew.
Simple things. How it would be all right.
Telling them to look at the lights of their village
at the top of the great cliffs of Santorini,
up in the dark among the stars.

Whole and Without Blessing

What is beautiful alters, has undertow.
Otherwise I have no tactics to begin with.
Femininity is a sickness. I open my eyes
out of this fever and see the meaning
of my life clearly. A thing like a hill.
I proclaim myself whole and without blessing,
or need to be blessed. A fish of my own
spirit. I belong to no one. I do not move.
Am not required to move. I lie naked on a sheet
and the indifferent sun warms me.
I was bred for slaughter, like the other
animals. To suffer exactly at the center,
where there are no clues except pleasure.

Together in Greece

I was sitting on the steps of the cinema
when he introduced his pretty friend.
The few bare bulbs showed how dark and barren it was.
I got up and left the town.
Went out with no attitude prepared.
I went to a winnowing ring in the fields and lay down,
where all day they ran horses and donkeys
over the barley, a farmer running with his hands tied
to them. Knew the air was cold and I saw myself there.
Realized I was strange.
When the moon wanted me to sing
with my mouth open, I refused.
I knew Jack was looking for me. Stayed silent.
Heard him calling my name in the village streets.
Finally came out of the fields
and walked toward him. Dark and huge.
My head ached from the sounds I did not make.
It was more frightening than living.
I went to him, with that singing in me.

Classicism

The nights are very clear in Greece.
When the moon is round we see it completely
and have no feeling.

Marilyn Hacker

Marilyn Hacker (1942–).   Born in New York City, Marilyn Hacker lives there and
in Paris. She has received fellowships from the Ingram Merrill Foundation, the
Guggenheim Foundation, the National Endowment for the Arts, and the Michael
Karolyi Memorial Foundation. Her collections of poetry include *Presentation Piece,*
which was the Lamont Selection of the Academy of American Poets and the winner
of the National Book Award in 1975, *Separations* (1976), *Taking Notice* (1980),
Assumptions (1985). The following is taken from *Love, Death, and the Changing of the
Seasons* (1986), a narrative sequence of sonnets and villanelles.

Bloomingdale's I

"If I weren't working, I'd sleep next to you
an hour or two more. Then we'd get the car

and drive a while, out of Manhattan, to
a quiet Bloomingdale's in Westchester.
If we saw anything we liked, we'd buy it!
We'd try things on, first, in one cubicle.
You'd need to make an effort to be quiet
when I knelt down and got my fingers full
of you, my mouth on you, against the wall.
You'd pull my hair. You'd have to bite your tongue.
I'd hold your ass so that you wouldn't fall.
Later, we'd take a peaceful walk along
the aisles, letting our hands touch every chance
they got, among the bras and underpants."

Lacoste IV

It's almost as if we're already there,
in the narrow stone house, me upstairs
writing at the splintery pine table,
you in the downstairs study, with its cradle
of a marriage bed, slit window looking
into the Buniols' herb garden. I'm cooking
a sonnet sequence and a cassoulet
with goose from Carcassonne, let *mijoter*
on the burner till nightfall. The vow
of silence breaks at seven. It's noon now.
Pleasure delayed is pleasure amplified
—I'll show you these bitch Welsh quatrains I've tried.
It's your turn to work outdoors in the sun
on the roof—your footsteps, and the last line's done.

Sharon Olds

Sharon Olds (1942–).   Born in San Francisco, she was educated at Stanford University and at Columbia University. She has received fellowships from the National Endowment for the Arts and from the Guggenheim Foundation. Her first book, *Satan Says* (1980), won the San Francisco Poetry Center Award; her second, *The Living and the Dead* (1984) won both the Lamont Poetry Selection of the Academy of American Poets and the National Book Critics Circle Award. *The Gold Cell* (1987) is her latest volume.

Sex Without Love

How do they do it, the ones who make love
without love? Beautiful as dancers,
gliding over each other like ice-skaters
over the ice, fingers hooked
inside each other's bodies, faces
red as steak, wine, wet as the
children at birth whose mothers are going to
give them away. How do they come to the
come to the   come to the   God   come to the
still waters, and not love
the one who came there with them, light
rising slowly as steam off their joined
skin? These are the true religious,
the purists, the pros, the ones who will not
accept a false Messiah, love the
priest instead of the God. They do not
mistake the lover for their own pleasure,
they are like great runners: they know they are alone
with the road surface, the cold, the wind,
the fit of their shoes, their over-all cardio-
vascular health—just factors, like the partner
in the bed, and not the truth, which is the
single body alone in the universe
against its own best time.

Ideographs

(a photograph of China, 1905)

The small scaffolds, boards in the form of
ideographs, the size of a person,
lean against a steep wall of
dressed stone. One is the simple
shape of a man. The man on it
is asleep, his arms nailed to the wood.
No timber is wasted; his fingertips
curl in at the very end of the plank
as a child's hands open in sleep.
The other man is awake—he looks

directly at us. He is fixed to a more
complex scaffold, a diagonal cross-piece
pointing one arm up, one down,
and his legs are bent, the spikes through his ankles
holding them up off the ground,
his knees cocked, the folds of his robe flowing
sideways as if he were suspended in the air
in flight, his naked leg bared.
They are awaiting execution, tilted against the wall
as you'd prop up a tool until you needed it.
They'll be shouldered up over the crowd and
carried through the screaming. The sleeper will wake.
The twisted one will fly above the faces, his
garment rippling.
Here there is still the backstage quiet,
the dark at the bottom of the wall, the props
leaning in the grainy half-dusk.
He looks at us in the silence. He says
Save me, there is still time.

Tess Gallagher

Tess Gallagher (1943–). Tess Gallagher's books of poetry include *Instructions to the Double* (1976), which won the Elliston Book Award; *Under Stars* (1978); *Willingly* (1985); and *Amplitude: New and Selected Poems* (1987). She has also written *A Concert of Tenses: Essays on Poetry* (1986), *Death of Horses by Fire* (1983), *The Lover of Horses and Other Stories* (1986). With her late husband, Raymond Carver, she wrote *Dostoevsky: A Screenplay* (1983). She introduced Raymond Carver's last book of poems, *A New Path the Waterfall,* and *Carver Country,* a book of photographs by Bob Adelman with whom she collaborated to compile letters and selections from stories and poems to accompany the photographs. Among her many awards and honors are fellowships from the National Endowment for the Arts and the Guggenheim Foundation. She taught at Syracuse University, and now lives in Port Angeles, Washington.

In "Black Silk," a mother figure finds an old silk vest, and they make their "hands / heavy until its shape . . . came back." So it is with her works, heavy hands giving shape back to the people she writes about. She has said that women must take what will not be freely given. These are poems that demand intimacy.

Black Silk

She was cleaning—there is always
that to do—when she found,
at the top of the closet, his old

silk vest. She called me
to look at it, unrolling it carefully
like something live
might fall out. Then we spread it
on the kitchen table and smoothed
the wrinkles down, making our hands
heavy until its shape against Formica
came back and the little tips
that would have pointed to his pockets
lay flat. The buttons were all there.
I held my arms out and she
looped the wide armholes over
them. "That's one thing I never
wanted to be," she said, "a man."
I went into the bathroom to see
how I looked in the sheen and
sadness. Wind chimes
off-key in the alcove. Then her
crying so I stood back in the sink-light
where the porcelain had been staring. Time
to go to her, I thought, with that
other mind, and stood still.

Black Pudding

Even then I knew it was the old unanswerable form of beauty
as pain, like coming, in that lost-Eden-way, onto a pair of herons
near the river mouth at dawn. Beauty as when the body
is a dumb stick before the moment—yet goes on,
gazes until memory prepares a quick untidy room
with unpredictable visiting hours.
So I brought you there, you who didn't belong, thinking to out-
    save
even memory by tearing the sacred from

its alcove. I let you see us, arms helplessly tender,
holding each other all night on that awkward couch
because our life was ending. And we fell again and again
into each other like spring water secretly in the wood, murmuring,
retelling our love in that blurted way between gusts of weeping.

Did I let you overhear those grey-blue dyings?
Or as I think now, like a Mongol tribesman, did I stop the horse
on its desert march, take the meal of blood

from its bowed neck to be heated. This then is my black pudding
only the stalwart know to eat. How I climbed
like a damp child waking from nightmare to find
the parents intimate and still awake.
And with natural animal gladness did rub my face against
the scald of their cheeks, tasting the salt
of the unsayable—but, like a rescuer who comes too late, too
fervently marked with duty, was unable to fathom

what their danger and passage had been for. Except
as you know now, even to glimpse this scene is intrusion enough
to insure that when there is nothing else to sustain, blood will be
thickened with fire. Not a pretty dish.
But something taken from the good and cherished beast on loan to
    us
who is muscled over in spirit and just strong enough to carry us
only as far as it can, there being advantage
to this meagerness, an unsavoriness that rations itself
and reminds us to respect even its bitter portion.
Don't ask me now why I'm walking my horse.

Yes

Now we are like that flat cone of sand
in the garden of the Silver Pavilion in Kyoto
designed to appear only in moonlight.

Do you want me to mourn?
Do you want me to wear black?

Or like moonlight on whitest sand
to use your dark, to gleam, to shimmer?

I gleam. I mourn.

Ellen Bryant Voight

Ellen Bryant Voight (1943–).   Ellen Bryant Voight grew up in Chatham, Virginia, and received a B.A. from Converse College and an M.F.A. from the University of Iowa. She teaches at the Warren Wilson M.F.A. program for writers. Among her awards are grants from the Guggenheim Foundation and the National Endowment for the Arts. Her books are *Claiming Kin* (1976), *The Forces of Plenty* (1983), and *The Lotus Flowers* (1987). She lives in Cabot, Vermont, with her husband and two children.

Bright Leaf

Like words put to a song, the bunched tobacco leaves
are strung along a stick, the women
standing in the August heat for hours—since first light—
under the pitched tin roof, barefoot, and at their feet
the babies, bare-assed, dirty, eating dirt.
The older children hand the leaves from the slide,
three leaves at a time, stalks upright, three handers
for each stringer, and three more heaped canvas slides
waiting in what little shade there is: it's ten o'clock,
almost dinnertime. They pull the pails of cold lunch
and Mason jars of tea out of the spring
when they see the farmer coming from the field, their men
stripped to the waist, polished by sweat and tired as mules.
By afternoon, the loose cotton dresses, even
the headrags are dark with sweat.
Still their fingers never miss a stitch,
though they're paid not by the stick but by the day,
and the talk—unbroken news of cousins and acquaintances—
unwinding with the ball of twine, a frayed snuff-twig
bouncing on one lip, the string paying out
through their calluses, the piles of wide green leaves
diminishing, until the men appear with the last slide
and clamber up the rafters of the barn
to line the loaded sticks along the tiers. It's Friday:

the farmer pays with a wad of ones and fives,
having turned the mule out to its feed and water,
hung up the stiffened traces and the bit. He checks
again the other barns, already fired, crude ovens
of log and mud where the crop is cured;
in that hot dry acrid air, spreads a yellowing leaf

across his palm, rolls an edge in his fingers,
gauging by its texture and its smell
how high to drive the fire.

His crew is quiet in the pickup truck—did you think
they were singing? They are much too tired to even speak,
can barely lick salt from the back of a hand, brush at flies,
hush a baby with a sugartit. And the man
who owns this land is also tired.
Everyday this week he's meant to bring home pears
from the old tree by the barn, but now he sees
the fruit has fallen, sees the yellow jackets feeding there.
He lights a Lucky, frames a joke for his wife—he'll say
their banker raised a piss-poor field this year.
And she will lean against the doorjamb
while he talks, while he scrubs his hands at the tin basin
with a split lemon and a pumice stone, rubs them raw
trying to cut the gummy resin, that stubborn
black stain within the green.

Sandra McPherson

Sandra McPherson (1943–).   Born in California, she was educated at San Jose
College and the University of Washington. Her volume *Elegies for the Hot Season*
(1970) was chosen as a Selection of the National Council on the Arts. She received a
grant from the Ingram Merrill Foundation and the Helen Bullis Prize from *Poetry
Northwest,* where she was later a guest editor. Her poems have appeared in numerous
magazines, among them, *Poetry,* the *New Yorker,* and *The Nation.*

Pregnancy

It is the best thing.
I should always like to be pregnant,

Tummy thickening like a yoghurt,
Unbelievable flower.

A queen is always pregnant with her country.
Sheba of questions

Or briny siren
At her difficult passage,

One is the mountain that moves
Toward the earliest gods.

Who started this?
An axis, a quake, a perimeter,

I have no decisions to master
That could change my frame

Or honor.
Immaculate. Or if it was not, perfect.

Pregnant, I'm highly explosive—
You can feel it, long before

Your seed will run back to hug you—
Squaring and cubing

Into reckless bones, bouncing odd ways
Like a football.

The heart sloshes through the microphone
Like falls in a box canyon.

The queen's only a figurehead.
Nine months pulled by nine

Planets, the moon slooping
Through its amnion sea,

Trapped, stone-mad . . . and three
Beings' lives gel in my womb.

Louise Glück

Louise Glück (1943–).   Born in New York City, she has taught at the University of Virginia, the University of North Carolina, and Goddard College. She has been awarded a Rockefeller Foundation grant and a National Foundation for the Arts grant. She lives in Plainfield, Vermont. Her volumes include *Firstborn* (1969) and *The House on Marshland* (1975).

Lamentations

1. The Logos

They were both still,
the woman mournful, the man
branching into her body

But god was watching.
They felt his gold eye
projecting flowers on the landscape.

Who knew what he wanted?
He was god, and a monster.
So they waited. And the world
filled with his radiance,
as though he wanted to be understood.

Far away, in the void that he had shaped,
he turned to his angels.

2. Nocturne

A forest rose from the earth.
O pitiful, so needing
God's furious love—

Together they were beasts.
They lay in the fixed
dusk of his negligence;
from the hills, wolves came, mechanically
drawn to their human warmth,
their panic.

Then the angels saw
how He divided them:
the man, the woman, and the woman's body.
Above the churned reeds, the leaves let go
a slow moan of silver.

3. The Covenant

Out of fear, they built a dwelling place.
But a child grew between them
as they slept, as they tried
to feed themselves.

They set it on a pile of leaves,
the small discarded body
wrapped in the clean skin
of an animal. Against the black sky
they saw the massive argument of light.

Sometimes it woke. As it reached its hands
they understood they were the mother and father,
there was no authority above them.

4. The Clearing

Gradually, over many years,
the fur disappeared from their bodies
until they stood in the bright light
strange to one another.
Nothing was as before.
Their hands trembled, seeking
the familiar.

Nor could they keep their eyes
from the white flesh
on which wounds would show clearly
like words on a page.

And from the meaningless browns and greens
at last God arose, His great shadow
darkening the sleeping bodies of His children,
and leapt into heaven.

How beautiful it must have been,
the earth, that first time
seen from the air.

5. Night Song

Look up into the light of th lantern.
Don't you see? The calm of darkness
is the horror of Heaven.

We've been apart too long, too painfully separated.
How can you bear to dream,
to give up watching? I think you must be dreaming,
your face is full of mild expectancy

I need to wake you, to remind you that there isn't a future.
That's why we're free. And now some weakness in me
has been cured forever, so I'm not compelled
to close my eyes, to go back, to rectify—

The beach is still; the sea, cleansed of its superfluous life,
opaque, rocklike. In mounds, in vegetal clusters,
seabirds sleep on the jetty. Terns, assassins—

You're tired; I can see that.
We're both tired, we have acted a great drama.
Even our hands are cold, that were like kindling.
Our clothes are scattered on the sand; strangely enough,
they never turned to ashes.

I have to tell you what I've learned, that I know now
what happens to the dreamers.
They don't feel it when they change. One day
they wake, they dress, they are old.

Tonight I'm not afraid
to feel the revolutions. How can you want sleep
when passion gives you that peace?
You're like me tonight, one of the lucky ones.
You'll get what you want. You'll get your oblivion.

Shirley Williams

Shirley Williams (1944–).   Educated at Brown University, she has taught at
the University of California at San Diego. Michael Harper writes of her poetry: "She

is a musician whose blues, comedy and heartbreak are a testimony to autobiography/history where both oral and literary Afro-American traditions touch and fuse." Her titles include *The Peacock Poems* (1975) and *Give Birth to Brightness* (criticism).

If He Let Us Go Now

let me strap.
the baby in the seat, just don't say
nothing all that while . . .
I move round to
the driver side of the car. The air
warm and dry here. Lawd know what it be
in L. A. He open the door for me
and I slide behind the wheel. Baby
facin me lookin without even
blinkin his eye. I wonder if he
know I'm his mamma that I love him
that that his daddy by the door (and
he won't let us go; he still got time
to say wait). Baby blink once but
he only five week old and whatever
he know don't show.
His daddy call
my name and I turn to him and wait.
It be cold in the Grapevine at night
this time of year. Wind come whistlin down
through them mountains almost blow this old
VW off the road. I'll be in
touch he say. Say, take care; say, write if
you need somethin.
I *will* him to touch
us now, to take care us, to know what
we need is him and his name. He slap
the car door, say, drive careful and turn
to go. If he let us go now . . . how
we gon ever take him back? I ease
out on the clutch, mash in on the gas.
The only answer I get is his back.

The Killing of the Birds

I member we went to the hospital that day.
    The only mirror in the house a small
    piece we keep in the kitchen window
    sill. Mamma barely tall

    enough to see in it but she stand in front
    of it puttin on red lipstick, water
    wavin her hair that she usual
    wear in braids. The light catch yo

    reflection so you really can't see
    so good but she stand there anyway
    and when she finish that she oil her legs
    wid vaseline and knot her stockins so they stay.

She put on a flowered dress that make
    her skin look shiny black.
    Miss Irma tease bout how fine
    she look, she say my husband back

    from the TB place; he out to the County
    now. When we get there me and Ruise
    and Le'rn went to play while Mamma
    and Jesmarie stand at the window by the trees
    and talk to Daddy. After while
    Jesmarie come to get us; it be time
    to go. At the window Daddy was screamin
    bout some man and Mamma was cryin.

Sandra Alcosser

Sandra Alcosser (1944–).   Sandra Alcosser's book, *A Fish to Feed All Hunger* (1986), won the Associated Writing Programs Award Series in Poetry in 1984. Her poems have appeared in the *New Yorker, Poetry,* the *American Scholar,* and the *Paris Review.* James Tate writes in his introduction to her book, "Each moment seems to have its just emphasis. In our daily lives, we are performing a series of rites for one another. And Alcosser's sense of ritual is keen. She gives meaning when it is most needed."

Cry

White legs and pink footpads, the black cat
loved me. It was summer, a perfect flush
of weeds and flowers. Mornings, he'd listen
for my kettle, the screen door snap, and he'd know
I'd come to breakfast in the asters. As I ate
my bowl of red berries, he'd burl and stretch
and claw about my hips.

One night as the cat and I watched the moon eclipse,
amidst the scuttling of bear and mice, there was a cry
from the forest, not seductive, but pained and wailing
like a siren. The next day the cat was gone. I'd heard
that even blackbirds broke veins in their throats
singing love songs. I stood by my window practicing,
trying to shape the feline song, to call him back.

My daughter was no different than a cat,
tapping the window glass over my bed,
crying at night till I rocked her frail ribs
against mine. Her hands on my breast,
dark curls sweated against her forehead,
tell me about the princess, she said, *the way
she slept in a blue dress, waiting.*

It was a month of heatstorms, lightning scratched
like Sanskrit across the valley. A boy came riding
our footpath. He wore black jeans, a sliver of green
malachite at his neck. The breathless afternoon,
the bees laid out on the red eyes of gaillardia.
Before she left my daughter cut off her long hair
and bleached it yellow.

There were years when I too turned from my mother's
cool white arms. First the pale boy, scarred
and silent, then my husband. We cleaned the ditches
together in spring, raking out the silt and dead branches.
He played a silver harmonica. A ring-boned pony
was what I had when we ran away. A field of salsify
and a black skillet.

Stretched out on the porch this noon, resting
my swollen legs, I'm tired of canning tomatoes,
the house thick with red steam and basil.
The bite of salt and vinegar, cucumbers
floating like green bathers in brine.
All that flesh I've tended gone to pulp.
All that mismatched tenderness.

One weed knows another and each animal has its own cry
and when it's right, it's easy. Easy as my husband
behind me now, holding open the black screen door.
He is drinking tea with honey and a halo of gnats
screams about his face. *Let's sneak down to the basement,*
he says, *where it's cool and dark.* He cracks a bead of ice
in his teeth and offers half to me.

Maura Stanton

Maura Stanton (1946–).   Born in Evanston, Illinois, Maura Stanton was educated
at the University of Minnesota (B.A.) and the University of Iowa (M.F.A.) She has
received two fellowships from the National Endowment for the Arts and one from the
Indiana Commission for the Arts. She has published books of poetry, *Snow on Snow*
(1975), winner of the Yale Series of Younger Poets Award, *Cries of Swimmers* (1984),
and *Tales of the Supernatural* (1988), and a novel, *Molly Companion.* Stanton's poems
haunt the reader with a reality at once surreal, immediate, beautiful, and terrible. She
teaches at Indiana University.

Wander Indiana

Introduced in January 1984, the "Wander" plates have been a cause for much unhappiness and
confusion—not only for Indiana residents, but also for motorists around the country. . . . Some
thought "Wander" was a county—a large one—somewhere in central Indiana.
                                                                —Newspaper Editorial

How did I come to be here? I suppose
I was like other girls at first, just shyer.
I used to stand outside the practice room
Listening to Chopin on the piano
With my eyes closed, imagining love.
I was a wise man in the Christmas play,
No lines to speak, but the whole stage to cross
Pretending to follow a light-bulb star.
I liked to spin the globe in my homeroom

After school, and stop it with my finger.
Then I grew up, got glasses, read thick books.
I saw the sights that all explorers see
When I began to travel, yet somehow
The pictures in the books were always brighter—
"Smiling mermaids, combing their yellow hair"
The caption said, but when I reached that shore
And saw the mermaids sprawled upon their rocks,
I saw how thin they were, how they shivered,
And tried to dry their wet tails with their hair.

I heard the rumors about Shangri-la:
Yes, most of them are true, the palms sway
And gentle unicorns crop the green grass
Below the snow-capped, shadowy mountains,
But people stopped me on broad avenues
To ask me a question: Was I ever happy
Down there where snow fell? If I said "Yes,"
They turned from me in shock, almost angry,
Swept up their gauzy robes, and walked away.
That's when I crossed the Iceberg Sea to Limbo
And disembarked in the ramshackle port.
It looked so ordinary, a town of bars
And rutted streets. Inside the "Rainy Daze"
I asked a sailor if he ever tried
To catch a glimpse of Heaven through the fog.
He shook his head, lifting his heavy stein.

But it was on my short voyage to Hell
That I first heard of Wander, Indiana.
I waited on the shore beside the Lethe
Among the mingling shades. I had no right
To passage on the ferry for the dead,
And the shades jostled me, mocking, annoyed.
I was loveless, hopeless, but I was alive,
Solid enough to weight the buoyant wood
Of the deck, remind them of their losses.
After the ferryman refused to take me
I pleaded with the dead. Where should I go?
Wander, Indiana some voices hissed
Above the groan of oars, the shrieks and moans.

And so I drove across the big prairie
Searching for the narrow road to Wander.

The sky was blue, the rustling corn uncut.
I passed the quarry and the water tower,
Drove into the county seat at twilight—
It looked real. I knew that strangers slept
Soundly at the Bide-a-Wee Motel,
Then drove away, never suspecting the trick:
The whole town, the whole enormous county,
Is made of drifting vapor, molecules
Combined—no one knows how—to resemble
Shapes of houses, hardware stores, and people.
None of us exist. We're clouds of matter
Driven by gusts of passion, lips dissolving
As we smile at you, and give you directions.

Ai

Ai (1947–).   Her volume of poetry *Cruelty* (1972) was published by Houghton-Mifflin in 1973. Her poems have appeared in leading periodicals including *American Poetry Review, Iowa Review, Ironwood, Lillabullero,* and *Renaissance. The Killing Floor* was published in 1978, and in that year Ai was awarded the Lamont Poetry Selection.

Abortion

Coming home, I find you still in bed,
but when I pull back the blanket,
I see your stomach is flat as an iron.
You've done it, as you warned me you would
and left the fetus wrapped in wax paper
for me to look at. My son.
Woman, loving you no matter what you do,
what can I say, except that I've heard
the poor have no children, just small people
and there is room only for one man in this house.

Child Beater

Outside, the rain, pinafore of gray water, dresses the town
and I stroke the leather belt,

as she sits in the rocking chair,
holding a crushed paper cup to her lips.
I yell at her, but she keeps rocking;
back, her eyes open, forward, they close.
Her body, somehow fat, though I feed her only once a day,
reminds me of my own just after she was born.
It's been seven years, but I still can't forget how I felt.
How heavy it feels to look at her.
I lay the belt on a chair
and get her dinner bowl.
I hit the spoon against it, set it down
and watch her crawl to it,
pausing after each forward thrust of her legs
and when she takes her first bite,
I grab the belt and beat her across the back
until her tears, beads of salt-filled glass, falling,
shatter on the floor.

I move off, I let her eat,
while I get my dog's chain leash from the closet.
I whirl it around my head.
O daughter, so far, you've only had a taste of icing,
are you ready now for some cake?

Twenty-Year Marriage

You keep me waiting in a truck
with its one good wheel stuck in the ditch,
while you piss against the south side of a tree.
Hurry. I've got nothing on under my skirt tonight.
That still excites you, but this pickup has no windows
and the seat, one fake leather thigh,
pressed close to mine is cold.
I'm the same size, shape, make as twenty years ago,
but get inside me, start the engine;
you'll have the strength, the will to move.
I'll pull, you push, we'll tear each other in half.
Come on, baby, lay me down on my back.
Pretend you don't owe me a thing
and maybe we'll roll out of here,

leaving the past stacked up behind us;
old newspapers nobody's ever got to read again.

Emily Hiestand

Emily Hiestand (1947–).   Emily Hiestand grew up in Tennessee. She paints at the
Vernon Street Studios and lives in Cambridge, Massachusetts. Jorie Graham, who
selected her *Green the Witch-Hazel Wood* (1989) for the National Poetry Series, writes
that "with her radical trust in description as a guide to the moral life . . . she works
reason—kneads it, assaults it really—till it explodes once again into the magic and
mystery it truly is . . . [Her book] crackles like some source of energy we had no idea
we had lived without and now—of course—would not."

Planting in Tuscaloosa

Three women are walking in Alabama.
My mother and I help my grandmother walk
around the field where she planted and raised.
As we circle the land I think of the way
women will sometimes stroke a belly with child.
My uncle's tractor combs the deep red clay.
        Now she wears a housecoat.

Summers, I stayed with her and rode the glider
on her porch—cement painted pink.
I watched her wave a paper fan printed
with pictures of Jesus in unbelievable colors.
She waved away the sulphur smells that blew
at night from the Warrior River paper mill.
Once a man reading Sunday papers
in my bed asked me if I had page twelve;
I said I didn't have it. Then he asked
for page fifty; I said I didn't have it.
Then he asked for page seventy-three
and I said, "Go fish," and we laughed
for ten minutes and made love and laughed.
Those laughs were courtesy of my grandmother.
She played Go Fish with me for hours,
managing a dumb wedge of cards
while I was mesmerized by the distinctions
between diamonds and hearts. How
could any adult love a child enough

to play a game like Go Fish for hours?
Now she calls us to her room.

Every summer another tree was covered
by the swarming kudzu vines that grew
taller and taller than the men with machetes.
A glass kept on her Bible magnified the word.
The women snapped beans in Sister's parlor
and watched "As the World Turns" on TV.
"Laura, was that Brian with you in church?"
Snap. Ping into the metal colanders.
I tried always to get the whole string off,
counting how many were right, two, then a goof.
How did she get the beans to snap so,
and always get the whole string off
and watch television and talk all the time.
Now she is heaped with gladiolas.

Two women are walking in Alabama.
My mother and I walk arm and arm in her field.
The tractor harrows and dust begins to rise.
I stand ankle-deep in the field.
I am given her porcelain pitcher to keep.
Bits of clay cling to my feet.

Heather McHugh

Heather McHugh (1948–).   Heather McHugh was born in San Diego, California, and educated at Radcliffe College (B.A.) and the University of Denver (M.A.). She has published four books of poetry, *Dangers* (1977) and *A World of Difference* (1981), *To the Quick* (1987) and *Shades* (1988), and two of translation, *D'Après Tout: Poems by Jean Follain* (1981) and with Niko Boris, *Because the Sea Is Black,* poems by Blaga Dimitrova (1989). She has received fellowships from the National Endowment for the Arts, the Rockefeller Foundation, and the New York Arts Council. She teaches half the year at the University of Washington, Seattle, and spends the other half in the island community of Eastport, Maine. A continuing member of the nonresidential M.F.A. program for writers at Warren Wilson College, she has also taught at Columbia University, the University of California, Irvine, SUNY Binghamton, and as a Holloway lecturer at the University of California, Berkeley. McHugh, a poet of dazzling wit, takes on the full emotional range of relationships with, as Seamus Heaney puts it, "Lots of impulse and energy, *Sprezzatura, bravura.*"

I Knew I'd Sing

A few sashay, a few finagle.
Some make whoopee, some
make good. But most make
diddly-squat. I tell you this

is what I love about
America—the words it puts
in my mouth, the mouth where once
my mother rubbed

a word away with soap. The word
was *cunt.* She stuck that bar
of family-size in there
until there was no hole to speak of, so

she hoped. But still
I'm full of it—the cunt,
the prick, short u, short i,
the words that stood

for her and him. I loved
the thing they must have done,
the love they must have made, to make
an example of me. After my lunch of Ivory I said

vagina for a day or two, but knew
from that day forth which word struck home
the more like sex itself.
I knew when I was big I'd sing

a song in praise of cunt—I'd want
to keep my word, the one with teeth in it.
Even after I was raised, I swore
nothing but nothing would be beneath me.

The Matter Over

It is better to say "I am suffering" than to say "This landscape is ugly."

—Simone Weil

From the piling's kelp I drew
the starfish with its five blunt fingers.

First I thought the creature
less than handsome, less of a hand

than I expected, rigid, with a stumpy gray
asymmetry of grasp. It wasn't soft. It hardly moved. So maybe

it was dead? I couldn't see
beyond myself, until I turned

the matter over, and beheld
billions of unfamiliar

facts—minute transparent
footlets, feelers, stems

all waving to the quick, and then
the five large radials beginning

gradually to flail, in my slow sight,
and then, in my thin air,

to drown. I'd meant
to send it, as a gift, to you

who were my missing part,
so far inland. Instead

to a world the sighted have no rights to,
to the dark that's out of mind,

I made myself resign it,
flinging the hand from my hand.

To Have To

is an odd infinitive, in which
compulsion and possession meet
and share a word together.

Both propose, and both accept;
to have because it wants to hold;
have to, because it has no will.

But then there is
no past or present either.
Coming's going, in this match.

It's odd because they're one
and endless, in the end, in their
capacity to be attached . . .

Olga Broumas

Olga Broumas (1949–).   Born in Greece, Broumas became a student in the United
States in 1967. She is the seventy-second winner of the Yale Younger Poets award for
her volume *Beginning with O* (1977). The poems presented here are from her recent
book, *Soie Sauvage* (1980). Her diction, revealing no trace of a learned language, is
precise and daringly inventive. Her themes mirror personal drama and nature in the
New World and also reach into the ancient world of Greek islands and mythological
figures. Her loves, sung with brutal accuracy, are directed to both men and
women.

Landscape with Leaves and Figure

Passionate Love Is Temporary
Insanity the Chinese
say that day
I walked nine miles in the bowl
the hill makes coming round
and round avoiding
the road in
sane I realized a whole
week later at the time
I sank my crepe

soles in the spread
of leaves grass needles
bedding down the path
I took describing
every tree bush fern each
stone leaf stick
isolate
detail in the mind
one woman / it was icy cold / my nose
froze in the air lichen were dancing
up hundred-footed trees the ivy
dirndling up like glitter
flint I stood
there planted
firmly and I could not feel
the cold
wind rain the ivy glinting
savagely like mirrors on the skirts
the six-armed goddess dancing
a storm / wet / it was wet inside
the forest though no rain
was falling it was
sliding
down and you
meanwhile clear
cross-country from the snow
packs of Vermont two weeks one half
a honeydew papaya moon
were eating
while I rimmed the bowl
the woods make in the penetrating
silence between rains in
Oregon in
sane I realized a whole
week later and I said
since you had not yet
left Because
I love you Yes
you said I know that
day

Landscape with Next of Kin

Imagine father that you had a brother were
not an orphan singly that you had a twin
who moved away when he got married had
a kid a similar career whom you had not seen
but heard from frequently for thirty years
imagine meeting him some evening somewhere
familiar to you both not in the village but by
the sea / perhaps / you have

been talking for hours
and for many days
at ease in the proprietor's
gaze—he is young you are old he could have been
a soldier in your regiment that northern province
not so long ago / perhaps he is / you are

here this evening you and your brother seated at the damp
alloy table rusting in some seaside
Patra of the mind identical sighting
the prow of the ferry from Brindisi / perhaps / a woman

bows out from the throng
of tourists very feminine and very strong
resemblance to this man your brother you have never
married / yourself / tonight
are you sipping

the weak milk of your ouzo
having heard everything / at ease / on the other side
of the customs waiting for his daughter your
first blood kin is there anything
in the love you feel
swimming towards him as you did
nine months one heartbeat

pounding like an engine in those waters / is
there anything you won't forgive
her / him

Olga Broumas (1949) and Jane Miller (1949)

The following is from an extraordinary collection of mostly prose poems *Black Holes, Black Stockings* (1985) co-written by Broumas and Miller.

> Remember how close we sat in Sifnos having dinner by the water? You said in your country once you put the table *in* the water. You began the meal, and then what a great idea to move it over a little, it would cool you, it was that calm. You rolled your pants to the knee and poured drinks all around, the fishbones back to the sea. Lizards climb the stone outside the kitchen by the sea. Weeds and flowers grow out of the stone; the relatives spill out of the kitchen. The daughter is well educated or about to be. She serves us with the happy face of one who is leaving. You lifted your skirt walking home in the dark over the pebbles to sit. One night we saw the only other lovers—they were both fair, she blond and he gray—and their eyes moved only to each other and the sea, these two destinations. Now the sea once in a while slips a wave up to their feet, because a boat passes or for no reason, now the yellow moon divides the sea into fields.

Jane Miller

Jane Miller (1949–).   Born in New York City, Jane Miller was educated at Pennsylvania State University (B.A., 1970), California State University (M.A., 1975), and the University of Iowa (M.F.A., 1977). She has taught at the University of Iowa; Goddard College; the Writer's Community in New York City; Freehand, a learning community in Provincetown; and is now on the faculty at the University of Arizona. Her four books of poetry are *Many Junipers, Many Heartbeats, The Greater Leisures,* which won the Open Competition of the National Poetry Series, *Black Holes, Black Stockings* (1985), which she wrote in collaboration with Olga Broumas, and *American Odalisque* (1987). The poems of Jane Miller have the classical clarity of Sappho—everything is cut with light. Her wonderful odd eye gives us a careful fury of cumulative images, passions, reflections.

Memory at These Speeds

I love these hours alone I do
    not
        like them. Like them, I am
slow to divine
        meaning from change, meaning
I love you & remembering
          waking next
to you like a white gull against a white sky

            become blue
I feel detached, although I realize
this is the drift of happiness it is not
            my choice
                        yes I like you
for it. Faith

            for this moment is living
with a fear
            I will lose you or myself,
   each arousing
                  the other,
eternity!
            that spectacular hour in the afternoon
      when you arrive & suck me
            as if it were through time
we are reconciled
                  or in dream,
      the desert we return to
         heaven
                  all that disappears
      when we look back,
                        for this time we are lovers we are
moved by the sea
                  in a studio with aqua floorboards
      & white lamps now like stars inhabiting a pattern
            now random.
Never let ourselves be subject
                        to either dependence again
or pain. Where once there were so many
   words we had to choose
                  between us,
your sentence effortless as mine is fair.

Tilt

I am on a peninsula
forty miles out in the Atlantic
and have driven my car to a mechanic
to replace its ball joints.

I left it in Wellfleet
and am walking every half mile
and crying and walking every other
the four miles out to the harbor.
When I get there I intend to
pace the pier and receive
the appreciation of the fishermen.
I have a mind to fuck
one for the afternoon.
This probably won't happen, and not
because I'm not good looking, and tender
in grief. Anyway the cry
has become more
like a detonation, dry, brief.
It's all right. I'm not doing this
to forget, and I feel great
humor and communion. Standing on this pier
where my own two feet had been
on similar docks in Amsterdam,
Biarritz, Nice, Athens, I remember my mind
wandered even then
from the two lovers I happened to
have, traveling the sun to serve
our ends. Tomorrow,
why the hell on earth
even bring it up, like a tide
brackish, effervescent, pink,
familial, I'll be back in town
with my freedom to come and go
geared to the misconception
I want to. I wrote a good
friend and fruit grower, Mary Fisher,
a few weeks ago, it's funny,
Mary, I'm on a red bedspread
in The White Horse Inn in America,
you're on the other soiled coast, California,
I'm talking *broke* and more beautiful
than that day you saw me leaving
my husband many lovers back,
feeling rummy. Christ: girls,
art, money, I'm thirty-three,

this isn't TV, and there's a war on.
Do you want to live
forever? Or is that poetry,
a wild iris I was sent,
wasted at The White Horse
powerless to a fault,
one for everyone.

Marianne Boruch

Marianne Boruch (1950–).   Educated at the University of Illinois, Urbana (B.S.,
1972) and at the University of Massachusetts, Amherst (M.F.A., 1979), Marianne
Boruch has taught at the University of Maine, Farmington, the University of Wiscon-
sin, Tunghai University at Taichung, and is now an associate professor of English and
director of the writing program at Purdue University. She has received grants from
the National Endowment for the Arts and the Wisconsin Arts Board. Her strong
poems capture at once the actuality of the waking world and a dreamscape in which
everything seems to be slipping into the past in the instant of its apprehension.

After Supper in Madison, Wisconsin

Where they come from, I do not know
these dead
walking off their old confusions, 1928
or 1941, the war
just beginning over Sunday dinner.
Here gables in high roost
over forsythia, the same drunken bluebells
slow the vibrant grass.

I am walking west, early May, toward the end
of the century. Silence.
The dead hear it, nothing
but birds
louder than cars. Like a small child
the street wanders: brick wood airy trees.
Whole families lost
in such houses where memory presses
its body back into doorways and rooms. *I've got to know,* the dead
hiss, rigid at the windows, correcting,
quarreling. Gradually
porchlights claim each landing anyway

calling *home home.*
Darkness sets adrift the rest.

It's spring and spring and spring—as though
a mystery
to be found at the bottom of a sack.
So what, the dead whisper. So I look past
the new railing—the girl
in the day-glo sweatshirt
leaning icily against the slate blue door.
I am polite
to these dead, say, it *is* the same girl,
1928, 1941, the one you hated or loved
or just didn't believe. Cars
creep down the boulevard,
barely hum. And yes—the same boy, sullen,
lingers on the steps.

Carolyn Forche

Carolyn Forche (1950–).   Born and raised in Detroit, Michigan, she was the eldest
of seven children. Her *Gathering the Tribes* (1976) won the Yale Younger Poets
award; *The Country Between Us* (1982) was the Lamont Poetry Selection of the Acad-
emy of American Poets. She translated Claribel Alegria's *Flowers from the Volcano*
(1982) and wrote the text of *El Salvador: The Work of Thirty Photographers* (1983).
Forche has received fellowships from the Guggenheim Foundation and the National
Endowment for the Arts. While living in Lebanon, she contributed to National Public
Radio's "All Things Considered." She has also lived in El Salvador and South Africa.

The Vietnam War "marked" her generation, she has said. Although "To write out
of such extremity is to incise, with language, that same wound," she asserts that "those
who perish at the hands of others must not be forgotten . . . the[ir] memory . . . remains
in very few hands. I can't let go of that work if I am of that number."

Selective Service

We rise from the snow where we've
lain on our backs and flown like children,
from the imprint of perfect wings and cold gowns,
and we stagger together wine-breathed into town
where our people are building
their armies again, short years after
body bags, after burnings. There is a man

I've come to love after thirty, and we have
our rituals of coffee, of airports, regret.
After love we smoke and sleep
with magazines, two shot glasses
and the black and white collapse of hours.
In what time do we live that it is too late
to have children? In what place
that we consider the various ways to leave?
There is no list long enough
for a selective service card shriveling
under a match, the prison that comes of it,
a flag in the wind eaten from its pole
and boys sent back in trash bags.
We'll tell you. You were at that time
learning fractions. We'll tell you
about fractions. Half of us are dead or quiet
or lost. Let them speak for themselves
We lie down in the fields and leave behind
the corpses of angels.

The Memory of Elena

We spend our morning
in the flower stalls counting
the dark tongues of bells
that hang from ropes waiting
for the silence of an hour.
We find a table, ask for *paella,*
cold soup and wine, where a calm
light trembles years behind us.

In Buenos Aires only three
years ago, it was the last time his hand
slipped into her dress, with pearls
cooling her throat and bells like
these, chipping at the night—

As she talks, the hollow
clopping of a horse, the sound

of bones touched together.
The *paella* comes, a bed of rice
and *camarones,* fingers and shells,
the lips of those whose lips
have been removed, mussels
the soft blue of a leg socket.

This is not *paella,* this is what
has become of those who remained
in Buenos Aires. This is the ring
of a rifle report on the stones,
her hand over her mouth,
her husband falling against her.

These are the flowers we bought
this morning, the dahlias tossed
on his grave and bells
waiting with their tongues cut out
for this particular silence.

1977

San Onofre, California

We have come far south.
Beyond here, the oldest women
shelling limas into black shawls.
Portillo scratching his name
on the walls, the slender ribbons
of piss, children patting the mud.
If we go on, we might stop
in the street in the very place
where someone disappeared
and the words Come with us! we might
hear them. If that happened, we would
lead our lives with our hands
tied together. That is why we feel
it is enough to listen
to the wind jostling lemons,

to dogs ticking across the terraces,
knowing that while birds and warmer weather
are forever moving north,
the cries of those who vanish
might take years to get here.

1977

Jorie Graham

Jorie Graham (1951–).   Jorie Graham grew up in Italy and was educated at the
Sorbonne, New York University, Columbia University, and the University of Iowa.
She has written the books *Hybrids of Plants and of Ghosts* (1980), which received the
Great Lakes Colleges Award for the Best First Book of Poetry, *Erosion* (1983), and
The End of Beauty (1987). She has been awarded fellowships from the Guggenheim
Foundation, the Merrill Foundation, and the Bunting Institute. She teaches at the
University of Iowa. Helen Vendler has praised the "haunting indwelling musicality"
of her work. Graham postulates that "poems are, after all, dialogues between the song
of man and the silences of God."

The Hiding Place

The last time I saw it was 1968.
Paris, France. The time of the *disturbances.*
We had claims. Schools shut down.
Three million *workers* and *students* on strike.

Marches, sit-ins, helicopters, gas.
They stopped you at gunpoint asking for papers.

I spent eleven nights sleeping in the halls. Arguments.
Negotiations.
Hurrying in the dawn looking for a certain leader,
I found his face above an open street fire.
No, he said, tell them *no concessions.*
His voice above the fire as if there were no fire—

language floating everywhere above the sleeping bodies;
and crates of fruit donated in secret;
and torn sheets (for tear gas) tossed down from shuttered win-
dows;
and bread; and blankets, stolen from the firehouse.

The CRS (the government police) would swarm in around dawn
in small blue vans and round us up.
Once I watched the searchbeams play on some flames.
The flames push up into the corridor of light.

In the cell we were so crowded no one could sit or lean.
People peed on each other. I felt a girl
vomiting gently onto my back.
I found two Americans rounded up by chance,
their charter left that morning, they screamed, what were they
going to do?

Later a man in a uniform came in with a stick.
He started beating here and there, found the girl in her eighth
month.
He beat her frantically over and over.
He pummelled her belly. Screaming aren't you ashamed?

I remember the cell vividly,
but is it from a photograph? I think the shadows as I
see them still—the slatted brilliant bits
against the wall—I think they're true—but are they from a pho-
tograph?
Do I see it from inside now—his hands, her face—or

is it from the news account?
The strangest part of getting out again was *streets.*
The light running down them.
Everything spilling whenever the wall breaks.
And the air—thick with dwellings—the air filled—doubled—
as if the open

had been made to render—
the open squeezed for space until the hollows spill out,
story upon story of them
starting to light up as I walked out.
How thick was the empty meant to be?
What were we finding in the air?

What were we meant to find?
I went home slowly, sat in my rented room.
   Sat for a long time the window open,

   watched the white gauze curtain sluff this way then that
a bit—
   watched the air suck it out, push it back in. Lung
of the room with street cries in it. Watched until the lights
   outside made it gold, pumping gently.
Was I meant to get up again? I was inside. The century clicked by.
   The woman below called down *not to forget the*

   loaf. Crackle of helicopters. Voice on a loudspeaker issuing
warnings.
   They made agreements, we all returned to work.
The government fell but then it was all right again.
   The man above the fire, listening to my question,

the red wool shirt he wore: where is it? who has it?
   He looked straight back into the century: no concessions.
I took the message back.
   The look in his eyes—shoving out—into the open—
   expressionless with thought:
no—tell them *no*—

Brenda Hillman

Brenda Hillman (1951–).   Brenda Hillman received a B.A. from Pomona College
and an M.F.A. from the University of Iowa. Her *White Dress* (1985) won the Delmore
Schwartz Memorial Award from New York University and the Norma Farber First
Book Award from the Poetry Society of America. She received a National Endow-
ment for the Arts Fellowship to work on her second volume, *Fortress* (1989). She
teaches at St. Mary's College and lives in Kensington, California.

   These selections are from a series of poems, "Death Tractates," which will be
published as a chapbook, and which is part of her forthcoming *Bright Existence.* Like
many of Emily Dickinson's poems, "Death Tractates" responds to the inadequacy of
orthodox theology in the face of death; Hillman writes, "—No, the male heavens
wouldn't do." Written when her closest female mentor died suddenly at a young age,
these lyrics invent a liturgy to take a woman through her grief for a woman. Hillman's
poems shift tones with skill and speed; they are versatile, funny, sad, wild, quiet,
profound.

Reverse Seeing

—A fox ran across your path—pure totem!
You would never see it again;
likewise the loved one:

you stared hard into the rusty aftermath.

But things kept coming through the panel of death:
doves took off
outside the window: click click click,
(click)—gosh, their wings needed oiling—then

no more them!

You want to be like your dead friend?
You are like her. Writing
is dying. But the war
was not about borders it was about surrender—

Split Tractate

But I feared that her soul didn't
miss me. Didn't miss spring. That she was pre-
occupied, like a tourist, maybe not
moving around in the mind
of god but in the onyx
market, which was the exact same thing—

Help, mockingbird! don't say no!
Maybe she has forgotten us,
she has given us this priceless gift,
she has let us go.

I looked for her in anger,
behind sunsets,
along the iron tracks of the personal;
I looked for her in planes of agony
and she was quite close by.

They said I had to let go of her.
She said so too. Let go she said from the
What.
The screen between me and her.

But still I held on; holding on
is my specialty. I held on to her image,
to the moment of death, to the problem
with pronouns; maybe I'd learn.

Spring could let go couldn't it.
Vireos hung upside down from the cottonwood.
The old calm towhee at the feeder—it did not tarry.
Beautiful, average mornings: the scattered actual: grief
changed them only slightly.
Mornings waiting for the triple A,
of neighbors standing by their cars and chatting,

one pink kleenex
in the street—or is it a camellia—

then a man climbs up the shining ladder to a phone pole,
takes the spool of insulated wire and threads it—
Where?
To the heaven of messy souls
behind the bright new consciousness
or to the old Baptist heaven with its silverware—

so many heavens! Which was she in.
I wished she'd speak more clearly when I asked her
who was noticing her now.
What was "this" to her.

And the mockingbird stayed all morning with its row
of checkmarks and the verse that sounded like
teacher-teacher-teacher
police! police!
Maybe that bird was her—
so versatile; it did not cling—

Let go said the
What.
Let go said everything.

Sweet afternoons of exhaustion. Trips to the library
with the other moms. Taking the books
to the chrome mouth of the book deposit
and hesitating
before letting the slender paperback slide down
on its very own bardo journey;
Maybe I should have warned it
not to attach itself to its travels,

not to identify with the suffering,
that is the main thing.

What is this so-called
death anyway. Fat chickadees hop up
the "dead" fennel. A little
cowlick sprouts from the "dead" place
in the pine. Petals die
and in a day, what looks like mascara brushes
fall from the birthday tulips.

Is the "falling" or are the tulips *it*.
What is this so-called
death what is it.

Let go said the so-called
What.
Let go said everything.

Even the poem said it.
Said it would come in its own good time
as I leaned forward to see death's face
though there was always this gap
between my hand and the page,

I had only to trace the pen
over the words;
the poem was already written—

Winged One

—Not unwillingly, but not with lightness either,
not sure of itself
but with great hope in its energy,
the mockingbird still sat there at the end of spring,
speckle-sided, flapping its wings up high,
stealing whole passages, like a young poet—

and what it could not discover
it was taught: break the rules
with your singing, don't be normal, shatter the plot.

You think her voice collided with yours?
All right. The voice collided.

But what if the outside voice wasn't true?
What if, despite your false calm,
your brokenness, your self-deception—
in fact, when you were most broken,
her heaven was you?—

Joy Harjo

Joy Harjo (1951–).   Born in Tulsa, Oklahoma, Joy Harjo grew up there and in
New Mexico. She is a member of the Creek tribe. She attended the Institute of
American Indian Arts in Santa Fe, and received a B.A. from the University of New
Mexico in 1976 and an M.F.A. from the University of Iowa in 1978. She is a
filmmaker, painter, tenor saxophonist, and associate professor of English at Arizona
State in Tucson. Her books include a chapbook, *The Last Song.* She has also had
published *Secret from the Center of the World,* with photographs by Stephen Strom, and
three books of poetry, *What Moon Drove Me to This?, She Had Some Horses,* and *In Mad
Love and War* (1990). Among her awards are an Academy of American Poets Award
at the University of New Mexico, a National Endowment for the Arts Fellowship, and
Arizona Commission on the Arts Fellowship.

Mercy

Mercy
       on this morning where in the air is a flash
of what could be the salvation of spring.
                         After all this winter

I mean, it wasn't just devil snow that rode us hard.
Mail me to Jamaica.
                        I want to lay out on steaming beaches.
Find my way back through glacier ice another way.
Forget the massacres, proclamations of war
                                    rumors of wars.
I won't pour rifle shot through the guts of someone
I'm told is my enemy.
                        Hell, my own enemy is right here.
Can you look inside, see past the teeth worn down
by meat and anger,
                can you see?
                        Sometimes the only filter
is a dead cat in the road.
                        Sucks your belly up to your teeth
in fear of what might happen to you; all your sins
chase you in the street,
                string what you thought was the only you
into a greasy field. I want to enter the next world
    filled with food, wine
                and the finest fishing.
Safe, so safe, like a beach in Jamaica
    where blood stains have already
soaked through to the bottom of the Caribbean
    so you don't have to see
                        unless this light
becomes a bayonet of sound, hands of fire
to lead you to yourself
                until you cry
                        mercy.

Rita Dove

Rita Dove (1952–).   Born in Akron, Ohio, Rita Dove is a graduate of the University of Miami (B.A.) and the University of Iowa Writer's Workshop (M.F.A.). She teaches at Arizona State University. Her books of poetry include *The Yellow House on the Corner* (1980), *Museum* (1983), *Thomas and Beulah* (1986), and *Grace Notes* (1989). She has also had published a book of short stories, *The Fifth Sunday* (1985). Among her honors and awards are the Pulitzer Prize for *Thomas and Beulah,* the Academy of American Poets 1986 Peter I. B. Lavan Younger Poets Award, and National Endowment for the Arts, Fulbright/Hays, and Guggenheim fellowships. Whether speaking for the ancient Chinese or Romans or the American slaves, Dove gives history flesh and breath in her powerfully empathic poems.

Someone's Blood

I stood at 6 A.M. on the wharf,
thinking: *This is Independence, Missouri.*
I am to stay here. The boat goes on to New Orleans.
My life seemed minutes old, and here it was ending.

I was silent, although she clasped me
and asked forgiveness for giving me life.
As the sun broke the water into a thousand needles
tipped with the blood from someone's finger,

the boat came gently apart from the wharf.
I watched till her face could not distinguish itself
from that shadow floated on broken sunlight.
I stood there. I could not help her. I forgive.

David Walker (1785–1830)

Free to travel, he still couldn't be shown how lucky
he was: *They strip and beat and drag us about*
like rattlesnakes. Home on Brattle Street, he took in the sign
on the door of the slop shop. All day at the counter—
white caps, ale-stained pea coats. Compass needles,
eloquent as tuning forks, shivered, pointing north.
Evenings, the ceiling fan sputtered like a second pulse.
Oh Heaven! I am full!! I can hardly move my pen!!!

On the faith of an eye-wink, pamphlets were stuffed
into trouser pockets. Pamphlets transported
in the coat linings of itinerant seamen, jackets
ringwormed with salt traded drunkenly to pursers
in the Carolinas, pamphlets ripped out, read aloud:
Men of colour, who are also of sense.
Outrage. Incredulity. Uproar in state legislatures.

We are the most wretched, degraded and abject set
of beings that ever lived since the world began.
The jewelled canaries in the lecture halls tittered,

pressed his dark hand between their gloves.
Every half-step was no step at all.
Every morning, the man on the corner strung a fresh
bunch of boots from his shoulders. "I'm happy!" he said.
"I never want to live any better or happier than
when I can get a-plenty of boots and shoes to clean!"

A second edition. A third.
The abolitionist press is *perfectly appalled.*
Humanity, kindness and the fear of the Lord
does not consist in protecting devils. A month—
his person (is that all?) found face-down
in the doorway at Brattle Street,
his frame slighter than friends remembered.

The House Slave

The first horn lifts its arm over the dew-lit grass
and in the slave quarters there is a rustling—
children are bundled into aprons, cornbread

and water gourds grabbed, a salt pork breakfast taken.
I watch them driven into the vague before-dawn
while their mistress sleeps like an ivory toothpick

and Massa dreams of asses, rum and slave-funk.
I cannot fall asleep again. At the second horn,
the whip curls across the backs of the laggards—

sometimes my sister's voice, unmistaken, among them.
"Oh! pray," she cries. "Oh! pray!" Those days
I lie on my cot, shivering in the early heat,

and as the fields unfold to whiteness,
and they spill like bees among the fat flowers,
I weep. It is not yet daylight.

The Abduction

The bells, the cannons, the houses black with crepe,
all for the great Harrison! The citizenry of Washington
clotted the avenue—I among them, Solomon Northrup
from Saratoga Springs, free papers in my pocket, violin
under arm, my new friends Brown and Hamilton by my side.

Why should I have doubted them? The wages were good.
While Brown's tall hat collected pennies at the tent flap,
Hamilton's feet did a jig on a tightrope,
pigs squealed invisibly from the bleachers and I fiddled.

I remember how the windows rattled with each report.
Then the wine, like a pink lake, tipped.
I was lifted—the sky swivelled, clicked into place.

I floated on water I could not drink. Though the pillow
was stone, I climbed no ladders in that sleep.

I woke and found myself alone, in darkness and in chains.

Louise Erdrich

Louise Erdrich (1954–).   Born and raised in Wahpeton, North Dakota, Louise
Erdrich is of German-American and Chippewa descent, and is a member of the Turtle
Mountain band of Chippewa. She was educated at Dartmouth College and lives in
New Hampshire with her husband/collaborator novelist Michael Dorris and their
children. Writing with accomplished authority, she ranges from learned theological
meditation to the milk, wonder, and muck of childbirth and children. In addition to
her two books of poetry, *Jacklight* (1984) and *Baptism of Desire* (1989), she has written
three highly acclaimed and best-selling novels, *Love Medicine, The Beet Queen* (1986),
and *Tracks* (1989).

Fooling God

I must become small and hide where he cannot reach.
I must become dull and heavy as an iron pot.
I must be tireless as rust and bold as roots
growing through the locks on doors
and crumbling the cinderblocks

of the foundations of his everlasting throne.
I must be strange as pity so he'll believe me.
I must be terrible and brush my hair
so that he finds me attractive.
Perhaps if I invoke Clare, the patron saint of television.
Perhaps if I become the images
passing through the cells of a woman's brain.

I must become very large and block his sight.
I must be sharp and impetuous as knives.
I must insert myself into the bark of his apple trees,
and cleave the bones of his cows. I must be the marrow
that he drinks into his cloud-wet body.
I must be careful and laugh when he laughs.
I must turn down the covers and guide him in.
I must fashion his children out of playdough, blue, pink, green.
I must pull them from between my legs
and set them before the television.

I must hide my memory in a mustard grain
so that he'll search for it over time until time is gone.
I must lose myself in the world's regard and disparagement.
I must remain this person and be no trouble.
None at all. So he'll forget.
I'll collect dust out of reach,
a single dish from a set, a flower made of felt,
a tablet the wrong shape to choke on.

I must become essential and file everything
under my own system,
so we can lose him and his proofs and adherents.
I must be a doubter in a city of belief
that hails his signs (the great footprints
long as limousines, the rough print on the wall).
On the pavement where his house begins
fainting women kneel. I'm not among them
although they polish the brass tongues of his lions
with their own tongues
and taste the everlasting life

The Glass and the Bowl

The father pours the milk from his glass
into the cup of the child,
and as the child drinks
the whiteness, opening
her throat to the good taste
eagerly, the father is filled.
He closes the refrigerator
on its light, he walks out
under the bowl of frozen darkness
and nothing seems withheld from him.
Overhead, the burst ropes of stars,
the buckets of craters,
the chaos of heaven, absence
of refuge in the design.
Yet down here, his daughter
in her quilts, under patterns
of diamonds and novas,
full of rich milk,
sleeping.

Sunflowers

When I walk into their bedroom at night
their cries fill my own mouth
so full of accurate misery,
heat flush, a stabbing in the gums,
something blind, with many hooks.
I drag the older one up into my arms
and talk until she opens her eyes.
The other
with her punishing beauty
ferments in a ball, soaked,
hot and vinegary.
I wash her.
The rag is sour.
But the talcum I shake into my palm
is dry and sweet.

Slowly, with both my hands,
I smooth along the hairline, throbbing with attention,
across the wishbone, the heart
vivid as a light,
down the arms, their tiny velvet muscles,
the arching torso, missing only the cleft
inside the diaper,
then the fat thighs, wet backs of the knees,
and the feet, small wooden apples.
Now their father brings the cold milk in bottles.
The doors shut.
We plunge into a dense sleep
that opens to a field of sunflowers,
each one of them a glowing clock,
turned, soft and bristling, to the bronze
face of the old god
who floats over us and burns.

Ninth Month

This is the last month, the petrified forest
and the lake which has long since turned to grass.
The sun roars over, casting its light and absence
in identical seams. One day. Another.
The child sleeps on in its capsized boat.

The hull is weathered silver and our sleep is green and dark.
Dreams of the rower, hands curled in the shape of oars
listening for the cries of the alabaster birds. But all
is silent, the animals hurled into quartz.
Our bed is the wrecked blue island of time and love.

Black steeples, black shavings of magnetized iron,
through which the moon parades her wastes,
drawing the fruit from the female body,
pulling water like blankets up other shores.

Then slowly the sky is colored in, the snow
falls evenly into the blackness of cisterns.

The steel wings fan open that will part us from each other
and the waves break and fall according to their discipline.

Breath that moves on the waters.
Small boat, small rower.

Birth

When they were wild
When they were not yet human
When they could have been anything,
I was on the other side ready with milk to lure them,
And their father, too, each name a net in his hands.

Cathy Song

Cathy Song (1955–).   Born in Honolulu, Hawaii, Cathy Song received her B.A.
from Wellesley College in 1977, and an M.A. in creative writing from Boston
University in 1981. Her first book, *Picture Bride,* was chosen for the Yale Series of
Younger Poets by Richard Hugo, who introduces it with high praise. *Frameless
Windows, Squares of Light* appeared in 1988. She lives in Honolulu with her husband
and two children.

The Youngest Daughter

The sky has been dark
for many years.
My skin has become as damp
and pale as rice paper
and feels the way
mother's used to before the drying sun
parched it out there in the fields.

   Lately, when I touch my eyelids,
my hands react as if
I had just touched something
hot enough to burn.
My skin, aspirin colored,
tingles with migraine. Mother
has been massaging the left side of my face

especially in the evenings
when the pain flares up.

This morning
her breathing was graveled,
her voice gruff with affection
when I wheeled her into the bath,
She was in a good humor,
making jokes about her great breasts,
floating in the milky water
like two walruses,
flaccid and whiskered around the nipples.
I scrubbed them with a sour taste
in my mouth, thinking:
six children and an old man
have sucked from these brown nipples.

I was almost tender
when I came to the blue bruises
that freckle her body,
places where she has been injecting insulin
for thirty years. I soaped her slowly,
she sighed deeply, her eyes closed.
It seems it has always
been like this: the two of us
in this sunless room,
the splashing of the bathwater.

In the afternoons
when she has rested,
she prepares our ritual of tea and rice,
garnished with a shred of gingered fish,
a slice of pickled turnip,
a token for my white body.
We eat in the familiar silence.
She knows I am not to be trusted,
even now planning my escape.
As I toast to her health
with the tea she has poured,
a thousand cranes curtain the window,
fly up in a sudden breeze.

Aliki Barnstone

Aliki Barnstone (1956–).   Born in New Haven, Connecticut, raised in Indiana, educated at Brown University (B.A. and M.A.) Aliki Barnstone is now in the Ph.D. program in English at the University of California, Berkeley. At present, she lives with her husband in Madison, Wisconsin, and teaches at Marquette University. She is author of the books *The Real Tin Flower* (with an introduction by Anne Sexton, 1968) and *Windows in Providence* (1981). She has traveled to Mexico, Guatemala, Spain, China, Burma, among other places, but most often to Greece, where she and her family live in a mountain village on the island of Seriphos.

Jack's Defeat Creek

My old flame lives by Jack's Defeat Creek
Where the privets are in flower, fragrant,
    Abundant with bees; three children tumble
In the yard; and a group of friends
Cooks outside, grabbing their bellies,

Laughing about how much they have to lose.
My old friend lives by Jack's Defeat Creek.
    He and his wife don't touch.
Their son pinches the heads of flowers
Because, I'm angry, he says.

If I saw them kiss it might be worse.
This is the house that Jack built
    Where I swing on the porch,
The guest the children sit beside.
My friends laugh, "No more hot peppers!"

Oh, we still have our appetite,
But can't stand the consequences.
    My old flame takes my hand.
We're here to do the work of love, he says,
And what is raising children but the work

Of love? I say I like being
Alone, but mean I want to be alone
    With someone on that first hill of passion
When we were all confused, when Jack
Fell down and broke his crown

And Jill came tumbling after her
Defeat. Oh, but who is Jack?
   Who fell in the creek in dire defeat
And was it by woe or by war?
It's Jack in Jack's Defeat Creek.

Sky Burial

Snowlands Hotel. Before dawn in one of the dormitories
David is up first, moving from bed to bed waking us gently.
We mount our clanking Flying Pigeon bikes and ride out of town

On the dusty road, telling each other our dreams.
Travelers' word is, if a fire's burning there will be a burial.
The fire burns. We park our bicycles by a shallow river

And roll up our pants. Water so icy that I bend over
On the opposite shore, breathing slowly, coaxing my feet
From the pain. Already a silhouette of vultures

Gathered on the mountain above us. A monk in yellow robes
Bright in the half-light chants, hits a tambourine and cymbal.
A young woman in an animal skin coat nurses a child,

The boy and girl beside her talk and laugh like spectators
At a Chinese soccer game. An older man spins something
Like a large, long, extravagantly decorated hat atop a broomstick;

Colored rings and ribbons float up, chime, and relax
With each turn. Now six men stamp out the fire and cross
To a large boulder where they undo two squarish bundles.

Two corpses roll out in fetal position, naked,
Their gender and age unintelligible. Laying them out
On their bellies, the men start their work. Sun

Begins to show us color on the ridges of the mountains,
Spreading, illuminating this rocky valley
Where starting at the necks the corpses are skinned,

The sheets of skin tossed to the men behind,
Who cut them into small squares;
The muscles are pulled from bone, limbs disjointed from body,

Bones crushed in absorbing white powder with a rock.
It is like a butcher shop. Pounding, hacking, slapping,
Hundreds of vultures wait on the rocks or circle

Or, swooping down to the boulder too early, are shooed away
By the corpse-cutters. I cringe when they get to the feet,
And keep looking back to my bicycle, which is delicate,

Dark, pretty by the whitened river. By now it is light;
The city is awake: trucks and tractors rumble,
Loudspeakers have resumed broadcasting political homilies.

I pass my waterbottle to friends. Some of us sit alone and stare.
Some of us hold each other. A few look through binoculars.
Everything is clicking, rhythmic:

Chanting; voices directing from the central government;
Chopping; the river hisses; vultures glide or preen;
Small reverent, nervous, or revolted gestures of tourists.

Supports and resistances move. For now and perhaps
For a while afterward my fears are merely furniture
I can walk around or discard. I will be

Like those two—dismembered, insensible, incomprehensible—
But—lucky accident—my flesh aches and lusts.
At last the corpse-cutter wraps the head in a cloth,

Holds it up to the sky, prays, places it in a hollow,
And smashes it with a rock.
Two others cross to the flat where we stand

And drive us back a few steps. Bloody hands and bloody knives.
One of them taps me with his blade.
I check my sleeve for a stain, but I'm clean.

I've read the ground here, frozen most of the year,
Is no good for burial. There's too little timber for cremation.
When the soul is gone, the body means nothing.

Sometimes the Tibetans leave their dead
In a river to be eaten by fish.
We say dust to dust. This is flesh to flesh.

Vultures, symbols of peace,
The carnivore self that does not kill,
Circle huge, horrible, beautiful, black-white in the blue.

The white V's of their bodies and their wingtip feathers
Spread like black fingers in the sky
Of turquoise the Tibetans wear. The vultures eat.

I must get my visa at the Nepalese consulate.
As we ride back together Anna says, "I felt we were no better
Than the vultures." "Really?" I say. I'm enjoying

The view of the Potala, people selling their wares,
My legs peddling, the clanking bike, the sun on my face.
I search for some guilt, but find nothing—

Only this happiness, wind, elation, breath circling.

August 2, 1985
Lhasa, Tibet

Ntozake Shange

Ntozake Shange (20th century). With a B.A. from Barnard College and an M.A. in American Studies from the University of Southern California, Shange has succeeded in accomplishing the most unlikely literary feat: bringing poetry to a mass audience of theatergoers in the Broadway production *For Colored Girls Who Have Considered Suicide, When The Rainbow Is Enuf* (1975) and at the same time using extravagant, elliptical black speech as the basic ingredient of her poetry. Her new volume is *Nappy Edges* (1978).

from For Colored Girls Who Have Considered Suicide When the Rainbow Is Enuf

at 4:30 AM
she rose
movin the arms & legs that trapped her
she sighed affirmin the sculptured man
& made herself a bath
of dark musk oil egyptian crystals
& florida water to remove his smell
to wash away the glitter
to watch the butterflies melt into
suds & the rhinestones fall beneath
her buttocks like smooth pebbles
in a missouri creek
layin in water
she became herself
ordinary
brown braided woman
with big legs & full lips
reglar
seriously intendin to finish her
night's work
she quickly walked to her guest
straddled on her pillows & began
      'you'll have to go now /
        i've
      a lot of work to do / & i
        cant
      with a man around / here
        are yr pants /
      there's coffee on the
        stove / its been

very nice / but i cant see
you again /
you got what you came
for / didnt you'
& she smiled
he wd either mumble curses bout crazy bitches
or sit dumbfounded
while she repeated
    'i cdnt possibly wake up / with
    a strange man in my bed / why
    dont you go home'
she cda been slapped upside the head
or verbally challenged
but she never waz
& the ones who fell prey to the
dazzle of hips painted with
orange blossoms & magnolia scented wrists
had wanted no more
than to lay between her sparklin thighs
& had planned on leavin before dawn
& she had been so divine
devastatingly bizarre the way
her mouth fit round
& now she stood a
reglar colored girl
fulla the same malice
livid indifference as a sistah
worn from supportin a wd be hornplayer
or waitin by the window
    & they knew
    & left in a hurry
she wd gather her tinsel &
jewels from the tub
& laugh gayly or vengeful
she stored her silk roses by her bed
& when she finished writin
the account of her exploit in a diary
embroidered with lilies & moonstones
she placed the rose behind her ear
& cried herself to sleep.

Roberta Hill Whiteman

Roberta Hill Whiteman (20th century).   Roberta Hill Whiteman grew up in Green Bay, Wisconsin, and worked for a year in Minneapolis in the Poets-in-the-Schools program. She has taught at Sinte Gleska College, Rosebud, South Dakota. Her poems have appeared in numerous magazines, among them, *American Poetry Review, Poetry Northwest,* and *Cut Bank,* and in collections of Native American poetry.

A Nation Wrapped in Stone
for Susan Iron Shell

When night shadows slipped across the plain, I saw a man
beside his horse, sleeping where neither man nor horse
had been. I've prayed
to a star that lied. The spirits near the ceiling of your room,
did they leave on horseback, turning dew into threads
by moonlight?
In wild stretch of days, you didn't fear ashes or weeping.
We, left behind, can't warm sunlight.
Isaac, you left with the wind.

The chokecherry grows slower. I held your trembling wife,
and windows trembled in our north room. The creek gnaws
remaining snow. Our blood runs pale.
You taught us to be kind to one another. Now we wake, ques-
    tioning
our dreams. Nighthawks in warm fog. A nation wrapped in stone.
What do nurses
know of hay, of scents that float broken between canyons,
of strength in a worn face? You wept love, not death.
Around your bed, owls stood.

The north wind hunts us with music, enough pain
to set fires in ancient hills. West winds growl
around Parmalee.
The tanned, uneven banks will hold more frost. Unlike dust
we cannot die from tears. You've settled
on a quiet prairie. Shrouded eyes
in thickets give a reason to contain
this heavy rind. We are left with grief, sinking boneward,
and time to watch rain soak the trees.

Depot in Rapid City

When the last bus leaves, moths stream toward lights
like litter in wind. One by one, bulbs dim. The ticket man
locks up, talks of ancestors pale from dreaming.
In this corner, sleep is ugly, the moon vigilant.
Here, hatred taps along sidewalks. He dreams
of wild buses and the one percent he cannot see. You look
down corridors, where building edges whirr at the night,
to find an aged Indian gnawing glass.
Businessmen rub the medicine stones, and wear
crisp smiles that wrinkle in daylight. Muffled,
the heartbeat continues, abandoned stars haunt
the reservations. Clear as tracks,
are callings and cold signals on the wind.

Lines for Marking Time

Women know how to wait here.
They smell dust on wind and know you haven't come.
I've grown lean walking along dirt roads,
under a glassy sun, whispering to steps.
Twenty years I've lived on ruin. When I escaped
they buried you. All that's left is a radio
with a golden band. It smells of heat,
old baseball games, a shimmering city inside.
The front door has stopped banging and the apple tree
holds an old tire strange children swing in.

This house with broken light has lost me
now when the sweet grass dries. Its scent lingers
in the living room among sewing and worn-out shoes.
In your silence, I grew visions for myself, and received
a name no one could live up to. Blood rises
on hot summer wind, rose petals trickle
past rough solemn wood. Hear the distant sobbing?
An Indian who's afraid of tears. She charms her eyes
to smiling, waits for the new blue star. Answers
never come late.

Look west long enough, the moon will grow
inside you. Coyote hears her song, he'll teach you now.
Mirrors follow trails of blood and lightning.
Mother needs the strength of one like you. Let blood
dry, but seize the lightning. Hold it like your mother
rocks the trees. In your fear, watch the road, breathe deeply.
Indians know how to wait.

Linda Bierds

Linda Bierds (20th century).   Linda Bierds grew up in Anchorage, Alaska. She has
written two books of poems, *Flights of the Harvest-Mare* (1985) and *The Stillness, the
Dancing* (1988). She has received a Pushcart Prize in Poetry and fellowships from the
National Endowment for the Arts and the Artist Trust Foundations of Washington and
edits the publications of the University of Washington's Women's Information Cen-
ter. She has taught poetry in the schools and was a docent at Seattle's Woodland Park
Zoo. Her poems, which are frequently in the third person and based on historical
events, explore the extraordinary interstices of past and present, the psyches of human
and horse. In her own words, "Here is the world of the world."

The Stillness, The Dancing

> *I am indefinitely capable of wonder.*   —Federico Fellini

Long ago, in the forests of southern Europe,
just south of Mâcon, a woman died in childbirth.
She was taken, by custom, to the small slate
lip of a mountain. Legs bound at the knees
she was left facing west, thick with her still child.

Century by century, nothing disturbed them

so that now
the bones of the woman cup the small bones
of the child: the globe of its head angled
there, in the paddle and stem of her hips.

It is winter, just after midday. Slowly,
shudder by civilized shudder, a train slips over
the mountain, reveals to its weary riders

something white, then again, something
white at the side of the eye. They straighten,

place their lips to the glass, and there, far
below, this delicate, bleached pattern,
like the spokes of a bamboo cage.

What, someone whispers, and What, What,
word after word bouncing back from its blossom
of vapor, the woman and child appearing,
disappearing, as the train slips down through the alders—

until they are brands on the eyelid, until they are
stories, until, thick-soled and silent,
each rider squats with a blessing of ocher.

And so there are stories. Mortar. A little stratum
under the toenails. A train descends from a mountain,
levels out, circles a field where a team of actors
mimics a picnic. The billowing children.
On the table, fruit, a great calabash of chilled fish.
And over it all, a beloved uncle, long mad,
sits in the crotch of an oak tree.

He hears to his right, the compressed blare
of a whistle—each sound wave approaching shorter, shorter,
like words on a window, then just as the engine passes,
the long playing out.
He smiles as the blare seeps over
the actors, the pasture, the village

where now, in the haze of a sudden snowfall,
a film crew, dressed for a picnic, coaxes a peacock
to the chilled street. Six men on their knees
chirruping, laughing, snow lifting in puffs
from the spotlights. And the peacock,
shanks and yellow spurs high-stepping, high-stepping,
slowly unfolds its breathless fan, displays
to a clamor of boxcars, clubcars—

where riders, excited,
traveling for miles with an eyeful of bones
see now their reversal.

In an ecstasy of color the peacock dips,
revolves to the slow train:
each rider pressed to a window,
each round face courted in turn.

Susan Howe

Susan Howe (20th century).   Susan Howe was born in Boston, and lives with her
husband and son in Guilford, Connecticut. Her daughter is a painter in New York
City. She herself began her career as a visual artist. Howe is the author of many books
of poetry, including *The Western Borders* (1976), *Pythagorean Silence* (1982), *Defenestra-
tion of Prague* (1983), *Articulation of Sound Forms in Time* (1987). Her work has been
influenced by concrete poetry. Her book of criticism *My Emily Dickinson* (1985) is one
of the most highly esteemed readings of Dickinson. Marjorie Perloff points out that
"in Howe's work there is virtually no 'I-centered' mode." Yet in her many historical
re-creations, the I-center is predominant. Perloff points out that the "emotive contours
[of her work] depend upon the collisions (and sometimes, it may be, collusions) of
three codes—the historical, the mythic, the linguistic—all three, it should be added,
as informed by an urgent, if highly individual, feminist perspective."

from Speeches at the Barriers

9.

Passion
and intellectual articulation

Truth and glory

as forms of beauty
Proteus

formlessness
Possibility of discovering

anything
anything

foreshadowed words of all
wandering

Full volumes
confederacies of volumes

near and far a fugue of fear

crisp aphorisms die out

the Seventy Interpreters
—old men who sail off

Measurable things
My beginning from beginning

pleasure of eden (eastward)
translation

Death
an opinion or imagination

Long lives of the Patriarchs

walkers on hills
language

Strides of the sun in golden
Inaccessible proof

Day falling and decaying

number of times in all things

from **Hope Atherton's Wanderings**

To Kin I call in the Iron-Woods
Turn I to dark Fells last alway

Theirs was an archheathen theme
Soon seen stumbled in lag Clock

Still we call bitterly bitterly
Stern norse terse ethical pathos

Archaic presentiment of rupture
Voicing desire no more from here

Far flung North Atlantic littorals

Lif sails off longing for life
Baldr soars on Alfather's path

Rubble couple on pedestal
Rubble couple Rhythm and Pedestal

Room of dim portraits here there
Wade waist deep maidsworn men

Cumbled masonry windwept hickory

Diana O'Hehir

Diana O'Hehir (20th century).   Growing up in Berkeley, California, Diana O'Hehir worked ten years in the labor movement, then earned an M.A. and Ph.D. from Johns Hopkins University. She is professor of English and Creative Writing at Mills College. Though she wrote poetry as a child and adolescent, she didn't write again for twenty years. She writes that she began "to write poetry late in life as a result of Plath, Shelley, Keats, Blake, and a year of life crisis":

I was drunk on personal emotional impact and on Shelley; his brilliant Italian landscape and my brilliant California landscape—I saw it all for the first time as if it were happening for the first time—the poetry and the real world were inextricably merged in my perception.

True to her description of her rediscovery of poetry, her poems are immediate, move swiftly, and contain striking images—they are an awakening. She is both a poet and a novelist. Her volumes of poetry are *Summoned* (1976), *The Power to Change Geography*, published in the Princeton Series of Contemporary Poets (1979), *Home Free* (1988); her novels, *I Wish This War Were Over* (1984) and *The Bride Who Ran Away* (1988).

Home Free

Inch by inch along the bed,
Growing more compact, his arms pulled up like bird's wings
(My father is almost ninety),
I love you, I say over and over,
Until I read in *Time* Magazine that saying this holds the dying
    back;
They get polite, they hang around to thank you.
I love you, I say,
Under my breath.

In Bangkok you can buy a bird in front of the temple
For twenty cents. It's not to eat
Nor to listen to nor to admire but to
Set free.
Spring the door with your plastic diner's card, wait for the
    scrabble, the
Head poked out the door, air by your face,
And up he goes.

Riding the San Francisco Train

Some day I'll go to San Francisco,
Climb on to the old red train,
Cross over the bridge to the far side,
And be different, simple, and plain.

Those shallow plain houses
Where nothing much ever happens,
Their panes of glass innocent as the back of a dog's eye.
People trudge upstairs in those houses, carrying wash.

Everyone knows his place,
God bubbles up through the evening beer,
The jukebox colors smell of candy,
The gold dust plant gets polished with car wax,
And God comes in again on the late movie,
Orders tomorrow's box lunch, orders no real pain,
Says put chocolate in the thermos.

I'll live there keeping my secret
Powerful as the magic grasshopper that creaked by the well.
No one will guess my true house:
Four floors of guilt, basement to attic,
Acres of garden, wet with confrontation,
Pain that goes stolid because everyone is thinking.

I'll live there, not ever thinking,
I'll have a son and a daughter,
Keeping my secret, until at seventy
I ride out to my own deep water.

Katha Pollitt

Katha Pollitt (20th century).   Born in New York City, where she now lives, Katha
Pollitt attended Radcliffe College and Columbia University. She is the recipient of
numerous grants and awards, including The Robert Frost Award from *The Nation* and
the Discovery Award from the Poetry Center of the 92nd Street Y. Her poems have
appeared in *Shenandoah, Atlantic Monthly,* the *New Yorker, Paris Review, Ploughshares,*
and *Poetry.* Her outstanding first volume of poems, *Antarctic Traveller,* was published
in 1982.

Happiness Writes White

So what good is it? Let's be sad,
wear melancholy like an old brown sweater
patched at the elbows and smelling of our own funk.
The coffee cups pile up on the little table,
pages turn, electric lights come on—
it would be good to have a dog, you think,
one with grave eyes and an understanding of life,
it would be good

to go down to the docks and watch the freighters
idly listing in the oily water,
to smoke a cigarette and look out at the sea
and then walk home in the gathering evening,
at a measured pace, still hearing the voice of the sea
that speaks to you like a friend, of serious things
so simply and quietly
you barely notice the sky blanch after rain
or the woman coming out of the subway

carrying an immense bouquet of white lilac
wrapped in white tissue paper, like a torch.

Mary Jo Salter

Mary Jo Salter (20th century).   Born in Grand Rapids, Michigan, Mary Jo Salter
was educated at Harvard and Cambridge universities. She has received a National
Endowment for the Arts Fellowship, a Discovery/*The Nation* prize, and has been
poet-in-residence at the Frost Place. Her book *Unfinished Painting* (1989), from which
the following poem was selected, was the Lamont Poetry Selection for 1988 of the
Academy of American Poets. Her first book was *Henry Purcell in Japan* (1985).

The Upper Story

As Emily Dickinson
would not come down, I'm
sorry, but I've felt the need to climb
the worn steps to her room,
winding up the stair
as if into her inner ear.

Art, as she once said,
is *a House that tries to be haunted,*
and as I stand
on the landing where she curled in shadow
to follow the piano
and soprano voice of Mabel Todd

(her editor years later—
who now graciously accepted
a poem and glass of sherry in place
of having seen her face),
this would become that House.
No trespass can erase

what she once made of it—
that gate she opened, resolute
to escape, and just as quickly shut:
*I think I was held in check by some
invisible agent . . .* And when she wrote
Again—his voice is at the door—

here is the door she meant.
Her room, probably Spartan
even when lived in, now holds but few
fabled artifacts: a snow-white
coverlet; a "sleigh bed," narrow
like a wooden shoe; a snipped

lily of a dress, limp in the closet;
a wilted hatbox; a woven basket
she'd lower, something like Rapunzel,
full of gingerbread.
Or so our guide has said. Yet
devoted to the genuine

as she was—first jasmine of the season,
hummingbird and snake—
I doubt she would have taken umbrage
when learned men in Cambridge
spirited off her writing table
to higher education. A double

(its surface little more
than two feet square, and where
poems commensurately small
were scrawled on backs of envelopes)
sits convincingly beneath the tall
window onto Main Street.

To shut our eyes is Travel,
and that table may as well
be anywhere as here.
She'd have held close whatever house
she was born in, as a squirrel
palms its acorn; but with a need

not wholly fed by fear.
At twenty-four, moving back
to her birthplace, she'd lived the thought
transposed: To travel, shut the eyes.
I supposed we were going to make a "transit,"
as heavenly bodies did . . .

She was truly half-
astonished at those carriages
and cartons—almost as if
she'd lived only in that other life,
unseen, in her upper story.
Touch Shakespeare for me,

she wrote to Mabel in Europe,
thinking her close enough.
Why had anyone expressed the hope
to see Emily, who'd compare in letters
her unmet friends to Peter's
Christ: "whom having not seen, ye love"?

Finding nothing and no time
impalpable, she'd call
attention to the Biblical
"house not made with hands" for all
who'd listen. Wasn't that her home
as much as this was? Fame,

a lower form of Immortality,
in the intervening century
has unpacked her cradle to restore
its place, steps from her deathbed.
There is no first, or last, in Forever . . .
To the West, across the field

from another window, lives the family
at The Evergreens, whom Emily
saw little more than I can: Austin
and dark sister-in-law Sue.
I would have come out of Eden
to open the Door for you . . .

but she hadn't had to.
Drumming down the stair,
my ears fill with the spirals of a fly
a poem let in and won't be shown the way:
as if that buzzing, when she died,
were here still amplified.

Gwen Harwood

Gwen Harwood (1920–).   Gwen Harwood's verse came to prominence in the late 1950s and she is now established as one of the most powerful lyric poets in Australia. A critic and anthologist, her poems have craft and freedom, whim and passion. Her volumes include *Poems* (1963) and *Poems, Volume Two* (1968).

The Lion's Bride

I loved her softness, her warm human smell,
her dark mane flowing loose. Sometimes, stirred by
rank longing, laid my muzzle on her thigh.
Her father, faithful keeper, fed me well,
but she came daily with my special bowl
barefoot into my cage, and set it down:
our love feast. We became the talk of town,
brute king and tender woman, soul to soul.

Until today: an icy spectre sheathed
in silk, minced to my side on pointed feet.
I ripped the scented veil from its unreal
head and engorged the painted lips that breathed
our secret names. A ghost has bones, and meat!
Come soon, my love, my bride, and share this meal.

Rosemary Dobson

Rosemary Dobson (1920–).   Rosemary Dobson was born in Sydney and has lived in both Canberra and London. Along with Gwen Harwood, she is of a generation of leading Australian poets. She is the author of *Child with a Cockatoo* (1955), *Cock Crow* (1965), and *Selected Poems* (1973).

The Three Fates

At the instant of drowning he invoked the three sisters.
It was a mistake, an aberration, to cry out for
life everlasting.

He came up like a cork and back to the river-bank,
put on his clothes in reverse order,
returned to the house.

He suffered the enormous agonies of passion
writing poems from the end backwards,
brushing away tears that had not yet fallen.

Loving her wildly as the day regressed towards morning
he watched her wringing in the garden, growing younger,
barefoot, straw-hatted.

And when she was gone and the house and the swing and daylight
there was an instant's pause before it began all over,
the reel unrolling towards the river.

Leslie Scalapino

Leslie Scalapino was raised in Berkeley, California, and was educated at Reed College
and the University of California at Berkeley. She teaches at the New College in San
Francisco and at San Francisco State University. Her books of poetry include *Consider-
ing how exaggerated music is* (1982), *That they were at the beach—aeolotropic series* (1985),
How phenomena appear to unfold (1990), *The Return of Painting, The Pearl, and Orion/A
Trilogy* (1991), and *Crowd and not evening or light* (1992). The following selections are
from a sequence entitled "hmmmm" and, as Scalapino writes, are " 'about the night
on which a man said he would spend a 100 dollars' . . . What is important in terms of
action is that it is not I who is sated, but someone else. The concentration is not on her
pleasure either. It is located in the city, which is 'past' her and which is outside my (the
speaker's) framework entirely."

From *Considering how exaggerated music is*

How can I help myself,   as one woman said to me about wanting

to have intercourse with strange men,   from thinking of a man

How can I help myself,   as one woman said to me about wanting
to have intercourse with strange men,   from thinking of a man
(someone whom I don't know) as being like a seal. I mean I see a
    man
(in a crowd such as a theatre) as having the body of a seal in the
    way
a man would, say, be in bed with someone, kissing and barking,
which is the way a seal will bark and leap on his partly-fused hind
    limbs.

Yes. Am I not bound, I guess, (I say to myself) to regard him tenderly,
to concentrate on the man's trunk instead of his face, which in this case,
is so impassive.   Seriously,   I am fascinated by the way a seal moves.

[EPILOGUE: *anemone*]

"About the night on which a man said he would spend a 100 dollars
on me," a woman described, (and he did use up most of it
simply on taxi fares), "I was able to describe my feelings:

"About the night on which a man said he would spend a 100 dollars
on me," a woman described, (and he did use up most of it
simply on taxi fares), "I was able to describe my feelings:
by saying it was like being an insect who puts its feelers
out into the flowers of a plant, and sucks from them, as we were
(sucking) from the restaurants and bars of the city
to which the taxi took us. All night we were surrounded by lights.
As I lay back inside the taxi, just waiting for the man to make
arrangements for me (in regard to *that* part of my feeling,
I would describe the taxi as being more like a buoy), I had the
feeling (thru-out it) of rising slowly, and of floating along side
particular spots in the city. By morning, naturally, I was sated."

From *The Return of Painting, The Pearl, and Orion*

the lightened white air. Wheeling oneself forward on a cart, a
sled—of the leg. On the sidewalk asking money of the
passersby—in it—on the sled.

it is free

for the one they think. for that other who's asking for the
money.

on the sled—it is.
a soldier affected by the unburied dead covered with the
buzzards in the valleys and not turn that inward.

and then he's in the light air

and not figure out how it unfolds
Wheeling on the sled—having slept in the indentation—deer
simply have ticks which become huge until they drop off.
a huge tick in the side of having waded.
they begin singing—soldiers she meets on the road are a choir
and they began singing.
into the area of just pulp—only that
One realizing I have to do this myself.
the leg is soaked. She goes on the sled. There's a sandbar out
along stretching on which are corpses the buzzards had encrusting
flapping. the light air is coming up. no planet. or orb. an orb
floating.
Now it's gone.
And out tangled in the yellow grass, on it. The woman wading.
There's a corpse in the grass the buzzards sapping it whirling. It's
far gone. in the light air.
it can't be that in the long yellow grass
the hams stretch out and running down the slope in the yellow
grass. arms twirling flapping being in the grass.
There are weeds. It's dawn. Encounters sensitive man. as in
trunk of seal lying on her, rearing—their coming. the light air is
coming up. entwined thrashing around. He puts it into her again.
Him rearing, on the trunk
He withdraws it, takes it out
the weeds are still
He puts it back in—on the trunk
Him having gotten an erection
the trunk, the bulb of it in her. after
the dawn

There was this crescent moon hanging with a bright planet in this
blue night sky. They were low
in it

the sack of corpse wavered bulb that was created by some
behavior
    they the orbs weren't held
    birds come glancing sucked and then released
    by the one or the people in their behavior
    it's completely irrelevant

Acknowledgments

We are grateful for the use of translations done by Aliki Barnstone and/or Willis Barnstone in association with Matei Calinescu, Nelson Cerqueira, and Elene Kolb.

Every effort has been made to trace copyright, but if any omissions have been made please let us know. We gratefully acknowledge the following permissions:

Ai. "Twenty-Year Marriage," "Child Beater," and "Abortion" from *Cruelty* by Ai. Copyright © 1970, 1973 by Ai. Copyright © 1971, 1972 by Florence Anthony. Reprinted by permission of Houghton Mifflin Company.

Sonja Åkesson. From "Autobiography" tr. Ingrid Claréus. English translation Copyright © 1980 by Ingrid Clareus and used with her permission.

Bella Akhmadulina. "The Bride" tr. Stephen Stepanchev and used with his permission. "Sleep-walkers," "Winter," and "Goodbye" tr. Barbara Einzig, originally appeared in *Russian Literature Triquarterly.* Copyright by *Russian Literature Triquarterly.* Reprinted by permission of *Ardis.* "Words Spoken by Pasternak During a Bombing," "A Dream," and "In the Emptied Rest Home" tr. Jean Valentine and Olga Carlisle and "The Names of Georgian Women" tr. Stanley Noyes and Olga Carlisle are from *Poets on Street Corners* edited by Olga Carlisle. Copyright © 1968 by Random House, Inc. Reprinted by permission of Random House, Inc. and Olga Carlisle. "Small Aircraft" and "Silence" tr. Daniel Halpern. "Silence" appeared originally in *The New York Review of Books.* "At Night" and "The Sound of Rain" tr. Daniel Halpern with Albert Todd. Copyright 1979 by Daniel Halpern. Reprinted by permission of the translators. "Autumn" tr. Barbara Einzig appeared originally in *Contemporary Literature in Translation.* Copyright © 1973. Reprinted by permission of the editor.

Anna Akhmatova. "He loved three things in life" tr. Barbara Einzig appeared originally in *Contemporary Literature in Translation.* Copyright © 1973. Reprinted by permission of the Editor. "How can you look at the Neva" and "Your lynx-eyes, Asia" tr. Stanley Kunitz with Max Hayward from *Poems of Akhmatova,* Selected, Translated and Introduced by Stanley Kunitz with Max Hayward. Copyright © 1967, 1968, 1972, 1973 by Stanley Kunitz and Max Hayward. By permission of Little, Brown and Co. in association with the Atlantic Monthly

Press. "Summer Garden" tr. Stephen Stepanchev is used by permission of the translator. "Lot's Wife" tr. Richard Wilbur from *Walking to Sleep,* translated and Copyright © 1969 by Richard Wilbur. Reprinted by permission of Harcourt Brace Jovanovich, Inc. and Faber and Faber Ltd. "What's worse than this past century" tr. Barbara Einzig first appeared in *Out There* Poetry Magazine. Reprinted by permission of Rose Lesniak, Editor. "Tashkent Breaks into Blossom" and the "Requiem" cycle of fifteen poems tr. Richard McKane from *Anna Akhmatova: Selected Poems.* © 1969 by Richard McKane. Published by Penguin Books Ltd. as part of Penguin Modern European Poets, 1969. Reprinted by permission of the publisher. "Alone" tr. Stephen Berg. Used by permission of the translator.

Yosano Akiko. "You never touch" and "Spring is short" tr. Geoffrey Bownas and Anthony Thwaite from *The Penguin Book of Japanese Verse* translated by Geoffrey Bownas and Anthony Thwaite (Penguin Poets, 1964). © Geoffrey Bownas and Anthony Thwaite, 1964. Used by permission of Penguin Books Ltd.

Anne-Marie Albiach. "Irreducible Geometer" tr. Keith Waldrop. Published originally by The Burning Deck Press. Used by permission of the translator.

Sandra Alcosser. "Cry" from *A Fish to Feed All Hunger,* University Press of Virginia. Copyright © 1986 by Sandra Alcosser. Reprinted by permission of the author.

Claribel Alegría. "Search," "Loneliness and July Ninth," and "Small Country" tr. Willis Barnstone. Used by permission of Editorial Universitaria, Universidad de El Salvador.

Julie Allen. "A sweet thing is marriage" tr. Julie Allen and used with her permission.

Betti Alver. Poems tr. Willis Barnstone and Felix Oinas and used by their permission.

Astrid Hjertenaes Andersen. "Before the sun goes down" tr. Nadia Christensen. © Astrid Hjertenaes Andersen. Reprinted by permission of H. Aschehoug & Co. and the translator.

Anyte. "Lounge in the shade . . ." "Alive, this man was Manes," and "I am Hermes" tr. Willis Barnstone from *Greek Lyric Poetry* translated by Willis Barnstone. Copyright © 1962, 1967 by Willis Barnstone. Reprinted by permission of Schocken Books, Inc.

Margaret Atwood. "Habitation" from *Procedures for Underground* by Margaret Atwood. Copyright © 1970 by Oxford University Press. "Elegy for the Giant Tortoises" from *Animals in That Country* by Margaret Atwood. Copyright © 1968 by Oxford University Press. Reprinted by permission of Little, Brown and Co. in association with the Atlantic Monthly Press and Oxford University Press. "Dream 2: Brian the Still-Hunter," "Daguerreotype Taken in Old Age," and "Death of a Young Son by Drowning" from *The Journals of Susanna Moodie* by Margaret Atwood. Reprinted by permission of Oxford University Press.

Ingeborg Bachmann. "The Firstborn Land," "You want the summer lightning," and "Days in White" tr. Daniel Huws first appeared in *Modern Poetry in Translation 3.* From *Die Gestundete Zeit* by Ingeborg Bachmann. Copyright © R. Piper & Co. Verlag, 1957 and *Anrufung Des Grossen Bären* by Ingeborg Bachmann. Copyright © R. Piper & Co. Verlag, 1956. English translation copyright Daniel Huws. Used by permission of Joan Daves and Daniel Huws. "Curriculum Vitae" tr. Jerome Rothenberg from *New Young German Poets* by Jerome Rothenberg. English translation Copyright 1959 by Jerome Rothenberg. Reprinted by permission of Joan Daves and Jerome Rothenberg. "Out of the corpse-warm vestibule . . ." tr. Janice Orion. Used by permission of the translator and Joan Daves. "Every Day" tr. Christopher Middleton appeared originally in *Modern German Poetry 1910–1960* edited by Michael Hamburger and Christopher Middleton, Grove Press. From *Die Gestundete Zeit* by Ingeborg Bachmann. Copyright © R. Piper & Co. Verlag, 1957. Used by permission of Joan Daves and the translator.

Mira Bai. Poems tr. Willis Barnstone and Usha Nilsson and used by their permission.

Aliki Barnstone. Poems used by permission of the author.

Bayati. "Love Songs" and "Death Songs" tr. Reza Baraheni and Zahra-Soltan Skokoohtaezeh. Used by permission of the translators.

Georgina and Ulli Beier. "Oh moon, oh moon!" tr. Marase, "Lament for a Husband" tr. Laycock, "Song for a Girl on Her First Menstruation" tr. Prentuo from *Words of Paradise* by Georgina and Ulli Beier. Copyright © 1973 by Georgina and Ulli Beier. Reprinted by permission of Unicorn Press, P.O. Box 3307, Greensboro, North Carolina 27402.

Ulli Beier. "Love Song" tr. H. Gaden, "Song" and "Three Friends" tr. Ulli Beier, and "Song of the Lioness for her Cub" tr. Thomas Hahn from *African Poetry: An Anthology of Traditional African Poems* edited by Ulli Beier. Reprinted by permission of Cambridge University Press.

Olga Berggolts. "To My Sister" tr. Daniel Weissbort and used with his permission. "Infidelity" and "To Song" tr. Daniel Weissbort from *Post-War Russian Poetry* by Daniel Weissbort, Penguin Books Ltd. Copyright © 1974 by Daniel Weissbort and reprinted with his permission.

Linda Bierds. "The Stillness, The Dancing" from *The Stillness, The Dancing.* Copyright © 1988 by Linda Bierds. Reprinted by permission of Henry Holt and Company, Inc.

Elizabeth Bishop. "The Imaginary Iceberg," "The Fish," "Late Air," "At the Fishhouses," "Insomnia," "Invitation to Miss Marianne Moore," "Sestina," "In the Waiting Room," "Crusoe in England," and "The Moose" from *The Complete Poems 1927–1979.* Copyright © 1979, 1983 by Alice Helen Methfessel. Copyright © 1940, 1946, 1947, 1948, 1949, 1951, 1956, 1971, 1972 and renewed 1974, 1976, 1979 by Elizabeth Bishop. Reprinted by permission of Farrar, Straus and Giroux, Inc.

Ana Blandiana. "I need only fall asleep" tr. Stavros Deligiorgis. English translation Copyright © 1980 by Stavros Deligiorgis. Used by permission of the translator.

Cecil Bødker. "Calendar" tr. Nadia Christensen and Alexander Taylor. © Cecil Bødker. From *Contemporary Danish Poetry,* Twayne Publishers/Gyldendal, 1977. Used by permission of Albrecht Leonhardt Aps and the American Scandinavian Foundation. "Self Portrait" tr. Nadia Christensen appeared originally in the *Scandinavian Review.* Reprinted by permission of Cecil Bødker and Nadia Christensen.

Louise Bogan. "Medusa" and "Women" from *The Blue Estuaries* by Louise Bogan. Copyright © 1923, 1968 by Louise Bogan. Reprinted by permission of Farrar, Straus, & Giroux, Inc.

Marianne Boruch. "After Supper in Madison, Wisconsin" from *Descendant.* Copyright © 1989 by Marianne Boruch. Reprinted by permission of Wesleyan University Press, University Press of New England.

Geoffrey Bownas and Anthony Thwaite. "On the Death of Emperor Tenji" by a Court Lady tr. Geoffrey Bownas and Anthony Thwaite from *The Penguin Book of Japanese Verse* translated by Geoffrey Bownas and Anthony Thwaite (Penguin Poets, 1964). Reprinted by permission of Penguin Books Ltd.

Gwendolyn Brooks. "Jessie Mitchell's Mother" from *The World of Gwendolyn Brooks.* Copyright © 1960 by Gwendolyn Brooks. Reprinted by permission of Harper & Row, Publishers, Inc. "My Dreams, My Works . . .", "Kitchenette Building," "Sunset in the City," "We Real

Cool," and "Boy Breaking Glass" from *Blacks*. Copyright © 1991. Published by Third World Press, Chicago.

Olga Broumas. "Landscape with Next of Kin" and "Landscape with Leaves and Figure" from *Soie Sauvage* by Olga Broumas. Copyright Olga Broumas. Published by Copper Canyon Press. Reprinted by permission of the author.

Olga Broumas and Jane Miller. "Remember How Close We Sat in Sifnos . . ." from *Black Holes, Black Stockings*. Copyright © 1985 by Olga Broumas and Jane Miller. Reprinted by permission of Wesleyan University.

Edith Bruck. "Birth" tr. Ruth Feldman and Brian Swann from *Italian Poetry Today* by Ruth Feldman and Brian Swann. Reprinted by permission of New Rivers Press and the translators. "You Hide" tr. Ruth Feldman and Brian Swann. Copyright © 1980 by Ruth Feldman and Brian Swann and reprinted with their permission.

Julia de Burgos. "To Julia de Burgos" tr. Grace Schulman from *The Nation,* October 9, 1972. Copyright 1972 The Nation Associates. "Poem to My Death" tr. Grace Schulman from *The Nation,* January 11, 1975. Copyright 1975 The Nation Associates. Reprinted by permission of The Nation Associates.

Marguerite Burnat-Provins. "The fruits you give me," "You told me," and "Sylvius, your hands . . ." tr. Cassia Berman. English translation Copyright © 1980 by Cassia Berman and used with her permission.

Constanta Buzea. "I'm not here never was" tr. Stavros Deligiorgis. English translation Copyright © 1980 by Stavros Deligiorgis. Used by permission of the translator.

Yvonne Caroutch. "Night opens like an almond" tr. Elene Kolb. English translation Copyright © 1980 by Elene Kolb. "Child of silence and shadow," "I come to you with the vertigoes of the source," and "The limb of forests rises up" tr. David Cloutier. English translation Copyright © 1980 by David Cloutier. Used by permission of the translators.

Nina Cassian. "Knowledge" tr. Michael Impey and Brian Swann. First published in *Mundus Artium* and reprinted with their permission. "Hills picking up the moonlight like . . ." tr. Stavros Deligiorgis. English translation Copyright © 1980 by Stavros Deligiorgis and used with his permission.

Rosalía de Castro. "Now all that sound of laughter" tr. John Frederick Nims from *Sappho to Valery: Poems in Translation* by John Frederick Nims. Copyright © 1971 by Rutgers University, the State University of New Jersey. Reprinted by permission of the Rutgers University Press.

Chao Li-Hua. "Farewell" tr. J. P. Seaton and used with his permission.

Chao Luan-luan. "Slender Fingers" tr. Kenneth Rexroth and Ling Chung from *The Orchid Boat: Women Poets of China*. Translated and edited by Kenneth Rexroth and Ling Chung. English language translation Copyright © 1972 by the editors. Used by permission of The Seabury Press, Inc.

Andrée Chedid. "What Are We Playing At?" tr. Samuel Hazo and Mirene Ghossem and reprinted by permission of *Mundus Artium.*

Tada Chimako. "Mirror" tr. Kenneth Rexroth and Ikuko Atsumi from *The Burning Heart: Women Poets of Japan*. Translated and edited by Kenneth Rexroth and Ikuko Atsumi. English language translation Copyright © 1977 by The Seabury Press, Inc. Used by permission of the publishers.

Ch'in Chia's Wife. "Ch'in Chia's Wife's Reply" tr. Arthur Waley from *Translations from the Chinese* translated by Arthur Waley. Copyright 1919 and renewed 1947 by Arthur Waley. Reprinted by permission of Alfred A. Knopf, Inc. and George Allen & Unwin (Publishers) Ltd. from *More Translations from the Chinese.*

Ch'iu Chin. "How many wise men and heroes" tr. Kenneth Rexroth and Ling Chung from *The Orchid Boat: Women Poets of China.* Translated and edited by Kenneth Rexroth and Ling Chung. English language translation Copyright © 1972 by the editors. Used by permission of The Seabury Press, Inc.

Chiyo. Poems tr. David Ray and used with his permission.

Cho Wen-Chün. "Song of Snow-White Heads" tr. Arthur Waley from *Translations from the Chinese* translated by Arthur Waley. Copyright 1919 and renewed 1947 by Arthur Waley. Reprinted by permission of Alfred A. Knopf, Inc. and George Allen & Unwin (Publishers) Ltd. from *More Translations from the Chinese.*

Inger Christensen. "Men's Voices" tr. Nadia Christensen first appeared in the *Scandinavian Review.* Reprinted by permission of The American-Scandinavian Foundation.

Chu Shu-chen. "Sorrow" and "Lost" tr. Kenneth Rexroth from *Love and the Turning Year: One Hundred More Poems from the Chinese.* Copyright © 1970 by Kenneth Rexroth. "Morning," "Alone," "The Old Anguish," and "Stormy Night in Autumn" tr. Kenneth Rexroth from *One Hundred Poems from the Chinese.* Copyright © 1971 by Kenneth Rexroth. All Rights Reserved. Reprinted by permission of New Directions.

Amy Clampitt. "A Baroque Sunburst" from *What the Light Was Like.* Copyright © 1985 by Amy Clampitt. "Archaic Figure" and "Margaret Fuller, 1947" from *Archaic Figure.* Copyright © 1987 by Amy Clampitt. Reprinted by permission of Alfred A. Knopf, Inc.

Lucille Clifton. "Miss Rosie," "The Lost Baby Poem," "Confession," "She Understands Me," "Cutting Greens" from *Good Woman: Poems and A Memoir 1969–1980.* Copyright © 1987 by Lucille Clifton. Reprinted by permission of BOA Editions, Ltd., 92 Park Ave., Brockport, NY 14420. "Island Mary," "Homage to My Hips," "There Is a Girl Inside," "I Once Knew a Man," "How He Is Coming Then," "Holy Night" and "Anna Speaks of Her Childhood" from *Two-Headed Woman.* Copyright © 1980 by the University of Massachusetts. Reprinted by permission of Curtis Brown, Ltd.

Vittoria da Colonna. "As When Some Hungry Fledgling Hears and Sees" tr. Barbara Howes first appeared in *Poems from Italy* edited by William Jay Smith, 1972 Thomas Y. Crowell. English translation Copyright 1972 by Barbara Howes and reprinted with her permission.

Jane Cooper. "In the House of Dying" from *Maps and Windows.* Copyright © 1968 by Jane Cooper.

Jayne Cortez. "I Am New York City" and "So Long" are reprinted with permission of *Mundus Artium.*

Sor Juana Inés de la Cruz. From "First Dream" tr. Samuel Beckett from *An Anthology of Mexican Poetry* edited by Octavio Paz. Reprinted by permission of Indiana University Press.

Marceline Desbordes-Valmore. "The Roses of Sa'adi" tr. Barbara Howes first appeared in *Poems from France* edited by William Jay Smith, 1967 Thomas Y. Crowell. English translation Copyright 1967 by Barbara Howes and reprinted with her permission.

Emily Dickinson. Poems #24, 211, 249, 365, 441, 505, 528, 569, 613, 642, 657, 670, 709, 722, 732, 754, 1071, 1072, and 1651 are reprinted by permission of the publishers and the Trustees of Amherst College from *The Poems of Emily Dickinson,* edited by Thomas H. Johnson, Cambridge, Mass.: The Belknap Press of Harvard University Press. Copyright © 1951, 1955 by the President and Fellows of Harvard College. #341, 376, 396, 599 are Copyright 1929 by Martha Dickinson Bianchi. Copyright © 1957 by Mary L. Hampson. Reprinted by permission of Little Brown and Co. Individually copyright poems are from *The Complete Poems of Emily Dickinson,* edited by Thomas H. Johnson.

Rosemary Dobson. "The Three Fates" is © Copyright 1978 Rosemary Dobson c/o Curtis Brown (Aust) Pty Ltd., Sydney, Australia and is reprinted with permission.

Hilde Domin. "Birthdays" tr. Tudor Morris is reprinted with the permission of *Mundus Artium.*

Ruth Domino. "A Sparrow in the Dust" tr. Daniel Hoffman and Jerre Mangione from *Sole Di Solitudine* (Calabria: La Procellaria Editrice). Copyright © 1976 by Ruth Domino Tassoni. Used by permission of Daniel Hoffman.

H.D. All poems from *Collected Poems of H.D.: 1912–1944,* edited by Louis L. Martz. © 1925 by H. D. © 1953, 1957, 1973 by Norman Holmes Pearson. © 1983 by Perdita Schaffner. Reprinted with permission of New Directions.

Akazome Emon. "I, who cut off my sorrows" tr. Kenneth Rexroth and Ikuko Atsumi from *The Burning Heart: Women Poets of Japan.* Translated and edited by Kenneth Rexroth and Ikuko Atsumi. English language translation Copyright © 1977 by The Seabury Press, Inc. Used by permission of the publishers.

Enheduanna. Poems adapted by Willis and Aliki Barnstone from the translation by William W. Hallo and J. J. A. van Dijk in *The Exaltation of Inanna.* Copyright © 1968 by Yale University. Used by permission of Yale University Press.

Louise Erdrich. "Ninth Month," "The Glass and the Bowl," "Fooling God," and "Sunflowers," from *Baptism of Desire.* Copyright © 1990 by Louise Erdrich. Reprinted by permission of HarperCollins Publishers.

Forugh Farrokhzad. "Once More" tr. Jascha Kessler with Amin Banani will appear in *Selected Poems of Farrokhzad* edited by Amin Banani and translated by Jascha Kessler with Amin Banani. Used by permission of Jascha Kessler. "On Earth" and "In the land of dwarfs" tr. Girdhard Tikku and used with his permission. "I'm Sad" tr. Reza Baraheni and used with his permission.

Rosario Ferré. "I Hear You've Let Go" tr. Willis Barnstone. Used by permission of Editorial Joaquin Mortiz and the author.

Angel Flores. "Song of the Ill-Married" tr. Patricia Terry and "Ballad of the Cool Fountain" tr. Edwin Honig from *An Anthology of Medieval Lyrics* edited by Angel Flores. Originally published by Random House (Modern Library), 1962. New Edition 1979 Gordian Press, Staten Island, New York 10304. © 1962 Angel Flores and used with his permission.

Carolyn Forche. "Selective Service," copyright © 1981 by Carolyn Forche. "The Memory of Elena," copyright © 1977 by Carolyn Forche. "San Onofre, CA," copyright © 1978 by Carolyn Forche. From *The Country Between Us* by Carolyn Forche. Copyright © 1982 by Carolyn Forche. Reprinted by permission of HarperCollins Publishers.

Lucia Fox. "Dream of the Forgotten Lover" tr. R. Maghan. Used by permission of the translator.

Isabel Fraire. "If night takes the form of a whale and" tr. Thomas Hoeksema. First published in *Mundus Artium* and reprinted with their permission.

Marie de France. "The Nightingale," "Honeysuckle," and "The Two Lovers" tr. Patricia Terry from *Lays of Courtly Love,* in verse translation by Patricia Terry. Copyright © 1963 by Patricia Terry. Reprinted by permission of Doubleday & Company, Inc.

Martha Paley Francescato. "Parody" and "Semen" tr. Willis Barnstone. Used by permission of the author.

Gloria Fuertes. Poems tr. Willis Barnstone from *Antologia Poetica 1950–1969* by Gloria Fuertes. Published by Plaza and Janis.

Tess Gallagher. "Black Silk" from *Amplitude.* Copyright © 1987 by Tess Gallagher. Reprinted by permission of Graywolf Press, Saint Paul, Minnesota. "Black Pudding" and "Yes" from *Moon Crossing Bridge,* February 1992, Graywolf Press. "Yes" originally appeared in *The New Yorker.* Reprinted by permission of the author.

Agnes Gergely. "Crazed Man in Concentration Camp" tr. Edwin Morgan first appeared in *New Hungarian Quarterly.* © Edwin Morgan and *New Hungarian Quarterly.* Reprinted from *Modern Hungarian Poetry* edited by Miklos Vajda. Copyright © 1977 by Miklos Vajda. Published by Columbia University Press, 1977. Reprinted by permission of the translator and Artisjus.

Sandra M. Gilbert. "My Grandmother in Paris" from *Blood Pressure* by Sandra M. Gilbert. © 1988 Sandra M. Gilbert. Reprinted by permission of W. W. Norton & Company, Inc.

Louise Glück. "Lamentations" first appeared in *The New Republic,* June 1978. Reprinted by permission of the author.

Leah Goldberg. From "Nameless Journey II, III," "Of Myself," and "Our Backs Are to the Cypress" tr. Ramah Commanday and used with his permission.

Natalya Gorbanyevskaya. "Here, as in a painting . . . ," "To I. Lavrentevaya," "Not because of you . . ." and "And there is nothing at all . . ." tr. Daniel Weissbort from *Post-War Russian Poetry* by Daniel Weissbort. Published by Penguin Books Ltd. Copyright © 1974 by Daniel Weissbort and reprinted with his permission. "This world is amazingly flat" tr. Barbara Einzig first appeared in *Russian Literature Triquarterly.* Copyright *Russian Literature Triquarterly.* Reprinted by permission of *Ardis.*

Jorie Graham. "The Hiding Place" from *Region of Unlikeness.* Copyright © 1991 by Jorie Graham. Published by The Ecco Press and reprinted by permission. Originally published in *The New Yorker.*

Linda Gregg. "Whole and Without Blessing," "Together in Greece" and "Classicism" from *Too Bright to See.* Copyright © 1981 by Linda Gregg. Reprinted by permission of Graywolf Press, Saint Paul, Minnesota.

Anna Hajnal. "Fear" and "Half Past Four, October" tr. Daniel Hoffman. "The Felled Plane Tree" tr. William Jay Smith. All from *Modern Hungarian Poetry* edited by Miklos Vajda. Copyright © 1977 by Miklos Vajda. Published by Columbia University Press, 1977. Reprinted by permission of the translators and Artisjus.

Young Woman of Harima. "If you go away" tr. Kenneth Yasuda from *Land of the Reed Plains* translated by Kenneth Yasuda. Published by the Charles E. Tuttle Co., Inc. of Tokyo, Japan and reprinted with their permission.

Joy Harjo. "Mercury" from *In Mad Love and War.* Reprinted by permission of Wesleyan University Press, University of New England.

Gwen Harwood. "The Lion's Bride" is Copyright © 1978 by *Antaeus.* Reprinted by permission of Gwen Harwood.

Anne Hébert. "Bread Is Born" tr. Maxine Kumin from *Poèms* by Anne Hébert. "The Alchemy of Day" and "Our Hands in the Garden" tr. A. Poulin, Jr., from *Eve* by Anne Hébert. English translations by A. Poulin, Jr., Copyright by *Quarterly Review of Literature,* Volume XXI, 3/4, 1980. Used by permission of the translators, *Quarterly Review of Literature,* and General Publishing Co. Limited. Other poems tr. WB and AB and by permission of General Publishing Co. Limited and Anne Hébert.

Judith Herzberg. "Reunion" and "Nearer" tr. Shirley Kaufman. Copyright © 1980 by Judith Herzberg and Shirley Kaufman. Used by permission of the author and translator.

Emily Hiestand. "Planting in Tuscaloosa" from *Green the Witch-Hazel Wood.* Copyright © 1989 by Emily Hiestand. Reprinted by permission of Graywolf Press, Saint Paul, Minnesota.

Roberta Hill. "A Nation Wrapped in Stone" and "Lines for Marking Time" from *Carriers of the Dream Wheel* edited by Duane Niatum. Published by Harper & Row, Publishers, Inc. Copyright © 1975 by Roberta Hill. "Depot in Rapid City" is Copyright © by Roberta Hill. Reprinted by permission of the author.

Brenda Hillman. "Reverse Seeing," "Split Tractate," and "Winged One" from *Death Tractates.* Copyright © 1992 by Brenda Hillman. Reprinted by permission of Wesleyan University Press, University Press of New England.

Empress Iwa No Hime. "Longing for the Emperor" tr. Geoffrey Bownas and Anthony Thwaite from *The Penguin Book of Japanese Verse* translated by Geoffrey Bownas and Anthony Thwaite (Penguin Poets, 1964). © Geoffrey Bownas and Anthony Thwaite, 1964. Reprinted by permission of the publisher.

Ryōjin Hishō. (Collected by Emperor Go-Shirakawa) "May the man who gained my trust . . ." tr. Geoffrey Bownas and Anthony Thwaite from *The Penguin Book of Japanese Verse* translated by Geoffrey Bownas and Anthony Thwaite (Penguin Poets, 1964). © Geoffrey Bownas and Anthony Thwaite, 1964. Reprinted by permission of the publisher.

Anselm Hollo. "Poem to Ease Birth" tr. Anselm Hollo from the Nahuatl (Aztec) and used with his permission.

Lady Horikawa. "Will he always love me?" tr. Kenneth Rexroth from *One Hundred Poems from the Japanese* by Kenneth Rexroth. All Rights Reserved. Reprinted by permission of New Directions.

Susan Howe. "To Kin I Call in the Iron Woods" from *In the Athenian Wanderings.* Copyright © 1991 by Susan Howe. Wesleyan University Press for permission to quote from *Singularities.*

Hsi-chün. "Lament of Hsi-Chün" tr. Arthur Waley from *Translations from the Chinese* translated by Arthur Waley. Copyright 1919; renewed 1947 by Arthur Waley. Reprinted by permission of Alfred A. Knopf, Inc., and George Allen & Unwin (Publishers) Ltd. from *More Translations from the Chinese.*

Hsüeh T'ao. "Spring-Gazing Song," "Weaving Love-Knots," and "Weaving Love-Knots 2" tr. Carolyn Kizer and used by her permission.

Huang O. "Every morning I get up," "You held my lotus blossom," and "A Farewell to a Southern Melody" tr. Kenneth Rexroth and Ling Chung from *The Orchid Boat: Women Poets of China.* Translated and edited by Kenneth Rexroth and Ling Chung. English language translation Copyright © 1972 by the editors. Used by permission of The Seabury Press, Inc.

Lady Ise. Poems, other than those tr. WB, tr. Etsuko Terasaki and Irma Brandeis and used with their permission.

Nana Issaia. "Sacrifice" and "Dream" tr. Helle Tzalopoulou Barnstone, English translation Copyright © 1980 by Helle Tzalopoulou Barnstone and used by permission of the author and translator.

Denise Jallais. "Lullaby for My Dead Child" tr. Maxine Kumin and Judith Kumin from *Poèsie I,* December 20, 1969. Used by permission of Maxine Kumin.

Ingrid Jonker. "This Journey," "I Am with Those," and "Time of Waiting in Amsterdam" tr. Jack Cope and William Plomer from *Selected Poems* by Ingrid Jonker translated from the Afrikaans by Jack Cope and William Plomer. Reprinted by permission of the Estate of Ingrid Jonker and Jonathan Cape Ltd.

June Jordan. "For My Mother" from *Things That I Do in the Dark: Selected Poetry* by June Jordan. Copyright © 1971 by June Jordan. By permission of Random House, Inc.

Lady Kasa. "I dreamed I held" and "I love and fear him" tr. Kenneth Rexroth from *One Hundred Poems from the Japanese* by Kenneth Rexroth. All Rights Reserved. Reprinted by permission of New Directions.

Lina Kasdaglis. "Traffic Lights" tr. Edmund and Mary Keeley from *Eighteen Texts: Writings by Contemporary Greek Authors* edited by Willis Barnstone. Copyright © 1972 by the President and Fellows of Harvard College. Reprinted by permission of Harvard University Press, Cambridge, Mass.

Shirley Kaufman. From *Looking at Henry Moore's Elephant Skull Etchings in Jerusalem during the War* by Shirley Kaufman. Copyright © 1978 by Shirley Kaufman. Reprinted by permission of Unicorn Press, P.O. Box 3307, Greensboro, North Carolina 27402.

Shiraishi Kazuko. "Phallus" appeared originally in *Modern Poetry in Translation.* Reprinted by permission of the International Writing Program of the University of Iowa and the author.

Anne-Marie Kegels. "Nocturnal Heart" tr. W. S. Merwin from *Selected Translations 1948–1968* by W. S. Merwin. English translation Copyright © 1961, 1968 by W. S. Merwin. Reprinted by permission of Atheneum Publishers and David Higham Associated Limited.

Delores Kendrick. "Canticle of a Black Lady," "Leah in Freedom," "Jenny in Love," "Julia, Carrying Water," and "Lucy Sleeps with Master Muford" from *The Women of the Plums.* Reprinted by permission of William Morrow & Company, Inc./Publishers, New York.

Karin Kiwus. "All Splendor on Earth" tr. Almut McAuley. Used by permission of the translator.

Nagase Kiyoko. "Mother" tr. Kenneth Rexroth and Ikuko Atsumi from *The Burning Heart: Women Poets of Japan.* Translated and edited by Kenneth Rexroth and Ikuko Atsumi. English language translation Copyright © 1977 by The Seabury Press, Inc. Used by permission of the publishers.

Carolyn Kizer. "The Intruder" and "Through a Glass Eye, Lightly" Copyright © 1961 by Indiana University Press. "Lines to Accompany Flowers for Eve" Copyright © 1964 by Shenandoah from *Midnight Was My Cry* by Carolyn Kizer. Reprinted by permission of Doubleday & Company, Inc.

Ono no Komachi. "The color of the flowers" tr. Kenneth Rexroth. Copyright © Kenneth Rexroth and used with his permission. "A thing which fades" tr. Arthur Waley from *Japanese Poetry: The Uta* by Arthur Waley is reprinted by permission of Oxford University Press. "Doesn't he realize" tr. Kenneth Rexroth from *The Burning Heart: Women Poets of Japan.* Translated and edited by Kenneth Rexroth and Ikuko Atsumi. English language translation Copyright © 1977 by The Seabury Press, Inc. Used by permission of the publishers. "So lonely am I" tr. Donald Keene from *Anthology of Japanese Literature* by Donald Keene. Copyright © 1955 by Grove Press. Reprinted by permission of the publisher and Donald Keene.

Korinna. All poetry from *Greek Lyric Poetry* translated by Willis Barnstone. Copyright © 1962, 1967 by Willis Barnstone. Reprinted by permission of Schocken Books, Inc.

Vénus Khoury-Gata. "The autumn made colors burn" and "your cheeks flat on the sand" tr. Willis Barnstone from *Terres Stagnantes* by Vénus Khoury-Gata. Copyright © 1968 by Editions Seghers and used with their permission.

Kshetrayya. "Dancing-Girl's Song" tr. Tambimuttu and R. Appalaswamy from *Indian Love Poems.* Reprinted by permission of Peter Pauper Press.

Maxine Kumin. "Together," from *The Nightmare Factory.* Copyright © 1970 by Maxine Kumin. Reprinted by permission of Curtis Brown, Ltd. "The Hermit Has a Visitor" from *Our Ground Time Here Will Be Brief.* Copyright © 1972 by Maxine Kumin. Reprinted by permission of Viking Penguin, a division of Penguin Books USA Inc.

Monique Laederach. "Leaving the island . . ." and "And so I speak" tr. Charles Guenther and used with his permission. From *Penelope* by Monique Laederach.

Emilia Lanier. "Eves Apologie" from *The Poems of Shakespeare's Dark Lady: Salve Deus Rex Judaeorum* by Emilia Lanier, introduced by A. L. Rowse. Reprinted by permission of Jonathan Cape Ltd.

Else Lasker-Schüler. "End of the World" and "A Love Song" tr. Michael Gillespie. "Hagar and Ishmael," "Jacob and Esau," and "Abraham and Isaac" tr. Rosemarie Waldrop. Used by permission of Kösel-Verlag and the translators.

Takako U. Lento. From "Glass," which appeared originally in *Modern Poetry in Translation* under the title "Between Two Cultures." Reprinted by permission of the International Writing Program of the University of Iowa and the author.

Denise Levertov. "Adam's Complaint" from *Relearning the Alphabet* by Denise Levertov. Copyright © 1970 by Denise Levertov Goodman. Reprinted by permission of New Directions and Laurence Pollinger Limited. "Overheard over S. E. Asia" and "To Antonio Machado" from *Footprints* by Denise Levertov. Copyright © 1971 by Denise Levertov Goodman. Reprinted by permission of New Directions. "Roamer" from *Poems: 1968–1972* © 1972 Denise Levertov. "Stepping Westward" from *Poems: 1960–1967* © 1967 Denise Levertov.

Li Ch'ing-chao. "melting in thin mist and heavy clouds" tr. J. P. Seaton and used with his permission. "Clear Bright" tr. Kenneth Rexroth from *The Orchid Boat: Women Poets of China.* Translated and edited by Kenneth Rexroth and Ling Chung. English language translation

Marula. "Meeting after Separation" tr. Tambimuttu and G. V. Vaidya from *Indian Love Poems* by Tambimuttu. Reprinted by permission of Peter Pauper Press.

Jenny Mastoraki. "Then they paraded Pompey's urn," "The Wooden Horse then said," "The Crusaders," "The Vandals," and "Prometheus" tr. Nikos Germanakos from *boundary 2,* Winter 1973. Reprinted by permission of the Editors. "The Death of a Warrior" tr. Kimon Friar appeared originally in *Mundus Artium* and is reprinted with permission.

Heather McHugh. "To Have To" from *Shades.* Copyright © 1988 by Heather McHugh. "I Knew I'd Sing" from *To the Quick.* Copyright © 1987 by Heather McHugh. Reprinted by permission of Wesleyan University Press.

Sandra McPherson. "Pregnancy" from *Elegies for the Hot Season* by Sandra McPherson. © 1970 by Sandra McPherson. Reprinted by permission of the author.

Cecília Meireles. "Ballad of the Ten Casino Dancers" tr. James Merrill from *An Anthology of Twentieth-Century Brazilian Poetry* by Elizabeth Bishop and Emanuel Brasil. Copyright © 1972 by Wesleyan University. Reprinted by permission of Wesleyan University Press.

Gabriela Melinescu. "time of fish dying" tr. Stavros Deligiorgis. English translation Copyright © 1980 by Stavros Deligiorgis and used with his permission.

W. S. Merwin. "When I was a good and quick little girl," "My spouse, Chunaychunay," "The bee-keeper kissed me," and "The Corpse Keeper" tr. W. S. Merwin from *Selected Translations 1948–1968* by W. S. Merwin. English translation Copyright © 1961, 1968 by W. S. Merwin. Reprinted by permission of Atheneum Publishers and David Higham Associates Limited.

Kanai Mieko. "The House of Madam Juju" tr. Christopher Drake from *Contemporary Japanese Literature: An Anthology of Fiction, Film and Other Writings Since 1945* edited by Howard Hibbett. Reprinted by permission of the translator.

Josephine Miles. "Memorial Day," "Before," "If You Will," and "Doll" from *Collected Poems.* Reprinted by permission of The University of Illinois Press.

Edna St. Vincent Millay. "Spring," "Sonnet LXVI," "Sonnet to Gath," and "Sonnet XXXI" are from *Collected Poems* by Edna St. Vincent Millay. Published by Harper & Row. Copyright 1921, 1923, 1928, 1949, 1951, 1955 by Edna St. Vincent Millay and Norma Millay Ellis. Reprinted by permission of Norma Millay Ellis, Literary Executor of the Estate of Edna St. Vincent Millay.

Jane Miller. "Memory at These Speeds" and "Tilt" from *American Odalisque.* Copyright © 1987 by Jane Miller. Reprinted by permission of Copper Canyon Press, P.O. Box 271, Port Townsend, WA 98368.

Gabriela Mistral. "Sister" tr. Langston Hughes from *Selected Poems of Gabriela Mistral* translated by Langston Hughes. English translation Copyright © 1957 by Indiana University Press. "Death Sonnet I," "Drops of Gall," "Dusk," and "Midnight" tr. David L. Garrison from the Aguilar edition of Gabriela Mistral's poems. Copyright 1922, 1938, 1954 by Gabriela Mistral; © 1964 by Doris Dana. English translations Copyright © 1980 by David L. Garrison. All reprinted by permission of Joan Daves.

Marianne Moore. "To a Steam Roller" and "Poetry" are Copyright 1935 by Marianne Moore, renewed 1963 by Marianne Moore and T. S. Eliot. "The Steeple-Jack" is Copyright 1951 by Marianne Moore. All are from *Collected Poems* by Marianne Moore and are reprinted by permission of Macmillan Publishing Co., Inc., and Faber and Faber Ltd. "Critics and Connoisseurs," "A Grave," "Marriage," and "Silence," from *Collected Poems* © 1935 by Marianne

Moore, renewed 1963 by Marianne Moore and T. S. Eliot. Reprinted with permission of Macmillan Publishers. "Paper Nautilus" © 1941, renewed 1969 by Marianne Moore. Reprinted with permission of Macmillan Publishers. "Avec Ardeur" from *The Complete Poems of Marianne Moore* © 1981 by Clive E. Driver, Literary Executor of the Estate of Marianne C. Moore. Used by permission of Viking Penguin, a division of Penguin Books USA, Inc.

Petra von Morstein. "1968," "Justice," "For one who says he feels," "Thing Poem," "Anthology Poem," and "In the Case of Lobsters," tr. Rosemarie Waldrop from *An Alle* by Petra von Morstein. © S. Fischer Verlag Gmbh, Frankfurt am Main, 1969.

Eva Mylonás. "Holidays" tr. Kimon Friar and used with his permission.

Ágnes Nemes Nagy. "Bird" and "Words to a Song" tr. Bruce Berlind appeared originally in *Green House.* Reprinted by permission of the translator. "I Carried Statues" tr. Bruce Berlind from *Modern Hungarian Poetry* edited by Miklos Vajda and published by Columbia University Press. Copyright © 1977 by Miklos Vajda. Reprinted by permission of the translator and Artisjus. Translations also from *Selected Poems: Agnes Nemes Nagy,* translated by Bruce Berlind, International Writing Program, the University of Iowa, 1980. Copyright © 1980 the University of Iowa.

Kaccipettu Nannakaiyar. "What She Said" tr. A. K. Ramanujan from *Interior Landscape* by A. K. Ramanujan. Published by Indiana University Press and reprinted with their permission.

Lorine Niedecker: "Easter Greeting," "Laundromat," "I Married," "Foreclosure," "Darwin," "My Friend Tree," "Well, Spring," "Old Mother Turns Blue," "What Horror to Awake at Night," "I Knew a Clean Man," "In the Great Snowfall," "Swept Snow, Li Po," "Newsaved," "Popcorn-can cover," "Get a load," "Now in One Year," "In Leonardo's Light," "As Praiseworthy," "As I Paint the Street," "Some Float Off on Chocolate Bars," "Poets Work," "To My Pressure Pump," and "Alcoholic Dream." Copyright © 1991 by Lorine Niedecker Literary Estate, Cid Corman, Sole Executor.

Diana O'Hehir. "Home Free" and "Riding the San Francisco Train" from *Home Free.* Copyright © 1988 by Diana O'Hehir. Reprinted by permission of Atheneum Publishers, an imprint of Macmillan Publishing Company.

Sharon Olds. "Sex Without Love" and "Ideographs" from *The Dead and the Living.* Copyright © 1983 by Sharon Olds. Reprinted by permission of Alfred A. Knopf, Inc.

Mary Oliver. "The Honey Tree" and "John Chapman" from *American Primitive* by Mary Oliver. © 1978, 1979, 1980, 1981, 1982, 1983 Mary Oliver. "John Chapman" first appeared in *American Scholar* (Spring 1982). Used by permission of Little, Brown and Company.

Rossana Ombres. "Flower Ensnarer of Psalms" tr. I. L. Salomon originally appeared in the *Michigan Quarterly Review.* Reprinted by permission of the translator.

Lady Pan. "A Present from the Emperor's New Concubine" tr. Kenneth Rexroth from *Love and the Turning Year: One Hundred More Poems from the Chinese* by Kenneth Rexroth. Copyright © 1970 by Kenneth Rexroth. All Rights Reserved. Reprinted by permission of New Directions.

Marge Piercy. "Song of the Fucked Duck" from *To Be of Use* by Marge Piercy. Copyright © 1969, 1971, 1973 by Marge Piercy. Reprinted by permission of Doubleday & Company, Inc. and Wallace & Sheil, Inc., 118 East 61st Street, New York, N. Y. 10021.

Florencia del Pinar. "Another Song of the Same Woman, to Some Partridges, Sent to Her Alive" tr. Julie Allen. English translation Copyright © 1980 by Julie Allen and used with her permission.

Ping Hsin. "Spring Waters" tr. Kai-yu Hsu from *Twentieth Century Chinese Poetry* edited and translated by Kai-yu Hsu. Copyright © 1963 by Kai-yu Hsu. Used by permission of Doubleday & Company, Inc. "The orphan boat of my heart" tr. Kenneth Rexroth and Ling Chung from *The Orchid Boat: Women Poets of China.* Translated and edited by Kenneth Rexroth and Ling Chung. English language translation Copyright © 1972 by the editors. Used by permission of The Seabury Press, Inc.

Christine de Pisan. "Alone am I, and alone I wish to be" tr. Julie Allen. Copyright © 1980 by Julie Allen and used with her permission. "Christine to Her Son" tr. Barbara Howes from *Poems from France* edited by William Jay Smith. Copyright © 1967 by Barbara Howes and used with her permission.

Thérèse Plantier. "Overdue Balance Sheet" tr. Maxine and Judith Kumin from *Poesie I.* English translation originally appeared in *Antioch Review,* Summer 1975. "Doors" tr. Willis Barnstone and Elene Kolb. Used by permission of the author and translators.

Sylvia Plath. "Daddy," copyright © 1963 by Ted Hughes. "Morning Song," copyright © 1961 by Ted Hughes. Both from *Ariel* by Sylvia Plath. Reprinted by permission of Harper & Row, Publishers, Inc. and Olwyn Hughes. *Ariel,* published in London by Faber and Faber Ltd., copyright © 1965 by Ted Hughes. "The Moon and the Yew Tree," copyright © 1963 by Ted Hughes. "Crossing the Water," copyright © 1962 by Ted Hughes. "The Arrival of the Bee Box," copyright © 1963 by Ted Hughes. "Poppies in October," copyright © 1963 by Ted Hughes. "Lady Lazarus," copyright © 1963 by Ted Hughes. "Sheep in Fog," copyright © 1965 by Ted Hughes. "Edge," copyright © 1963 by Ted Hughes. All from *Collected Poems of Sylvia Plath,* edited by Ted Hughes. Reprinted by permission of HarperCollins Publishers. "The Eye-Mote" from *The Colossus and Other Poems.* Copyright © 1960 by Syliva Plath. Reprinted by permission of Alfred A. Knopf, Inc.

Ezra Pound and Noel Stock. "With candor I confess my love," "The swallow sings 'Dawn, Whither fadeth the dawn?'" "Pleasant Songs (I, II, and III)," "The pomegranate speaks" and "I find my love fishing" tr. Ezra Pound and Noel Stock from *Love Poems of Ancient Egypt* by Ezra Pound and Noel Stock. Copyright © 1962 by Noel Stock. Copyright © 1962 by New Directions Publishing Corporation and reprinted by permission of New Directions.

Marie-Françoise Prager. "I'll act out a weird dream" tr. Willis Barnstone and Elene Kolb from *La Poèsie Feminine,* Paris, Seghers, 1966. Copyright Editions Chambelland Paris. Used by permission of the publisher and the translators.

Praxilla. "You gaze at me teasingly . . ." and "Most beautiful of things I leave . . ." tr. Willis Barnstone. Reprinted from *Greek Lyric Poetry* translated by Willis Barnstone. Copyright © 1962, 1967 by Willis Barnstone. Used by permission of Schocken Books, Inc.

Kathleen Raine. "The Wilderness" from *Collected Poems* by Kathleen Raine. Published by Hamish Hamilton Ltd. and reprinted with their permission.

Knud Rasmussen. "Far inland" tr. Knud Rasmussen and adapted from that translation by Willis Barnstone. Used by permission of the heirs of Knud Rasmussen and Rudolf Sand and William Bentzen.

Dahlia Ravikovitch. "Poem of Explanations" and "The Everlasting Forests" tr. Channa Bloch. Copyright The Sheep Meadow Press and reprinted with their permissions.

Kenneth Rexroth and Ling Chung. "After kicking on the swing" by Anonymous Courtesan tr. Kenneth Rexroth from *The Orchid Boat: Women Poets of China.* Translated and edited by Kenneth Rexroth and Ling Chung. English language translation Copyright © 1972 by the editors. Used by permission of The Seabury Press, Inc.

Adrienne Rich. "Peeling Onions" from *Snapshots of a Daughter-in-Law, Poems, 1954–1962* by Adrienne Rich. Copyright © 1956, 1957, 1958, 1959, 1960, 1961, 1962, 1963, 1967 by Adrienne Rich Conrad. Reprinted by permission of W. W. Norton & Company, Inc., Chatto and Windus and the author. "IV" and "XX" from "Twenty-One Love Poems" from *The Dream of a Common Language,* Poems 1974–1977, by Adrienne Rich. Copyright © 1978 by W. W. Norton & Company, Inc and reprinted with their permission.

Muriel Rukeyser. "This Morning," "Darkness Music," and "Eyes of Night-Time" from *Collected Poems,* 1978. Reprinted by permission of William L. Rukeyser.

Jerome Rothenberg. "Young Woman's neo-aramaic jewish persian Blues" tr. Jerome Rothenberg from *A Big Jewish Book* edited by Jerome Rothenberg. Copyright © 1978 by Jerome Rothenberg. Reprinted by permission of Doubleday & Company, Inc.

Nelly Sachs. "But Perhaps" tr. Ruth and Matthew Mead from *The Seeker and Other Poems* by Nelly Sachs. Translated from the German by Ruth and Matthew Mead and Michael Hamburger. Copyright © 1970 by Farrar, Straus and Giroux. Reprinted by permission of Farrar, Straus and Giroux Inc. "In the blue distance," tr. Ruth and Matthew Mead, "Line Like," "The Sleepwalker," and "White Serpent" tr. Michael Hamburger from *O The Chimneys* by Nelly Sachs. Translated from the German by Ruth and Matthew Mead and Michael Hamburger. Copyright © 1967 by Farrar, Straus and Giroux, Inc. Reprinted by permission of Farrar, Straus and Giroux, Inc. "In flight in escape" and "The last one" tr. Arthur Wensinger from *Fahrt Ins Staublose. Die Gedichte der Nelly Sachs.* © Suhrkamp Verlag Frankfurt am Main 1964. English translations copyright © 1980 by Arthur Wensinger. Used by permission of Kurt Bernheim for Suhrkamp Verlag.

Lady Ōtomo of Sakanone. "Sent from the Capital to Her Elder Daughter" tr. Geoffrey Bownas and Anthony Thwaite from *The Penguin Book of Japanese Verse* translated by Geoffrey Bownas and Anthony Thwaite (Penguin Poets, 1964). © Geoffrey Bownas and Anthony Thwaite, 1964. Reprinted by permission of the publisher.

Mary Jo Salter. "The Upper Story" from *Unfinished Painting.* Copyright © 1989 by Mary Jo Salter. Reprinted by permission of Alfred A. Knopf, Inc.

Sappho. Poems tr. Willis Barnstone and reprinted from *Greek Lyric Poetry* translated by Willis Barnstone. Copyright © 1962, 1967 by Willis Barnstone. Reprinted by permission of Schocken Books, Inc.

Fumi Saitō. "The palm of the hand" tr. Edith Marcombe Shiffert and Yuki Sawa from *Modern Japanese Poetry* translated by Edith Marcombe Shiffert and Yuki Sawa. Reprinted by permission of Charles E. Tuttle Co., Inc. of Tokyo, Japan, the publishers.

Leslie Scalapino. "how can I help myself" and "[EPILOGUE: Anemone]" from *Considering how exaggerated music is.* "lightened white air" from *The Return of Painting, The Pearl, and Orion.* Used by permission of the author and North Point Press Estate.

Grace Schulman. "Burial of a Fisherman in Hydra" from *Burn Down the Icons. Poems by Grace Schulman.* Copyright © 1976 by Princeton University Press. Reprinted by permission of Princeton University Press.

Armand Schwerner. "Dirge" tr. Armand Schwerner from *Journal of the Polynesian Society,* 1953 in a transcription by M. H. Pukui and E. S. Cragill Handy. "Song of the Old Woman" adapted by Armand Schwerner from *Poèmes Eskimo* by Paul Emile Victor, Paris, Seghers, 1958. Adaptation Copyright © 1972, by Armand Schwerner. Used by permission of the translator.

Maura Stanton. "Wander Indiana" from *Tales of the Supernatural,* published by David R. Godine in 1988. Copyright © 1988 by Maura Stanton.

Lydia Stephanou. "A 'Case of Assault' " tr. Kimon Friar. By permission of the author and translator.

Ruth Stone. "Winter" and "Repetition of Words and Weather" first appeared in *Green House.* Copyright Ruth Stone. Reprinted by permission of *Green House* and the author. "Years Later" first appeared in *Poets-on-Loving.* Copyright Ruth Stone. "Dark Conclusions" Copyright © 1980 by Ruth Stone. Reprinted by permission of the author. "Room," "Whose Scene," and "Codicil" from *Cheap: New Poems and Ballads* by Ruth Stone. Copyright © 1975 by Ruth Stone "On the Mountain," "The Talking Fish," "Dénouement," and "Liberation" from *Topography and Other Poems* by Ruth Stone. Copyright © 1971 by Ruth Stone. Reprinted by permission of Harcourt Brace Jovanovich, Inc.

Alfonsina Storni. "I Am Going to Sleep," "Lighthouse in the Night," "My Sister," and "They've Come" tr. Willis Barnstone from *Antologia Poetica* by Alfonsina Storni. Used by permission of Alejandre Alfonso Storni.

Woman of Suminoe. "How I wish I had known" tr. Kenneth Yasuda from *Land of the Reed Plains* translated by Kenneth Yasuda. Reprinted by permission of Charles E. Tuttle Co., Inc. of Tokyo, Japan, publishers.

Sun Yün-feng. "On the Road Through Change-te" and "The Trail up Wu Gorge" tr. Kenneth Rexroth from *The Orchid Boat: Women Poets of China.* Translated and edited by Kenneth Rexroth and Ling Chung. English language translation Copyright © 1972 by the editors. Used by permission of The Seabury Press, Inc.

May Swenson. "Women" from *Iconographs* by May Swenson. Copyright © 1970 by May Swenson. Reprinted with permission of the author.

Wislawa Szymborska. "I Am Too Near" tr. Czeslaw Milosz from *Post-War Polish Poetry* translated by Czeslaw Milosz. Copyright © 1965 by Czeslaw Milosz. Reprinted by permission of Doubleday & Company, Inc.

Mitsuhashi Takajo. "The hair ornament of the sun" tr. Kenneth Rexroth and Ikuko Atsumi from *The Burning Heart: Women Poets of Japan.* Translated and edited by Kenneth Rexroth and Ikuko Atsumi. English language translation Copyright © 1977 by The Seabury Press, Inc. Used by permission of the publishers.

Ise Tayü. "The clear water of the imperial pond" tr. Kenneth Rexroth and Ikuko Atsumi from *The Burning Heart: Women Poets of Japan.* Translated and edited by Kenneth Rexroth and Ikuko Atsumi. English language translation. Copyright © 1977 by The Seabury Press, Inc. Used by permission of the publishers.

Telesilla. "O Artemis and your virgin girls" tr. Willis Barnstone from *Greek Lyric Poetry* translated by Willis Barnstone. Copyright © 1962, 1967 by Willis Barnstone. Reprinted by permission of Schocken Books, Inc.

Elsa Tió. "I am furious with myself" tr. Willis Barnstone and used by permission of the author.

T'sai Yen. "From 18 Verses Sung to a Tatar Reed Whistle—Verses I, II, VII, and XIII" tr. Kenneth Rexroth and Ling Chung from *The Orchid Boat: Women Poets of China.* Translated and edited by Kenneth Rexroth and Ling Chung. English language translation Copyright © 1972 by the editors. Used by permission of The Seabury Press, Inc.

Kiyoko Tsuda. "To be a mistress" tr. Edith Marcombe Shiffert and Yuki Sawa from *Modern Japanese Poetry* translated by Edith Marcombe Shiffert and Yuki Sawa. Reprinted by permission of Charles E. Tuttle Co., Inc. of Tokyo, Japan, the publishers.

Marina Tsvetayeva. "We Shall Not Escape Hell" tr. Elaine Feinstein from *Selected Poems* by Marina Tsvetayeva translated by Elaine Feinstein and Angela Livingstone, © Oxford University Press 1971. Reprinted by permission of Oxford University Press. ". . . I'd like to live with you" and III, V, VII, VIII, IX, XI, and XII from "The Daughters of Jairus" tr. Paul Schmidt and used by his permission. "Ars" tr. Willis Barnstone and Edward Brown. Appeared originally in the *New York Review of Books.* Used by permission of the translators.

Nadia Tuéni. "Nothing but a man" and "Would you come back if I said the earth" tr. Willis Barnstone from *Poemes Pour Une Histoire* by Nadia Tuéni. Reprinted by permission of Editions Seghers.

Tzu Yeh. Poems from "Five Tzu-Yeh Songs" tr. Arthur Waley from *Translations from the Chinese* translated by Arthur Waley. Copyright 1919 and renewed 1947 by Arthur Waley. Reprinted by permission of Alfred A. Knopf, Inc. Also by permission of George Allen & Unwin (Publishers) Ltd. from *More Translations from the Chinese* by Arthur Waley.

Julia Uceda. "2976" and "Time Reminded Me" tr. Willis Barnstone from *Poemas de Cherry Lane* by Julia Uceda. Used by permission of Concha Lagos and Agora, Madrid.

Ruth M. Underhill. "I'd run about" and "Owl Woman's Death Song" transcribed by Ruth M. Underhill from *Papago Indian Religions* by Ruth M. Underhill. Reprinted by permission of Columbia University Press and Ruth M. Underhill.

Eleni Vakalo. "My Father's Eye" tr. Kimon Friar appeared originally in *Modern European Poetry* edited by Willis Barnstone. Reprinted by permission of the poet and the translator.

Jean Valentine: "Foraging," "The One You Wanted to Be . . ." and "The Free Abandonment of Blues." Reprinted by permission.

Blanca Varela. "The Things I Say Are True" tr. Donald Yates appeared originally in *Mundus Artium.* Reprinted by permission of *Mundus Artium.* All Varela poems by permission of the author.

Ellen Bryant Voigt. "Bright Leaf" from *The Lotus Flowers: Poems* by Ellen Bryant Voight. © 1987 Ellen Bryant Voigt. Reprinted by permission of W. W. Norton & Company, Inc.

Diane Wakoski. "Blue Monday" from *Emerald Ice: Selected Poems 1962–1987.* Copyright © 1968 by Diane Wakoski. Reprinted by permission of Black Sparrow Press.

Arthur Waley. "A very handsome gentleman" and "Widow's Lament" tr. Arthur Waley from *Book of Songs* by Arthur Waley. Reprinted by permission of Grove Press, Inc. and George Allen & Unwin (Publishers) Ltd. "Cold, cold the year draws to its end," "At the beginning of winter a cold spirit comes," and "The bright moon, oh how white it shines," tr. Arthur Waley from *Translations from the Chinese* translated by Arthur Waley. Copyright 1919 and renewed 1947 by Arthur Waley. Reprinted by permission of Alfred A. Knopf, Inc. Reprinted from *More Translations from the Chinese* by Arthur Waley by permission of George Allen & Unwin (Publishers) Ltd.

Wang Ch'ing-hui. "Now the lotuses in the imperial lake" tr. Kenneth Rexroth and Ling Chung from *The Orchid Boat: Women Poets of China.* Translated and edited by Kenneth Rexroth and Ling Chung. English language translation Copyright © 1972 by the editors. Used by permission of The Seabury Press, Inc.

Wang Wei. "Seeking a Mooring" tr. Kenneth Rexroth and Ling Chung from *The Orchid Boat: Women Poets of China.* Translated and edited by Kenneth Rexroth and Ling Chung. English language translation Copyright © 1972 by the editors. Used by permission of The Seabury Press, Inc.

Geoffrey Waters. "Parting Is Hard," "There is a soldier on a battlefield," and "Written on a Leaf" by Anonymous Palace Women, ca. 700, 730, 790 tr. Geoffrey Waters. Used by permission of the translator.

Martina Werner. "Monogram 4," "Monogram 23," and "Monogram 29" tr. Rosemarie Waldrop. © Suhrkamp Verlag Frankfurt am Main 1965, Alle Rechte vorbehalten. Used by permission of the publisher and the translator.

Shirley Williams. "The Killing of the Birds" and "If He Let Us Go Now" from *The Peacock Poems* by Shirley Williams. Copyright © 1975 by Shirley Williams. Reprinted by permission of Wesleyan University Press.

Anne Winters. "Night Wash" and "The Stethoscope . . .: (from: 'Elizabeth Near and Fair')" from *The Key to the City.* Reprinted by permission of the University of Chicago Press.

Wu Tsao. "In the Home of the Scholar Wu Su-chiang . . . ,'" "Bitter rain in my courtyard," and "On your slender body" tr. Kenneth Rexroth and Ling Chung from *The Orchid Boat: Women Poets of China.* Translated and edited by Kenneth Rexroth and Ling Chung. English language translation Copyright © 1972 by the editors. Used by permission of The Seabury Press, Inc.

Elinor Wylie. "The Eagle and the Mole" and "Down to the Puritan marrow of my bones" from "Wild Peaches" Copyright 1921 by Alfred A. Knopf, Inc.; renewed 1949 by William Rose Benet. "Sanctuary" Copyright 1949 by William Rose Benet. "Prophecy" Copyright 1923 by Alfred A. Knopf, Inc. Reprinted from *Collected Poems of Elinor Wylie* by permission of Alfred A. Knopf, Inc.

Kenneth Yasuda. "Even though my hands" tr. Kenneth Yasuda from *Land of the Reed Plains* translated by Kenneth Yasuda, Charles E. Tuttle Co., Inc. of Tokyo, Japan, publisher. Reprinted by permission of the publisher.

Sachiko Yoshihara. "Madness" tr. James Kirkup and Shozo Tokunaga appeared originally in *Mundus Artium* and is reprinted by permission.

Yüeh-Fu Shih. "I think of him" tr. Wai-lim Yip. English translation Copyright © by Wai-lim Yip and used with his permission.

Yü Hsüan-chi. All tr. Geoffrey Waters. Copyright © 1980 by Geoffrey Waters and used with his permission.

Katha Pollitt. "Happiness Writes White" originally published in *Grand Street* #8:2, Winter 1989. Copyright © 1989 by Katha Pollitt. Reprinted by permission of the author.

Index of Poets

Ada, 487–89
Ai, 721–23
Akazome Emon, 170–71
Åkesson, Sonja, 362–66
Akhmadulina, Bella, 406–19
Akhmatova, Anna, 373–85
Albiach, Anne Marie, 224
Alcosser, Sandra, 717–19
Alegria, Claribel, 276–81
Alver, Betti, 370–72
Andal, 66–67
Andersen, Astrid Hjertenaes, 361
Anonymous (Amharic), 106
Anonymous (Anglo-Saxon), 431–33
Anonymous (Apache), 423–24
Anonymous (Arabic), 100–102
Anonymous (Catalan), 245–46
Anonymous (Chinese), 110–11,
  115–16
Anonymous (Chinese, Music Bureau),
  117
Anonymous (Chinese, Palace Women),
  122–23
Anonymous (Chinese, Tzu Yeh songs),
  120–21
Anonymous (Chippewa), 423
Anonymous (Egyptian), 11–15
Anonymous (Eskimo), 426–27

Anonymous (French), 185, 200–201
Anonymous (Greek, Moirologia),
  48–49
Anonymous (Hawaiian), 425–26
Anonymous (Hebrew, *from* Song of
  Songs), 20–23
Anonymous (Hottentot), 105
Anonymous (Japanese), 158–59,
  167
Anonymous (Kshetrayya), 79–80
Anonymous (Latin), 59–60, 61
Anonymous (Nahuatl), 420–21
Anonymous (Neo-Aramaic), 29
Anonymous (Nyasa), 104
Anonymous (Pampa), 422
Anonymous (Papago), 424–25
Anonymous (Papuan), 427–29
Anonymous (Provençal), 184
Anonymous (Quechua), 421–22
Anonymous (Spanish, ballads),
  248–50
Anonymous (Spanish, *jarchas*), 247
Anonymous (Spanish, songs), 250–56
Anonymous (Turkish), 87–89
Anonymous (Yoruba), 104–5
Anyte, 43–44
Atwood, Margaret, 694–99
Ava, Frau, 314

Bachmann, Ingeborg, 333–40
Banus, Maria, 348–49
Barnstone, Aliki, 753–56
Barreno, Maria Isabel, 296–99
Behn, Aphra, 447–49
Berggolts, Olga, 400–402
Bertken, Sister, 343–44
Bierds, Linda, 761–63
Bishop, Elizabeth, 572–95
Blandiana, Ana, 354
Bødker, Cecil, 366–68
Bogan, Louise, 554–55
Boruch, Marianne, 733–34
Bradstreet, Anne, 438–46
Brontë, Emily, 462–63
Brooks, Gwendolyn, 606–10
Broumas, Olga, 727–30
Browning, Elizabeth Barrett, 460–61
Bruck, Edith, 311–12
Burgos, Julia de, 271–74
Burnat-Provins, Marguerite, 218–19
Buzea, Constanta, 353

Caroutch, Yvonne, 221–23
Cassian, Nina, 351–52
Castellanos, Rosario, 268–70
Castro, Rosalia de, 257–59
Céu, Sor Violante do, 294
Chao Li-hua, 147
Chao Luan-luan, 121
Chedid, Andrée, 243–44
Ch'in Chia's wife, 113–14
Ch'iu Chin, 153–54
Chiyo, 173–74
Cho Wen-chün, 112
Christensen, Inger, 368–69
Chu Shu-chen, 143–46
Clampitt, Amy, 611–15
Clifton, Lucille, 679–84
Coleridge, Mary Elizabeth, 490–91
Colonna, Victoria da, 305–6
Cooper, Jane, 631–32
Cortez, Jayne, 673–76
Court Lady, A, 157
Cruz, Sor Juana Inés de la, 262–68

Deborah, 17–20
Desbordes-Valmore, Marceline, 217
Dickinson, Emily, 467–87

Die, Countess Beatritz de, 183–84
Dobson, Rosemary, 771–72
Domin, Hilde, 324–25
Domino, Ruth, 308–9
Doolittle, Hilda [pseud. H.D.],
    521–31
Dove, Rita, 744–47
Droste-Hüishoff, Annette Von, 314–16

Enheduanna, 1–8
Erdrich, Louise, 747–51
Eristi-Aya, 10

Farrokhzad, Forugh, 83–86
Ferré, Rosario, 275–76
Fonte Boa, Maria Amália, 302–3
Forche, Carolyn, 734–37
Fox, Lucia, 284
Fraire, Isabel, 270–71
France, Marie de, 186–200
Fuertes, Gloria, 259–61

Gallagher, Tess, 707–9
Gergely, Ágnes, 360
Gilbert, Sandra M., 685–87
Glück, Louise, 712–15
Goldberg, Leah, 24–27
Gorbanyevskaya, Natalya, 402–6
Graham, Jorie, 737–39
Gregg, Linda, 702–4

H.D. *See* Doolittle, Hilda
Hacker, Marilyn, 704–5
Hadewijch, 341–43
Hajnal, Anna, 356–58
Hannah, 16–17
Harima, Young Woman of, 159
Harjo, Joy, 743–44
Harwood, Gwen, 771
Hébert, Anne, 229–40
Herbert, Mary Sidney, Countess of
    Pembroke, 434–35
Herzberg, Judith, 344–45
Hiestand, Emily, 723–24
Hill, Roberta, 759–61
Hillman, Brenda, 739–43
Honnamama, 69–70
Horikawa, Lady, 172–73
Horta, Maria Teresa, 296–99

Howe, Susan, 763–64
Hsi-chün, 113
Hsüeh T'ao, 123–24
Huang O, 147–49

Inib-sarri, 9
Isanos, Magda, 349–50
Ise, Lady, 162–67
Ise Tayú, 172
Issaia, Nana, 53
Iwa no Hime, Empress, 156
Izumi Shikibu (Lady Izumi), 167–70

Jahan, Nur, Empress, 82
Jallais, Denise, 228–29
Jana Bai, 71
Jonker, Ingrid, 107–9
Jordan, June, 677–79

Kaccipettu Nannakaiyar, 65–66
Kanai Mieko, 181–82
Kasa, Lady, 161
Kasdaglis, Lina, 52–53
Kaufman, Shirley, 625–26
Kegels, Anne-Marie, 225–26
Kendrick, Dolores, 637–41
Khansa, Al-, 92–97
Khirniq, Al-, 91
Khoury-Gata, Vénus, 242–43
Killigrew, Anne, 449–51
Kiwus, Karen, 332–33
Kizer, Carolyn, 632–35
Korinna, 44–45
Kumin, Maxine, 635–37

Labé, Louise, 204–17
Laederach, Monique, 227
Laila Akhyaliyya, 98–99
Lal Ded, 80–81
Lanier, Emilia, 435–38
Lasker-Schüler, Else, 316–19
Lento, Takako U., 180
Levertov, Denise, 626–31
Li Ch'ing-chao, 133–42
Li Chü, 155
Lisboa, Henriqueta, 300–301
Lorde, Audre, 666–68
Lowell, Amy, 491–97
Loy, Mina, 497–519

McHugh, Heather, 724–27
McPherson, Sandra, 711–12
Mahādēvi, 67–69
Mahodahi, 63
Maillard, Claude, 228
Malancioiu, Ileana, 352–53
Mansour, Joyce, 220–21
Marias, The Three, 296–99
Marula, 64
Mary, Mother of Jesus, 46–47
Mastoraki, Jenny, 54–56
Mechain, Gwerfyl, 429–30
Meireles, Cecilia, 299–300
Melinescu, Gabriela, 354–55
Mello Breyner Andresen, Sophia de, 295
Miccolis, Leila, 301–2
Miles, Josephine, 595–98
Millay, Edna St. Vincent, 552–54
Miller, Jane, 730–33
Mira Bai, 72–79
Mistral, Gabriela, 291–93
Mitsuhashi Takajo, 175
Montagu, Lady Mary Wortley, 451–52
Morstein, Petra von, 329–32
Moore, Marianne, 533–52
Mukta Bai, 70
Mylonas, Eva, 54
Murasaki Shikibu (Lady Murasaki), 171

Nagase Kiyoko, 175
Nagy, Ágnes Nemes, 358–59
Niedecker, Lorine, 557–71

O'Hehir, Diana, 765–67
Okkur Macatti, 65
Oku, Princess, 157
Olds, Sharon, 705–7
Oliver, Mary, 671–73
Ombres, Rossana, 313
Ono no Komachi, 161–62
Ōtomo of Sakanone, Lady, 159–60

Paley Francescato, Martha, 289–90
Pan, Lady (Pan Chieh-yu), 114
Philips, Katherine, 446–47
Piercy, Marge, 676–77
Pinar, Florencio del, 256

Ping Hsin, 154–55
Pisan, Christine de, 201–4
Plantier, Thérèse, 219–20
Plath, Sylvia, 654–66
Pollitt, Katha, 767–68
Porumbacu, Veronica, 350
Prager, Marie-Françoise, 224–25
Praxilla, 43

Rabi'a the Mystic, 90
Raine, Kathleen, 571–72
Ravikovitch, Dahlia, 27–28
Rich, Adrienne, 646–54
Rossetti, Christina, 463–64
Rukeyser, Muriel, 598–600
Ryōjin Hishō, 172

Sachs, Nelly, 319–24
Sagami, Lady (Sagami Shikibu), 170
Saitō, Fumi, 175–76
Salter, Mary Jo, 768–70
Sappho, 30–42
Schulman, Grace, 693–94
Sexton, Anne, 641–46
Shange, Ntozake, 757–58
Shikishi, Princess, 173
Shiraishi Kazuko, 177–79
Sila, 63
Sitwell, Edith, 531–33
Smith, Charlotte, 452–53
Smith, Stevie, 556–57
Solt, Mary Ellen, 615–24
Song, Cathy, 751–52
Spaziani, Maria Luisa, 309–10
Spivack, Kathleen, 691–93
Stampa, Gaspara, 306–8
Stanton, Maura, 719–21
Stephanou, Lydia, 51–52
Stone, Ruth, 600–605
Storni, Alfonsina, 285–88
Sulpicia, 57–59
Sumangala's Mother, 71

Suminoe, Woman of, 158
Sun Yūn-feng, 150–51
Swenson, May, 610–11
Szymborska, Wislawa, 346–47

Tada Chimako, 176–77
Telesilla, 43
Tió, Elsa, 274–75
Ts'ai Yen, 118–20
Tsuda, Kiyoko, 176
Tsvetayeva, Marina, 386–99
Tuéni, Nadia, 240–42
Tzu Yeh. *See* Anonymous (Chinese, Tzu Yeh songs)

Uceda, Julia, 261–62

Vakalo, Eleni, 50
Valentine, Jean, 669–71
Vallana, 64
Varela, Blanca, 281–84
Velho da Costa, Maria, 296–99
Vidya, 62–63
Voight, Ellen Bryant, 710–11

Wakoski, Diane, 687–91
Wang Ch'ing-hui, 146–47
Wang Wei, 149–50
Werner, Martina, 325–28
Wheatley, Phillis, 453–65
Williams, Shirley, 715–17
Winters, Anne, 699–702
Wu Tsao, 151–53
Wylie, Elinor, 519–21

Yosano, Akiko, 174
Yoshihara Sachiko, 179–80
Yü Hsüan-chi, 124–33
Yüeh-fu shih. *See* Anonymous (Chinese, Music Bureau)

Zeb-un-Nissa, Princess, 82

Index of Translators

Allen, Julie, 203–4, 256
Appalaswamy, B., 79–80
Atsumi Ikuko, 161, 170–72, 175–79

Banani, Amin, 85
Baraheni, Reza, 84, 87–89
Barnstone, Aliki, 1–8, 47, 57–59, 207, 211, 238–40, 257–58, 263–66, 274, 277–81, 285–88
Barnstone, Helle Tzalopoulou, 53
Barnstone, Willis, 1–10, 15, 20–24, 30–48, 57–64, 66–67, 69–83, 90–102, 106, 134–37, 157–58, 160, 163, 167–70, 183–85, 202–3, 205–17, 219–22, 225–26, 232–35, 238–43, 246–47, 249–66, 269–70, 274–83, 285–90, 294–95, 300–305, 314–17, 341–44, 348–51, 355, 370–72, 388, 423–24, 426–27, 429–33
Beckett, Samuel, 266–68
Beier, Ulli, 104–5
Berg, Stephen, 384–85
Berlind, Bruce, 358–59
Berman, Cassia, 218–19
Bloch, Chana, 27–28
Bownas, Geoffrey, 156–57, 159–60, 172, 174

Brandeis, Irma, 163–66
Brown, Edward, 388

Calinescu, Matei, 348–51, 355
Carlisle, Olga, 410–11, 415–18
Cerqueira, Nelson, 295, 300–304
Christensen, Nadia, 361, 366–69
Chung Ling, 118–21, 142, 146–55
Claréus, Ingrid, 362–66
Cloutier, David, 222–23
Commanday, Ramah, 24–27
Cope, Jack, 107–9

Deligiorgis, Stavros, 352–55
Desmore, Frances, 423
Drake, Christopher, 181–82

Einzig, Barbara, 374, 402–4, 408–10, 414
Eoyang, Eugene, 133

Feinstein, Elaine, 386–87
Feldman, Ruth, 310, 311–12
Friar, Kimon, 50, 51–52, 54, 56

Gaden, H., 103
Garrison, David, 291–93
Germanakos, Nikos, 55–56

Ghossem, Mirene, 243–44
Gillespie, Michael, 316–17
Guenther, Charles, 227

Hahn, Thomas, 105
Hallo, William W., 2–8
Halpern, Daniel, 407, 411–14
Hamburger, Michael, 321–22
Hayward, Max, 376
Hazo, Samuel, 243–44
Hoeksema, Thomas, 270–71
Hoffman, Daniel, 309, 356–57
Hollo, Anselm, 420–21
Honig, Edwin, 248
Howes, Barbara, 202, 217,
    305–6
Hsu, Kai-yu, 154–55
Hughes, Langston, 291
Huws, Daniel, 334–36

Impey, Michael, 351–52

Kaufman, Shirley, 344–45
Keeley, Edmund, 52–53
Keeley, Mary, 52–53
Keene, Donald, 162, 173
Kessler, Jascha, 85
Kirkup, James, 179–80
Kizer, Carolyn, 123–24
Kolb, Elene, 48–49, 219–20, 222,
    225, 341–43, 431–33
Kumin, Judith, 220, 228–29
Kumin, Maxine, 220, 228–32
Kunitz, Stanley, 376

Lane, Helen R., 296–99
Laycock, Don, 428

McAuley, Almut, 332–33
McKane, Richard, 375–84
Maghan, R., 284
Marase, Mari, 428
Mead, Matthew, 320–21
Mead, Ruth, 320–21
Merrill, James, 299–300
Merwin, W. S., 226, 245–46, 251,
    421–22
Middleton, Christopher, 339–40
Milosz, Czeslaw, 346–47

Mongione, Jerre, 309
Morgan, Edwin, 360
Morris, Tudor, 324–25

Nawfal, Tony, 97
Nilsson, Usha, 72–79
Nims, John Frederick, 258–59
Noyes, Stanley, 415–16

Oinas, Felix, 370–72
Orion, Janice, 333

Plomer, William, 107–9
Poulin, A., Jr., 235–37
Pound, Ezra, 11–14
Prentuo, Joe, 428–29

Ramanujan, A. K., 65–69
Rasmussen, Knud, 426–27
Ray, David, 173–74
Rexroth, Kenneth, 114, 118–21,
    138–55, 161–62, 170–73, 175–77
Rothenberg, Jerome, 29, 336–39

Salomon, I. L., 313
Sawa, Yuki, 176
Schmidt, Paul, 387–99
Schulman, Grace, 271–73
Schwerner, Armand, 425–27
Seaton, J. P., 142, 147
Shiffert, Edith Marcombe, 176
Smith, William J., 357–58
Stepanchev, Stephen, 375,
    418–19
Stock, Noel, 11–14
Sun Chu-chin, 134–37
Swann, Brian, 311–12, 351–52

Tambimuttu, 64, 79–80
Taylor, Alexander, 366–68
Terasaki, Etsuko, 163–66
Terry, Patricia, 186–201
Thwaite, Anthony, 156–57, 159–60,
    172, 174
Tikku, Girdhard, 83–86
Todd, Albert, 412–14
Tokunaga, Shozo, 179–80

Underhill, Ruth, 424–25

Vaidya, G. V., 64
Valentine, Jean, 410–11, 416–18
Van Dikj, J.J.A., 2–8
Victor, Paul Emile, 427
Vitiello, J., 306–8

Waldrop, Keith, 224
Waldrop, Rosemarie, 317–19, 325–32
Waley, Arthur, 110–16, 120–21,
   161–62

Waters, Geoffrey, 122–33
Weissbort, Daniel, 400–402, 404–6
Wensinger, Arthur, 323–24
Wilbur, Richard, 373–74

Yasuda, Kenneth, 158–59
Yates, Donald, 283–84
Yip, Wai-lim, 117

Zahra-Soltan, Shokoohtaezeh, 87–89

Index of Titles and First Lines

A *Baroque Sunburst,* 611
A basket of dirty clothes, 605
A bright moon illumines the
night-prospect, 115
A *"Case of Assault,"* 51
A *Curse on Uruk,* 6
A *Dream,* 417
A *Farewel to Worldly Joyes,* 450
A *Farewell to a Southern Melody,* 148
A few sashay, a few finagle, 725
A flower of waves, 164
—A fox ran across your path—pure
totem, 740
A free woman. At last free, 71
A *Grave,* 550
A leaf floats in endless space, 149
A *Letter to Her Father,* 9
A *Letter to Her Mother,* 10
A Light exists in Spring, 476
A loon? No, 423
A *Love Song,* 316
A *Lovely Young Moor,* 249
a lyric elixir of death, 500
A narrow Fellow in the Grass, 476
A *Nation Wrapped in Stone,* 759
A new volcano has erupted, 585
A *Present from the Emperor's New
Concubine,* 114

A *Rapier of Treason,* 101
A *Sparrow in the Dust,* 309
A star crashes in a small plaza and a
bird loses its eyes, 283
A story, a story, 641
A *Sunset of the City,* 608
A *Tailor Called Sorrow,* 370
A Tatar chief forced me to become his
wife, 118
A thing which fades, 161
A thousand women's eyes, 504
A very handsome gentleman, 110
A *Weary Song to a Slow Sad Tune,*
141
A Word made Flesh is seldom, 486
Abortion, 721
Abraham and Isaac, 318
Abraham built a town of sod, 318
Abraham's children played with shells,
318
Abysmal corners will dis (be) located,
302
Adam's Complaint, 627
Afraid of the sun, I hide behind my
sleeve, 125
After a long winter, giving, 173
After an age when thunderbolts and
hail, 213

After great pain, a formal feeling comes, 470
After having slain very many beasts, 214
After he stripped off my clothes, 64
After kicking on the swing, 142
After noon, in the plaza, cries, shrill yells, running and breaking, 595
After Supper in Madison, Wisconsin, 733
after the all been done and i, 684
Against Love, 447
Alcoholic dream, 563
Alive, this man was Manes, a common slave, 44
All Greece hates, 522
All night I could not sleep, 121
All seas are seas in the moon to these, 699
All Splendor on Earth, 332
All the while, believe me, I prayed, 37
All things within this fading world hath end, 440
all those heads those ears those eyes, 427
All through the march, besides bag and blanket, 360
Alone, 144
Alone, 384
Alone am I, and alone I wish to be, 203
Already I am no longer looked at with lechery or love, 608
Although he has no form, 70
Although I cry and though my eyes still shed, 212
Although I was her pupil, 45
Although it is a cold evening, 577
An Old Woman, 515
And call ye this to utter what is just, 434
And Hannah prayed, and said, 16
And in conclusion I'll say, 408
And now the riverbank. For the last time, 391
And now the riverbank. I cling, 389
And so at last I climbed, 673
And so I speak, 227
And there is nothing at all—neither fear, 404
And Time would be set back, 511

Andromache's Wedding, 37
Andromeda, 42
Anna Speaks of the Childhood of Mary Her Daughter, 683
Another Song of the Same Woman, to Some Partridges, Sent to Her Alive, 256
Answering Li Ying Who Showed Me His Poems About Summer Fishing, 126
Anthology Poem, 331
Antiphonal Hymn in Praise of Inanna, 7
Appeal to the Moongod Nanna-Suen to Throw Out Lugalanne, the New Conqueror of the City of Uruk, 5
Apricot Tree, 349
Archaic Figure, 612
Arrangement by rage, 514
Ars, 388
As Emily Dickinson, 768
As for me, my Nanna ignores me, 6
As I paint the street, 562
As if I didn't have enough, 411
As if somebody ordered it, 375
As praiseworthy, 561
As soon as I lie down in my soft bed, 209
As When Some Hungry Fledgling Hears and Sees, 305
As when some hungry fledgling hears and sees, 305
At dawn of the day the Creator (for Whom . . .), 306
at 4:30 AM, 757
At last love has come. I would be more ashamed, 57
At Night, 412
At Tauba's death I swore, 98
At the beginning of winter a cold spirit comes, 116
At the Door of the House, 504
At the End of Spring, 125
At the Fishhouses, 577
At the Holi festival of color, 77
At the instant of drowning he invoked the three sisters, 771
At the time when blossoms, 120
Autobiography, 362
Autumn, 408
"Avec Ardeur," 547
Avoid the reeking herd, 519

Balancing Everything, 703
Ballad of the Cool Fountain, 248
Ballad of the Ten Casino Dancers, 299
Banishment from Ur, 4
Be happy for me, girls, 201
bear's blood, 352
Because I could not stop for Death, 477
Because we suspected, 164
Before, 596
Before the Birth of One of Her Children, 440
Before the Pacific, 282
Before the sun goes down, 361
Behind you, 279
Belly Dancer, 687
Better not go to these deep woods, 232
Bird, 359
Birth, 311
Birth, 355
Birth, 751
Birthdays, 324
Bitter rain in my courtyard, 151
Black lake, black boat, two black cut-paper people, 660
Black Pudding, 708
Black Silk, 707
Blameless as daylight I stood looking, 658
bled, 327
Bloomingdale's I, 704
Blossoms crowd the branches: too beautiful to endure, 123
Blue Monday, 688
Blue of the heaps of beads poured into her breasts, 688
Boudoir Lament, 131
Boy Breaking Glass, 609
Bread Is Born, 229
Bright Leaf, 710
Burial of a Fisherman in Hydra, 694
But I feared that her soul didn't, 740
But Perhaps, 320
But perhaps, 320
But Venus first, 266
By day she woos me, soft, exceeding fair, 464
—By your breasts, 296

Calendar, 366
Cambridge Songs, from the, 59
Camel, 99
Camoes and the Debt, 295
Can these movements which move themselves, 687
Canticle of a Black Lady, 637
Carmina Burana, from the, 61
Carrefour, 495
Child Beater, 721
Child of silence and shadow, 222
Ch'in Chu's Wife's Reply, 113
Chippewa Love Song, 423
Christine to Her Son, 202
Christmas Mass for a Little Atheist Jesus, 228
Classicism, 704
Clear Bright, 139
Coal, 667
Codicil, 602
Cold, cold the year draws to its end, 115
Cold in the earth, and the deep snow piled above thee, 462
Colors shifting, 355
Come at dawn, good friend, 251
Come, holy tortoise shell, 31
Come let's go climb on that jasmine-mantled rock, 65
Come slowly—Eden, 479
Come to me in the night—we shall sleep closely together, 316
Coming home, I find you still in bed, 721
Condemning the Moongod Nanna, 6
Confronting a longing, 272
Consider at the outset, 564
Conversation between the Chevalier de Chamilly and Mariana Alcoforado, in the Manner of a Song of Regret, 296
Cordilleras to climb—Andean, 568
Correspondence, 165
Country of hunchbacks!—where the strong, straight spine, 553
Crazed Man in Concentration Camp, 360
Crimes of Lugalanne, 5
Critics and Connoisseurs, 551
Crossing the Water, 660
Crown of Happiness, 233

Crusoe in England, 585
Cry, 718
Cry out for Sakhr when a dove with
   necklaces, 92
Cuckoo, noisy among the Shenbaka
   flowers, 66
Curie, 500
curling them around, 681
Curriculum Vitae, 336
Cutting Greens, 681

Daddy, 655
Daguerreotype Taken in Old Age, 696
Daily the wind-flowers age, and so do I,
   123
Dancing-Girl's Song, 79
Dare you see a Soul *at the White Heat,*
   480
Dark Conclusions, 603
Darkness Music, 599
Darkness reigned, 53
Darling, I won't be your hot love, 57
Darwin I-V, 567–70
Daughters of Jairus, from, 389
David Walker (1785–1830), 745
Days in White, 335
Dear one   at your mercy,
   512
Death, become a shewolf, 233
Death of a Young Son by Drowning, 698
Death Songs, 88
Death Sonnet I, 293
Deep lane, poor families, I have few
   friends, 125
Dénouement, 601
Depot in Rapid City, 760
Dirge, 425
Diving into the Wreck, 647
Do you have a sweet thought,
   Cerinthus, 58
Doesn't he realize, 161
Doll, 597
Don't blame me, ladies, if I've loved.
   No sneers, 216
Don't dress for it, 173
Don't sing a song, 292
Don't suppose that the weightless
   phantom, 371
Doors, 219

Dream, 53
Dream of the Forgotten Lover, 284
Dream 2: Brian the Still-Hunter, 695
Dreams in War Time, from, 496
Dress me in green, 253
Drops of Gall, 292
Dürer would have seen a reason for
   living, 535
During the holidays, 54
Dusk, 293
Dust, 691
dying asks a question: she gives an
   answer, 637

Earlier, when I remember: a small, 596
Earthworms, 289
Easter Greeting, 565
Edge, 665
Eighteen, 349
Elegy for Her Brother Sakhr, 92
Elegy for the Giant Tortoises, 697
Elegy for the Wife of a Friend, 130
*Elegy: Ise Lamenting the Death of Empress
   Onshi,* 166
Elizabeth Near and Far, 701
End of the World, 317
Evadne, 523
Even in my dreams, 164
Even the sun-clouds this morning
   cannot manage such skirts, 662
Even then I knew it was the old
   unanswerable form of beauty, 708
Even though my hands, 158
Every Day, 339
Every morning I get up, 148
Every morning, in the dust, 309
Every peak is a crater. This is the law of
   volcanoes, 652
Eves Apologie, 436
Eyes of Night-Time, 598
Eyes shut tight, 179

Fallen leaves are scattered by evening
   rain, 132
Far inland, 426
Farewel to Unsubstantial Joyes, 450
Farewell, 147
Fear, 356
Fear the one, 105

Feeling the urge my mother, 311
Final Notations, 654
Final Prayer, 7
Fineness of midnight, 291
First Dream, from, 266
First having read the book of myths, 647
FitzRoy blinked, 568
Flower Ensnarer of Psalms, 313
Fooling God, 747
Foolish men who accuse, 264
For a moment I saw a surging river, 81
For a Neighbor Girl, 125
For authorities whose hopes, 546
For Colored Girls Who Have Considered Suicide When the Rainbow Is Enuf, from, 757
For Hidden Mist Pavilian, 124
For Kuo Hsieng, 127
For My Mother, 678
for my mother, 678
For one who says he feels, 330
For years I had not seen such a town, 344
Foraging, 1, 2, 669
Foreclosure, 567
Forgot to mail my letter to my friend Death, 220
Forsythia, 619
Fountain, coolest fountain, 248
Free to travel, he still couldn't be shown how lucky, 745
Friend, don't be angry, 72
Friend, how can I meet my Lord, 72
Friends, 62
From Brooklyn, over the Brooklyn Bridge, on this fine morning, 579
From darkness, 167
From 18 Verses Sung to a Tatar Reed Whistle, 118
From moonwater, from mirror mist, a slender porcelain, 348
From narrow provinces, 590
From One Who Stays, 495
From that first flash when awful Love took flame, 207
From the House of Yemanjá, 667
From the icy niche where men placed you, 293

From the piling's kelp I drew, 726
From the slopes of the mountain, 139
Funeral Lament (Kommos) From Epiros, 48

Gertrude Stein, 500
Get a load, 561
Gift Hour, 348
Glass, 180
God exists, though he doesn't exist, 177
Goodbye, 408
Grandfather, 563
Greatly shining, 496
Green things grow, 513
Grim monarch! see, depriv'd of vital breath, 457
Grotesque, 494

Habitation, 696
Hagar and Ishmael, 318
Hail, happy bride, for thou are truly blest, 452
Hail, happy day, when, smiling like the morn, 457
"Half-cracked" to Higginson, living, 647
Half of our borders, rivers and mountains were gone, 152
Half Past Four, October, 257
Hanging from the branches of a green, 163
Hannah's Thanksgiving, 16
Happiness Writes White, 767
Hardly Spring, with ice, 174
Hari helps his people, 76
Hari, look at me a while, 75
Harvesting Wheat for the Public Share, 155
Have you heard? The troubles, 59
he accepts the circle, speech and so, 224
He and I sought together, 525
He come, 641
He loved three things in life, 374
He, who navigated with success, 698
He wore a tin pot for a hat, in which, 672
Headless in East Berlin, no goddess, 612

Hear, 564

Helen, 522

Heliodora, 525

Hence Cupid! with your cheating toys, 447

Here are fine gifts, children, 39

Here, as in a painting, yellow noon burns, 405

Here Follows Some Verses upon the Burning of Our House July 10th, 1666. Copied Out of a Loose Paper, 444

Here in the mountain woods, 629

Here in this world, 170

Hermes came to me in a dream. I said, 41

Hesperos, you bring home all the bright dawn disperses, 41

Hidden immortal, 164

hills picking up the, 352

His being gone is a gift to my people, 431

His holy, 567

His trousers are wind, 106

Hold, hold it tight, 428

Holidays, 54

Holy angels, in envy I cast no sigh, 307

Holy Night, 684

Homage to My Hips, 682

Home Free, 766

Honestly I wish I were dead, 34

Honeysuckle (Chevrefoil), 190

Hope Atherton's Wanderings, from, 764

How can I call out? How can I shout, 412

How can you look at the Neva, 376

How did I come to be here? I suppose, 719

How do they do it, the ones who make love, 706

How do you make bread talk, this old treasure all wrapped, 229

How do you recognize death, 300

How empty seems the town now you are gone, 495

How He Is Coming Then, 684

How I wish I had known, 158

How many evenings in the arbor by the river, 133

How many wise men and heroes, 153

How will you cross, 157

Human Geography, 260

I am a bunch of red roses, 87

I am a king's daughter, you a king's wife, 10

I am a skinny girl, 234

I am a widow, robed in black, alone, 203

I am a young girl, gay, 185

I am afraid I may be Ilia, 356

I am always aware of my mother, 175

I am furious with myself, 275

I am Going to Sleep (Suicide Poem), 288

I am Hermes. I stand in the crossroads by a windy, 44

"I Am in Danger—Sir—", 647

I am leading a quiet life, 362

I am my lover's and he desires me, 23

I Am New York City, 674

I am new york city, 674

I am of this world, 157

I am on a peninsula, 731

I am reminded of the vestment, 353

I am still bitter about the last place we stayed, 602

I am the centre, 506

I am the jealous storehouse of the candle-ends, 511

I Am Too Near, 346

I am too near to be dreamt of by him, 346

I Am with Those, 108

I am with those, 108

I am yours, 314

I argue, 298

I came by the way, 81

I came too late to the hills: they were swept bare, 571

I can not invent it, 529

I can only say I have waited for you, 107

I can't appease Ashimbabbar, the moon god An, 5

I can't break with the Dark One, 74

I Carried Statues, 358

I carried statues on the ship, 358

I catch the movement of his lips, 389

I caught a tremendous fish, 573

I come, 423

I come home from you through the
early light of spring, 652

I come to you with the vertigoes of
the source, 223

I could not hope, 32

I crawl up the couch leg feeling, 601

I did not know where you kept your
heart, 51

I died for Beauty—but was scarce, 471

I don't care, 513

I don't sleep. All night, 77

I don't want to be a nun, 256

I drag a boat over the ocean, 80

I dreamed I held, 161

I dreamt of the old house, 401

I dug a grave under an oak-tree, 496

I dwell in Possibility, 482

I feel my heart melting, 293

I felt a Funeral, in my Brain, 468

I find my love fishing, 14

I first tasted under Apollo's lips, 523

I flee the city, temples, and each place,
213

I get up. I am sick of, 145

I had come to the house, in a cave of
trees, 554

I had eight birds hatcht in one nest,
441

I had three friends, 104

I have done it again, 662

I have no embroidered headband, 39

I Hear You've Let Go, 275

I hear you've let go, 275

I heard a Fly buzz—when I died, 472

I heard my love was going to
Yang-chou, 121

I hold my honey and I store my bread,
607

I knew a clean man, 559

I Knew I'd Sing, 725

I know I change, 696

I Korinna am here to sing the courage,
44

I left my hills, 168

I let the incense grow cold, 139

I like to see it lap the Miles, 473

I live on this depraved and lonely cliff,
305

I live where darkness, 70

I love and fear him, 161

I love these hours alone I do, 730

I loved, 61

I loved her softness, her warm human
smell, 771

I make this dirge for you Miss Mary
Binning I miss you, 425

I make this song sadly about myself,
432

I married, 566

I member we went to the hospital that
day, 717

I must become small and hide where
he cannot reach, 747

I need only fall asleep, 354

I never believed that in my broken
life, 119

I never wanted to be a star, 83

I Once Knew a Man, 683

i once knew a man who had wild horses
killed, 683

I ordered this, this clean wood box,
660

I painted my eyes with black antimony,
103

I put out the worship plate, 76

I raise the curtains and go out, 144

I reckon—when I count at all, 481

I Remember, 556

I remember, he said, 570

I remember you in young peaches like
jade, 130

I run away, 638

I sat before my glass one day, 490

I saw no Way—The Heavens were
stitched, 473

I see a man who is dull, 100

I see bodies in the morning kneel,
626

I shall lie hidden in a hut, 520

I sleep but my heart is awake, 22

I stood at 6 A.M. on the wharf, 745

I suppose there is nothing, 565

I think of him, 117

I, too, dislike it; there are things that
are important beyond all this, 534

I took a piece of the rare cloth of Ch'i,
114

I wake up in your bed, I know I have been dreaming, 651

I walk down the garden paths, 491

I walk in loneliness through the greenwood, 185

I want to be in a garden with my love, 100

I want to be with my love in a garden, 101

I wanted this morning to bring you a gift of roses, 217

I wanted to see you, 301

I was born in a time of peace, 118

I was born with a song in my tongue—but would, 388

I was foretold that on a certain day, 214

I was sitting on the steps of the cinema, 704

I was sleepless. I was awake all night, 95

I was the Moor Moraima, 249

I who cut off my sorrows, 170

I will carry my coat and not put on my belt, 121

I will make love, 247

I wish to paint my eyes, 15

I wish you would come, 169

I would not paint—a picture, 480

I write to make you suffer, 226

I'd like to live with you, 387

I'd run about, 424

Ideographs, 706

If again in the Spring, 163

If ever two were one, then surely we, 440

If He Let Us Go Now, 716

If I could linger on his lovely chest, 211

if i stand in my window, 680

"If I weren't working, I'd sleep next to you, 704

If it is you, there, 166

If my nipples were to drip milk, 41

If my torch goes out it will be dark, 277

if night takes the form of a whale and, 270

If snow falls on the far field, 158

If you go away, 159

If you have no time, 169

If you love me, 169

If you really care for me, 247

If you take the moon in your hands, 524

If You Will, 596

I'll act out a weird dream, 225

I'll always dress in black and rave, 202

I'll greet the sun once more, 85

I'll keep your shirt white, 88

I'm always, 329

I'm Nobody! Who are you, 469

I'm not here   never was, 353

I'm Sad, 84

I'm sad, 84

I'm the snow on mountains, 89

Imagine father that you had a brother were, 729

Impermanence, 81

In an orchard a little fountain flows, 200

In Death's Field, 93

In death's field, in morning distress, 93

In flight in escape, 323

In gold sandals, 32

In Leonardo's light, 561

In Memory of My Dear Grandchild Anne Bradstreet Who Deceased June 20, 1669, Being Three Years and Seven Months Old, 444

In my bed at night, 21

In Progress, 464

In Reference to Her Children, 23. June 1656, 441

In shaping the snow into blossoms, 154

In silent night when rest I took, 444

In that ancient time—in eternity, 410

In the blue distance, 321

In the Case of Lobsters, 331

In the censer the coals are high, 7

In the Emptied Rest Home, 416

In the gathering dew, 170

In the great night my heart will go out, 424

In the great snowfall before the bomb, 559

In the Home of the Scholar Wu Su-chiang From Hsin-an, I Saw Two

In the Home (*cont.*)
Psalteries of the Late Sung General Hsieh Fang-tê, 152
In the House of the Dying, 631
in the house with the tortoise chair, 420
In the laboratory waiting room, 633
In the land of dwarfs, 85
In the mountain where you are unworshiped, 4
In the night there was murder in the street, 350
In the sky there is a moon and stars, 495
In the Snowfall, 429
In the Waiting Room, 582
In this her thirty-seventh year, the Italy, 613
In using there are always two, 676
In Which She Satisfies a Fear with the Rhetoric of Tears, 263
In Worcester, Massachusetts, 582
Inanna and An, 2
Inanna and Ebih, 4
Inanna and Enlil, 2
Inanna and Ishkur, 3
Inanna and the Anunna, 3
Inanna and the City of Uruk, 4
Inanna and the Divine Essences, 2
Inch by inch along the bed, 766
Infidelity, 400
Insomnia, 576
Interior Landscape, 259
Into her mother's bedroom to wash the ballooning body, 606
Invitation to Miss Marianne Moore, 579
Iron Heaven, 372
is an odd infinitive, in which, 727
Is it true that black birds infinitely dispersed, 67
is the total black, being spoken, 667
Island Mary, 684
It has no wings, 278
It is a year of good harvest, 155
it is all blood and breaking, 681
It is an ancestral castle, 240
It is the best thing, 711
It was easy to see that he was not an ordinary merchant, 530

It was my bridal night I remember, 556
it will not be simple, it will not be long, 654
It would be wrong for us. It is not right, 41
It's a madman, I said, 53
It's all familiar, 417
It's almost as if we're already there, 705
It's nice that though you are casual about me, 58
It's ten. Evening. The room is in half light, 285
Its trunk as of dead silver cast, 357
I've been free, 563
I've been thinking—mean, cogitating, 547
I've moved here to the Immortal's place, 133
I've seen a Dying Eye, 473
I've stitched my dress with continents, 351

Jack's Defeat Creek, 753
Jacob, 317
Jacob, a bull among his herd, 317
Jacob and Esau, 319
Jean, death comes close to us all, 645
Jessie Mitchell's Mother, 606
John Chapman, 672
joseph, i afraid of stars, 684
Journey in the Orient, 310
Justice, 329

Kingfisher blue along a tangled bank, 128
Kiss me again, rekiss me, kiss me more, 214
Kiss me and hug me, 254
kitchenette building, 607
Kithairon sang of cunning Kronos, 44
Knowledge, 351
Kypros, 37

Lacoste IV, 705
Lady Lazarus, 662
Lady Murasaki says, 171
Lady of all the essences, full of light, 2

Lady of the Ferry Inn, 430
Laila Boasting, 98
Lament after Her Husband Bishr's Murder, 91
Lament for a Husband, 428
Lament of Hsi-Chün, 113
Lamentations, 713
Lamenting Tauba, 98
Landscape with Leaves and Figure, 727
Landscape with Next of Kin, 729
Last, 137
Last night I saw your corpse, 221
Last year at the Feast of Lanterns, 144
Lately I've felt a grave concern, 183
Laundromat, 566
Leah: in Freedom, 638
Leave Krete and come to this holy temple, 36
Leave the window open, 88
(Leaving the island, she believes, to go to the child . . .), 227
Let Joy go solace-winged, 513
Let me see you, 78
let me strap, 716
Let no girl wait on you that day when you bind your wild, 235
Let others pray for the passenger pigeon, 697
Let the flowers make a journey, 643
Let us bring out those heavy dice, 355
Letters of the Unliving, 499, 516
Letting My Feelings Out, 131
Liberation, 601
Life in the Castle, 240
Light mist, then dense fog, 141
Lighthouse in the Night, 287
Lightly forsaking, 163
Like a dragon you have filled the land, 2
Like a flight of arrows the wind, 143
Like a madwoman and almost alone, 259
Like a mountain whirlwind, 32
like a pot turned on the straw, 684
Like a ravaged sea, 164
Like a sweet apple reddening on the high, 37
Like cutting the dry rot out of a potato, 603

Like Gulliver, 351
Like Gulliver pulling a hundred ships, 351
Like Halley's comet, bending on its tail, 701
Like words put to a song, the bunched tobacco leaves, 710
Line Like, 322
Line like, 322
Lines, 488
Lines for Marking Time, 760
Lines to Accompany Flowers for Eve, 634
Loneliness and July Ninth, 278
Long ago, in the forests of southern Europe, 761
Long is the night, 336
Longing for the Emperor, 156
Look at my continent containing, 260
Looking at Henry Moore's Elephant Skull Etchings in Jerusalem During the War, 625
Lord, this woman who fell into many sins, 47
Lost, 144
Lot's Wife, 373
Lounge in the shade of the luxuriant laurel's, 43
Love—bittersweet, irrepressible, 35
Love has seven names, 341
Love in the peaceful u.s.a., 692
love set you going like a fat gold watch, 657
Love Song, 103
Love Songs, 87
Love Songs to Joannes, from, 510
Love—the permanent littérateur, 514
Love u.s.a., 692
Love's Witness, 449
Lucy Sleeps with Master Muford, 641
Lullaby for My Dead Child, 229
Lute, companion of my calamity, 211

Madness, 179
Mama, 325
Man looking into the sea, 550
Margaret Fuller, 1847, 613
Marriage, 538
Marriage, 621
Marriage is not, 696

Mary Magdalene, 47
Master of blood I am yours, 226
May the man who gained my trust yet did not come, 172
Me from Myself—to banish, 482
Medusa, 554
Meeting after Separation, 64
Melting in this mist and heavy clouds, 142
Memorial Day, 595
Memory at These Speeds, 730
Men's Voices, 369
Men's voices in the darkness, 369
Mercy, 743
Mercy, 743
Midnight, 291
Mine—by the Right of the White Election, 481
Minor Elegy, 300
Mira is dancing with bells tied, 73
Mirror, 176
Miss Rosie, 679
Monogram 4, 325
Monogram 23, 327
Monogram 29, 328
Montalbert, from, 452
Moonshot Sonnet, 617
More than the gems, 159
Morning, 145
Morning Song, 657
Morning and evening, drunk and singing, 127
Most beautiful of things I leave is sunlight, 43
Mother, 175
Mother darling, I cannot work the loom, 37
Mother, I want to go, 250
Mother Mother shave me, 104
Mother's Song, 158
Moving in Winter, 650
Moving out, 330
Much Madness is divinest Sense, 471
My Anthis, although our dear Anaktoria, 33
my boat goes west, yours east, 147
My body is like, 165
My brother has on, 160
My brother was not a camel driver, 96

My camel kneels at Ibn Marwan's door, 99
My desire for revenge, the bitterness, 302
my dreams, my works, must wait till after hell, 607
My eye cried and woke me, 93
My eyes are thirsty, 75
My father had a glass eye, 50
My father used to say, 552
My Father's Eye, 50
My friend tree, 558
My Grandmother in Paris, 685
My hated birthday is here, and I must go, 58
My heart is an oil lamp, 101
My heart is on my fist, 238
My heart's friend, will you tell me who this mischievous youngster is, 79
My husband is the same man, 63
My lady Carenza of the lovely body, 184
My life closed twice before its close, 474
My Life had stood—a Loaded Gun, 485
My life is engraved on my poems, 25
My Lord has departed, 156
My love has gone down to his garden, 22
My love is in my house, 75
My love is white and ruddy, 23
My lover capable of terrible lies, 65
My love's eyes are red as the sargasso, 603
My man loved me so much, 675
My mirror is always a little taller than I am, 176
My mother always said, 31
My mother had two faces and a frying pot, 667
My Mother—preferring the strange to the tame, 632
My old flame lives by Jack's Defeat Creek, 753
My passion is like turbulence at the head, 100
My people have married me, 113
My poor body is also unworthy, 113
My room is so small, 24

My Sister, 285
My soul magnifies the Lord, 46
My spirit leans in joyousness tow'rd
    thine, 488
My spouse, Chunaychunay, 421

Nameless Journey, 24
Near a Waterfall at Ryūmon, 164
Nearer, 345
nevertheless I prefer, 329
New-sawed, 560
News of the palace, 165
Night opens like an almond, 222
Night Wash, 699
Nights bring you the fever, 569,
    763
Nineteen Old Poems, from, 115
. . . 1968 . . ., 329
Ninth Month, 750
No day was sad as the day Sakhr, 93
No one can hurt me. They've tried to
    kill me, 384
No one has sung "Let the world
    know," 7
Nobody will open the door for you,
    282
Nocturnal Heart, 226
Noisy politicians confuse the world,
    128
Not because of you, not because of me,
    just that, 405
Not to sigh and to be tender, 449
Not Ulysses, no, nor any other man,
    205
—Not unwillingly, but not with
    lightness either, 743
Not waking, in my dreams, my dreams,
    400
Not working, not breathing, 408
Nothing, 274
Nothing but a man, 241
Now all that sound of laughter, sound
    of singing, 258
Now I don't have to leave this place
    not for anybody, 670
Now in my, 42
Now in my Samarkand of blue enamel,
    310
Now in one year, 561

Now the lotuses in the imperial lake,
    146
Now they're pillaging the last coast, 56
Now we are like that flat cone of sand,
    709

O Artemis and your virgin girls, 43
O blazing Sun, how happy you are
    there, 215
O cloud that wants to be the sky's
    arrow, 270
O dream from the blackness, 40
O eye, weep for a rider, 97
O eyes clear with beauty, O tender
    gaze, 210
O flowers of Mekhmekh, give us
    peace, 12
O Gongyla, my darling rose, 39
O handsome chestnut eyes, evasive
    gaze, 206
O interminable desires, O futile hope,
    206
O my hornbill husband, you have a
    bad smell, 428
O my lady, the Anunna, the great
    gods, 3
O my Lord, if I worship you from fear
    of Hell, 90
O my Lord, the stars glitter and eyes
    of men are closed, 90
O people who live in the world, 66
O Suen, the usurper Lugalanne means
    nothing to me, 5
O, winter, your gesture, 409
O you, 495
Of Autumn, 350
Of Course—I prayed, 470
Of Myself, 25
Of Petronilla Lucia Letizia Felicita, 506
Often when alone I liken my lord, 307
Oh moon, oh moon, 428
Oh, oh, you will be sorry for that word,
    553
Oh to be a bride, 418
Old Mother turns blue and from us,
    558
On Being Brought from Africa to America,
    455
On Death, 449

On Death's domain intent I fix my
   eyes, 458
On Earth, 83
On Her Brother, 96
On Her Brother Sakhr, 93
On nights when hail, 167
On Seeing the Field Being Singed, 165
On the Death of Emperor Tenji, 157
On the Death of Mrs. Bowes, 452
On the ground are my sketches of the
   contours, 371
On the holy day of your going out to
   war, 63
On the last year's trip I enjoyed this
   place, 150
On the Mountain, 603
On the Road Through Chang-te, 150
On the roads at night I saw the glitter
   of eyes, 598
On this winter night, 170
On your dazzling throne, Aphrodite, 35
On your slender body, 151
Once again a public wedding, 566
Once he puts out the light, 636
Once More, 85
Once my parents were older, 174
One need not be a Chamber—to be
   Haunted, 483
One year there were too many, 366
Only to have a grief, 651
Orange leaves are gone, 169
Other men are thorn, 68
Our Backs Are to the Cypress, 27
Our backs are to the cypress, 27
Our Hands in the Garden, 237
Our last bridge, 392
Our love was pure, 112
Our roofs are adjacent, 88
Out of the corpse-warm vestibule of
   heaven steps the sun, 333
Outside, the rain, pinafore of gray
   water, dresses the town, 721
Overdue Balance Sheet, 220
Overheard over S.E. Asia, 627
Owl Woman's Death Song, 424

Paris. 1900. A sky of corrugated iron.
   Snow and mud, 685
Parody, 289

Parting, a thousand cups won't wash
   away the sorrow, 128
Parting Is Hard, 122
Parting is hard, I'll tell you twice, 122
Parturition, 506
Passionate Love Is Temporary, 727
—Past factory workshops, empty, 395
Patterns, 411
Pear Tree, 522
Peeling Onions, 651
Penelope, from, 227
People, 69
Perception of an object costs, 486
Phallus, 177
Photo after Pogrom, 514
Planting in Tuscaloosa, 723
Pleasant Songs, 12
Please keep an eye on my house for a
   few moments, 62
Poe, 500
Poem of Explanations, 27
Poem to Ease Birth, 420
Poem to My Death, 272
Poem to the Tune, "Riverbank Willows,"
   128
Poetry, 534
Poet's work, 563
Popcorn-can cover, 560
Poppies in October, 662
Pregnancy, 711
Prometheus, 56
Prophecy, 520
Proportion, 495
Psalm 58: Si Vere Utique, 434
Puberty Rite Dance Song (Traditional),
   423
Publication—is the Auction, 484

Rain. A heavy mane, 398
rain down, 620
Rain to the Tribe, 97
Rana, I know you gave me poison, 74
Rana, why do you treat me, 74
Rattan, 134
Rebecca's maid: a girl come from afar,
   319
Red lotus incense fades on, 140
Regretful Thoughts, 132
Relaxed, nothing to do, 131

Remember how close we sat in Sifnos having dinner by the water? You, 730

Remembrance, 462

Repetition of Words and Weather, 605

Requiem 1935–1940, 377

Reunion, 344

Reverse Seeing, 740

Rhyming a Friend's Poem, 127

Rhyming with a Friend, 128

Riding the blue sapphire mountains, 67

Riding the San Francisco Train, 766

Room, 600

Root and grape, pear and bean, 253

Rowing, 641

Sacrifice, 53

Sad music from vermilion strings, 129

Saddle and Cell, 298

San Onofre, California, 736

Sanctuary, 519

"Sappho, if you do not come out," 33

Search, 277

Search. Search. Seek. Seek, 141

Seated on her bed legs spread open, 221

See the young man I've laid out, 48

Seeing the Plum Blossoms by the River, 163

Seeing the Returning Geese, 163

Seeking a Mooring, 149

Seldom   Trying for Love, 512

Selective Service, 734

Self-Portrait, 368

Selling Ruined Peonies, 124

Semen, 290

Sent from the Capital to Her Elder Daughter, 159

Sent to Wen T'ing Yün on a Winter Night, 129

September rain falls on the house, 581

Sestina, 581

Set me as a seal on your heart, 23

Seven years I have kept him, dead, 245

Sex without Love, 706

Shall I pull the curtains against the coming night, 596

She Attempts to Refute the Praises That Truth, Which She Calls Passion, Inscribed on a Portrait of the Poet, 263

She is dead, 324

She Proves the Inconsistency of the Desires and Criticism of Men Who Accuse Women of What They Themselves Cause, 264

She rose to His Requirements—dropt, 484

She saying, You don't have to do anything, 670

She Understands Me, 681

she wanted rain, 691

She was cleaning—there is always, 707

She was my staff and I am blind, 71

Shedding our petty pruderies, 514

Sheep in Fog, 665

Sheltered from the Spring wind by, 144

Sigh, in the wind fall flowers, their petals dance, 124

signs of wear, 328

Silence, 407

Silence, 552

Silver dust, 522

Since I entered the inner rooms, 122

Since I'm a girl, 255

Since life is nothing in your philosophy, 274

Since that night, 168

Since the night is dark, 254

Sir Beezlebub, 531

Sister, 291

Sky, 136

Sky Burial, 754

Sleepless, 95

Sleepwalkers, 414

Slender, delicate, soft jade, 121

Slender Fingers, 121

Slight unpremeditated Words are borne, 449

Small Aircraft, 411

Small Country, 279

Small space, 304

Snowlands Hotel. Before dawn in one of the dormitories, 754

So lonely am I, 162

So Long, 675

So once again, hearing the tired aunts, 631

So what good is it? Let's be sad, 767

Some day I'll go to San Francisco, 766
Some float off on chocolate bars, 562
Some people, 627
Some people know how to love, 27
Some say cavalry and others claim, 31
Someone else, 168
Someone, I tell you, 42
Someone in the next apartment, 600
Someone passes, 171
Someone's Blood, 745
Son, of great fortune I have none, 202
Song, 104
Song for a Girl on Her First Menstruation, 428
Song of Snow-White Heads, 112
Song of Songs (The Shulamite), from, 20
Song of the Ill-Married, 200
Song of the Lioness for her Cub, 105
Song of the Fucked Duck, 676
Song of the Old Woman, 427
Song to a Lover, 106
Sonnet to Gath, 553
Sorrow, 145
Spawn of Fantasies, 510
Speeches at the Barriers, from, 763
Split Tractate, 740
Spring, 552
Spring flowers and autumn moon enter poems, 124
Spring-Gazing Song, 123
Spring has come to the Pass, 138
Spring is short, 174
Spring Thoughts Sent to Tzu-an, 130
Spring Waters, from, 154
Stars in the sky are as big, 88
Staying on the Mountains in Summer, 133
Stepping Westward, 630
Still Falls the Rain, 532
Still falls the Rain, 532
Still in October, the woodcock, 603
Stop! Don't touch me, 254
Storms lend you wings, destroyer of the lands, 2
Stormy Night in Autumn, 143
struck through such a dome, 611
Summer Garden, 375
Sunflowers, 749
Sweet Mountains—Ye tell Me no lie, 484

Swept snow, Li Po, 560
Swift fleet the billowy clouds along the sky, 452
Sylvius, your hands near my mouth are heady flowers, 219

Tashkent Breaks into Blossom, 375
Teeth of flowers, hairnet of dew, 288
Tell 'em to take my bare walls down, 567
Tell me though safest End of all our Woe, 449
Telling My Feelings, 129
Ten dancers glide, 299
Ten years ago it seemed impossible, 464
That conversation we were always on the edge, 653
That Day, 644
That man entered through my eyes, 284
The Abduction, 747
The Alchemy of Day, 235
The Arrival of the Bee Box, 660
The Author to Her Book, 446
The autumn made colors burn, 242
The bee-keeper kissed me, 251
The bells, the cannons, the houses black with crepe, 747
The blossoms have fallen, 173
The Board of War has quelled the mutiny, 126
The Bride, 418
The chemist creates, 565
The Child Bearers, 645
The clear water of the imperial pond, 172
The cloth-plant grew till it covered the thorn bush, 111
The color of the flowers, 162
The coming of that limpid Star is twice, 208
The Corpse-Keeper, 245
The Crusaders, 55
The day time failed began as usual, 694
The day will come when I will, 148
The days grow and the stars cross over, 599
The Death of a Warrior, 56

The death of a warrior, 56
The Diary of Izumi Shikibu, from, 167
The Eagle and the Mole, 519
The Everlasting Forests, 28
The everlasting forests won't last forever, 28
The Eye-mote, 658
The father pours the milk from his glass, 749
The Felled Plane Tree, 357
The first horn lifts its arm over the dew-lit grass, 746
The first lady of the throne room, 8
The Firstborn Land, 334
The Fish, 573
The Fisherman's Wife, 496
(The Floating Poem, Unnumbered), 653
The florist was told, cyclamen or azalea, 634
The Flowering of the Rod, 530
The Free Abandonment Blues, 670
The fruit on the trees is aging fast, 359
The fruits you give me are more savory than others, 218
The Fury of Flowers and Worms, 643
The Glass and the Bowl, 749
The glow and beauty of the stars, 32
The great fish's eyes never shut, 269
The Great Fountains, 232
The hair ornament of the sun, 175
The Hermit Has a Visitor, 636
The Hiding Place, 737
The hills step off into whiteness, 665
The Honey Tree, 673
The House of Madam Juju, 181
The House Slave, 746
The Imaginary Iceberg, 575
The Intruder, 632
The just man followed then his angel guide, 373
The Killing of the Birds, 717
The Lady's Resolve, 451
The Last Day of the Year (New Year's Eve), 314
The last Night that She lived, 475
The last one, 323
The last time I saw it was 1968, 737
The limb of forests rises up, 223
The Lion's Bride, 771

The Lost Baby Poem, 680
The Magnificat, 46
The man I saw in the forest, 695
The Matter Over, 726
The Memory of Elena, 735
The monk sat in his den, 556
The Moon and the Yew Tree, 659
The moon in the bureau mirror, 576
The Moon in Your Hands, 524
The moon of Id came, 82
The moon rises, a vengeance on anguish, 414
The Moose, 590
The mountain road is steep, the stone steps are dangerous, 130
The Names of Georgian Women, 415
The needy were lined up by order of famine, 233
The Night, 93
The Nightingale, 186
The nights are very clear in Greece, 704
The Offended, 233
The Old Anguish, 144
The One You Wanted to Be Is the One You Are, 670
The orphan boat of my heart, 155
The Other Side of a Mirror, 490
The Painter in the Lion Cage, 371
The palm of the hand, 176
The Paper Nautilus, 546
The past has come apart, 515
The people are saying that I am your enemy, 271
The pomegranate speaks, 13
The present implies presence, 516
The prig of passion, 514
The Prologue, 438
The Restoration of Enheduanna to her Former Station, 8
The Risk, 643
The Roamer, 628
The Roses of Sa'adi, 217
The skin-sack, 510
The Skinny Girl, 234
The sky a black sphere, 287
The sky has been dark, 751
The Sleepwalker, 321
The sleepwalker, 321

The small scaffolds, boards in the form of, 706

The Song of Deborah, 17

The Soul selects her own Society, 469

The Sound of Rain, 413

The sound of rain like a lute, 413

The square stone room makes a shape in the air, 702

The Steeple-Jack, 535

The Stillness, The Dancing, 761

The story I shall tell today, 186

The sun sets. The wind moans, 119

The swallow sings "Dawn . . .", 12

The Tale of Genji, from, 171

The Talking Fish, 603

The Taxi, 496

The ten o'clock train to New York, 604

The Things I Say Are True, 283

The Three Fates, 771

the time I dropped your almost body down, 680

The Titans, 371

The Tomb of the Kings, 238

The trail climbs in zig-zags, 150

The Trail Up Wu Gorge, 150

The train's french horn sighs, sheds a few tears, 406

The Two Lovers, 194

The Upper Story, 768

The Vandals, 56

The voice of my darling, 20

The water closing, 636

The waves surge higher still, 166

The Weak Monk, 556

The white moon gleams through scudding, 145

The Wife's Lament, 432

The Wilderness, 571

The wind stuffs the scum of the white street, 511

The woman is perfected, 665

The Wooden Horse then said, 55

The World, 464

The world comes back to me, 628

The year at its turn, 314

The Youngest Daughter, 751

Their life, collapsed like unplayed cards, 650

Then I said to the elegant ladies, 35

Then sang Deborah and Barak the son of Abinoam on that day, 17

Then they paraded Pompey's urn, 55

There are, 331

There are caverns, 625

There came from Normandy an old, 194

There in the flower garden, 251

There is a crying in the world, 317

there is a girl inside, 682

There is a great amount of poetry in unconscious, 551

There is a flower blossoming out of season, 313

There is a Languor of the Life, 471

There is a morn by man unseen, 478

There is a pain—so utter, 474

There is a soldier on a battlefield, 122

There on the sea sails wandered, 415

There's a bird perched on my shoulder, 359

There's a certain Slant of light, 467

These birds were born, 256

These days I get up with the birches, 335

these hips are big hips, 682

They are rebuilding, 165

They say that plants don't talk, nor do, 257

They shut me up in Prose, 482

They unfold before the sky, 219

They were both still, 713

They were dancing as if, 180

They've Come, 287

They've opened up a road in the jungle and found, 262

Thing Poem, 330

Thinking hard, hunting rhymes, humming by my lamp, 129

This afternoon, my love, speaking to you, 265

This institution, 538

This is my letter to the World, 479

This is the bricklayer; hear the thud, 519

This is the desk I sit at, 644

This is the last month, the petrified forest, 750

This is the light of the mind, cold and planetary, 659

This Journey, 107

This journey that obliterates your image, 107

This lay, a favorite of mine, 190

This Morning, 599

This morning I woke, 349

This world, 402

Those eyes, 506

Thou ill-form'd offspring of my feeble brain, 446

Thou large-brained woman and large-hearted man, 461

Though I am dark, 255

Though I am Laila of the Persian romance, 82

Though the willows bent down to shelter us where we played, 597

Though we lived in the same lane, 126

Though you have never possessed me, 501

Three Friends, 104

Three Moments in Paris, 501

Three Poems, 269

Three women are walking in Alabama, 723

Through a Glass Eye, Lightly, 633

Till Death Do Us Part, 302

Till now your indiscretion sets us free, 436

Tilt, 731

time of fish dying, 355

Time of Waiting in Amsterdam, 107

Time Reminded Me, 261

Time to garden, 565

Tiny snow of the stunningly cold black day, 429

'Tis not that Dying hurts us so, 469

Title divine—is mine, 486

To a Gentleman and Lady on the Death of the Lady's Brother and Sister, and a Child of the Name Avis, Aged One Year, 454, 458

To a Lady on the Death of Her Husband, 456

To Antonio Machado, 629

To be a mistress, 176

To demolish it, 332

To fall, like an apple, no mind, 416

To George Sand: I. A Desire, 461

To George Sand: II. A Recognition, 461

To Have To, 727

To heal you Hieronymus I had brought you, 352

To honor the return of sparkling sun, 212

To I. Lavrentevaya, 406

To Julia de Burgos, 271

To Kin I call in the Iron-Woods, 764

To know there are rhododendrons on the slopes of the Himalayas, 345

To Krishna Haunting the Hills, 67

To lose it all at once, 396

To make a prairie it takes a clover and one bee, 474

To me he seems like a god, 30

To My Dear and Loving Husband, 440

To my firstborn land, in the south, 334

To My Pressure Pump, 563

To My Sister, 401

To remember is not always to go back to what was, 261

To S. M., a Young African Painter, on Seeing His Works, 459

To show the lab'ring bosom's deep intent, 459

To sing of wars, of captains, and of kings, 438

To Song, 400

To the Minister Liu, 126

To the Right Honorable William, Earl of Dartmouth, His Majesty's Principal Secretary of State for North-America, etc., 457

To Tzu-an, 128

To what purpose, April, do you return again, 562

Today, 512

Today I saw a place no one has seen, 372

Today I saw a woman plowing a furrow. Her hips are, 291

Today my mother and sisters, 287

Together, 636

Together in Greece, 704

Tradition, I, II, 565

Traditional Funeral Songs, 48

Traffic Lights, 52
Tribute to the Angel, from, 529
True genius, but true woman! dost deny, 461
Tsu Yeh Songs, 120
Turning, following the arrows through, 181
Twas mercy brought me from my Pagan land, 455
Twenty-One Love Poems, from, 651
Twenty-Year Marriage, 722
Twice I have written you that I am unhappy, 9
Twilight. By now the genial sea of dusk, 357
Two Gifts, 346
Two hearts: two blades of grass I braid together, 123
Two Springs, 138
2976, 262
Two Tile Beaks, 304

Under the oak tree, oak tree, 252
Unknown love, 160
Upon Her Soothing Breast, 463
Upon her soothing breast, 463

Vitality, 302
Voice of a Dissipated Woman Inside a Tomb, Talking to Another Woman Who Presumed to Enter a Church with the Purpose of Being Seen and Praised by Everyone, Who Sat Down Near a Sepulcher Containing This Epitaph, Which Curiously Reads, 294

Wake as you will, but wake in me, 400
Wake, child, 77
Waking this morning, 599
Wander Indiana, 719
War is not declared anymore, 339
Warm, 135
Wasn't your mother a woman, 69
We are going down a long slide, 625
We are the Akhail. Our youth persists, 98
We are things of dry hours and the involuntary plan, 607

We dream—it is good we are dreaming, 473
We got this idea, 237
We have come far south, 736
We ladies sense it is the cuckoo builds no nest, 601
We might have coupled, 511
We might have lived together, 513
We Real Cool, 608
We real cool. We, 608
We rise from the snow where we've, 734
we rise up early and, 683
We see each living thing finally die, 208
We Shall Not Escape Hell, 386
We shall not escape Hell, my passionate, 386
We spend our morning, 735
Weaving Love-Knots, 123
Weaving Love-Knots 2, 123
We'd rather have the iceberg than the ship, 575
Weeds grow shamelessly, 368
Well, spring overflows the land, 558
Wet streets. It has rained drops big as silver coins, 349
What am I in the place of nourishment, 6
What Are We Playing At, 243
What are you doing here in this strange world that goes on and off, 52
What can I send you under the earth, 48
What can melt a traveler's grief, 127
What else can we do, 243
What good is it to me if long ago, 216
What grandeur makes a man seem venerable, 215
What Her Girlfriends Said to Her, 65
What horror to awake at night, 558
What is beautiful alters, has undertow, 703
What is green in me, 630
What is weaker than a god? It groans hungry, 269
What it felt like, 669
What She Said, 65
What you see here is a colorful illusion, 263

Whatever happens with us, your body, 653

What's worse than this past century, 374

WHEN, 531

When a daughter tries suicide, 643

When before those eyes, my life and light, 308

When he sailed into the harbor, 45

When I am alone, 496

When I go away from you, 496

When I lie in bed thinking of those years, I often, 703

When I perceive your blond and graceful head, 210

When I said "You have grown thin," 64

When I strip, 225

When I walk into their bedroom at night, 749

When I was a girl, 246

When I was a good and quick little girl, 422

when i watch you, 679

When I went into my garden, I found, 343

When night shadows slipped across the plain, I saw a man, 759

When our two souls stand up erect and strong, 460

When the birds sang, 255

When the fifth month comes, 163

When the last bus leaves, moths stream toward lights, 760

When they were wild, 751

When we are two drunk suns, 222

When you broke from me, 169

When you Love, or speak of it, 448

Where they come from, I do not know, 733

Whilst thirst of praise and vain desire of fame, 451

White cups white, 87

White legs and pink footpads, the black cat, 718

"White phosphorus, white phosphorus, 627

White Serpent, 321

White serpent, 321

White Venus limpid, wandering in the sky, 207

Who am I? I am a lady faithful to the ways, 430

Who was it that took away my voice, 407

Whole and Without Blessing, 703

Whose broken window is a cry of art, 609

Whose Scene, 601

Why did you keep finding me where I was? 669

Why do the lilies goggle their tongues at me, 494

Widow's Lament, 111

Wild Crab, 618

Wild Nights—Wild Nights, 479

Will he always love me, 172

Will you sleep forever, 45

Wind and Silver, 496

Wind is thin, 59

Winged One, 743

Winter, 409

Winter, 604

Wishing for roses, I walk through the garden, 375

With a Blessing Rather Than Love Said Nietzsche, 702

With a handful of weeds I weep in the slanting sun, 131

With candour I confess my love, 11

With every note, 167

With troubled heart and trembling hand I write, 444

Women, 555

Women, 610

Women, 610

Women have no wildness in them, 555

Women know how to wait here, 760

Women, whoever wishes to know my lord, 307

Words Spoken by Pasternak during a Bombing, 410

Words to a Song, 359

Would a circling surface vulture, 68

would write a letter with, 29

Would you come back if I said the earth, 241

Written On a Leaf, 122
Wulf and Eadwacer, 431

Year after year I have watched, 138
Years . . . balancing, 570
Years Later, 604
Years later my eyes clear up, 604
Yellow blood on the dunes, 282
Yes, 709
Yesterday I was, 331
Yesterday in drizzling rain, 370
Yogi, don't go away, 76
you, 228
You asked me to enter the holy
    cloister, 4
You came. And you did well to come,
    38
You do not do, you do not do, 655
You fool yourself and live a crazy day,
    294
You gaze at me teasingly through the
    window, 43
You have spoken your holy command
    over the city, 4
You held my lotus blossom, 149

You Hide, 312
You hide in the ostrich egg, 312
You intimidated me. I was thrown into
    hell without a trail, 601
You keep me waiting in a truck, 722
You lay in wait, 40
You never touch, 174
You shouldn't be afraid of the dark,
    229
You strike everything down in battle, 3
You told me: "I am not worthy of
    you." And you hid, 218
You told me it was, 168
You vilify me, but I rise above grief, 91
You want the summer lightning, throw
    the knives, 335
You wear the face, 168
You'll go to the plaza. To ask, 295
*Young Woman's neo-aramaic jewish
    persian Blues,* 29
Your cheeks flat on the sand, 242
Your handkerchief should be blue, 87
Your love turned my body, 83
Your lynx-eyes, Asia, 376